This volume provides a history of the Crow Indians that demonstrates the link between their nineteenth-century nomadic life and their modern existence. The Crows not only weathered and withstood the dislocation and conquest that was visited upon them after 1805, but acted in the midst of these events to construct a modern Indian community – a nation. Their efforts sustained the pride and strength reflected in Chief Plenty Coups's statement in 1925 that he did "not care at all what historians have to say about the Crow Indians," as well as their community's faith in the beauty of both its traditions and its inventions.

Frederick Hoxie demonstrates that contact with outsiders drew the Crows together and tested their ability to adapt their traditions to new conditions. He emphasizes political life, but also describes changes in social relations, religious beliefs and economic activities. He profiles the skilled tribal leaders who bridged the worlds of the buffalo and the era of automobiles, and links Indians to other ethnic groups in American history. His concluding chapter discusses the significance of the Crow experience for American history in general.

Parading through history

CAMBRIDGE STUDIES IN
NORTH AMERICAN INDIAN HISTORY

Editors
Frederick Hoxie, The Newberry Library
Neal Salisbury, Smith College

Also in the series

RICHARD WHITE   *The Middle Ground: Indians, Empires, and Republics in the Great Lakes Region, 1650–1815*
SIDNEY L. HARRING   *Crow Dog's Case: American Indian Sovereignty, Tribal Law, and United States Law in the Nineteenth Century*
COLIN G. CALLOWAY   *The American Revolution in Indian Country: Crisis and Diversity in Native American Communities*

Parading through history

The making of the Crow nation in America, 1805–1935

FREDERICK E. HOXIE
The Newberry Library

CAMBRIDGE
UNIVERSITY PRESS

Published by the Press Syndicate of the University of Cambridge
The Pitt Building, Trumpington Street, Cambridge CB2 IRP
40 West 20th Street, New York, NY 10011–4211, USA
10 Stamford Road, Oakleigh, Melbourne 3166, Australia

First published 1995

Printed in the United States of America

Library of Congress Cataloging-in-Publication Data
Hoxie, Frederick E., 1947–
Parading through history: the making of the Crow nation,
1805–1935 / Frederick E. Hoxie.
p.   cm. – (Cambridge studies in North American Indian
history)
Includes index.
ISBN 0–521–48057–4 (hardback).
1. Crow Indians – History.   I. Title.   II. Series.
E99.C92H69   1995
973'.04975 – dc20   94–40757
CIP

A catalog record for this book is available from the British Library.

ISBN 0–521–48057–4 Hardback

For Holly, my partner in the parade

Contents

Prologue:
Why are there no Indians in the
twentieth century?

I do not care at all what historians have to say about the Crow Indians.

Plenty Coups, August 5, 1925[1]

I am an invisible man. No, I am not a spook like those who haunted Edgar Allen
Poe; nor am I one of your Hollywood-movie ectoplasms. . . . I am invisible, understand, simply because people refuse to see me. . . . When they approach me they see
only my surroundings, themselves, or figments of their imagination – indeed, everything and anything except me.

Ralph Ellison, *Invisible Man*[2]

I

The opening lines from Ralph Ellison's searing novel of black dispossession
have haunted American readers for nearly half a century. It is perhaps jarring
to begin a book about American Indians with an observation about African-
Americans, for ever since the founding of Jamestown where John Rolfe married
an Indian woman while laying the foundations of an economy based on African
slavery, commentators have emphasized the different experiences of the two
groups. The cultural traditions of African-Americans and Native Americans
were formed on separate continents and have run through largely separate
chronologies, but they converge in one essential element: conventional understandings of their separate histories have been shaped by the refracting mirror
of racial fantasy and the narrow lens of economic need. According to Ralph
Ellison, African-Americans are invisible because their fellow citizens refuse
either to see their humanity or to confront the tragic dimensions of their
historical experience. American Indians have suffered a similar fate.

---

[1] Memorandum of Conference . . . August 5, 1925, "Inspector's Reports, 1924–1925," Item 15, Box
60, Records of the Crow Indian Agency, Federal Records Center (hereafter cited as RCIA-FRC,
Seattle).
[2] Ralph Ellison, *Invisible Man* (New York: Vintage Books, 1972), 3. Originally published by
Random House, 1952.

The invisibility of Native Americans is a by-product of their military defeat and economic dispossession. Conventional history teaches that Indians lost control of the continent because they resisted economic development and rejected the ideology of American progress. In this view, the passing of native power was a tragic but unavoidable chapter in the evolution of North American civilization. By extension, modern Indians are typically viewed as noble relics: descendants of a proud race who had the misfortune to be born to a losing cause. Death figures prominently in popular histories of Indian communities, and the horrors of the Native American past count as evidence of cultural demise. "Almost overnight," the standard history of the nineteenth-century Indian wars declares, for example, "a whole way of life had vanished, and thus whole clusters of habits and customs, activities, attitudes, values, and institutions lost relevance and meaning and likewise began to vanish." Odd to read this statement in an age that has watched a revival of Jewish culture follow closely on the heels of genocide, and witnessed the persistence or reemergence of "extinct" ethnicities within the borders of modern nation states.[3]

The American public's willingness to accept the cultural death of Indian people is the reason for the group's modern invisibility. A generation ago, Sioux historian Vine Deloria Jr. devoted a chapter of his best-selling manifesto, *Custer Died for Your Sins*, to the distorted pictures of Indian life emanating from academia. Anthropologists, he declared, insist that "Indians are a folk people, whites are an urban people, and never the twain shall meet. . . . These insights," Deloria added, "propounded every year with deadening regularity . . . have come to occupy a key block in the development of young Indian people. . . . They are crutches by which young Indians have avoided the arduous task of thinking out the implications of the status of Indian people in the modern world." So long as Indians are defined as people whose histories end with the triumph of industrialization, Deloria explained, they will be invisible members of American society.[4]

The opposite of this statement should also be true: turning away from a foreordained story of defeat offers us an opportunity to connect modern Indian people with the past through the medium of history. "We cannot turn the clock back," Deloria has written, "but we can certainly make note of the past as a prologue to the future."[5] In order to make that connection, however, a historical narrative must begin from a new premise.

Instead of viewing the confrontation of Native Americans and Euro-

---

[3] Robert M. Utley, *The Indian Frontier of the American West, 1846–1890* (Albuquerque: University of New Mexico Press, 1984), 236. Textbook portrayals of Native Americans regularly reflect these popular attitudes. For a discussion of this phenomenon, see Frederick E. Hoxie, "Historians Versus the Textbooks: Is There Any Way Out?" *D'Arcy McNickle Center Occasional Papers in Curriculum*, No. 1 (Chicago: Newberry Library, 1984), 25–28.

[4] Vine Deloria Jr., *Custer Died for Your Sins: An Indian Manifesto* (New York: Avon, 1969), 87–88.

[5] Vine Deloria Jr., "Foreword," in Michael L. Lawson, *Dammed Indians: The Pick-Sloan Plan and the Missouri River Sioux, 1944–1980* (Norman: University of Oklahoma Press, 1982), xvii.

Americans as a tragic but inevitable episode in the triumphal growth of the United States, chroniclers of the past should recognize that the consequences of an encounter between two cultural traditions, while dramatic, are not fore-ordained. Such meetings are unprecedented, and therefore unpredictable. As they encounter one another, divergent cultural traditions enter a historical no-man's land where expectations are disappointed, messages are misunderstood, and innovation becomes commonplace. Anthropologist Marshall Sahlins puts it this way: "In the clash of cultural understandings and interests, both changes and resistance to change are themselves historic issues." In such a setting, the future is open-ended.[6]

Once one sets aside the historical scripts that reduce cross-cultural interaction to simplistic melodrama, a range of new subjects present themselves. One finds more than befeathered, male warriors riding into purple sunsets. Turning away from ideologically driven scripts ("the end of the frontier," "the rise of the industrial state" or "the triumph of democracy") and focusing on the complicated interaction of cultural systems allows historians to identify human actors whose lives trace a path from the past to the present; these lives allow us to imagine events from the perspective of all those who participated in them.

Bringing Indian actors to the center of a historical narrative promises to transform the conventional treatment of native people. Objects become subjects; Native Americans cease to be faceless, tragic victims of "progress" or anonymous representatives of "lost" civilizations. Instead they are people who initiate, adapt and win as well as suffer and lose. In sum, they create a legacy that is independent of conventional, nationalistic narratives. Viewed in three dimensions, these Native Americans can drop their feathers, dismount from their ponies, join their families and enter the human arena that is history. They can thus become visible.

II

Parading Through History makes visible a story historians and the public have long ignored. Like all historical narratives, it begins with "facts" that seem to cry out for explanation. The first of these is the surprising survival of an Indian community whose demise has been predicted confidently for more than a century. Writing in 1855, a representative of the American Fur Company who worked the Missouri River observed that his principal trading partners, the Crow Indians, were doomed to extinction. The group suffered from disease, raids launched by neighboring tribes and pressure from Anglo-American settlers. "Situated as they now are," Edwin Thompson Denig reported, "the

[6] Marshall Sahlins, *Historical Metaphors and Mythical Realities: Structure in the Early History of the Sandwich Islands Kingdom*, Association for the Study of Anthropology in Oceania, Special Publication, No. 1 (Ann Arbor: University of Michigan Press, 1981), 68.

Crows cannot exist long as a nation." Nearly 150 years later, there are more Crows in the Yellowstone valley than there were in 1855; most of them speak the Crow language and occupy a self-governing tribal homeland. Other features of their community life contradict Denig's predictions: the persistence of a lively indigenous art tradition, the emergence of new forms of religious expression and a relatively low rate of intermarriage with non-Indians. One of their number has recently enrolled at Oxford University as a Rhodes scholar.[7]

Second, contemporary Crows reject the proposition that they are heirs to an anachronistic social tradition. Rather than represent a modern version of a "stone age" culture, they insist that their reservation is, in many respects, a modern nation. Crow faith in this self-image is strong despite decades of insistent instruction to the contrary. Missionaries, teachers, government officials and business interests have long taught that Indian ways could not survive in the modern world. But governed by a general assembly, regulated by a tribal court, educated by their elders and represented effectively by lobbyists and attorneys, the Crow community insists that it maintains "government to government" relationships with the state of Montana and the United States of America.

Conventional views of Native American history can not explain these surprising outcomes. Instead of being overwhelmed by events or swept away by the tide of progress, this community has been deeply engaged in countless interactions with the outside world. Apparently something occurred after their confinement on their reservation that derailed the confident expectations of outside observers and made possible the survival of a distinctively Crow community occupying a distinctively Crow homeland. That "something" is the subject of this book. Its contents exchange rhetorical generalizations for an intimate portrait of worthy, but forgotten, Americans.

The description of Crow life that follows has a broad ambition. In addition to making the invisible visible, it explores the accuracy of anthropologist Sherry Ortner's bold assertion that "history is not simply something that happens to people, but something they make – within, of course, the very powerful constraints of the system within which they are operating." Few groups appear to have had as much history "happen" to them as Plains Indians, and few eras seem as dominated by powerful, impersonal "forces" than the first decades of the twentieth century. To follow historical actors belonging to a beleaguered group of Native Americans through an age when cities "rose" and the frontier "ended" should illuminate the process by which ethnic and racial groups experienced the onset of an industrial society. Their history might also suggest how it was that a group of forgotten men and women helped "make" the historical moment we all now occupy.[8]

[7] Edwin Thompson Denig, *Five Indian Tribes of the Upper Missouri*, edited and with an introduction by John C. Ewers (Norman: University of Oklahoma Press, 1961), 204.

[8] Sherry Ortner, "Theory in Anthropology since the Sixties," *Comparative Studies in Society and History*, 26 (1984), 126–166, at 159.

Between 1880 and 1920 the population of the United States doubled while the nation's urban areas tripled in size. The history that "happened" to millions of Americans who lived their lives in those decades is reflected in those crude statistics – that history established the social fabric of our own time and defined the political loyalties and ethnic identities that continue to mobilize our communities. In this sense, events and processes that took place a century ago forged our sense of who we are as Americans. The received narratives of this era – marked by plots of national progress, cultural homogenization or environmental decline – are less than satisfying because most people, whatever their background, find it difficult to connect them to their own experiences or the experiences of their families.

Tied to the question of how individual experiences relate to conventional narratives is the question of how individual experiences relate to each other. Did the Crows' passage through the early twentieth century, for example, bear any resemblance to the confused and uncertain voyages of the millions who journeyed to the United States from abroad during the same period? Did Indians and immigrants share common hopes and a common nostalgia for an irretrievable world they saw slipping away behind them? Or might the Crow experience more closely resemble the shorter trips African-Americans made from plantations to sharecroppers' cabins in Georgia, Mississippi and Alabama? Perhaps Indian suffering mirrored the oppression of blacks in the Jim Crow South – or perhaps the Crow experience was unique. Such musings can only end when we have a clear grasp of each community's history. Only then can one find both the areas of overlap and the corners of distinctiveness in the lives of those who shaped our world.

III

The central metaphor of *Parading Through History* is drawn from both ethnography and autobiography. As plains hunters whose prosperity and survival demanded flexibility and mobility, the Crow communities of the eighteenth and nineteenth centuries frequently moved their camps in grand, mounted processions. "A Crow migration is a festive occasion," wrote one anthropologist who interviewed tribal members in the first years of this century. "Scouts ride far in advance to warn of enemies. Police guard the flanks. The chiefs and old men lead the procession. The various families follow with their horses, dogs and household possessions, the women dressed in their finest apparel. A moving column sometimes extends for several miles." The group moved forward in their world by arranging themselves self-consciously into a coherent unit and proceeding together. This practical parade was at once coherent and mobile, organized and adaptive. News of a buffalo herd would cause a shift in direction; the appearance of enemies would bring the group to a halt.[9]

Other types of parades have punctuated more recent accounts of Crow life. According to anthropologist Robert Lowie, for example, returning warriors would parade through camp, waving the spoils of victory and shouting flamboyant accounts of their comrades' bravery. Peter Nabokov has also demonstrated how processions form part of community ritual, most prominently in tribal celebrations of the Crow Tobacco Society. Parades have also become a favored way for Crow families to display their costumes and prize possessions at powwows and fairs. Today, parades are a typical feature of community celebrations and historic commemorations.

A historian's own experiences can transform ethnographic details into significant themes. The bulk of this book was written on the outskirts of Chicago. My green, suburban environment in the center of the table-flat heartland bears no resemblance to the rolling, brown prairies and heart-stopping peaks of eastern Montana, but our town's central avenue is the site of an annual, and widely celebrated, Fourth of July parade. Every year we join with our neighbors and thousands of visitors to watch the procession of old cars, floats and marching bands pass down Central Street in celebration of Independence Day. The event recalls the parades I witnessed as a child in a distant, rural community. There, national holidays were celebrated along a three-block-long main street. Perhaps five hundred people witnessed the largest of those parades, and easily half of them shuttled back and forth to their seats from turns with the Boy Scouts, the VFW or the Little League. These were the only occasions during which our one fire truck and police car flashed their lights and sounded their sirens. In memory, screaming fire engines and flashing emergency lights celebrate our persistence and the survival of our remote social order.

The link between Crow ethnography and my autobiography was forged in the summer of 1990 when my family and I pulled off I-90 at the "Crow Agency" exit after an early morning drive from Sheridan, Wyoming. We were on our way to visit friends and to witness the inauguration of a new tribal leader who had just been elected after a bitter political struggle. The atmosphere was tense; it was hot; we were late. But we never made it off the exit ramp. Traffic was backed up, and the people ahead of me had left their cars and started walking ahead to the foot of the grade. The inaugural parade was just stepping off – and it included a screaming fire engine.

This book is a description of a people who paraded, both literally and figuratively, into American history at the start of the nineteenth century. It begins with a description of the founding of the modern Crow Reservation in 1884,

---

[9] George Peter Murdock, *Our Primitive Contemporaries* (New York: Macmillan, 1934), 267. I am grateful to Peter Nabokov for bringing this quotation to my attention.

but quickly backpedals to describe the events that led the tribe to that place at that time. The narrative then starts forward again, tracing the community's history into the era of the New Deal. Throughout these events, the narrative will demonstrate that the Crows have maintained their tradition of marching together. Their insistence on this practice, like a childhood memory, is insignificant in itself, but it signals to those who pay attention that a group can maintain its traditions and its identity through a staggering era of change. Indeed, as the narrative to come will demonstrate, the Crows not only weathered and withstood the dislocation and conquest that was visited upon them after 1805, but acted in the midst of these events to construct a modern Indian community – a nation. Their efforts sustained the pride and strength reflected in Chief Plenty Coups's statement in 1925 that he did "not care at all what historians have to say about the Crow Indians," as well as their community's faith in the beauty of both its traditions and its inventions.

Part One

Into history, 1805–1890

In time, then, words will not stand still. Moralistic theories of history . . . dwell on [a] timeless pattern of being, not process, and therefore deal in absolutes. But a concern with process, becoming, ousts the language of fixity for the language of movement – the language of relativism. Absolutism is the parochialism of the present, the confusion of one's own time with the timeless. . . . This is the confusion one fosters when he judges other times by his own criteria. . . . No one has the norm of norms.[1]

While their relations with Europeans were frequently tense and occasionally marked by violence, the Crow Indians never launched a wholesale attack on the United States or its colonial predecessors. Unlike the Cheyenne, Sioux and Blackfeet with whom they fought, the Crows' passage into the reservation era was not marked by a bloody confrontation or a dramatic, battlefield defeat. Nevertheless, the transition to this new chapter in their history began with a single event: the relocation in April 1884 of the tribe's agency headquarters from a mountainous area in the Stillwater valley to the flatland alongside the Little Bighorn River. Prior to that event, the Crows were relatively free from the daily intrusions of white settlers and cattlemen; afterwards they lived amidst rail traffic, cattle drives and enterprising farmers. Before the relocation, missionaries and government schoolmasters were infrequent visitors; afterwards, missions and boarding schools became fixtures within the community. And before the agency moved to the prairies south of the Yellowstone, the tribe had been free to range across a large area in search of game and enemy raiders; afterwards the entire population was expected to locate permanently on a gradually shrinking reservation. Part One begins with a description of the events surrounding the agency's relocation.

But the need to understand how the Crows understood and experienced their new reservation home requires more than an account of a single event. A narrative constructed to counteract the simplistic tales of the past and to engage the experiences of long-neglected actors must move in at least three additional directions. First, the tale must move backwards. Where did this journey to a new reservation home begin? What bound the group together? Who were its leaders, and why were they followed? Answering these questions forces the

---

[1] Joseph R. Levenson, *Confucian China and Its Modern Fate: A Trilogy* (Berkeley: University of California Press, 1958, 1964, 1965), Part Three, 87.

narrative back from 1884, the subject of Chapter 1, to Chapter 2, which describes the Crows as they first appeared to non-Indians nearly eighty years earlier. Subsequently, Chapters 3 and 4 will trace the experiences of the group through the intervening periods of trade, warfare and diplomacy. These descriptions will clarify the extent to which merchants, American military officials, rival tribes and the relentless demographic pressures unleashed by white settlement affected the people who marched down from the Stillwater to take up new homes on the Montana prairies.

Second, an observer must move forward: what did this journey produce for this community? What was the nature of the "progress" the Crows experienced in the immediate aftermath of their relocation? Did it mark a sharp break with the past, the first step downward in a spiral of defeat, or something resembling the development witnessed in other parts of the Yellowstone valley during the early years of Montana statehood? Chapter 5 answers these questions as it traces the tribe's initial reaction to the reservation environment.

And finally, one must move outward. In what ways did the process initiated by the procession of the Crows to their new homes resemble the journeys of the 23,000,000 who immigrated to the United States in the forty years after 1880 or the additional millions who moved across other of the continent's boundaries and borderlands during the same period? Do passages across cultural and geographical barriers generate similar changes in the life of a community? Do they affect a group's structure as well as its idea of itself, and do those aspects of life evolve towards some common form? How many similar voyages might one identify, and how might the effort to understand them on their own terms illuminate an understanding of American social history? Such questions will remain on the outskirts of our discussion until the end of Part Three, but they will continue within sight, disrupting moralistic theories of history before they can grow too persuasive, protecting our narrative from both parochialism and the temptation to pronounce the Crow story, the "norm of norms."

1

Immigration in reverse

This earth was all covered with water. Old-Man-Coyote alone was going around on the water. Then a little coyote met him. "I am alone, I am looking for a companion, I'll meet one," he had said. Then they met. There was no living thing then. They went around together. "We are alone; it is bad; let us make the earth." "All right, how shall we make it?" After some time ducks came flying. "You dear younger brothers, dive here," he said. "How shall we do it?" "Dive into the water, bring earth, we'll make the world," he said. They brought some. "Is there any?" "Yes." "Go, bring some."
Four times they brought some, he took it and made the earth.[1]

I

Running at a diagonal from Canada, down along the Idaho–Montana border, turning south across Wyoming and trailing deep into central Colorado, the Rocky Mountains form the western border of the northern Great Plains. Their ranges mark the edge of the rolling grasslands of the Missouri River drainage and form a dramatic marker of climatic and environmental change. Through the centuries their cloud-like peaks have also formed a border between cultural realms. For two thousand years before the arrival of Europeans in North America the region to the west of the Rockies – the arid ranges and high plateaus of the Great Basin – supported gathering peoples who felt the influences of communities located to their south, along the Colorado River and the Rio Grande. They received tools, artistic motifs and trade goods that passed northward from the villages in what would become modern Arizona and New Mexico. East of the mountains, groups of hunters and river-based farmers developed communities under the influence of migrants from the moist and heavily wooded prairies of the Mississippi valley and the Great Lakes. People travelled across the Rocky Mountain barrier, but their passage came at the expense of a shift in cultural tradition.

In the eighteenth and nineteenth centuries these dramatic ranges created a

---

[1] Robert H. Lowie, *Myths and Traditions of the Crow Indians* (Lincoln: University of Nebraska Press, 1993), 17, originally published in 1918.

similar borderland between the ranges of European exploration. Spanish settlers along the Rio Grande pushed north into modern Utah and east into Texas, but their sphere did not extend across the Rocky Mountain divide, onto the northern Great Plains. Similarly, adventurers in New France struggled west across Lake Superior and past Thunder Bay to Lake Winnipeg, but they stopped short of the Rocky Mountain front. Englishmen and Americans followed suit, so that it was not until the 1840s that travellers could contemplate regular passage over – and substantial settlement across – the mountains. Significantly, when explorers and fur traders breeched the divide, they frequently claimed that they had found a new "empire" in Oregon and California. Even after the newcomers had conquered and mapped them, the mountains continued to mark the border between regions and lifeways.

At a point in the Rocky Mountain chain near the spot where the modern states of Idaho, Wyoming and Montana meet – where geysers and waterfalls announce the Yellowstone River's departure for the Missouri River and the Gulf of Mexico – one massive arc of granite shifts eastward and thrusts itself into space. For nearly three hundred miles, the Gallatin, Beartooth and Bighorn ranges abandon the great diagonal from Canada to Colorado and run off on their own towards the East and the South. These wayward peaks form a giant crescent that enfolds central Wyoming to its south and creates a dramatic backdrop for the prairies of eastern Montana. Around the base of these mountains . the Yellowstone River bends its way to the Missouri and the Gulf, widened by a series of icy, north-flowing tributaries: the Stillwater, Clark's Fork, the Bighorn, the Powder and the Tongue Rivers. Together these errant ranges form a peninsula of pine and alpine meadows that juts out into the plains, accentuating the border it marks between regions and cultural traditions.

In early April 1884, 130 families began a journey across that border; they moved down from the foothills of the Beartooth range to the flatlands of the Bighorn and Little Bighorn valleys. Over 900 people, accompanied by wagons and guarded by federal agents, began their passage in the shadow of 12,000 foot Granite Peak, the highest point in modern Montana, and moved eastward out of the Stillwater valley. Within a few days they crossed Red Lodge and Rock Creeks, forded Clark's Fork of the Yellowstone, and trailed onto the spring-green prairie. Picturesque but only beginning to sprout, the landscape provided little food for their horses. Few animals emerged from the cottonwoods or muddy ravines. The company carried only the most meager provisions, so that by April 12 when they reached the banks of the Little Bighorn River, they were exhausted and hungry. There the pioneers pitched their tents, watered their animals, and began making preparations for spring planting. Like countless others who had passed across the barrier of the mountains, they came to the flatland with the expectation that their new homeland, while demanding new skills, would open a door to a new way of life. Thrilled by this prospect, the

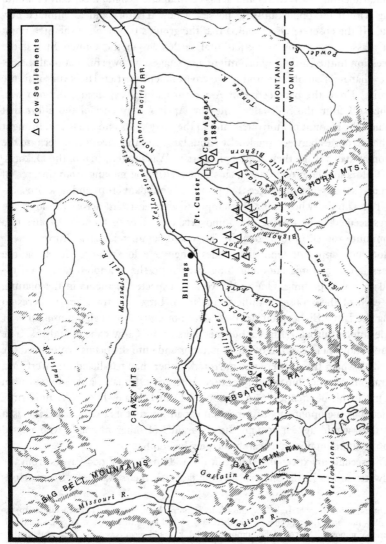

Map 1. Crow settlements, 1884.

group's leader noted excitedly, "It seems as if I had lived a year and a half in the past six weeks."[2]

A modern American observer of this procession might imagine that its route through melting snow drifts and across a dramatic geographical border would bring with it the opportunity to possess a new territory and to embrace new habits. If the observer also recalled that the group's trip came at the high point of a massive expansion of agricultural settlement in the United States, the procession to the Little Bighorn might also suggest a powerful, national theme: the exchange of an old, unproductive environment for rich lands full of fertile promise. From the perspective of American national expansion, the 900 who pushed off from the Stillwater valley on April 1 were part of the effort that doubled the amount of cultivated land in the forty years after 1875 and brought all the territories between the Rocky Mountains and the Missouri River into the Union as states. Like their fellow pioneers in Washington, Idaho, the Dakotas, and Colorado, these 900 Montanans appeared to be moving from an area of marginal subsistence to a place that promised abundant crops and new prosperity. The families who trailed the supply wagons eastward across the lowering ridges seemed to be leaving old, impoverished homes to found new ones in a community rooted in individual initiative and commercial agriculture.

But such apparent familiarity fades when one looks more closely at the procession of 900 migrants marching away from the Beartooth range and towards a new beginning. One sees several unexpected elements in the picture, and each of them raises a difficult question. First, the travellers who rested along the Little Bighorn on April 12 were not eager Norwegian immigrants or single-minded urban refugees, but members of the Crow tribe of Indians. The group's movement east out of the mountains and onto the plains symbolized the extent to which their experience mirrored, rather than paralleled, the westward migrations of other nineteenth-century Americans. Indians, after all, had been cast in the role of enemies from the time of Daniel Boone. They were uniformly depicted as the opponents of American expansion, not its exemplars. How is it that they would appear to join the thousands of other migrants who passed across the mountains in a search for new beginnings?

The second unexpected element in the 1884 passage of 900 Crows from the Stillwater to the Little Bighorn was the fact that theirs was not a spontaneous

---

[2] Eight days after their arrival along the Little Bighorn, Agent Armstrong issued rations to 130 families numbering 907 people. While there was no roll taken of the Crow migrants (and it is therefore impossible to verify the number exactly), it would seem reasonable to assume that the total drawing weekly rations (which varied little over the next several weeks) would be approximately the same as the number of people who made the initial journey. See "Issue Book, April 20 to . . . ," Item 39, Box 171, Records of the Crow Indian Agency, Federal Records Center, Seattle, Washington (hereafter cited as RCIA-FRC, Seattle). For Armstrong's comment on the journey, see Armstrong to Commissioner of Indian Affairs, May 7, 1884, Item 3, Box 10, RCIA-FRC, Seattle.

act. At the head of the wagon train rode Captain Henry Armstrong, an army officer, temporarily assigned to the Office of Indian Affairs. A crusty career officer from Kansas, Armstrong had not been elected or hired by the migrants the way most trail bosses had been in the days of the Oregon Trail. He sympathized with the tribe's predicament – he even claimed to have Native American ancestors – but he reported to superiors in Washington, D.C., rather than to the Indians who followed him. He disbursed supplies on the order of the Office of Indian Affairs rather than in response to community need.

Finally, even though the Crow migration to the Little Bighorn ended with the organization of a new town, their pioneer settlement was not formed to aggregate individual landholdings or focus entrepreneurial ambition. Instead, Crow Agency, Montana, was established to house Captain Armstrong and his staff and to provide a central location for their educational and missionary work among the tribe. The new town did not embody a community's desires for the future as Plymouth or Dedham, Massachusetts, had done in the seventeenth century (or, indeed, as the African-American "exoduster" settlements in western Kansas were doing at that very moment); it was not an expression of the community's optimism and freedom. Instead the collection of government offices and warehouses that quickly took form along the Little Bighorn reflected a bureaucrat's dream; it was an instrument of social control.[3]

The Crows had passed across a cultural and geographical border, suggesting in the process the movement from one stage of existence to another, but the tribe's migration resembled neither the prehistoric diffusions of cultural traits that had characterized their ancestors lives in the distant past, nor the more recent, westering epics of their American neighbors. It fit neither script and raises more questions than it answers. Was the journey significant? If so, what did it mean? The first question is easily answered. The relocation of the Crow Indians to permanent homes on the eastern Montana prairies marked their confinement within the permanent boundaries of a modern reservation. Before 1884 the tribe could imagine that their life as a hunting people persisted; the founding of Crow Agency marked the beginning of the days after the buffalo had gone away and when other game could not sustain them. It also marked the onset of an administration that enforced its orders that they stay "at home," take up new occupations and send their children to the white man's schools. Their arrival on the banks of the Little Bighorn marked the moment when they would have to begin heeding collectively the brutal demand, mouthed by windy politicians from Helena to Washington, D.C., that they "root hog or die."

While the Crow procession marked a turning point in their history, its significance is far from self-evident. It fits none of the master narratives with which one normally understands American migrations or national expansion.

---

[3] See Armstrong to C. H. Barstow, May 8, 1884, Item 3, Box 10, RCIA-FRC, Seattle.

Did it mark the end of Crow history – or was it the beginning of some sort of transformation? Where had the Crows come from? Where were they going? The journey from the Stillwater fits neither the model of neutral, prehistoric culture change nor the epic of upward, westward "progress." Many would argue that it follows yet another well-worn narrative: the decline and fall of a proud people. "For generations," Sioux historian Vine Deloria Jr. has written, "it has been traditional that all historical literature on Indians be a recital of tribal histories from the pre-Discovery culture through the first encounter with the white man to about the year 1890. At that point the tribe seems to fade gently into history, with its famous war chief riding down the canyon into the sunset." Such a tableau, Deloria notes, symbolizes "not living people but the historic fate of a nation overwhelmed by the inevitability of history."[4]

The ride of the 900 might well fit this stereotypical narrative, but, just as the Crow riders in 1884 rode into the sunrise rather than the sunset, events do not square with a preconceived narrative of cultural defeat. Accepting that image not only denies the significance of Crow peoples' experience during the preceding century, but it ignores their community's modern existence. It suggests that modern Crows are at best ghosts – shadows of their authentic ancestors – or, at worst, fakes: people trying to pretend that they belong to a distinctive and ancient cultural tradition. After all, the Crow tribe continues to this day, challenging its white neighbors in court, joining with them to elect members of the state legislature, worshiping beside them in churches and the out-of-doors, while teaching its language and religious ideas to its children and grandchildren. Theirs was not a journey into oblivion.

The 1884 journey invites us to set aside our master narratives and to imagine instead the experience of the Crow migrants from the perspective of their own history, rather than from the perspective of national expansion or cultural adaptation. It also suggests that this tribe's experience is linked to a broader process, for its journey out of the mountains occurred in an age of other journeys that crisscrossed North America. The first steps in our narrative must be cautious. Stepping back only a few years will clarify the events in the Crow world of 1884; stepping forward a few weeks will suggest where they lead. Both movements help set a context for the larger tale of what this event meant, both in Montana and the United States at large. Like the ducks in the Crow creation story who retrieved a piece of earth from the primordial sea, these initial descriptions provide the space from which a larger narrative can be launched. In a historian's dreams, as in mythic time, a tiny incident, like a tiny spot of land might mark our emergence into an entirely new world of historical understanding. For now the narrative should remain at the scale of the duck and his lump of mud.

[4] Vine Deloria Jr., *God is Red* (New York: Delta, 1973), 41.

II

What started the Crow journey? From the time of his arrival at the Indian Office's Stillwater valley agency, Agent Henry Armstrong had believed that a crucial moment in the history of the 3,000-member Crow tribe was at hand. In his first monthly report, sent to Washington in January 1882, Armstrong wrote that he had assumed control of the agency "at a time that may be said to be the crisis in the history of the Crows." Almost immediately he had solicited advice from his fellow officer, the commander at nearby Fort Custer, at the mouth of the Little Bighorn River, asking if the river valleys to the east of his headquarters were, as he had been told, "far superior to the country around the agency."

Before his first year in Montana was over, Armstrong had developed a plan for the agency's relocation. Having compared the mountainous terrain surrounding his offices with the rolling prairies along the Bighorn, he concluded that there was no alternative to a wholesale move. Writing in July 1882, he noted that he might "presume too much" by making this request after only six months on the job, but he added that "having watched other Indian tribes during the first 20 years of my life I feel that the first, greatest and most important question affecting the Crows today is to locate them permanently on the best portion of their country ... and then settle the whites around them as closely and as quickly as possible. ...." Armstrong believed this resettlement was an essential preparation for the changes he saw coming to eastern Montana. If the Crows did not adapt, Armstrong warned, they would "become extinct."[5]

Armstrong's proposal travelled up the chain of command to the office of Secretary of the Interior Henry Teller, a former Colorado senator who had risen to power in part on the strength of his stalwart support for the removal of all tribes from that state. Sensing controversy – *any* relocation of western Indians would surely bring protests – and noting that Armstrong's proposal would require new legislation reallocating humanitarian support already earmarked for the tribe (and promised to the usual government contractors), the secretary stalled. He sent the agent's request back down the bureaucratic mountain with the suggestion that Armstrong consult local whites and secure the tribe's formal consent before proceeding.[6]

Teller's tactic stretched the process of approval into 1883, but events in the new year persuaded the Crow agent that his charges had even less time to move out of the mountains than he had previously supposed. While he waited for

---

[5] H. J. Armstrong to Commissioner of Indian Affairs, January 31, 1882, RCIA-FRC, Item 3, Box 9; H. J. Armstrong to commissioner of Indian Affairs, July 20, 1882, Letters Received, 14191–1882, Records of the Office of Indian Affairs, Records Group 75, National Archives, Washington, D.C. (hereafter cited as LR-OIA, RG 75, NA).

[6] Commissioner of Indian Affairs to Secretary of the Interior, November 16, 1882, Letters Received, 20928–1882, LR-OIA, RG 75, NA.

approval from Washington, the Northern Pacific Railroad completed the last pieces of its transcontinental line and began to transport new settlers to the Yellowstone valley in unprecedented numbers. Billings, founded in 1882 as a rail depot and named for the president of the line, was an instant metropolis. Within months it sported churches, schools, rival newspapers and a street railway. The town was sure to grow and form a center of opposition to Crow landholding. Armstrong also understood the impact of the Northern Pacific on what remained of the region's buffalo population. Both the disruption of railroad construction and the influx of new settlers doomed what little game remained in the Yellowstone valley area. Writing in the fall of 1883, Armstrong was categorical (and accurate) about the fate of what had been the basis for Crow subsistence for more than a century: "There is no game left upon their reservation at all worth speaking of and we shall have to have a much larger quantity of supplies than have been allowed us for the present fiscal year or the Crows will starve or go over the [reservation] line."[7] To Armstrong, either outcome would have been disastrous, for Montana Territory's burgeoning population resented the tribe's vast reserve of land and would have seized on any off-reservation hunting expeditions as evidence of the Indians' hostile intent.

Out of concern for the tribe's livelihood (as well as its safety), Armstrong struggled to interest his charges in farming. During this first year in office he cultivated an agency garden, using what funds he had available to hire Crows to cut logs for fencing and putting his agency staff to work in the fields. Once the soil was prepared, he assigned small sections to individuals who promised to grow potatoes and hay under his supervision. A few tribesmen pitched in. Most of these were families of "headmen," individuals recognized by Armstrong as leaders of groups who drew rations together and hunted in the same territory. The headmen formed a pivotal group that aspired to recognition by both the government and their kinsmen. Their numbers included most of the men who would figure prominently in the community's history over the next half-century.

The headmen who farmed with Armstrong in 1882 included Old Onion, Wolf Bow and Long Otter, three distinguished warriors who had served as scouts during the Sioux wars that had been fought near the Yellowstone over the preceding two decades. These three were joined by two younger warriors whose careers as tribal leaders lay largely in the future: Pretty Eagle and Plenty Coups. Coaxed by Armstrong, worried about how to fulfill their obligation to provide for the members of their bands, these hard-working chiefs and their families tried their hand at Armstrong's farm. The agent reported nervously that these new farmers "want to work together" in family groups rather than as

---

[7] Armstrong to Commissioner of Indian Affairs, September 15, 1883, Letters Received, 17631–1883, LR-OIA, RG 75, NA.

The young warrior Plenty Coups, photographed in 1880, not long before he indicated to Agent Armstrong that while he was willing to settle his band at Pryor Creek, he did not wish to sell any more lands or to divide the Crow reserve into individual farms. Courtesy of Smithsonian Institution.

competing individuals, but he encouraged their efforts and by fall their kinsmen were storing their crop in bales and at the agency root cellar.[8]

Armstrong was determined to develop his farming program as well as to keep the Crows away from both hostile white settlers and restive neighboring tribes. He reported regularly on Blackfeet raiders who swept south across the Yellowstone to steal horses, frequently asking the commander at Fort Custer to block Crow retaliation raids or to head off small groups that set off towards the Powder River in response to rumors of errant buffalo or south to the Wind River range in search of smaller game. Faced with these thankless (and often futile) requests, the commander at Fort Custer asked in return that the Interior Department issue an order prohibiting all travel by Indians outside the reservation. Again, the request moved slowly up the bureaucracy, and no action was taken.[9]

In the fall of 1883, a new set of requests began to accumulate at the door of the Indian Office. Because these came from important white voters and not obscure government employees, they required a response. Western politicians and stockmen demanded that federal officials recognize the destruction of the region's game population by seizing the Crow's hunting territory and confining the tribe to a small, agricultural reservation. "These people cannot hold such an extent of country as they now do very much longer," a worried Armstrong wrote his superiors that winter. In addition, Armstrong sensed that the tribe was on the verge of starvation. In the past, only a few dozen Crows had remained at the government's isolated agency during the winter; most bands gathered up their supplies and dispersed to favorite hunting grounds in sheltered valleys and river bottoms to the east and south. By the first months of 1884, however, it was clear that the absence of game and the hostility of local whites had caused most Crows to stay close to Armstrong's warehouse. The agent reported in February that supplies were running short.

From his snowbound headquarters, Armstrong again pleaded for permission to relocate the tribe. He wrote that "the selection of the location for the permanent home of the Crows and the removal of this agency is the starting point of all affairs pertaining to the civilization of these people. . . ." He dismissed Secretary Teller's requirement that the Indians give their consent to a move. "The time has come, he replied, "when the Indians ought to be *governed* and there is no way to govern them but by force."[10]

The migration of the Crows out of the Rocky Mountains was not the

---

[8] Armstrong to Commissioner of Indian Affairs, March 31, 1882, Item 3, Box 9, RCIA-FRC, Seattle; see also Mary 10, 1882, June 6, 1882, August 15, 1882, September 1, 1882, October 5, 1882, and November 6, 1882, RCIA-FRC, Seattle.

[9] For correspondence related to Crow hunters raising protests from ranchers and the Indian Office, see Secretary of War to the Secretary of the Interior, June 9, 1883, Letters Received, 10648–1883, LR-OIA, RG 75, NA, and July 13, 1883. Letters Received, 12905–1883, LR-OIA, RG 75, NA.

[10] Armstrong to Commissioner of Indian Affairs, December 12, 1883, February 5 and February 24, 1884, Item 4, Box 11, RCIA-FRC, Seattle. Emphasis in original.

migration of eager, landless peasants to a land of promise, but the forced retreat of landed hunters to a tiny corner of a rapidly developing federal territory. The families who travelled out of the mountains with Captain Armstrong were not coming to America; America was coming to them. It was immigration in reverse.

Armstrong believed the Crows' march to the Little Bighorn would begin a process of cultural transformation. Leaving their mountain retreat and settling along the well-watered valleys to the east would bring the tribe to a "starting point" comparable to the one reached by European peasants who disembarked at eastern ports or fresh-faced farmers who located their homesteads on the windswept prairies of the Dakotas or eastern Colorado. The agent wrote his superiors in Washington that the tribe's migration might cause an increase of expense, "but it is better to stand this increase for a couple of years than to continue the reservation system 25 years." He added, "If any man can take a tribe of wild Indians and make anything out of them, I can."[11]

While Armstrong's cocky words help us see beneath the surface of events in the spring of 1884, it would be a mistake to trade one cliché for another. The tribe did not make its journey eagerly, but neither did it leave the Stillwater at the point of a gun. In fact, Armstrong's two-year campaign for agency reloca-tion had been punctuated by frequent references to Crow leaders who were willing, even eager, to move east onto the lowlands. Long famous on the plains for their friendliness to whites, many Crow leaders appeared willing to cooper-ate with Armstrong's relocation scheme. The tribe had never joined other tribes in wholesale attacks on American settlers or soldiers. They had refused to join the Sioux during the Powder River war of the 1860s and a decade later had denied requests for help from their old Nez Perce comrades under Chief Joseph as they fled through Crow country on their way from Oregon to Canada. Most loyal of all were the men who had served as scouts for the U.S. Army over the preceding two decades. Because the army still called on them from time to time, many of these men camped near Fort Custer at the confluence of the Bighorn and Little Bighorn Rivers, one hundred miles east of the agency at Absarokee. Armstrong could therefore legitimately claim that the scouts and their families wanted to settle down in the lowlands.

Early in 1882 the agent had noted that five large families had resettled voluntarily along the Bighorn River. Among the heads of these families were two men who had served the military since the Red Cloud war and were con-sidered the most trustworthy of the group. Iron Bull and War Man had worked closely with several military commanders and had long adapted themselves to working for cash and mediating between the demands of the government and the needs of their followers. They were joined by a young white adventurer, Thomas Leforge, who had become a part of the Crow community by marrying

[11] Ibid.

the Crow widow of Mitch Bouyer, Col. George Custer's half-Sioux scout who had died with his commander at the Little Bighorn in 1876. Each of these family heads expressed an interest in gaining individual title to land and a willingness to try farming along the river. Before long they were joined by a veteran of Armstrong's agency farm: Pretty Eagle, a widely respected warrior and band leader who had also served the army as a scout. Like the others he appeared eager to farm and, perhaps, had the idea of selling hay to local cattlemen.[12]

In the fall of 1882, Agent Armstrong reported to the commander at Fort Custer that he had just received permission to have the lowland areas around his post surveyed. He added that he hoped to be laying out farms for the Crows the following spring. Soon he wrote again reporting that "some influence" was delaying things. The survey would be postponed.[13] Despite these bureaucratic ups and downs, the agent continued to believe that a substantial number of Crow families would be willing to settle on the lowlands. In the summer of 1882, War Man, one of the former scouts who had worked at the agency farm under Armstrong's direction, asked a visiting U.S. senator to write to the Indian Office on his behalf to request a deed for land along the Bighorn. Late in 1882 a visiting Indian Office inspector conveyed a similar request from Bear In The Water, another young band leader. Speaking "to his Great Father" in Washington, Bear In The Water said, "I want to settle down in the Bighorn country."[14]

In the summer of 1883, Thin Belly, another band leader and former scout who had settled near Fort Custer, testified before a visiting delegation from the U.S. Senate's Committee on Indian Affairs. The chief told the leader of the congressional delegation, Henry Dawes of Massachusetts, that he wanted title to a tract of land along the Little Bighorn.

"What do you want to do with this land yourself?" Dawes asked.

"I want to farm on it," Thin Belly replied.

"Why don't you take more?"

"The reason is that I want to keep near the agency and don't want to go far away from it. . . . I want the Great Father to give me everything the white man has. I want chickens and animals."[15]

[12] H. J. Armstrong to Commissioner of Indian Affairs, March 24, 1882, 6491, LR-OIA, RG 75, NA. For information on Leforge and his family, see Joseph Medicine Crow and Herman J. Viola, "Introduction," to Thomas H. Leforge, Memoirs of a White Crow Indian (Lincoln: University of Nebraska Press, 1974), p. viii.

[13] Armstrong to John Hatch, September 18, 1882, Item 3, Box 9, RCIA-FRC, Seattle, and October 9, 1882, Item 3, Box 9, RCIA-FRC, Seattle.

[14] War Man's request is contained in Beck to Commissioner of Indian Affairs, September 6, 1882, 16898–1882, LR-OIA, RG 75, NA. See also Statement of Bear In The Water, January 21, 1883, 1986, LR-OIA, RG 75, NA.

[15] "Report of the Select Committee to Examine the Condition of the Sioux and Crow Indians," Senate Report 283, 48th Congress, 1st Session (Serial 2174), 9.

Dee-Kit-Shis or "Pretty Eagle"
Copy-Hillers

Pretty Eagle, a band leader and former army scout who settled voluntarily in the Bighorn valley in the early 1880s. This photograph was taken in 1880 when the chief travelled to Washington, D.C., as part of a tribal delegation. Courtesy of Smithsonian Institution.

These men and their bands did not even accompany the wagon train as it descended, rounding the hillside into the river valley. While Armstrong was marching his column east from the hills, Iron Bull and Bear In The Water were already settled into the Bighorn valley, accompanied now by at least thirty-five other families. Armstrong's march to the Little Bighorn might appear to some to have been an act of coercion, but Iron Bull, Bear In The Water, Thin Belly and their families were not among the people being forced out of the mountains. By the spring of 1884 the total Bighorn group numbered over 200 people.

Another group of Crow headmen appeared willing to cooperate with Armstrong, but for reasons that had little to do with farming or the cash economy. Most prominent among them was Plenty Coups, a noted warrior in his middle thirties who had fought with General Crook at the Battle of the Rosebud in 1876, but who now stood on the brink of a political career that would last more than half a century. Plenty Coups's battle exploits meant nothing to Armstrong, but he had been impressed by the young man's willingness to raise oats at the old agency in 1882. The young chief surprised his agent, however, by refusing to follow the other former scouts to the Bighorn valley. Instead, he told Armstrong that he and his band of some twenty families would prefer to establish "a ranch" near his birthplace along Pryor Creek, about midway between Absarokee and the Little Bighorn. Plenty Coups and his followers promised the agent they would soon build permanent homes along the stream which flowed north out of the Bighorns, but they were not interested in farming or in settling near the proposed new headquarters. "I have asked him to look around and select some nice place nearer to the agency," Armstrong reported, "but he says it is no use for him to do so; that he is well acquainted with every part of his country and that there is no other place where he wants to live and have his home."[16]

While they had not instigated the move, men like Plenty Coups apparently had concluded that ranching provided a possible solution to the disappearance of game from the Crow homeland. The young chief also insisted that the moment had arrived when he and his followers should stake a claim to a significant portion of the reservation. Thus, while War Man, Iron Bull and other former scouts – generally older men in their forties and fifties – concluded that maintaining good ties to federal officials required them to cooperate with Armstrong's agricultural program (although they appeared determined to avoid the Little Bighorn), Plenty Coups was looking to the future. Some marched

[16] For the size and composition of the Iron Bull, Bear In The Water and Plenty Coups bands, see Item 156, "Record of Indian Bands," RCIA-FRC, Seattle. The census, which is undated but which was probably taken in 1885, lists heads of households, sizes of families and band membership. On Plenty Coups's desire to relocate to Pryor, see Henry Armstrong to Commissioner of Indian Affairs, June 30, 1882, Item 3, Box 9, RCIA-FRC, Seattle.

with Armstrong because they were starving, others because they believed there was space within his scheme to carve out a new life for themselves.

Henry Armstrong's correspondence and monthly reports indicate that by the spring of 1884 the subject of relocating the agency had produced four distinct positions within the tribe. One group, which constituted most of the 900 who marched with the agent from the Stillwater to the new agency, was composed of people who were refugees: hungry, dependent and cooperative. The second group, made up of headmen such as Thin Belly, War Man, Iron Bull and the other former scouts, consisted of families who camped near Fort Custer and along the Bighorn. They were, the agent noted, "disposed to settle down and become good citizens. This party has been trying to farm in a small way for two or three seasons." The agent added that Thin Belly "said he wanted his home near to the agency."

Considerably less enthusiastic were Plenty Coups and, apparently, Pretty Eagle. While aware that the time had come to alter their traditional hunting way of life, these men saw no reason to relocate the Crow agency to the prairie or to assign tribesmen to individual tracts of land. This group, Armstrong noted, "want[s] the Crows to spread out and take up and hold all the valleys on their reservation." They knew the time had come to adopt a new way of life, but they wanted to proceed on their own terms. "All the Indians that live on the prairies and wear the breech clout are fools," Plenty Coups had told Senator Dawes in 1883, adding that "none of the Crows are fools yet. . . . We want houses and farms along the creeks, and if the Great Father will give us cattle we will raise them."

Men like Plenty Coups apparently feared that settling in one location to raise crops like wheat or oats, or gathering around a new tribal agency would encourage reliance on government handouts and prompt whites to demand that the tribe sell the "unused" portions of their reserve. The young chief from Pryor Creek had himself travelled to Washington, D.C., in 1880 as the junior member of a tribal delegation and he was familiar with the way local settlers could pressure the government to acquire tribal land. He and his colleagues were also aware of the potential of their land for grazing. His one summer raising oats seemed to have convinced him that cattle would be a far better basis for tribal subsistence than farming. He declared that he was willing to move to a permanent home on the reservation because he refused to be a "fool." At the same time he saw no reason to conform to the agent's plan for his future.

Finally, Agent Armstrong and all the other observers of the Crows noted that there was a substantial group within the tribe who adamantly opposed any change in their lifeways. Not surprisingly, Armstrong described this group as "thoroughly wild" and willing to "fight before they . . . work. . . . Nothing can satisfy them," he reported, "but to have the government provide for them always. . . ." This group included Crazy Head and Bear Wolf, two warriors in their mid-forties who each led bands of ten to fifteen families each, and an outspoken, ambitious young comrade named Spotted Horse. Spotted Horse (whom the agent sometimes referred to as "Spot") was a decade younger than the other two men and leader of a smaller band. None of these men had served significant tours as government scouts or employees and most had relied on the dwindling buffalo herds for as long as possible.

The pragmatism of some Crows seemed only to harden these men's resolve. For example, in the spring of 1882, when Armstrong began to press the younger band leaders to begin farming, Spotted Horse apparently had told him he would kill anyone who complied. A few weeks later, all of these "wild" bands dismantled their lodges near the agency and headed east to hunt buffalo along the Powder River.[17]

Crazy Head, Bear Wolf, Spotted Horse and a number of their allies (including a reclusive older warrior named Deaf Bull) regularly hunted along the Little Bighorn River and Armstrong often suspected them of following game (and cattle) south into Wyoming or further east to the old Sioux hunting grounds along the Powder River. Their association with the eastern edge of the reservation was so strong, in fact, that they attempted to charge white sheepmen a fee for crossing "their" valley and refused to recognize grazing permits granted by the agent, even if these permissions brought income to the tribe. Instead they insisted that the government recognize that they were the leaders of the tribe's eastern division. In 1883, one agency employee told a group of visiting senators that Spotted Horse and Crazy Head had come to the position that their bands were the sole proprietors of the Little Bighorn valley and that they would not permit a relocation of the agency. They refused to cooperate with Armstrong and were rarely mentioned in the agent's optimistic reports.[18]

Thus, groups within the tribe seem to provide evidence for several versions of their migration from the Stillwater. First, we can imagine that hungry and defeated Crows marched with Armstrong because they had no choice. They were in desperate straits and had become dependent on government subsidies. They imply a narrative of defeat. Second, loyal scouts agreed to preserve their good relations with the government by taking up farms along the Bighorn River, thereby ensuring steady incomes and retaining their positions as auxiliaries for the army post at Fort Custer. Third, ambitious young chiefs sought to make the best of what was probably an inevitable train of events. They left

---

[17] Henry Armstrong to Commissioner of Indian Affairs, May 10, 1882, June 6, 1882, and June 20, 1884, Item 3, Box 9, Armstrong to Commissioner, September 15 and 26, 1883, Item 1, Box 1, all in RCIA-FRC, Seattle. For Plenty Coups' statement, see *Senate Report 283*, 6.

[18] The description of the three "parties" among the Crows is in Armstrong to Commissioner of Indian Affairs, December 6, 1882, Item 3, Box 9, RCIA-FRC, Seattle. The report of Spotted Horse's claim is in *Senate Report 283*, 21 (testimony of George Milburn). One piece of evidence also indicates that the opponents of resettlement had discussed their complaints with the Sioux. See V. T. McGillicuddy to Commissioner of Indian Affairs, December 13, 1883, 23277, LR-OIA, RG 75, NA. For Spotted Horse's behavior during 1883 see also Henry Armstrong to Commissioner of Indian Affairs, February 26, 1885, 4791–1885, LR-OIA, RG 75, NA.

the mountains to defend the interests of their bands and their tribe. By securing their claim to every part of their eight-million-acre reserve, this third group of Crows believed they might accomplish what white westerners frequently spoke of – they could make a new start for themselves and their families. They and the settlement of scouts along the Bighorn suggest a story of pragmatism and adaptability. Finally, there were groups of Crows who refused to resettle or remain within the boundaries of their reservation. By resisting Armstrong's efforts, and condemning those who cooperated with him, they occupy the center of a tale of defiance and conflict.

An event – the resettlement of a tribe in a new setting at a new agency in an age of rapid social change – was sure to produce dramatic consequences for the Crow community, but the meaning of the event itself remains obscure. The people involved in it are not only distant in time, but they participated in a cultural tradition that was only vaguely understood by the people who recorded their words and their actions. Something happened, but its content appears neither uniform nor immediately accessible. Can one understand the event in terms that reflect rather than flatten its complexity?

III

A few days after the Crow caravan entered the Little Bighorn valley, an incident occurred that embodied the complexity of what had just taken place. "When we arrived in the valley," Henry Armstrong wrote, "we found that Spotted Horse with his band had preceded us. He did not come to our camp immediately, but sent us word that he was going to have the entire valley for himself and his band." Armstrong ignored these warnings and began to build a temporary warehouse near the road running north along the river to Fort Custer.

A few days later, the agent announced that he would distribute horses and tools to those who had made the trip from the Stillwater and that cabins would soon be built for the band leaders who had agreed to relocate near the new agency. On the day that Armstrong began to issue these supplies, however, Spotted Horse and all of the men in his band, "marched into camp in the form of a platoon of cavalry." The agent tried to ignore the young chief as he had for the previous two years, but, determined to force a confrontation, Spotted Horse stepped forward in front of the assembly and ordered the proceedings to halt. Advancing on the agent, he announced that he and Crazy Head were the owners of the entire Little Bighorn valley and that neither the agent nor the other band leaders the government called "chiefs" could remain there without his permission.[19]

[19] Henry Armstrong to Commissioner of Indian Affairs, February 26, 1885, 4701–1885, LR-OIA, RG 75, NA.

This confrontation vividly reveals the distance between the conventional narrative of a tribe "riding down a canyon into the sunset" and the events that transpired among the Crow. Rather than riding into obscurity, Armstrong's charges were engaged in a struggle over the control of their lands. Those who cooperated with him were implicitly accepting the power of the Indian Office to establish a new agency on their lands and to organize their lives around a new subsistence pattern. Those who did not asserted their prior claim to the Little Bighorn. The struggle entailed several groups of tribal members and the resident agent of the United States. Spotted Horse's declaration revealed the presence of several narratives within what Armstrong had hoped would be a simple scene.

The agent reported what happened next: "Another chief, Bull Nose, stepped in between us and putting out his left hand toward me told me not to listen to Spotted Horse, that he was crazy, and putting out his right hand toward Spot he said, 'Now you strike me if you want to.'" Sixty-five years old and a former scout, Bull Nose was both a generation older than Spotted Horse and a man with an established position in the tribe as a warrior and the head of an extended and numerous family. He had led one of the refugee bands that had travelled from the Stillwater with Armstrong and he was clearly committed to the success of the agent's program. In the face of this intervention – stated boldly by a senior warrior and backed implicitly by the soldiers at Fort Custer – Spotted Horse withdrew and the distribution of supplies continued.[20]

The confontation between Armstrong, Spotted Horse and Bull Nose reveals issues in the relocation of the Crow agency that have little to do with westward migrations, anthropological theories or government dreams about the "civilization" of the tribe. An aggressive young Crow leader, speaking for a group of bands that previously had lived and hunted in the Little Bighorn valley, asserted that their claims to ownership and authority preceded the rights of the U.S. government and the authority of the assembled tribal "chiefs." In the face of this, another Crow leader came forward and identified himself with both the agent and the tribe's need for food and a new home. Playing the role of Armstrong's protector, Bull Nose asserted his own claim to influence and defended the authority of headmen like himself who supported the idea of cooperation with the government.

While the entire Crow tribe eventually settled on its Montana reservation and thus shared the consequences of the white man's growing presence on the northern plains, there was considerable variation in the way individuals behaved during the events that marked the American advance into their homeland. This variation, together with the tensions revealed in the confrontation

---

[20] Ibid. Interestingly, when the distribution went forward Spotted Horse and two other family heads in his band received cabins from the government.

of Spotted Horse and Bull Nose, indicate that external events affected, but did not eliminate, an ongoing struggle over community leadership. The group's passage out of the mountains and into the valley of the Little Bighorn had also brought a number of difficult issues forward for consideration. Who were the Crows? Were they hunters, warriors, farmers, ranchers or all four? Was their community distinct? Could there be a Crow community in the new, reservation environment? If so, who would be this new community's leaders? And how could both leaders and followers identify themselves in a setting where they would soon be outnumbered by powerful outsiders? In short, what was their future as a people in this new land?

The story of the Crow Indians' struggle to answer these questions encompasses both the dreams of Henry Armstrong and the confrontation between Bull Nose and Spotted Horse. It requires us to examine both the internal workings of this distinctive, tribal community and the external conditions that shaped and oppressed it. Like the story of the 1884 agency relocation, an exploration of the tribe's history in the late nineteenth and early twentieth centuries launches us into an inquiry that rejects stereotypical conceptions of "Indians" and "whites" and opens issues that are at the heart of both modern Crow and modern American social history. For like the Europeans and Asians who travelled to North America throughout the nineteenth century, these Montana migrants came to realize that the modern world brought with it both coercion and opportunity. The future would pose new problems of subsistence, leadership and community definition, while intensifying the familiar quest for a stable community leadership and a coherent cultural identity that both honored the past and served the future. And through it all, the Crows, like other twentieth-century Americans, would be forced to inhabit an environment imbued with an ideology of industrial progress that both shaped their experience and distorted their history.

What set the Crows and other Indian people apart, of course, was that they were already undeniably Americans. As other powerful residents of the United States attempted to mold them into an alien model of citizenship, the Crows resisted with an integrity few could deny. The ensuing struggle over what kind of Americans these hunting bands would become was therefore a contest − played out in one tiny location − over the nature of their social life in the century to come. To the extent that this struggle produced new ways of organizing their lives and presenting themselves to outsiders, it resonates with, and perhaps prefigures, similar battles waged elsewhere among widely different groups in every corner of the continent.

As for the Crows, one cannot understand the meaning of their migration if it is viewed solely in terms of how successfully the tribe matched or resisted the rigid expectations of outsiders. For as the confrontation of Spotted Horse and Bull Nose reveals, even an apparently defeated and suffering community could avoid descent into passive self-doubt. It is therefore necessary to explore the way the actions we can observe in 1884 grew out of the community's distinctive experience, as well as to investigate how these "Crow" events fit into the larger story of a North American Indian tribe's transition to the modern age.

The anthropologist Marshall Sahlins has written that culture is "a gamble played with nature."[21] For the Crows, as well as for other Americans, this has frequently been true. The tribe's migration from the foothills of the Beartooth range to the banks of the Little Bighorn River was instigated by events and people the group could not predict or control: the ambition of white politicians, the technology of the railroad, the dreams of non-Indian settlers and the fantasies of a strong-willed government agent. Nevertheless, none of these forces could determine the Crow reaction to the event: some leaders were willing to relocate, others were not, still others had mixed feelings. New, unpredictable conditions channeled but did not create ideas, rivalries and tensions within the tribe. The interplay of the events produced by these conditions with the community's ongoing traditions defined the group's history and created the modern version of its culture.

The creation of the modern Crow Reservation, which was initiated by the movement of the agency headquarters from the Stillwater valley to the Little Bighorn, marked a dramatic acceleration of the tribe's transition to modern self-consciousness. New conditions forced members of the group to confront unprecedented problems of leadership, social organization, religious belief and economic subsistence. Wrestling with these problems while maintaining a coherent Crow community produced new definitions of both the tribe and its relationship to the outside world. Managing internal tensions while adapting to externally generated events, Crow people came to a new sense of themselves, their institutions and their traditions. This "gamble with nature" produced the modern Crow nation just as, in a larger and more complex way, it produced the modern American nation as well. The story of how this occurred is the subject of this book.

But before the narrative can go forward, it must stop and move back.

---

[21] Marshall Sahlins, *Islands of History* (Chicago: University of Chicago Press, 1985), ix.

2

Parading into history

They are excellent marksmen with bow and arrow, but poor shots with the gun, but they practice dayly as of late years they have more ammunition than usual. They have never had any traders with them, the[y] get their kettles guns, ammunitions &c from the Mandans and Big Bellys' in exchange for horses, robes, leggins & shirts, they likewise purchase corn pumpkins and tobacco from the Big Bellys' as they do not cultivate the ground themselves.

François Antoine Larocque, 1805[1]

I

On June 25, 1805, at about one o'clock in the afternoon, the Crow Indians paraded into written history. Some 654 men, wearing brightly decorated buckskin clothing, carrying painted rawhide shields, and sitting astride their prize ponies, filed solemnly through three Hidatsa and Mandan villages that hugged the south shore of the Knife River, not far from where that muddy stream once flowed into the Missouri River. The villages sat in the middle of the northern Great Plains at a point about midway between the North Dakota Badlands and the site of that state's modern capital, Bismarck. The Crow warriors rode proudly among the village Indians' dome-shaped earth lodges before turning back to the elegant tipis and warm campfires the women of their tribe had set up just west of the settlements.

Even though the Crows paraded before the Hidatsas and Mandans without any special ceremony, their arrival caused a sensation. The Hidatsas craned their necks to catch a better sight of the visitors' elegant costumes and to examine their magnificent ponies. Quickly, the welcoming villagers fell into step behind the Crows and followed the procession back to their tipis. Within minutes, one witness noted, "there did not remain 20 persons in the village, men, women and children all went to the newly arrived camp, carrying a quantity of Corn raw and cooked which they traded for Leggings, Robes and dried meat."[2]

---

[1] François Antoine Larocque, "Yellowstone Journal," in W. Raymond Wood and Thomas D. Thiessen, eds., *Early Fur Trade on the Northern Plains: Canadian Traders Among the Mandan and Hidatsa Indians, 1738–1818* (Norman: University of Oklahoma Press, 1985), 215. Remarkably, despite his Quebec origins, Larocque kept his journal in English.
[2] Ibid., 170. On Crow tipis, see Walter Stanley Campbell, "The Tipis of the Crow Indians," *American Anthropologist*, n.s. 29 (1927), 87–104.

A Crow warrior drawn by George Catlin near the Hidatsa villages during the artist's trip up the Missouri River in the summer of 1832. Catlin wrote at the time that "no part of the human race could present a more picturesque and thrilling appearance on horseback than a party of Crows rigged out in all their plumes and trappings – galloping about and yelping, in what they call a war-parade. . . ." Courtesy of The Newberry Library.

The witness who recorded the Crow entry into the Missouri River villages was a well-educated French Canadian fur trader named François Antoine Larocque. Son of a merchant family from the outskirts of Montreal (and later, one of the founders of the Bank of Montreal), Larocque observed the excitement of the Crow parade with considerable envy. The young man had recently arrived from his post at Fort Montagne a la Bosse on the Assiniboin River in what is now southern Saskatchewan, and he was making a second, frustrating journey to the Missouri. Larocque was looking for business for the British Northwest Company. His first trip had taken place seven months earlier, during the winter of 1804–5, when he had ventured into what appeared to be a relatively unexploited area in search of new sources of pelts and stronger ties between the Missouri River tribes and his company's traders. He had hoped to create the kind of excitement that surrounded the Crow procession.

Instead he had found indifference and competition. On his arrival in November 1804, Larocque discovered that rival Hudson's Bay Company agents were already established among the Missouri River villages, and that the local villagers were preoccupied with another set of visitors who had recently arrived from the south. When the Canadian sought out Toussaint Charbonneau, a free trader whom he hoped would serve the Northwest Company as interpreter, emmisary and aide, he was told the Frenchman was "with some Americans, below the Mandan villages." The "Americans" turned out to be Meriwether Lewis and William Clark, who were attracting a great deal of attention as they settled in for the winter at their newly constructed fort about ten miles downsteam. The men from Washington, D.C., appeared to have beaten the Canadian to the punch. Undaunted, Larocque, who spoke fluent English, sought out the American expedition and asked for permission to accompany them on their westward journey. Lewis and Clark were friendly but firm. They fed Larocque, gave Charbonneau permission to work for him (temporarily) – they even fixed his broken compass – but they would not take him upriver. They reminded the ambitious young trader-to-be that he was operating within the boundaries of the United States and that his business fell within an area of American jurisdiction. Larocque observed dryly that the young officers had "a very grand plan." In February 1805, while the Americans prepared to embark for the falls of the Missouri (guided there by Charbonneau and his wife, Sacajawea), the disappointed trader retreated north to the Assiniboin River. He had little to show for his journey.[3]

When Larocque returned to the Missouri in June, he had a new plan. In eastern North America the Europeans had penetrated the native trade network by erecting trading posts and market towns at strategic locations between rival groups or at the edges of a large resource area. Thus, Albany, Montreal and New Orleans became gathering grounds for native traders and villages at Green Bay, Mackinac, La Pointe and Kaskaskia funneled furs and trade goods back and forth across a vast and permeable frontier. No doubt part of Larocque's initial hopes had ridden on the fact that the Knife River villages were ideally placed to capture the trade of the Great Plains. A man of his imagination could foresee that the networks emanating from the Missouri villages could be extended

[3] Larocque recorded the Crow parade at the Big Hidatsa village site, near the confluence of the Knife River and the Missouri, about fifty miles upriver from the site of modern-day Bismarck, North Dakota. For the background to the Larocque expedition, see Edwin C. Bearss, *Bighorn Canyon National Recreation Area*, Montana-Wyoming, History Basic Data, Vol. 1 (Washington, D.C.: Office of History and Historic Architecture, Eastern Service Center, February 1970), 28–29. The motives for Larocque's journey are also described in Wood and Thiessen, *Early Fur Trade*, 18–32. The passage describing Larocque's arrival in November 1804 and his meetings with Lewis and Clark are in his "Missouri Journal," in Wood and Thiessen, *Early Fur Trade*, 136–140, and 151–152. The Crow entry into the Hidatsa village is in Larocque, "Yellowstone Journal," 170. For a general introduction to this early period of trading on the Missouri River, see John C. Ewers, "The Indian Trade of the Upper Missouri Before Lewis and Clark: An Interpretation," *Bulletin of the Missouri Historical Society*, 10, 4 (July 1954), 429–446.

Lewis spent an entire day in late January repairing the fur trader's compass. Nevertheless, relations were strained between the French Canadian and the Americans. See Wood and Thiessen, *Early Fur Trade*, 140, 151–152.

westward to the Rockies and north to Saskatchewan. Now, a more subdued
Larocque reasoned that with the villages so crowded and the Americans so
fixated on the Pacific, he might be able to attach himself to another group whose
home lay closer to a source of furs. Perhaps there was a new tribe that could be
persuaded to trade exclusively with the Canadians.

Larocque began an account of this second journey to the Missouri by naming
it "a voyage of discovery to the Rocky Mountains." In June 1805, after he
arrived and greeted his former hosts, he announced that the goal of his summer
visit would not be trade, but "to smoke a pipe of peace and amity with the
Rocky Mountain Indians and to accompany them to their lands." He reasoned
that people who lived at a distance from the villages might help him tap into
new sources of fur and avoid his American rivals. People who lived near the
mysterious mountains would likely have access to hunting grounds other traders had not yet reached. The Crows, marching proudly in from the West barely
two weeks after Larocque's arrival, fit perfectly into his scheme. The young
trader fell quickly into step behind the crowds that flocked to their camp.[4]

But the Hidatsas barred his way. Unlike previous travellers who had sighted,
or inadvertantly met, members of these "Rocky Mountain Indians" as early as
1716, the merchant from Montreal had a long-term interest in the Crows. He
did not intend to make a few naive observations and return to his old haunts.
Thus, as soon as his hosts understood his interest in face to face contact, they
began to discourage him. They knew that an expansion of Larocque's network
would only come at the expense of their own. At first Larocque found the
Hidatsas were "extremely troublesome" to sell him their horses. After the
indifference of the previous winter, he was confused, but the trader soon
understood that the Hidatsas "would wish us to have no more goods when those
(Rocky Mountain) Indians arrive, so as to have the whole trade to themselves."[5]

Hidatsa hostility only redoubled the trader's resolve. He refused to purchase
anything in the Missouri villages and he told the local leaders that he would not
part with any of his goods until he had visited the Crows in their home country.
One chief quickly arose and "made a long harangue to dissuade me from going
there. . . . He gave the worst character possible to the Rocky Mountain Indians,
saying they were thieves and liars." At a later council Larocque endured a

[4] Wood and Thiessen, *Early Fur Trade*, 160, 165.
[5] See ibid., 165–166. For a discussion of possible Crow contact with Hudson Bay traders, see ibid.,
18–19. James Knight, who directed the Hudson's Bay Company activities from a post at the
mouth of the Nelson River, reported in 1715 that a group of "Mountain Indians" arrived to trade.
When they returned the following year they were accompanied by Crows. In his discussions with
the Crows, Larocque referred to a man named Menard who had previously lived with the tribe
and had apparently been ill-treated. Like most free traders, Menard was illiterate; he left no
written record of his years with the Crow. For more on Menard, see Jean Baptiste Trudeau,
"Trudeau's Description of the Upper Missouri (1796)," in A. P. Nasatir, ed., *Before Lewis and
Clark: Documents Illustrating the History of the Missouri, 1785–1804* (Lincoln: University of
Nebraska Press, 1990), Vol. 2, 381, originally published by St. Louis Historical Documents
Foundation, 1954.

second speech in which his hosts "made use of all their art to induce me not to go, representing the journey as dangerous to the last degree and [adding] that the Rocky Mountain Indians would not come." Another Canadian trader, Alexander Henry, visiting the Missouri River villages one year after Larocque, recorded a comment in his journal that might well have reflected the Montrealer's reaction to this outrageous speech. "It was disgusting," Henry wrote, "to see how those impious vagabonds . . . keep those poor inoffensive Crows in subjection, making their own price for horses and everything else." Larocque's spoken reply was simpler. He told his hosts he would make the trip "or die."[6]

On June 27, Larocque, acting on his own, invited the visiting Crow leaders to a council. When they assembled, he spread a pile of axes and knives on the ground before them and asked permission to follow the group home. In addition to offering presents, the trader acknowledged the diplomatic etiquette of the plains by offering his guests "smoke in a stem," telling them it was "that of the Chief of the White people who was desirous of making them his Children and Brethren." The Crow responded by presenting Larocque an equivalent collection of goods: buffalo robes, dressed elk skins, saddles, leggings and the pelt of a mountain lion. Next the trader took an unexpected step. As the opening protocols concluded, he turned and insulted the people he had just met. He declared that his superior in Canada "knew they were pitiful, and had no arms to defend themselves from their enemies, but that they should cease to be pityful [sic] as soon as they made themselves brave hunters." When no one stood up to denounce him for calling them "pitiful," Larocque went on to assure the Crows that if they "behaved well towards us and kill beavers, otters and bear, they would have white people on the lands in a few years who would winter with them and supply them with all their wants."[7]

Larocque's acuity and candor carried the day. The Crows accepted his invitation and the Hidatsas, realizing that the trader would indeed visit the Rockies, now presented themselves as the trader's sponsor and partner. The villagers held an extensive farewell council with the Crows, endorsed Larocque's expedition, and two days later travelled with the trader and his new hosts as the group departed, heading southwest towards the headwaters of the Heart River. Larocque spent the next three months with the Crows, sharing their camp and recording his experiences in his journal. His descriptions of tribal life and the territory he visited have all the precision of a shareholder's prospectus. The Larocque journal offers a remarkably vivid portrait of the Crows as they entered an age the Europeans called the nineteenth century.[8]

---

6 Larocque, "Yellowstone Journal," 165, 168; Elliot Coues, ed., *New Light on the History of the Greater Northwest: The Manuscript Journals of Alexander Henry and David Thompson, 1799–1814* (New York: Francis P. Harper, 1897), 399.
7 Larocque, "Yellowstone Journal," 171.
8 Wood and Thiessen, *Early Fur Trade*, 171, 172.

II

François Antoine Laroque's description begins with a scene of celebration and good fellowship at the Knife River. The Crows arrived in peace and friendship and their hosts literally ran out their front doors to greet them. The trader also noted that during his negotiations with the tribe's leaders, "the ceremony of adoption was going on," adding to the festive quality of the visit. Despite the tension over his plan to travel with the Crows, it appeared that this summer visit was a well-established part of the region's economic life. Western Indians arrived with horses, hides, dried meat and clothing which they exchanged for corn and other foodstuffs. It was also clear to Larocque that the protocol of the trade required the familial greetings he saw going on around him. (One of his Hidatsa hosts noted that "his adopted son" was a Crow chief.) But Larocque was not told that when he began his journey west on June 29, he was reenacting the group's initial journey onto the plains, a journey that began hundreds of years before his arrival.

The trader's new hosts traced their origins as a people to the village-dwelling Hidatsas, a people who had migrated westward from the Mississippi valley. According to modern archaeologists, these ancient people had leap-frogged from Lake of the Woods to Devils Lake to the James River in a series of migrations that may have begun more than a thousand years before Larocque's visit. The reasons for that original migration from the East are lost to history, but the advent of agriculture in North America at approximately the time of Christ and the development of corn cultivation which came in the centuries afterward must have played a major role. Northern Flint corn was an important motive for expansion to the upper Missouri. More resistant to drought and cold, this seed variety encouraged a transition from marginal horticulture to full-time farming and allowed the region's increasingly sophisticated agriculturalists to exploit the fertile bottom lands north along the Missouri, into territories with severe winters and relatively short growing seasons.

Even as new technologies drew communities west, they made it possible for farming people to produce surpluses and to trade those surpluses to neighbors who relied primarily on hunting or other forms of subsistence. As a consequence, Missouri River farmers over the centuries balanced their reliance on agricultural products with dried meat and hides they gathered themselves or received from the region's nomadic tribes. Farming villages like the ones along North Dakota's Knife River gradually became centers of exchange where groups would meet and supply one another with food, skins and other manufactured goods. During the period Europeans called the Middle Ages, while people in modern-day France, Germany and Italy were establishing trade networks among farmers and craftsmen in market towns, the people of the Great Plains were developing economic alliances that linked riverine farming villages to distant hunters and craftsmen. Rocky Mountain obsidian (ideal for knife blades), Knife

River flint, pipestone from modern-day Minnesota, dressed skins, dried corn, pottery vessels and a variety of bone and stone tools would change hands at festive meetings which were always punctuated by gift giving and dancing and frequently sealed with adoptions and marriages. By the time of the Columbus voyages at the end of the fifteenth century, clusters of earth lodges, each housing an extended family, stood at the center of a web of trade that radiated in all directions from their cozy perches overlooking the Missouri.[9]

In the seventeenth century, as European settlers were beginning to form communities along the Atlantic Coast of North America, villages like the one Larocque visited in 1805 began to take their modern form. The Crow's Hidatsa ancestors were joined by the forerunners of modern Mandan Indians who had worked their way gradually northward, up the Missouri River, at about the same time their new neighbors had been moving west. Their villages were characterized by clusters of spacious, dome-shaped dwellings constructed of cottonwood logs covered by layers of grass and dirt. These earth lodges housed extended family groups who shared a common central fire and slept on platforms arranged around the periphery of the building. Some were home to as many as three dozen people. The villages generally sat on a bluff and were surrounded by cornfields laid out along the floodplain below. Frequently the lodges were surrounded by pallisades made of driftwood and brush.

Families and extended clan networks organized life within these villages – from religious ceremonies that punctuated an elaborate calendar of community events, to the more spontaneous activities of warriors and hunters. Groups of relatives, usually a cluster of sisters and their husbands, shared a lodge, contributing its members to village ceremonies and joining in communal hunting and gathering. Farming was the primary responsibility of women who planted corn, beans and squash in the spring, harvested their crops in the late summer, and dried their surpluses in the fall. Men hunted individually and in large summer and fall expeditions and took primary responsibility for organizing religious and healing rituals. While villages frequently appeared to be a jumble of lodges, food drying racks and work areas, they all contained a broad, central plaza where visitors were received and where community events took place. It was through these plazas that Larocque's Crow hosts had paraded in the summer of 1805.

In the seventeeth and eighteenth centuries, the upper Missouri offered village dwellers an abundant life. Their fields yielded steady crops of corn, beans and squash, and both trade and communal forays onto the nearby plains produced

---

[9] This description is based on Preston Holder, *The Hoe and the Horse on the Plains: A Study of Cultural Development Among North American Indians* (Lincoln: University of Nebraska Press, 1970), Bison Books edition, 1974, chap. 2; Michael Gregg, *An Overview of the Preshistory of Western and Central North Dakota* (Billings, Mont.: Bureau of Land Management, Cultural Resources Series, No. 1, 1985), 4–67, and W. Raymond Wood, "Plains Trade in Prehistoric and Protohistoric Intertribal Relations," in W. Raymond Wood and Margot Liberty, eds., *Anthropology on the Plains* (Lincoln: University of Nebraska Press, 1980), 98–109.

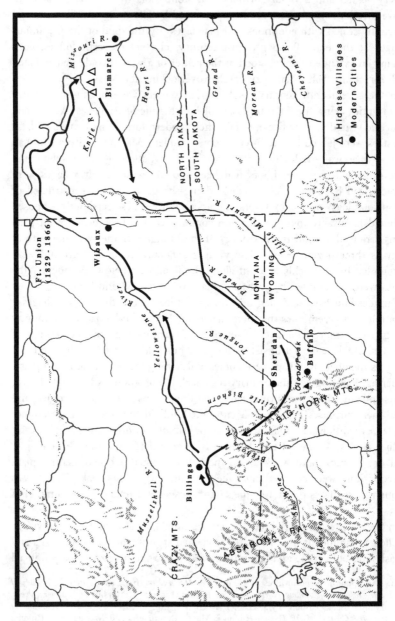

Map 2. François Antoine Larocque's route, 1805.

all the meat the hunters and their dogs would need. Despite this bounty, however, some villagers found life in regimented farming communities unattractive. For these people, the surrounding, ocean-like plains offered much more appeal. According to anthropologist Alfred Bowers, one such restless group was known as the Awatixas, relatives of the Hidatsas who arrived on the Missouri in the sixteenth century and who moved on to the plains after only a brief stay. Bowers argues that this group formed the nucleus of a new tribe, a group who lived permanently on the prairies, but who returned regularly to trade. There is a great deal of evidence to support Bowers's claim.

Archaeologists, for example, point to an abandoned village called the Hagen Site near the confluence of the Yellowstone and Missouri Rivers. Located near modern Glendive, Montana, nearly 150 miles west of the Knife River villages, the Hagen Site was occupied in the seventeenth century by a group who erected an earth lodge overlooking the Yellowstone, but who ringed that single structure with a number of smaller, temporary dwellings. While researchers have found evidence of corn agriculture at the village, deer and bison remains are so plentiful that they believe its occupants relied primarily on hunting for their livelihood. Archaeologists have been unable to establish a firm tie between the Hagen Site and the ancestors of the "Rocky Mountain Indians" who appeared before François Antoine Larocque in 1805, but both the date of the village's occupation and the fact that it sits astride the migration route identified in Crow traditions as the pathway from their ancestral homeland in North Dakota to the tribal domain along the east side of the Rocky Mountains create a powerful circumstantial case.[10]

Other late prehistoric sites in the area between the upper Missouri and the Rocky Mountains contain similar mixtures of materials that suggest occupancy in the two or three hundred years before Larocque's journey by people who combined hunting and sedentary ways of life. Most impressive of these are a series of buffalo processing areas located and analyzed by archaeologist George Frison. Frison has shown that locations near modern Buffalo and Sheridan, Wyoming (on the eastern flank of the Bighorns) were occupied in the sixteenth and seventeenth centuries by people who used a type of pottery similar to that found in farming communities along the Missouri. In addition, the sites contained evidence of large gatherings of individuals who used massive cooking pits to remove marrow from animal bones as well as to tan hides. These materials suggest summer gatherings by hunting bands who were probably moving onto the plains in small groups, but coming together for large-group activities much as they had done when they had been farmers. It is likely, then,

---

[10] William T. Mulloy, *The Hagen Site, University of Montana Publications in Social Science, 1.* Peter Nabokov summarizes the literature on this early transitional phase of Crow history in "Cultivating Themselves: The Inter-play of Crow Indian Religion and History" (Ph.D. Dissertation, University of California, Berkeley, 1988), chap. 3. See also Gregg, *An Overview*, 31–48.

that Bowers's Awatixas (or some other group of farming people) were moving west toward the Bighorn mountains in the sixteenth and seventeenth
centuries.[11]

Crow oral tradition also confirms that Larocque's journey west from the
Knife River repeated an earlier pattern. A number of stories recorded in the
twentieth century explain that the tribe separated from the Hidatsas after a
group of villagers refused to share meat from a buffalo that wandered into
camp. They note that the soon-to-be Crows lived in a separate section of the
Hidatsa farming village and that they were offended by their kinsmen's selfish-
ness. In one version a wife comes home to tell her husband, "These people
brought some meat . . . (and) they have not given me any." After some discussion a neighbor says, "I do not like those people. Let us move camp without
them." The group then packs up and moves out onto the plains.[12]

The rituals associated with the Crow Tobacco Society underscore the message of these stories. These rituals require the members of a voluntary organization to carry out a dramatic reenactment of the tribe's separation from the
Hidatsas and its procession onto the plains. The Tobacco Society's members
believe that the ritual planting and harvesting of *Nicotiana multivalvis*, a rare
variety of tobacco, fulfills the vision of No Vitals, an ancient leader who received
the seeds for the original plant from a spiritual guardian. The gift came to the
Crows at the Missouri River and was carried by the first migrants onto the
plains as a sign of divine guidance and protection. Each year the society adopted
new members into its ranks through a series of ceremonies leading to a spring
or summer festival highlighted by a solemn procession from a ceremonial lodge
to an adoption lodge containing an altar-like replica of a tobacco garden. In the
words of anthropologist Peter Nabokov, this procession "reenacts the hegira of
the proto-Crow." Taken together, he adds, "Tobacco society ritualism is a
unified dramatization of Crow historical origins and territorial claims."[13]

---

[11] George Frison, "Archaeological Evidence of the Crow Indians in Northern Wyoming: A Study
of a Late Prehistoric Buffalo Economy" (Ph.D. Dissertation, University of Michigan, 1967). See
esp., 16–35, 40–60, 175–181.

[12] Robert H. Lowie, *Myths and Traditions of the Crow Indians*, Bison Book Edition (Lincoln:
University of Nebraska Press, 1993), 272, 273, originally published by American Museum of
Natural History, 1918. See also Robert H. Lowie, *Crow Texts* (Berkeley: University of California
Press, 1960), 423–432.

The Crow–Hidatsa separation has generated considerable discussion. The major elements of
the debate are contained in W. Raymond Wood and Alan S. Downer, "Notes on the Crow–
Hidatsa Schism," in W. R. Wood, ed., *Trends in Middle Missouri Prehistory: A Festschrift Honoring the Contributions of Donald Lehmer*, Memoir 13, *Plains Anthropologist*, 22, 78, part 2 (1977),
83–100, and "Symposium on the Crow–Hidatsa Separation," *Archaeology in Montana*, 20, 3
(September–December, 1979), 1–126.

[13] Peter Nabokov, "Cultivating Themselves: The Inter-play of Crow Indian Religion and History"
(Ph.D. Dissertation, University of California, Berkeley, 1988), 320, 395. This brief reference does
not do justice to Nabokov's vast, complex discussion of Tobacco Society ritualism and its meaning
for Crow people. For a brief overview of the Tobacco Society, see Robert H. Lowie, *The Crow
Indians* (Lincoln: University of Nebraska Press, 1983), 274–296, originally published in 1935.

As significant as the theme of migration is, however, Crow literature also describes a tradition of friendship and intercourse that emerged once the separation of Larocque's new hosts and the Hidatsas was complete. In one tale, a group of Hidatsas steal up on what they thought was an enemy camp only to hear their own language being spoken within its tipis. They entered the village calling out, "My dear friends," and the Crows replied, "They are our relatives, let them come." The story ends: "Thus they found each other. From that time until today they have regarded each other as relatives. In the summer and winter the Crow would pack their horses, go to the Hidatsa and bring corn."[14]

As Larocque and his colleagues watched the cottonwoods along the Missouri River disappear behind them, they entered a rolling sea of grass and sagebrush it would take weeks to cross. Alone on the trail, their hosts began to talk more openly about themselves. They explained, for example, that the Crows consisted of "about 2,400 persons dwelling in 300 tents," but that prior to the arrival of a strange illness, "they counted 2,000 lodges . . . in their camp when all together." According to Larocque's informants the disease (probably smallpox) "raged among them for many years successively and as late as three years ago." His group of less than 700 thus represented about a third of the entire membership.[15]

While his hosts did not (or perhaps could not) describe the size and location of other Crow bands in detail, it is apparent from Larocque's journal that the entire tribe was probably composed of two other similarly sized subgroups and that there was enough interaction among these three divisions to spread diseases and information. Evidence gathered later in the nineteenth century suggests that the trader was travelling with a group of Mountain Crows, the largest of the three divisions, whose annual migrations were centered in the Yellowstone valley. Larocque did not encounter the Kicked In The Bellies, a subgroup of the Mountain Crows who had left the main body a generation or two before the trader's arrival and who spent the bulk of the year near the Shoshone River on the south side of the Bighorn range. The trader also missed the River Crows, a band which spent virtually all of its time north of the Yellowstone River.

While many early visitors like Larocque tended to assume that the "Rocky Mountain Indians" travelled regularly through the Bighorns and up to the headwaters of the Yellowstone, later arrivals learned that the third major subdivision of the tribe lived almost entirely alongside the vast buffalo herds who

[14] Lowie, *Myths and Traditions of the Crow Indians*, 273, 274.
[15] Larocque, "Yellowstone Journal," 206. Raymond Wood, building on the work of archaeologist Donald J. Lehmer, reports that the first smallpox epidemic to hit the Missouri River settlements came in 1781. Wood also notes that an earlier epidemic may have reached the area in 1751. Wood and Lehmer also argue that epidemic diseases killed as many as two-thirds of the people who lived in these villages and caused the Mandans to move their villages north from the site of modern-day Bismarck to the area near the Hidatsa settlements at the Knife River. See Wood and Thiessen, *Early Fur Trade*, 6.

roamed the banks of the upper Missouri. This division spoke the same language as the fur trader's hosts, but they ranged far to the north of their kinsmen
and developed close ties to Gros Ventres and other groups who lived on the
prairies near the 49th parallel. Subsequent archaeological research has confirmed this fact, with some modern scholars even suggesting that the river
group separated independently from the mountain bands. Based on the analysis
of data from both the Missouri River sites and hunting sites in modern-day
Wyoming and Montana, these scholars believe that the River Crows were
descendants of a second wave of disaffected Hidatsa farmers who migrated onto
the plains and took up hunting on a full-time basis about 1700, two hundred
years after the first group of Awatixas had left the Missouri River villages for
the Bighorns.[16]

In the early days of the summer Larocque also observed some of the more
superficial results of the tribe's indirect contact with Europeans. Most obvious
to any observer of the tribe's magnificent costumes and grand public style, was
the horse. While certainly established on the plains prior to the arrival of
horses, the Crows had benefitted greatly from their presence. The Spanish,
who used horses to assist their conquest of Mexico and Peru, had brought the
animals into the Rio Grande valley when they forced their way into the region
in 1540. A permanent Spanish colony was established there in 1598 and the
local horse herds began to grow. The authorities were careful not to allow these
mounts to be distributed, however, for they would naturally convey a military
advantage to their subjects. Nevertheless, the Pueblo tribes resisted the Spanish
presence and finally rose up in a coordinated revolt in 1680. While the priests
and settlers who survived the uprising retreated south, the Pueblo peoples and
their allies quickly seized the horses that were left behind. Within a generation,
descendants of these animals were carrying Crow hunters amidst the herds of
buffalo that blackened the plains of eastern Montana.

Larocque saw immediately that the Crows were "very fond" of their horses.
"Everybody rides," he reported, "men, women and children. The females ride
astride as the men do. A child that is too young to keep [in] his saddle is tied
to it . . . he . . . gallops or trots the whole day if occasion requires." Later visitors learned that the tribe had first acquired its mounts from the Comanches, a
group that ranged the territory between the Rio Grande valley and the plains of
southern Colorado. In addition to dramatically raising their food production,
these new acquisitions were also valuable as trade items, sometimes being
offered in lots of one hundred or more for equal numbers of guns. Larocque
discovered their price when he purchased a new mount by giving its owner a
gun, 200 musket balls, some knives and other clothing. He also learned that

[16] The Bowers interpretation is ably summarized in Nabokov, "Cultivating Themselves," 78–79.
See also Gregg, *An Overview*, 43–46; and an excellent series of articles edited by Leslie B. Davis
in *Archaeology in Montana* 20, 3 (September–December 1979).

favorite horses could not be had at all: "No price will induce a man to part with a favorite horse on whom he places confidence for security either in attack or flight."[17]

By the end of their third week on the trail, Larocque and the Crows had passed near the spot where the future border between North and South Dakota would intersect the eastern boundary of Montana. Passing over prairies that less than a century later would be covered with Texas longhorns, heading up the trail to the railroad depots that would be constructed at modern Wibaux and Miles City, the trader and his hosts began to see "plenty of buffaloes" and evidence of beaver in most of the creeks and streams. On July 27 they struck the Powder River and began to move upstream along its banks. With elk and beaver readily at hand, the journey fell into a lazy routine. The trader hunted buffalo with his hosts and admired the countryside, even as he kept his official duties in mind. At one point he assembled the camp and "dressed" two beaver "to show them how to do it." He reported a few days later that his hosts were now "felling" the animals on their own and that "the women were busily employed in dressing and drying the skins." As August began Larocque's journal was filling up with descriptions of camp life.[18]

The trader understood that he was part of a hunting band made up of several dozen lodges or households. He was assigned to one family that gave him space in their tipi and fed him at mealtime, and he fell under the jurisdiction of the camp chief. He had joined a consensual, kinship society in which membership was defined by family and authority derived from one's standing in the community rather than from externally imposed, written rules. A half-century after Larocque's adventure, the pioneer anthropologist Lewis Henry Morgan explained this social environment in a journal he kept of his own expedition up the Missouri. After interviewing Indians and fur traders in the summer of 1862, Morgan reported that the Crows were divided into "tribes" whose members were forbidden from marrying each other. These subgroups – which Morgan's successors would call clans – were defined maternally. Children belonged to their mother's clan. "An interesting fact," the amateur scholar noted, "because it is followed out by all of its logical consequences. The son does not follow his father as chief. It descends in the tribe and is bestowed in reward of merit." By definition, then, bands such as the one Larocque accompanied contained more than one extended clan group (since husbands would belong to different clans than their wives), and groups like his would meet periodically with others so

---

[17] Larocque, "Yellowstone Journal," 213, 183. For Crow participation in horse trading, see Ewers, "Indian Trade of the Upper Missouri," 439. The story of acquiring the first horses from the Comanches comes from Leslie A. White, ed., *Lewis Henry Morgan: The Indian Journals, 1859–1862* (Ann Arbor: University of Michigan Press, 1959), 197. The Morgan journals also indicate that the horse's forage requirements pressed the Crows to complete their conquest of the Yellowstone from the retreating Shoshones.

[18] Larocque, "Yellowstone Journal," 175, 177, 178.

young people could seek out new partners and clan relations could gather together.[19]

While belonging to their mother's clan, Crow children were also obligated to their father and his kin. The Crow term for clan, *ashammaleaxia*, translates "as driftwood lodges," referring to the way logs intertwine and bundle together along the rivers of the northern plains. One's siblings and maternal relations were conceived of as a group that could be called on for economic aid, political support or social endorsement. Alternatively, the term for paternal relation is *aassahke*, often translated as "respected clan aunts and uncles." The relationship with one's father's clan appears to have been more reverential, with children offering their fathers and his clan relations obedience and honor, expecting respect and encouragement in return. In addition, this entire universe of kin relations was modified by the age of one's relatives; older individuals generally receiving greater deference, while younger people often played the role of companions and critics. Finally, because clan relationships were pervasive in Crow society, individuals acquired new obligations and associations as they married, made friends and participated in tribal activities. As the anthropologist Robert Lowie wrote in describing one nineteenth-century leader, he had "fairly specific relations with a very large proportion of his tribesmen."[20]

Larocque, having begun the summer with scenes of adoption along the Missouri River, and having travelled and lived in a lodge with an individual (unnamed) family, appreciated intuitively the significance of kin ties to the Crows. Lewis Henry Morgan, interested in recording tribal customs rather than acquiring new trading partners, was more explicit. He noted, for example, that within a family children received their name from their father's kinsmen rather than from their immediate parents. A senior relative of the father would place aromatic roots on a fire and, taking the child, "announces the name which he gives the child. He raises him up gently in the rising smoke towards heaven and invokes the Great Spirit to give him many days with success in war, in horse stealing, and a happy life." Other significant moments were celebrated in a similar fashion. Relatives would lead the praise for a successful warrior or hunter, mourn most prominently at funeral services for the dead and even offer unmarried sisters as substitutes to a brother-in-law to replace a fallen spouse. Morgan reported that one of his informants, a Scotsman who had lived with the tribe for nearly forty years, had told him that "in their domestic relations the Crows are our superiors. They are kind, respectful, obliging, sociable, and generous, and live together in harmony."[21]

[19] Ibid., 182; Morgan, *The Indian Journals*, 168.
[20] Robert H. Lowie, *Social Organization* (New York: Rinehart, 1948), 358. For discussions of clan relationships, see Rodney Frey, *The World of the Crow Indians* (Norman: University of Oklahoma Press, 1987), 3–4, 44–46; and Lowie, *The Crow Indians*, 8–12, 18–20.
[21] See Morgan, *Indian Journals*, 169, 170, 172. Morgan approved the fur trader's statement but added, "But the men are allowed to beat their wives, and the women do not dislike polygamy."

On August 4, standing at a spot just east of modern Sheridan, Wyoming, François Antoine Larocque caught his first glimpse of the Rockies. As he and his hosts skirted the eastern flank of the Bighorn Mountains and began the slow descent into the Yellowstone valley, other Crows began to appear in camp and the trader began to witness some of the tensions in tribal society. Amidst his notes of beaver habitats in the streams he passed, was the observation on August 19 that "since we are close to the mountain many women have deserted with their lovers to their fine tents that are across the mountains." The trader's comment underscores for modern readers the extent to which women in a matrilineal society were remarkably independent. Because couples often began their marriages in the lodges of the woman's parents, and because their children belonged to the woman's clan, husbands were not essential to social stability. Men provided the family with meat, but because its distribution, preservation, and storage were the responsibility of their wives and in-law women, it was not surprising that females were generally considered to be the owners of the larder. In addition, women owned the tipi itself and most of its contents. Asserting one's independence, then, was something women could do without necessarily endangering themselves or their livelihood. And Larocque's experience suggested that women asserted that independence frequently. The trader observed upon his return to Canada, for example, that "jealousy seems to be their predominant passion."[22]

Larocque's journal contains almost no mention of daily activities shared by men and women. Most household duties were gender specific. On their way to the Bighorns, for example, the trader had noted that groups of Crow men rode forward to kill elk and buffalo. They were followed swiftly by women "dressing and drying the skins." Women made leggings and dried meat, while men guarded the camp and scouted the surrounding country for enemies. "Women do most of the work," Larocque observed, "but as they are not so wretchedly situated as those nations who live in forests, the women . . . are more at ease." It was not cooperative men who provided their comfort, however, but bountiful surroundings and the ever-present horse: "The women are indebted solely to their having horses for the ease they enjoy more than their neighbors."[23]

The departure of several women for their lovers' tipis across the Bighorns (possibly to join a village of Kicked In The Bellies who typically lived south of the mountains) inflamed more than jealousy. Because there were no explicit sanctions against such behavior, the band's male leaders could not decide how to respond. Larocque reported that Spotted Crow, the chief "who regulates our movements," had ordered the entire band to pursue the women. Other leaders,

---

[22] Larocque, "Yellowstone Journal," 208. For an overview of Crow women's experience in this period, see Martha Harroun Foster, "Of Baggage and Bondage: Gender and Status Among Hidatsa and Crow Women," *American Indian Culture and Research Journal*, 17, 2 (1993), 121–152.

[23] Larocque, "Yellowstone Journal," 178, 209.

unconcerned by the defection, disagreed. Larocque wrote that "the chiefs of the other bands are for following our old course" toward the Yellowstone. The trader understood that the camp's senior leader had complete authority over the group's movements, as he and his companions had been prevented from leaving on a hunt a few weeks earlier by "a party of their soldiers" who feared their wanderings would disturb a nearby buffalo herd. The incident also impressed the trader with the power of the all-male soldier societies – groups of warriors who fought and hunted together and wore common regalia and were appointed by the village chiefs to police and protect the camp. The trader had been told that a camp chief was selected by a group of men who had gained prestige in battle and the hunt and that his orders were swiftly enforced by the soldiers. Larocque had assimilated all of this information, but he had not before witnessed a public conflict among the chiefs.[24]

After three days of desultory movement reflecting obvious indecision within the group, Laroque was called to witness a council of the unhappy camp chiefs. There, he reported, "Spotted Crow resigned his employment of regulating our marches, [and] another old man took the office upon himself." The new chief told the trader that "he intended to pursue their old course to the River aux Roches Jaune [Yellowstone]." The next day the camp was underway again, and by evening they were settled on the banks of what was probably Lodge Grass Creek, a tributary of the Little Bighorn. The line of movement was now deliberate and clear; the group moved a short way down the Little Bighorn and then struck west across the low buttes and dry tablelands that stood between them and the Bighorn River. Larocque reported no dissension or recrimination following the change of command. After all, Spotted Crow was a chief, *bats é* (literally: good man), a term that denotes social standing rather than formal office; to sulk or scheme for revenge would diminish his standing within the community. His resignation illustrated perfectly the words of the great scholar of the Crows, anthropologist Robert Lowie, who noted that a camp chief "was neither a ruler nor a judge and in general had no power over life and death."[25]

Two days after Spotted Crow's fall the Crows demonstrated to Larocque how little the recent leadership dispute had affected their sense of solidarity. One of the young soldiers who guarded the camp reported that three unidentified Indians had been sighted nearby. Thirty men – probably other members of the guard's soldier society who shared the responsibility of protecting the main group – saddled their ponies and disappeared towards the Bighorn. Within a few hours they returned to report an enemy war party. "In less time than the courier could well tell his news," Larocque noted, "no one remained in the

[24] Ibid., 171, 184.
[25] Ibid., 185; Lowie, *The Crow Indians*, 5.

camp but a few old men and women." The trader followed the pursuers and witnessed a remarkable scene. As scouts in the distance signaled the direction of the enemies' flight with their robes, members of the chief's council "harangued" the band and ranks of warriors formed, wearing their "best cloths," followed immediately "by their wives who carried their arms." When the speeches were over "everyone set off the way he liked best, and pursued according to his own judgement."[26]

Before long, two warriors, later identified as Assiniboins, were surrounded and killed. By the time Larocque arrived on the scene the intruders had already been scalped. As the band gathered around the bodies, it shifted its attention from combat to celebration. "Everyone was desirous of stabbing the bodies to show what he would have done had he met them alive," the French-Canadian noted. "In a short time the remains of a human body was hardly distinguishable, every young man had a piece of flesh tied to his gun or lance with which he rode off to the camp." The victors danced all night, "and the scalp carried in procession throughout the day." Two days later the festivities continued, despite the fact that the band was now moving itself closer to the Bighorn River: "The young men paraded all day with the scalps tied to their horses' bridles, singing and keeping time with the Drum and . . . rattle." Three days later Larocque reported that the celebration continued: "The singing and dancing of the scalps prevented any sleep being had."[27]

The capture of the Assiniboin warriors brought two facts about warfare home to the young trader. First, he saw that the Crows were acutely aware of threats posed by hostile neighbors. The epidemics that had killed perhaps as many as 14,000 Crows in the late eighteenth century had dramatically altered the power balance in the region. All across the plains, groups were in motion as weakened tribes sought out new allies and those who had eluded the invisible killer pursued territorial ambitions at the expense of their decimated neighbors. In the northern area, for example, relative newcomers such as the Lakota, who were retreating from the better-armed Ojibwes who had driven them out of the western Great Lakes region, had largely escaped the ravages of epidemic disease. New to the region, but considerably larger than many of the decimated neighbors, these western Sioux began to harass farming villages that were anchored to river courses and to sweep across the rich hunting grounds of the Tongue, Powder and North Platte River valleys. At the same time, nervous Blackfeet, Assiniboin and Crow war parties sought to expand their own spheres of influence by pushing the last of the Shoshones (whom Larocque referred to as "Snakes") out of modern-day Montana and engaging each other in running

[26] Larocque, "Yellowstone Journal," 186.
[27] Ibid., 186–187.

battles over access to the buffalo along the Yellowstone and upper Missouri. The decade prior to Larocque's arrival was, in the words of one modern scholar, a time of "profound transition" for all of the groups in the area.[28]

Second, the excitement generated within the Crow camp by the alarm and the exuberant celebration following the death of the two enemy warriors offered Larocque compelling evidence of how important warfare was in the lives of his hosts. Almost constantly in motion, and surrounded by neighbors who were as uncertain of their future as the Crows were of their own, the trader's new partners could not rely on rigid religious and political hierarchies like those that governed the pallisaded villages along the Missouri River. Hunters like the Crows could prosper only by being flexible, mobile and opportunistic. They could not rely upon written laws or a fixed order of priests and generals, because their situation was both precarious and unprecedented. Groups like the Crows therefore valued military leaders whose bravery was unquestioned and whose exploits would stir and mobilize community support. Flamboyant, even reckless young men embodied the community's fears as well as its dreams, for the men and women who mutilated the two Assiniboin raiders and paraded for days with bits of scalp on their bows revealed both an obsession with security and a tireless devotion to martial glory. The tribesmen who followed them reinforced the warriors' standing and endorsed their values. "None can become chiefs," Lewis Henry Morgan wrote, "unless he has first distinguished himself in war . . . Merit is the source of office."[29]

It is possible that one of the young men who joined in the excitement Larocque witnessed was a Crow warrior remembered by his descendants as Long Hair or Red Plume. His career illustrates how important flamboyance and military vision were in the first moments of the tribe's recorded history. According to Little Face, an elderly Crow chief who recounted the warrior's exploits to an army officer in the 1870s, Red Plume was supremely self-confident. As a boy he had predicted he would be a great warrior even though he had accomplished nothing. Skeptical fellow tribesmen called the outspoken youth "Fool-boy," but he ignored them and travelled frequently to the mountains to pray to the Great Spirit for guidance and assistance. According to Little Face, people continued to taunt the boy until he announced that he would go to war, adding that "when I return I shall return successful and bring something back to prove to you who laugh at me that my medicine is strong."

Once Fool-boy returned in triumph, the narrator noted, "Great was the

---

[28] Anthony McGinnis, *Counting Coups and Cutting Horses: Intertribal Warfare on the Northern Plains* (Evergreen, Colo.: Cordillera, 1990), 10. As one demonstration of the extent of this arena of conflict, one French trader in modern South Dakota, more than 500 miles from the Yellowstone, noted in 1795 that he had recently encountered a group of Arikaras carrying "the scalp of a man of the Crow nation. . . ." "Journal of Truteau on the Missouri River, 1794–5," in Nasatir, *Before Lewis and Clark*, 295.

[29] Morgan, *Indian Journals*, 168.

The Swiss artist Karl Bodmer captured a group of Crow warriors in this pencil sketch he made in 1833. Bodmer, who accompanied the German naturalist Prince Maximilian on his expedition up the Missouri River, encountered the Crows at the Mandan villages near modern Bismarck, North Dakota. Courtesy of The Newberry Library.

wonder in the village . . . and while people were speaking his praises [a] sign appeared which the Great Spirit had promised him." His hair, which had previouly been thin and short, began to grow. The young warrior adopted a new name, refused to cut his hair (even after it touched the ground.), and "many young warriors flocked to join him. . . . From this time forward," Little Face concluded, "Long Hair was foremost in war and never failed to triumph over his enemies. His expeditions were beyond number and such a warrior was never seen among the Crows before."[30]

Seeking help from guardian spirits was a well-established theme in Crow folklore long before Larocque visited the tribe. Traditional Crow stories are filled with spiritual actors who shape events and the plains environment, and elders frequently reminded their listeners that the tribe's migration onto the plains was assisted by visionaries such as No Vitals, the recipient of the first tobacco seeds, and his spiritual guardians. "It is customary," one fur trader wrote in 1834, "for every tribe . . . to have some instrument or article to pay homage to and invoke, but no nation . . . are so devoutly devoted to their talismans as the Crow nation – it is their life – their very existence." Not surprisingly, when the fur trader, a young adventurer named Zenas Leonard, met Long Hair that same year he noted that the chief "uses every precaution to preserve his hair . . . he worships it as the director or guide of his fate through life – never rising or laying down without humbly and devoutly adoring this talisman. . . ."[31]

Red Plume's exploits would have been difficult to duplicate in earlier periods of the group's history. Coming of age at the turn of the nineteenth century, Fool-boy/Long Hair vaulted to prominence by protecting his kinsmen from their proliferating ranks of enemies and demonstrating his mastery of the recently acquired horse and gun. Bolstered by divine support, he was just the kind of success to whom people in a dangerous and fluid world would flock; once he had succeeded, it didn't matter that people once thought him a fool. And even though his success had come on the battlefield, he had become an influential person whose prestige might affect other arenas of tribal life.

By the end of the last week of August, the victory celebrations had diminished

[30] "Story of Long Hair as Told by Little Face, Bradley Manuscriopt – Book F," *Contributions to the Historical Society of Montana*, 8 (1917), 224–225. For more on Long Hair/Red Plume, see Joseph Medicine Crow, "Bits of Information on Chief Long Hair," an unpublished manuscript held as part of the Plenty Coups Papers, Plenty Coups Museum, Pryor, Mont. A modern physician has examined what is purported to the Red Plume's hair and concluded that the chief glued lengths of hair together to achieve his dramatic appearance. See Edward F. Corson, "A Final Note About 'Long Hair,'" *Archives of Dermatology*, 83 (1961), 852–853.
[31] Crow, "Bits of Information On Chief Long Hair," 3–4; Zenas Leonard, *Narrative of the Adventures of Zenas Leonard*, original 1839 edition edited by Milo Milton Quaife (Lincoln: University of Nebraska Press, 1978), 228–229. The fervor and individualism of Crow religion is discussed in a comparative context in Margot Liberty, "Priest or Shaman on the Plains: A False Dichotomy?" *Plains Anthropologist*, 15 (1970), 73–79.

and Larocque's hosts struck the "broad, deep and clear water" of the Bighorn. The trader sensed he was near the center of the band's homeland. Village elders told him that they spent each spring and fall along the Bighorn and Yellowstone Rivers; they left only to winter in small, family-sized camps among the foothills of the Rockies and to venture out onto the plains during midsummer in large groups. Here along the river they had ready access to water, firewood and small game, and were within easy striking distance of the buffalo that migrated up the Yellowstone valley. François Larocque – ever the careful market analyst – noted dryly that there were "plenty of buffalo" in the area; it was left to the American explorer William Clark, who floated down the Yellowstone the following summer, to reveal the scale of the valley's resources. "For me to . . . give an estimate of the different species of wild animals on this river," Clark wrote in July 1806, "particularly buffalo, elk, antelope and wolves, would be incredible." He called the herds passing by his camp "immense."[32]

The richness and grandeur of this heart of "Crow country" may have lain behind the one moment during the summer with the Crows when François Laroque lost his accountant's composure. That moment came on the afternoon of August 31 when the curious trader set out to explore the mouth of the Bighorn canyon. Clambering up the rocky embankment where twentieth-century engineers would later anchor a massive hydroelectric dam, the young trader saw the flow of the Bighorn suddenly pinched between two granite walls. His hosts told him the river did not originate in the canyon, but passed through it (and over a massive falls guarded by a "Manitou or Devil") from headwaters far to the south. Larocque reported that the boiling water passing beneath him "makes one giddy . . . so that I did not dare to look down." The surrounding canyon walls were "bare and naked." They were "as smooth and perpendicular as any wall and of an amazing height." Overcome by this splendor, the young explorer lost track of his two languages. "The tout ensemble," he wrote, "is grand and striking."[33]

The next day, September 1, Larocque's party moved downstream and encountered a disturbing visitor. "A Snake Indian arrived," the trader reported. "He had been absent since the spring," and he had been to see other Shoshones "who trade with the Spaniards." While the Canadian did not object to the presence of a rival merchant in camp, it was clear that he understood the significance of the Shoshone's arrival: his Crow hosts had entered a new commercial orbit. The Indian trader showed the Crows a Spanish bridle, an ax, "a large thick blanket" (presumably of wool), and a supply of blue beads. These items had no doubt passed from Mexico, through Texas or New Mexico, to the

[32] Larocque, "Yellowstone Journal," 190; Meriwether Lewis and William Clark, *Original Journals of the Lewis and Clark Expedition, 1804–1806*, Reuben Gold Thwaites, ed. (New York: Dodd, Mead, 1905), Vol. 5, 290, 294.
[33] Larocque, "Yellowstone Journal," 188.

southern plains where they had been exchanged for hides or horses with
Comanche, Kiowa and Shoshone hunters until they crossed modern Colorado
and entered the Bighorn basin of central Wyoming. From there they had
travelled across the Bighorn range to the Crow camp. A century earlier, this
southern network had brought the Crows horses; now it brought them tools,
weapons and European manufactured items. Larocque made no direct comment
on the incident, but he bought some sample blue beads to show his superiors in
Canada.[34]

The day the Shoshone trader arrived, Larocque noted in his journal that "the
leaves begin to fall." He was reminded that despite his exciting surroundings,
the company men back on the Assiniboin River expected a report before winter.
There would be no more sightseeing; Larocque's mission did not include describing the landscape or reporting on other trade networks. He had reached
the end of his provisions and the outer limit of an area that could reasonably be
served from Northwest Company warehouses. To move further south would be
to begin competing with the Spanish in Santa Fe, Taos and El Paso; to move
west would bring him hard against the Rocky Mountain front and spark a
confrontation with the Hudson's Bay Company men who operated beyond it.
In the course of the summer, the French Canadian must have learned from his
hosts that another trade route led into the Yellowstone from the plateau country
of modern-day Washington and Oregon. Nez Perce and Flathead bands brought
horses as well as beadwork and foodstuffs across the Rockies as gifts and items
for trade.[35]

As his hosts continued to move up the Yellowstone valley, passing Pryor
Creek and camping near the site of modern Billings, Larocque grew impatient.
The trader purchased beaver skins offered him, questioned his hosts about their
future plans, and tried to keep note of future trapping sites. One day he
persuaded a group of young men to escort him north to see the Yellowstone,
but the party encountered a small group of buffalo and the trader failed to keep
the group on course. They returned to camp "with meat, but with rain" and
without having reached their destination. His hosts eventually made their way
to the river, striking it above the modern city of Billings, but the trader's
enthusiasm was on the wane. Finally, on September 14, as the band camped on
the riverbank near what would be a century later a tangle of rail yards surrounding Laurel, Montana, Larocque called the band's elders together to announce
his departure.[36]

---

[34] Ibid., 189. His purchase of sample Spanish beads took place on September 13; see ibid., 192.

[35] For a classic overview of precontact trade patterns on the plains, see John C. Ewers, "The Indian
Trade of the Upper Missouri Before Lewis and Clark: An Interpretation," *Bulletin of the
Missouri Historical Society*, 10 (July 1954), 429–446. Trade between the Nez Perces and Crows
is described at 437–438.

[36] Larocque, "Yellowstone Journal," 190–192.

The Canadian conducted his farewell council as if he were reading from a salesman's manual. He told the Crow chiefs that he was grateful for their hospitality and promised to return to their country in twelve months. In the meantime, he told the Crows they should "kill beavers and bears" and dress their skins as he had demonstrated. He left them with the same blunt talk he had used at their first meeting in June. He noted that there were "many reasons . . . [why] it was in their interest to hunt beavers. . . ." No doubt his weeks with the Crows had helped him compile these "reasons." Beavers could be exchanged for rifles and knives the tribe could use against their enemies; furs could purchase tools to ease the rigors of camp life, or luxury items that might enhance the standing of a chief or warrior. Beaver could also be traded for blankets, food and tobacco. Thinking, perhaps of the accounts he would have to settle with his employers when he returned to Canada, Larocque concluded the journal of his adventure with the prediction that his summer would pay rich dividends in the future: "The presents I made them I thought were sufficient to gain their good will in which I think I succeeded." The trader added, "I never gave them anything without finding means to let them know it was not for nothing." The 122 beaver furs purchased during the summer were not of good quality, but they would direct European trade goods "into the most deserving hands, that is the less lazy."[37]

On this commercial note – and carrying a Crow pledge not to steal his horses – Larocque departed. Three weeks later he was back at the Hidatsa villages. While he never returned to the northern plains, the Northwest Company man's journey to the Yellowstone heralded the onset of an era in which Crow tribesmen would encounter non-Indian fur traders on a regular basis. During the summer Larocque spent travelling in the shadow of the Bighorns, Meriwether Lewis and William Clark reached the Pacific Ocean and Zebulon Pike searched deep into the forests of north central Minnesota for the headwaters of the Mississippi. Lewis and Clark's return to St. Louis in 1806, together with Pike's trip across the southern plains a year later, provided American merchants and adventurers with both the information and the encouragement they needed to plunge into a new arena of commercial activity. During the next two decades, traders from Montreal and Santa Fe were shouldered aside by the men who followed in the wake of Lewis and Clark. While representing a different group of white men, the St. Louis traders offered as many enticements as Larocque. They presented the Crows and their neighbors with weapons, tools and foodstuffs in exchange for exquisite, processed hides of beaver, bear and otter.

The first American description of the Yellowstone valley was written by William Clark in 1806. Temporarily separated from his partner Meriwether Lewis, the explorer descended the river on his return journey to St. Louis,

[37] Ibid., 192–193.

listing geographical features and potential resources as he passed. Clark's tales of vast buffalo herds along the Yellowstone stirred his companions, so much so that even before the reunited expedition had returned to the American settlements, one of their most loyal men – Virginian John Colter – asked permission to leave the company and return to Montana to hunt and trap. After wintering near the mouth of the Clark's Fork, Colter formed a partnership with Manuel Lisa, a St. Louis trader who had come north in response to Clark's glowing (and now-public) report. Lisa and Colter built a two-room cabin at the mouth of the Bighorn and dubbed it Fort Raymond. While wary of the newcomers, the Crows were enthusiastic about the possibilities of the trade. Speaking years later, one elderly member of the tribe rememberd those early contacts, noting that "before this they had never dressed more robes than they needed for themselves." Once the traders had arrived, however, "every lodge had from sixteen to eighteen robes to sell. . . ."[38]

Others followed in their wake. Fort Raymond was abandoned in 1811 and the War of 1812 brought a lull in American activity, but a new trading post was erected in 1821, and in 1822 the Missouri Fur Company dispatched 300 traders to the Rockies. In 1829, a competing outpost was established by the American Fur Company to the east of Crow country at the confluence of the Yellowstone and Missouri Rivers. Fort Union would be the principal supply depot and gathering place for traders and their Indian hosts until the arrival of the railroads made it obsolete.[39]

By the 1820s traders travelled regularly up and down the Missouri, even though they were frequently harrassed by Arikaras and others who attempted to blockade the middle stretch of the river in an attempt to exact tolls and tribute from the merchants. Ironically, these efforts only increased the number of Americans bound for the Yellowstone because a second group of traders began avoiding the river altogether by sending their supplies overland, following the course of the Platte River to the eventual site of Fort Laramie in modern Wyoming. There (and at rendezvous sites in the Bighorn basin and along the Green River) they would exchange manufactured goods for furs from the Bighorns and the Wind River range. Within two decades, traders began reporting that the Rockies' seemingly limitless supply of beaver pelts was giving out.[40]

[38] Testimony of Little Face in "Historical Sketch of the Crows, from the Journal of James H. Bradley," *Contributions to the Historical Society of Montana*, 2 (1896), 200. For Clark's report on the Yellowstone, see his entries for July 15 to July 29, 1806. Comments about "incredible" game and "immense" herds of buffalo are included in the entries for July 24 and 25. See Lewis and Clark, *Original Journals*, 290, 294.

[39] For a concise and informative history of the fur trade on the plains, see William R. Swagerty, "Indian Trade in the Trans-Mississippi West to 1870," in Wilcomb E. Washburn, ed., *Handbook of North American Indians: Volume 4, History of Indian–White Relations* (Washington, D.C.: Government Printing Office, 1988), 351–375.

[40] See, e.g., Donald McKay Frost, *Notes on General Ashley, the Overland Trail and South Pass* (Barre, Mass.: Barre Gazette, 1960), 12–26.

As agents of the fur trade industry reached the outskirts of Crow territory, they triggered new dreams of wealth and power. In the eighteenth century, as the Crows acquired horses and completed their migrations from the Missouri, the various bands that made up the group seemed absorbed with internal affairs. Except for new diseases and the arrival of individual (and unrecorded) traders, outside events rarely intruded into the daily lives of Crow people, and there was little incentive to control additional territory. The great leaders from this period appear to have been valued primarily for their spiritual powers or their skill as warriors. As they entered the nineteenth century, however, the Crows grew more expansive.

Traders continued to welcome the Crows who brought their furs to the Missouri River villages, but in the years immediately following Larocque's journey, Crow hunters ranged from the Judith and Musselshell Rivers on the upper Missouri to the Green River basin. In each of those areas the tribe's efforts to control the flow of furs and hides provoked increasingly violent confrontations. They battled the Blackfeet along the upper Missouri, the Lakota Sioux and Cheyenne to the south, near the headwaters of the Platte, and the Shoshone along the Wind River range and in the Green River country of what is now southern Wyoming. The most dramatic of these confrontations occurred in 1822 or 1823 when a party of as many as 1,000 Sioux warriors surprised a Crow village near the Yellowstone and destroyed several hundred lodges. According to an oral version of the event recorded years later, half of the village's population was killed in the attack.[41]

The fur trade offered the possibility of greater wealth as well as access to the power represented by steel knives, hatchets, pack horses and rifles. In the orbit of the trade, bands could kill more game, transport more possessions over a larger area, build larger lodges and devote more energy to military competition. Already established in the mobile lifestyle of equestrian hunters, the Crows of the early nineteenth century adapted quickly to take maximum advantage of these opportunities. As the trade increased, their lodges grew larger. More men took second or third wives, both because their rising wealth made this

---

[41] Generalizing about chiefs who lived before the nineteenth century is difficult, but the men listed in a modern tribal publication as among the "All Time Great Chieftans" from that era were largely valued for their skill in battle or their religious insight. These include Paints His Body Red, Red Fish, One Heart, One Eye (or Raven Face) and White Moccasin Top. See Joe Medicine Crow, "All Time Great Chieftans of the Crow Indians, 1600–1904," in Eloise Whitebear Pease, ed., *Crow Tribal Treaty Centennial Issue* (Crow Agency, Mont.: Crow Tribe, 1968), 29–30. An excellent summary of fur trade activity among the Crows in this period can be found in Bearss, *Bighorn Canyon*, 42–70. For a geographical analysis of Crow culture change in this period, see John W. Stafford, "Crow Culture Change: A Geographical Analysis" (Ph.D. Dissertation, Department of Geography, Michigan State University, 1972), esp. chaps. 2 and 3. For an account of the Sioux attack, see "Bradley Manuscript – Book F," 238–244. Other evidence of wide-ranging fighting in this period can be found in Charles L. Camp, ed., *James Clyman: Frontiersman* (Portland, Oreg.: Champoeg Press, 1960), 19, 36.

possible, and because the trade required larger households to process buffalo and beaver skins. At the same time, band leaders arose who could articulate the community's new dreams of wealth and who could manage the era's rapidly shifting conditions and values.[42]

Sore Belly, who was a teenager when Larocque visited the Yellowstone valley, epitomized the powerful and savvy leaders of the early fur trade era. The Canadian visitor probably did not see Sore Belly in 1805, because the young man was a River Crow who spent most of his time north of the Yellowstone. At about the time of the fur trader's journey, Sore Belly carried out his vision quest in the Crazy Mountains at the headwaters of the Musselshell River. While fasting near the rugged, 11,000 foot peaks of this range that stands midway between modern Billings and Great Falls, Montana, Sore Belly was suddenly confronted by a terrifying thunderbird, a spirit creature who spouted lightning and made a terrible roar. But instead of harming the young warrior, the thunderbird offered him instructions in the art of war. Thunder became Sore Belly's guardian spirit and his contemporaries reported this association allowed him to manipulate the weather as well as to see into the future.[43]

Sore Belly rose to prominence because of his powerful vision and his skill as a warrior, but his military prowess was usually displayed in struggles over control of trading areas and resources. For example, he was noted for his ability to capture large herds of horses from neighboring tribes and then use those herds to amass great wealth. He also urged his followers to trade for guns and ammunition first and to shun less practical items. His engagement in the fur trade and his ambition that the Crows should eliminate rivals prompted him to lead war parties as far south as the Arkansas River in modern Oklahoma and as far north as Fort McKenzie in the heart of Blackfeet country. Sore Belly understood that the Crows were in an advantageous position for trade, but that their wealth made them attractive targets. The trader Edwin Thompson Denig noted that Sore Belly urged his followers "to trade for more guns and ammunition, established regular camp sentinels night and day, and used such vigilance that during his life the hostile neighbors could make no headway either against his people or their animals."[44]

[42] For a summary of Crow social life in the nineteenth century, see Robert H. Lowie, *Social Organization* (New York: Holt, Rinehart, 1948), 349–352. Lowie's full description is in "Social Life of the Crow Indians, " *American Museum of Natural History, Anthropological Papers*, Vol. 9 (1912), 309–444. The crucial role of women as processors of skins is described in the memoirs of fur trader Zenas Leonard: *Narrative of the Adventures of Zenas Leonard*, 252.

[43] For profiles of Sore Belly, see *Crow Social Studies: Baleeisbaalichiwee History – Teacher's Guide* (Crow Agency, Mont.: Bilingual Materials Development Center, 1986), 44–47.

[44] Edwin Thompson Denig, *Five Indian Tribes of the Upper Missouri*, edited and with an introduction by John C. Ewers (Norman: University of Oklahoma Press, 1961), 162–163. See also Sore Belly, *Crow Social Studies*, 44–45.

III

Ever the assiduous merchant, Francois Antoine Larocque prepared a summary report on the Crows after he returned to Canada. His "Observations" promised to provide future Northwest Company traders with a capsule sketch of his hosts, a description of their homeland, and a list of Crow words and phrases. While it is filled with useful, intimate details, the trader's briefing paper began with a misperception. "This nation," Larocque wrote, was divided into "three principal tribes."[45]

The Crows of 1805 were a dispersed community of hunters and their families who had few formal institutions to unify them. They spoke a common language, but they dispersed themselves across an immense, borderless landscape, and they had no centralized leadership. Even though some neighbors, such as the Hidatsas, were considered relatives and others were sworn enemies, membership in the Crow community did not appear to require any particular ritual or formal proceeding. (Some traders followed Larocque's approach of holding themselves aloof from the group, while others married into their hosts' families; a few made their home with the Crows and never returned to the East.) Without a written language, the Crows sustained no bureaucracy and functioned without a set of governing statutes. Larocque's hosts belonged to a polity – a self-governing community – and their numbers, wealth and military power clearly warranted a respectful label, but the Crows of 1805 were not a modern nation.

What were they? Social scientists have tried to define categories of political organization across cultural boundaries for decades. Their efforts have produced a proliferating list of terms, but little agreement. Human inventiveness has simply defied those who have strained to pack community patterns into neat boxes. For every definition, there is an exception. When one adds the element of time, the complexity of this task increases still further. As anthropologist Elizabeth Colson has observed, "Political associations can be combined in various ways . . . they should not be thought of as integrated systems where the various elements mutually reinforce each other." In this environment, it is fruitless to seek an absolute definition or universal term. "At such an impasse," historian Francis Jennings has written, "one sends for Humpty Dumpty" and joins him in declaring that descriptive terms "mean what I say they mean in this book."[46]

On the other hand, as Humpty Dumpty might also testify, the process of

---

45 François Antoine Larocque, "A Few Observations on the Rocky Mountain Indians with Whom I Passed the Summer," in Wood and Thiessen, *Early Fur Trade*, 206.
46 Elizabeth Colson, "Political Organization in Tribal Societies," in *American Indian Quarterly*, 10 (Winter 1986), 15; Francis Jennings, *The Ambiguous Iroquois Empire* (New York: Norton, 1984), 38.

historical change cannot be denied. Events occur, and communities, like individuals (even make-believe ones) cannot be restored to their previous condition of wholeness, even when that condition was contradictory to begin with. It might be fruitless to seek an absolute definition for the descriptive labels we apply to the Crows of 1805, but it is useful nonetheless to use labels to describe the process of historical change we can observe in the ensuing decades. For the Crows, this change followed a clear path. Beginning in the early nineteenth century with the extension of the fur trade to the Yellowstone, the community was gradually incorporated into a national state, the United States of America. That incorporation had a variety of consequences for the internal life of the group. The group lost some of its powers of self-government as it entered into a formal association with the national government. It developed new institutions of leadership. It adopted new religious forms and conducted some of its business in English. Community boundaries were fixed and subsistence practices changed.

Looking forward from the summer François Antoine Larocque spent with the Crows, it would not be accurate to describe the incorporation process, in which the group lost its autonomy, as a fall from nationhood. Because it did not enter written history as a nation in the conventional, European sense of the term, it would not be logical to define its subsequent history as a movement away from nationhood. Neither would it be accurate to characterize that history as the decline of a "tribe" (the second term the trader used to describe his hosts). While that term came into modern usage as an instrument for describing kin-based, stateless societies such as the one Larocque observed in 1805, modern anthropological scholarship has demonstrated that little unites those to whom the label has been applied other than their status as subjects of Western imperial powers. Without common definitions of boundaries, comparable origins or similar political systems, communities lumped together as "tribes" share only a common rung on an imagined evolutionary ladder of cultures, a step midway between disorganized, savage hordes and sophisticated urban states. As a consequence, most scholars today can only agree with anthropologist Colson who declared, "I do not know what is meant by 'tribal societies.' "[47]

By freeing ourselves from both Larocque's misperception and the confusion of anthropologists, we can draw closer to an understanding of the Crow predicament in 1805. While "nation" and "tribe" are suggestive – the one of the Crows' power and the other of their statelessness – both terms cast the group's experience into scenarios that distort its political history. Larocque's observations make clear that his hosts were not nations in decline or exotics in innocence, but a community of people who shared a language, system of kinship,

[47] Colson, "Political Organization in Tribal Societies," 5; see also June Helm, ed., *Essays on the Problem of Tribe* (Seattle: American Ethnological Society, 1968), esp. 14.

complex set of social traditions, distinctive religious outlook and collective commitment to self-defense and dreams of prosperity. They occupied a precarious spot on the northern plains: surrounded with abundance, yet besieged by rivals and threatened with technological change. Their future was not predictable just as their past was not obvious.

Calling the group Larocque encountered a "band" is helpful for a number of reasons. A band is an organized group bound together by kinship and obligation. Bands generally do not operate by written statutes or charters but by custom, and their leaders are produced by social tradition. Bands are flexible and their members do not necessarily share a primordial (or permanent) attachment to one another. But most significant for an understanding of Crow experience, the term does not suggest a membership composed of an entire ethnic or language group. Trader Larocque travelled with a large band of Crows; he understood that he had not accompanied "the" Crows to the Yellowstone. He gathered information about the entire group, but he was only vaguely aware that while he was exploring the Yellowstone, another major band was travelling along the Milk River near the 49th parallel, and another hunted in Wyoming's Bighorn basin. These groups drew together periodically, but there were few traditions that compelled them to gather regularly or permanently as a single unit. And finally, the major bands were in a constant state of flux as smaller groups of hunters departed, families veered off on their own for various periods, captives married into the community and visitors arrived expecting friendship and hospitality.

François Antoine Larocque's journey with a Crow band does more than record the conditions of life at the outset of the tribe's encounter with written history. By allowing readers of his journal to look over his shoulder as he travelled to the Yellowstone, the trader makes it possible for others to look past the labels and categories so often assigned to Native Americans and other "unfamiliar" people. Seeing the Crows on their own terms and in their own country, we can better understand that their lifeways do not fit a neat, ethnographic summary and that their future was not fixed. Nevertheless, Larocque's summer exploration of the Crow homeland also makes clear that in the years ahead the forces of incorporation in the form of traders, military enemies, government agents and new technologies would begin to bind the Crows together, drawing them steadily into a new and common history.

3

Life in a tightening circle

The Crow country is a good country. The Great Spirit has put it exactly in the right place; while you are in it you fare well; whenever you go out of it, whichever way you travel you fare worse.

Arapooash (Sore Belly), c.1830[1]

I

Prior to the arrival of Europeans in North America, the histories of indigenous communities were marked by gradual change and a remarkable aversion to centralization. Major technological innovations such as the introduction of maize horticulture or the invention of the bow and arrow profoundly affected cultural traditions across vast areas, but their impact seems to have been diffuse and gradual rather than direct and abrupt. It is difficult to identify many groups in the precontact world that exerted an immediate influence on their neighbors, or to trace a swift sequence of influence among cultural entities. Similarly, the rise of large population centers and the growth of intensive trade networks seem to have been balanced by tugs in the opposite direction; communities pulled apart as frequently as they fell together. Across the continent, the center of cultural life continued to exist within village squares and council houses rather than following the Asian and European tendency to concentrate authority in large political, economic or religious institutions.

For centuries, life on the northern plains reflected these continental patterns, as groups passed innovations on to their neighbors and formed new communities by separation rather than colonization. Just as the Crows had gradually "hived off" from the Hidatsas, other groups emigrated to new environments, adapted to new resources and split off to form new entities. While larger groups maintained a tradition of unity in their literature and religious beliefs, they placed few limits on their members and exerted little control over their actions. Without Europeans, it is likely that hunting societies such as the Crows might have eventually dispersed and formed new subgroups or reversed their westward migrations and returned to their prior, horticultural ways.

But the Europeans came. Diseases, horses, trade goods, weapons and iron

---

[1] "Lieut. James H. Bradley Manuscript," *Contributions to the Montana Historical Society*, 9 (1923), 306.

tools heralded their arrival during the sixteenth, seventeenth and eighteenth centuries, and individual traders and explorers appeared in their wake. In the first decades of the nineteenth century, face-to-face visits from people like François Antoine Larocque became a regular feature of Crow life, and delegations travelling east to the Missouri River or south to the Platte could count on exchanging their furs and horses for manufactured goods and foodstuffs. The magnet of new technologies, together with the rivalries they inspired, quickened the pace of change in the region, drawing groups like the Crows together with unprecedented force while raising the significance of the boundaries between themselves and other groups.

By midcentury, the Crows found themselves wealthier and more powerful than they had been when Larocque and his partners first saw them, but the group was also more constrained by its enemies and more dependent on powerful strangers. As Sore Belly's statement suggests, "Crow country" became both a focus of community pride and a refuge from hostility. By 1870 tribal life had grown richer and more intense, but it was taking place within a tightening circle of danger.

II

From the perspective of Andrew Jackson's White House, the northern plains was a lawless and unruly region. While willing to tolerate American explorers and trade with American merchants, the native peoples who lived north and west of St. Louis in the 1820s did not care that they lived within the boundaries of the United States of America. In the spring of 1823, for example, when Col. Henry Leavenworth and a force of nearly 1,000 soldiers, fur traders and Sioux allies shelled an Arikara village that had blockaded the Missouri River and stopped American commerce, its residents simply withdrew into their sturdy earth lodges and waited for the frustrated infantrymen to go away. On the upper Missouri, the Blackfeet spoke openly of their preference for Hudson's Bay traders and ignored the Americans' pretentious demands. It seemed clear to policy makers in the nation's capitol that if American interests were going to be promoted in the West, its military forces would have to make a show of force there.

The 1825 Atkinson–O'Fallon expedition was conceived as just such a measure. Consisting of nine, hand-powered paddle boats and a regiment of nearly five hundred men, the enterprise had been urged on the army by Missouri Senator Thomas Hart Benton, an ardent anglophobe and defender of the St. Louis fur traders, who had served in the Upper House since his state entered the Union in 1821. Commanded by two officers who would later see service in the Black Hawk war, the party carried orders to contact every major tribe along the river north of Council Bluffs, Iowa, and to invite them to sign treaties in which they pledged their loyalty to the United States.[2]

Henry Atkinson and Benjamin O'Fallon's arrival at the Hidatsa villages in August 1825 – at a point not far from where Francois Antoine Larocque first met the "Rocky Mountain Indians" twenty summers earlier – marked the first instance when the United States displayed its military prowess before the Crows. And while the treaty signing was a fiasco, it signaled the onset of a period of interplay between external authorities and local leaders that would produce a sharper sense of Crow identity even as it promised to reduce the group's autonomy and independence.

As his troops neared the Hidatsa villages, Atkinson ordered a few men to carry gifts of tobacco to a large encampment of Crows who were waiting nearby. As they had for decades, the bands had come to the Missouri to trade. The military commander's message urged the leaders of these villages to visit him at his headquarters on the river. On August 1, after he had waited for a reply for five days, Atkinson sent a second detachment to renew his request. The Americans should not have worried, for on the morning of August 3 a large body of Crows rode into the American camp on their ponies. Dressed in buckskin and arrayed behind a brilliantly decorated leader, the band presented itself to the president's representatives. The group was lead by Red Plume, the distinguished Mountain Crow warrior, who indicated that he was prepared to accept the Americans' presents and friendship. The visitors appeared united, but they had actually left another large body of warriors behind in their camp. That group, made up largely of River Crows and lead by Sore Belly, refused to meet the white soldiers. There was a comic quality to the ensuing negotiations – conducted with an eye to the absent Sore Belly by illiterate fur trader-interpreters – but the people involved and the actions they took foreshadowed the pressures and events the Crows would face in the decades ahead.

Prepared in advance of the Crow arrival (and, indeed, written to match other agreements signed earlier in the summer further downstrem), the 1825 treaty of friendship between the United States and the Crows appeared to demand nothing of the tribe but pleasant words. The document declared that the Crows acknowledged the supremacy of the United States and promised to remain loyal to the U.S. government and its licensed traders. In return the U.S. government vowed to protect the tribe from unscrupulous merchants and to return to the Indians any horses or other belongings that might be stolen from them in the future. Atkinson and O'Fallon also presented the visiting Crows with an array of trade goods as both an expression of goodwill and a tangible sign of what was

[2] For background to the expedition, see Francis Paul Prucha, *The Great Father: The United States Government and the American Indians*, 2 vols. (Lincoln: University of Nebraska Press, 1985), 132–134, and Russell Reid and Clell G. Cannon, eds., "Journal of the Atkinson–O'Fallon Expedition," *North Dakota Historical Quarterly*, 4 (1929–30), 5–56.

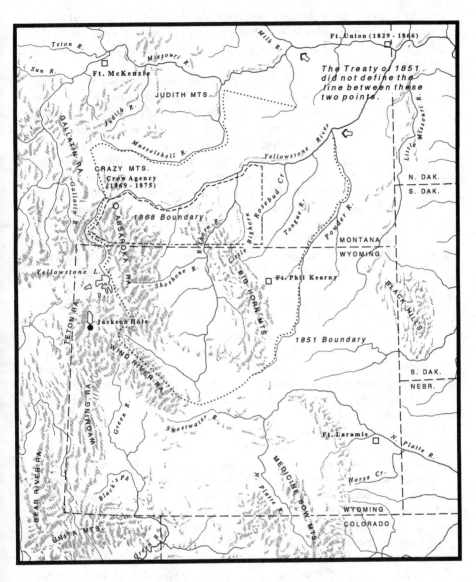

Map 3. Crow country in the fur trade era.

available from Senator Benton's supporters downriver. Red Plume and fifteen other Crow chiefs quickly indicated their assent. They made their marks on the document at the end of the first day's meeting, collected their booty, and prepared to depart.

But Atkinson stopped them. He invited the group to reassemble on the following morning of August 4 and, after some discussion, Red Plume and his followers agreed. At this second meeting, the expedition's deputy commander, Benjamin O'Fallon, called on the Crow chiefs to provide hard evidence of their newly pledged friendship. He demanded the return of two "Iroquois prisoners" supposedly being held by Red Plume's people. Since Iroquois Indians from the East often worked with the American fur traders, this demand might well have been an attempt on the part of the several St. Louis traders present to rein in a pair of renegade employees. Nevertheless, Red Plume and the others were insulted by the request from their new "friends." The Indians declared they had no such prisoners among them. A group of young warriors in the group was so angered by the Americans' threatening tone and the looming presence of their canon that they proceeded to spike the deadly weapon with handfuls of dirt.

As the young men attacked the Americans' artillery, Red Plume and the other chiefs rose to gather up their presents and leave, but a panicky O'Fallon stepped forward, swinging the butt of his pistol at the heads of his guests. With the sounds of a full-scale brawl emanating from the council grounds, General Atkinson, who had left the meeting for his midday meal, hustled back and ordered his men to disperse and the Crows to be patient. "This probably saved blood-shed," the expedition journal noted. The next day Atkinson tried to smooth over the incident by visiting Red Plume's camp and distributing additional presents, but suspicion was high on both sides.[3]

Deeply offended by the indignity of an American official striking tribal leaders while gathered in council, and perhaps eager to put distance between himself and the cooperative Red Plume, Sore Belly and his River Crows started for home as soon as they heard what had happened on August 4. His followers later reported that the chief used his ability to control the weather to bring a violent hail storm down on the Mandan villages in retaliation for the incident, and he vowed never to deal with the United States. While Sore Belly lived for another decade and had frequent meetings with American traders, he remained deeply suspicious of them and he must have pressed his position onto his followers, for he spent the bulk of his later years in the remote areas northwest of the Yellowstone, fighting the Blackfeet and trading frequently with the representatives of the Hudson's Bay Company.[4]

[3] Reid and Cannon, "Journal of the Atkinson–O'Fallon Expedition," 36.
[4] For the Atkinson–O'Fallon negotiations, see *American State Papers, Class II. Indian Affairs* (Washington, D.C.: Grales and Seaton, 1834). Vol. 2, 602–607.

Because he regularly wintered in the Bighorn basin and was familiar with a number of American traders, Red Plume must have sensed that he could not be so arbitrary. He and his followers depended on the Americans for weapons, tools and other items and he could not alienate them. Red Plume was also aware that both the eastern flank of the Bighorns and the southern rim of his hunting grounds in modern-day Wyoming and Colorado were attracting growing numbers of Lakota, Cheyenne and Arapaho bands. These groups were not only a military threat; their presence compelled the Crows to maintain a steady supply of American weapons and tools. It is not surprising, then, that on the day after O'Fallon's attack on the Crow chiefs, Red Plume and his men assured the Americans that Atkinson's diplomacy had been sufficient to pacify them. They stated that "their wounds were covered and they would throw all that had passed behind them." When the general paid a final courtesy call on the Mountain Crow chief, he once again was assured of the band's friendly intentions.[5]

The events that produced the Crows' first treaty with the United States contained several elements that affected both the power and the nature of community life during the middle decades of the nineteenth century. First, of course, was the power of the United States – laughable in 1825, but clearly greater than it had been in 1805 and capable of orchestrating the efforts of both fur traders and military men. General Atkinson had had difficulty even locating the Crows as his expedition moved northward, but once the groups met face-to-face, Red Plume and his fellow chiefs could see that the Americans were potential allies and dangerous foes. Men like Sore Belly could be contemptuous of the blue-coated soldiers in their hand-powered boats, but other Crow leaders must have imagined that their grandchildren would not have that luxury. In the future they would have to gauge their actions with increasing reference to the military strengths of the United States.

Second, from the perspective of Red Plume and the Mountain Crows, a significant part of the Americans' power was their association with the St. Louis–based fur traders. The waves of new weapons that had swept into the region during the past twenty years had forced them to calculate carefully the distance between their campfires and the next supply post. To be short of ammunition or knives on the northern plains was to be vulnerable to attack by rival groups or unable to process the hides and pelts that visiting traders would exchange for coffee, beads, blankets and other goods. In 1825 traders were present on both sides of the council ground: men from St. Louis travelled with Atkinson, while Edward Rose, an African-American free trapper, accompanied Red Plume.

---

[5] Reid and Cannon, "Journal of the Atkinson–O'Fallon Expedition," 36. In Plains Indian societies, injuries are frequently "covered" by giving gifts to the injured party. An additional account of this incident and further evidence for the separate geographical realms of Red Plume and Sore Belly can be found in the "Journal of James H. Bradley," *Contributions to the Historical Society of Montana*, 2 (1896), 180–182.

Their involvement demonstrated how deeply intertwined military and economic motives had become in the region and underscored the fact that tribal
leaders could not escape continued contact with foreign traders.

Third, while the 1825 treaty contained only vague pledges of friendship, it
implied a set of territorial boundaries for all who accepted it. After all, Atkinson
had negotiated identical treaties with tribes along the entire length of the upper
Missouri, implying an American recognition that each group held sway over a
particular territory. From the Crow perspective, Americans could reasonably be
expected to support the group's current interests; these were geographical as
well as economic and military. American friendship might well counterbalance
the hostility of surrounding tribes, for example, no matter how vague the
borders between the Crows and those groups might be. At the same time, the
fact that the United States concluded agreements with all of the plains tribes in
1825 suggested that the maintenance of boundaries would be an important
aspect of intergroup relations in the years to come.

Finally, the sudden intrusion of American military power amplified internal
tensions within Crow political life that could easily undermine the community's
own, rather tentative sense of solidarity. The arrival of powerful strangers, no
matter how foolish, posed a problem for Crow leaders. Chiefs like Red Plume
and Sore Belly were forced to decide whether to accept or oppose the visiting
diplomats. Would they spurn the American offer of friendship and turn exclusively to the British traders from Hudson Bay? Would they link themselves
more formally to the traders from St. Louis? Would they turn south to the
Spanish and Mexicans? Or was it possible to follow some course in between
those extremes or to balance one off against another?

To complicate matters further, a decision by a band leader to befriend one
group of outsiders might well cause his rivals to side with their opponents.
After all, why should ambitious young men go along with the decisions of their
elders (particularly in a society that rewarded initiative and had little tradition
of hierarchy and deference)? The appearance of new and potentially powerful
actors like Atkinson and O'Fallon introduced an array of unprecedented political questions into Crow political life. Like Larocque's Hidatsa hosts who
wrestled with the problem of whether or not to introduce the trader to the
visiting "Rocky Mountain Indians" twenty years before, Red Plume, Sore Belly
and their contemporaries would have to consider where to position themselves
in a new landscape of power and economic rivalry.

The Atkinson–O'Fallon expedition marked the end of a period of informal,
long-distance contact between Crows and outsiders and the onset of an era in
which the presence of Americans and intensified rivalries between tribes would
have a direct and sustained impact on community life. Between 1825 and 1870,
change would cease to be gradual and diffuse. The Great Plains would witness
the impact of traders, military conflict and American expansion, and the Crows

would learn that living in the "right place" would require that they strengthen their ties to their territories and each other. Life within the shrinking borders of their homeland would be shaped by the fur trade, the ambitions of their Indian neighbors, the shifting structure of their own traditions and the expanding power of the U.S. government.

III

After 1825, the expansion of the American fur trade had a powerful and constricting effect on the location and leadership of Crow bands. Men who developed close ties to the traders rose to prominence, and important trading posts became pole stars around which groups of hunters would travel in an annual cycle of commerce. At first the introduction of horses, guns and other trade items had enabled Crow bands to inhabit a wider hunting territory. Supported by new technologies, they had ranged from Colorado to the Canadian border and from the Missouri River to the Continental Divide. But as band leaders became concerned with maintaining access to tools and weapons, they decided to stick with particular suppliers and to remain within a prescribed area. By the 1850s, deepening ties with American fur traders had regularized the Crows' relationship with the outside world and sharply defined the tribe's territory.

While Crow leaders could engage in the fur trade with a considerable degree of independence – accepting or rejecting offers made to them by traders whom they usually outnumbered and could generally overpower – their supplies came from a limited number of sources. The chiefs would be enriched by the trade only as long as they bent their annual travels to coincide with the location of fur trade posts. Several small "forts" were conveniently erected in the Yellowstone valley at the beginning of the century, but few of them were long-lived. Manuel Lisa's initial outposts were abandoned during the War of 1812, but these were followed by two "forts" erected by the American Fur Company: Fort Benton, erected in 1822, and Fort Cass, which appeared in 1832. Both stood at the mouth of the Bighorn River, but each survived for only a few years. They were replaced by Fort Alexander, which stood on the north side of the Yellowstone from 1842 to 1850, and Fort Sarpy, erected near Rosebud Creek immediately afterward. In 1855 this first Fort Sarpy was abandoned. Two years later a second Fort Sarpy arose near the mouth of the Bighorn. It survived for only two years. A description exists of this second Fort Sarpy. It was apparently somewhat larger than its predecessors, but it followed a similar design: it was a 100-foot-square cottonwood pallisade erected close to the banks of the Yellowstone River. The traders built small sheds against the inner walls of the fort. They used the sheds for shelter and storage and perched on their sod roofs to watch over the surrounding countryside. W. F. Raynolds, a visiting American military officer, noted in 1859 that the fort was "a decidedly primitive affair" but that it was "amply sufficient . . . to protect its inmates against the schemes and martial science of the Indians" who came to trade there. Raynolds also reported that while visiting Crows "take constant and . . . most disagreeable liberties, . . . prying into everything accessible," the fort's heavy gate "was carefully closed at night" so as to separate the traders from their customers.[6]

As Raynolds's report suggested, the fur posts were a mecca for Crow bands, particularly during the winter months when animal pelts were thickest and both Indians and traders were eager to relieve the tedium of living in cramped quarters during severe weather. An itinerant Swiss artist, Rudolph Friederich Kurz, recorded in his diary in the early 1850s, for example, that a series of Crow chiefs began to appear at his Missouri River station in late October, and by late December there were so many visitors that two chiefs were sharing his room. By January he felt overwhelmed, noting that "if we were required to entertain everyone who comes . . . we should soon have nothing but visitors – no trade, no compensation; consequently we should soon go to ruin, or, in other words, be literally eaten out of business." By February, guests usually had begun to disperse. Four years after Kurz wrote his description, trader James H. Chambers reported a similar pattern of visitation. In November he noted that his post was "full of Crows [come] to receive their presents." Two months later the band was still present: "Cold morning. Fort full of Crow loafers. No robes – dull times." His guests left during the first week of March.[7]

The Yellowstone valley forts such as Sarpy and Cass were popular with the Crows because they had been erected well within their traditional hunting territory, but as time went on the bulk of the supplies that reached the tribe came from three relatively distant sources: Fort Union, constructed at the confluence of the Yellowstone and Missouri Rivers in 1829; Fort Laramie, built in 1834 on the north branch of the Platte River; and the fur traders' rendezvous which was held south of the Wind River range that cut across what is now west central Wyoming. These three locations were at the borders of the Crows' most frequently travelled buffalo grounds, so that trade goods frequently came to the tribe via middlemen. Leaders with large followings like Red Plume and Sore

[6] U.S. Senate, *Senate Executive Document 77*, 40th Congress, 2nd Session, 1867 (Serial 1317), "Report on the Exploration of the Yellowstone River by Bvt. Brig. Gen. W. F. Raynolds," 50, 48. For information on the history of Fort Sarpy, see "Notes and References," *Contributions to the Historical Society of Montana*, 10 (1940), 282–283. The forts erected in Crow country were Fort Raymond (or Fort Lisa), 1807–1813; Fort Benton, 1822–1824?, Fort Cass, 1832–1838; Fort Van Buren, 1839–1842; Fort Alexander, 1842–1850; and Fort Sarpy (two of them), 1850–1855 and 1857–1860. See Edwin C. Bearss, *Bighorn Canyon National Recreation Area*, Montana-Wyoming, History Basic Data, Vol. 1 (Washington, D.C.: Office of History and Historic Architecture, Eastern Service Center, February, 1970), 60–106.

[7] Rudolph Friederich Kurz, *Journal of Rudolph Friederich Kurz*, J. N. B. Hewitt, ed., Myrtis Jarrell, trans., Bureau of American Ethnology Bulletin No. 115 (Washington, D.C.: Government Printing Office, 1937), 240, 251, 269; "Original Journal of James H. Chambers, Fort Sarpy," *Contributions to the Historical Society of Montana*, 10 (1940), 149, 155, 158.

Fort Union, erected by the American Fur Company in 1829, quickly supplanted the Mandan and Hidatsa villages as a Missouri River trade center. Frequented by Assiniboin, Crow, Blackfeet and others, the post became a regular stop in the annual migrations of hunting bands. This view of Fort Union was painted by Karl Bodmer during the summer of 1833 and included in Prince Maximilian's report of his expedition to the upper Missouri. Courtesy of The Newberry Library.

Belly might journey to Fort Union or the Green River rendezvous, but most band leaders relied upon traders who shuttled between the external supply points and individual hunting bands. As Army Lieut. James Bradley noted after interviewing aging Montana mountain men in the 1860s, "In former times the Crows had been supplied with goods in their camps by mountain trappers who resorted every summer to Fort Union to the number of sixty or eighty to sell the proceeds of their trade and trappings and procure supplies." As a consequence of this arrangement, most Crows of the 1830s and 1840s had relatively little direct access to – or influence on – the open marketplace.[8]

[8] "Affairs at Fort Benton from 1831 to 1869 from Lieutenant Bradley's Journal," *Contributions to the Historical Society of Montana*, 3 (1900), 262. Trader William Marshall Anderson described the arrival of Sore Belly's band at the 1834 rendezvous: "Like flies on a sugar barrel or nigers [*sic*] at corn shucking, the redskins are flocking to the trading tents." William Marshall Anderson, "Anderson's Narrative of a Ride to the Rocky Mountains in 1834," Albert J. Partoll, ed., *Frontier and Midland*, 19 (Autumn 1934), 62.

Because they were so dependent on outsiders and their goods, many Crow chiefs developed close ties to individual traders. Both merchants and Indians understood that it was most advantageous to establish regular contacts with each other and to concentrate on predictable items of exchange. Thus, beginning early in the nineteenth century, most Crow bands welcomed non-Indian traders who sought to live among them and readily agreed to focus their attention on the resources of their immediate surroundings. Few of these resident traders left written accounts of their activities, but several early travellers reported on the presence of men such as Edward Rose, a black trader who moved in with a Crow family after a dispute with Manuel Lisa in the 1810s, and a Scot named Robert Meldrum, who spent more than thirty years with the Crows (and married six Crow women) before his death in 1865. A few of the "mountain men" recorded their exploits. Among them were James Beckwourth, son of a Virginia slave woman and her master who – by his own account – became a "chief" of the Crows in the 1820s, and Zenas Leonard, a Pennsylvania farm boy who spent several winters with the tribe in the 1830s. Their accounts describe a mutually rewarding relationship that tribal leaders seemed willing to sustain. Relationships of this kind were probably on the increase as the trade itself expanded.[9]

A number of travellers commented on the close ties between traders and Crows. For example, in 1862, Army Capt. James L. Fisk, who had been dispatched to the upper Missouri to scout a route to the Montana gold fields, was impressed by a chief named White Hair who showed him two faded and tattered American Fur Company banners that he had kept for decades in a case attached to his saddle. After unwrapping the banners from their holder, White Hair told the visitor that the flags demonstrated the company's "high appreciation of the constancy of his friendship for the white man. . . ." Robert Meldrum later confirmed the chief's statement, telling Fisk he had known White Hair for twenty years and that "he has never forfeited his title to the good name accorded to him by these testimonials." Rudolph Friederich Kurz was more cynical, but equally certain about the ties between Crow chiefs and fur traders when he wrote in 1851 that "a redskin thinks twice before he murders his trader; he is aware of his dependence on the fur traders and of the reciprocal interest that unites them."[10]

Mountain man Zenas Leonard recounted that Crows and traders were both

---

[9] See James P. Beckwourth, *The Life and Adventures of James P. Beckwourth* (Lincoln: University of Nebraska Press, 1972), originally published in 1856; and Zenas Leonard, *Narrative of the Adventures of Zenas Leonard* (Lincoln: University of Nebraska Press, 1978), originally published in 1934. On Meldrum, see Keith Algier, "Robert Meldrum and the Crow Peltry Trade," *Montana: The Magazine of Western History* (Summer 1986), 36–47.

[10] U.S. Congress, House of Representatives, *House Executive Document No. 80*, 37th Congress, 3rd Session, "Expedition from Fort Abercrombie to Fort Benton," 1863 (Serial 1164), 22: Kurz, *Journal of Rudolph Friederich Kurz*, 215.

sociable and dependent on each other's services. Arriving at a Crow camp near the Wind River range in December 1834, Leonard reported that "the Crow chiefs were made presents of some small articles of merchandise," before "we commenced bartering with them for their furs and buffalo robes." The bartering went well, Leonard noted, for "as soon as they had sold out their present stock, they left us all highly pleased with their success and commenced hunting for more." Despite the fact that they had purchased all they could from the white men, the Crows pleaded with them to stay for the winter. Leonard agreed and spent a relatively comfortable few months with the band; its members scurried through the snows in search of more furs while Leonard and his colleagues stayed in camp, eating their host's food and enjoying the warmth of their lodges. His description hardly fits the popular image of a frost-bitten mountain man starving his way through a Rocky Mountain winter. "We occupied our time in hunting and trapping a little ourselves," Leonard recalled later, "but deriving our principal profits by trading with the Indians for robes which they would bring into our camp as fast as they could dress them."[11]

Leonard's account also suggests that the Crows of the 1830s were moving from the individualistic beaver trade to traffic in heavy – and more reliable – buffalo hides. Other traders confirmed that shift. Osborne Russell, who travelled through the Bighorn valley in 1838, reported, for example, that "the Crows had destroyed nearly all the beaver" in the surrounding mountains and that the Blackfeet had similarly exhausted the area north of the Yellowstone. There were no such reports regarding the buffalo. In fact one of the most dramatic descriptions of bison herds in Crow country was penned in 1859 by Brig. Gen. W. F. Raynolds who crested the Wolf Mountains on the eastern edge of the Little Bighorn valley and reported that "the entire tract of 40 or 50 square miles was covered with buffalo. . . ." He added, "I will not venture an estimate of their probable numbers." With such rich herds to draw upon, the Crows had little incentive to travel great lengths in search of the disappearing beaver. Writing from Fort Union in 1851, Swiss artist Rudolph Friederich Kurz confirmed this preference for buffalo. "The Absaroka are famous for their

---

[11] Leonard, *Narrative of the Adventures of Zenas Leonard*, 256. It is significant as well that when James Beckwourth was captured and "adopted" by the Crows in the winter of 1825–1826, he spent the bulk of his time trapping. After he had worked for several months, a party from his village took both Beckwourth's furs and their own to the Mandan villages. It is not clear from the mountain man's autobiography what he received in return. He did write the following: "I was pacifically engaged in trapping during the ensuing winter, and the season being open and pleasant, I met with great success. Could I have disposed of my peltry in St. Louis, I should have been as rich as I coveted." Beckwourth, *The Life and Adventures of James P. Beckwourth*, 163. Even so hostile a chief as Sitting Bull made exceptions to his antiwhite philosophy when it came to traders. Throughout his career as a war leader, the Hunkpapa warrior maintained friendly relations with traders, even working at one point as their agent. See Robert M. Utley, *The Lance and the Shield: The Life and Times of Sitting Bull* (New York: Henry Holt, 1993), 64, 72, 73–74.

robes," the visiting painter reported. "In no other nation are the dressed skins so soft and pliable."[12]

In his reports from Fort Union, American Fur Company agent Edwin Thompson Denig echoed Kurz's descriptions of Crow buffalo robes and praised the tribe's willingness to concentrate on the Yellowstone valley's apparently limitless resources. Denig noted that early in the century the tribe "hunted nothing but beaver," but that by midcentury they had shifted to bison. He pointed out that the Indians' passage from the beaver trade "tended considerably to constrict their wandering habits." Rather than disappear into the Rockies in search of the elusive beaver, Crow bands would locate within reach of a trading post and spend the fall and winter taking animals from the immense herds and dressing their skins. The result was not only long-term relationships with traders such as Denig, but the formation of relatively large bands that would follow regular patterns of movement.[13]

Linked ever tightly to traders and their goods, midcentury Crows oscillated within relatively limited areas. Mountain Crow leaders were most frequently encountered near the buffalo herds which ranged the Bighorn basin south of the Bighorn range. They returned in the summer to the Yellowstone valley, but they spent the bulk of their time between the Bighorns and the Wind River range and relied upon the traders who participated in the Green River rendezvous or drew their supplies at Fort Laramie. The Kicked In The Bellies, who were closely associated with the Mountain Crows, kept roughly to this same pattern, although they were usually found further to the east, along the Little Bighorn, Powder and Tongue Rivers, and they occasionally appeared at Fort Union. River Crow leaders operated along the Yellowstone for part of the year, but moved north along the Judith and Musselshell Rivers during the winter. Their contacts were principally with the traders at Fort Union.[14]

IV

During the 1830s and 1840s, the locations of Crow bands were also determined by the presence of powerful Indian neighbors, particularly the Sioux and their allies to the east and south, and the Blackfeet to the north and west. The effect of conflicts with these tribes was the Crows' gradual withdrawal from the eastern reaches of the Yellowstone valley and the southern portions of

---

[12] Osborne Russell, *Journal of a Trapper*, Aubrey L. Haines, ed. (Portland: Oregon Historical Society, 1955), 82; Kurz, *Journal of Rudolph Friederich Kurz*, 250.

[13] Edwin Thompson Denig, *Five Indian Tribes of the Upper Missouri*, edited and with an introduction by John C. Ewers (Norman: University of Oklahoma Press, 1961), 185. As was the case with other Plains tribes, the shift to buffalo robes also encouraged polygamy among the Crows.

[14] For descriptions of Crow locations, see (for 1832) Washington Irving, *The Adventures of Captain Bonneville* (Boston: Twayne, 1977), 117, originally published in 1837.

modern-day Wyoming, and the isolation of the River Crow bands who retreated north to the upper Missouri.[15]

The Lakota Sioux and their allies were the Crows' most frightening adversaries. When the first Sioux bands encountered Europeans in the seventeenth century, they lived in central Minnesota, at the eastern edge of the plains. The group quickly entered the Great Lakes fur trade, establishing firm ties to French traders and growing reliant upon the guns and tools they acquired from the East. At the opening of the eighteenth century, however, the search for new hunting grounds and the growing militancy of the Ojibwe (who were positioned closer to the French) caused the westernmost bands of Sioux to emigrate westward onto the prairies. One set of hunting bands pursued the buffalo across what is now central South Dakota in the direction of the Black Hills and became known as the Teton, or western branch of the tribe. Another group followed the beaver, moving north and west and forming a division called the Yanktonai. The movement of both divisions was of course greatly facilitated by their acquisition of horses and guns which occurred at the same time.[16]

The westward movement of the Teton Sioux (also referred to as "Lakota," the name of their common Sioux dialect) was contested by the wealthy and well-fortified farming peoples along the Missouri, as well as the Kiowas, Cheyennes and Arapahoes. The Teton groups were formidable rivals for this territory, however, since they were securely tied to eastern traders and were themselves desperate; they were being pushed westward by the expanding sphere of white settlement which they could not stop.

François Antoine Larocque alluded to conflicts between the Sioux and his hosts in 1806, but these had been scattered and confined to the eastern reaches of the Yellowstone valley. Lewis and Clark's journals, compiled at about the same time, give a similar impression. Writing from the Mandan villages during the winter of 1804–5, William Clark reported that the Sioux, whom he called "the pirates of the Missouri," claimed lands running west *to* the Missouri as

---

[15] The following discussion of Crow rivalries with neighboring tribes takes strong exception to the view that through warfare "the Crow produced a high degree of consistency and coherence in their culture." For that point of view, see Fred W. Voget, "Warfare and the Integration of Crow Culture," in Ward H. Goodenough, ed., *Explorations in Cultural Anthropology* (New York: McGraw-Hill, 1964), 489. The narrative to follow takes a historical approach to Plains Indian warfare. It rests heavily on the writings of Frank Raymond Secoy and Colin Calloway. See Frank Raymond Secoy, *Changing Military Patterns on the Great Plains*, Monographs of the American Ethnological Society, Vol. 21 (Locust Valley, N.Y.: J. J. Augustin Publisher, 1953); and Colin G. Calloway, "'The Only Way Open to Us: The Crow Struggle for Survival in the Nineteenth Century,'" *North Dakota History*, 53 (Summer 1986), 25–34.

[16] The best summary of this history can be found in Richard White, "The Winning of the West: The Expansion of the Western Sioux in the Eighteenth and Nineteenth Centuries," *Journal of American History*, 65, 2 (September 1978), 319–343. Like Professor White, I have tried in this description to keep in mind that the divisons of the Teton Sioux – the Oglala, Hunkpapa, Brule, Sans Arcs, Blackfeet, Two Kettle and Minneconjou – functioned as autonomous units for most of the nineteenth century.

well as the Cheyenne and White Rivers; he made no mention of the Yellowstone.
A report of a peace agreement between the Crows and Teton bands from 1816
to 1817 confirms this picture of two groups occupying competing, but adjacent,
territories.[17]

Reports of fighting in the Yellowstone valley began to appear about 1830. At
first these were raids that the Crows could repell. In 1834, for example, the
Crows scored a dramatic victory over a Sioux raiding party that had invaded
the Bighorn valley. According to an account compiled from tribal members at
the end of the century, the Sioux had surprised Sore Belly's band and were
on the verge of victory when the chief, wearing an eagle feather war bonnet
whose tail floated six feet behind him, rode forward to lead a last-minute rout
of the invaders. Six years later, Father Pierre-Jean DeSmet, a Belgian priest
who was returning from a historic journey to Rockies where he had founded a
series of Catholic missions among the Flatheads and other mountain tribes,
reported that the Crows continued to rule the Yellowstone. "The Crows are
considered the most indefatigable marauders of the plains," he wrote in his
journal. "Their country seems to stretch from the Black Hills to the Rocky
Mountains, embracing the Wind River mountains and all the plains and valleys
watered by that stream, as well as by the Yellowstone and Powder Rivers. I rode
with this camp for two days," he concluded; "they had plenty of everything."[18]
Soon after the Belgian priest's visit, however, the tide of victory turned dramatically against the Crows. In 1850, fur traders near Fort Laramie and Fort
Union reported a growing number of Sioux bands in the area and a rising level
of conflict between the tribes. Veteran warriors interviewed a generation later
by whites recalled that the American traders encouraged the Sioux to drive the
Crows from the Platte and Missouri. In 1859, an army exploration detachment
placed the border with the Sioux at the Powder River and noted that the Crows
"thus far have been able to maintain their independence and defend their
territory." The commander's report went on to observe, however, that "at the
time of my visit . . . they evidently feared the effect of this constant pressure
and expressed a dread of being ultimately overpowered." Red Bear, a Mountain
Crow band leader told these American visitors that the Sioux "are making war
on us all the time."[19]

---

[17] For Larocque on the Sioux, see François Antoine Larocque, "Yellowstone Journal," in W.
Raymond Wood and Thomas D. Thiessen, eds., *Early Fur Trade on the Northern Plains:
Canadian Traders Among the Mandan and Hidatsa Indians, 1738–1818* (Norman: University of
Oklahoma Press, 1985), 206, 218. Clark's comments can be found in "Fort Mandan Miscellany,"
The Journals of the Lewis and Clark Expedition, 6 vols. (Lincoln: University of Nebraska Press,
1987), Vol. 3, 418.

[18] William A. Allen, *Adventures with Indians and Game: Twenty Years in the Rocky Mountains*
(Chicago: A. W. Bowen, 1903), 95–99; Pierre-Jean DeSmet, S. J., *Life, Letters and Travels of
Father Pierre-Jean DeSmet, S. J.*, Hiram Martin Chittenden and Alfred Talbot Richardson, eds.
(New York: Francis P. Harper, 1905), Vol. 1, 238.

[19] "Journal of James H. Bradley," 182–183; U.S. Senate, *Senate Executive Document 77*, 40th
Congress, 2nd Session, 16, 38, 51.

There were many reasons for the success of the Sioux after 1840, but chief among them was the impact of European diseases on their enemies. While detailed evidence is sketchy, it is clear that epidemics of smallpox reached as far north as the Mandan and Hidatsa villages in 1781. Larocque himself reported in 1806 that smallpox had "raged among them for many years" and reduced their population by as much as 80%. During the nineteenth century, waves of epidemics weakened the plains groups and reduced their ability to resist the Sioux onslaught. The Sioux also suffered from these diseases, but their longer exposure to Europeans seemed to give them a greater ability to survive. In 1837 a disastrous epidemic ignited by an outbreak of smallpox in the Missouri River villages cut the entire Plains Indian population by as much as 50% and eliminated the Mandan and Hidatsa tribes as significant actors in the region's commerce. The Crows were affected by all of these epidemics, but their more isolated location and their tactic of scattering into family-sized bands at the first news of the disease saved them from extinction. Only marginally affected by the disease, and eager to capitalize on the new demand for buffalo robes, the Sioux quickly moved west of the Missouri to fill the vacuum left by the demise of the Hidatsas and Mandans. They became eager customers at the American Fur Company's Missouri River forts and bitter enemies of rival tribesmen who tried to compete with them.[20]

The actions of the Cheyenne and Arapaho were closely related to the expansion of the Teton tribes. These tribes were themselves being pushed west and south by white settlement, and they frequently joined forces with the Sioux in order to preserve a position for themselves in a rapidly shifting environment. For example, the trader William Bent, who lived among the Cheyenne during much of the early nineteenth century, reported a series of clashes between his clients and the Crow west of the Black Hills during the 1820s. Crow accounts tell of bloody battles between the two tribes during the same period, all south of the Yellowstone. Clearly, the Cheyennes were being pushed into conflict with Crows who hunted to their north and sought to prevent anyone from entering the Wind River territory.[21]

In 1825, when the disgusted chief Sore Belly left the American emissaries at the Mandan villages, he moved his River Crow bands north and west, away from both whites and the expanding Sioux and into the relatively isolated area of the upper Missouri. He knew he would find other enemies there, but he was confident that he could defend his followers from harm. This region had long been a contentious borderland between the Crows and their northern neighbors the Blackfeet, Assiniboin and Cree, but in recent years the wealth of the early fur trade era made conflicts with the Blackfeet the most troublesome. Sore Belly

[20] For Larocque, see "Yellowstone Journal," 206. White describes the impact of disease on Sioux expansion at 325, and 329–335.
[21] George Hyde, Life of George Bent Written from His Letters, ed. Savoie Lottinville (Norman: University of Oklahoma Press, 1968), 20–30.

himself had risen to prominence in the tribe for a brilliant daylight attack on a Blackfeet village sometime in the 1810s.

The Blackfeet had first acquired firearms from the British in the eighteenth century, and because of that connection the tribe had resisted the spread of American fur traders into their country. Armed by their friends in Canada, Blackfeet war parties raided River Crow camps along the Musselshell and Yellowstone throughout the first decades of the nineteenth century, but like the Sioux during the same period, they did not succeed in dislodging their enemies from their Montana hunting grounds. American explorer Benjamin Bonneville noted in 1832, for example, that despite the fact that the Crows ruled the prairies as far as Nebraska, "their incessant wars with the Blackfeet . . . are gradually wearing them out."[22]

At first the rivalry between the Blackfeet and Crow was transferred to the American mountain men as well, for those who were friendly to the Crows were regularly rebuffed in their attempts to trap and barter among the Blackfeet, while the Blackfeet's allies were regular objects of Crow hostility. The centralization of the fur trade under American control eventually won out, however, for in 1831 the American Fur Company (operating from its new base at Fort Union) erected a temporary Blackfeet trading post at the mouth of the Marias River. The following year a permanent facility, Fort McKenzie, was built nearby, on a spot forty miles below the great falls of the Missouri. When the River Crow leader Sore Belly learned about the construction of Fort McKenzie, he vowed that he would destroy the fort and its Blackfeet customers. He told the American fur traders that it would be disastrous for him if his enemies had a source of military supplies so close at hand. Not only the Blackfeet, but any of the western tribes contemplating a raid against Sore Belly and his followers could be sure of fresh supplies of guns and ammunition before heading south to attack.

A party of Crow warriors set out for the upper Missouri in the summer of 1834. The chief knew that only a skeleton crew would be present at Fort McKenzie during June and July because the Blackfeet were trading at the Canadian posts to the north and the American Fur Company had sent a number of its employees downriver to Fort Union with the spring shipment of furs. Sore Belly's men captured the fort's horses and laid seige to the outpost for a month, but the American trader in charge would not surrender. As the garrison faced starvation, a party of 800 Blackfeet lodges suddenly returned from Canada. The Crows retreated. Unable to fulfill his promise of victory over the enemy, Sore Belly refused the path of discretion. He died charging a band of Blackfeet warriors during the group's retreat south.[23]

[22] Irving, *The Adventures of Captain Bonneville*, 118.
[23] The principal account of Arapaoosh's seige of Fort McKenzie and death is found in Denig, *Five Indian Tribes of the Upper Missouri*, 177–184.

Destructive battles with the Blackfeet continued for the next half-century despite the fact that the Crows could no longer enlist individual fur traders on their side. Struggles over access to the buffalo herds, rivalries over trade and simple revenge fueled round after round of attack and counterattack. A group of Crow elders apparently tried to negotiate a peace between the groups in the late 1830s, but this was short-lived. As the trader Zenas Leonard reported when he travelled with a hunting party that accidentally came upon a party of Blackfeet in the fall of 1834, these were the Crows' "implacable enemies." "War," Leonard added, "was now their only desire."[24]

Smaller, more distant tribes frequently allied themselves with the Crows against the Blackfeet, Sioux and Cheyenne. Before 1837 these included the river tribes, the Hidatsa and Mandans, who wanted to maintain their trade relationship with the Crows and who had an interest in stopping the westward expansion of the Tetons and the Cheyennes. Similarly, the Shoshone, who had been trading partners of the Crows since the arrival of the horse in the early eighteenth century, continued to maintain generally peaceful relations with their northern neighbors despite occasional tensions over hunting territory in the Bighorn basin. Finally, plateau peoples such as the Nez Perce and Flatheads, who had become accustomed to crossing the Rockies on horseback to hunt buffalo and trade, found that friendly relations with the Crows preserved their access to the Yellowstone and protected them against the Blackfeet. These groups sought out the Crows for refuge as well as to buy and sell horses, furs, handicrafts and foodstuffs.[25]

The shifting power relationships on the northern plains, like the fur trade itself, fixed the Crows into a tightening geographical circle. Families continued to camp, hunt and travel together much as they had in Larocque's day, but these bands were increasingly hemmed in by powerful Indian adversaries just as they were tied to particular traders or trading sites. Pressures from other tribes increased during the 1840s, leading to the virtual separation of the River and Mountain Crows. Rarely could Crow camps feel confident enough to gather in large groups or to travel without posting guards and dispatching scouts to detect oncoming attacks. But despite growing Crow vigilance, Blackfeet raids

[24] Leonard, *Narrative of the Adventures of Zenas Leonard*, 237. For a discussion of the alliance and its failure, see Katherine M. Weist, "An Ethnohistorical Analysis of Crow Political Alliances," *Western Canadian Journal of Anthropology*, 7, 4 (1977), 39. Further information on Crow relations with the Blackfeet is in Calloway, "The Only Way Open to Us," 30.

[25] For a discussion of these alliances, see Wiest, "An Ethnohistorical Analysis of Crow Political Alliances," 39, and Larocque, "Yellowstone Journal," 218. These alliances were not permanent. For example, Pierre Jean DeSmet, the Jesuit missionary who travelled up the Missouri in 1840, described a battle between the Flatheads and the Crows. See "DeSmet's Oregon Missions and Travels over the Rocky Mountains, 1845–1846," in Reuben Gold Thwaites, ed., *Early Western Travels, 1748–1846* (Cleveland: Arthur H. Clark, 1906), Vol. 29, 330–335. DeSmet also described a friendly 1840 meeting between Crows and Flatheads where horses were purchased. See DeSmet, *Life, Letters and Travels of Father Pierre-Jean DeSmet*, 233.

and Teton expansion continued. By the decade of the 1850s the Sioux had pushed west of the Powder River country and were regularly raiding the Bighorn valley, while Blackfeet incursions from north of the Yellowstone disrupted life in Bighorn and Little Bighorn valleys.

In 1859 the last of the Yellowstone River trading posts, the second Fort Sarpy, was abandoned and burned. A fur company official noted that with the Blackfeet making "constant warlike incursions into Crow territory" and the Sioux raiding the from the east, "it became difficult finally to induce men to go to such a dangerous locality, and this was one of the principal causes of the withdrawal from the country." As eastern Montana became the center of constant warfare between desperate tribes, the best the Crows could do was defend themselves against intruders and maintain their ties to the supply posts at Fort Union and Fort Laramie. The era of vague borders and friendly mountain men was over. "As the country now stands," trader Edwin Thompson Denig wrote from Fort Union, "it is destitute of traders."[26]

<h1 style="text-align:center">V</h1>

Despite the hardships that warfare and traders brought them, the Crows neither retreated from their adversaries nor scattered in panic. In the words of government inspector Gideon Matlock in 1847, they and their neighbors endured the new pressures exerted upon them by "tenaciously adhering to all the ferocious customs and miserable expedients of savage life." Other, less hostile observers described the tribe as having a distinctive and a strong "national" identity. Among the customs frequently noted by travellers was a preoccupation with the acquisition of trade goods. The tools and weapons available from whites made the trade and traders essential to the tribe's livelihood. Crow hunters were regular customers at the trading posts, exchanging furs for supplies when they had some, and pleading for assistance when they had none. When these pleas were ignored, they "captured" supplies where they could; to be without guns, blankets and ammunition in the Yellowstone in the 1850s was suicide.[27]

Crows also placed increasing emphasis on military success in the training of

---

[26] Alexander Culbertson quoted in "Affairs at Fort Benton from 1831 to 1869 from Lieutenant Bradley's Journal," *Contributions to the Historical Society of Montana* 3 (1900), 261–262; Denig, *Five Tribes of the Upper Missouri*, 204. In his overview of the northwestern plains area, John C. Ewers concluded that the Crows of midcentury were "in the most desperate military position. . . ." John C. Ewers, "Was There a Northwestern Plains Sub-Culture? An Ethnographic Appraisal," *Plains Anthropologist*, 12 (1967), 172–173.

[27] *Annual Report of the Commissioner of Indian Affairs* (hereafter cited as *ARCIA*), 1847 (Serial 503), 851. For a description of the Crows' "national" behavior, see Leonard, *Narrative of the Adventures of Zenas Leonard*, 250–252.

DEATH OF A-RA-POO-ASH.

A fanciful illustration of the death of Sore Belly, contained in the memoirs of the African-American fur trader James P. Beckwourth. Beckwourth claimed that at the moment of his death the Crow chief appointed the trapper to succeed him, and this engraving was included in *The Life and Adventures of James P. Beckwourth* when it was published in 1856 in order to bolster the claim. Courtesy of The Newberry Library.

their young people and the selection of their leaders. Bravery and the ability to lead war parties had always been important, but in the mid-nineteenth century they were essential to the group's survival. George Catlin, a Philadelphia lawyer who travelled up the Missouri in the early 1830s to study the region's tribes, was among the first to remark that attacks from their Indian enemies seemed to doom the Crows. He estimated that there were "two or three women to a man in the nation; in consequence of the continual losses sustained amongst their men in war. . . ." In this atmosphere, he reported only warriors could aspire to be leaders. As fur trader Osborne Russell reported in 1839, "Their government is a kind of democracy. The chief who can enumerate the greatest number of battle exploits is unanimously considered the supreme ruler."[28]

Emphasis on warfare not only limited the avenues to community leadership, but also helped sustain an atmosphere in which bands were in a constant state of miliary readiness. The River Crow warrior Two Leggings, who dictated his life story in the early twentieth century, recalled his youth spent fighting the Blackfeet as a time of excitement. Insulated by five decades from the desperation of those days, Two Leggings remembered spending his boyhood "listening to the stories of our warriors and medicine men. I wanted to be just as brave and honored," he remembered, adding that in the aftermath of a story session he "would train . . . that much harder, running and riding and playing war games with my friends." For men of Two Leggings's generation, the tribe assigned levels of value to particular acts of bravery, from capturing an enemy horse to touching an enemy warrior, and the community kept close watch over individual achievement. "Whenever one person exceeds the existing chief in these deeds," Zenas Leonard reported, "he is installed into the office of chief of the nation, which he retains until some other ambitious, daring brave exceeds him." The result, the trader noted, was that "there is more personal ambition and rivalry existing among this tribe than any other I became acquainted with. . . ."[29]

Despite the forces at work encouraging individual battlefield bravado, Crow communities maintained a remarkable degree of military discipline. A young adventurer who came to live among them in the 1860s amidst the worst of the Sioux wars remembered years later that the tribe "had among themselves law and order more effectively prevalent than among any community of white people I have known." Village life was regulated by councils of elders whose decisions were enforced by warrior societies composed of young men who could demonstrate their martial skills by maintaining control over the population.

---

[28] George Catlin, *Letters and Notes on the Manners, Customs, and Conditions of the North American Indians* (New York: Dover, 1973), 43, originally published in 1844; Russell, *Journal of a Trapper*, 146.

[29] Peter Nabokov, ed., *Two Leggings: The Making of a Crow Warrior* (New York: Thomas Y. Crowell, 1967), 6; Leonard, *Narrative of the Adventures of Zenas Leonard*, 232.

These "soldiers," Zenas Leonard reported, ensured that there were "seldom" any disturbances; they were "always ready to chastise and punish" any disruptive conduct.[30]

The young Crow policemen of the 1850s would certainly have been recognizable to their grandparents who regulated trader Larocque's hunting forays and guarded his hosts, but contact with both whites and intruding Indian tribes had elevated the group's loyalty to these military units. In the process the flamboyant chiefs of the early fur trade period were replaced by hardened military veterans who demanded rigid loyalty from their followers. Long Hair and Sore Belly were noted for their long-distance travelling and raiding – activities that took them from the Canadian border to the Arkansas River – but the men who succeeded them led a far more circumscribed existence. A tribal profile prepared in the 1870s from interviews with Crow elders confirms this view, for it declared in its conclusion that "the real authority rests in the soldiers who band together to enforce order in the camp and preserve unity of action."[31]

Among the River Crows, Sore Belly was succeeded by a series of men who emulated his military success but operated in a smaller arena. First among these successors were Twines (or Twists) His Tail and Bear's Head. Both were born sometime in the first decade of the nineteenth century and died before 1870. They rose to prominence following Sore Belly's death in 1834, carrying on that leader's struggles with the Blackfeet and trading regularly along the Yellowstone and at Fort Union. The Swiss artist Rudloph Friederich Kurz was present at the latter site in the fall of 1851 when Twines His Tail, "their leader on this side of the mountains," arrived with several packs of buffalo robes. The painter wrote that despite his plain dress – the chief wore "gray leggings but no shirt, no vest, neither neckcloth nor hat" – he had the bearing of a nobleman. His resemblance "to Louis Philippe of blessed memory struck me at once," Kurz wrote in his journal, "the same capable expression of citoyen, the same shrewd look of a merchant, the same official mien." A few months later when the chief reappeared with a request for advance payment for his next shipment of buffalo robes, the Swiss visitor switched similes, declaring the chief was "a Yankee; he is Smart."[32]

Like Sore Belly, Twines His Tail and Bear's Head based their military decisions on a sense of divine mission, claiming that supernatural guides advised

---

[30] Thomas LeForge, *Memoirs of a White Crow Indian* (Lincoln: University of Nebraska Press, 1974), 142, originally published in 1928; Leonard, *Narrative of the Adventures of Zenas Leonard*, 233.

[31] Much of the discussion in this and succeeding paragraphs draws on the ideas in Tom E. Roll, "Crow Chieftanship: A Study of Status Acquisition," in Leslie B. Davis, ed., *Lifeways of Intermontane and Plains Montana Indians* (Bozeman: Montana State University Occasional Papers of the Museum of the Rockies, No. 1, 1979), 99–107.

[32] Kurz, *Journal of Rudolph Friederich Kurz*, 212, 268. After delivering "heavy bundles" in October, Twines His Tail returned in late December with 130 additional robes; see ibid., 251.

them and protected them from their enemies. Like Red Plume, who had been known as Fool-boy when young, Twists His Tail began his career as a poor, orphaned child. He carried out his first raid in response to insults from a well-connected young man who later stood shame-faced as Twines His Tail and his victorious war party paraded his captured horses through camp. According to one version of the story, the crowd who witnessed the warriors' return asked, "Who is the leader of these . . .? . . . Why it is Twined-tail! How is it he is so handsome!"[33]

A generation younger than Twines His Tail and Bear's Head were a series of band leaders who headed River Crow war parties in the 1860s and 1870s and were numbered among the reservation "headmen" who rode with Henry Armstrong into the Little Bighorn in 1884. These included Horse Guard, Big Ox, Hunts The Enemy, One Pine (or Lone Tree) and Long Horse. Like their elders, these chiefs spent the bulk of their time in the Yellowstone valley and on the plains to the north and rose to prominence on the strength of their military service. Their names appear frequently in the journals of Fort Union. Each man could command a following among the younger warriors when they announced that they were going to lead a raid or a revenge attack. Most survived the warfare of the 1860s and 1870s; the exception was Long Horse, who died battling the Sioux in the Judith River basin in 1875.[34]

By midcentury the Mountain Crow were being referred to as the "main body" of the tribe. Perhaps because of their size, or in response to increased military pressure from the Sioux, these bands experienced a proliferation of war leaders during the 1840s and 1850s. Red Bear and Two Face were the principal leaders among this group, rising to prominence immediately after the death of Red Plume. The trader Edwin Thompson Denig estimated in the 1850s that Two Face led more than 200 lodges of Mountain Crow. If this is correct, he would have been the leader for nearly half of all Crows. An account written in

[33] Robert Lowie, *The Crow Indians* (Lincoln: University of Nebraska Press, 1983), originally published in 1935, 169. For Bear's Head, see Denig, *Five Indian Tribes of the Upper Missouri*, 143. Bear's Head was also described briefly in Ferdinand Hayden's report, which itself was based on information gathered from Denig in the middle 1850s. See Ferdinand V. Hayden, "On the Ethnography and Philology of the Indian Tribes of the Missouri Valley," *Transactions of the American Philosophical Society*, 2, 3 (1862), 394. The "orphan motif" in Crow folklore, in which a powerless youth is befriended by a guardian spirit who brings him to prominence, is quite common. See, for example, the discussion in Peter Nabokov, "Cultivating Themselves: The Inter-play of Crow Religion and History" (Ph.D. Dissertation, Department of Anthropology, University of California, Berkeley, 1988), chap. 4. Bear's Head also appears as an agent of the Fort Union traders in "The Yellowstone Expedition of 1863: From the Journal of Captain James Stuart," *Contributions to the Montana Historical Society*, 1 (1876), 152.

[34] For profiles of these younger chiefs, see Edward Curtis, *The North American Indian*, 20 volumes (New York: 1909–1903), Vol. 4, 197–210. For Long Horse, see Bernardis, *Crow Social Studies: Balleeisbaalichiwee History, Teacher's Guide* (Crow Agency, Mont.: Bilingual Materials Development Center, 1986), 49–50. Horse Guard provides an example of a chief whose name appears in the journals of fur traders. Trader James Chambers noted in 1855 that when Horse Guard appeared at Fort Sarpy he always received coffee because "he is a chief and leads a camp of fifty lodges." See "Journal of James H. Chambers," 113.

1859 by Gen. W. F. Raynolds from his camp on the Yellowstone River conveys the flavor of Two Face's chiefly status. According to the visiting officer, Two Face "rode into camp in full court costume, announcing his name by the expressive procedure of touching his face and holding up two fingers. He calmly took temporary possession of the largest tent, making himself completely at home."[35]

It is from the ranks of the Mountain Crow soldiers who fought with Red Bear and Two Face that the American military recruited its first Crow scouts. These warrior leaders included Iron Bull (or White Temple), Pretty Eagle, Bull Chief and Wet. Iron Bull was the senior member of this group. He was so successful in his dealings with whites that he earned a reputation as the wealthiest man in the tribe; his hospitality and generosity were famous additions to his leadership on the battlefield. He and his wives enjoyed entertaining visiting army officers and traders, treating them to lavish meals and long discussions of politics and military tactics. Most of these younger chiefs survived into the reservation period. It is not surprising that Henry Armstrong turned to many of them to help plan the relocation of the government agency to the Little Bighorn in the early 1880s and to stand with him against dissenters like Spotted Horse.[36]

During the 1860s and 1870s, the dominance of military men in tribal affairs was reflected not only in the leadership of the two major tribal divisions, but also in the internal life of the Kicked In The Bellies. Their principal leader during the 1840s was a chief the whites called "Big Robber" or "Big Robert." Big Robber led a band which established close ties to the American traders on the Platte River and who spent the bulk of their time east and south of the Bighorns. Because of their location, the Kicked In The Bellies were almost constantly at war with the Sioux; not surprisingly Big Robber himself was killed by Teton warriors in 1858.[37]

Following Big Robber's death, Blackfoot, or Sits In The Middle Of The Land, an accomplished warrior who was about the same age, rose to prominence. Like Big Robber, Blackfoot had won most of his military honors in battles with the Sioux (one of his wives was a Sioux captive). He also continued Big Robber's practice of allying himself as much as possible with the American government and the traders at Fort Laramie. Blackfoot was one of the tribe's principal representatives during the Sioux war of 1866–8, and he was a member

---

[35] For Two Face, see Denig, *Five Indian Tribes of the Upper Missouri*, 143; and Hayden, "On the Ethnography and Philology of the Indian Tribes of the Missouri Valley," 394. The description by General Raynolds is in W. F. Raynolds, "Report on the Exploration of the Yellowstone," *Senate Executive Document 97*, 40th Congress, 2nd Session (1859), 47. Red Bear's deeds are described in Curtis, *The North American Indian*, Vol. 4, 52; and Bernardis, *Crow Social Studies*, 48–49.

[36] For Iron Bull, Pretty Eagle and Wet, see Bernardis, *Crow Social Studies*, 52–54; for Bull Chief, see Curtis, *The North American Indians*, Vol. 4, 197. For an account of Iron Bull's hospitality, see James D. Lockwood, *Life and Adventures of a Drummer Boy* (Albany: John Skinner, 1893), 168–174

[37] See Denig, *Five Tribes of the Upper Missouri*, 143, 194; and Curtis, *North American Indian*, Vol. 4, 105. For Big Robber's death, see *ARCIA*, 1858 (Serial 919), 443–444.

of the first group of Crow leaders to visit Washington in 1873. When the young
white adventurer Thomas LeForge was adopted into the tribe in 1868, he
reported that Blackfoot "was the chief of my band." The chief died of pneumonia in central Wyoming in 1877.

During the war-torn decades of midcentury, two ancient Crow institutions
operated to reinforce the group's political unity and military discipline. In
different ways, warrior societies and the tobacco ceremonies helped the Crows
defend themselves from outside aggression by checking the traditional tendency
towards fragmentation and providing networks to hold scattered band members
in line.

Warrior societies were clubs that had a long history. They were responsible
for keeping order in camp and in guiding the band when it was on the move.
During the nineteenth century, however, these clubs increasingly resembled
guilds devoted exclusively to the rituals and achievements of war. Open to
promising youngsters, guided by celebrated veterans, and marked by distinctive
regalia and rituals, these societies appear to have proliferated during the early
years of the century, offering a path of upward mobility and a vehicle for
mobilizing Crow manpower on a large scale. As pressure on the group increased, however, the societies consolidated; by the 1860s there were only two,
the Foxes and Lumpwoods. The reduction in numbers increased their military
spirit, for the two societies were intensely competitive. They tried to outdo each
other's battlefield exploits and to humiliate anyone who questioned their tactics.
Competition between the societies also stretched from horse racing to wife
stealing.[38]

Contemporary Crows often teach that No Vitals, the first tribal leader after
the group separated from the Hidatsa, "received a vision from the spirit world
which showed him that the life of the Crows was to find its future at the place
where the sacred tobacco seeds grew." Ultimately, "the Crow people found the
sacred tobacco seeds here where the Crow people now live." Different versions
of this story suggest varying routes the migrating Crows followed on their way
to the Yellowstone and Bighorn valleys, and there is additional disagreement over
whether the group brought the seeds with them or found them on their arrival.
Despite these uncertainties, however, tobacco planting among the Crows was
universally associated with the group's special claim to the area immediately
surrounding the Bighorn Mountains. Moreover, the historic record indicates
that this association was a prominent feature of nineteenth century tribal life.[39]

Like other Plains Indians, the Crows incorporated tobacco and smoking into

---

[38] For Blackfoot, see Bernardis, *Crow Social Studies*, 50–52; and Leforge, *Memoirs of a White Crow Indian*, 90. For a description of the warrior societies and their many activities, see Lowie, *The Crow Indians*, 172–214.

[39] Quoted in Nabokov, "Cultivating Themselves," 111–112. For a discussion of the various versions of the origins of the Tobacco Society, see also chap. 5.

many aspects of daily life: greetings, discussions, diplomacy and prayer. François Antoine Larocque observed that his hosts were "most superstitious with regard to the pipe which is the object of their most sacred regard." Leaders were called "pipeholders," men who would carry their pipes before them as they directed the band to new hunting grounds or charted the way for a war party. The Crows were unique in the region, however, in maintaining a ceremony in which they planted a variety of "short" tobacco each spring and harvested it each fall. This ritual activity was under the control of the Tobacco Society made up of men and women who would supervise the multiple rituals accompanying the annual cycle. The society was so extensive that several chapters operated among the group. The "short tobacco" was never smoked; society leaders would store seeds, plant them and organize a fall harvest. All of these activities memorialized and celebrated No Vitals's original vision and recalled the tribe's common claim to its homeland.[40]

References to tobacco planting appear repeatedly in accounts of mid-nineteenth century Crow life. James Beckwourth, the mountain man who lived with the tribe during the 1820s, was disappointed that the cultivated leaf was "unfit to chew," but he reported that it was planted "by the prophets and medicine men; after which a great feast is provided, and a general time of dancing and rejoicing follows." Similarly, the veteran fur trader Edwin Thompson Denig wrote that "this nation has from time immemorial planted tobacco . . . They believe that as long as they continue to preserve the seed and have in their homes some of the blossom they will preserve their national existence." The society even functioned through the military struggles of the 1860s and 1870s. Two Leggings, a young warrior who came of age in that chaotic world, identified his adoption into the Tobacco Society by Bull That Goes Hunting as the turning point in his life. The ceremony began with an image of tribal unity: "The next morning the Mountain Crows broke camp and went down Elk [Yellowstone] River to meet the River Crows for the planting of the tobacco." Afterwards, he declared, "I was very happy."[41]

VI

During the first half of the nineteenth century, external events – the advent of the fur trade and the intrusion into their homeland of rival tribes – dramatically

[40] Larocque, "Yellowstone Journal," 211. Robert Lowie offers a summary of the ritual in *The Crow Indians*, chap. 15; Peter Nabokov's dissertation, "Cultivating Themselves," provides a compelling description of the ritual's history down to the present and argues for the centrality of the ritual in Crow cosmology.
[41] Beckwourth, *The Life and Adventures of James P. Beckwourth*, 259; Denig, *Five Indian Tribes of the Upper Missouri*, 189; Nabokov, *Two Leggings*, 144.

affected Crow life. Despite these disruptions, however, Crow bands continued to organize their lives according to inherited traditions and to operate outside the direct authority of any other group. Individuals would certainly have preferred fewer deaths in battle and more freedom to travel beyond their shrinking domain, but shifts in circumstance neither dissolved their traditions nor severed their ties to their kinsmen. In fact, these external threats drew the group more tightly together. During the 1860s and 1870s, however, conflicts associated with the rising power and presence of the U.S. government and its citizens caused restrictions on the group's freedom to reach a new level of intensity.

It is striking that even as late as 1851, when the United States called for a general Plains Indian peace conference to be held at Fort Laramie along the North Platte River, the Americans were a peripheral force in the region. Concerned for the safety of emigrants who were now passing across the prairies each summer on their way to the new territories of Oregon and California, government officials invited representatives of all the major tribes to meet for a general peace conference. Ten thousand Crow, Sioux, Cheyenne, Arapaho, Shoshone, Arikara and Assiniboin people responded. Also present were representatives of the forces which had provoked such profound changes in the region during the previous half-century: fur traders (including the famous Jim Bridger and the Crows' Robert Meldrum), a Catholic priest (Father DeSmet), and a detachment of American soldiers.

Fearful that the assembled Indians would attack if they were not fed and entertained properly, Thomas Fitzpatrick and David D. Mitchell, the American representatives, moved the meeting to nearby Horse Creek, a site where the grass and water was more plentiful. They also promised all the delegates that presents were soon to arrive. The government's men had no ability to question the credentials of tribal delegates or to force the assembled leaders to accept unpopular treaty provisions. They hoped that friendly visiting and speech making would strengthen the paper loyalties contained in General Atkinson's 1825 treaties and lay the groundwork for a series of renewed alliances between native groups and the American government.[42]

Within a week the conference produced a treaty promising safe passage for whites in exchange for federal recognition of tribal territories. Tribal leaders also promised to maintain peace among themselves. Throughout these proceedings the Crows were represented by Big Robber and the trader Robert Meldrum. Comfortable with American fur traders and worried primarily about the Sioux,

---

[42] For a description of the Fort Laramie negotiations and the Crow's role in them, see Edwin Bearss, *Bighorn Canyon National Recreation Area*, 103–105, and Anthony McGinnis, *Counting Coup and Cutting Horses: Intertribal Warfare on the Northern Plains* (Evergreen, Colo.: Cordillera, 1990), 85–88; an overview of government relations during this midcentury period can also be found in Keith Algier, *The Crow and the Eagle: A Tribal History from Lewis and Clark to Custer* (Caldwell, Idaho: Caxton, 1993), 129–197.

Big Robber agreed to protect white migrants and to accept the present Mountain Crow hunting grounds as the tribal domain. According to the treaty, "Crow country" ran from the Continental Divide on the west to the Musselshell River on the north, from the mouth of the Musselshell to the Powder River on the east and south to the Rattlesnake range in what is now central Wyoming. No River Crow leaders were present at the Fort Laramie conference, so it is not surprising that their hunting grounds along the Judith and Milk Rivers were forgotten in Big Robber's speeches. The abandonment of the lands east of the Powder, which Larocque had visited with his hosts in 1805 but which were now dominated by the Sioux, was also made without comment.

For the Crow, however, the absence of any enforcement provisions for these new boundaries was more disturbing than the location of specific boundaries. Despite a brief effort on the part of some Teton Sioux bands to coexist peacefully with Big Robber's Crows in the Powder River country, raids by warriors from other branches of both tribes continued unabated, and the strip of land from Fort Laramie to Fort Union, roughly the western boundaries of modern North and South Dakota, continued as a battleground between Crows defending their buffalo herds and the oncoming Sioux and Cheyenne. The Blackfeet were not at the Fort Laramie proceedings, so conflict with them was unaffected by the 1851 agreement. Within a few years it was clear that U.S. officials could not police the intertribal borders created in the treaty. The Crow were on their own.[43]

Big Robber and others who might have defended the Fort Laramie agreement pointed out that even though the United States failed to enforce the new treaty, it had promised to distribute $50,000 worth of supplies each year to the tribes. Presumably such supplies would include weapons for self-defense, and tribes violating the agreement would be cut off from future subsidies. Such expectations were naive. The "annuities" rarely reached the Crow. They were delivered in 1854, but in 1855 pressure from hostile tribes was so intense that the American Fur Company abandoned its Yellowstone outpost, the first Fort Sarpy. The following year the Indian Office representative in the area announced that deliveries of treaty goods would no longer be made; anyone desiring a share of the promised supplies was told to report to Fort Union. In succeeding years, small bands of Crows came there and to the trading posts on the North Platte River, but they were never free from attack and the full amount of the promised annuities was never delivered. Band leaders such as

---

[43] For a description of the peace between the Sioux and the Crows, see Kingsley M. Bray, "Lone Horn's Peace: A New View of Sioux–Crow Relations," *Nebraska History*, 66, 1 (1985), 28–47. In the 1860s, during the Red Cloud war, U.S. Army Col. Henry B. Carrington asked a group of Cheyenne chiefs why they claimed to own land which belonged to the Crows. "We stole the hunting grounds of the Crows because they were the best," was the reply. "We fight the Crows because they will not take half and give us peace with the other half" (quoted at 38).

Two Face regularly protested this failure when they met with American officials, but the fur traders' gradual withdrawal from the Yellowstone in the 1850s made it impossible to supply them on their home turf. When the second Fort Sarpy was abandoned in 1859, all pretense of fulfilling the promises made at Fort Laramie was dropped.[44]

Big Robber's authority within the tribe plummeted in the wake of the 1851 agreement. Government agents wanted him to serve as the Crows' representative in all future negotiations, but because he failed to bring peace or security to his followers (as well as the fact that he was leader of no more than one-third of the community), they abandoned him. "He is now despised by the other bands," Edwin Thompson Denig reported in 1856. In general, the 1850s and 1860s were characterized by a gradual descent into poverty and the onset of perpetual war. The fur trade, which had been in decline, all but ended; unreliable – and then nonexistent – government subsidies were the only source of weapons. tools and ammunition.

At the same time, the Crows' military enemies, pressed by white settlement and the American military in Kansas, Nebraska and the eastern Dakotas, were increasingly forced to retreat into the Yellowstone valley in search of food and security. This was particularly true following the military expeditions that rampaged across the northern plains in the wake of the 1862 Minnesota Sioux uprising. Led by Gen. Henry H. Sibley and Gen. Alfred Sully, units of soldiers and eager volunteers pursued every band that offered them resistance, whether they had been involved in the Minnesota events or not. The effect of their indiscriminate actions was to scatter the Sioux and Cheyenne bands who hunted along the upper Missouri and drive them even closer to their western neighbors.[45]

Not unrelated to the Sibley–Sully expedition was the fact that gold strikes in 1862 in Idaho and western Montana began to draw prospectors and adventurers north from the well-trod path to Oregon. So many non-Indians appeared in Crow country that within a year of the initial discoveries, the government's agent in the area reported that "the whites are now overrunning their whole country." These newcomers, another local official reported, "are not to be considered the purest spirits the world affords by any means." When the gold fields inevitably disappointed these impure spirits, they turned to other methods

[44] Before it ratified the 1851 agreement, the U.S. Senate reduced the pledge from fifty to fifteen years. *ARCIA*, 1854 (Serial 777), 292–293; *ARCIA*, 1856 (Serial 853), 10; Bearss, *Bighorn Canyon National Recreation Area*, 107–108; *ARCIA*, 1857 (Serial 942), 417–421; *ARCIA*, 1858 (Serial 997), 438–447. The Indian Office report for 1858 called the Crows "insolent, audacious and lawless" (447). The 1864 report noted that the year's Crow annuities were aboard a steamer which was attacked by Sioux before it reached Fort Union. The surviving goods were distributed only to individuals who came to Fort Union; most Crows were reported to be "above Milk River on the Musselshell"; *ARCIA*, 1864 (Serial 1220), 288, 407.

[45] For a masterful account of the Sibley–Sully campaign, see Alvin M. Josephy Jr., *The Civil War in the West* (New York: Knopf, 1991), 122–154.

of subsistence. Many decided to try their hand at farming, while others became wolfers, cattlemen or teamsters. Their dreams of finding wealth on the region's endless prairies received a boost in the summer of 1866 when Nelson Story arrived in Montana with 600 Texas longhorns that he had driven north across Colorado and along the eastern flank of the Bighorns. The transition of the region's economy was confirmed a year later when Fort Union, no longer profitable as a fur trade center, was sold and abandoned.[46]

The ironic last step in the annihilation of the promises made in 1851 at Fort Laramie came in 1866 when the Teton bands loyal to Red Cloud and Crazy Horse declared war on the United States for opening the Bozeman Trail, a road that ran from Fort Laramie to the Montana gold camps at the upper end of the Yellowstone valley. The trail crossed land guaranteed to the Crows under the 1851 treaty, but the Sioux attacked the United States anyway, claiming that the Yellowstone was now their land. Equally remarkable, the Crows, whom the Sioux and the Americans had forced to retreat to the west and north, remained at peace. In a council with military officials early in 1866, Twines His Tail and Blackfoot explained that they had been invited by the Sioux to join their war parties then gathering near the Tongue River, but that their first priority was preserving their alliance with the Americans in order to expel the Lakota from the Yellowstone. The Crows rejected joining what one chief called a "war of extermination against the whites," pledging instead to send their young men to help the U.S. Army win back their traditional hunting grounds.[47]

The Red Cloud war was largely a prolonged siege of the government posts erected to guard the Bozeman Trail. It began in the fall of 1866 and ended with the abandonment of those forts in the summer of 1868. During 1866 the Sioux and their allies succeeded in cutting off much of the traffic on the Bozeman Trail and isolating the various units that had been dispatched to guard it. Fighting was sporadic and inconclusive until December 21, when Captain William Fetterman and a detachment of eighty soldiers and volunteers rode out of Fort Phil Kearny on the eastern flank of the Bighorns in pursuit of Sioux and Cheyenne warriors who had been harassing a wood-cutting crew. A few miles from the walls of the fort, Fetterman and his entire command were lured into a hollow and wiped out. Their sensational defeat electrified the American public, signaling how serious the Bozeman Trail conflict would be. But with

[46] *ARCIA*, 1863 (Serial 1182), 375; 1862, 324. For a recent account of the Sibley–Sully expedition and its impact on the Sioux, see Utley, *The Lance and the Shield*, 51–53. A detailed history of the white exploration of Crow country in the 1850s and 1860s can be found in Merril G. Burlingame, "Historical Background for the Crow Indian Treaty of 1868," prepared for the Indian Claims Commission, Docket 54, March 1, 1956. See also Bearss, *Bighorn Canyon National Recreation Area*, 109–134.

[47] Margaret Irvin Carrington, *Absaraka: Home of the Crows*, (Lincoln: University of Nebraska Press, 1983), 130–133, originally published in 1868. Half Yellow Face recalled a decade after the war that the Sioux had invited him and his colleagues to join "a war of extermination." See "Bradley Manuscript–Book F," *Contributions to the Montana Historical Society* 8 (1917), 223.

Appomattox a recent memory, there was little interest in Congress or among
the military leadership in waging large-scale war on the plains. Eager to demo-
bilize the army and trim the federal budget, Congress responded to Fetterman's
defeat by calling for a new peace conference with the region's tribes. A joint
resolution created an Indian Peace Commission in early 1867, ordering it to
begin negotiations on all outstanding issues with all the plains groups as quickly
as possible. Commissioner of Indian Affairs Nathaniel G. Taylor was named
chair of the group.[48]

After concluding a treaty with southern plains tribes at Medicine Lodge
Creek in Kansas in the fall of 1867, Taylor and his fellow commissioners moved
on to Fort Laramie and invited representatives of the region's tribes to meet
with them there. The Sioux stayed away, but Blackfoot and a band of nearly
300 Kicked In The Bellies and Mountain Crows responded. Their arrival at the
fort was recorded by Louis Simonin, a young French mining engineer then
touring the Rockies. Simonin wrote that the proceedings were to begin at ten
o'clock on the morning of November 14 and that soon after the appointed hour,
a parade of Indians appeared, "adorned in their finest costumes. Some were on
horseback. These forded the Laramie River, while others came by the bridge,
followed by their women and children, squaws and papooses." They were led
by Blackfoot, who rode up before the commission and "made a sign for his
braves or warriors to line up."

"After being lined up," Simonin reported, "the sachems intoned a song of
their nation, solemn and somber, mingled with discordant cries and sometimes
sharp yelpings." Dressed in war paint and feathers, the group then came forward in single file, declaring that they were prepared to meet the president's
representative. "Never," the Frenchman declared, "had the athletic form and
majestic figure of the Crows appeared more dignified." When the group assembled in a military storehouse that had been turned over to the commission for
the occasion, they were welcomed by an army medical doctor and self-taught
linguist, Washington Matthews. He attempted to set a tone of candor and
friendship for the proceedings: "Here are the commissioners sent from Washington to make peace with you, and you will see if I have told you lies,"
Matthews declared. A chief named Bear Tooth responded to this greeting by
offering his pipe to the government's representatives and inviting them "Smoke,
father, and have pity on me."[49]

Facing the Crow chiefs was Nathaniel Taylor, a former congressman and
Methodist preacher from Tennessee, who offered the group a scaled-down

[48] For a description of the Peace Commission's work, see Francis Paul Prucha, *The Great Father*,
2 vols. (Lincoln: University of Nebraska Press, 1985), 488–492.
[49] Louis L. Simonin, *The Rocky Mountain West in 1867*, translated and annotated by Wilson O.
Clough (Lincoln: University of Nebraska Press, 1966), 100–104. A shorter version of Simonin's
account was also published: see Louis L. Simonin, *Fort Russell and the Fort Laramie Peace
Commission in 1867*, translated and annotated by Wilson O. Clough, Sources of Northwest
History, No. 14, State University of Montana, 1931.

version of the agreement made by Big Robber in the same place fifteen years earlier. Taylor promised the assembled chiefs that the government would recognize about 25% of the Crow homeland described in 1851 as a permanent refuge for the tribe. "We wish to separate a part of your territory for your nation where you may live forever," he told them, adding that this area would be a place where the "Great Father in Washington and the commission will not allow any whites to settle."[50]

Taylor's words were translated for the Crows by Pierre Chien, a fur trader who had come up the Missouri in the 1840s and lived with the Mountain Crows as an agent for the American Fur Company. Again, Bear Tooth made the initial response, shaking the commissioner's hand and urging them "to do me justice," adding "I am a poor man." He urged the commissioners to consider the suffering of the Crows. "Your young men have devastated the country," he reminded them; "have pity on me." With that Bear Tooth presented Taylor with a pair of moccasins and urged him to take them and "keep your feet warm." Then Blackfoot, who would be the principal Crow speaker for the remainder of the conference, rose to address the commissioners. The chief laid out what would be the consistent position of the Mountain Crows and Kicked In The Bellies for the next decade.[51]

After repeating Bear Tooth's benign performance of shaking hands with each of the assembled commissioners, Blackfoot ceremoniously placed his own buffalo robe around the shoulders of Commissioner Taylor. "Keep this robe," he purred, "because by accepting it you recognize that you are my brother." The chief begged the white diplomats "to hear him with patience and with an attentive ear." Then, after "going to the middle of the council and with his hands throwing back his long, black locks, which fell halfway to his waist," Blackfoot turned on the commission in a cold fury.[52]

"Do not speak to us of confining us in a corner of our territory!" he declared. "First give up the route of Powder River. Recall your young men . . . and all those who seek gold there." Blackfoot recited the promises made in 1851 and never kept. He observed that the Crows had spurned the repeated invitations of the Sioux to join with them against the Americans. The Crow had remained loyal to the United States, Blackfoot noted, but he emphasized that no one in the tribe had forgotten the past. "We are not slaves," he shouted at the Commissioner; "we are not dogs!"[53]

---

[50] M. Simonin, "Fort Russell and Fort Laramie Peace Commission in 1867," Ayer 2, M76, No. 14, Newberry Library, 9.

[51] Simonin, *The Rocky Mountain West in 1867*, 106–109.

[52] Ibid., 109.

[53] Ibid., 111. Another account (which includes the incident with the buffalo robe) appeared in the *New York Times*, November 23, 1867, 8. This is quoted in A. Glen Humpherys, "The Crow Indian Treaties of 1868," *Annals of Wyoming*, 43 (Spring 1971), 78. Information on the life of Pierre Chien is drawn from an unpublished history of the Chien/Shane family, dated February 1987 by Mardell Hogan Plainfeather.

The meeting adjourned the next day. The Crows accepted gifts and supplies from the commission and promised to return for more negotiations in the spring, but they would not agree to a new treaty. Some chiefs said they would wait until the Sioux were willing to make peace, while others insisted that the government abandon its forts along the Bozeman Trail as a sign of good faith. When the Crows and the commission met again in May 1868, Blackfoot and his comrades received presents of food, clothing and ammunition along with the news that the government had decided to abandon the Bozeman Trail forts. They also learned that all of the Sioux bands other than those loyal to Red Cloud and Sitting Bull had agreed to terms and had promised to settle on reservations in the new Dakota Territory. Accompanying this information was a proposal for a new treaty between the United States and the Crows which would drastically reduce the tribal domain established in 1851. All of the Crow lands in the new state of Wyoming would be ceded to the United States and the Yellowstone would become the tribe's northern border. Despite the fact that these new boundaries reduced the tribe's holdings from over 38 million acres to 8 million, the assembled chiefs were inclined to accept them.[54]

There were several reasons for them to be cooperative. First, the transcontinental railroad was nearing completion in southern Wyoming and its presence doomed the remaining buffalo herds in the Bighorn basin. Second, the River Crows, who hunted north of the Yellowstone, were not represented at the proceedings; Blackfoot and the other leaders expected that their northern kinsmen's lands would be protected in a separate agreement. The area promised the Mountain bands contained their principal buffalo hunting grounds and appeared adequate. Third, the new treaty promised to correct a major flaw of the 1851 agreement by stipulating that annuities would be distributed from a government agency to be located within the boundaries of the new Crow territory. Blackfoot and his colleagues could now expect to involve the Americans directly in the task of removing the Sioux from the Yellowstone valley.

After discussing the agreement among themselves and with Pierre Chien, Blackfoot and ten others signed it on behalf of the Crows. While they had little choice, the signers were probably among the most trusting members of the tribe. Six of the ten had previously scouted for the Army or befriended the commanders at the Bozeman Trail forts. They had assessed the military situation first hand and would have reasonably concluded that this was the best treaty they could hope to achieve.[55]

North of the Yellowstone, the River Crows spent most of the 1860s in

---

[54] Simonin, *The Rocky Mountain West in 1867*, 116-117. For terms of the 1868 agreement, see Humphreys, "The Crow Indian Treaties of 1868," 83-84, and Charles J. Kappler, ed., *Indian Affairs: Laws and Treaties* (Washington: Government Printing Office, 1904), Vol. 2, 998-1012.

[55] The co-signers of the 1868 agreement whose previous association with the military can be identified are Pretty Bull, White Horse, Wolf Bow, White Forehead, The Swan and probably Shot In The Face (referred to in one source as Shot In The Jaw). Their identification was derived from the following: "Diary of William Templeton," Newberry Library, entry for August

retreat. Sioux expansion and their ongoing rivalry with the Blackfeet drove them increasingly into the arms of the Gros Ventres who occupied the lands north of the Missouri in what is now central Montana. Like the River Crows, the Gros Ventres were being pushed north by larger tribes to their east and west. Evidence for this association appears repeatedly in various government reports for the middle years of the decade. In 1863, for example, an army scouting party reported that the two tribes were "living together almost indiscriminately," while the following year Henry H. Reed, an Indian Office official sent to investigate the condition of the upper Missouri tribes, reported that when his steamboat arrived at the mouth of the Milk River in what was considered Gros Ventre country, "we came across about fifty lodges of Crows." Reed learned that these people "dare not go up into their own country on the Yellowstone . . . They have been for years fighting Sioux; . . . for the past few years the Sioux encroach on their lands and annoy them almost constantly." The association with the Gros Ventres continued. Another official reported in 1865 that the two groups were again together on the Milk River, "constantly moving to avoid the Sioux, as well as to follow the buffalo." In 1866, the government reported that each group was "in as bad a fix" as the other.[56]

After the establishment of the Peace Commission to settle the Red Cloud war and other plains disputes, the Indian Office offered to negotiate new agreements with all groups occupying lands along the Missouri River above Fort Union. Special Agent W. J. Cullen was dispatched to meet them. After surveying the situation in Montana, Cullen reported that an expanding white settler population and ongoing intertribal violence made it "important that these Indians be dealt with promptly." His solution was to "place the Indians out of harm's way" by granting them a protected area as a tribal home. Nathaniel Taylor

28, 1866 (Pretty Bull and White Horse); ibid., entry for January 1–5, 1867 (Shot In The Face); and ibid., entry for October 23, 1867 (White Forehead); Bearss, *Bighorn Canyon National Recreation Area*, 211 (The Swan); and ibid., 214 (Wolf Bow).

The River Crows repeatedly complained that Wolf Bow's signature on the 1868 treaty was taken by the United States as a sign of their consent to the agreement. A suit in the Court of Claims was based on this point and lost. Despite the legal defeat, however, the historical record is clear. Twines His Tail, the principal River Crow leader, was not present at (or probably even aware of) the proceedings, and Wolf Bow was a relatively minor band leader who spent a good deal of time with his Mountain Crow kinsmen. Thomas LeForge, a white man who lived with the tribe during this period testified in a 1929 deposition that Wolf Bow "was there [at Fort Laramie] on a visit and he went there and just signed the same as the rest did." LeForge's version of events followed testimony by Round Rock, a Mountain Crow who was also deposed in 1928. Round Rock claimed that Wolf Bow was selected to go to Fort Laramie at a council held near Pompey's Pillar prior to the treaty negotiations, but he agreed that the River Crow chief did not represent that division of the tribe. See Records Group 123, Records of the U.S. Court of Claims, General Jurisdiction Case Files, H-248, *Crow Nation v. United States*, Box 3356, file no. 50867–63698, 131 (LeForge), and 51–52 (Round Rock).

[56] U.S. Congress, House of Representatives Document No. 80 (Serial 1164), 22; *ARCIA*, 1864 (Serial 1220), 407; 1865, 411; 1866 (serial) 203. See also *ARCIA*, 1867 (Serial 1326), 254. For the Gros Ventre–Crow rapprochement, see also McGinnis, *Counting Coup and Cutting Horses*, 105.

preferred a single location for the River and Mountain Crow bands, "but," he admitted, "this, in view of the distance between them, may be impracticable." In July 1868, Cullen negotiated agreements with the Gros Ventre and River Crows which established a large tract for them along the Milk River.[57]

Between 1868 and 1870 several factors conspired to invalidate the River Crow agreement and drive this part of the tribe south to the Yellowstone. First, the Indian Office failed to win ratification of the Cullen treaties. Local settlers and their representatives in the new territorial government believed the agreements were too generous. The Indian Office was inclined to agree, the commissioner of Indian affairs noting in 1869 that if the River Crow treaty were not ratified, the group "can doubtless be induced to settle upon the reservation provided for the other band." Other federal officials, aware of the tribe's weakness and the opposition of local whites to extensive land grants to Indians, pointed out that the Crows could not really oppose being concentrated in one location. It is a tribe "disposed to do what is right," the veteran Indian fighter Lt. Col. Alfred Sully wrote the commissioner. Having used Crow scouts in his battles with the Sioux, Sully added knowingly, "I think I will have no difficulty in persuading them to join the Mountain Crows on their reservation."[58]

The River Crows were also victims of the resettlement of other plains groups, most significantly the Assiniboins. The Assiniboins were increasingly drawn south to the Missouri to receive government rations and seek protection from the Blackfeet and Sioux. While friendly with the Gros Ventres, this group had long been military rivals of the Crows. Their arrival thus sparked further calls for the removal of the River Crow bands. Finally, the continued failure of the government to deliver promised supplies to the River Crows reduced them to poverty and set many of them off in search of food. "Unless I can be furnished with some provisions and goods," the government's agent at Milk River wrote in 1869, "it will be difficult for me to prevent [the Indians] from carrying out their threats to join the hostile Sioux and Arapahoes." Writing at about the same time from a lonely trading post in the Judith basin, Peter Koch, a young Danish immigrant, confirmed the agent's judgement, noting that the River Crows "were much poorer than their brethren of the mountains, had fewer horses, fewer good arms and took much less pride in their dress and general appearance."[59]

Government agents also reported that the Sioux now laughed at the Crows.

[57] W. J. Cullen, quoted in *ARCIA*, 1868 (Serial 1366), 682; Taylor in ibid., 684; treaty discussed in ibid., 449. For a general treatment of the Cullen treaties, see Humphreys, "The Crow Indian Treaties of 1868," 86–87. Samuel N. Latta, the government's agent for the upper Missouri tribes, also called for a separate River Crow reservation. See *ARCIA*, 1863 (Serial 1182), 281.

[58] Letter to Commissioner of Indian Affairs, September 23, 1869, quoted in *ARCIA*, 1869 (Serial 1414), 733.

[59] *ARCIA*, 1869 (Serial 1414), 469, 733, 741, 742; Peter Koch, "Life at Musselshell in 1869 and 1870," *Contributions to the Historical Society of Montana*, 2 (1896), 296.

"Look at us," they called; "we are rich and ride fat horses and have plenty, while you are friends to the whites and are poor and have no horses." Faced with a choice between a dangerous alliance with the Sioux, poverty along the Missouri River or a retreat within the boundaries established at Fort Laramie, River Crow bands decided to stick with their kinsmen.

The River Crow desire to move south was reinforced in 1869 and early 1870 when smallpox swept first through the Gros Ventre camps and, later, the nearby lodges of the River Crows. Fleeing the disease, the bulk of the Crows moved west into the Judith basin, but approximately 20% of the group travelled south during 1870 to rejoin the Mountain Crow band. At the same time, the Indian Office was constructing a government storehouse on Mission Creek, eight miles east of modern-day Livingston, Montana. Built of cottonwood logs and located as far from the Sioux as possible, the new agency appeared to provide the entire Crow tribe a secure source of supplies and food.[60]

VII

In the forty-five years since Red Plume and Sore Belly had encountered the American emissaries at the Mandan villages, contact with outsiders had intensified, and the Crows had been drawn into a web of increasingly uneven military, economic and political relationships. As they lost the ability to act independently and freely, band leaders found themselves anchored to a narrowing geographical environment and forced together with unprecedented force. The fur trade had kept them close to traders and their posts, and the expansion of other tribes had confined them to a shrinking portion of their aboriginal hunting grounds, but never before had their movements been so restricted. Legal agreements between band leaders and the United States now bound them to a large, but precisely defined territory the government called a "reservation" for the Crow "tribe." Once an agency had been created within the boundaries of that reservation, the circle of "Crow country" – which had been contracting for nearly half a century – had a acquired a new centerpoint.

[60] *ARCIA*, 1870 (Serial 1449), 656; and Bearss, *Bighorn Canyon National Recreation Area*, 291–293.

4

Refugees at the agency

A fierce storm was coming fast. The sky was black with streaks of mad color through it. I saw the Four Winds gathering to strike the forest, and held my breath . . . . I shielded my own face with my arm when they charged! I heard the Thunders calling out in the storm, saw beautiful trees twist like blades of grass and fall in tangled piles where the forest had been. . . . Only one tree, tall and straight was left standing where the great forest had stood. The Four Winds that always make war alone had this time struck together, riding down every tree in the forest but one. Standing there alone among its dead tribesmen, I thought it looked sad. "What does this mean?" I whispered in my dream.

Plenty Coups[1]

I

In the summer of 1866, Capt. Nathaniel C. Kinney led two companies of regular army troops north from Fort Phil Kearney, a fortified outpost erected to guard the prospector's road from the Platte River to the Montana gold fields. His troops kept the broad slopes of the Bighorn range to their left as they rounded the flank of the mountains and headed west across the Little Bighorn valley. Kinney's assignment was to construct the last of the Bozeman Trail forts, ensuring emigrants safe passage across what was still officially recognized as Crow country. With the aging mountain man Jim Bridger as his guide, Kinney and his men rode past the future sight of Sheridan, Wyoming, and crossed the line separating Wyoming and Montana Territories. When they reached the Bighorn River, the captain decided to locate his installation near the mouth of the Bighorn canyon, the spectacular spot François Antoine Larocque had explored and admired some sixty years before. With little heavy timber at hand, Kinney's troops erected kilns and began producing adobe bricks for the fort's walls. As Fort C. F. Smith took shape, his soldiers could see that their commander had chosen well. From the guard posts their eyes could sweep the entire countryside. They could see the frequently used ferry crossing that sat just west of them on the Bighorn River, the rocky canyon cliffs that twisted their way southward towards Wyoming and the prairies that stretched north to

[1] Linderman, Frank, *Plenty Coups: Chief of the Crows* (Lincoln: University of Nebraska Press, 1962), 65–66, originally published in 1930.

the Yellowstone and east to the brown hills that separated their outpost from the Little Bighorn valley.

On August 28, as Kinney's troops sweated at their tasks, a noisy band of Indians rode boldly up the valley in pursuit of a wounded buffalo bull. They were a party of Crows, accompanied by the trader Pierre Chien. After cornering and dispatching their prey, the warriors rode up to Captain Kinney "singing their songs." Kinney and one of his lieutenants, a Pennsylvania-born Civil War veteran named George Templeton, welcomed the group and invited them to sit and share information. Templeton later recorded the day's events in his diary. He and Kinney were curious about the location of a hostile Sioux camp that had recently been reported east of them on the Tongue River and which might well be headed in the direction of the Bighorn. The ever-gregarious Iron Bull was the most outspoken of the Crow leaders present that day, but he was accompanied by a jovial group that included a young warrior named Pretty Bull and an elderly man named Boy Chief. Iron Bull quickly confirmed that a large camp of Oglala Sioux was camped on the Tongue and added that the group had been urging young Crow warriors to join them in their battle against white encroachment into Montana. Speaking through Chien, the war leader also noted that these invitations had not tempted the Crows; their objective continued to be the expulsion of the Sioux from their hunting grounds. In Templeton's retelling, this unexpected meeting between Kinney and the Crows was entirely friendly until the hunters suddenly rose to leave. The abrupt action made the young officers nervous. Had they offended their guests? Templeton described what happened next:

> The Boy Chief took my hat off and putting his arm around my neck repeated something entirely unintelligible to me and I didn't know but he was saying that he hoped he would have the pleasure of scalping me at some future time. However, the interpreter [Chien] said that he was saying that he loved me so much and wanted me to love him in the same way. He then repeated this ceremony with the other officers and said he had had his say. . . .[2]

The fear and irony in this brief encounter typify the Crows' odd status within the official boundaries of their homeland during the 1860s. The bulk of the territory "reserved" by them, and recognized by the United States as their tribal territory in both the 1851 and 1868 treaties, was simultaneously being overrun by white prospectors and invaded by the Sioux. Oglalas under Crazy Horse and Red Cloud and Hunkpapas and Minneconjous under Sitting Bull continued to follow the dwindling buffalo herds west from the Powder River, while gold seekers travelled north into the region along the Bozeman and Bridger Trails (the latter road running across the Bighorn basin and down

---

[2] George Templeton Diary, August 28, 1866, Ayer Manuscript Collection, Newberry Library.

Clark's Fork of the Yellowstone) and south from the Missouri River steamboat landings at Fort Benton. Across the northern plains the number of American settlers grew so large during the 1860s that Congress established territorial governments in Wyoming, Montana and the Dakotas, and the newcomers began thinking of the windy prairies as their home. In the midst of these invasions, the Crows tried to maintain their previous patterns of life. They hunted as they could, and traded buffalo robes for food and ammunition, but the rising presence of outsiders – both Indian and non-Indian – forced retreating bands of Crows into corners of their vast estate and drove them literally into the arms of men like Captain Kinney and Lieutenant Templeton.

During the 1870s, the feelings of fear and isolation that spurred Boy Chief's embrace of the U.S. Army officers at Fort Smith would intensify. White emigrants continued to stream into the area, so that by 1880 Montana Territory's white population of 39,000 was roughly equal to the combined population of its resident Indian tribes. At the same time, eastern tribes fleeing white settlement in the Dakotas continued to congregate in the Yellowstone valley and to prey upon dwindling buffalo herds. Crow band leaders like Iron Bull could still ride their ponies across the prairie and subsist on buffalo and elk, but they could no longer survive alone. Not only did they need the supplies available from fur traders, but they were beginning to rely as well on the rations distributed by the Indian Office and the military protection offered by the army. By 1880, the tribe's scattered bands had become refugees on their own reservation. The "Four Winds" Plenty Coups had seen in his vision had begun to blow.[3]

II

River Crow bands suffered the cruelest dislocations during the 1870s. Their leaders had been hundreds of miles away when Blackfoot and the other Mountain Crow chiefs agreed to the 1868 reservation boundaries, and yet by the end of the decade they had been forced to relocate their families south of the Yellowstone. In May 1868, all who were present at Fort Laramie assumed the River Crow bands would be covered by a separate treaty to be drawn up near their home on the Missouri River later in the summer. In fact, a separate treaty was signed in July 1868 at Fort Hawley on the Missouri River, but it was not submitted to Congress until the lame duck session at the end of the year. At

---

[3] Crows joined the white buffalo hunters who destroyed the vast northern herd during the 1870s. Absence of alternative sources of income and starvation encouraged the tribe's hunters to trade as many as 7,000 robes in 1879, together with a larger number of wolf and bear skins. See Edwin Bearss, *Bighorn Canyon National Recreation Area*, Montana-Wyoming, History Basic Data, Vol. 1 (Washington, D.C.: Office of History and Historic Architecture, Eastern Service Center, February, 1970), 314. In 1880 the tribe's agent reported that he was only able to provide four months' worth of rations to the tribe. See *ARCIA*, 1880 (Serial 1959), 230.

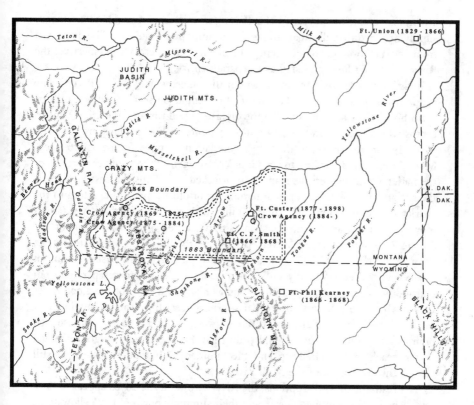

Map 4. The Crow Reservation, 1868–1890.

that point, with legislators eager to wrap up business, the River Crow agreement was literally buried and forgotten. It never came up for a vote. And as had been the case in California a decade earlier, the combination of a rapidly multiplying settler population and gold fever turned white Montanans firmly against reserving any more lands for Indians. By the end of 1868, the moment when the Crows might have had two preserves in the new territory had passed.

In the aftermath of Congress's failure to ratify the River Crow treaty, the Missouri River division of the tribe was left without a home. Ever logical if not wise, local and federal officials began thinking of the 1868 Fort Laramie treaty as *the* Crow treaty and the lands reserved by it as *the* Crow Reservation. In the summer of 1869, when the first agency buildings were erected for the Crows on Mission Creek near modern Livingston, Montana, the territory's superintendent of Indian affairs predicted that the division of the tribe into two groups would die out, "when they are brought together on *their* reservation on the Yellowstone." Amnesia of this kind was routine during the 1870s, for no further attempts were made to ratify the River Crow treaty. Government officials simply declared that all tribal rations and annuity payments would be dispensed from the Yellowstone valley agency. From the bureaucracy's perspective, the River Crows no longer existed as a separate entity.[4]

Invisible to the government on whom they increasingly relied, River Crow bands began to move to a place where they could be seen. Smallpox pushed them first. In the summer of 1869 the disease ripped through the Gros Ventres camps which had begun to cluster in the vicinity of Fort Belknap on the Milk River. In a matter of weeks, the tribe's population dropped from 2,000 to 1,300. More disastrous, according to the Gros Ventre agent, "the younger portions of the nation were the persons principally attacked. . . . Thus the best hunters of the nation have died, leaving a large number of old people and children to the charity of the government." Long familiar with the disease, the River Crows moved south of the Missouri as soon as they learned of their ally's plight.

The River Crows were relatively safe during the following winter, but in the summer of 1870, a Crow woman reportedly picked up the disease from an infected Gros Ventres family and carried it home. Her kinsmen separated from one another immediately, and in the end as many as a third of the 2,000 River Crows who were still north of the Missouri came south to the Mountain Crow agency. The balance of the group moved west, seeking refuge in the isolated prairies along the Musselshell and Judith Rivers. Only a few lodges remained within reach of Fort Belknap and the "immense" buffalo herds which still ranged the area north of the Milk River.[5]

As a result of these disruptions, the River Crows in the 1870s appear to have established a new routine. They spent their summers north of the Yellowstone, but in winter, instead of coming in to Fort Belknap or one of the other northern posts, they moved south to collect rations at the Mission Creek agency. In 1871, the tribe's new agent, a former fur trader named Fellows D. Pease, reported hopefully that approximately 1,400 River Crows would be drawing flour, beef and other supplies at the agency headquarters and that the leaders he had met expressed a "strong desire" to relocate there permanently. The following year, however, on the heels of a devastating Sioux attack on his outpost, Pease reported only occasional visits from the north. In 1873 fifty lodges of River Crows spent the winter at the agency, while the bulk of the group – perhaps as many as a hundred other families – remained north of the Yellowstone.

In the summer of 1873, the continuing failure of the River Crow bands to move south, together with the steady influx of both white settlers and the Sioux onto Mountain Crow lands, caused tribal leaders and federal officials to meet at agency headquarters to discuss finding a place where the entire tribe might live

[4] *ARCIA*, 1869 (Serial 1414), 732, emphasis added.
[5] *ARCIA*, 1870 (Serial 1449), 654 (on Gros Ventre epidemic), 664 (on River Crow relocations and buffalo on Milk River) and 662 (report of arrival of River Crows at Mountain Crow Agency).

in peace. Gathered that August amidst the twenty-five adobe storehouses, office buildings and cabins that made up the Mission Creek agency were the principal band leaders of the tribe, the Crow agent and two men from Washington, D.C.: Felix R. Brunot and Gen. Eliphalet Whittlesey. Brunot, a pious Pittsburgh industrialist, and Whittlesey, a Civil War veteran who now taught at the capital's all-black Howard University, represented the Board of Indian Commissioners. The board was made up of "Christian humanitarians" who acted as advisors to the Indian Office and advocates of peaceful negotiations between the government and the tribes.[6]

All who participated in the Mission Creek council were acutely aware of the Sioux and white invasions. The government men insisted that the best solution to these onslaughts was simply to forget the old treaties and create a new refuge in a place that was safe from prospectors, cattlemen and homesteaders, and would give the Crows sufficient space so that they could begin learning to raise their own crops. Brunot, a reformer who once wrote that America's Indian policy was marked by "the tragedy of war and the farce of treaty," argued forcibly for a fresh start. He told the assembled chiefs that "we want you to have lands that you can keep." He reminded them that a railroad – the Northern Pacific – was heading for the Yellowstone, dooming the northern buffalo herds. The shaggy beasts "are going away and soon will be all gone," Brunot decared, so the tribe must learn to live "on the white man's food." The commissioner suggested resettling the tribe in the Judith River basin near Fort Benton. The new reservation would be close to the River Crows, far away from the Sioux, and north of the major areas of white settlement. It also lay outside the boundaries of the Crow "homeland" defined in the tribe's 1868 treaty with the United States.[7]

Speaking for the Crows at Mission Creek were Blackfoot, who had led the tribal delegation five years earlier at Fort Laramie, Iron Bull and Long Horse, prominent warriors who had served as army scouts during the Sioux wars. These three were eager to maintain their positions as trusted diplomats and leaders, but they were equally concerned that their fellow tribesmen understand that they would not automatically support the government's demands. Blackfoot reminded his audience that the Sioux "took me by the arm" and tried to persuade him to join them, "but I pulled loose from them and would not do so." He also condemned what was said at Fort Laramie in 1868 as "all lies" and added that promises made then by the government to protect the buffalo herds and expel the Sioux from the Yellowstone were never incorporated into the

[6] See Prucha, *The Great Father*, 506–507. For a description of the Mission Creek agency, see "Journal of James H. Bradley," 157.
[7] An account of the negotiations is contained in *ARCIA*, 1873 (Serial 1601), 484–511; for Brunot's opening speech, see 500. Brunot's comments on Indian policy are quoted in Prucha, *The Great Father*, 529.

treaty. "I am ashamed about it," the chief confessed, noting that even the few annuity goods that had actually gotten to the Crow bands were inadequate: "They send us tin kettles; we go to get water to carry to our lodges; we dip the water, but it all runs out again. This is what we get for our land."[8]

Joining Blackfoot, Long Horse and Iron Bull at the council were a series of individuals the federal officials called "headmen" – family heads and warriors who spoke for smaller groups within the tribe. "They seem to have degrees of rank among them similar to the officers of an army," one observer of the proceedings wrote. "In time of war they have one head-chief, and all the rest command squads under him . . . In time of peace the tribe is divided into parties or bands, under the leadership of the various chiefs." Caught between war and peace, the assembled headmen appeared willing to let Blackfoot and the others speak for them, but the presence of these lesser leaders suggested a variety of interests would have to be accommodated within the tribe once the external threat from prospectors and the Sioux subsided. "The chiefs hold their position by an exceedingly precarious tenure," another visitor noted; "their popularity, and consequently the numerical strength of their following, fluctuates as good or evil results attend their undertakings." These words would be dramatically confirmed a decade later when two of the headmen present in 1873, Thin Belly and Old Dog, would accompany Captain Armstrong on his trek down from the Stillwater agency while a third, Crazy Head, would await them along the Little Bighorn, urging his followers to resist the agent's advance.[9]

The parties present on Mission Creek in 1873 were united by crisis; it was the reason both for the agreement made there and for its failure. Crisis prompted the government men to offer the tribe a new haven, safe from the warfare that rampaged through the Yellowstone, even though the area was claimed by the Blackfeet and had already witnessed the arrival of Sioux war parties. (Long Horse would be killed there by the Sioux the following year.) Crisis also allowed three men to speak for the entire assembly, relying on their past ties to the U.S. government for their authority rather than drawing support from kinsmen and fellow warriors. Despite the fact that witnesses testified that among the Crows "each lodge forms a little community in itself," Blackfoot and his two principal colleagues put themselves forward in 1873 as annointed leaders who could bargain away the tribe's traditional homeland. Their attitude was revealed in an exchange between Commissioner Brunot and Blackfoot at the outset of the council. When asked where the River Crow leaders were, the Mountain Crow chief declared, "The River Crows belong to me."[10]

[8] Edwin J. Stanley, *Rambles in Wonderland: Up the Yellowstone and Among the Geysers and Other Curiosities of the National Park* (New York: D. Appleton, 1878), 31, 32.
[9] Ibid., 27; Earl of Dunraven, *The Great Divide: Travels in the Upper Yellowstone in the Summer of 1874*, second edition (London: Chatto and Windus, 1876), 69.
[10] Earl of Dunraven, *The Great Divide*, 98; *ARCIA*, 1873 (Serial 1601), 492.

A group of Crow chiefs, photographed at the Mission Creek Agency in 1872. Blackfoot, the outspoken leader of the Fort Laramie councils in 1867 and 1868, is second from the left. The other men, all considered "headmen" by the government, included Old Onion (extreme right) and – wearing a peace medal – He Shows His Face. Courtesy of The Newberry Library.

But crisis could not sustain the new treaty. Despite the fact that the chiefs and headmen assembled at Mission Creek approved a document calling for the creation of a new Crow reserve on the Judith River, the agreement was never approved. Officials realized other tribes would also lay claim to the territory and no doubt instigate a new round of fighting, while local politicians protested that wagon roads and trading posts were quickly "settling" the area. As happy as they were to abolish the old Crow Reservation, white Montanans did not support the creation of a new one, even if it was only one-third its predecessor's size. The isolated refuge Brunot had imagined when the Crow council first gathered was displaying all the problems of the tribe's current reservation. In the face of these criticisms – and in the aftermath of the bankruptcy of the Northern Pacific in October of the same year – the Indian Office decided not to press for congressional approval of the agreement, allowing it to die in committee without a vote.

The failure of the 1873 negotiations marked the end of a time when federal negotiators could bargain with the tribe in the hope of moving it to unoccupied lands far from white settlement. Despite the fact that neither the 1868 boundaries or the proposed 1873 borders had ever been enforced by federal power, both agreements attempted to establish a preserve where traditional tribal life could continue for at least a short period. For the River Crow bands, the second failure to establish a Crow homeland north of the Yellowstone and the obvious reluctance of federal officials to oppose white settlement in the territory spelled the end of their hope for an existence apart from the Mountain Crows. At first the northerners appeared briefly at the Mission Creek Agency, pausing only to draw rations and·visit with their kinsmen, but their stays gradually grew longer. By 1878, Agent George Frost wrote from the Yellowstone that while the two groups "keep up separate organizations," they were intermarrying at a growing rate and "both tribes now profess to be attached to their agency and call it their home."[11]

The experiences of individual River Crow families confirm this general picture of suffering and relocation during the 1870s. Undercut by federal negligence and the ambitions of Mountain Crow leaders, small groups of River Crows spent the decade dodging both hostile tribes and oncoming settlers. As game grew scarce and the pace of change quickened, they had no choice but to

---

[11] *ARCIA*, 1875 (Serial 1680), 803; *ARCIA*, 1876 (Serial 1749), 492 (on Ft. Peck); *ARCIA*, 1878 (Serial 1850), 580. The agent's report from Fort Belknap for 1881 reveals that the movement south was not simply a function of wanting to be with kinsmen. He noted that the Gros Ventres under his charge were spending an increasing amount of time south of the Missouri, much of it in the company of the Crows. See *ARCIA*, 1881, 176. See also Dexter Clapp to H. Keiser, January 18, 1875, Item 1, Box 1, RCIA-FRC, Seattle. The assertiveness of the upper Missouri tribes – particularly the Assiniboin – also drove the River Crows south. For the latter point, see Anthony McGinnis, *Counting Coup and Cutting Horses: Intertribal Warfare on the Northern Plains* (Evergreen, Colo.: Cordillera, 1990), 159.

heed the government's order to move south. Amos Spotted, for example, recalled in 1928 that his River Crow family came to the Yellowstone Agency for
"rations and clothes and other presents like that and they went back [north]
again after they received the goods." After two or three years of this practice,
Spotted noted, the agent "sent some white people that could talk Crow down
there to bring them and to tell them that if they did not come they would use
some other means to bring them . . . they would make them move camp at night
to get them over there. . . ."[12]

Survivors of the River Crow relocation also recalled that the agent threatened
to keep their children in the new government boarding school if they did not
move voluntarily to the Yellowstone. Despite the fact that the school enrolled
no more than a hundred students during the 1870s, the agent's threat had a
powerful impact. Yellow Face, who was a young father during the decade, was
still angry when asked about the relocation fifty years later. "We love our
children," Yellow Face declared, "and the government grabs them and forces
them into the schools and the reason we stayed [on the Yellowstone] was that
we love our children." One of the men sent to persuade the River Crows to
relocate south was Thomas Leforge, a white cowboy who attached himself to a
Crow family in the years immediately following the Red Cloud war. He remembered that the process of moving the northern bands to the Yellowstone continued "all of ten years," and he added that these groups never moved willingly.
"They said," Leforge reported, " 'we grew up here, and died here; our people
died here; they are buried here.' "[13]

Thomas Leforge also recalled that the relocation produced tensions between
River Crow bands and the Mountain Crows who had preceded them at the
Mission Creek Agency. He reported, for example, that early in 1874 a River
Crow man was accidentally killed by an unknown rifleman who was out taking
target practice. The victim's family accused Tom Kent, the agency butcher, of
the murder and threatened to attack the government stockade in retaliation.
According to Leforge, after he heard of the incident, he, the agency interpreter
and "a Mountain Crow" went out to the River Crow camp, offering "concil-
iatory presents" as would have been customary under tribal etiquette. A man
approached them with his bow drawn, shouting "I'd like to kill both of you
white men," but the nameless Mountain Crow stepped forward to defend them.
"He called them fools and told them if they should harm any one there, the
white soldiers would come from Fort Ellis and kill many of their people." His
threat ended the confrontation, as the victim's widow shouted "Accident!" and
Horse Guard, one of the most distinguished River Crow war leaders, told the

[12] Deposition of Amos Spotted, U.S. Court of Claims General Jurisdiction Case Files, H-248,
   Crow Nation v. U.S., Records Group 123, Stack 5, Row 26, Box 3356, 60–61.
[13] Thomas Leforge, *Memoirs of a White Crow Indian* (Lincoln: University of Nebraska Press, 1974),
   originally published in 1928, 135, 131.

would-be assailant, "If you kill them, you will have to kill me." After hand-shakes and pledges of presents for the widow, the River Crow soldier society members "pony-whipped the mob into quiet" while Leforge and his compan-ions withdrew.[14]

Coming at a time when the River Crows found themselves without any refuge but the Mountain Crow agency, this incident clarified both the divisions between the two wings of the tribe and the relationship between both groups and the government. While Leforge is the only source for this incident, it would seem that the Mountain Crow who defended him was attempting to strike the same pose Blackfoot had in 1873 when he told the delegation from Washington that the River Crows "belonged" to him. As refugees with no-where else to go, the River Crows could either be defiant or, like Horse Guard, they could put themselves forward as defenders of white authority. By resolving the crisis as they did, Horse Guard and his soldiers prefigured the actions of Bull Nose and the "loyal" headmen who stepped forward to support Henry Armstrong when he was challenged by Spotted Horse in 1884. They asserted their authority over recalcitrant River Crows by siding with LeForge and blocking the Mountain Crow's assertion of leadership. In any event, Leforge's tale indi-cates that despite their common cultural roots, Mountain and River Crow bands at the new agency were divided both by unfamiliarity and by competiton for supremacy in their relationship with white authority figures.

III

While the River Crows were the most obvious refugees along the Yellowstone in the 1870s, the intensity of intertribal warfare during the decade left the Mountain Crow bands only marginally better off. In the early 1870s, the chief threat to Mountain Crow security remained the Sioux, who, no longer con-strained by the Bozeman Trail forts, pushed up the Yellowstone with renewed vigor. In September 1872, the Sioux struck the agency on Mission Creek, over a hundred miles west of the Bighorn, killing four people and capturing all the agency livestock. The following summer, much of the discussion about relocat-ing the Crows to the Judith River was punctuated with pleas from Mountain Crow leaders for help in fending off the Sioux. "When you whip the Sioux," Blackfoot taunted the treaty commissioners, "come and tell us of it. You are afraid of the Sioux. . . . You ought not to give the Sioux guns and ammun-ition," the leader added; "you should wipe them all out; you should throw a bad disease on them."[15]

[14] Ibid., 52–53.
[15] ARCIA, 1873 (Serial 1601), 501, 509.

The memoirs of Crow leaders indicate not only that the number of conflicts was rising in the early 1870s, but that their scale was also on the rise. Battles were no longer simply raids of one camp on another; there were increasing reports of set battles between large forces of heavily armed warriors. Thomas Leforge described one of the largest of these contests at the mouth of Pryor Creek in the summer of 1873 (it may have occurred just prior to the Judith River negotiations). After their scouts reported a large Sioux camp heading towards them from the Little Bighorn, a group of 2,000 Crows and an allied group of 200 Nez Perces formed a classic half-circle defensive perimeter with their backs to the river. When the Sioux appeared the following morning, Iron Bull and Pretty Eagle divided the Crow warriors into separate units and commanded them to hold their defensive positions. Throughout the day Sioux riders tried to lure the Crow out of their formation. Several skirmishes took place and the two sides taunted each other mercilessly, but the defenders stood their ground. Near sundown, according to Leforge, "we heard among them an unusual shouting of orders . . . their women went away out of sight while their wariors opened an extraordinary fusillade of gun-fire." The Sioux were attempting a retreat. At this point, the Crow warriors rushed after the fleeing enemy, pursuing them as far as the Bighorn River, thirty miles away. "This had been the most extensive battle between Crows and Sioux since the advent of guns." Leforge noted.[16]

Such conflicts also cemented the bond between the American military and the Crows, for the Sioux were considered enemies wherever they appeared. In 1874, for example, the young chief Plenty Coups recalled that a group of Mountain Crows arrived at Fort Maginnis on the Judith River with the intention of trading buffalo robes for supplies. They found that a Sioux war party had just escaped with the post's mounts. A group of more than a hundred Crows under Long Horse set off in pursuit. They captured the horses and returned them to the post, but Long Horse was killed in the battle. The soldiers happily identified their horses and thanked the Crows for their help. The Crows repeated this service many times, despite the cost of losing an important war leader, because they understood that they were fulfilling their obligations as allies and the alternative was to face the Sioux alone. In his memoirs dictated decades after the incident, Plenty Coups recalled the loss of Long Horse and the despair that accompanied it. "We did not care what horses [the Sioux] took, or what they gave us for bringing them back," he remembered. "Long Horse

---

[16] Leforge, *Memoirs of a White Crow Indian*, 95, 96. The battle is described on 83–96. Plenty Coups describes a similar battle fought near Arrow Creek at about the same time. See Linderman, *Plenty Coups: Chief of the Crows*, 255–265. For an account of a Crow raid on Sitting Bull's camp on the Powder River, see Joseph DeBarthe, *The Life and Adventures of Frank Grouard* (St. Louis: Combe Publishing, 1894), 103–104.

our great war-chief, was no longer with us, and we could think of nothing else."[17]

Pressure from prospectors and territorial politicians, as well as a desire to place the tribe near more favorable agricultural lands, led the government to relocate the Crow Agency to the Stillwater valley in June 1875. A stockpile of food, weapons and animals so close to the Bighorn was too appealing for the Sioux to ignore, and raids began on the new outpost within weeks of its completion. When the attacks subsided in August 1875, the agency had lost its horses and oxen, eight residents and any hope that the Crows would wish to settle near their new "home." "As long as they are harassed and driven from point to point," Agent Dexter E. Clapp reported in September, "there is no use in asking them to settle down and farm."[18]

Instead, Agent Clapp issued his charges bullets and carbines, and Mountain Crow hunters ventured into the Bighorn valley with renewed confidence. When a detachment of regular army troops encountered Blackfoot, Iron Bull and a large body of followers on Pryor Creek in the summer of 1875, the chiefs boasted that they would recapture the Bighorn if they "had to kill all the Sioux Nation" to do it. Clapp continued to pepper his superiors with pleas for help, writing in March 1876, for example, that "the Sioux are now occupying the eastern and best portion of their reservation, and by their constant warfare, paralyzing all efforts to induce the Crows to undertake agriculture. . . ." Not surprisingly, then, when the U.S. Army launched its attacks against the Sioux and Cheyenne in the spring of 1876, Crow warriors were an integral part of their plans. West Pointers like Lieutenant Colonel Custer might not have agreed with the man who said the Crows were "worth a regiment of cavalry," but they understood the tribe's leaders were committed to act in support of the American campaign.[19]

Two of the central battles of the 1876 offensive – Crook's standoff at the Rosebud and Custer's disastrous assault on the allied village at the Little Bighorn – occurred within the Crows' traditional hunting grounds, and Crow auxiliaries were involved in both. The largest group, 175 warriors, rode with Crook as he worked his way north from Wyoming in early June. When a war party led by Sitting Bull and Crazy Horse struck at Crook on June 17, they found a Crow screen between their warriors and the American troops. The

[17] Linderman, *Plenty Coups: Chief of the Crows*, 284. The entire incident is described on 277–284. Elsewhere in the memoir, Plenty Coups indicated that he was twenty-nine when Custer was killed (180). His statement that he was twenty-seven when Long Horse was killed would put this incident in 1874. For a general discussion of the Crow military predicament in the 1870s, see McGinnis, *Counting Coup and Cutting Horses*, 142–145.

[18] *ARCIA*, 1875 (Serial 1680), 805.

[19] *ARCIA*, 1876 (Serial 1749), 491; Dexter Clapp to Commissioner of Indian Affairs, March 10, 1876, Item 1, RCIA-FRC, Seattle. Clapp summarized recent Sioux activity in a letter to the commissioner, dated March 4, 1876 (Item 1, RCIA-FRC, Seattle).

Crows blunted the Sioux attack, giving the bluecoats time to reorganize and defend themselves. A week later, a small contingent of Crow scouts helped Custer find the hostile village on the Little Bighorn but were unsuccessful in their attempts to dissuade him from attacking. Crow scouts served regularly in the fighting that flickered across eastern Montana during the following year. In 1877 and 1878, as Sioux and Cheyenne leaders surrendered or fled to Canada, the Crows felt justified in claiming some credit for the American victories and reasserting their claims to their homeland.[20]

On June 25, 1877, exactly one year after Custer's defeat, Lt. Col. George Buell and a detachment of workmen selected a site for a military post that would stand barely ten miles from the Little Bighorn battlefield where the Sioux and Cheyenne had vanquished the American hero. Located at the confluence of the Bighorn and Little Bighorn Rivers, the site of modern-day Hardin, Montana, Fort Custer received its first troops the following October. It stood as a deterrent to hostile leaders who might have been tempted to leave their reservations and follow the rapidly dwindling buffalo herds of north central Montana, while to the Crows it appeared to be the first tangible sign that the government was willing to secure their homeland for them.[21]

Before the new post was itself a year old, Col. Nelson A. Miles, the aggressive young officer who had blocked Chief Joseph's flight to Canada in 1877 and who would one day become U.S. Army chief of staff, came to the Bighorn valley to meet with Crow leaders and celebrate the defeat of the Sioux. "The Crows were overjoyed" at the outcome of the war, Miles later recalled, and they assembled a camp of some 700 lodges for a victory celebration. "At a signal given by firing a rifle," Miles wrote, "the whole body of warriors shouted and moved forward, following their leader in columns of twos." The columns passed through the center of an immense village the young officer guessed held 3,500 people: "The horses were careering and prancing and the men were shouting, singing war songs and firing their rifles in the air." As they passed before Miles and Blackfoot the marchers saluted their leaders "with every mark of respect. In all my experience with Indians," Miles added, "I have never seen such a display of decorations."[22]

Unfortunately, the construction of Fort Custer and the friendship of military men like General Miles did not guarantee that Crow territory would now be left to them alone. Within a few years, conflicts with both Indians and whites would undermine the security that drove Blackfoot's men to celebrate with Miles

[20] Robert Utley, *The Lance and the Shield: The Life and Times of Sitting Bull* (New York: Henry Holt, 1993), 139–142, 146–7.
[21] The construction of Fort Custer is described in Bearrs, *Bighorn Canyon National Recreation Area*, 309–313.
[22] Nelson A. Miles, *Personal Recollections and Observations of General Nelson A. Miles* (Chicago: Werner, 1896), 283, 284.

in the shadow of the new post. The defeat of the Sioux did not stop the decline of their fortunes.

With the Crows' eastern frontier now secure, the tribe found itself increasingly at odds with its northern neighbors the Blackfeet, Yanktonais and Assiniboin. These conflicts grew more intense as the buffalo herds retreated north of the Yellowstone, as the struggles for game in that area grew more desperate and as Crow raiders ranged as far north as the the Blackfeet reserves in Canada. Following the construction of Fort Custer there were no opportunities for the large-scale fighting that had characterized the Sioux–Crow battles of the early 1870s. Battles were usually small-scale raids to capture horses or supplies or to retaliate for past wrongs. When two Yanktonais warriors were killed in a battle with Crows in the fall of 1881, for example, the agent at Fort Peck declared that "the origin of the existing feud dates so far back that the oldest Indians in the camp cannot tell from what it originated."[23]

Despite their modest size, these raids added substantially to the tribe's growing hardships. Not only were Indian families constantly on guard against attack, but assaults from other tribes drained away precious resources. In the spring and summer of 1882, the Blackfeet carried off "several hundred" Crow horses from the Stillwater valley. According to the agent, families who remained near the government agency were likely to "lose all their property." Nevertheless, the agent reported, "The Crows have retaliated in one instance only." He noted in August that there had been five major raids at the agency since January. Not even the Crow scouts at Fort Custer were immune. When a band of Blackfeet rode off with their ponies in the fall of 1882, the post commander heard one of the raiders shout, "We are going to steal the Crows poor this winter!"[24]

Erected as a symbol of order, Fort Custer was also a beacon of "civilization" for thousands of white settlers who understood the army's arrival as a sign that the northern plains were finally open for farming and ranching. As early as 1872, the Crow agent reported that whites were coming onto the reservation by the hundreds, "killing and driving the game; . . . destroying the best of their grazing country by bringing into the country herds of cattle and horses; roaming at will from one end to the other; [and] searching for gold and silver mines. . . ." Ironically, the perception that eastern Montana was now "safe"

[23] N. S. Porter to Commissioner of Indian Affairs, January 26, 1882, 2920–1882, LR-OIA, RG 75, NA. For an account of a retaliatory raid by Crows in 1880 that crossed the boundary with Canada, see John L. Tobias, "Canada's Subjugation of the Plains Cree, 1879–1885," *Canadian Historical Review*, 64 (1983), 529. See also McGinnis, *Counting Coup and Cutting Horses*, 168, 159–160.

[24] Henry Armstrong to Commissioner of Indian Affairs, March 31, 1882, Item 3, Box 9, RCIA-FRC, Seattle; H. J. Armstrong to Major Lewis Merrill, August 24, 1882, 21403–1882, LR-OIA, RG 75, NA; Henry Armstrong to Commissioner of Indian Affairs, August 15, 1882. Item 3, Box 9, RCIA, FRC, Seattle; John Hatch to Adjutant General, November 14, 1882, 21928–1882, LR-OIA, RG 75, NA. Se also H. J. Armstrong to Gen. A. H. Terry, October 31, 1882, 21201–1882, LR-OIA, RG 75, NA.

from attacks by the Sioux succeeded in undermining the peace of the region, for conflicts with newcomers – both on and off the reservation – were a central feature of Crow life in the 1870s and 1880s.[25]

Just as conflicts between small bands of Indians sometimes lead to bloodshed, so did unexpected meetings betweens Crows and whites. The difference, however, was that attacks by warriors on settlers or their cattle were considered acts of war, while violence originating with whites was considered self-defense. These unequal standards also fit the white perception of reservation borders. Most ranchers and settlers believed the boundaries around Crow lands were temporary and should not exclude whites, while at the same time they felt that tribal members should remain on their lands at all times and not be allowed to exercise their right to hunt on public lands.

An incident in the summer of 1881 illustrates these skewed perceptions. In early August nine young Crow men crossed the Yellowstone above the Stillwater River and rode north twenty miles to hunt antelope. The group divided into three smaller parties of three men each. One party encountered two cowboys who accused the hunters of stealing a horse; the cowboys shot one Crow hunter and hid his body in the underbrush. The Crow agent reported that all the white men in the area had "banded together" and declared their intention to "kill any Indian on sight found in the country. . . ." He added that "no respect" was paid to Indians in the area. "It is deemed no crime to kill an Indian but rather an act of heroism."[26]

Indian hunting parties were repeatedly accused of stealing horses and killing stock belonging to white ranchers whose lands adjoined the reservation. There may have been some truth to these reports of cattle killing, for dozens of them were filed with the Indian Office during the years after 1876, a period when it was also clear that the supply of game in the region was dropping precipitously. Nevertheless, the uniform testimony of the tribe's agents and the commander at Fort Custer was that the Crows were innocent. Col. Edward Hatch at Fort Custer wrote in early 1882, for example, that while quarrels with whites were bound to occur, "such frays are unlikely to be espoused by the tribe. The rough element among the whites on this frontier is very hostile to the Indians." Agent Armstrong wrote in the summer of the same year that while Crows occasionally begged for food, they had not done "any great wrong since my arrival at this agency." The following spring, Hugh L. Scott, a young lieutenant who would later rise to the rank of general, was dispatched to capture a group of

[25] *ARCIA*, 1872 (Serial 1959), 834.

[26] A. R. Keller to Commissioner of Indian Affairs, August 13, 1881, 15011–1881, LR-OIA, RG 75, NA. Earlier that same year Keller had come upon a group of stockmen who were driving "many hundred" cattle across tribal land in the upper Yellowstone valley. Writing that it was "useless to prosecute them," the agent reported the he "got from them all I could without litigation. I have succeeded so far in collecting $500. . . ." A. R. Keller to Commissioner of Indian Affairs, March 7, 1881, Item, 3, Box 9, RCIA-FRC, Seattle.

"renegades" who were hunting near the Little Missouri River. Upon his return to his post, Lieutenant Scott reported that "there are no more inoffensive people in the United States of any color than are these Crows."[27]

The experience of Crazy Head's band illustrates the extent to which conflict with local whites made it virtually impossible for Crow hunters to follow what little game remained in the Yellowstone valley. Born about 1837, Crazy Head grew up in the increasingly violent middle decades of the nineteenth century. He was closely allied with Iron Bull and other Mountain Crow chiefs who generally hunted in the Little Bighorn and Powder River valleys and, for that reason, frequently fought with the Sioux. In fact, Crazy Head was remembered in the twentieth century as having been one of the warriors who "kept the Sioux away." It is not surprising, then, that the chief befriended Cap. Kinney and his men at Fort C. F. Smith in 1867, providing the Americans with men to act as couriers and passing on information about the location of Crazy Horse, Sitting Bull and other hostile leaders. After their enemies were dispersed in 1877, Crazy Head and his followers returned to their old hunting grounds, unconcerned that much of their territory lay beyond the boundaries established by the Fort Laramie treaty.[28]

For a few years, the now-middle-aged chief hunted on the Powder River each summer and fall, visiting the Mission Creek Agency in winter to draw supplies and bring his buffalo robes to the nearby traders. By the early 1880s, however, the growth of white settlement disrupted this pattern. In the spring of 1881 a buffalo hunter named McMurdy complained that a group of Crows had come into his camp just east of the reservation line and accused him of hunting on their reservation. McMurdy reported that the Indians had cut up 180 buffalo hides and seized 60 deer skins. A River Crow leader named Spaniard told Agent Armstrong that Crazy Head and another River Crow leader had been in the area where the incident took place, but the agent was reluctant to

[27] Col. Hatch to Adjutant General, February 16, 1882, 4892–1882, LR-OIA, RG 75, NA; Henry Armstrong to Commissioner of Indian Affairs, June 23, 1882, 12066–1882, LR-OIA, RG 75, NA; Lt. Hugh L. Scott to Post Adjutant, Fort Meade, D. T., May 29, 1883, enclosed with John Tweedale, Chief Clerk to the Secretary of War to Secretary of the Interior, July 13, 1883, 12905–1883, LR-OIA, RG 75, NA. Accusations against the Crows can be found in Armstrong to Commissioner of Indian Affair, April 7, 1882, 7643–1882, LR-OIA, RG 75, NA; Secretary of Interior to Commissioner of Indian Affairs, January 14, 1882, 1042–1882, LR-OIA, RG 75, NA; Governor Hoyt to Secretary of the Interior, June 12, 1882, 10918–1882, LR-OIA, RG 75, NA; Secretary of War to Secretary of Interior, June 12, 1882, 11009–1882, LR-OIA, RG 75, NA; Secretary of War to Secretary of the Interior, June 9, 1883, 10648–1883, LR-OIA, RG 75, NA; and William Hale, Governor of Wyoming, to Commissioner of Indian Affairs, November 9, 1883, 20708–1883, LR-OIA, RG 75, NA.

[28] For references to Crazy Head's association with Fort Smith, see Bearss, *Bighorn Canyon National Recreation Area*, 197, 210. For Crazy Head's reputation as a warrior who opposed the Sioux, see testimony of Antelope, Box 3356, U.S. Court of Claims, General Jurisdiction Case Files, H-248, *Crow Nation vs. U.S.*, Records Group 123, National Archives, Washington, D.C., 63.

take action. He suspected McMurdy was "attempting to do something that was not legitimate" and he recognized that hunting remained the most reliable source of food for the tribe.

The following winter, Crazy Head was again hunting beyond the reservation boundaries when Agent Armstrong received a complaint from local whites. This time the president of the Wyoming Stock Grower's Association reported that Crazy Head and thirty-five lodges of followers had been on the Powder River in Wyoming Territory for several months. Other correspondents from the area accused Indians from several tribes of stealing cattle and horses from local ranchers, but insisted that "the Crows are the worst offenders in every respect." Again, the agent defended his charges. "There is no doubt," Armstrong wrote, "that the whites have committed greater depredations on those Indians than the Indians have on the whites." He noted that Crazy Head had recently lost 200 horses to a group of whites "and when the Indians went after the horses the white men killed one of the Indians, a brother of the chief." (The chief later reported that the horse thieves shot his brother, Round Iron, while the man was shaking hands with them.) No action was taken to punish the murderer.[29]

Despite Armstrong's support, the killing of Crazy Head's kinsman (variously reported as his brother, son and brother in law) evidently convinced the chief that he could not expect protection from the Indian Office. In February 1883 he set off for the Little Missouri with a group that included two River Crow band leaders (Horse Guard, now quite elderly, and a former scout named Two Belly), together with a small Mountain Crow band led by an ambitious young warrior named Spotted Horse. According to the commander at Fort Custer, these were "the discontented people of the tribe." Despite his sympathy for the Indians, Hatch added that Crazy Head was "a bad man . . . If his people need food, he will allow them to kill cattle, and may cause alarm along the whole frontier." What had previously been an annual spring hunt was coming to be considered an act of rebellion.[30]

To support of Colonel Hatch's assertion that Crazy Head was apparently

[29] Henry Armstrong to Commissioner of Indian Affairs, March 31, 1883, 6469–1883, LR-OIA, RG 75, NA; Moreston Frewen to General O. O. Howard, May 25, 1883, enclosed with 10648–1883, LR-OIA, RG 75, NA (a letter from General Phil Sheridan appended to Frewen's complaint dismissed the rancher as a "greedy, grasping Englishman").

[30] See Col. Hatch to H. J. Armstrong, April 9, 1883, and Col. Hatch to Assistant Adjutant General, April 10, 1883, both enclosed with 12905–1883, LR-OIA, RG 75, NA. Hatch refers to the murdered Indian as Crazy Head's brother in law. The individual is referred to as Crazy Head's son in George Milburn to H. J. Armstrong, July 20, 1883, 3466–1883, LR-OIA, RG 75, NA. The details of the murder were related to Lt. Hugh Scott when he contacted Crazy Head in May. See his report contained with 12905–1883, LR-OIA, RG 75, NA. Much of this material is also filed in Records Group 393, National Archives, U.S. Army Commands, Department of Dakota, Letters Received, Box 59. See also Arden Smith to Commissioner of Indian Affairs, February 13, 1883 (file 2545), and John Hatch to Assistant Adjutant General, April 10, 1883 (file 2609).

shifting from loyal scout to "bad man," the army command at Fort Snelling, Minnesota, ordered a "strong force" of soldiers from Fort Meade in the Black Hills to ride north and return the entire group to the reservation. But upon their arrival at Crazy Head's camp, the detachment found not rebels, but refugees. Lt. Hugh Scott reported that he overtook Crazy Head and his followers on the afternoon of May 10. The chief and his band of forty-nine lodges received the orders to return home "in a very mild and submissive manner and informed me that they were on their way to Fort Custer as fast as the condition of their stock would permit." Instead of raiding local ranches, this group of approximately 250 people had been living off the carcasses left behind by white buffalo hunters.

Desperate as he was for food, Crazy Head clearly understood that he would be safer within the boundaries of the reservation. Communicating through a young black man called "Smokey" who had attached himself to the band, Scott noted that Crazy Head did not intend to challenge the authority of the Indian Office. He added that the chief "desired me to report that he intends to farm next spring and to build a log house and live in it like a white man and cease wandering about." After receiving a similar pledge from Two Belly, Lieutenant Scott told his superiors that placing these men behind bars would be "a great injustice." The "rebels" were ready to come home.[31]

By the end of July 1883, Agent Armstrong could report that "all chiefs of bands are now on the reservation." Apparently some members of Crazy Head's and Spotted Horse's groups ("stragglers") remained east of the Little Bighorn, but the vast majority of the tribe was accounted for. Fifteen years after the Fort Laramie negotiations, the Crows had been relocated to the lands reserved by them in the 1868 treaty. Unfortunately, those lands could no longer support them. As Henry Armstrong reported to the Indian Office three months after Crazy Head's return to the reservation, "It is a mistake . . . to suppose that there is any game on this reservation for the Crows to hunt. There is none and they have to go outside to get elk and deer." The dilemma was clear: leave and be hunted down by the military or live at the agency as refugees.[32]

A few months after Crazy Head's return from the Powder River country, a visiting Indian Office inspector indicated which unattractive alternative federal authorities would insist that the Crows follow. Inspector George Milburn, dispatched to Crow Agency to investigate the causes of Crazy Head's "outbreak," noted that "probably all of the Crows were at the agency for their annuity goods," but added that reports of "depredations" against white ranchers

---

[31] See Lt. Hugh Scott to Post Adjutant, May 29, 1883, enclosed with 12905–1883, LR-OIA, RG 75, NA.

[32] Armstrong to Commissioner of Indian Affairs, July 27, 1883, 13920–1883, LR-OIA, RG 75, NA; Henry Armstrong to Commissioner of Indian Affairs, November 20, 1882, 21658–1883, LR-OIA, RG 75, NA.

were continuing. Milburn felt the solution to this problem was clear: enforced dependency on the local agent. He wrote, "The committal of one or two Indians to the penitentiary would do a great deal to stop the evil."[33]

IV

On the eve of the tribe's resettlement along the Little Bighorn River, Crow country appeared to be empty of animals. Agent Armstrong reported during the winter of 1883–4 that "the only way" the tribe had survived in recent years had been by leaving the reservation to hunt. But the coming year would be different. More than 250,000 buffalo hides had been shipped out of the area in the preceding five years. Crazy Head, a loyal scout, had been hunted down when he ventured eastward in search of game. Itchy-fingered ranchers routinely trespassed on their lands and attacked families who crossed the reservation's borders to hunt for food. Armstrong reported the consequences: "Usually there have been not more than forty or fifty Indians remaining at the agency; but this winter we have had about two-thirds of the tribe at the agency or near enough to come in and draw their rations regularly. Consequently," he added, "we have exhausted the supply of coffee, sugar, and baking powder." He pleaded that without supplementary appropriations from Congress, the tribe would starve.[34]

Like other communities of refugees, the inhabitants of the Crow Reservation in 1884 found themselves powerless in a familiar setting. The defeat of their tribal enemies had not brought prosperity to the tribe. Instead, it had opened the floodgates of white emigration, destroying the buffalo and ringing the group's territory with desperate rival tribes and hostile settlers. The "Crow lands" (which had been reserved in a formal treaty proceeding but which Mountain Crow leaders had never expected would accommodate the entire group) now marked the limits of Crow mobility. The daily life of tribal households and bands remained largely under the control of Crow men and women, but individual authority was circumscribed both by poverty and the American military. Nowhere were these circumstances more evident than in the political life of the tribe.

Writing from the Stillwater valley in the summer of 1879, Agent A. R. Keller reported that he could detect no political order within the tribe. According to

[33] George Milburn to Commissioner of Indian Affairs, November 7, 1883, 20843–1883, LR-OIA, RG 75, NA. Four Crows were imprisoned in December after attempting an unauthorized "visit" to Standing Rock Agency. See Armstrong to Commissioner of Indian Affairs, December 10, 1883, 23143–1883, LR-OIA, RG 75, NA. The men were Bear Wolf, Three Irons, Big Eye and Wolf. One of the members of Bear Wolf's band was a young man named Wraps Up His Tail who would lead a Crow "uprising" in November 1887.
[34] Henry Armstrong to Commissioner of Indian Affairs, January 7, 1884, Item 2, Box 1, RCIA-FRC, Seattle. The count of buffalo hides shipped from Miles City is from Agnes Jones, *Crow Country* (Billings, Mont.: BPI Foundation, n.d.), 13.

Keller the Crows were "wild tribes without acknowledged leaders . . . the whole tribe [is] broken up into bands of from ten to thirty lodges. But little authority is exercised or possessed by any chief over his followers." While certainly colored by ethnocentrism and limited by ignorance, Keller's observation contained a grain of truth. As the experience of Crazy Head illustrates, even the most independent leaders among the Crow had little opportunity to exercise their power and authority in the early 1880s. Once they had been relocated and confined, tribal leaders could not recruit a following by traditional means. Increasingly, warfare, hunting and trading were impossible, and there were no other avenues open to community influence.

For Crow political leaders in the early 1880s, the only immediate source of power was the tribe's resident federal agent and the commander at Fort Custer. And because these officials were now intent on establishing their authority, the only way to share in their power was to cooperate with them on a piecemeal basis. Spiritual and religious authority was always available to individual Crows, but secular authority now emanated from the United States.

Early in 1880, Indian Office officials, responding to demands from white Montanans for a reduction in the size of the Crow domain, proposed a general council with the tribe. While this was a standard government procedure, its use at this time and for this purpose created a new forum for community decision making, one that both clarified the tribe's dependent status and opened new opportunities for tribal unity. When they assembled on March 23, the River and Mountain Crow leaders must have understood that they were treading new ground. With the River Crow bands now resettled at the Stillwater, and with most families drawing rations at the agency, the gathering promised to bring together an unprecedented number of band leaders. The presence of federal officials armed with demands and packaged arguments challenged the gathering to devise a response to the insistence that it approve the sale of Crow lands. Because so many prospectors had settled along the headwaters of the Yellowstone, it was clear in 1880 that the tribe could not continue to assert complete control in the area. In the weeks before the conference, Agent Keller had suggested that the tribe agree to part with the areas they could no longer occupy, thereby moving the western boundary of Crow lands east, perhaps as far as Clark's Fork of the Yellowstone. While he claimed his plan would prevent further conflict with miners by ridding the Crows of "all the region upon which valuable minerals are known to exist," Keller also believed that the sale would assist the tribe's transition to farming by eliminating uncultivated territory and providing them with capital for tools and seeds.

When the council opened, Keller found more than fifty chiefs and headmen arrayed before him. Blackfoot, the principal speaker at both Fort Laramie and the Judith basin negotiations had died in 1877. In his place stood Iron Bull, the gregarious former scout who had long served as friend to white officials. Iron

Bull declared that "we are all willing to learn" to farm, but he resisted the notion of a large land cession. His lead was followed by other chiefs who pledged their friendship – one enthusiastic man declared, "I am going to shake the white man's hand until I die" – but refused to sell. The most remarkable feature of this first session, however, was the appearance of a thirty-one-year-old Mountain Crow warrior named Plenty Coups. The 1880 land sale conference was the occasion for his initial speech before a tribal council; the first appearance in what would be a fifty-year career in tribal politics.[35]

Plenty Coups came to the council with a substantial record of military achievement. A small, athletic man, Plenty Coups had played a prominent role in several battles with the Sioux (he was one of the leaders of the famous Crow charge that turned aside Sitting Bull's attack on Crook at the Rosebud in 1876), and he had acquired significant religious authority through a series of visions and successful sun dances. His personal courage was beyond question, and he had devoted himself to accomplishing all the war deeds expected of him. In this sense he was completely conventional. Recalling Long Horse, Iron Bull and his other mentors years later, Plenty Coups exclaimed, "How they inspired me, a boy, aching for age and opportunity."[36]

But Plenty Coups had unconventional ambitions. In autobiographical memoirs dictated at the end of his life, the chief revealed that despite his earlier devotion to warfare, he had had two visions while only twenty years old which indicated that he should cooperate with the oncoming whites and become a peace chief and political leader. In the first vision, Plenty Coups saw himself as a tiny chickadee riding out a violent wind storm by sitting in its nest. As he watched the storm in his dream, a voice declared, "The lodges of countless bird people were in that forest when the Four Winds charged it. Only one is left unharmed, the lodge of the Chickadee-person. Develop your body but do not neglect your mind," the voice continued. "It is the mind that leads a man to power. . . ." In the second vision, the young Plenty Coups watched herds of cattle replace the buffalo ranging near his home on Pryor Creek. When the cattle appeared, the buffalo went away: "There was not one in sight anywhere. . . ." By the time of the 1880 conference, the young man had decided to act on his visions.[37]

When he rose to speake before Agent Keller, Iron Bull and the assembled headmen, Plenty Coups struck a pose of humility. "I have a heart and I thought I had a mind," he was reported to have said. He added, "The white men think

---

[35] The council proceedings for the March 23, 1880, gathering are contained in "Special Case 52, Crow Cessions to Relinquish Western Part of Reservation in Montana," Records Group 75, National Archives, Washington, D.C. (hereafter cited as RG 75, NA).

[36] Linderman, *Plenty Coups: Chief of the Crows*, 50.

[37] Ibid., 67, 63. The visions are also a prominent part of Plenty Coups, "Autobiography," mss. at National Museum of the American Indian, chaps. 5 and 6.

for me. I do what the white men want me to do." Despite such self-deprecation, however, the council was not impressed; it did not approve the proposed land sale. Keller responded to this decision by announcing that a delegation of six chiefs would be sent to Washington, D.C., to speak directly with the president. According to Plenty Coups, he was the first member of the delegation to be selected; he asked Two Belly, the senior River Crow leader, to accompany him. To round out the group, Keller selected four additional Mountain Crows: Pretty Eagle, an accomplished warrior in his middle thirties; Medicine Crow, a highly decorated war leader who was only twenty-nine; Long Elk, who was leader of a band with several members who had married white traders and agency employees; and Old Crow, the eldest delegate, who was a respected band leader in his middle forties.[38]

The 1880 delegation left for Washington almost immediately. It was remarkable for its youth, its disproportionate number of Mountain Crows, and its failure to include men who had participated in the 1868 or 1873 negotiations and been outspoken in their opposition of further white settlement – Crazy Head, Horse Guard and Spotted Horse. It also excluded – perhaps because of the rigors of the journey – Iron Bull, the tribe's most experienced diplomat. Once in the capital city, however, the delegation showed remarkable spunk. It resisted pressure from the president and the secretary of the interior; while acknowledging that some territory would have to be ceded, the Crow delegates refused to authorize the sale of any lands east of Clark's Fork. Finally in June 1880, the group agreed to a provisional treaty (in part because the Crows believed they would be held as hostages in Washington until they did so) and promised to urge its adoption by their kinsmen back home. The Indian Office then allowed the group to return to the Stillwater.[39]

Significantly, when the delegates presented their agreement to a tribal gathering on June 12, Iron Bull took the floor to oppose it. The old chief and his supporters insisted that no land be sold west of Clark's Fork. Instead of using that river as a boundary, they suggested recognizing only the area where mining claims were now outstanding. Boulder Creek, seventy miles west of the Clark's Fork, would be the new border. "Finally," the agent who chaired the session reported, "the chiefs, *including the delegation*, voted with one voice against the [provisional] proposal." Under Iron Bull's guidance, the council then voted to sell the government 1.6 million acres west of Boulder Creek – the minimum necessary to satisfy the clamor for Crow land.[40]

---

[38] An account of the March 23 Council is contained in A. R. Keller to Commissioner of Indian Affairs, June 14, 1880, Special Case 52, LR-OIA, RG 75, NA.

[39] Plenty Coups, "Autobiography," chap. 17.

[40] See Agent Keller to Commissioner of Indian Affairs, June 14, 1880. For a description of the Crow delegation's visit to Washington, see C. Adrian Heidenreich, "The Crow Indian Delegation to Washington, D.C., in 1880," *Montana: The Magazine of Western History*, 31, 2 (1981), 54–67.

The friendly opposition of Iron Bull and his allies to the Clark's Fork boundary postponed approval of the 1880 land sale until 1882 and delayed the arrival
of much needed financial assistance, but the agreement demonstrated that skil-
ful leaders could calibrate their accommodation to American power, appearing
friendly while resisting the white man's demands. This tactic of appeasement
did more than keep the government at bay; it also heightened the prestige of
tribal leaders. Delay and piecemeal agreements forced government negotiators
to return repeatedly to tribal leaders for additional rounds of negotiations, and
each repetition of these proceedings underscored the authority of the Indian
participants. What was a routine meeting for a harried government bureaucrat
was a public endorsement for a struggling tribal politician. Even though Plenty
Coups was rebuked by his tribesmen when he returned from Washington in
1880, he had proven himself an honest broker between Iron Bull and the agent,
and he had learned a valuable lesson: acquiescence did not bring political
power. As he continued to follow his vision of himself as a political leader, both
his moderation and his toughness would win him support from his tribesmen
and influence with federal officials.

Other issues tumbled forward in the early 1880s, providing an excellent
forum for ambitious politicians and their rivals. Would the tribe approve a right
of way through its lands for the Northern Pacific Railroad? Would the tribe
consent to the settlement of a band of Cheyennes on public lands adjoining
theirs? Would the tribe agree to lease part of their land to Montana cattlemen?
Would tribal leaders agree to send their young people east to school? For each
of these questions, Indian Office administrators wanted a discussion with Crow
representatives and a decision which would allow federal programs to go forward. For tribal leaders, the form of these meetings was as important as their
substance. The repetition of formal encounters between Americans and Indian
headmen became a ritual for the transfer of authority from outsiders to the
tribe. By the end of 1882, Henry Armstrong described an innovation that Crow
leaders had devised to create additional proceedings. "It is customary," he
wrote to his superiors, "to hold a general council the day previous to the annual
issue of annuity goods, at which time the chiefs state their grievances if they
have any, and if not, their wishes for the future."[41]

In the fall of 1880 the Northern Pacific Railroad, now out of bankruptcy and
determined to push west of Bismarck where it had been stranded for nearly a
decade, began moving up the southern bank of the Yellowstone River. The line
had survived Jay Gould and a host of other enemies, but its officials were still
unprepared for the reception they received as they crossed onto the Crow
Reservation. J. J. Moore and his survey party were thunderstruck when Spotted

---

[41] Henry Armstrong to Commissioner of Indian Affairs, November 9, 1882, Item 3, Box 9, RCIA-
FRC, Seattle.

Horse and a band of young warriors met them near Arrow Creek and told them to leave their land. Spotted Horse told the retreating engineer he intended to yank out his survey stakes and burn the Crow hay he had gathered for his horses. While Spotted Horse never acted on these threats, it was clear to both company and government officials that a successful council with tribal leaders would be necessary if they wished to meet their construction goals during the 1881 season.[42]

Crow leaders and government officals held three councils on the Northern Pacific right of way during 1881. At the first session in May, Iron Bull made it clear that the matter could not be disposed of quickly. "When we get together and talk this matter over, we will know what to say," he told the agent. "We all ought to talk it over one with another first . . . if we say anything today the rest of the camp may not like it." The agent recessed the group until June, then postponed the meeting again until August when the group of leaders who assembled was too small. Agent Keller was also interested in using these sessions to promote leaders whom he found cooperative. In May, for example, he sent a transcript of the council to Washington with the comment, "the remarks of the young chief Medicine Crow are especially commended."[43]

When the full Crow council finally assembled in August, Agent Keller began by asking Iron Bull to speak. Before he could begin, however, Enemy Hunter stepped forward and "pulled Crazy Head and Two Belly upon the floor, stating that he wanted them to talk for the Crows." Neither man objected to the road (Crazy Head asked for food and Two Belly for "plenty of pay"), but both used the opportunity to present themselves as community leaders. When they were done, Thin Belly, one of Iron Bull's comrades from his days at Fort C. F. Smith, called out, "There is no tribe with only two chiefs. We all want to say something about this matter." At that, a parade of men – but not Iron Bull – came forward and added their assent to the right of way.

After several band leaders had delivered their addreses, Plenty Coups brought the matter to closure. "I will touch the pen and sign for all the Crows," the thirty-two year old warrior said evenly, "if you will pay us $30,000." When the government officials offered $25,000, Crazy Head called it "good." A bargain had been struck at the end of an elaborate series of public declarations, and apparently, the young warrior had positioned himself as the voice of consensus.

---

[42] J. J. Moore to J. T. Dodge, Engineer, Yellowstone Division of the Northern Pacific Railroad, November 10, 1880, 2767.5–1880, Special Case 82, "Northern Pacific Railroad Through Crow Reservation," LR-OIA, RG 75, NA. Another letter in the same file describes another threatening visit by Crazy Head in August. See J. T. Dodge to Nelson A. Miles, August 5, 1880, 2241–1880, Special Case 82, LR-OIA, RG 75, NA.

[43] See council proceedings, May 16, 1881, Item 3, Box 9, RCIA-FRC, Seattle; A. R. Keller to Commissioner of Indian Affairs, May 26, 1881, Item 3 Box 9, RCIA-FRC, Seattle. The council proceedings are in Keller to Commissioner of Indian Affairs, May 28, 1881, 9744–1881, Special Case 82, LR-OIA, RG 75, NA.

The result was both an agreement with the railroad and a roster of Crow leaders led by Plenty Coups who would receive credit for bringing it about. As the August meeting was about the adjourn, however, Spotted Horse could not resist one of his characteristically dramatic finales. The council proceedings indicate that as the group began to disperse, the man who less than a year earlier had confronted the survey party on Arrow Creek "drew his knife and wanted the commissioners and agent to swear that no timber should be cut (by the construction crews)."[44]

Within a week of the council, most band leaders had left the agency in search of food. Most of these men were accompanied by families who travelled with them through the winter. While in many respects these bands resembled the groups who hosted François Antoine Larocque in 1805 – they were composed of extended families and contained both elders and young people – their cohesion was greatly affected by their leader's standing within the new reservation environment. Diplomatic headmen such as Plenty Coups and Medicine Crow could expect to provide greater protection and assistance to their followers than could those like Spotted Horse who were identified as "troublemakers." This new dynamic was partially reflected in a report sent to Washington by Agent Keller two weeks after the August council. "Before leaving the agency the heads of several bands of the tribe visited me," Keller noted. The agent had indicated that he would build some cabins for the Crows during the coming year, and the chiefs wanted to be sure that they "and their following" would receive one. Keller added that the entire band "usually accompanied their chief to give force to their requests." Finally, the agent observed that "some jealousy" had emerged between those who were cooperating with his effort to contain the tribe on the reservation and "the wild element . . . the latter being under the leadership of Crazy Head: a restless and ambitious chief."[45]

Other encounters between federal authorities and tribal leaders in the early 1880s produced similar patterns of rivalry and competition. Prominent Mountain Crow headmen such as Iron Bull, Medicine Crow, Plenty Coups and Thin Belly cast themselves as the government's allies. They were willing to be co-

---

44 See Report on Council of August 22, 1881, 16006–1881, Special Cases 82, LR-OIA, RG 75, NA. Spotted Horse's declaration was not purely rhetorical, for the rail line repeatedly cut Crow hay and timber without permission. In addition, tribal leaders insisted that they had been promised free passage on the company's trains and the Special Cases file cited above contains numerous complaints from Crows who had been tossed off trains for refusing to buy a ticket. See also Ronan Agent to Commissioner of Indian Affairs, March 19, 1884, 5301–1884, LR-OIA, RG 75, NA, and Robert Harris to Commissioner of Indian Affairs, April 17, 1884, 5378–1884, LR-OIA, RG 75, NA, for correspondence involving a visit by twenty Crows to the Flathead Reservation. When they were ready to come home, the group apparently boarded a train and demanded free passage back to the Yellowstone. The president of the line in New York City ordered the local agent to let them through.

45 A. R. Keller to Commissioner of Indian Affairs, September 3, 1881, Item 3, Box 9, RCIA-FRC, Seattle.

operative, they insisted, but they told the agent that they deserved concessions and assistance in return. One example of this assertive form of friendship was the response of a general council called by Agent Keller to discuss the resettlement of the Northern Cheyennes on the Crow Reservation. Speaking first, Iron Bull warned that "the Great Father thinks he knows these people but he don't, we know them." He added that if the plan were implemented the newcomers would "do things the whites will lay to us." Medicine Crow was equally insistent. "We want to be friendly with the whites," he declared; "we don't want the Cheyenne with us."[46]

Individual band leaders were often torn between their desire to benefit from cooperation with the government and their traditional obligation to respond to the needs of of their followers and family members. As a result, all of the men who spoke up as government allies during these early councils followed independent and often unpredictable courses. Pretty Eagle, for example, was a senior Mountain Crow leader who cut hay along the Yellowstone in the summer of 1882 in expectation that he would be able to sell it to local ranchers. When fall rains made it impossible for him to carry the hay across the Yellowstone, the agent agreed that he should leave the reservation to go hunting and then tried to sell the crop for him. During the same year, Takes Wrinkle and his band pleaded for permission to hunt off the reservation, but then slipped away when he said no. Even Plenty Coups, whom agents in the 1880s came to rely upon for support, insisted on remaining aloof from the agency at his camp along Pryor Creek.[47]

V

By the end of 1882, as Henry Armstrong began planning for the relocation of his agency headquarters from the Stillwater to a "permanent" site on the Little Bighorn, tribal leaders and their families had come to realize that "Crow country" was a reservation. Because the buffalo were now nearly extinct and their Sioux and Piegan enemies were rapidly being replaced by American farmers and ranchers, they knew that crossing the Yellowstone or travelling south into Wyoming or east to the Powder River country would bring them into a hostile and barren land. Because they had served with the army units who expelled the Sioux and Cheyenne from the buffalo grounds of eastern Montana, they knew

---

[46] Proceedings of Council of July 19, 1881, Item 3, Box 9, RCIA-FRC, Seattle. The proposal was dropped, but a reservation was created for the Northern Cheyennes (who also opposed settlement with the Crows) in November 1884.

[47] Henry Armstrong to Commissioner of Indian Affairs, November 2, 1882 (on Pretty Eagle); Henry Armstrong to Nelson Story, May 2, 1882 (on Takes Wrinkle); and Henry Armstrong to Commissioner of Indian Affairs, June 30, 1882 (on Plenty Coups); all in Item 2, Box 9, RCIA-FRC, Seattle.

that the post at Fort Custer represented a force they could not destroy. And because they were so often hungry and without protection, they understood that the ignorant and wilful men who dispensed food and supplies from the adobe-walled agency represented a power that had somehow to be accommodated and turned to their advantage.

But while the contours of this new reservation life were clear, the shape of the community that inhabited it was not. In fact the "tribe" of 1882, despite its rapid accommodation to the government's desire for general councils, consisted of twenty-six loosely structured bands of fifteen to forty lodges each. While linked by clan and kin ties, these bands were units that gathered rations together, but migrated according to their own preferences and inclinations. Their leaders were largely independent from one another, even though it was clear that both the government and several ambitious chiefs were eager to establish some form of centralized leadership for the group. Others resisted this trend. As Henry Armstrong reported to his superiors in Washington at the end of 1882, some Crows were angry with him "because I refused to acknowledge them as chiefs." Alternatively, some young men had abandoned the band leaders who cooperated with the government and were planning to create a new roster of leaders. "These young men," the agent wrote, "want to form new bands which they call prairie bands composed entirely of Indians who oppose all civilizing influence. Of course I oppose such a movement in every possible way," he noted. That "way" was usually through withholding food, clothing and tools. Armstrong added that when an old chief died, "I put forward men who are disposed to settle down to farming."[48]

Similarly, despite the brutality local Montanans and the U.S. government might bring to bear on the Crows or their Indian neighbors, the Americans' specific objectives for the reservation's residents were far from clear. American expansion and military might had turned the Crows into refugees, but federal and state officials had few goals for the Indians beyond having them live an "orderly" existence. In the same report that contained his promise to promote cooperative tribal leaders, Henry Armstrong reminded his superiors of the reality of reservation life:

> I believe the hearts of the Crows will average as good . . . as the hearts of any other people, but there are some very mean ones among them. The best of them – even those who have travelled down to Washington and seen what a great country we have – have many superstitious notions and heathenish customs which they give up very reluctantly. There are many discouraging features connected with this service, not the least of which is

---

[48] Armstrong to Commissioner of Indian Affairs, December 6, 1882, Item 3, Box 9, RCIA-FRC, Seattle. Armstrong also discussed the emergence of "prairie bands" in another letter to the Commissioner, found at the same location and dated November 5, 1882.

the feeling that the government is not doing what it might and ought toward settling the Indians down upon homes of their own. The powers of an agent in such weighty matters are very limited indeed.[49]

In the preceding decade, as Crow bands and their leaders made ever more regular calls on the agency, the tribe's various agents had attempted to launch an educational program for the community children and to bring farming instruction to its adults. Participation in both efforts had been sporadic. Some agents reported as many as a hundred Crows in the tribal school in the 1870s, but Henry Armstrong confided in 1883 that with valiant effort, the school was a success "except in regard to numbers." As a result, he added, "not one of the chiefs or headmen can speak our language at all." Armstrong was certain that this failure was a product of active resistance. "I am certain," he commented in another of his reports, "their people talk to them and teach them to act so and persuade them not to learn to speak our language.[50]

Not surprisingly, despite several agents' excited reports of warriors cutting hay and following the plow, no Crows had become devoted farmers. Leaders frequently struck a cooperative pose, and agency employees managed to raise crops for themselves and their families, but the bulk of the tribe continued to subsist on rations and the dwindling supply of game. Several individuals expressed an interest in raising cattle, but Agent Keller noted in 1882, "A large number of Crows look upon the whites with suspicion [and] cling to the life to which they are born." Mission activity found a similar response. Few Crows actively opposed the arrival of Methodist clergy at the agency in 1873, but the tribe's indifference, together with the rising tide of violence in the Yellowstone valley as a whole, soon persuaded the missionaries to withdraw.[51]

Looking back on his and his predecessors' campaigns to "civilize" the tribe, Henry Armstrong wrote in January 1883 that "nearly all the Crow Indians hate the white man's language and the white man's mode of life." Outsiders like the earnest agent had succeeded in altering the Crows' environment and economy; they continued to nurture ambitions for the future. And many in the refugee bands which lay scattered across the reservation must have thought that they had reached the end of their life as members of a Crow community. But the encounter between the Crows and outsiders had yet to reach the group's central values, traditions and institutions, while the tribe's resistance continued to

---

[49] Armstrong to Commissioner of Indian Affairs, November 5, 1882, Item 3, Box 9, RCIA-FRC, Seattle.
[50] Henry Armstrong to Commissioner of Indian Affairs, January 3, 1883, Item 3, Box, 9, RCIA-FRC, Seattle; ARCIA, 1883 (Serial 2191), 157; ARCIA, 1882 (Serial 2100), 162.
[51] A. R. Keller to Commissioner of Indian Affairs, May 5, 1882, Item 3, Box 9, RCIA-FRC, Seattle. For discussions of the farming program, see ARCIA, 1876 (Serial 1749), 592; ARCIA, 1881 (Serial 2018), 172; ARCIA, 1883 (Serial 2191), 156. The short-lived Methodist mission is described in ARCIA, 1874 (Serial 1639), 570, and ARCIA, 1881 (Serial 2018), 172.

manifest itself in the daily life of both leaders and their constituents. As they packed their belongings in anticipation of the move to the Little Bighorn, the Crows were not preparing for the end of their tribal existence, but for its transformation and rebirth.[52]

[52] Henry Armstrong to Commissioner of Indian Affairs, January 3, 1883, Item 3, Box 9, RCIA-FRC, Seattle.

5

A new home

Nothing happened after that. We just lived. There were no more war parties, no capturing of horses from the Piegans and the Sioux, no buffalo to hunt. There is nothing more to tell.

Two Leggings, 1919[1]

I

In the spring of 1884, the Crows who paraded behind Captain Armstrong from the Stillwater valley to the Little Bighorn River entered a new world of record keeping as well as a new arena of experience. Unprecedented poverty and suffering lay before them, but the ordeal to come would take place in the most intensively recorded period in Crow history. Unlike other North American Indians who faced epidemic diseases and the effects of domination in isolation, or whose suffering was hidden by embarrassed officials, the Crows setting along the flatlands of their reservation moved into a new home where clerks and inspectors would track their words and tally their actions in minute detail. In the half-century following the tribe's migration out of the mountains, the Crows would generate a Mt. Everest of records and reports which have been preserved in archives and libraries across the United States.

But like the journey from the Stillwater itself – a trip which demanded more of the tribe than a simple shift in location – the Crows' arrival in the land of bureaucratic record keeping offers the opportunity to view the community's adjustment to a new environment. While the rich documentary record of the early reservation years contains unparalleled written accounts of tribal life, its insights rest on a bedrock of forms and lists. The lists are the most intriguing and the most impenetrable. There are, for example, lists of agency employees, lists (and dimensions) of government buildings, lists of tools issued and lists of arrests made. With these one can often find lists of children who attended school, lists of children who died, lists of Crows who were baptized and lists of Crows who married. Tribal census lists contain thousands of names in both Crow and English, together with lists of family members, lists of birthdays,

---

[1] Peter Nabokov, *Two Leggings: The Making of a Crow Warrior* (Lincoln: University of Nebraska Press, 1982), 197, originally published in 1967.

and, sometimes, lists of jobs held and crops produced. Although poorly educated white missionaries, teachers and government officials compiled most of these lists, they are surprisingly accurate. The problem is that they are mute. They contain few words and no narrative. They mark ten thousand moments, yet each is isolated from every other. Rather than opening the tribe's experience to its modern heirs and others wishing to study its culture, these lists have become a wall separating observers from the intimate moments they record.[2]

Knowing that they are unparalleled – but perhaps useless – documents of a tragic time in Crow history, one sifts through the records of this new, reservation existence and wonders in reply to Two Leggings's despondent statement: what happened? What themes are hidden here? How can the tiny threads of lives running through them be knit together? How can the moments they record be reconnected so they can speak to us and tell us their story? And once reconnected, what will these moments reveal – and what will they hide – about Two Leggings and his kinsmen, people who "just lived" on the reservation that had once been theirs alone?

The problem is not only one of quantity. When François Antoine Larocque and Jim Beckwourth came to live with the Crows, record keeping and history making were tasks taken up by the community's elders and religious leaders. Their stories were the archive; their memory was the tribal history. When other forms of record keeping arose – or were imposed – it was not clear what meaning should be attached to these new and alien pieces of paper. How might one hear a Crow voice when the mountain of records that contained it was constructed by outsiders?

As the tribe took up life along the Little Bighorn, events and pressures multiplied so dramatically that the tribe's traditional record-keeping practices were overwhelmed by both the number and the power of the newcomers. As leaders like Blackfoot and Iron Bull learned at the Judith River negotiations in 1873, it had become increasingly impossible for Crows to win a hearing for their version of events, just as it was impossible for traditional methods of record keeping to match the capacity of the white man's written lists. So the lists drowned out the voices of the elders. Can they be transformed now? If so, how can bureaucratic documents unlock the voices they silenced a century ago? Can they illuminate the tribe's passage into the modern era, or can they only document a series of tragic and unrelated moments that tell only a story of victimization and chaos?

What follows in this and succeeding chapters will provide increasingly precise answers to these questions. As the narrative of the reservation era unfolds, however, it will be important to understand that the immense documentary

---

[2] The problems associated with archival research in this area are discussed in Frederick E. Hoxie, "The View from Eagle Butte: National Archives Field Branches and the Writing of American Indian History," *Journal of American History*, 76, 1 (June 1989), 171–180.

record available for the Crow community at best provides imperfect evidence for the tribe's modern history. Even if one assumes that the inevitable errors and language problems contained in written records can all be overcome and one might somehow reconstruct the life story of every Crow Indian who was present along the Little Bighorn in 1884, we would still be gazing through a clouded and distorted lens. The fact that we can know when people were baptized, how they performed in school and where they sold their cattle has a limited impact on our effort to understand how Crow men and women viewed the course of their community's life at a pivotal moment in their history.

For example, less than two weeks after his arrival at the site of the new Crow Agency, Agent Henry Armstrong made his first issue of rations to the 900 people who had accompanied him on the journey from the mountains. For the occasion he started a new list in a standard, Indian Service notebook. Barely four inches wide, the book slipped easily into the agent's pocket and formed a handy guide to the pioneers who had come with him to the Little Bighorn valley. In one column, Armstrong recorded the ration ticket number of the family head who presented him- or herself for the one-pound-per-person allotment of beef. In the other he noted the number of rations issued. One of those who appeared for that first distribution was a man named Old Dog, who drew rations for his family of six people, a group which probably included two wives. Subsequently, Armstrong noted that Old Dog was the leader of a band of a dozen families, at least three of whom lined up with their headman for beef that first April morning.

Twenty-six other men were recognized as band leaders by Henry Armstrong. Like Old Dog, they appeared repeatedly in the agent's lists and the records of the new agency. Less than a month after his first distribution of rations, for example, Henry Armstrong ordered special brands to be made for Old Dog and the other headmen so that he could distribute a shipment of government horses. He hoped to use these brands so deserving headmen could keep track of their pony and cattle herds.[3]

Seven months later, in January 1885, Old Dog appeared on another list: he was recorded as favoring the use of a portion of the tribal treasury for supplementary food distributions. Other documents contain brief transcripts of his comments at council meetings. On one occasion, for example, he welcomed the arrival of rent-paying cattlemen on the reserve and praised the system of leasing tribal land to generate income. In the 1890s, Old Dog settled down with his children and their families on a tract of land south of the new agency town. By the time of his death in summer of 1917, he and Well Known Rock, his wife of

---

[3] For Armstrong's discussion of the twenty-seven bands, see Armstrong to Commissioner of Indian Affairs (hereafter cited as CIA), November 24, 1884, Item 3, Box 10, RCIA-FRC, Seattle.

more than three decades, had spent half of their lives as reservation residents. How can they speak to us? What did their lives signify?[4]

Answering these questions, like tracing Crow history through the reservation era, requires that we both use and question the written records compiled by Old Dog's white contemporaries. We could not know these details of the headman's life without the overlapping lists that contain his name and the names of his kinsmen, but we cannot know the import of Old Dog's experience unless we can set aside the assumptions of the original record keepers and seek out intimations of Old Dog's motives and, perhaps, his dreams. We must look for hints of coherence and continuity in a life that seems at first glance to be filled with suffering and disjunction. We must listen for his voice and we must watch the behavior of his neighbors and relatives during his lifetime and afterwards as the perspectives and ideas he nourished were passed on and reflected in the history of his community.

When we find, for example, that Old Dog acquired a piece of property in the 1890s, we should not assume with the clerk who recorded the transaction that the event marked the seventy-year-old man's debut as an enterprising Montana rancher. While coerced to live on an individual plot of land, Old Dog, like Plenty Coups and the men who voluntarily cut hay at the Stillwater agency in 1882, may have had his own reasons for agreeing to his agent's orders. Despite its choice location downstream from the village of Lodge Grass, on the banks of the Little Bighorn River, Old Dog's farm might represent something more than a chance to participate in commercial agriculture. We might ask, for example, "Who were his neighbors?" And we should not be surprised to learn that Old Dog's land lay near his daughter's, next to that of his wife, and adjoining a tract of land belonging to The Bread. In 1884, The Bread had belonged to Old Dog's band and had probably travelled with him from the Stillwater. Like his band leader, The Bread had also received a special brand – and a horse – from Henry Armstrong in the first month of their relocation. The Bread's property was also alongside land owned by Stoops To Charge, his wife

---

[4] Armstrong's issue book is Item 39, Box 171, RCIA-FRC, Seattle. Old Dog held ration ticket 404, a fact which is recorded in "Record of Indian Bands," Item 21, Box 156, RCIA-FRC, Seattle (Old Dog is listed as the head of family 165 and the leader of his band). Armstrong's intention to distribute horses and special brands to a group which included Old Dog is made clear in Henry Armstrong to C. H. Barstow, May 8, 1884, Item 3, Box 10, RCIA-FRC, Seattle. Old Dog's residence near Lodge Grass is established by his listing in the "Round Up, June 1889," Item 42, Box 174, RCIA-FRC, Seattle, and the location of his allotment. The latter is noted in the "List of Crow Allotments," Item 53, Box 199, RCIA-FRC, Seattle. Old Dog and his spouse are listed in the first complete census of the Crow tribe, compiled in 1887, and in the subsequent federal censuses of 1900 and 1910. (The 1887 census is Item 17, Box 154, RCIA-FRC, Seattle. Old Dog's death is recorded in "Register of Crow Deaths, 1902–1921," on July 17, 1917. Item 44, RCIA, FRC, Seattle.)

Old Dog's statements at various tribal council meetings can be found in 1249–1885 and 15835–1890, both in LR-OIA, RG 75, NA.

of more than twenty years. One wonders, if these old comrades viewed their property as two adjoining homesteads or one, continuous refuge. How did they use it, and what did they tell their families about it?[5]

Old Dog and the other band leaders who settled on the flatlands with their families and kinsmen carried many features of their old life with them into what Captain Armstrong was hoping would be a new, sedentary existence. Conflicts with other tribes continued, despite the fact that, like the Crow, the Blackfeet, Assiniboin and Gros Ventre tribes were also constrained by the disappearance of game and the arrival of soldiers and railroads. People in the Crow community also continued to value the leadership of their elders and warriors, despite the fact that warfare was prohibited by the American military and outlawed by the government's new, written rules. Happily, none of those rules outlawed the Crow belief in maintaining one's allegiance to family and clan members, and in the first years of the new agency, the government paid little attention to individual behavior. In 1884 there was still no resident missionary on the reservation and only the beginnings of a boarding school. With so many tasks before them, the government's beleaguered employees had relatively little time to devote to undermining the tribe's traditions.

In the course of the 1880s, however, as movable lodges were replaced with more permanent camps, the lists and documents help us outline the new life the Crows could not avoid. Raiding and warfare against other tribes ended. Missionaries and other outsiders began to attack old patterns of belief and loyalty. Federal officials began to exercise a new kind of authority, favoring some band leaders and attempting to undercut others. Three years after the move to Crow Agency, these pressures produced the worst political crisis in the group's modern history and threatened to shatter both the tribe's leadership and its social traditions. As that crisis passed, Crow leaders like Old Dog, acting in concert with others in native communities taking root across the reservation, began to lay the foundations for a new version of their tribal culture. These reconstruction efforts would take decades to complete, but they ensured the group's survival in the coming century and transformed its refugee bands into a new political entity: the Crow nation.

II

A dramatic decline in tribal population underlay the events of the 1880s. It is possible that the Crows had lost more people at other times in their history, but the generation experiencing the 1884 relocation had nothing with which to compare the carnage they witnessed.

[5] See allotments 1200, 1201, 1202, 1203 and 1204, Township 5 South, Range 35 East, in Crow Agency Plat Drawings, Item 66, Box 190, RCIA-FRC, Seattle.

Captain Armstrong's replacement as agent to the Crows, a former military officer named Henry Williamson, conducted the first systematic census of the tribe in the summer of 1887. He wrote the commissioner of Indian affairs that his enumeration (which had been compiled with the assistance of extra interpreters so as to make it *"absolutely accurate"*) had "been taken very carefully and with much labor." His final report that there were 2,456 Crows on the reservation was the first systematic enumeration of a group whose numbers had been estimated by various travellers for nearly a century. Williamson noted that the tribe was divided into 630 families; all but 82 of them regularly drew rations at the agency.[6]

In 1805, François Antoine Larocque had recorded that, according to his hosts, smallpox epidemics in the eighteenth century had reduced the Crows from 2,000 lodges to 300. Larocque noted that "lodges" contained an average of 8 people (an unusually high estimate) and guessed that a few generations prior to his visit there may have been as many as 16,000 Crows. According to his informants, that number had declined to about 2,400 by the time of his visit. Because Laroque appears to have been unaware of the existence of the River Crows, we should accept his figure as the population of the Mountain Crows alone and consider Lewis and Clark's 1806 estimate of 3,500 for the entire tribe (based on interviews with the Hidatsas and Mandans) as plausible. Both Larocque and Lewis and Clark may have underestimated, but given the presence of so many other competing tribes in the region, it is unlikely that there were more than 5,000 Crows on the northern plains in 1800.[7]

Estimates of Crow population generally placed their number in the range of 3,500 to 5,000 until Williamson conducted his 1887 census. Edwin Thompson Denig, the American Fur Company trader who lived on the upper Missouri from 1833 to 1856, wrote in his memoirs that the Crows "were formerly about 800 lodges or families, but from the usual causes of diminution, sickness and war, are now reduced to 460 lodges." Depending on whether one accepts Larocque's estimate of 8 people per lodge or uses a more modest guess of 4, this would correspond to a population of between 3,200 and 6,400 (whenever "formerly" was), to between 1,800 and 3,600 in the 1850s. Like Larocque, Denig believed the worst devastation from epidemics had occurred in the eighteenth century, before actual contact with whites. The trader noted, for example, that

---

[6] Henry Williamson to Commissioner of Indian Affairs, December 27, 1886, file 41, LR-OIA, RG 75, NA; Henry Williamson to Commissioner of Indian Affairs, June 30, 1887, file 17921, LR-OIA, RG 75, NA. On the subject of interpreters, see Henry Williamson to Commissioner of Indian Affairs, June 23, 1886, file 16992, LR-OIA, RG 75, NA.

[7] For Larocque's estimate, see his "Observations on the Rocky Mountain Indians," in W. Raymond Wood and Thomas D. Thiessen, eds., *Early Fur Trade on the Northern Plains* (Norman: University of Oklahoma Press, 1985), 206. Lewis and Clark's report is in Reuben Gold Thwaites, ed., *Original Journals of the Lewis and Clark Expedition, 1804–1806* (New York: Dodd, Mead, 1905), vol. 6, 82.

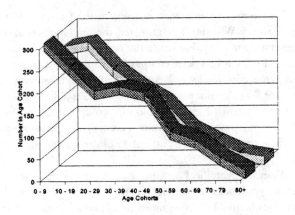

Figure 1. Age distribution, Crow tribe, 1887.

the great smallpox epidemic which destroyed the Missouri River trading villages in 1837 had little impact on the Crows (presumably they had developed
some immunity).[8]

Between 1865 and 1887, figures for Crow population come principally from
the annual reports of the commissioner of Indian affairs. These estimates were
usually contained in reports from field agents or military officers and were
based on requests for rations and annuities, as well as comparisons with other
groups. (Agents noted that the Crows were less numerous than the Sioux, more
numerous than the Hidatsa, etc.) Using these crude techniques, the Indian
Office usually maintained an estimate of 3,500 for Crow population during the
eighteen years between 1865 and 1882.[9]

The fact that Crow population estimates were generally the same for thirty
years after Denig's estimate of 1856 does not mean the tribe experienced a
period of tranquility. Infectious diseases were common afflictions throughout
these years, and there were certainly periods of intense suffering and dislocation
caused by epidemic episodes. It is remarkable, however, that during most of the
nineteenth century, when the Mandans and Hidatsas nearly became extinct,
and other groups such as the Shoshones and Blackfeet suffered significant
reductions, the Crows appeared to hold their own. This impression is confirmed by an examination of the tribe's age composition in 1887 as displayed in
Figure 1. The relatively even "pyramid" shape of this population indicates no

[8] For Denig's comments on Crow population, see Edwin Thompson Denig, *Five Indian Tribes of
the Upper Missouri*, John C. Ewers, ed. (Norman: University of Oklahoma Press, 1961), 142, 185,
186. Note also Dr. Ewers's comments on Denig's estimates.

[9] See *ARCIA*, 1865 (Serial 1248), 193; *ARCIA*, 1882 (Serial 2100), 162. The highest estimate for
this period is 5,000 in 1868 (*ARCIA*, [Serial 1366], 813); the lowest estimate is 2,600 in 1876
(*ARCIA* [Serial 1749], 492).

severe gaps caused by epidemic episodes. (Epidemics frequently will virtually eliminate an age cohort such as the elderly or a large percentage of the infants and children.) It would seem that, while embattled, Crow society had remained relatively intact during the middle decades of the nineteenth century.

The available population figures provide vivid evidence that the relative demographic stability the Crows had enjoyed at midcentury disappeared during the 1880s. Assuming the accuracy of the census figures after 1887 (if anything, they *over*report the size of tribal population as individuals hid the death of family members in order to continue receiving their ration), the tribe appeared to enter a period of rapid population decline. Since the estimate of 3,500 made in 1882 cannot be verified, it is impossible to know exactly how rapidly the population had dropped to reach the 1887 figure of 2,456. From that date forward, however, one can be more confident. In 1894 the agent reported a population of 2,126, a loss of 10% in seven years. Nine years later there were 1,941 Crows, a reduction of 9% in nine years.

The Crow population continued to decline into the second decade of the twentieth century, but the precipitous drop of the early reservation years was unique. Nearly one-third (31%) of the 2,461 individuals recorded on the 1887 census were reported to have died during the 1890s. The worst of these years was 1890, with the agency recording 165 deaths in its logs during twelve months, more than 3 a week. The horror of that year is compounded if one examines the age distribution of those who passed away. More than half of the 1890 dead were under the age of twenty. The decimation of the tribe's youngest generation spared no one. Long and Slides Down Well Known, the adopted son and daugher of Old Dog, were among those who died during the 1890s. According to the agency census records, both of the children listed in the band leader's household in 1887 were dead by 1893.[10]

Figure 2 makes clear that while the tragedy of the first reservation years may have faded after 1900, its effects lasted well into the new century. In contrast to a normal "pyramid" pattern of age distributions in which younger age cohorts would gradually give way to older ones, this description of age distribution within the tribe reveals that twenty-year-olds were vastly underrepresented in the 1910 census. These were people born between 1881 and 1890, the first years of the agency relocation. That gap offers inexact but striking evidence that the Crow people suffered the loss of almost an entire generation of young people at the same time that Agent Armstrong and his successors were launching them on the path to "civilization." This conclusion is reinforced by an examination of the 726 Crow children who were twelve years old or younger when the census of 1887 was conducted. Of this number, 224 – one third – were dead by 1900.

[10] The manuscript copy of the 1887 census at the Federal Records Center in Seattle contains notations giving the dates of death of approximately half the people listed in the enumeration. Old Dog's family is recorded in the census at 56.

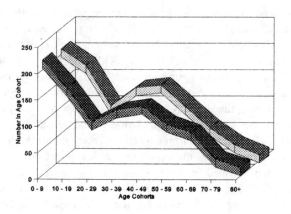

Figure 2. Age distribution, Crow tribe, 1910.

A final indication of the general ill health of the tribe during the 1880s emerges from the annual reports of government agents. These self-serving letters to Washington generally avoided unpleasant news in favor of reports that the government was making headway in the campaign to alter the Crows' way of life. New agents were usually the most optimistic. Henry Williamson reported on his arrival in 1886, for example, that he found "the great majority of the Indians very tractable." After a few years on the job, the tone frequently changed. Henry Armstrong's third report, for example (filed two years before Williamson's optimistic note quoted above), declared that "these Indians hate the white man's way of life in their hearts. . . ." Despite their shifting tone, however, the reports for the 1880s consistently referred to severe illnesses that afflicted the tribe.[11]

In 1884, Agent Armstrong reported that 1,168 cases of "illness" had been recorded at the agency; similar figures appeared in 1886, 1887 and 1890. Between 1891 and 1895 the agents reported half that number, between 400 and 600 "sick" tribesmen per year. According to the annual reports, a large percentage of those who were sick suffered from gastric disorders, either "constipation" (1886), "acute diarrhea" (1891) or "gastric obstruction" (1893). It is impossible to be precise about the causes of such disorders, but the tremendous loss of life suffered during these same years strongly suggests that the Crows suffered from a series of infectious diseases, possibly related to the government's efforts to alter tribal lifeways. Prominent among these were the practice of slaughtering and issuing beef to the tribe from the agency headquarters on the Little Bighorn River and the attempt to house Crow families in permanent dwellings along the same waterway. As agent Briscoe noted in 1888,

[11] *ARCIA*, 1886 (Serial 2467), 396; 1884 (Serial 2278), 155.

"Hereditary diseases and the abrupt change from a nomadic life and an all-meat diet to living in houses and an almost vegetable diet is causing the enormous death rate." Among the specific culprits that may have caused the death are diptheria and tuberculosis (which thrive in cramped and unsanitary dwellings) and various water-borne infections such as typhoid fever that can spread rapidly through the sedentary camps. Henry Armstrong placed the slaughterhouse for the new Crow Agency on the banks of the meandering Little Bighorn River. This placement might well have aided the spread of dangerous infectious diseases near the government offices. While settlements along Pryor Creek and the Bighorn were less concentrated, the clustering of families along a single water course and their permanent location at a single site would have produced similar results.[12]

Population loss was a fact of life at the new agency. Public activities of many kinds took center stage during the 1880s, but sickness and early death could not have been far from their minds. These conditions created a backdrop of crisis for political maneuvering and rivalry, and they made the maintenance of tribal traditions and values more dear. During their first decade in their new homes the Crows struggled to be a settled community in a setting marked by desperation.

III

Despite the loss of many young men and women, and the imposition of new restrictions on their movements, the reservation Crows maintained their affection for military activity and the glory that came with raiding and warfare. Crow warriors continued to capture horses from neighboring tribes and to retaliate against those who attacked them. Nevertheless, during the 1880s, as the authority of the Indian Office and the American military expanded, the tribe's contacts with other Indian communities took new forms. As leaders began to recognize their common predicament, raiding gave way to peacemaking and visiting. Men who had been enemies on the battlefield found they

---

[12] See *ARCIA*, 1884 (Serial 2278) 155; 1886 (Serial 2467), 395; 1887 (Serial 2542), 220; 1890 (Serial 2841), 122; 1891 (Serial 2934), 275; 1892 (Serial 2953), 290; 1893 (Serial 3210), 182; and 1894 (Serial 3306), 171. The diagram of Crow Agency is from the Reports of the Field Jurisdiction of the Office of Indian Affairs, National Archives Microfilm 1070, Reel 8, frame 261. Despite their reports of the number of Indians sick at the agency, none of the officials used the term "epidemic" to describe conditions at the agency. Moreover, a comparison of the notations on the manuscript of the 1887 census cited above with the annual reports of births and deaths contained in the agents' annual reports indicates that the government officials either did not know about or did not report the extent of the suffering going on around them. In 1890, for example, the year the census notations indicate 165 people died, Agent Wyman reported 4 deaths on the reservation. Agent Briscoe's comment can be found in *ARCIA*, 1888 (Serial 2637), 153.

could encourage one another in a new age of dislocation and defeat, and experiment with new forms of intertribal leadership.

In the summer of 1886 a visitor from the East toured the new Crow communities along the Little Bighorn and, while praising the tribe's "peaceful nature," noted that "they still cling with tenacity to all the traditions of the past, and have not deviated in dress, habits or pursuits from the tribe of fifty years ago." Many outsiders agreed with that assessment, frequently citing the tribe's apparent desire to continue its nomadic way of life and avoid both "civilization" and hard work. Despite their recent relocation to good farmland, the Billings *Gazette* observed at the end of 1885 that many Crows "still continu[e] to roam about the country at large depredating the ranges and the settlements."[13]

In 1885 and 1886 it appeared that this was indeed the case. The government operated only one small school, and the tribe actively opposed sending its children away to the Indian Office's new boarding institutions in the East. "The Indians are unwilling to part with their children," Henry Armstrong wrote in 1885. The following year a Unitarian mission school was begun near the Yellowstone, north of Fort Custer, while a group of Jesuit missionaries began making plans for a mission in the Bighorn valley; still, there would be no year-round Christian outpost among the Crows until at least 1887.[14]

For government agents, military officers and local journalists, however, the best measure of the slow progress of "civilization" among the Crows was the continuation of intertribal warfare. With the decline of the Sioux presence in the Yellowstone valley in the 1880s, it seemed to many in the tribe that they could turn their attention back to their old rivals, the Assiniboin and the Blackfeet or Piegans. These targets were particularly inviting as years of peace and the decline of the buffalo allowed them to expand their pony herds, and the dullness of reservation life became evident. The Piegans were cited most frequently as instigators of horse-stealing raids and as the target of Crow war parties. "These raids," an exasperated Henry Armstrong reported in the fall of 1885, "are no new thing at all. They have been going on every summer since I have been in charge of this agency."

Intertribal conflicts provided steady work for the military, as post commanders across Montana dispatched troops to recover horses and capture the young men who left their agencies without authorization. Unfortunately for the soldiers, it was also frustrating duty, for by the time the cavalry investigated an alleged theft or raid, the trail had usually run cold. In the case of the Piegans, who occupied a reservation that straddled the border with Canada, the frustration was frequently compounded by the fact that their war parties sought refuge with kinsmen north of the line. In 1885, for example, a Piegan leader named

[13] Billings *Gazette*, July 5, 1886, 3; ibid., December 17, 1885.
[14] *ARCIA*, 1886 (Serial 2467), 347–348; ibid., 1887 (Serial 2542), 394.

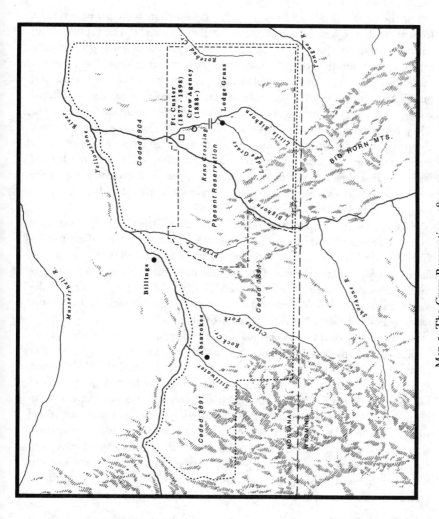

Map 5. The Crow Reservation, 1890–1904.

White Calf told a young captain from Fort Shaw, that "all the horses that were taken from the Crows from time to time went north as fast as received, and were sold to the Blackfeet, Bloods and North Piegans." The chief declared his willingness to "make friends" with the Crows but he warned that it would be "hard to find" any of the missing stock.[15]

For the Crows, these incidents represented something more than a diversion from their dreary new life or an attack on their property. The capture of an enemy's horse had long been recognized as a war honor on a par with the touching or "counting coup" on an individual in battle. For that reason, a person suffering the loss of a horse had experienced a personal defeat and humiliation. Alternatively, successfully retaliating against an enemy offered young men a way of enhancing their standing within their bands and clans. They could repair their pride and win war honors for themselves and their companions. For established band leaders or headmen, these retaliatory raids were also a way of reassuring their followers that they still recognized the old ways and that they had not become simple puppets of the agent. Despite the opposition of the government, Crow leaders insisted that they had to pursue those who attacked their property.

Henry Armstrong told his superiors that he "always tried" to keep his charges from retaliating on their own, but he admitted in 1885 that his pleas usually failed to alter Crow behavior. He wrote that when he ordered the Crows to stay home, "they have accused me of making slaves of them and even of inducing the Piegans to come steal their horses." Clearly, giving in to the agent's demands in this area would undercut a headman's authority with his own band, rendering him a "slave" in the eyes of his followers.[16]

But for most whites, the continuation of raiding and horse stealing was an indication of Crow "backwardness" and a threat to law and order. A rancher from Miles City, which lay northeast of the reservation on the Yellowstone, wrote in the spring of 1884, for example, that a friend of his had spotted one of his own ponies in a Crow herd and had tried to recover it only to have a group of Indians "cut the rope and [say] that they would not give up the horses, [they] would fight first." Agent Armstrong had refused to intervene and the cattleman was furious: "We think the agent in charge of the Crows should have, and exercise, sufficient authority over [them] to settle these troubles without our having to come to Washington with our grievances." Complaints from cattlemen as far south as the Bighorn basin in Wyoming and as far north as Choteau,

[15] Armstrong to Gen. Dudley, September 24, 1885, Item 5, Box 12, RCIA-FRC, Seattle; Exhibit A, Captain Edward Moale to Acting Assistant Adjutant General, Fort Shaw, October 29, 1885 (11), enclosed with Secretary of War to Secretary of Interior, November 28, 1885, 5712–1885, LR-OIA, RG 75, NA.
[16] Armstrong to Gen. Dudley, September 24, 1885. For a discussion of Crow war honors, see Robert H. Lowie, *The Crow Indians* (Lincoln: University of Nebraska Press, 1983), originally published in 1935, 216 and chap. 10.

Montana (less than a hundred miles from the Canadian border) contained similar sentiments. "Agent Armstrong now tells our representatives . . . that he cannot control the Indians," the secretary of the Wyoming Stock Growers Association wrote in 1885, adding that the Indian Office should now ask the army "to do what the agent cannot."[17]

Despite his brave predictions of "progress" at the new agency, it is clear from reports of Henry Armstrong and his successors that the persistence of intertribal raiding represented a direct challenge to his authority. Typically, the agents responded to this affront with a renewed call for discipline. Even when crop failures left the tribe "pretty hungry," Armstrong insisted there was no need for expanded government support. Instead, the agent lectured the tribal headmen to keep their people at home and at work. He believed that those who left the reservation should be jailed and punished. "The sooner they learn that there is some law in this country which they cannot violate without suffering," he wrote, "the better it will be." He added, "A little starving will be good for them."[18]

Such hostility placed band leaders and headmen in a declicate position. If they ignored the agent's orders they would lose the protection and supplies that were becoming increasingly central to their status in the community. It was equally clear that siding with the agent would alienate their followers whom the government expected would learn by "a little starving." This tension infused raids and off-reservation hunting trips with added political and cultural signifi-cance. Both established leaders and ambitious young men recognized that raid-ing offered an opportunity to challenge white authority as well as to demonstrate one's skill as a warrior and one's allegiance to Crow ways. At the same time, band leaders quickly learned that even the most successful raid could not escape criticism. During the 1880s, while tribal leaders were frequently tempted to defy the agent and his military supporters, they gradually shifted the emphasis of their encounters with other tribes from warfare to diplomacy. Crow leaders began the practice of "visiting" their rivals, meeting with them peacefully, to socialize and to discuss common problems. There was little in these new gath-erings that violated the government's rules of conduct. As the decade wore on, these seemingly innocuous meetings replaced raiding as the focus of intertribal contact.

[17] Scott and Company to Henry M. Teller, April 1, 1884, 7046–1884, LR-OIA, RG 75, NA; Petition from Meeteetse, Wyoming, April 18, 1884, 12295–1884, LR-OIA, RG 75, NA; Petition from Choteau, Montana, May 21, 1885, 2890–1885, LR-OIA, RG 75, NA; Thomas Sturgis to Commissioner of Indian Affairs, April 18, 1885, 8879–1885, LR-OIA, RG 75, NA.

[18] Armstrong to Commissioner of Indian Affairs, June 4, 1884, 11016–1884, LR-OIA, RG 75, NA. That Crows also chafed under the leadership of cooperating chiefs is also hinted at by the fact that Spotted Tail and a group of scouts from the Little Bighorn refused to pursue some Piegan raiders who had apparently stolen horses belonging to Plenty Coups. See C. H. Barstow to Commander, Fort Custer, October 23, 1885, Item 4, Box 12, RCIA-FRC, Seattle.

A turning point with the Piegans came in the fall of 1885 when Henry Armstrong dispatched Bull Nose (the man who had defended him a year earlier – "one of my best chiefs") and twelve others (including two agency policemen and the young band leader Medicine Crow) to the Blackfeet Agency to meet with army officers and tribal leaders. The agent gave no reason for his action, but he may have responded to complaints from local cattlemen, or he might have felt that intervening to control the young warriors in both tribes would ensure that the recent Cree and Metis rebellion in Saskatchewan did not spread south of the international boundary. Armstrong might also have viewed a peace conference as a way to elevate "his" loyal band leaders in the eyes of their kinsmen. At any rate the Crow delegation was taken seriously. When word first reached the Blackfeet camps that Crows were approaching to recover their horses, several hundred armed warriors assembled in front of the agency to defend themselves. The officers accompanying the Crow delegation quickly informed the nervous hosts that the group's intentions were peaceful, however, and two Blackfeet leaders, White Calf and Little Dog, came out to welcome them. According to White Calf, the Blackfeet had decided to receive their old foes as guests. "It was plain," he said, "they did not come for anything else."[19]

Greatly calmed, the Crow visitors, nearly two dozen Blackfeet leaders, three interpreters and a brace of cavalry officers crowded into the agency schoolhouse the next afternoon for a council. According to one of the army men who was present, "The whole tenor of their words were that they were all desirous of having peace in the future, and they were not satisfied that it had been duly made. They claimed that many horses had been stolen on both sides. . . ." White Calf and other Blackfeet speakers insisted that the raiding was in retaliation for the Crow murder of two Piegans in the Judith basin in 1880. This action had broken a peace concluded five years earlier in Saskatchewan's Cypress Hills. "The Crows," the note-taking officer reported, "never . . . said one word about the stealing of horses, but merely about making friends." The Blackfeet requested permission to "give the Crows a dance" to seal the peace, but the army refused and the two sides parted, promising to "be friendly forever again."[20]

Raiding did not end with the Crow–Blackfeet council. Piegans and their

---

[19] Edward Moale to Acting Assistant Adjutant General, Fort Shaw, October 29, 1885, enclosed with Secretary of War to Secretary of Interior, November 28, 1885, 5712–1885, LR-OIA, RG 75, NA.

[20] Captain Moale's report of October 29, 1885, cited above, contains all of these descriptions. Moale appended the transcript of an interview with White Calf and Little Dog to his report. The Crow desire for peace might also have been a case of war weariness. Another military observer, writing from Fort McKinney in September 1885, reported, "The truth is, the Piegans have gotten the Crows so demoralized that anything they see is Piegan." Quoted in Gen. Alfred Terry to Adjutant General, Department of Missouri, October 22, 1885, enclosed with Secretary of War to Secretary of Inteior, 27176–1885, LR-OIA, RG 75, NA.

Blood kinsmen from north of the international boundary were reported again in the Yellowstone valley in 1886, and periodic clashes broke out the same year with Sioux and Yanktonais raiders from the reservation near Fort Peck, Montana. But increasingly, these raids had the appearance of uncoordinated attacks mounted by young men. They were focused on achieving momentary glory and did not reflect a larger military strategy. The attackers generally avoided the large number of white settlers who now lay in their path, concentrating instead on their enemies' ponies. As one commander wrote in the fall of 1886, "Although the northern and southern Indians raid and steal from each other . . . the occasions are very rare when horses or property belonging to the settlers are stolen or disturbed."[21]

While intertribal raiding continued as an annoyance to both the army and the established reservation headmen, it remained an enticement to the restless young Crow men who believed they had been born too late to share in the glories of the Sioux wars. As the decade wore on, however, serious diplomatic gatherings gradually replaced the capturing of enemy ponies. In November 1883, for example, as Agent Armstrong prepared his charges for their movement to the new agency, the Crows had "the first friendly visit . . . on record" from a delegation of forty-five Oglala Sioux. Led by Red Cloud's old comrade, Young Man Afraid of His Horse, the group appeared in the Stillwater valley in full regalia and war paint. They stood abreast of one another on the outskirts of the Crow camp, before beginning a dramatic – and clearly well-rehearsed –

---

[21] General Ruger to Assistant Adjutant General, September 21, 1886, 26694–1886 (copy), LR-OIA.

For evidence of continued raiding, see Henry Williamson to CIA, July 14, 1886, 19095–1886, LR-OIA; Alfred Terry to Adjutant General Office, September 20, 1886, 28306–1886 (copy), LR-OIA; General Ruger to Assistant Adjutant General, October 13, 1886, 28358–1886 (copy), LR-OIA; General Ruger to Assistant Adjutant General, November 10, 1886, 31786–1886 (copy), LR-OIA; all in RG 75, NA. See also Henry Williamson to Commander, Fort Custer, November 10, 1886, Item 4, Box 13, RCIA-FRC, Seattle.

In October 1886 a Crow raiding party killed a Sioux woman near Fort Peck. There were nineteen men in the group. Of the thirteen whose ages could be determined from other sources, the eldest was thirty-one; only three others were over twenty-five. The youngest Crow raider was seventeen.

For the Fort Peck killing, see H. Heth to Henry Williamson, August 30, 1886, 24401–1886, LR-OIA, RG 75, NA; and Henry Williamson to H. Heth, October 11, 1886, Item 4, Box 13, RCIA-FRC, Seattle. The latter correspondence contains a roster of the nineteen members of the Crow raiding party. One of the raiders, Knows To Fight, died of consumption in early 1887. Thirteen of the eighteen others appear on the 1887 tribal census. They are (with ages in parentheses): Long Tail (28), Louis Bompard (21), Takes Among Enemy (25), Fire Bird (23), Gives Away (27), Old Rabbit (22), The Bird (16 or 17, two listed), Plenty Hoops (21), Onion (30), Dont Run Away (Don't Run, 19), White Woman (26), Old Bear (31) and The Other Bull (17 or 21, two listed).

Two Crows – Piegan (not on 1887 census) and Fire Bird, age 23 – were subsequently charged with murder in this case. Presumably they were the leaders of the party. Charges against these men were dismissed in the fall of 1887. See Henry Williamson to CIA, Item 2, Box 2, RCIA-FRC, Seattle.

ritual. First the group "came forward in one platoon with military precision dressed out with all their finery and paints." Then with two of their chiefs remaining in the lead and resting in their saddles, the entire group dismounted in unison, walked forward four or five paces and "knelt down with their heads bent forward until they almost touched the ground." According to Armstrong, the Sioux "remained in that position a moment, then arose, returned to their horses, squatted or sat down in a row in front of the horses and began shouting and making speeches."[22]

The Sioux visitors' extraordinary invitation to peace was denounced by one (unnamed) Crow chief, but the offer appeared to have struck a positive chord. The dissenting Crow leader threatened to attack the visiting delegation single-handedly, but Armstrong intervened and ordered him away. With the remainder of the tribe apparently standing by without objection, the rest of the Crow leaders welcomed their old enemies into their lodges. The following spring, Two Moon and Roman Nose, heroes of the Custer fight and other plains battles in the 1860s and 1870s, led similar delegations of Cheyennes to the Little Bighorn. During 1885 and 1886, traditional allies like the Hidatsas from Fort Berthold also appeared to renew old ties and pledge their friendship. By the summer of 1886, one military officer could report that, "the Crows have made peace with all the different bands of Sioux" as well as with their other neighbors.[23]

Traditional etiquette demanded that these visitors be housed and fed and that the Crow hosts reciprocate by visiting their new friends. Agent Armstrong observed this pattern when he wrote in 1884 that departing delegations "carry away a good many presents and the Crows then feel that they ought to return the visits to receive presents." Armstrong and his colleagues at other agencies also saw that this rising tide of intertribal visiting was possibly a graver threat to federal authority than horse stealing. The Crow agent wrote, "I think it is a

[22] The visit of Young Man Afraid of His Horse is in Henry Armstrong to Commissioner of Indian Affairs, November 13, 1883, Item 2, Box 1, RCIA-FRC, Seattle. For a description of a similar ceremony in an encounter between the Omahas and Yankton Sioux, see Ella Deloria, *Waterlily* (Lincoln: University of Nebraska Press, 1988), 107–110. I am grateful to Raymond J. DeMallie for pointing out this reference. The visit is also referred to briefly in Anthony McGinnis, *Counting Coup and Cutting Horses: Intertribal Warfare on the Northern Plains* (Evergreen, Colo.: Cordillera Press, 1990), 178.

[23] Two Moon and Roman Nose are discussed in Armstrong to Capt. E. P. Ewers, June 26, 1884, Item 3, Box 10, RCIA-FRC, Seattle; Visits of Gros Ventres are discussed in Armstrong to "Gifford," October 7, 1884, Item 3, Box 10, RCIA-FRC, Seattle, and Henry Williamson to A. J. Gifford, February 22, 1886, Item 4, Box 12, RCIA-FRC; on Crow peacemaking, see H. Heth to CIA, September 1, 1886, 24401–1886, LR-OIA, RG 75, NA. Visits from Bannocks (which suggests other plateau-dwelling people continued to visit from across the Continental Divide) are described in C. H. Barstow to A. M. Quivey, October 19, 1881, and Indian Agent, Lemhi Agency, October 22, 1881, both in Item 3, Box 9, RCIA-FRC, Seattle. The end of intertribal warfare is also discussed in McGinnis, *Counting Coup and Cutting Horses*, 182–183.

better policy to keep alive the traditional enmities and jealousies between these tribes than for us to try to get them to be friends." The more divided they remained, he added, the more easily "controllable" they would be.[24]

IV

Despite the risks involved in diplomatic visits to other tribes, several chiefs welcomed the opportunity to establish friendly ties with people who now shared their fate. Not surprisingly, the popularity of this new diplomacy quickly attracted government concern, for intertribal contacts naturally encouraged Crow leaders to resist the more authoritarian aspects of reservation life. The tribe's diplomats and visitors were quickly perceived by the government's representatives as the tribe's principal "troublemakers." Spotted Horse, for example, who had hunted frequently in the valleys to the east of the reservation, welcomed the opportunity to make peace with the Sioux who had so often opposed him there. His encounters with Oglala and Hunkpapa Sioux leaders grew more frequent and more friendly following the relocation of the agency into "his" valley, and he frequently turned eastward when he needed additional support in his struggles with Armstrong and his successors. Crazy Head and Deaf Bull, the other band leaders who claimed to have a prior claim on the Little Bighorn valley, also travelled to Dakota Territory to visit their old enemies at the Pine Ridge and Standing Rock Reservations. Bear Wolf, whose mother was Sioux, was the most dramatic headman in this group. In the fall of 1883, he openly defied a prohibition against leaving the reservation and set out with his followers to visit the Sioux agencies. His attempt landed him in the Fort Custer guardhouse, but when he was released early in 1884 he tried again. This time he was successful, and he spent the bulk of that summer travelling to the Pine Ridge and Cheyenne River Sioux agencies as well as to the Northern Cheyenne settlements east of the Little Bighorn valley. Soon after the chief's return in the fall of 1884, delegations from both Pine Ridge and Cheyenne River appeared at Crow Agency.[25]

The tribe's first winter at the new agency pitted Agent Armstrong against this ambitious group of increasingly active diplomats. Bear Wolf, Spotted Horse, Crazy Head and Deaf Bull seemed to draw confidence from their Sioux and

[24] Armstrong to E. P. Ewers, June 26, 1884, Item 3, Box 10, RCIA-FRC, Seattle, and Armstrong to Commissioner, November 13, 1883, Item 2, Box 1, RCIA-FRC, Seattle.
[25] Armstrong to Colonel George B. Sanford, Ft. Custer, August 25, 1884, and September 7, 1884; Armstrong to Commissioner of Indian Affairs, September 20, 1884; all in Item 3, Box 10, RCIA-FRC, Seattle. Armstrong described Bear Wolf as "half-Sioux" in Armstrong to Commissioner of Indian Affairs, February 26, 1885, 18, Item 3, Box 10, RCIA-FRC, Seattle.

Cheyenne friends. They opposed any discussion of farming or the assignment of individual homesteads to tribal members, and they spoke out against the use of tribal money to further the government's "civilization" program. During the first year following the relocation to the Little Bighorn, Spotted Horse would brandish a Sioux war club at councils and tell his followers that all the equipment at the new agency actually belonged to the Indians. Armstrong reported that the chief would "urge them to help themselves whenever they want anything." Bear Wolf also struck a defiant pose, riding up and down the lines of family heads waiting for rations condemning the government "in a loud voice."[26]

Early in 1885, two issues came before the tribe that gave Spotted Horse and his followers an opportunity to campaign openly against Henry Armstrong's reservation policies. First, a pair of amendments to the Crows' 1880 land sale agreement were brought before a general council of "chiefs and headmen" for approval. They called for using tribal funds to increase rations and to build irrigation ditches in the Bighorn and Little Bighorn valleys. According to Armstrong, Spotted Horse worked actively in opposition to both ideas. The agent claimed that the angry young chief used "every endeavor inclusive of threats to prevent the better disposed element of the tribe from following their inclincations." Despite those efforts, however, the first of the two proposals – which involved only $5,500 – was approved.[27]

The second amendment would increase the tribe's expenditure for "permanent improvements" on the reservation from $30,000 to $90,000. Because these funds would be drawn from the $750,000 the Crows had received for the sale of their western lands in 1880, its effect would have been to exhaust their account in seven rather than twenty-five years. When Armstrong asked for approval of this proposal Spotted Horse's threats turned to action. According to Armstrong, the chief began "driving" his fellow tribesmen "out of the house" that had been set aside for the signing of the agreement. The meeting broke up without taking action.[28]

Immediately on the heels of this failure, a committee of cattlemen from the Board of Trade in nearby Billings arrived to protest the leasing of tribal lands to a group from Colorado. Armstrong had rented a vast tract of grazing land to outsiders in the fall of 1884 as another way of expanding his budget and demonstrating the viability of stock raising to the Crows The rental had been approved by a small group of band leaders (including Plenty Coups), but the group from Billings claimed that Armstrong had threatened to cut off rations

---

[26] Henry Armstrong to Commissioner of Indian Affairs, February 26, 1885, Item 3, Box 10, RCIA-FRC, Seattle.
[27] See petition dated January 8, 1885, Item 3, Box 10, RCIA-FRC, Seattle. The second is filed with Armstrong to Commissioner, February 27, 1885, 4492–1885, LR-OIA, RG 75, NA.
[28] See Armstrong to Commissioner, February 27, 1885, 4492–1885, LR-OIA, RG 75, NA.

to anyone who refused to go along with him. The secretary of the interior dispatched Inspector Henry Ward to the Little Bighorn to investigate. Ward began hearing testimony at Crow Agency on January 28, 1885.[29]

The Board of Trade presented Ward with 129 Crows who opposed Armstrong's action, but it did not take the inspector long to evaluate their testimony. He reported that 89 of the witnesses's "were very young men who had not before participated in councils. Some were boys, and all were members of Spotted Horse's band." Many of the remainder "were plainly intimidated by Spotted Horse." Like the soldier societies who once enforced discipline on a buffalo hunt, Spotted Horse and his followers seemed intent on bringing the tribe under their authority. Bear Wolf joined in the attack on the new lease arrangement, and Deaf Bull was reported to have said that he would kill the first person who took the proffered money. Ominously, the inspector also forwarded a report that the "inflamed" chief Spotted Horse was "the captain of the dog soldier element."[30]

Inspector Ward exonerated Armstrong and dismissed the Billings cattlemen's hearing as "a farce." He also recommended that "discipline" at the agency demanded the immediate arrest of the outspoken chiefs by army units from Fort Custer. The recently organized agency police would be useless, he noted: "I do not think the whole force could or would arrest Deaf Bull." Armstrong greeted the recommendation enthusiastically. In a separate letter to headquarters he claimed that Spotted Horse had "put a rope around" the neck of the agency clerk and had provoked the agent himself into drawing his revolver during an argument. He also claimed that Deaf Bull, frustrated at not receiving furniture from the agency, had grabbed Armstrong near his office and tried to drag him off "to Spotted Horse [sic] camp." Bear Wolf had apparently threatened the agent with a knife. But more than these particulars, Armstrong warned that the troublemakers were undermining his authority over the tribe: "Spotted Horse says he is a chief. I think it is high time a little discipline was administered to him and the other two Indians I have mentioned and I ask what sort of a government have we if such men are allowed to go on from bad to worse unrebuked and unpunished?" Spotted Horse and Bear Wolf were arrested on February 21, 1885, and imprisoned at Fort Custer. The soldiers had orders to apprehend Deaf Bull as well, but he apparently fled the reservation. Five days later, with the opposition neutralized, the second proposed amendment to the 1880 Crow land sale was signed and approved by 254 Crow men. By the time Spotted Horse and Bear Wolf were released in late May, Agent

---

[29] See Reports of Inspection of the Field Jurisdiction of the Office of Indian Affairs, Crow Agency, National Archives Microfilm 1070, Reel 8, frames 183–241, for Ward's report (hereafter cited as as MM1070, Reel 8).

[30] Ibid., frames 223, 230, 231. The report of Deaf Bull's threat and the reference to Spotted Horse as a "dog soldier" are from an affidavit filed by the Agency Clerk, C. H. Barstow.

Armstrong had reported that he had "never seen the Crows better natured than they are today, or more willing to work."[31]

In the ensuing months, unsettling spasms of assertion and defiance flashed across the reservation. The agency's confident reports of improvement in school attendance and the construction of new facilities were punctuated with complaints of stolen horses and absent young warriors. In October 1885, Henry Armstrong reported to Agent Valentine McGillicuddy at Pine Ridge that fifty or sixty "of your Indians" had been visiting at Crow for over a week. "I object to large parties of Indians coming here at any time for any reason," he declared. Nevertheless, the Crows quickly organized a return visit, and the following spring yet another delegation of Oglalas appeared on the Little Bighorn.[32]

Also in October 1885, George Milburn, an attorney from nearby Miles City, appeared on the reservation carrying orders from Washington to begin assigning homesteads to individual Crows. His arrival marked the first application of the government's allotment policy to the tribe. Armstrong and his predecessors had long suggested that certain Crows were willing to start individual farms, but Milburn's orders were to assign a portion of the reservation to every tribal member. This comprehensive approach was popular with white westerners and it was gaining strength in Congress. The tribe's agent hoped that allotment would "save great trouble, annoyance and discontent," within the tribe by giving every Crow an opportunity to "make his home his castle in every respect." But there were other reasons for allotment's popularity. Everyone knew that the

---

[31] Ward's statement that the "hearing" was a farce is in MM1070, Reel 8, frame 228. Armstrong's assessment of Crow attitudes is in a letter from him to the Commissioner, dated April 17, 1885, 9166–1885, LR-OIA, RG 75, NA.

Armstrong's letter to the commissioner, dated February 26, 1885, cited above, contains his charges against all three men. Clerk Barstow's statement regarding Spotted Horse can be found in C. H. Barstow to Henry Armstrong, 4792–1885, LR-OIA, RG 75, NA. Armstrong's report on the successful January council is with Armstrong to Commissioner, January 13, 1885, 1249–1885, LR-OIA, RG 75, NA. See also Armstrong to Commanding Officer, Fort Custer, February 3, 1885, Item 3, Box 10, RCIA-FRC, Seattle, which contains the agent's initial request for military assistance.

The report of the arrest of Spotted Horse and Bear Wolf is in Secretary of War to Secretary of the Interior, February 28, 1885, 4499–1885, LR-OIA, RG 75, NA. It is puzzling that Bear Wolf's "mark" appears on the February 28 document, because he was in jail on that day. The marks of Spotted Rabbit, Deaf Bull and Crazy Head do not appear. The order for the troublemakers' release from Fort Custer is in Alfred Terry to Adjutant General (copy), 3744–1885, LR-OIA, RG 75, NA.

[32] Henry Armstrong to V. T. McGillicuddy, October 8, 1885; and Henry Williamson to V. T. McGillicuddy, May 8, 1886, both Item 4, Box 12, RCIA-FRC, Seattle. A series of letters from Fort McKinney, Wyoming, and Fort Assiniboine, Montana, forwarded to the Indian Office and filed as 9697–1885, LR-OIA, RG 75, NA, contains reports from nervous commanders about the possibility of a joint Crow–Sioux–Shoshone offensive against the Blackfeet in the summer of 1885. The reports proved false, but a Lt. C. C. Compton wrote from Fort McKinney in March that "Indians from the different reservations have been for more than a year past roaming hither and thither, camping here and there, in parties of from one to fifteen lodges, and I suppose there has been much random talk between them and the settlers . . . occasioning among the timid an anxiety which upon being talked of and harped upon, produces a state of alarm. . . ."

assignment of 160 acres to each tribal member would leave millions of "surplus" acres eligible for sale to whites. (Giving each of 2,500 tribal members a homestead of 160 acres would require less than half a million of the tribe's 5-million-acre reserve.) It was not surprising, then, that the Billings *Gazette* welcomed Milburn's appointment, remarking that "the sooner" the Crows were allotted, "the better for themselves, and for the nation; particularly for the citizens of Montana."[33]

Milburn began his work among the bands who had settled in the Little Bighorn valley, but he learned quickly that the Crows did not share the enthusiasm of the Billings editorial writers. He reported that the Indians in Lodge Grass had removed the survey markers needed to locate homestead boundaries. In February 1886, Milburn wrote from the Bighorn valley that he had no more completed the assignment of an entire "village" than "the Indians deserted their houses and camped near the agency," treating his pleas to return "with contempt." He also noted that the government's plan to allocate different amounts of land to household heads and unmarried individuals and children did not fit with conditions in the tribal settlements. "A man today gets 80 acres, tomorrow he may become head of a family, but he has had allotted to him only 80 acres of land, while another man is to-day head of family and gets 160 acres, but tomorrow he 'throws away' his squaw or she dies and the children, if any, vanish . . . but he has 160 acres of land nevertheless."[34]

Milburn was replaced in mid-1886, but the new allotting agents did not appear to fare any better. Like their predecessor, they concentrated their work among the friendliest bands camped near the agency and at Fort Custer, and delayed work at the more distant settlements such as Plenty Coups's home along Pryor Creek. Despite this strategy they found a great many of the survey markers left by earlier crews had been destroyed or damaged. "I anticipate that the labor of the gentlemen . . . will be very difficult and prolonged," the Crow's agent reported. Resistance to white intruders also seemed to be spreading, for the Billings *Gazette* reported in March that Crows were setting fire to their grazing land to keep trespassing white stockmen off their ranges. The paper declared that these actions presented "another strong argument for settling [the Crows] on lands in severalty and promptly reducing the reservation, which has become an intolerable nuisance and a constant menace to the white settlers outside of its boundaries."[35]

---

[33] Henry Williamson to Commissioner of Indian Affairs, March 24, 1886, 8984–1886, LR-OIA, RG 75, NA; Billings *Gazette*, October 23, 1885, 2. Armstrong's early enthusiasm for allotment can be found in his letter to the CIA, December 1, 1884, Item 3, Box 10, RCIA-FRC, Seattle.

[34] George Milburn to Commissioner, November 5, 1885, 26805–1885, LR-OIA; and February 25, 1886, 6429–1886, LR-OIA, both in RG 75, NA.

[35] *ARCIA*, 1886 (Serial 2467), 394; Billings *Gazette*, March 24, 1886, 2. It is also worth noting that city officials in Billings hired a group of Crows to perform at the town's Fourth of July celebration but were disappointed when Deaf Bull and Old Dog intercepted the group enroute to town and turned it back. See Billings *Gazette*, July 5, 1886, 1.

Efforts to "civilize" the tribe seemed equally mired in both passive and active resistance. Jesuit missionaries had begun spending the summer months with bands in the Bighorn valley, but in 1886 plans for a mission station remained vague. More promising was a small boarding school constructed in July and August by Henry F. Bond, a Unitarian missionary from Boston. The Bond School was completed in September 1886, but its only students during the fall were visitors interested in a square meal. The agency school had only a handful of students (many of them orphans), and the agent's annual report – a document usually full of hopeful statistics – noted that in 1886 the tribe did not contain a single church member.[36]

On August 28, 1886, this cast of ambitious and competing chiefs, restless young men, frustrated missionaries and acquisitive cattlemen heard news that multiplied all the delicate tension that had been building over the preceding eighteen months: Sitting Bull and a party of a hundred Sioux were on their way to the Little Bighorn for a "visit." The visionary genius who had vanquished Custer, eluded capture by the U.S. Army and thumbed his nose at the government by greeting socialites in the company of Buffalo Bill expected to spend several days camping with his Crow "friends." Agent Henry Williamson, who had replaced Armstrong the previous December, telegraphed his protests eastward, but there was no reply. He then wrote the Hunkpapa leader's government supervisor and begged him to send couriers out to recall the old warrior to his reservation. "My Indians are peculiarly situated at the present time," Williamson complained. "They are peculiarly susceptible to any outer influence for either good or evil." Horrified by what was coming, he added, "Should the Indians you mention visit the Crows there would probably be several hundred Crows who would insist on returning such visit. . . ."[37]

Sitting Bull arrived in mid-September and stayed about two weeks. He seems to have remained in the Little Bighorn valley and visited the valley battlefield with its newly erected monument to Custer and his troops. According to a reporter who was present, that event produced a remarkable statement which foreshadowed the extent to which the new diplomatic ties between tribes could be turned to the Indians' advantage. The charismatic old warrior turned to his hosts after viewing the Seventh Cavalry's resting place and declared, "Look at that monument. That marks the work of our people":

---

[36] See Michael E. Engh, S. J., "Peter Paul Prando, S. J., 'Apostle of the Crows,'" *Montana: The Magazine of Western History*, 34, 4 (Autumn 1984), 24–41; Margery Pease, "A Worthy Work in a Needy Time: The Montana Industrial School for Indians," n.p.; and *ARCIA*, 1886 (Serial 2467), 395.

[37] The circumstances leading up to the visit are in Williamson to Commissioner, September 27, 1886, 26353–1886, LR-OIA, RG 75, NA. The agent's pleading letter to McLaughlin was dated September 7, 1886, Item 4, Box 13, RCIA-FRC, Seattle.

See how the white men treat us and how they treat you. We get one and
one half pounds of beef per ration, while you receive but one half pound.
You are kept at home and made to work like slaves, while we do no labor
and are permitted to ride from agency to agency and enjoy ourselves.

"Imagine the outcome of this," the reporter added. When Sitting Bull departed, he promised to return the following spring.[38]

It is clear from the reports of Sitting Bull's visit that the Sioux leader spent
a great deal of time talking about the evil of allotment. He told the Crows that
the headmen at "his" agency in Dakota Territory had opposed the division of
their lands and that the agent had obediently agreed to "defer" carrying out the
new policy. Speaking within sight of his most famous battlefield triumph,
Sitting Bull insisted that authentic tribal leaders would never cooperate with
the American government. To do so would be to surrender one's personal
authority and sacrifice one's followers to the whims of petty officials. The
allotting agents who were at work during Sitting Bull's visit were terrified.
After meeting with the Sioux leader on September 26, they wrote that he had
"convinced the Crow chiefs that their influence with their people will be destroyed and lost in proportion as their people learn to look to the agent for
guidance and control instead of to them. . . . His visit here," they concluded
darkly, "was mainly for the purpose of inducing the Crows to take common
action in opposition [to allotment] and thus toughen his position at home."[39]

Agent Williamson agreed, warning that further contact with Sitting Bull
would destroy what little discipline existed on the reservation. "During the
talk," Williamson recalled of the council on the 26th, "several of the Crow
chiefs who had never before uttered one word against the allotments . . . came
forward and took the same stand that Sitting Bull said *he* had taken at *his*
agency. Among the Crows speaking after this manner was Spotted Horse. . . ."
Significantly, when the young chief came forward he repeated the claim made
first in 1884 when Henry Armstrong had arrived with his wagon train at the site
of Crow Agency and which he had been repeating with growing conviction for
two years: "this country was his and he would put the Crows on places where
he wished them to live etc. etc." As Sitting Bull started back towards the
Missouri, Williamson predicted ominously that "passive resistance would be
made" to the government's program.[40]

In the twelve months following Sitting Bull's visit, however, events would

---

[38] Billings *Gazette*, June 10, 1887.
[39] Walker and Howard to Commissioner, September 27, 1886, 26352–1886, LR-OIA, RG 75, NA.
[40] Williamson to Commissioner, September 27, 1886, 26353–1886, LR-OIA, RG 75, NA. Not
surprisngly, Spotted Horse was also supported by his fellow "disaffected" headmen who had
themselves spent a good deal of time visiting the Dakotas. Among these men were Crazy Head,
Bear Wolf and Deaf Bull. See C. H. Barstow to J. G. Walker, October 7, 1886, Item 4, Box 13,
RCIA-FRC, Seattle.

crowd away the possibility of passive resistance. Struggles for leadership within the tribe, together with continued opposition to the federal government's actions, produced a series of confrontations that brought all parties rapidly into the open.

V

Despite the fact that councils between government officials and tribal leaders had been the basis for formal dealings between the United States and the Crows since 1825, these forums rose in prominence during the 1880s. With the tribe confined to a single location and the community receiving rations in bands, such conferences gained greater attention within the Crow community. More people participated and the decisions reached affected everyone on the reservation. As the Little Bighorn agency established itself, the councils also appeared to embody a natural system of representation. Membership at councils changed frequently, but a group of designated band leaders and headmen usually formed the core of the gathering. As the agenda for the meetings grew longer, they became more frequent. Councils approved the sale of Crow lands in 1880 and the following year granted the Northern Pacific Railroad the right to run its tracks across the reservation between Miles City and Billings. Following the move to the Little Bighorn, additional councils were called to discuss cattle leasing, allotment and reservation administration. In 1887 the expansion of the councils reached its peak when a succession of closely followed meetings took up a proposal for a new railroad right of way and a strategy for renting tribal lands to cattlemen.[41]

Throughout these proceedings, tribal leaders moved cautiously into dangerous territory. Both the railroad and leasing issues pitted Crow headmen against outside business interests. If the council fashioned agreements that benefitted the tribe, the headmen who spoke there might rise in influence; if not, these men risked appearing as "slaves" of the Indian Office. The restless young men who had gloried in Sitting Bull's visit, and who looked forward to a season of raiding in 1887, would be watching their elders' performance with interest, scrutinizing them for signs of weakness.

The issue of cattle on Crow lands had arisen repeatedly during the 1880s, but the tribe and the Indian Office had never agreed on a procedure for renting out pastures and keeping squatters off the reservation. In the fall of 1885 the tribe had agreed to the controversial Wilson and Blake lease that opened reservation

---

[41] For a general discussion of this process, see Joseph Medicine Crow, "The Development of Crow Tribal Government" (a report presented to the Crow Tribal Council, 1976, in partial fulfillment of the Crow tribe's report to the American Indian Policy Review Commission), Bilingual Materials Development Center, Crow Agency, Montana, 2–3.

land to a group from Colorado, but pressure from local ranchers caused the Interior Department to withold its approval. By 1887 the growth of Montana's cattle herds and the dwindling size of the territory's public range continued to fuel demands for some method of opening tribal lands for grazing. For their part, tribal leaders – who were perfectly aware of the income they were losing to illegal grazing – also demanded some kind of lease policy. Agent Henry Williamson wrote his superiors in September 1886 – days before Sitting Bull was to arrive – that he was "receiving almost daily applications to graze stock on the reserve," adding that he hoped that "the Department will come to some decision in this matter at as early a day as possible."[42]

When the government failed to respond, Williamson reported that the "leading men of the tribe" (a group which included Plenty Coups, Two Belly, Spotted Horse, Pretty Eagle and Old Dog – all band leaders) summoned a local stockman, James A. Campbell, to the agency. Gathered in his office (Williamson wrote that it was "full of Indians"), the leaders announced that they wanted Campbell to have exclusive use of the range lands to the east of the Little Bighorn. In return the rancher would pay rent and keep all trespassers off tribal land. In addition to his cattle interests, Campbell served as captain of Crow scouts at Fort Custer. He was a man these headmen knew and trusted. Promising that he "knew nothing about the matter until the Indians came to me," Williamson recommended approval.[43]

The Indian Office accepted the agent's suggestion, but the clamor for leases in other parts of the reservation was undiminished, and tribal leaders continued to demand some control over the matter. Finally, in the spring of 1887, Williamson called for a tribal council to address the grazing issue on all parts of the reserve. On April 23, 350 Crows gathered at Crow Agency. The men who had crowded into his office the previous November once again took the initiative. The entire group first met "for some hours" in a closed session at the agency school. "Having arrived at a conclusion satisfactory to all present," Williamson later reported, "they sent for me and I entered the council." At this point a formal session began. Crazy Head, Plenty Coups and Spotted Horse spoke for the tribe.[44]

The three chiefs repeated their request that James Campbell have exclusive use of the lands on the eastern border of the reserve. They added that Nelson Story of Bozeman, one of Montana's largest cattlemen and a man who had first

[42] Williamson to Commissioner of Indian Affairs, September 11, 1886, Special Case 133, 24960–1886, LR-OIA, RG 75, NA. For a review of lease proposals for Crow pastureland, see Secretary of the Interior to Commissioner of Indian Affairs, June 20, 1887, 15620–1887, LR-OIA, RG 75, NA.

[43] Williamson to Commissioner of Indian Affairs, November 19, 1886, Item 2, Box 1, RCIA-FRC, Seattle.

[44] Williamson to Commissioner of Indian Affairs, May 6, 1887, Special Case 133, 12645–1887, LR-OIA, RG 75, NA.

befriended the Crows while carrying supplies to Fort C. F. Smith in the 1860s, be granted a similar right to the western end of the reservation. "Put stock on the reservation," Spotted Horse declared, "and when we want them off, put them off." When the agent asked for a vote on the matter, 350 hands shot up. Following the meeting, Williamson dutifully forwarded a report to Washington with a recommendation that the tribe's wishes be granted.[45]

As the summer of 1887 began, events in two distant cities conspired to thwart Spotted Horse and the united Crow headmen. First, in the territorial capital of Helena, U.S. Attorney Robert Smith began prosecuting local cattlemen for trespassing on Crow lands and illegally cutting firewood along the south bank of the Yellowstone. With the prosperous Nelson Story apparently on the verge of obtaining the exclusive use of tens of thousands of acres of tribal land, the protests from those who were about to be excluded (and fined) were both predictable and furious. The Montana *Stock Gazette* declared that "class privileges" were "about to be confirmed and made legal on the Crow Reservation."[46]

At the same time, Secretary of the Interior Lucius Quintus Cincinnatus Lamar vetoed the tribal council's April resolutions. Faced with protests over similar grants to "cattle barons" in Indian Territory and the Dakotas, the secretary, who was a former senator from Mississippi, declared that the Story and Campbell permits would only be allowed to run until November 1, 1887. After that date, permission to graze would be granted by the government after "public advertisement." Decisions on who would receive these permits would be made in Washington, not at a tribal council meeting.[47]

Stung by these actions, Williamson filed a long protest with the Indian Office. Insisting that his superiors held "an erroneous view" of the matter, the agent pleaded for a reconsideration and predicted that the peaceful Crows would not accept the proposed procedure. "I feel great hesitancy," he noted delicately, "in making to them any proposals which may tend to set aside the determination arrived at by them *in council.* . . ." James Howard, the surveyor who had begun allotting homesteads to the Crows and who was witness to the events of the past year, added his own unsolicited opinion, warning the politicians in Washington about what might lie ahead. Giving voice to Williamson's

---

[45] "Proceedings of a Council of the Crow Indians Held at Crow Agency, Montana Territory, Friday, April 23, 1887" enclosed with Williamson to Commissioner of Indian Affairs, May 6, 1887, Special Case 133, 12645–1887, LR-OIA, RG 75, NA.

[46] The convictions for trespass were reported in Frank Armstrong to Secretary of the Interior, October 27, 1887, MM1070, Reel 8, frame 302. The Montana *Stock Gazette* quotation is enclosed in Special Case 133, 18924–1887, LR-OIA, RG 75, NA, and dated July 1, 1887. The Billings *Gazette* also carried articles and numerous letters to the editor condemning the "special privileges" being granted wealthy cattlemen, e.g., July 6, 1887.

[47] Secretary of Interior to Commissioner of Indian Affairs, June 20, 1887, Special Case 133, 15620–1887, LR-OIA, RG 75, NA.

unspoken fears, Howard noted that Lamar's decision to select the lessors in Washington fulfilled "the bad predictions of Old Sitting Bull who when here last fall told them 'that the white man only wanted to squat them down on a small piece of land and take the balance from them in some way.' They have never gotten over that."[48]

Six weeks after 350 Crows gathered at Crow Agency to discuss cattle on their reservation, "over three hundred" tribal members reassembled to consider a request from the Rocky Fork and Cooke City Railway Company for a right-of-way across lands west of the Clark's Fork of the Yellowstone. The road promised to connect mining operations southwest of Billings to the Northern Pacific line and was enthusiastically supported by local merchants and civic boosters. Again, the Crows discussed the proposal among themselves for two hours before summoning the agent to the council room and beginning a public dialogue. Plenty Coups, who identified himself as the "chief" of the Indians living on the western end of the reserve, spoke first. While agreeing to the proposal, the thirty-eight-year-old band leader made it clear that his approval came with conditions. He insisted that no further roads be laid out in the area and that the agent negotiate as high a price as possible from the road. "I want you to get all the pay you can for us," he declared.

The remainder of the council speakers were from the eastern end of the reservation. They too agreed to the new railway line, but they used the occasion to spell out their expectations for the future. Old Dog, for example, spoke up here to emphasize that he wanted less, rather than more, contact with whites. "Don't ask us for anything else," he warned. "Don't ask us for anythng more. We don't want any more roads on our land anywhere." He added that they needed larger rations. As it was, "we don't get enough." The usually contentious Spotted Horse agreed. "We are hungry," he declared; "you issue us rations to last seven days and they don't last half of that time." He asked the agent to look at the young men who sat silently before him: "You don't see one fat one among them all."[49]

Once they had recorded their complaints, Plenty Coups, Old Dog, Deaf Bull and Spotted Horse led fifty-nine headmen and "representative leaders" forward to approve the right-of-way agreement. When he forwarded news of the tribe's approval to Washington, Williamson urged that the weekly beef ration be increased to demonstrate that the Crows had been "immediately and particularly

[48] Williamson to Commissioner of Indian Affairs, July 9, 1887, Special Case 133, 18588–1887, LR-OIA, RG 75, NA, emphasis in original; James Howard to Commissioner of Indian Affairs, August 7, 1887, Special Case 133, 21371–1887, LR-OIA, RG 75, NA. Howard added that Lamar's actions "would be promptly resisted and [would] defeat the object for which I am sent here to accomplish."

[49] Report of council held with the Crow tribe of Indians at Crow Agency, Montana Territory, on the 4 June, 1887, dated June 13, 1887, 15182–1887, LR-OIA, RG 75, NA. See also Billings Gazette, editorial of February 19, 1887.

benefited," but as summer ended it seemed that the accommodations reached at the Crow council grounds had not defused the tensions surrounding the reservation. The head of the Wyoming Stock Growers Association was once again complaining that Crows were killing white-owned cattle south of the Bighorns, and local politicians were insisting that the government "confine these Indians to their reservation." A few weeks later, those tensions exploded into gunfire.[50]

VI

Shortly before sunset on Friday afternoon, September 30, twenty-one brightly painted warriors rode into the agency compound on the Little Bighorn and brought the political jostling of the previous three years to a climax. Skirting a long line of freight wagons that were being unloaded in preparation for the next day's distribution of rations, this tiny band of young Crows guided their ponies into the horseshoe formed by the government's shops, houses and offices and began firing their weapons into the air. Henry Williamson and his wife, who were sitting on the front porch of their quarters with the day's mail before them, watched the charge and listened to the "pop" of pistols. In a few minutes the advancing men reached the agency office. Their leader, a twenty-five-year-old youth called Sword Bearer, reached forward and thrust his gun into the belly of Tom Stewart, the agency interpreter who had been lounging near the front door. Just as quickly as Sword Bearer had lunged forward, however, he raised his pistol into the air and fired. Sword Bearer and his followers then rode toward Williamson, shooting at the roofs of nearby buildings and shattering several bricks in the chimney over their heads. The group then turned back and rode off to the south in the twilight, leaving the agent frozen and slack-jawed, his unopened mail still resting in his lap.[51]

Sword Bearer's party was a cross-section of the tribe's young men. They ranged in age from seventeen to thirty and were drawn from ten different bands and eighteen different extended families. The immediate explanation for their noisy ride through the agency was that it was a celebration of a successful horse-stealing raid against the Piegans. On the surface at least, the "attack" was an

---

[50] For Williamson's recommendation, see Williamson to Commissioner of Indian Affairs, June 7, 1887, Item 2, Box 2, RCIA-FRC, Seattle. For complaints of Crow "depredations" and the recommendation to confine the tribe, see Joseph M. Carey to Commissioner (and enclosure), September 9, 1887, 24498–1887, LR-OIA, RG 75, NA.

[51] The best primary account of the original incident is James Howard to Commissioner of Indian Affairs, October 7, 1887, filed with 27964–1887, LR-OIA, RG 75, NA. Secondary accounts include Brian Jones, "A Battle at Little Bighorn: Being an Account of the Crow Outbreak of 1887," *The Brand Book* (publication of the English Westerners' Society), 17, 3–4 (April–July 1975), 27–55; Colin G. Calloway, "Sword Bearer and the 'Crow Outbreak' of 1887," *Montana: The Magazine of Western History*, 36, 4 (Autumn 1986), 38–51; and McGinnis, *Counting Coup and Cutting Horses*, 188–190.

exuberant re-creation of an ancient public ritual. Once he regained his composure, however, Henry Williamson did not accept this version of the event. As
he sent his agency policemen down the trail to Fort Custer for help, the agent
began to formulate his own interpretation of the young men's actions. By ten
o'clock that night, when the first soldiers arrived at Crow Agency, he had struck
a tone of outrage that was reflected in the Billings *Gazette*'s editorial for the
following Monday morning, "The time for mawkish sentiment in these matters
has gone by and the stern hand of the law should never relax its hold on these
Indians." Williamson's reaction also set the tone for events to come; Sword
Bearer's harmless gunfire quickly produced an unprecedented demonstration of
federal power on the Crow Reservation that put the community's embattled
band leaders squarely on the spot. They had somehow to maintain their dignity
and the support of their kinsmen while deciding how to respond to an onslaught of well-armed bluecoats. When the crisis had passed, the Crows had
entered a new chapter of their history.[52]

Sword Bearer embodied the defiant independence that Sitting Bull had called
up among the Crows in 1886. Originally named Wraps Up His Tail, he was a
member of Bear Wolf's band when the government first began issuing rations
at the new agency. As a teenager, Wraps Up His Tail may have travelled with
his half-Sioux band leader on his unauthorized visits to the Dakota reservations, but the first written record of his travels has him journeying east in the
spring of 1887 to attend a Cheyenne sun dance. He received a powerful vision
there, and to honor this blessing, the young man's hosts gave him a ceremonial
sword and a new name: Sword Bearer. Through the summer of tribal council
meetings and rumors of conflict with ranchers and railroad men, Sword Bearer
gravitated towards Spotted Horse, Crazy Head and the other "discontented"
leaders from the Little Bighorn. Like these men, Sword Bearer welcomed new
friendships with the Sioux and encouraged visits between Crow Agency and the
agencies at Standing Rock, Pine Ridge and Rosebud.[53]

One such visit had occurred in June 1887, when a party from the Rosebud
reserve was given permission to travel to Montana. Williamson protested, saying the visit "means two or three weeks of dancing, war paint and feathers," but
the group came anyway. When they arrived, a squad of soldiers and Indian

---

[52] For the members of Sword Bearer's group, see Frank Armstrong to Commissioner of Indian
Affairs, November 4, 1887, 30413–1887, LR-OIA, RG 75, NA. Ages for all individuals save one
(The Bank) were derived from the 1887 tribal census, Item 17, Box 154, RCIA-FRC, Seattle.
Billings *Gazette*, October 3, 1887, 2.

[53] According to Crow historian Joe Medicine Crow, Wraps Up His Tail found his sword in the
Bighorn Mountains. While not repeated in other published accounts of the incident, Medicine
Crow's version has greater logic. The author is not aware that the presentation of a sword was
ever a part of the Cheyenne sun dance. Mr. Medicine Crow's version is generally supported by
the account of White Man Runs Him recorded by Gen. Hugh L. Scott and contained in Box 2,
Hugh L. Scott Papers, Manuscript no. 4525, National Anthropological Archives, Washington, D.C.

Frederick Remington executed this illustration of the Wraps Up His Tail incident for
the November 5, 1887, edition of *Harper's Weekly*. Because Remington worked from
press reports, it should not be surprising that his Crows were taking careful aim and
apparently firing at targets rather than shooting wildly into the sky as the youthful
offenders had done. Courtesy of The Newberry Library.

policemen met them at Reno Crossing south of the agency and attempted to
turn them back. As Lt. Frank Edwards spoke to the group, a large party of
Crows began to gather, declaring that they would not move until the visitors
were allowed to proceed. The Crows were lead by Crazy Head and his noisy
son, Knows His Coups; also in the crowd was Sword Bearer. Edwards later
reported that the young "medicine man," who posed before the crowd, "can do
as he wishes, notwithstanding all the soldiers at Fort Custer. The Agency
people say he is crazy . . . but at the same time he is gaining quite a following
and may at some time be troublesome." When Sword Bearer rode past
Williamson's front porch on September 30, the agent no doubt recognized
Knows His Coups riding behind him. More disturbing, he might also have
noticed the young sons of Long Otter, a cooperative band leader, and Old
Snake, a former army scout at Fort Custer, riding along too.[54]

[54] Williamson to Commissioner of Indian Affairs, June 8, 1887, Item 2, Box 2, RCIA-FRC, Seattle;
Jones, "A Battle at Little Bighorn," 31. Another account of the June incident at Reno Crossing
is contained in Thomas H. Ruger to Assistant Adjutant General, November 30, 1887, 33393–
1887, LR-OIA, RG 75, NA.

Despite his charismatic appeal, it was clear from the first night of the crisis that Sword Bearer's actions would not trigger a general uprising. When the first eight soldiers arrived from Fort Custer on the evening of the 30th, they were quickly surrounded by a surging group of excited young Crows. Outnumbered and on the verge of panic, the soldiers were quickly surrounded by Medicine Crow, Bull Nose, Fringe and a few other headmen who drove the crowd back with their riding quirts and allowed the soldiers to take up their positions. A few minutes later, Knows His Coups and an eighteen-year-old named Big Hail rode up to the agency store, demanded ammunition and began firing through the building's windows. Agency policemen and soldiers drove them off, but for the remainder of the night the young men (in one observer's words) "kept up . . . their shooting tour around the agency buildings . . . making the night hideous with their yells." Significantly, however, no one from the camps stretching north and south along the river rode out to join them.[55]

The next day Sword Bearer and his group retreated to a rise east of the agency and challenged the now-reinforced troops to attack them. The soldiers stood their ground and held their fire. By evening the "rebels" had moved up the Little Bighorn, leaving the bulk of the tribe (and its headmen) camped near the agency. James Howard, the allotting agent, wrote a week later that the situation was stable, at least for the moment. Sword Bearer was out "planting the seeds of discord" among the tribe," but most Crows had come in to camp along the Little Bighorn "waiting to see what will be the result." Howard added that "some of the old Indians are coming in daily, trying to apologize for the conduct of these beligerent bucks."[56]

For the next four weeks Sword Bearer eluded capture. Initially he benefitted from the Fort Custer commander's reluctance to send his troops into the field without a clear command from Washington (an attitude shaped in part by ongoing sniping between military and civilian officials over how best to "manage" Indians). By the middle of October it appeared that the rebel leader had left the reservation. Rumors circulated that he had gone south to the Bighorns to "make medicine" or that he was visiting the Sioux in search of support.

Despite its customary insistence that civilian agents were best suited to Indian administration, the potentially wide scale of the Sword Bearer uprising persuaded the Indian Office that the Crow rebel should be met with force. On October 11, Secretary Lamar dispatched Inspector Frank Armstrong, a veteran internal investigator, to the scene. When he arrived several days later, Armstrong

---

[55] James Howard to Commissioner of Indian Affairs, October 7, 1887, 27964–1887, LR-OIA, RG 75, NA. White Man Runs Him, a former scout who recounted the story of Sword Bearer years later for Gen. Hugh Scott, noted that "not very many" people followed the young man. He added, "Some of the fellows went in with him for the sake of the fight. I do not believe many believed in him. They thought he was rather foolish on the subject." Box 2, Hugh L. Scott Papers, Manuscript no. 4525, National Anthropological Archives, Washington, D.C.
[56] James Howard to Commissioner of Indian Affairs, October 7, 1887.

reported that the raiding and visiting that had been going on in the region was responsible for this unrest. "Sitting Bull and other visiting Indians have done much harm here by bad advice and boasting talk," Armstrong observed. He recommended that Sword Bearer and his band "should be arrested as soon as possible." Lamar forwarded copies of Armstrong's cables to the War Department with the comment that the inspector was "a prudent and sagacious man" and the request that the military carry out "the suggestions contained in his telegram."[57]

Just as Armstrong's recommendations were reaching Washington, the government agent for the Northern Cheyennes wired headquarters that Sword Bearer and fifty of his followers had arrived at the Lame Deer Agency. The rebel leader was accompanied by Deaf Bull and others who had a history of travelling east to Sioux country and was reportedly having success winning new adherents to his movement. Officials at the Rosebud Agency also reported that "runners" had arrived with news of the Crow incident, and Sword Bearer's supporters were "urgently soliciting passes" so they could travel to Montana. Military commanders now had hard evidence to confirm their fears of a multitribal revolt. As they considered how to respond, their discussions must have echoed the reasoning of the Billings *Gazette*'s editorial writer who observed that "the Indians are few now and well scattered, but when the numbers at the different agencies in eastern Montana and western Dakota are figured up it is found that a general outbreak among them would result very seriously unless it was promptly nipped in the bud."[58]

On October 20, orders finally issued from the secretary of war. He directed Gen. Alfred Terry, the Civil War veteran who commanded the Division of the Missouri to "take such action at once as may be considered necessary . . . to prevent an outbreak." During the last week in October troops began pouring in to the Little Bighorn from Fort Missoula in western Montana, Fort McKinney in Wyoming and the Yellowstone valley posts, Fort Custer and Fort Keogh. By November 1, sixteen troop and infantry companies had been assembled in the vicinity of Crow Agency. Some units erected earthworks and barricades around the town, while others took up positions to prevent the "hostiles" from fleeing.[59]

Sword Bearer would receive no reinforcements. His Cheyenne hosts rejected his invitation to join in an uprising, and from Dakota Territory came word that

[57] Armstrong to Secretary of Interior, October 17, 1887, 27841–1887, LR-OIA; ibid., October 17, 1887, 27842–1887, LR-OIA; and Secretary of Interior to Secretary of War, October 18, 1887, 27842–1887, LR-OIA; all in RG 75, NA. Armstrong began his journey to Crow Agency on October 11, but the secretary had been trying to reach him since the 8th. The inspector was at the Pottawatomie Agency in Kansas, beyond the reach of the telegraph, and so did not learn of his appointment until he read it in a newspaper on the 10th. See Armstrong to Secretary of Interior, October 11, 1887, 27252–1887, LR-OIA, RG 75, NA.

[58] Upshaw to Commissioner of Indian Affairs, October 21, 1887, 1887–28087, and 1887–27985; and Spencer to Commissioner of Indian Affairs, October 20 ("1:50 AM"), 1887, 27900–1887, all in LR-OIA, RG 75, NA; Billings *Gazette*, October 17, 1887, 2.

[59] Secretary of War to Secretary of Interior, October 20, 1887, 28073–1887, LR-OIA, RG 75, NA.

Sitting Bull himself was cooperating with the allotment of his reservation. Twenty Gros Ventre warriors riding south near Fort Custer were intercepted and turned back, and agents across the region prohibited anyone from leaving their reservation. The spirit of rebellion seemed to be flagging.[60]

With overwhelming military superiority now assured, the Interior Department's Armstrong turned his attention to isolating Sword Bearer and Deaf Bull from the remainder of the Crow tribe. Medicine Crow, Bull Nose, Old Dog and other prominent men from the Little Bighorn continued to assure the authorities that they would not assist the rebels. By the end of the month, Pretty Eagle had arrived from the Bighorn with others from that area who too pledged loyalty. Spotted Horse was frequently rumored to be among Sword Bearer's supporters, but the outspoken leader remained quiet in his camp. Plenty Coups, who had figured so prominently in the tribal councils of the previous summer was the only major figure other than the rebel leaders themselves who was not in evidence at the agency. It was reported that his wife had died and he was alone in the mountains near Pryor Gap, grieving.[61]

On Monday, October 31, Inspector Armstrong decided the time had come for a showdown. He ordered all Indians to report to Crow Agency by Friday, November 4. Most of the tribe obediently assembled just north of the agency. Plenty Coups sent word that he did not sympathize with the rebels and that he was on his way from Pryor Creek, sixty miles to the west. Even Sword Bearer was present, riding through the Crow camps and promising to use his medicine to destroy the massed soldiers. Troops of infantry and cavalry and two Hotchkiss gun detachments drew up around the agency to await orders.

On Saturday morning, November 5, the military commander at the scene, Brig. Gen. Thomas Ruger, met with a group of ten band leaders, including Pretty Eagle, Crazy Head and probably Spotted Horse. Ruger demanded the surrender of Sword Bearer and seven of those (including Crazy Head's son) who had participated in the gunplay on September 30. The Crow chiefs were in a difficult position. They could not deny young Sword Bearer's charisma and power. "He is a great man," Pretty Eagle declared; "all things bend before him and the very ground is shaking before he does his great deeds." On the other hand, the chiefs knew that armed resistance was futile. Crazy Head's presence with the loyal chiefs spoke volumes. Pretty Eagle spoke for the group when he

---

[60] See Secretary of War to Secretary of Interior, October 26, 1887, 30562–1887 (copy), LR-OIA, RG 75, NA; Billings *Gazette*, October 28 and November 4, 1887.

[61] Spotted Horse's reasons for siding with the authorities in the Sword Bearer incident are unclear. The proceedings of the 1887 councils indicate that he was increasingly allied with Plenty Coups. He may have decided that he enjoyed the position of "responsible" tribal leader. There is also evidence that Spotted Horse's sister had been killed by the accidental discharge of Plenty Coups's pistol in 1872. Apparently, however, Spotted Horse was also related to Plenty Coups through marriage at the time and was prevented from seeking revenge. Perhaps the two men continued to identify themselves as relatives. See James Carpenter to Robert H. Lowie, December 2, 1933, Incoming correspondence, Robert H. Lowie Papers, University of California, Berkeley.

said, "The Crows do not want to fight." Nevertheless, the leaders' reply to Ruger was equivocal. They promised to turn over Sword Bearer, but added "We cannot give up the others that are wanted." The general gave Pretty Eagle and his comrades ninety minutes to comply with his orders.[62]

As Ruger's deadline expired, groups who wished to escape the impending fighting moved north of the agency. In their wake were groups of warriors who arrayed themselves on the plain just west of the Little Bighorn. Cavalry units positioned themselves between the "hostiles" and the government buildings, and a Hotchkiss unit took aim from the low bluffs on either side of the valley. In the center of this tableau rode Sword Bearer, haranguing his followers and displaying his paint, his battle finery and his ceremonial sword.

A volley from Sword Bearer's supporters brought two troops of cavalry up the valley at full gallop. After another round from the warriors (which killed one soldier), the cavalrymen dismounted, formed a skirmish line and began to move forward, all the while firing on the Crow positions. The Hotchkiss guns crackled overhead, striking a Crow lodge. After a few minutes of this intense fire, the rebels began retreating in a southwesterly direction towards the Big-horn valley. They disappeared for a few minutes, then reemerged under a white flag. As the bulk of Sword Bearer's men surrendered and began moving north away from the fighting, the defeated prophet and a few remaining loyalists scrambled to escape southward.[63]

They didn't get far. Sword Bearer was apparently wounded during the fighting with the soldiers, but following the surrender of his troop, he was still able to ride. Like the others who were fleeing towards the south, the young warrior struck off on his own and tried to stay under cover. As he crossed the Little Bighorn, however, Sword Bearer suddenly encountered Fire Bear, a member of the agency police force. The medicine man was unarmed and he offered no resistance to the policeman, but Fire Bear drew his pistol and fired, striking his target in the head.[64]

[62] Pretty Eagle's comments on Sword Bearer are in the Billings *Gazette*, November 7, 1887, 2; the report of the council with Ruger is in ibid., November 6, 1887.

[63] Accounts of the "battle" are best summarized in the articles by Jones and Calloway, cited above. The chief government source for the incident is the "Special Report of Inspector Frank C. Armstrong on the Affairs at Crow Agency, Montana, November 9, 1887," MM1070, Reel 8, frame 312.

[64] There are many accounts of Sword Bearer's death, most summarized in Calloway, "Sword Bearer," 47. Joe Medicine Crow, the Crow tribe's historian says that Pounded Meat, Sword Bearer's father, captured his son and was returning him to the agency when Fire Bear shot him. See Bearss, "Bighorn Canyon National Recreation Area," 357. In 1913, Grey Bull, by then an old man, told the anthropologist Robert Lowie that Sword Bearer (whom he called "the prophet") sought out his death. He claimed the rebel leader asked Agent Williamson to kill him before the final battle and that Fire Bear was the only Crow willing to do so. Gray Bull also told Lowie he "never heard" the cause of the uprising. See 1913 Notebook, Robert H. Lowie Papers, American Museum of Natural History. There is also an account of Sword Bearer's actions in Notebook no. 8 (1911), dated July 26, 1911, in the same collection.

The Crow "rebels" pictured shortly after Sword Bearer's death on November 5, 1887. Wearing leg irons, the young prisoners are flanked by Deaf Bull, the band leader who had urged them to resist federal authorities and who would now accompany them to prison at Fort Snelling, Minnesota. Courtesy of Montana Historical Society.

Remarkably, despite the fact that Sword Bearer died alone and abandoned, his violent end transformed him into a tribal hero. Carried from the riverbank to a hastily constructed arbor on the flatlands south of the agency, Sword Bearer lay in state for the remainder of the day and into the night; he was still decorated with war paint and dressed for battle. The entire tribe came to see him and to pay their respects. Over a century later, the daughter of a girl who was taken to see the dead warrior that day could still recall her mother's oft-repeated description of the scene:

> Men and women cried ... mourning for him and my mother's grand-
> mother said, "come on little girl, let's go over there and I'll cry for him
> too." And she took my mother and stood there by the body. ... He laid
> there dead. And the grandmother pulled my mother over and said, "now
> you go, touch him, touch him and come back. ... And my mother told me,

"I went and touched the man. He is a medicine man; he is holy. You touch him and you will be alright."

So she said she touched that man and came back to her grandma and her grandma was crying. And then they went home.[65]

Equally dramatic, the assembled soldiers had no more arrested the men responsible for the September 30 shooting, than the headmen who had refused to join Sword Bearer now came forward to request the rebels' release. Plenty Coups, who finally arrived at Crow Agency two days after the fighting, told Inspector Armstrong that it was time to "commence anew" by forgetting the troubles just past. "We have some crazy men with us but they are gone," he declared. Speaking of the men being shipped east to prison, he added, "You have got them. After they have been away for a while, we would like to have you send them back. . . . They will listen to what people say to them, and they will not be crazy any more." Before he departed for his home on Pryor Creek, Plenty Coups also called on James Howard, the tribe's allotting agent and asked for his help in securing the prisoners' release. Pretty Eagle struck a similar pose. "We would like to see their faces," he told Armstrong.[66]

The only vendetta within the tribe which lasted involved the tribal policemen. Fire Bear became a pariah after Sword Bearer's death, and the Crow headmen asked Armstrong to dismiss the entire force. Plenty Coups declared, "We want the policemen to be taken away. They have blood on their hands." He added that the assembled headmen would select "some strong men" to take their places. This argument, that the policemen had betrayed the Crows by killing Sword Bearer, would be used repeatedly in the years ahead to justify placing the appointment of new officers in the hands of tribal headmen. Two years later, for example, the captain of the tribal police force testified that after Fire Bear's action, "all the Indians wanted us discharged. They never like us since then." Spotted Horse answered for the head men: "*We* want to pick out all the policemen."[67]

Ironically, while it sowed seeds of discord that would remain with the tribe for years to come, the Sword Bearer incident marked the beginning of a new

---

[65] Interview with Lillian Bull Shows Hogan, August 12, 1987. Mrs. Hogan was born in 1905; her mother was five years old at the time of Sword Bearer's death.

[66] Statements from Plenty Coups and Pretty Eagle are in the "Special Report of Inspector Frank C. Armstrong," frames 329–330. An account of Plenty Coups's approach to Howard is in James Howard to Commissioner, February 28, 1888, 5716–1888, LR-OIA, RG 75, NA. Plenty Coups renewed his request the following spring, prompting a local official to report that Plenty Coups had told him that "the releasing of the two men will give him a stronger position with his people which I know to be true, and believe it will result in good." See Col. Dudley to Col. Howard, April 14, 1888, 11297–1888, LR-OIA, RG 75, NA.

[67] See Proceedings of Council, June 30, 1889, Special Case 133, 21254–1889, LR-OIA, RG 75, NA (emphasis added). Agent M. P. Wyman's commentary on that council (in which he describes the tribe's "ill will" towards the police force) is in Wyman to Commissioner of Indian Affairs, July 25, 1887, Item 2, Box 2, RCIA-FRC, Seattle.

Fire Bear, the agency policeman who killed Sword Bearer on November 5, 1887. Following this incident, other Crows shunned Fire Bear and agency employees claimed that he remained on the agency payroll in order to protect him from revenge seekers. This picture was taken nearly twenty years after the "uprising" by Billings photographer Richard Throssel. Courtesy of American Heritage Center, University of Wyoming.

reservation leadership. By casting themselves both as cooperative leaders who accepted federal authority and as guardians of Crazy Head's memory, headmen like Plenty Coups, Spotted Horse and Pretty Eagle turned the prophet's defeat into a launching pad for their own political authority. The tribal councils which had sputtered and fumed earlier in the year might now be seen as credible assemblies with authority to speak for the entire group. The restless young men who had spurned those gatherings were now defeated, and the ambitious young chiefs who struggled to control them now had the ear of the authorities. To remain effective, Plenty Coups, Pretty Eagle and the other leaders would have to respect the tribal values Sword Bearer seemed to have embodied, while they avoided direct confrontations with the Indian Office. Their followers, worn down by hunger and disease, overawed by American military might, but living in families and communities that continued to inspire loyalty to Crow ways, were willing to support these leaders so long as they provided protection and a measure of economic support. "Grandma was crying," the little girl remembered, "and then they went home."

VII

Two days after Sword Bearer's death, Inspector Frank Armstrong assembled the "leading men" of the tribe at the agency compound. Plenty Coups spoke first for the Crows. He deplored the recent fighting and declared that he and the other chiefs wanted "to commence anew and be a new kind of people and be good. I do not want to be hungry," he added. "I want to live well, and we want no more blood on our hands." With pledges like these ringing in his ears, Armstrong sat down the same afternoon to reassure his superiors. "Everything," he wrote, "is settled permanently and effectively."[68]

The Crows' "leading men" moved quickly to take advantage of their new status as battle-tested government allies. As Deaf Bull, Crazy Head and six of Sword Bearer's young followers were transported to a military prison at Fort Snelling, Minnesota, Plenty Coups, Pretty Eagle, Spotted Horse and their colleagues stepped forward to assert their primacy in reservation affairs. Their demand that the tribal police force be overhauled was quickly rejected by Armstrong and Williamson, but their outspoken attacks on the agent's administration and their insistence that cattle leases go to their friends were apparently agreed to. Williamson resigned later in the month and Armstrong agreed

---

[68] "Special Report of Inspector Frank C. Armstrong," frame 329; Armstrong to Secretary of the Interior, November 7, 1887, Letters Received by the Office of the Adjutant General, Microfilm 689, Reel 557, RG 75, NA.

to allow James Campbell, Nelson Story and a few other Crow favorites to remain on the reservation.[69]

The following March, a gathering of headmen led by Plenty Coups, Pretty Eagle, Old Dog and the recently rebellious Bear Wolf repeated their request that Campbell, Nelson Story, and the Hardin Cattle Company be granted grazing permits and that the Indian Office drop its plan to award leases on the basis of public bids. When the Washington authorities agreed, the prestige of these band leaders, and the tribal council they dominated, rose correspondingly. The practice of awarding grazing permits to companies associated with particular headmen also bolstered the standing of individuals. Plenty Coups, for example, testified in 1890 that in addition to his payments to the Indian Office, Nelson Story "has given me and my people food for *three winters*." Others noted that followers of prominent men like Plenty Coups and Pretty Eagle were regularly employed by the cattlemen as cowboys and teamsters.[70]

The council of headmen also asserted itself on the issue of railroad rights-of-way. Early in 1888, Plenty Coups announced that "we will not consent" to the idea of a rail line running up Clarks Fork. "Our young men live there," the chief told the lame-duck Agent Williamson, "and they are trying to make a living." (The road would also have disrupted Nelson Story's cattle operations.) A second request in December was also turned down, and in 1889 the tribe opposed the construction of another line up the Bighorn valley into Wyoming. When the Crows approved an extension of the Burlington Railroad from Wyoming to the Yellowstone in 1891, it attached a variety of conditions and complaints to their action. At the close of that decision, Medicine Crow warned off other entrepeneurs. "We are against any more railroads and surveys," he announced.[71]

Less than six months after Sword Bearer's death, the first of his followers were ordered released from prison. By the end of 1888 all but Deaf Bull were free. Deaf Bull was held longest because of his past hostility and because he

---

[69] On imprisonment, see Thomas H. Ruger to Assistant Adjutant General, November 30, 1887 (copy), 33393–1887, LR-OIA, RG 75, NA. On the November 7 council, see "Special Report of Inspector Frank Armstrong," frames 325–329. Williamson's letter of resignation is quoted in Jones, "A Battle at Little Bighorn," 46.

In its final editorial on the outbreak, the Billings *Gazette* noted on November 8, 1887, that "the main good is that the disturbing element among the Crows, all the chiefs and restless disturbers of the peace, are now in the Fort Custer guard house with iron shackles riveted on their moccasined feet. The leaders who are left are disposed for peace. . . ." (2).

[70] Report of remarks by Plenty Coups, made to the agent on February 20, 1890," 7432–1890, LR-OIA, RG 75, NA; comments by Bell Rock in "Report of Council with the Crow Tribe of Indians," March 15, 1890, Item 2, Box 2, 98, RCIA-FRC, Seattle.

[71] Plenty Coups to Agent Williamson, February 4, 1888, Item 2, Box 2, RCIA-FRC, Seattle; *ARCIA*, 1889 (Serial 2725), 37–38; M. P. Wyman to Commissioner, November 25, 1889, Item 2, Box 2, RCIA-FRC, Seattle; Report on Council of Crow Tribe, August 2, 1890, Item 2, Box 3, RCIA-FRC, Seattle; Council Proceedings, August 28, 1891, Item 2, Box 3, RCIA-FRC, Seattle.

attacked his fellow prisoners with a knife during the first winter of their incarceration. Nevertheless, he finally came home in the summer of 1889. When he returned, Deaf Bull found that the leaders who had remained peaceful in 1887 were now considered the tribal chiefs. Contacts with other plains agencies had ended and there were no more youthful pony-stealing raids on the Piegans and Assiniboins. Game was no more plentiful than it had been two years earlier, but the number of white settlers in the Yellowstone valley had increased. The result was more pressure for white access to the tribe's "unused" lands.[72]

Afflicted with rheumatism and stripped of his support, Deaf Bull accepted an allotment south of Crow Agency near the site of the camp where he had counseled and encouraged young Sword Bearer. During the years ahead, as he watched the progress of the allotment program, the growth of the government's schools and the proliferation of Christian mission outposts across the Crow reserve, Deaf Bull was a witness to the consequences of the young rebel's defeat. Not only had Sword Bearer represented a brief moment of Crow defiance; his futile ride through the agency had typified the common opposition all Plains Indians felt to the "slavery" of reservation life. His isolation and defeat spelled the end of direct confrontations, but it also demonstrated the impossibility of building an intertribal leadership on the diplomacy of the 1880s. For the Crows to survive as a community in the years ahead, they would have to build institutions and leaders of their own. They could not rely upon the charisma of old warriors like Sitting Bull or rally behind young visionaries like Sword Bearer. The men who rose to prominence in Deaf Bull's wake would have to look inward, making their new, reservation home the seat of their nation.[73]

---

[72] The first pardons went to Bank and Sees With His Ears; see Secretary of War to Secretary of the Interior, April 18, 1888, 1888–10527, LR-OIA, RG 75, NA; a copy of Deaf Bull's release order is 23287–1889, dated August 14, 1889, LR-OIA, RG 75, NA.

[73] Deaf Bull's allotment was no. 1209. He did not appear on the 1900 census and so probably died during the 1890s.

Part Two

Making a nation, 1890–1920

Friends, this is our home, this is our domain and this is our country. . . . The
paramount duty of all Indians as I see it, regardless of tribe, condition or location,
Crows included, is to unite in a new effort to fight for personal and tribal liberties,
and the creation of a real democracy among every tribe in the United States.

Robert Yellowtail, 1934[1]

The Crows' entry into history had taken place quickly. Barely eight decades
separated François Antoine Larocque's summer in the Bighorns and the death
of Sword Bearer. In little more than a single lifetime, the community had
migrated from a position where its activities and traditions were largely irrelevant to the United States to the status of federal wards, people whose every
action passed beneath government scrutiny. Yet the swiftness of the domination
process ensured that the Crows would enter American society with their memories intact. Whether they were exchanging visits with their old adversaries or
raising up the legacy of Sore Belly or Blackfoot, tribal people applied their old
traditions to new realities.

The events of the 1880s persuaded the Crows that firm limits now existed in
their world. In the aftermath of Sword Bearer's defeat, the tribe's agents and
missionary guardians came forward with a growing list of forbidden activities –
a list the rapidly expanding white population of Montana was determined to see
enforced. But while enforcement was possible, external pressure could not
dictate the contours of daily life. Specific actions might be outlawed, but outsiders could not remake the community's habits of mind, erase its collective
memory, or obliterate its values.

The story of the decades immediately following the prophet's demise cannot
be encompassed by a description of tribal "success" or "failure" in following the
white man's road. Events ran on more than a single track. In the early twentieth
century the Crows built a new community. Rooted in the past, that community
took shape in what tribal leader Robert Yellowtail would later call "the effort to
fight for personal and tribal liberties." That "effort" encompassed family life,
politics, religion and economic enterprise. In the end their struggles produced
their own "domain" and their own "country."

In 1920, the Crows were still living in the Yellowstone valley, and despite

---

[1] Hardin *Tribune*, August 3, 1934.

167

continuing hardships they had won a series of important victories. They had fended off the strangers who had questioned their values, denigrated their beliefs and coveted their land, and they had developed an array of habits and institutions that fit them to their new home. After four decades of reservation life, they had fashioned ways of translating their love for Crow country into a broad set of initiatives. These initiatives began with the persistence of tribal men and women in communities across the reservation, but their principal advocates were the leaders who rose to power in the aftermath of Sword Bearer's defeat and a younger generation of politicians, many of whom had attended the American's dreary boarding schools. Foremost among this new group of politicians was Robert Yellowtail: cattleman, Baptist, self-taught attorney, Republican, federal employee and advocate of "real democracy" in Montana and elsewhere.

6

Searching for structure:
Crow families in transition

There is no question but that both kin and clan affinities are extensive and inclusive, and the result is mutual and wide affection throughout the whole tribe. Tribal unity and harmony is thus maintained. . . . the influence of the whites has not yet affected this kinship system. School children who had been away would return and try to disassociate themselves from tribal customs and traditions, but invariably would be reclaimed through the kinship route. It is so affectionate, so real and embracing that before they know, it has melted their individualistic tendencies into the Indian nature which is sympathetic, understanding and philanthropic.

Joseph Medicine Crow, 1939[1]

I

In the summer of 1868, as Sioux and Cheyenne raiders passed through the Yellowstone valley, attacking Crow bands and threatening their buffalo herds, an eighteen-year-old trail hand from Ohio named Thomas Leforge befriended a Crow boy named Three Irons. As the weather turned warm, Leforge left his parents' home in the Gallatin valley and travelled to the upper Yellowstone, where he hunted and trapped with Three Irons and his many relatives. By September it had become apparent to Leforge's Crow hosts that their guest wanted to stay for the winter. Since he liked Leforge and valued his abilities as a horseman and hunter, Three Irons's father, Yellow Leggings, called his fellow band members together and announced that he wanted to sponsor a feast in the boy's honor. When they had assembled, he declared that his son's new friend was now his son. "There," Yellow Leggings added, pointing to his wife, "there is his mother."[2]

"Thus I became a Crow Indian," Leforge later recalled; he had become "a brother of Three Irons and a son of Yellow Leggings." His reception into the tribe underscored the extent to which nineteenth-century Crows understood membership in their community to be a function of kinship rather than legal

[1] Joseph Medicine Crow, "The Effect of European Culture upon the Economic, Social and Religious Life of the Crow Indians (M. A. Thesis, Department of Anthropology, University of Southern California, 1939), 25. A copy of the thesis is in the Little Big Horn College Archives.
[2] Thomas B. Marquis, *Memoirs of a White Crow Indian* (Lincoln: University of Nebraska Press, 1974), 26, originally published in 1928.

certification. One was not a Crow because of particular political rights or economic standing, but because one belonged to a household and was willing to assume the obligations associated with family living. Most of these obligations were defined by gender: men would hunt and provide military security; women would build and maintain the household dwelling, process food and make clothing. Other obligations were a function of age: children would defer to elders; elders would provide guidance and instruction in traditional skills; mature individuals would provide food and security. In addition, each household member would fulfil the community's expectations for the behavior of a spouse, child, in-law, parent or sibling.[3]

While this structure would have been generally familiar to Leforge – tasks in his own family were probably distributed along gender lines, and family ties were no doubt important in his hometown – the Crow social system he entered in 1868 also contained some elements that had not been a part of his midwestern childhood. Gender-specific tasks, for example, could be performed by anyone who dressed and lived appropriately. *Batée*, men who lived and dressed as women, were frequently praised for their skill at hide tanning and handicrafts; there was no stigma attached to transvestism or homosexuality. And just as the structure of gender-specific tasks was more important to the Crows than the actual biological construction of the person performing it, so the structure of family life took precedence over its membership. Couples frequently separated and formed new households. As with homosexuality, such behavior was tolerated so long as the individuals involved fulfilled their social obligations.[4]

The Crow family was remarkably resilient. The values and practices Leforge described in 1868 conform to those François Antoine Larocque observed a half-century earlier. When the young fur trader visited the Crows in 1805, he noted almost immediately that as they entered the Hidatsa villages on the Missouri River, the "Rocky Mountain Indians" called to their hosts in familial terms and sealed their trading bargains with ceremonies of adoption. As Larocque travelled with the Crows that summer, he had lived with families in their lodges, noting frequently that his hosts believed kin relations and loyalty to be the fundamental glue that held an organized society together. Throughout the nineteenth century, friendly strangers who came among the Crows, whether they were Indian or non-Indian, made similar observations. They were customarily greeted with food, tobacco and hospitality. They joined in the life of the household and the band. If they stayed, they were attached to a family as Leforge was – there was nothing else to do with them.[5]

[3] A summary of those obligations is contained in Robert H. Lowie's discussion of relationships in his "Social Life of the Crow Indians," *Anthropological Papers of the American Museum of Natural History*, 9 (1912), 207–215.

[4] See ibid., part 2, 220–226.

[5] See François Antoine Larocque, "Yellowstone Journal," in W. Raymond Wood and Thomas D. Thiessen, eds., *Early Fur Trade on the Northern Plains: Canadian Traders Among the Mandan and Hidatsa Indians, 1738–1818* (Norman: University of Oklahoma Press, 1985), 169–172.

The kinship terms Crows used to describe one another also made it clear that their ideas of family membership were far more extensive than those held by Europeans. Individuals did not think of themselves as members of a nuclear unit – parents, children and siblings – but of an extended set of kin relations that began with their mothers and passed through their female descendants, crossing both generational lines and household borders. In the late nineteenth century, these extended networks defined thirteen Crow clans, each of which was represented in the Mountain, River and Kicked In The Belly divisions of the tribe. It was these thirteen clans, as much as individual conjugal units, that were the "families" of the Crow tribe.

Clans multiplied a Crow individual's kinship ties. For example, children would call their biological mother and all of her sisters "mother." All maternally linked cousins (who were therefore members of both mother's and child's clan) were addressed as "brother" or "sister." While a father belonged to a separate clan from his child, he would receive the respectful title "father," as would his brothers and all paternally linked cousins. Crow youngsters would therefore be surrounded by several "mothers" and "fathers" and numerous "brothers" and "sisters." It was a community rich with intimate relatives.[6]

The persistence of family structures and distinctive social values meant that, in 1884, the people who gathered with Captain Armstrong at the site of the new Crow Agency still identified with their clan-based extended families. In the ensuing decades, as the outside world impinged on them in new and dramatic ways, Crow men and women continued to define themselves as members of an extensive and distinctive kinship system. They sustained that system despite the efforts of outsiders who insisted that Crows conform to Anglo-American standards and the disruptive consequences of the buffalo's disappearance. By 1920, Crow men and women had translated traditional household tasks and kinship obligations to a new setting, sustaining the "extensive and inclusive" kinship ties that tribal historian Joe Medicine Crow described at the opening of this chapter.

II

The increasingly rigid boundaries of the Crow Reservation set a grim context for the community's family life. While Crow agents had worked to enforce limits on the movement of the tribe throughout the 1880s, it was not until the death of Sword Bearer that the boundaries of the reservation had a major impact on tribal behavior. Not only did the events of 1887 clarify the military capacity of the United States, but the rising hostility of local whites promised

---

[6] See Lowie, "Social Life of the Crow Indian," 186–196; see also Joseph Medicine Crow, *From the Heart of Crow Country* (New York: Orion, 1992).

Table 1. *Crow population, sex ratio, fertility ratio, birth and death rates,*
1880–1930

	1880	1891	1900	1910	1920	1930
Total population	3,470	2,208	1,875[a]	1,740[a]	1,719	1,963
Ratio of men to women	.97	.90	.99	1.01	1.02	1.02
Ratio of births to deaths	n.a.	.85	.71	.75(1911)	1.03	n.a.
Deaths per 1,000	n.a.	28.1	43.9[b]		45.4	36.3	n.a.
Births per 1,000	n.a.	n.a.	36.6[c]		44.3	40.0	n.a.

[a] Based on U.S. Census.
[b] 1902 rate (82 deaths in population of 1870).
[c] 1903 rate (68 deaths in population of 1857).
Sources: Office of Indian Affairs Tribal Census, *Annual Report of the Commissioner of Indian Affairs* (1880, 1891, 1900, 1920, 1930), and Record of Crow Deaths, Item 44, Records of the Crow Agency, Federal Records Center, Seattle, Washington.

to confront individual Crows whenever they strayed beyond their borders. The pattern of intertribal visiting established in the 1880s continued – with or without the agent's permission – but without the political overtones it carried prior to Sword Bearer's death. It became exceedingly difficult to adopt or marry people from other tribes or to mobilize allies from other reservations. After 1890 it was clear to the Crows that the bulk of their lives would be lived between Pryor Creek and the Little Bighorn.

Within the formal boundaries of the Crow homeland, the disastrous demographic trends that became evident in the 1880s continued. As Table 1 indicates, the period from 1880 to 1930 witnessed the nadir of tribal population. Additional statistics presented there offer a broad explanation for this decline. The rising ratio of men to women indicates that women were making up a dwindling percentage of the population. On the other hand, the increasing ratio of births to deaths and the rise in the tribe's birth rate indicate that a shrinking number of Crow women were bearing a growing number of children. Finally, the decline in the tribal death rate (which impressionistic evidence suggests continued on into the 1920s) allowed the tribal population to increase. Only the maintenance of extraordinarily high birth rates prevented the tribe from dropping into oblivion.

The extinction of the tribe was frequently predicted. A woman who grew up at Crow Agency in the years before World War I recalled that traditional tree burials continued to be a feature of tribal life and that coffins sat in the high branches of cottonwoods all across the reservation. "One could not observe the horizon in any direction without seeing one silhouetted against the sky." In

1915, the local agent repeated the now-familiar prediction: there was "a mathematical certainty when the Crow Indian will sing his death song and cease to exist."[7]

As the size of the Crow population declined and the government bureaucracy grew more efficient, medical assessments of Crow health proliferated. While unable to reverse dramatically the tide of death that swept across the reserve, these reports offer an explanation of its causes. Tuberculosis was becoming better known by the turn of the century and government officials could now identify its presence with growing frequency. "Consumption has a strong hold on them," Agent Samuel Reynolds observed in 1906. Poor sanitation, crowded living conditions and severe weather helped strengthen the disease's grip. In 1911, the government estimated that 9% of the tribe (approximately 150 people) were sick with TB. In addition, the reports of agency personnel regularly noted that quarantines had been established or reservation schools closed because of epidemics of other dangerous infectious diseases. These included outbreaks of smallpox in 1900, 1901, 1903 and 1907 and individual reports of spinal meningitis in 1906 and infantile paralysis in 1916.[8]

While the population of adults within the tribe was declining markedly for most of the early reservation era, the number of children in the community was on the rise. Table 2 shows that the ratio of living children to married women aged 15–44 increased sharply between 1891 and 1910, from 1.13 to 1.74. It would seem from these figures that women were having more children in 1910 than they were in 1891, although it is possible that a drop in child mortality was also under way. This shift also confirms the report of a rising birth rate within the tribe during these same two decades (see Table 1). Even though the absolute size of the Crow community was shrinking – and the proportion of the tribe in the prime child-bearing years was declining as well – the number of children was rising. There were 386 Crows under the age of 10 in 1891 (17% of the total); in 1910 this group of young children had risen to 412 (22% of the tribe).

A brief excerpt from the memoirs of a teacher at Crow Agency conveys the flavor of this new, child-rich environment. Janette Woodruff recalled that

---

[7] Carolyn Reynolds Riebeth, *J. H. Sharp Among the Crow Indians, 1902–1910* (El Segundo, Calif.: Upton and Sons, 1985), 90; Superintendent's Annual Narrative Report, Crow, 1915, 9, RG 75, NA.

[8] The estimate of the tuberculosis infection rate is in *ARCIA*, 1911 (Serial 6222), 144. Smallpox is reported in J. E. Edwards to Commissioner of Indian Affairs, March 15, 1900, Item 2 Box 5, RCIA-FRC, Seattle; ibid., March 14, 1901, Item 2, Box 6, RCIA-FRC, Seattle; Fred Miller to Commissioner of Indian Affairs, February 17, 1903, Item 2, Box 6, RCIA-FRC, Seattle; Samuel Reynolds to Fred Foster, June 14, 1905, Item 4, Box 23, RCIA-FRC, Seattle; Reynolds to O. P. Benefiel, December 9, 1907, Item 14, Box 24, RCIA-FRC, Seattle. For notices of school closings and quarantines, see *ARCIA*, 1900 (Serial 4101–5) 268 (TB): *ARCIA*, 1906 (smallpox, spinal meningitis) (Serial 5118), 254; Circular to Employees and Residents of Crow Agency and Reservation, August 16, 1916, Plenty Coups Papers, Plenty Coups Museum, Pryor, Montana (infantile paralysis).

Table 2. *Fertility of married Crow women aged 15–44, 1891–1910*

| Year | n | \multicolumn{11}{c}{Number of children reported living} |
		0	1	2	3	4	5	6	7	8	9	R[a]
1891	357	116	123	87	17	12	2	0	0	0	0	1.13
1900	319	90	84	88	37	12	4	2	1	1	0	1.46
1910	268	87	60	45	32	25	6	6	4	1	2	1.74

[a] Ratio of total children reported to number of married women, ages 15 to 44.
Source: 1891 – Bureau of Indian Affairs Annual Enumeration; 1900 and 1910 – U.S. Census.

during her tenure at the Crow Agency boarding school during the first decade of the twentieth century, spring visiting day was the highpoint of the season. On a designated Saturday afternoon parents would arrive on foot and by wagon, carrying hampers of food and trailing children and dogs. "Each family sat as a unit," Woodruff recalled, "apparently concerned with nothing but family affairs. . . . Before the assembling had hardly been completed, baskets and boxes were opened, and the children entertained at a royal feast. . . . The Crows were never stingy when it came to gift-giving, and nothing was too good to bestow upon the offspring on visiting day."[9]

                                    III

As Crow families struggled through the demographic pressures of the early twentieth century and looked about for a place to settle, they faced a crucial decision. How would they settle this new environment? The Northern Pacific Railroad's arrival in 1883 had brought the nearby city of Billings to life and had stimulated commercial agriculture along the length of the Yellowstone valley. In the 1890s, this process accelerated despite the onset of hard times. The army closed Fort Custer in 1898, marking the region's transfer to civilian authority, and the following year the sale of all the reservation lands between the fort and the Yellowstone opened additional farming and stock-raising areas to whites. During the decade of the 1890s two new rail lines cut through the reservation. The first, along Clark's Fork west of Pryor, and the second running the length of the Little Bighorn valley, from Sheridan, Wyoming, to the Yellowstone. (By

[9] Janette Woodruff, as told to Cecil Dryden, *Indian Oasis* (Caldwell, Idaho: Caxton Printers, 1939), 58.

the time the Clark's Fork line was completed, the sale of the tribe's western rangelands placed it outside the boundaries of the preserve.)

The availability of transportation increased the value of reservation lands and hastened a movement away from cattle ranching and towards farming. This transition also brought new legions of settlers to the area. By 1907 the combination of economic ambition and settler energy brought a town into being at the confluence of the Little Bighorn and Bighorn Rivers. Fittingly, the principal figure in the land company which controlled the real estate in the new hamlet of Hardin, Montana, was John Rankin, a man who developed his taste for Yellowstone valley rangeland a decade earlier during his service as allotment agent on the Crow Reservation. In 1912, Hardin became the seat of Bighorn County, a branch of state government which asserted its jurisdiction over the entire Crow Reservation.

As the non-Indian population rose in size and drew closer to their borders, the Crow residents of the reservation formed themselves into five major communities. While initiated by the Indians themselves, this process was supported by government action: a succession of agents subdivided the preserve into five districts and created agency branches in each. By 1920, this process had created five self-contained communities across the 350 square miles of what was now Crow country. The core of each was a collection of government offices, stores and supply shops.

The communities – and the districts which formed around them – began as camps gathered around an important leader or group of leaders. Along the western end of the preserve, for example, Plenty Coups had settled along the upper reaches of Pryor Creek even before the move to Crow Agency. Similarly, decisions by Pretty Eagle and Iron Bull to settle near the mouth of Rotten Grass Creek in the Bighorn valley had brought others to the area. Further down the river – and at the lower end of the Little Bighorn valley – a community of River Crows and former scouts gathered near Fort Custer. Referred to as "Black Lodge," the tribal name for the River Crow bands, the people along this northern border of the reservation looked to headmen like Two Belly, Young Onion and Two Leggings for leadership. At the head of the Little Bighorn, Medicine Crow, Old Dog, Spotted Horse and Crazy Head attracted a number of families to the place where Lodge Grass Creek enters the river. A final district, called "Reno" after the creek where Custer's lieutenant scrambled for his life in 1876, surrounded the site of Crow Agency itself. Among the band leaders settled there were Bull Goes Hunting and Takes Wrinkle.

Agency personnel were assigned to these five communities as early as 1888, but it wasn't until 1892 that traders were licensed to operate at the mouth of Rotten Grass Creek and at Fort Custer, and not until 1894 that rations began to be issued at Pryor and in the Bighorn valley. In the ensuing decade schools were started at Pryor, Lodge Grass and at Rotten Grass Creek, adding to the sense that these communities were branches of the main reservation town at Crow Agency. In 1907, the tribe's agent reported that 450 Crows lived at Lodge Grass, 400 at Pryor, 400 at Bighorn, 200 at Black Lodge and 150 at Reno.[10]

Settled originally by the 150 members of Plenty Coups's band in the early 1880s, the community of Pryor was sixty miles by horse or buggy from Crow Agency. Despite its distance from local authorities, however, Pryor was not isolated. It lay less than thirty miles from Billings, and following the sale of the tribe's western lands in 1890, it was adjacent to white-owned ranchland and a rail line leading south from the Yellowstone into Wyoming. The skill of the community's leader, together with its access to whites other than Indian Office personnel gave Pryor an independent air. When a subagent was appointed to take up permanent residence there in 1894, he was cautioned by his superiors that the Crows of Pryor "have been allowed greater liberty than those residing in other districts." The new officer should therefore be careful to see "that the changes in their management . . . shall not be too abrupt."[11]

The center of the Pryor community was the two-story frame home built for Plenty Coups by the Indian Office shortly after the relocation of the agency to the Little Bighorn. Placed amidst a grove of cottonwoods overlooking Pryor Creek, the house was an ideal meeting place for both Indians and local ranchers. From his comments in the formal councils called to consider grazing leases, it was clear that Plenty Coups cultivated good relations with local cattlemen like Nelson Story and with the growing number of sheep men (such as Charles M. Bair) who were coming into the region. In addition, the chief operated a "store" at his home, a place where local residents could come for supplies and food. Since Plenty Coups had no trader's license or capital, his operation was more likely a kind of distribution center where presents from local ranchers and the leader's own crops and supplies could be retailed to the community. Surviving records suggest that Plenty Coups extended easy credit to his neighbors and followers; his goal did not appear to be the maximization of profit. In addition, Plenty Coups regularly intervened with the agent on questions arising from the allotment of land or the sale of livestock. It was not with too much exaggeration that a white visitor wrote in 1930 that the house "was the home of a great and famous man, the ruler of a people, an avowed sovereign." Not everyone was so

---

[10] For the 1888 farming districts, see Inspector's Reports (microfilm 1070), reel 8, September 15, 1888, frame 404, RG 75, NA; for the establishment of agency offices in the districts, see *ARCIA*, 1892 (Serial 2953), 287; *ARCIA*, 1894 (Serial 3306), 167; and for population estimates, see Reynolds to CIA, March 4, 1907, Item 2, Box 7, RCIA-FRC, Seattle. A slightly higher estimate for the Little Bighorn districts is contained in another district estimate filed in 1903. It lists the district populations as follows: Pryor, 400; Bighorn, 400; and 1,200 for the entire Little Bighorn valley. See Samuel Reynolds to Commissioner of Indian Affairs, April 6, 1903, Item 2, Box 6, RCIA-FRC, Seattle.

[11] J. W. Watson to W. H. Steele, June 11, 1894, Item 5, Box 27, RCIA-FRC, Seattle.

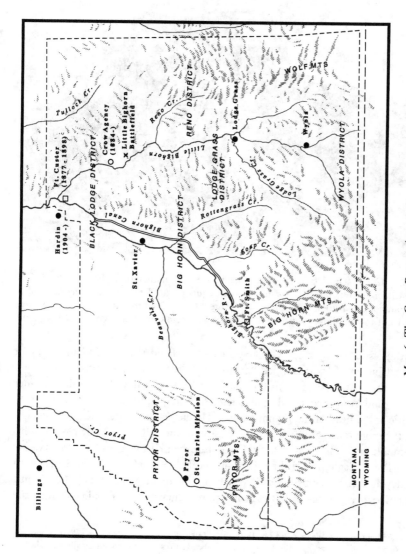

Map 6. The Crow Reservation, 1904–.

Plenty Coups standing at the front of his house in a photograph taken about 1900. The first floor of the chief's Pryor home was frequently used for district meetings and to accommodate visitors. The chief also operated a store from the storage rooms that were a part of the building. Courtesy of American Heritage Center, University of Wyoming.

enthusiastic. In 1912 the Crow agent had declared that the Indians of Pryor ("that bunch of Indians") had "grown impatient of all restraint."[12]

In the years just prior to the relocation of the agency, Iron Bull, a former scout and respected tribal spokesman, had frequently expressed a desire to settle at the head of the Bighorn valley. He died shortly after the migration out of the mountains, however, and leadership in the valley generally passed to his comrade and fellow scout Pretty Eagle. For the first two decades of reservation life, Pretty Eagle played the role of the local chief as effectively in the Bighorn valley as Plenty Coups did at Pryor. From his home along Woody Creek, just ten miles over the nearby buttes from Crow Agency, the chief could communicate

[12] Glendolin Damon Wagner and Dr. William A. Allen, *Blankets and Moccasins: Plenty Coups and His People, the Crows* (Lincoln: University of Nebraska Press, 1987), 276, originally published by Caxton Publishers, 1933; W. W. Scott to Commissioner of Indian Affairs, December 24, 1912, Item 14, Box 54, RCIA-FRC, Seattle. Wagner and Allen refer to Plenty Coups's store. The Plenty Coups Papers, housed at the Plenty Coups Museum in Pryor contain files of correspondence between the chief and various government officials regarding the affairs of Pryor Indians, as well as copies of orders for merchandise and invoices for the purchase and sale of horses.

with local residents as well as government officials. Some flavor of his effective-
ness is suggested by an order that went out to the local subagent in the spring
of 1903. "Any time Pretty Eagle interferes with any orders that you give,"
Agent Reynolds wrote his man in the Bighorn, "send him to this agency."
Referring to the chief's thirty-four-year-old son who was currently serving as
a tribal policeman, Reynolds added, "And the first time Holds The Enemy
disobeys an order you give him you send him to this agency also, and I will
remove his star. . . ."[13]

Despite the prominence of Pretty Eagle and Holds The Enemy, the 400 or
more residents of the Bighorn valley spread themselves for twenty miles along
the river, from the entrance of the Bighorn canyon in the south, to the flatland upstream from Fort Custer. This tendency to disperse accelerated after
the elder chief's death in 1903. Among the variety of people to settle in the
valley during the 1890s was Spotted Rabbit, a young man who had ridden
through Crow Agency with Sword Bearer in 1887, but who had escaped imprisonment on the promise that he would avoid trouble and take up farming.
Soon after his arrival, Spotted Rabbit married a young widow named Medicine
Tobacco whose son and eighteen-year-old brother had just died. Medicine
Tobacco's only surviving son, Philip Iron Head, came with her as she and
Spotted Rabbit took an allotment near his father, within sight of the now-
deserted Fort C. F. Smith. Closer to Pretty Eagle was Sits Down Spotted, only
twenty-one when Crow Agency was founded in 1884 and still listed as a
member of his stepfather's household. Within three years, however, two of Sits
Down Spotted's four siblings would die and he would leave to begin farming
along the Bighorn. By 1890 he was the owner of a house, a wagon, a plow and
a variety of farming tools.[14]

Among the River Crow families settling at Black Lodge, near Fort Custer at
the lower end of the Bighorn and Little Bighorn valleys, was Three Irons,
probably the same man who had become Tom Leforge's "brother" in 1868. As
a member of Bear Wolf's band, Three Irons had been one of the last Crows to
relocate to the reservation, preferring to travel with his kinsmen, visiting Sioux
and Assiniboin camps in Montana and the Dakotas. A term in the Fort Custer
guardhouse in 1883 probably persuaded him to stay put, and he apparently
established a camp on the prairies between the army post and the new agency.
During the 1890s, Three Irons wife, mother-in-law and two of his three children died, leaving him alone with the care of a son. Nearby, another family with

[13] Samuel Reynolds to T. J. Connelly, May 8, 1903, Item 5, Box 28, RCIA-FRC, Seattle.
[14] Spotted Rabbit is listed in the 1887 census as living with his father, Shot In The Hand; Medicine
Tobacco was listed as widowed and living with her two children and two brothers. His allotment
was no. 1786. Sits Down Spotted was also listed in the 1887 census; his allotment was no. 312.
For allotments, see List of Crow Allotment, Item 53, Box 199, RCIA-FRC, Seattle. Sits Down
Spotted's possessions are recorded in a file called "Round Up Record," Item 42, Box 174, RCIA-
FRC, Seattle.

roots outside the reservation was making its home. Louis Bompard was the twenty-two-year-old son of an Assiniboin woman and a white man (perhaps a French-Canadian trader), when he first appeared on the agency records as a young horse raider in 1887. Like Three Irons, Bompard lost two family members during the 1890s, but he and his new wife, a Crow woman who took the confusing name Lois Bompard, had two children and began farming.[15]

In addition to being the home of River Crows, former scouts and other relative newcomers to the Crow Reservation, Black Lodge also contained people who worked at Fort Custer or the new agency. Accusations of liquor selling – still relatively rare before 1900 – were usually aimed in this direction, as were complaints that residents were begging for food from soldiers and traders. Agency policemen – most notably the River Crow officer Big Medicine – also were frequently drawn from Black Lodge.

South of Crow Agency lay the Reno district, a collection of Mountain Crow camps scattered across the rich bottomland of the Little Bighorn. Like Black Lodge, Reno was too close to the reservation headquarters to develop an independent leadership. Among its more prominent residents were Boy That Grabs, the chief of the agency police force until his death in 1903, and Bull Goes Hunting, a respected, older band leader and religious figure. As a young man, Bull Goes Hunting had married Medicine Crow's widowed mother and brought the young man into his home. The young leader considered the old man his father.[16]

Like Bull Goes Hunting, many Reno residents had close ties to tribal members who lived further up the valley. The greatest concentration of these people appeared near the "Forty Mile" stage crossing where Lodge Grass Creek entered the Little Bighorn. People here were in easy reach of the Bighorn and Wolf Mountains and were less exposed to outsiders and government officials than their kinsmen down on the flatland of Reno and Black Lodge. Among them was Spotted Horse, who had always claimed the area as his own. Following Sword Bearer's death, Spotted Horse apparently decided to live at Lodge

[15] Three Irons is listed as the head of family 265 in the 1887 census roll and is also listed in the 1900 and 1910 federal census schedules. His son was listed as Drinks All The Time in the 1900 census and Victor Three Irons in the 1910 census. His term in the Fort Custer guardhouse is described in John P. Hatch to Henry Armstrong, December 10, 1883, 23143–1883, LR-OIA RG 75, NA.
  A "Mrs. Bompard," presumably Louis Bompard's mother was listed as a resident of the Absarokee Agency in the 1884 band enumeration of the Crows. Louis Bompard does not appear until 1887 where he is described as the head of family 604. Listed with him are a brother, sister and niece, all of whom were dead by 1902. The 1900 census lists Louis Bompard's mother as Assiniboin and his father as white; his wife Lois is listed as Crow. Their children Peter and Rosa were nine and four years old respectively in 1900.
[16] Bull Goes Hunting was listed as a band leader in the 1884 band census and, he was allotted just south of Crow Agency alongside fellow band member Spotted Buffalo. Boy That Grabs is listed as the head of family 209 in the 1887 enumeration. Bull Goes Hunting's tie to Medicine Crow is described in Peter Nabokov, *Two Leggings: The Making of a Crow Warrior* (New York: Crowell, 1967), 73.

Grass in peace. The uprising had apparently convinced him that further resistance was futile. Medicine Crow, however, usually represented the area at tribal gatherings. A veteran war leader, Medicine Crow was only thirty-six when the Sword Bearer crisis ended. He seemed to lack Plenty Coups's ambition for tribal leadership, but he matched his contemporary from Pryor in his ability to unify the residents of his district.[17]

The grasslands and river bottoms south of Lodge Grass also attracted a group of newcomers. These were mixed-blood families who had originally settled on the tribe's western lands near the city of Billings. When these lands were sold in 1890, and opened to white settlement two years later, tribal members had the option of remaining on their homesteads (now off the reservation) or claiming lands within the reduced boundaries of the preserve. Among those who relocated was the family of James B. Cooper, a white railroad worker from the East, and his Crow wife, Margaret Wallace. Their household also included three grown children of Margaret Wallace's prior marriage to Fellows D. Pease, a fur trader and an early Crow agent.

The local agent called Cooper and others like him "squaw men" and made every effort to exclude them from tribal life. The Cooper/Pease settlers in Lodge Grass were eager to exploit the farming and ranching country around them, however, and they quickly established themselves in the area. The Coopers ranched at the headwaters of Rottengrass Creek and were frequently involved in Lodge Grass affairs. As James Cooper passed from the scene, his eldest son, Joe – who had been one of the earliest students at the Crow Agency boarding school – took his place as outspoken defender of the family's interests. His half-brother, George Pease, settled near the Coopers for a time before moving on to Lodge Grass, where he opened the town's first store in 1900.[18]

The mix of its location along the new rail line connecting Wyoming to the Yellowstone, the presence of tribal elders like Spotted Horse and young, relatively sophisticated mixed-blood leaders like Joe Cooper gave Lodge Grass a unique personality. While they did not reject the presence or activities of

---

[17] Spotted Horse was the first Lodge Grass resident to sign a petition asking for an issue station to be started at Lodge Grass in 1902. See Edwards to Commissioner of Indian Affairs, March 11, 1902, 75047–1902, LR-OIA RG 75, NA. Also signing were Old Dog, Medicine Crow, Yellowtail and approximately eighty others. Medicine Crow is listed as head of family 268 in the 1887 census.

[18] The Cooper/Pease household (minus James Cooper) is listed as family 612 in the 1887 census. James Cooper is described as "the most troublesome of that class of men known as Squaw Men," in E. P. Briscoe to Commissioner of Indian Affairs, December 1, 1888, Item 4, Box 14, RCIA-FRC, Seattle. For an example of James Cooper's enterprising nature, see James Cooper to Commissioner of Indian Affairs, December 16, 1885, 30570–1885, LR-OIA, RG 75, NA. For an early example of Joe Cooper's similar attitude, see Joe Cooper to Secretary of Interior, December 25, 1893, 1155–1894, LR-OIA, RG 75, NA. For information on Fellows D. Pease and the Pease/Cooper genealogy, see Helen Pease Wolf, *Reaching Both Ways* (Laramie: Jelm Mountain Press, 1989), 21.

outsiders, community members were interested in charting their own course. There was little of the isolation of Pryor or Bighorn and perhaps less intimidation than was often felt by the residents of the two districts adjacent to Crow Agency itself. Not surprisingly, the residents of Lodge Grass were the first group on the reservation to submit a petition to Indian Office to protest the firing of a popular agent.[19]

A final mark of Lodge Grass's independence was the formation by its residents of a sixth reservation community in the years just before World War I. Recognized as a promising agricultural area, the area near Pass Creek at the southern end of the Little Bighorn valley had few Crow residents before 1910. The local agent reported in 1909 that there were about thirty people in the area. During the next five years, however, a group which included both mixed-blood Crows and the son of Spotted Horse moved into the area near the rail station at Wyola. Before long they were petitioning for the creation of a subagency in their new district and electing their own representatives to attend meetings of the tribal council.[20]

IV

Like an empty stage set, a description of the early reservation's basic social geography tells us little until we observe the movement of families across it. Similarly, a roster of names cannot by itself reconstruct a family system. Like the Crows who searched in the early twentieth century for opportunities to maintain their social traditions in a modern setting, modern researchers must seek out the human decisions that shape the meanings embedded in a census report. Understanding what influenced such decisions – the decisions to take up residence in a particular location or to choose a particular mate – should help illuminate the social values that persisted into the reservation era. The object of such a search is a pattern of behavior that describes the social relationships that held Crow people together as they entered the twentieth century.[21]

It is plain that households made up of grandparents, parents, children and

[19] Forty Mile Indians to Commissioner of Indian Affairs, December 31, 1901, 75437–1901, LR-OIA, RG 75, NA.

[20] See Henry Armstrong to Commissioner of Indian Affairs, November 22, 1884, 22905–1884, Special Case 190, LR-OIA, RG 75, NA for an early description of the Wyola area. The estimate of thirty Indians in 1909 is in Samuel Reynolds to Commissioner of Indian Affairs, Item 2, Box 8, RCIA-FRC, Seattle; and the petitions for services and representative election results are in, respectively, Commissioner of Indian Affairs to W. W. Scott, April 24, 1913, Item 14, Box 52, "Industries," and election results with Telegram to Farmers, March, 1920, Item 15, Box 78, both in RCIA-FRC, Seattle.

[21] For a more detailed discussion of the material presented in this section, see Frederick E. Hoxie, "Searching for Structure: Reconstructing Crow Family Life During the Reservation Era," American Indian Quarterly, 15 (1991), 287–309.

other relatives formed the basis for Crow family life in the reservation era. Crows continued to gather in these traditional family groups even though conditions had changed. Nevertheless, it is less clear what the nature of these households was after 1884. It is necessary, then, to trace changes within these households during the first decades of the reservation in order to generate an accurate portrait of life in the reservation's five districts during the first decades of the twentieth century.

Census enumerations provide one way to track the behavior of Crow households through time. There are many reasons for this. First, they are numerous. Beginning in 1887, federal officials conducted an annual census of the tribe. In 1900 and 1920, the U.S. Census Bureau added special schedules for Indians to its regular inventory, providing modern researchers with a wealth of "extra" questions to examine. Second, very few tribal members left the reservation before World War II. (Indeed, as a legacy of the 1880s, Crows could be jailed for leaving their communities without the permission of their agent until World War I.) Viewed as a group, these censuses hold out the possibility of tracing individuals (or groups of individuals) through several enumerations and linking them to create a portrait of social behavior.

Two areas are most helpful in presenting a picture of Crow family and household life in the early reservation years: residence and marriage. Where did people settle when the reservation was established? Who settled with them? What kinds of structures emerged in their new settlements? Marriage can have many culturally specific meanings, but for purposes of analysis we can call it the process by which people select mates and form households. Whom did people marry and for how long did they remain together? What did Crows believe about marriage and household formation?

Five tribal enumerations provide some answers to these questions. The first of these censuses, undated but probably written in 1883 or 1884, is a "Record of Indian Bands." It is contained in four small notebooks that list 401 households. The "head" of each household is named along with a record of the number of men, women and children in the group. In addition, the census identifies each unit according to a list of twenty-seven "bands." The 1884 census provides a picture of prereservation social structure. We know that all the people listed by name in that census were the heads of households, and we know that at least some of the people grouped together in a band were affiliated in some way.

The second document is the 1900 federal census. While the federal census does not provide information regarding the location of individual residences, it does contain information on spouses, children and marital status.

Third is the roster of Crow allotments prepared following the completion of the first general division of the reservation into individual homesteads in 1905. This list provides the precise location of assigned residences as well as the location of allotments assigned to other family members. Agents frequently reported that Crows did not live on their allotments, but a family's allotments were generally made together and located in the district of their residence. The allotment list can therefore be used as an general indicator of family residence.

Fourth is the 1910 federal census, which contained information parallel to that in the 1900 enumeration. Fifth is a census of "Adult Crow Indians" prepared by the agency superintendent in 1920. This list indicated the home district of Crow adults and listed husbands and wives together.

As a set, these records provide five "snapshots" of Crow households taken at intervals over a thirty-six-year period. While sharing the flaws of any bureaucratic document prepared by outsiders, they can be checked against each other to eliminate many errors. Linking individuals in these records allows a modern observer to trace the consequences of a process by which individuals and other members of their households shifted from a migratory hunting subsistence to a pattern of permanent residence in an agricultural community.

An initial comparison of the 1884 and 1900 censuses produces a list of 183 individuals who appeared in both. That is, there were 183 Crows who were listed as heads of a household before the establishment of modern Crow Agency and who were still household heads in 1900. Of the 183 people who appeared in the first two censuses, 135 were identifiable on the 1905 allotment roll. These were the "First Families of the Crow Reservation." They and their immediate kin can be identified in the federal census, their allotments can be located, and they can be tied to a prereservation social affiliation. Moreover, because they were heads of households throughout the first twenty years of reservation life, we can imagine they formed the backbone of Crow society in that period.

Several prereservation bands settled together and formed the core of a reservation district. The Plenty Coups band, for example, settled predominately along Pryor Creek, while Old Crow's and Spotted Horse's groups preferred the Little Bighorn. In addition, it appears that once settled in an area, families persisted there. For example, Figure 3 traces the behavior of two households from the Plenty Coups band during the first four decades of the reservation era. It presents in simple form the location of several first families and their offspring. The figure indicates that even though Three Bears left his wife (or she left him) and moved to the Little Bighorn district to marry Old Beaver, he returned to Pryor following her death. Following his departure, his second wife, Twin Woman, married Pretty Coyote and remained in the district.

The Back Of The Neck family presents a similar picture. Following Back Of The Neck's departure for Bighorn, his wife, Corn Woman, remained at Pryor with their children. In addition, Goes To House, listed as a member of their family in 1900, also remained in Pryor and married a local man. The women of the Back Of The Neck family stuck together and persisted in their original location.

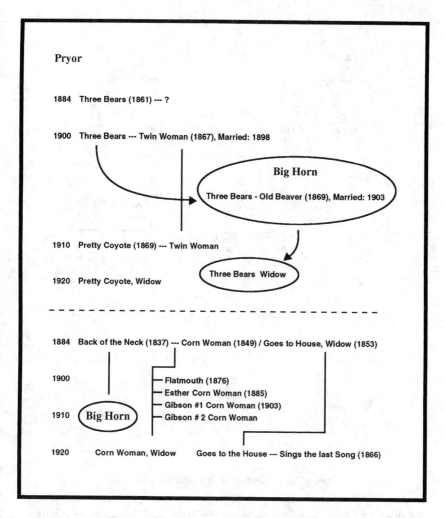

Figure 3. Plenty Coups first families, 1884–1920.

Figure 4 and Table 3 describe a similar phenomenon for the Medicine Crow band. Here nine of the band families were traced through time and across the three districts where they made their homes. Three families began in Pryor, four in the Bighorn, and two in the Little Bighorn. Only Alex Crane, child of The Crane and Kills With Horses, sought a spouse outside his district, and only Knows War, the son of Little Wolf, left his district to take up residence elsewhere.

While one's band affiliation appears to have had varying degrees of influence on an individual's decision about where to settle, it is clear that once located in

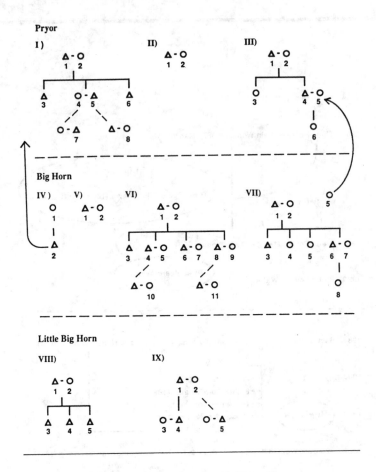

Figure 4. Nine Medicine Crow families, 1884–1920.

a district, a family remained there over time. Apparently, there was a structure, either in the Crows' nineteenth-century culture or in the emerging reservation community that fostered persistence in these separate districts. Several elements of this structure suggest themselves. First, in none of these cases – or in any of dozens of other family genealogies – is there an example of members of one band marrying the offspring of fellow band members. These data confirm that Crow bands were exogamous. Children of the Crow first families – particularly the men who are most easily traced and are therefore overrepresented in the documents – sought spouses from outside their band but within their district. As a result, there was relatively little movement away from the places where first family members had originally settled.

Table 3. *Nine Medicine Crow families, 1884–1920*

I.
1. Snake Bull (1852)
2. Strikes The Arm (1852)
3. Is Sweet Now (1895)
4. Plain Cedar (1890)

5. R. Spotted Arm (1880)
6. B. Bull Snake (1904)
7. P. Bird Hat (1887), second husband
8. Pretty Medicine (1877), second wife

II.
1. Sharp Horn (1842)

2. Woman with Eyes Open (1842)

III.
1. The Crane (1857)
2. Kills with Horses (1860)
3. "daughter"

4. End of Trail/Alex Crane (1886)
5. Weasel High Up (1891?)
6. Gretchen Crane (1910)

IV.
1. Little Wolf (1842)

2. Knows War (1879)

V.
1. Skins A Wolf (1842)

2. Has Horses (1849)

VI.
1. The Iron (1860)
2. Pretty Medicine Rock (1862)
3. Little Shield/Ernest Iron (1892)
4. Woodpecker's Child/Robin Iron (1885)
5. Minnie Iron (1888)
6. Good Coos/Albert Iron (1895)

7. Good Hearted Ground (1875?)
8. Gets Down Well Known/Edward Iron (1887)
9. Magdalene Medicine Mane (1892)
10. Emma Runs Between (1875), second wife
11. Angela Brass (1895), second wife

VII.
1. The Horn (1845)
2. All Alone (1855)
3. Goes After Spotted Horse (1884)
4. Mr. William Blaine (1874)

5. Florence Blaine (1895), granddaughter?
6. James Blaine (1890), grandson?
7. Ethel Plentyhawk (1890)
8. Josephine Blaine (1909)

VIII.
1. Medicine Crow (1851)
2. Medicine (1855)
3. Young Badger (1889)

4. Goes Pretty/Leo Medicine Crow (1894)
5. Chester Medicine Crow (1898)

IX.
1. Three Irons (1844)
2. Kills Many Men (1857)
3. Kills The Boy (1893)

4. Drinks All The Time/Victor Three Irons (1892)
5. John Wallace (?), #2's second husband

It is also apparent from other sources that Crow bands in the 1880s generally contained members of more than one clan. The Plenty Coups band, for example, contained three prominent warriors in addition to its famous leader. Three Bears and Bell Rock belonged to the Without Shooting They Bring Game clan, while the headman and Hunts To Die were Sore Lips people. Similarly, Old Dog, the band leader who settled at Lodge Grass, was a member of the Sore Lips clan, while two other prominent leaders in his band belonged to two other kin groups. The Bread was a Whistling Waters clan member and Arm Around The Neck belonged to the Newly Made Lodges group.

Each newly settled district contained members of several Crow clans. Certain clans might predominate in one area (Not Mixed or Filth Eating at Black Lodge, Sore Lip or Burnt Mouth at Pryor, Whistling Waters at Lodge Grass), but members of other clans would also be present. What government agents saw as settled farming communities were actually re-creations of Crow band settlements. Nothing in the otherwise alien reservation environment disrupted the clan system. On the contrary, the clan system served to enforce the Crows' ties to their new districts by regulating marriage and providing a source of loyalty and support at a time of intense suffering. The traditional taboo against marrying within one's clan continued, thereby reinforcing old rules and ensuring that new marriages would continue to link a wide network of Crow households. While there was a great deal of visiting between districts on the reservation, there was no necessity for children of the community's first families to leave home to find a suitable spouse. Even though they might live in a crowded log cabin in a remote section of one district, household members could maintain their ties to kinsmen in every part of the reservation.

V

The preceding description of household formation and family persistence would have puzzled George W. Frost. When Frost was superintendent of the Crow Reservation in 1877, he reported that there was *no* structure to Crow social behavior. "Perhaps the worst feature of the Crow tribes," he wrote in his annual report that year, "is the almost perfect disregard of marital rights. Polygamy is common, a man taking all the wives that he can support, and, in their language, 'throwing them away' at pleasure. . . . They consider adultery no crime, and . . . for its commission there is no punishment." A decade later as the new Crow Agency boarding school was being established, one of Mr. Frost's successors, Henry E. Williamson, suggested that a twelve-foot-high board fence be erected around the new buildings. "There is now only a wire fence," he reported to Washington, so that "every Indian from the camp who wishes to can converse with the pupils and it cannot be prevented." The evil to be avoided was obvious: "The scenes of camp life . . . are detrimental to the pupils."[22]

An analysis of the 1900 and 1910 federal census returns for the Crow Reservation presents a different view. Crows continued to marry within the tribe and to maintain their tribal language as the favored method of communication. While the percentage of the population reporting "100% Indian blood" declined from 91 to 77% between 1900 and 1910, the tribe continued to be overwhelmingly Crow in ancestry and orientation. Of all reservation residents, 98% were Crows, and two-thirds of them spoke only their tribal language.

When one turns to marriage statistics, there are two striking patterns. First, Crows valued marriage. (The term "marriage" is used here even though it is clear that the Crow respondents and federal census takers had different definitions of the term. Both understood the concept of a stable, long-term unions of men and women.) Over 90% of all adult Crows were either married or widowed, according to the federal censuses of 1900 and 1910. Moreover, Crows appear to have married for long periods. Of the 53 people aged 60–69 who were married in 1900, they reported marriages lasting an average of more than thirty years.

Second, the census figures reveal that Crows married with extraordinary frequency. In an era when some divorces still required legislative approval, 20% of the Crow tribe reported that they had been married four times or more. One might think that Agent Frost's condemnations were based on something concrete. But a careful examination of these data demonstrates Frost's myopia. For both men and women, the length of *last* marriage for individuals married in excess of five times indicates that the ideal of a long-term stable union had not been abandoned, even by those who married frequently. For men in their sixties, despite the fact that they had been married an average of eight times apiece, they had probably lived with their current spouse since sometime in their early forties.

Just as the persistence of district communities indicated the persistence of clan and family allegiances across the reservation, so the juxtaposition of outraged agents and extended marriages suggests a continuation of traditional Crow standards for individual conduct. Because Crow society was perceived as an amalgam of clans, marriages were more significant as alliances of extended families than they were as unions of individuals. For Crow men and women, the formation of a household brought together several generations and a large network of kin. When consolidated into an extended family containing children, this marriage created a complex web of social loyalties and social obligations. In

---

[22] *ARCIA*, 1877 (Serial 1800), 529; and 1887 (Serial 2542), 219.

the words of one modern anthropologist, "Crow women are not passive vehicles, but active *partners*."[23]

"Tell me of your marriage ... Did you fall in love?" Montana historian Frank Linderman asked an elderly Crow woman in the 1920s. "No," she replied, "young women did not then fall in love, and get married to please themselves, as they do now. They listened to their fathers, married the men selected for them." Other reports confirm Pretty Shield's answer. Suitors sought the approval of their intended's family through a process of gift giving which the girl's parents would control. In most cases these parents would play a major role in negotiating the terms of their daughter's marriage. If the marriage proved unsuccessful, the girl's parents would also supervise the dismissal of the man, even resorting in extreme cases to destroying their son-in-law's property and burning his lodge. The Anglo-American idea of romantic love – the idea that prompted Linderman's question in the first place – was not the central focus of Crow family life. Pretty Shield's reply suggests that in the twentieth century as in the nineteenth, other concerns took first priority.[24]

While sexual intercourse would seal and confirm a Crow marriage, individual sexual behavior was as irrelevant to the negotiations that led to the formation of a household in the reservation context as it had been in Leforge's day. Marriage partners were generally expected to be faithful, but little premium was placed on abstinence or virginity. Crow children were encouraged to think of marriage partners at an early age, Crow girls were not condemned for sexual experimentation, and Crow boys were frequently told that "women were like a herd of buffalo." Indeed, one feature of the rivalry between Crow warrior societies in the nineteenth century was wife kidnapping. This practice – which Larocque had witnessed in 1805 – was supported by a warrior ethic that encouraged stealth by attackers and stoicism among a raid's victims. Even though warrior societies declined in importance after the founding of Crow Agency, young men and women continued to participate in considerable sexual experimentation. In the tribal courts, virtually all prosecutions for "adultery" were of men and women under 25. That fact, coupled with the statistics of marriage and divorce, indicated that "traditional" practices continued into the reservation era.[25]

---

[23] Martha Harroun Foster, "Of Baggage and Bondage: Gender and Status Among Hidatsa and Crow Women," *American Indian Culture and Research Journal*, 17, 2 (1993), 142.

[24] Frank B. Linderman, *Pretty Shield: Medicine Woman of the Crows* (Lincoln: University of Nebraska Press, 1972), 130, originally published in 1932. See also Robert H. Lowie, *The Crow Indians* (Lincoln: University of Nebraska Press, 1983), originally published in 1935, 50–61; and (on the punishment of errant sons-in-law) M. P. Wyman to Commissioner of Indian Affairs, November 22, 1890, Manuscript 3653, National Anthropological Archives, Washington, D.C.

[25] On attitudes towards sex and wife kidnapping, see Lowie, *The Crow Indians*, 48, 49–52, 186; and Robert H. Lowie, "Social Life of the Crow Indians," 220–230. On adultery before the tribal courts, see Frederick E. Hoxie, "Towards a 'New' North American Indian Legal History," *American Journal of Legal History*, 30 (1986), 351–357. See also Walter J. Hoffman, "Childbirth and Abortion Among the Absaroka (or Crow) and Dakota Indians," Peter Bolz, ed., *European Review of Native American Studies*, 1, 1 (1988), 9–10.

An unidentified Crow couple, photographed inside their tipi shortly after the turn of the century. The woman appears to be carving a wooden pipestem. Courtesy of American Heritage Center, University of Wyoming.

VI

The persistence of distinctively Crow concepts of gender provides a final indication of the nature of Crow family life in the reservation era. Thanks to the preference of the U.S. government for male political leaders and the dominance of men in the cash economy, Crow males were able to sustain an image of themselves as warriors and providers. Chiefs and headmen now rose before a general council and conducted verbal battles with the government – a faint echo of the old war parties, but still an opportunity to display bravado and win over younger followers. In a similar way, the Indian Office's preference for hiring males as teamsters and policemen and the neighboring cattlemen's need for cowboys provided men a chance to exercise economic independence and provide for their families. While Crow women had less support from external authorities, the tribe's traditional ideas about females were surprisingly evident in the twentieth century.

Unlike Europeans, Crows did not believe that the creator made women after men or that women were derived from men. Instead, all the versions of the tribal creation story that have been collected indicate that the two genders were made at the same time and from the same materials. One story has Old Man Coyote and his companion, "the little coyote," make "people," while another has Old Man Coyote make men and women out of mud before telling them "to have intercourse" to produce the first people. Crow mythology describes females as sharing equal status with men and having a comparable level of autonomy. Wives leave their husbands when neglected or mistreated, and women even dispute with mythical heroes like Old Man Coyote. In one famous story, two girls refuse to marry Old Man Coyote and trick him when he comes back to them to seek revenge. Being biologically female did not in itself prevent Crow women from participating in any activity.[26]

Crow traditions made clear the distinction between biology and one's social role. Not only did the tribe accept men who dressed and lived as women, they acknowledged the achievements of women who chose to take on the male role of warrior. For example, when Pretty Shield was interviewed in the 1920s, she recalled two women who fought with the Crow warriors at the Battle of the Rosebud. After describing their exploits, she told her interviewer, "Ahh, the men did not tell you this; but I have. And it's the truth. Every old Crow, man or woman, knows that it is the truth." The anthropologist Robert Lowie reported a berdache living in the Bighorn district of the reservation in the first decade of the twentieth century. He reported that the government had repeatedly tried to have the man dress in male clothing but his neighbors refused, "saying that it was against his nature." In both instances, the successful fulfillment of one's social obligations was far more significant to the Crow community than an individual's anatomical makeup.[27]

In the reservation setting, Crow women were expected to conform to Anglo-American standards of behavior. Not only were men considered preeminent in politics and economic activity, but government officials placed restrictions on the Crow tradition of shifting marriage partners frequently at a young age. Women were expected to conform to their husbands desires rather than to maintain the level of autonomy they had enjoyed in the nineteenth century. Countering these pressures were the persistence of clan affiliation and the tradition of matrilineal descent within the clans, the pattern of frequent marriage and sexual experimentation noted above, and a personal sense of autonomy and individual power. While the latter is difficult to document, a set of

---

[26] For creation stories, see Robert H. Lowie, *Myths and Traditions of the Crows* (Lincoln: University of Nebraska Press, 1993), originally published in 1918, 16, 17; for women getting the better of Old Man Coyote, see Lowie, "Old Man Coyote and the Berrying Girls," *Myths and Traditions of the Crows*, 43–45.

[27] Frank Linderman, *Pretty Shield*, 230; Lowie, *The Crow Indians*, 48. See also, Walter L. Williams, *The Spirit and the Flesh: Sexual Diversity in American Indian Culture* (Boston: Beacon, 1986), 178–180.

A marriage ceremony performed by missionary James Gregor Burgess at Crow Agency in the first decade of the twentieth century. The bride and groom are surrounded by boarding school students in uniform and members of Burgess's family. Courtesy of Sallie W. Curtis.

twenty-three wills dictated by tribal members in the years just prior to World War I provide one kind of insight.

Fifteen of these wills – all filed with the agent between 1910 and 1914 – were written or dictated by women. Of the fifteen women, only three left anything to their husbands; other relatives usually took precedence. But even for the three women who remembered their spouses, the meaning of the gift was not obvious. One woman, for example, Goes First, left 48 acres of land to her husband and 77 acres to another man "who has lived with me and helped care for me. . . ." Among the others who left their husbands nothing were three who added language similar to that in Sarah Shane Williams's will. "I do not wish my husband . . . to have any share in my estate," Mrs. Williams wrote, "For reason that he deserted me several years ago and has since given nothing toward my support." These statements provide powerful evidence that Crow women continued to believe that marriage was an alliance of equals. Their allegiance to their family and clan relations did not require them to embrace Victorian morality; they continued to inhabit and sustain a distinctively Crow set of social structures that functioned within the limits of the reservation environment.[28]

During the first two decades of the twentieth century, the persistence of distinctively Crow patterns of kinship, marriage and family life established the underpinnings for community life. The "extensive" and "inclusive" relationships that Joseph Medicine Crow observed while growing up near Lodge Grass in the 1910s and 1920s were inherited from the people who had belonged to bands that had hunted buffalo in the Yellowstone country a century before. At the same time, the "harmony" and "tribal unity" Medicine Crow saw in his village were products of his relatives' ability to adapt inherited ideas about kinship to new conditions. The households he inhabited and visited, the relatives he counted within his extended family and the distinctive sense of social role and social obligation he carried into adulthood were all twentieth-century phenomena. They had been produced by men and women who lived as Crows despite the opposition of the government and the indifference of their white neighbors. Their achievement was no less a contribution to the new Crow nation than the council speeches of male politicians or the labors of the community's ranchers and farmers.

[28] These wills are filed as Item 58, Box 187, RCIA-FRC, Seattle.

7

New gods in Crow country:
the development of religious pluralism

When a missionary asked the Crows if they would like to have a white man come
here and live with them and learn their language and pray with and for them,
[Medicine Crow] rose up and replied that they did not let a day pass by without
praying to the Great Spirit to take care of them.[1]

I

Medicine Crow's reply to the missionary's inquiry, recorded by Agent Henry
Armstrong in the winter preceding the tribe's relocation to the Little Bighorn,
illustrates the equanimity with which nineteenth-century Crows greeted the
news of a new god's arrival in their homeland. As the young chief tried to
explain to his guest, the Crows had always believed that spiritual power was
deeply intertwined with their community's daily life. Important personal quali-
ties such as generosity and loyalty to kin were understood to be rooted in
tradition and endorsed by divine powers. The tribe's elders taught that crucial
events in the Crow past – from the visions of No Vitals that first brought
tobacco seeds to the tribe, to the victories of young warriors in battle – were
made possible by benevolent guardian spirits who pitied tribal members and
cast blessings upon them.

Spirits also expected to be remembered in daily ceremonies and prayers.
Crows celebrated spiritual power by repeating the mythical stories of creation,
honoring their traditions, and maintaining a flexible but demanding ceremonial
calender. Faith was a practical and reciprocal enterprise; it was based on neither
scripture nor orthodoxy. Medicine Crow's statement reflects the fact that
he and his kinsmen did not separate the world into believers and outcasts;
they believed spiritual power might come to them from many sources. In
the nineteenth century, both external pressures and a rising level of self-
consciousness hardened the Crows' commitment to their tribal beliefs. In an
atmosphere of rising military conflict, religious and ceremonial activity was an
important source of community strength. Most prominent among the tribe's

[1] Armstrong to Commissioner of Indian Affairs, January 11, 1884, Item 2, Box 1, RCIA-FRC,
Seattle.

rituals were those of the Tobacco Society, but a number of other ceremonies – the sun dance, the sacred pipe dance, the bear song dance – were also maintained by a shifting cast of healers, visionaries and community leaders. The Crows never supported a fixed religious hierarchy or believed that the tribe's salvation lay with a single cult. As a consequence, the divisions and dislocations of the immediate prereservation years did not weaken the links between Crow people and their gods.[2]

The arrival of Christian missionaries on the reservation in the mid-1880s injected a new element into the tribe's experience of religion. By insisting on conversion from "paganism" to a "genuine" faith, Christian missionaries introduced the Crows to the idea that salvation had a single source. Rooted in the belief in one creator, one savior and a single code of moral conduct, Christian teachings called on tribal members to consider their personal beliefs and actions before fulfilling their social obligations to fellow tribesmen. Because scripture stipulated a particular model of conduct, converts were urged to practice "good" behavior, shunning those who continued "bad" ways. To please the Christian god, one would be required to exist apart from traditional community relationships, placing one's new faith ahead of the Crow deities.

From the Christian missionary perspective, the task on the Crow Reservation was straightforward: to convert individuals from paganism to the truth. For the objects of this effort, the situation was more complex. Because of their belief in visions and their tolerance for multiple approaches to spirituality, Crow leaders were not inclined to reject missionary teaching out of hand; it deserved to be heard and evaluated. On the other hand, leaders who might accept Christianity risked alienating themselves from fellow Crows and undermining the social fabric which bound their community together. In the generation following the establishment of permanent Christian missions in Crow country, these competing perspectives presented grave risks for tribal members. As in the area of family life, contact with the outsiders' ideas was unavoidable, but conformity to their standards could well destroy the tribe's traditions. Nevertheless, as was true of the structure of reservation society, the religious landscape shaped by Crows in the early twentieth century adapted to new conditions even as it preserved the central values of the past. The religious pluralism that became evident on the reservation in the 1920s formed another major motif in the mosaic of modern Crow nationalism.

In the same letter in which he described Medicine Crow's reply to the missionary who offered instruction in prayer, Henry Armstrong acknowledged that it would be difficult to eradicate completely the tribe's traditional religious ideas and practices. "We cannot change the whole life of these people by simply

[2] For a description of these tribal rituals, see Robert H. Lowie, *The Crow Indians* (Lincoln: University of Nebraska Press, 1983), originally published in 1934, 264–327.

issuing a decree," he wrote. "We have got to lift them up and substitute other amusements and other ways of living in the place of those that they have always had and which they consider to be innocent." He wrote these words at the onset of the time when missionaries (backed up by the military and the Indian Office) insisted that individuals participate in Christian worship and adhere to Christian standards of conduct and dress. But his letter recognized that whatever conversion to these new ways occurred, it would probably not be total. And he was correct.

In response to missionary efforts, tribal community leaders defended traditional social arrangements and a few significant tribal ceremonies. As the twentieth century began, this two-sided contest grew more complex as different Christian sects began competing with one another for converts and new, aggressive native organizations – the peyote faith and a reinvigorated Tobacco Society – entered the scene. To these were added the efforts of formally organized (and quasi-religious) traditional dancing societies who wished to perpetuate both ancient practice and modern innovations. By the middle of the 1920s it had become clear not only that "conversion" to Christianity would not be immediate or complete, but that the Crows had succeeded in preserving their fundamental commitment to a practical faith rooted in individual choice. As had been the case in the nineteenth century and before, no single deity or ritual could encompass the religious ideas of the tribe.

Crow beliefs and practices frustrated, and ultimately defeated the Christian missionaries who wanted to bring doctrinal order to eastern Montana. But the tribe's victory – if that is what it was – did not transport the community back to their nineteenth-century rituals. Instead it reinvigorated the link between the Crows' daily life and their religion and opened a variety of new avenues for the expression of traditional religious ideas. Christian sects learned to coexist with one another, as did the various non-Christian religious groups which now functioned on the reservation. Moreover all of these religious communities linked themselves to the social life of the reservation's districts and villages. By 1920, with more than three decades of adjustment and struggle behind them, the Crows appeared to have successfully assimilated Christianity into their reservation nation. Crow religious expression could once again reinforce the community's social values and relationships.

II

On October 27, 1887, as troops gathered at Crow Agency for the final confrontation with Sword Bearer and his band of "hostiles," Agent Henry Williamson dutifully responded to a circular from the commissioner of Indian affairs. The inquiry had asked for a report on "the activities of the church, missionary and educational societies among the Crow Indians."[3]

His response could be brief. The legendary Jesuit missionary, Father Pierre-Jean DeSmet, had visited the Bighorn valley and preached to the Crows during his first cross-country trip in 1842, and a pair of Lutherans had wintered in the Bighorns in 1859–60, but otherwise there had been no resident missionary with the tribe during the preceding eight decades of contact with white Americans. A Methodist pastor had arrived at the Absarokee Agency on the Stillwater in 1873, but his stay was brief and his congregation consisted mostly of agency employees. Williamson would have little reason to revise a predecessor's report from 1875: "The Crows are thoroughly wild Indians. They have seen very little of any whites, except wolfers and outcasts from civilization. . . . They are very religious and very intense in their heathen prejudice and worship. They sacrifice all of their most valuable possessions to the sun, the river and the earth."[4]

But Williamson wrote at a time when conditions appeared to be changing. Not only were the Crows being forced to settle permanently on their reserve, but for the first time missionaries had arrived who settled in with them. Early in 1887 a Catholic mission had been started in the center of the Bighorn valley. Williamson, a Protestant, expected big things from the new outpost of St. Xavier. "The Jesuit priests go around and visit the Indians at their homes and labor among them," he wrote; "services are held on Sundays at the school." At almost the same time, a Unitarian preacher named Henry F. Bond and his wife had come to Crow country to found the Montana Industrial School to "lift the whole red man, physical, intellectual, moral, spiritual."[5]

St. Xavier and the Montana Industrial School provided the structural foundation for the imposition of Christianity on the Crows. In each case the new missionaries acted with the support of the military and the agent; each became the focus of both curiosity and serious attention from Indian leaders. During the next two decades, St. Xavier on the Bighorn would be the center of Catholic activity while the Little Bighorn would develop an attachment to Protestantism. By the first decade of the new century, Christianity had been imposed on the Crows.

Catholic missionary activity began in the summer of 1880 when a Mexican Jesuit, Father Peter Barcelo, briefly visited the Bighorn country. He returned the following year and lived for a time with Iron Bull's family in a log house

[3] Henry Williamson to Commissioner of Indian Affairs, October 27, 1887, Item 2, Box 2, RCIA-FRC, Seattle (copy). The original of the letter is 1887–29037, Special Case 143, Crow Agency, LR-OIA, RG 75, NA.

[4] Dexter Clapp to Commissioner of Indian Affairs, April 25, 1875, Item 1, Box 1, RCIA-FRC, Seattle.

[5] Williamson to Commissioner, October 27, 1887; Marjorie Pease, *Worthy Work in a Needy Time: The Montana Industrial School for Indians* (Boise, Idaho: n.p., 1986), 11. The Bond school opened in 1886, but it didn't have a significant number of Crow students until 1887.

constructed for the chief by the U.S. government. The old scout and tribal spokesman, who had recently announced that he would settle permanently near the mouth of the Bighorn canyon, was a natural host for the newcomer. Iron Bull's relationship with the priest grew more intense in 1882, however, when Barcelo baptized the band leader's brother while the man lay gravely ill. "Next day," Barcelo recalled, "the dying man got up cured." Later, Iron Bull's brother made the rounds of the Crow camp "speaking with great praise of Father Barcelo and of baptism as a strong medicine the great spirit gave to the Black Gown."[6]

Barcelo made two brief return visits to the area before coming back for a longer stay in August 1883. This time he arrived with a brother Jesuit, Father Pierpaolo Prando, an energetic, thirty-seven-year-old Italian who came to the Yellowstone valley from the St. Ignatius Mission in western Montana. Prando and Barcelo arrived at Stillwater Agency on August 4, and as they entered the grounds, Prando recalled, they "were astonished to see over four hundred lodges of this miserable people around the Agency." The lodges were arranged by band, presumably in anticipation of an issue of rations, and the two priests quickly sought out Iron Bull's group. The chief welcomed the priests, gave them a tent to sleep in and complied with their request that he begin making the sign of the cross before eating.[7]

Barcelo and Prando decided to focus their attention on their host and his family. Prando, who had been trained in medicine in his native Italy, attempted to treat some of the illnesses he encountered. He was particularly successful in treating rheumatism with a liniment he concocted with local herbs. The eager young priest also conducted a census of the Iron Bull band's twenty-two lodges (discovering "four polygamists" among them) and began visiting each one daily to preach and treat the sick. Writing to his superiors barely a week after his arrival, the bespectacled priest predicted that he would "make a complete cleansing of all the children that I find; thus I will baptize all the youths from seven years up."[8]

Barcelo's and Prando's attachment to Iron Bull typified the Catholic approach to the Crows. From the outset, the priests made it clear that they focused on the leader "knowing if we get the chief then it would be easy to get the whole tribe." Iron Bull was a fortuitous contact. Not only had he been a

---

[6] Fr. Pierpaolo Prando to Cataldo, September 26, 1883, Oregon Province Archives, Society of Jesus, Gonzaga University (hereafter cited as "OPA, Gonzaga").

[7] Ibid.

[8] Paul C. Phillips, *Medicine in the Making of Montana*, published by the Montana Medical Association (Missoula: Montana State University Press, 1962), 39; Prando to Fr. Cataldo, August 12, 1883, OPA, Gonzaga. The following discussion of conversion benefitted greatly from "A Medieval Model of Church: A History of the Catholic Church Among the Crow People, 1880–1921," by Karen Watembach (Master's Thesis, Department of History, Montana State University, 1985).

prominent speaker in councils with the whites, but he had earned the respect of both Indian and white military men during the battles with the Sioux, and he had been a stout supporter of Henry Armstrong's plan to relocate the agency headquarters in the Little Bighorn valley.[9]

By September 1883, the two priests could report considerable success. Prando, who had diligently studied the Crow language from the moment of his arrival, wrote proudly that he spoke with Iron Bull every day. He soon baptized the chief's wife ("a very intelligent old woman and pious") and discussed the roads to heaven and hell with his family. Early in September, after Iron Bull had sent away a young girl who had been brought to him, apparently as a gift, Prando decided the chief was "sufficiently instructed." He baptized the old warrior on September 14 and afterwards "blessed the marriage of the great chief with his wife." The priest noted in his report that he had given Iron Bull the name Joseph and had named his wife Mary, adding prayerfully, "I hope the Blessed Virgin and Saint Joseph will take care of these new children because with their new influence they can do a great deal of good for the tribe." Prando ended his account of the chief's baptism on a note of high optimism. Using his uncertain English, he predicted that the tribe's "good disposition" would bring the church "about three thousand Indians very fervent; . . . so I think and hope," he concluded, "the Crows will soon be change[d] into doves."[10]

From the outset, Father Prando's interest in the Crow language reinforced his strategy of winning entire families and bands over to the church. Rather than separate converts from their homes and kin, Prando sought to reach them on their own turf. After only six weeks in the Stillwater valley, the priest reported that his struggles to acquire a few words of the language "pleases the Indians." He added that "with a few words well understood, well pronounced, and said with ease they think that I already know the whole language." Prando even composed a hymn in Crow, reporting that it had "caused some excitement" and was well received. Prando requested that in the future a fellow Italian, Father Peter Bandini, should be added to their mission because "with his music [he] would lead the Crows around by the nose. The Crows are mad for music."[11]

By mid-October 1883, it was clear that the priests' concentration on Iron Bull and their unique commitment to the Crow language was paying results. Completing their conversion of Iron Bull's band, they proceeded to Pretty Eagle – another Bighorn valley resident – and persuaded him and many of his

[9] See Prando to Cataldo, September 26, 1883, OPA, Gonzaga. In the fall of 1883, while the priests were in residence, Iron Bull was asked to participate in the ceremonies accompanying the completion of the Northern Pacific Railroad in Billings.
[10] Ibid.
[11] Prando to Cataldo, September 20, 1883, OPA, Gonzaga. Traditionally, songs were "owned" by individuals and were frequently obtained from visionary experiences. The priests' ability to both compose and share their songs probably had a significant impact on their hosts.

followers to join their congregation. As the bands began to disperse to their winter camps, the two men reported that the Indians were "beginning to show an enthusiasm for religion." Prando estimated on October 18 that "the number of baptized Crow is now 255."[12]

The relocation of Crow Agency to the Little Bighorn and Prando's temporary assignment elsewhere delayed the Jesuit return to the Crows until February 1887. When they reappeared, Iron Bull was gone, having died the previous year, and Barcelo, whose nervous personality had irritated Prando, was not present. The Mexican priest had opted for the nearly Northern Cheyenne Reservation where he died in 1888. Accompanying Prando this time was the musical Peter Bandini. The two Italian priests walked through deep snow drifts from Custer Station on the Little Bighorn, up the Bighorn valley to a spot near Pretty Eagle's cabin on Rotten Grass Creek where they pitched a tent in a small clearing and took up their work.

Coming as they did in the depths of winter, the priests must have been confident that their old friends among Iron Bull's and Pretty Eagle's bands would welcome them. The location of the new mission had been determined by the proximity of those two bands, as well as by the agent's desire to keep the Catholics away from the Little Bighorn. Despite the harsh weather, Prando and Bandini set to work gathering materials for a school and a chapel. Their school opened in October, and within a year the local agent reported the two priests "are rapidly increasing the capacity of their buildings and filling them with pupils." In the summer of 1889 the St. Xavier Mission had room for 150 pupils, three times the number that could be accommodated at Crow Agency.[13]

It seemed clear from the outset that tribal leaders in the Bighorn and Pryor districts saw good reasons to cooperate with the "black robes." Unless they were directly opposed, Father Prando and his colleagues were solicitous of local chiefs and headmen. Their goal, the historian of St. Xavier has written, was to make the mission a "model of a perfect Christian world built into one perfect Christian community – paradise regained." Agency policemen and soldiers could be summoned in an emergency, but the priests had long-term goals. They hoped that St. Xavier would function without external interference and that the community's children would gradually convert their parents. Local band leaders understood on their part that so long as they avoided direct

[12] Prando to Cataldo, October 18, 1883, OPA, Gonzaga.
[13] *ARCIA*, 1888 (Serial 2637), 153; see *ARCIA*, 1889 (Serial 2725), 225. Before his death, Barcelo had negotiated with Henry Armstrong for permission to settle on the Bighorn. Part of his difficulty in securing the government's approval was the prior assignment of the Crows to the Methodist church. Barcelo had to clarify that the old peace policy doctrines had been set aside and Indians were now available to all missionaries. See Watembach, "A Medieval Model of Church," 25–26, and Barcelo to Cataldo, September 7, 1884, Barcelo Correspondence, 1890–1894, Montana Historical Society, Helena, Montana.

confrontations with the priests, they could maintain their social standing and avoid any drastic changes in their daily habits.[14]

School attendance was an early topic of contention between local headmen and the priests. Fathers Prando and Bandini wanted Crow children for their school, and Bighorn residents complied, but only on the condition that they be allowed to camp nearby and visit regularly. Not only did this arrangement fulfill a natural desire to see and touch one's children, but it allowed parents and band leaders to monitor missionary conduct and keep their children close to home. It is no coincidence, for example, that reports from St. Xavier contain no reports of corporal punishment. It is also not surprising that Father Bandini would conclude in 1893 that "the only drawback to the learning of the children comes from their parents who do not yet appreciate the benefits of education. . . ."[15]

Crow parents and grandparents wanted time with their children and relief from the regimentation of a boarding school routine. The first they obtained quickly as the priests put aside one day a week for picnics, horseback rides and fishing. In addition, the director of the school began inviting parents to the school to hear students sing and recite. He noted proudly that parents attended these recitations "with evident signs of gratification and even delight." (The fact that parents were also fed at these gatherings no doubt added to their enthusiasm.) The priests' commitment to learning the Crow language and translating Christian rituals into Crow also ensured that students would retain their language and continue to use it when speaking to their parents or other elder kinsmen.

Tribal leaders in the Bighorn valley quickly learned to strike the pose of piety in order to win concessions from U.S. government officials. This approach was particularly effective when the local agent was at odds with the priests, for here a local chief could claim to be above the conflict and exempt from coercive action. In the summer of 1892, for example, Acting Agent C. H. Barstow ordered men from the Bighorn district to cut wood in the nearby mountains and haul it to Fort Custer. Apparently a majority of Bighorn residents refused "on account of Pretty Eagle telling them to move up to the mission." According to Pretty Eagle, Father Crimont, the director of the mission school, had called a week-long conference with the Indians. Agent Barstow confessed to be operating "somewhat blindly" in the face of this opposition, but he pleaded with the priest for assistance. In the end, the Indians did haul some wood, but the incident illustrated the variety of power sources on the reservation and the way a skillful leader could place himself between them for maximum advantage.[16]

Alternatively, local leaders were also ready to exact a price from the priests for their loyalty to the church. Plenty Coups, for example, refused baptism

[14] Watembach, "A Medieval Model of Church," 23.
[15] ARCIA, 1893 (Serial 3210), 181.
[16] C. H. Barstow to Fr. Crimont, June 21, 1892, Item 4, Box 16, RCIA-FRC, Seattle.

until late in his life, dangling this prize before the priests when he needed a favor or concession. At St. Xavier, Pretty Eagle regularly negotiated with school authorities over vacation schedules and the release of children who wished to return to their families.[17]

An illustration of the collaboration of Catholic missionaries and local leaders despite their divergent goals was the founding of St. Charles Mission at Pryor in 1893. Plenty Coups and a group of other leaders from Pryor came to St. Xavier first in 1891 to request a school. He wanted to avoid sending his community's children sixty miles away to the Crow Agency boarding school, and he was curious about the men who attached themselves so firmly to the people along the Bighorn. A church was started in Pryor that same year, and a school opened its doors in 1893. The children in Plenty Coups's district would no longer be shipped away to live in the dormitories at Crow Agency.[18]

The independence of Catholic schools appealed to leaders like Plenty Coups, but not to congressmen and senators. Hostile to Catholics in general, and determined to make the government's expanding federal school system work, Congress reduced, then ended, federal appropriations for sectarian institutions during the 1890s. Nevertheless, by the turn of the century the Catholic fathers had imposed their religious institutions on the Bighorn and Pryor districts and were seeking beachheads in the other three districts.

Many Crows saw the church as a potential protector against the authoritarian federal government and as an institution that might be integrated into their new lives. The priests' commitment to learning the Crow language was unique among all the missionaries and government officials then working on the reservation. Catholic Crows also appreciated the priests' effort to present the new faith in Indian terms. These efforts included equating religious medals with Indian medicine bundles and giving the newly baptized a Christian name just as young men often acquired new names in celebration of a successful hunt or raid. The most enthusiastic of the tribe's converts joined the "red gown" society, a lay organization, which organized major celebrations and assisted in worship services.[19]

Running parallel to the Catholic effort at St. Xavier and Pryor were the Protestant missions of the Little Bighorn. While initially less successful than the Catholics, these outposts also had a long-term impact on reservation life.

---

[17] See Watembach, "A Medieval Model of Church," 76–77 and 107.
[18] Ibid., 63–64; *ARCIA*, 1893 (Serial 3210), 181; *ARCIA*, 1894 (Serial 3306), 171.
[19] Watembach, "A Medieval Model of Church," 57 (baptism); 81 (Red Gowns); 111 (medicine bundles). The potency of the language issue was revealed in an angry letter Agent Wyman wrote to Washington in 1891, responding to a request from the priests at St. Xavier to hold Crow language services at the government boarding school. "If they are addressed in their own tongue on such an important subject and on such an important day as the sabbath," Wyman wrote, "it will be very detrimental to the efforts made in our schools to have only English spoken." Wyman to Commissioner of Indian Affairs, May 19, 1891, 11663–1891, LR-OIA, RG 75, NA.

While hampered by uncertain financial support and shifting personnel, the Protestants had the endorsement of the reservation agent and his corps of Indian policemen. Lessons in "moral conduct" could therefore be reinforced with government power.

Missionaries in the Little Bighorn valley were comfortable with the use of force because their principal concern was the transformation of individual behavior. While their Catholic colleagues were equally ready to use force when a confrontation arose, the Protestants believed Crow converts should abandon everything of their old life before they could embrace "civilization" and Christianity. A typical example of this approach was an agent's letter, dated July 15, 1889, which reported on Grey Blanket and another man who had gone to the mountains "to dream and make medicine." The men were arrested and confined to Fort Custer "for several days." Protestant missionaries and government officials cared neither to learn the Crow language nor to apply the principles of due process to such examples of "immoral" behavior.[20]

The first Protestant mission in the Little Bighorn was the Montana Industrial School, founded by a group of New England Unitarians who dispatched one of their number, Henry F. Bond, to the West in 1886. A veteran of forty years in the pulpit, Bond had served briefly as agent to the Colorado Utes between 1874 and 1876. By midsummer of 1886, the preacher had selected a site for his school at the lower end of the Bighorn valley, thirty miles from Crow Agency and far from any Indian camp. Construction began at once and the buildings were ready for students by November. With eastern boarding schools like Hampton and Carlisle in mind, Bond assured his Boston backers that his institution would "elevate the whole man." With one eye obviously fixed on the competition at St. Xavier, he declared "We do not expect or desire simply to lug the Indians into our church, and give them the name Christian before the reality can possibly exist."[21]

During its nine-year existence the Bond school struggled to bring a new "reality" to the Crow Reservation. Its harsh methods attracted few students. Its early scholars were either the mixed-blood children of white fathers and Indian mothers, or delivered to the schoolmasters by the Indian police. Moreover, the Unitarians remained aloof from reservation life. Bond gave in to local custom and allowed visiting parents to smoke on the school grounds, and he grudgingly agreed to feed parents who brought their children to him, but he never sought out the kind of alliance that the Jesuits enjoyed. His goal was to cut his charges off from their past and transform them into Christians. He declared in an 1890 report, for example, that "corporal punishment has always been forbidden," but he added that "shutting up, sending to bed, trying hands or feet together,

[20] M. P. Wyman to Commissioner of Indian Affairs, July 15, 1889, Item 2, Box 2, RCIA-FRC, Seattle.
[21] Marjorie Pease, A Worthy Work, 10, 11–12.

depriving of privileges have been tried, and latterly bread and water diet or some extra hard work have been resorted to."[22]

Bond was most successful with mixed-blood children. He hired George Pease from Lodge Grass to serve as an interpreter and recruiter, and Pease brought several of his Cooper relatives (including the teenaged Joe Cooper) to the school. These students could more easily be separated from camp life and would be more willing to comply with the school's requirement that "English speaking by the children is a rule rigidly insisted on." Despite its success with this group, however, the school was too small and too far from the centers of tribal population to survive. It never attracted more than fifty or sixty students. It was transferred to government control in 1895 and finally closed in 1897.[23]

The second Protestant effort in the Little Bighorn was launched by the American Missionary Association, which was granted land at Crow Agency in the summer of 1895. James Gregor Burgess arrived in 1896 and attempted to build a congregation among the students at the government boarding school and the Crow families who lived nearby. His close association with government officials, however, and his insistence on "civilized" dress and English-only services limited his followers to Indian Office employees and a few tribesmen who had become Christians while away at boarding school.

The most forceful source of Protestant teaching in the 1890s was the agency boarding school. When he inaugurated the Crow Agency facility in 1885, Agent Armstrong made it clear that Indian parents would be expected to surrender their children to him. "I have already notified several of the chiefs," he wrote that year, "that there would be no issue of annuity goods this fall until they gave us thirty children. . . ." Once surrendered, the children would have no contact with their homes. Vacations were brief, especially for older children. Every effort was made to urge children to live apart from their parents. The most extreme example of this attitude appeared in the reservation school superintendent's report for 1887. H. M. Beadle requested funds to erect a board fence around the school grounds to replace the wire mesh enclosure that still allowed parents camped nearly to "converse with the pupils."[24]

During the 1890s, most children were brought to the agency by force and subjected to a harsh disciplinary routine. Officially secular, the school did not

---

[22] For a description of the early recruits, see Pease, *A Worthy Work*, 13–14, 16, 20; *ARCIA*, 1890 (Serial 2841), 121. Another example of Bond's disinterest in forming alliances with local leaders can be found in his relationship to Sorrel Horse. In the fall of 1886, this band leader came to the school and promised to send his children there in exchange for food. Bond apparently did not agree to the proposal, for the children did not come, and five years later the missionary's successor was assured that the chief and a friend would "be punished for their conduct at your school." Wyman to A. A. Spence, April 8, 1891, Item 4, Box 15, RCIA-FRC, Seattle.

[23] On Pease and the Cooper children, see Pease, *A Worthy Work*, 20; on English, see *ARCIA*, 1891 (Serial 2934), 275; on closing, see *ARCIA*, 1895 (Serial 3382), 188.

[24] *ARCIA*, 1885 (Serial 2379), 348; *ARCIA*, 1887 (Serial 2542), 220.

maintain a missionary on its staff, but children were marched off to the Burgess church each Sunday, and the cultural lessons presented during services were reinforced by the government's schoolmasters during the week.[25]

In the decade following the agency's relocation to the Little Bighorn, Christianity was imposed on the Crows. Resident missionaries set up churches on their land, opened schools which their children were forced to attend and called on the entire community to adopt Christian standards of behavior and belief. Some tribal members – Bighorn residents and mixed bloods – willingly accepted the new teachings, but there is little evidence that Christianity won a broad following, or that its adherents rejected all their other gods when they accepted Jesus.

III

Following the turn of the century, there was a dramatic change in the religious atmosphere of the Crow Reservation. While the agency boarding school grew for a time, mission boarding schools declined in significance. With this loss of influence over Crow children (and their parents), the missions became less influential and their dreams of converting the Crows shrank correspondingly. At the same time, a small number of tribal dances and ceremonies formed themselves into a new annual cycle of traditional Crow cultural and religious activity. People in every district found ways of maintaining older practices without incurring the wrath of the agency police. And finally, a new religious movement associated with the peyote ceremony arrived at the Crow Reservation and won many adherents. By the early 1920s, the Christian sects which had imposed themselves on the tribe were battling for survival in a pluralistic religious arena.

Enrollment at the Catholic boarding school began to decline within a decade of its founding. Beginning in 1895, the Indian Office gradually reversed its long-standing practice of paying religious organizations on a per capita basis to educate children on reservations, and this loss of support doomed the Jesuits' ambitious plans. From a peak of 175 students in 1891, St. Xavier's enrollment fell to 68 in 1903, the year the mission lost its federal subsidy. The Bond school also cited financial problems when it shifted to government control, but there was more to these two failures than dollars. Parents resisted sending their children away to school, fearing both disease and the alienation which was sure to result from a Christian education. "The Crows are bitterly opposed to sending their children to school," agent John Edwards wrote in 1897, "and they invent all

[25] *ARCIA*, 1890 (Serial 2841), 120 (on prohibition against tribal dancing); *ARCIA*, 1892 (Serial 2953), 289 (on vacations); *ARCIA*, 1897 (Serial 3641), 166 (on Sunday school attendance and enrollment of students by force).

kinds of excuses to get the children out or to keep them from sending them to school."[26]

Another perspective on boarding schools is provided by a remarkable letter written to Plenty Coups in early 1905 by Holds The Enemy, the outspoken son of Pretty Eagle who had been an early supporter of the St. Xavier Mission. Acknowledging the Pryor chief's growing prominence in the Crows' dealings with the U.S. government, Holds The Enemy urged Plenty Coups to "talk about" his concerns with the authorities. The younger man declared, "this mission school is no good." He continued:

> The only good thing of them is they feed the children well. That is alright. The rest they are no good. They want to pray so much that they keep me from not [sic] dancing. When they are sick he keeps them until they are very bad and he gives them back but they do not get well.

The delicate negotiations of the 1880s had given way to heavy-handed authoritarianism, and leaders like Holds The Enemy could no longer see an advantage in supporting the Jesuits' work.[27]

Ironically, the one successful mission of the early twentieth century, the Baptist church in Lodge Grass, owed its success to the Crows' adamant opposition to boarding schools. In 1902, the Indian Office began constructing a new boarding school at Pryor Creek to replace the Catholic mission which would soon lose its subsidy. No such plans were under way for Lodge Grass, however, and it seemed clear to parents in the upper end of the Little Bighorn that their children were bound to attend the soon to be expanded institution at the reservation headquarters. Perhaps this is why the delegation from Lodge Grass which travelled to Sheridan, Wyoming, in the summer of 1903 called for the establishment of a mission and a day school in their community.

Rev. William A. Petzoldt undoubtedly came to Lodge Grass in the winter of 1903–4 for religious reasons, but when he opened a mission that included a day school for the Crows in September 1904, he was offering tribesmen their first opportunity to have their children educated while living at home. The formula proved popular. Three years later another Baptist day school opened at Pryor. The new Wyola district established a third branch of the mission in 1910, and

---

[26] *ARCIA*, 1897 (Serial 3641), 164; for school attendance figures, see *ARCIA*, 1891 (Serial 2934), 275; *ARCIA*, 1903 (Serial 4645–5, 4646–5), 190–191. The Catholics held themselves aloof from the agency, but they did turn to the tribal police to assist in capturing escaped students. See Watembach, "A Medieval Model of Church," 76.

In the summer of 1904 the Crow agent wrote to the superintendent of Carlisle that he had no students to send East. "Our reservation schools have been depleted in the past by a custom that was in vogue here of marrying off the school girls at the age of 13 and allowing the boys at 15 and 16 to leave school on the pretext of helping their parents in their farm work." Reynolds to Captain W. A. Mercer, August 19, 1904, Item 4, Box 23, RCIA-FRC, Seattle.

[27] Holds The Enemy to Plenty Coups, February, 1905, Plenty Coups Papers, Plenty Coups Museum, Pryor, Montana.

a Bighorn outpost was established in 1917. Petzoldt's approach was so successful that when the Congregational missionary at Crow Agency died in 1921, his
church, together with its subsidiaries at Black Lodge and Reno, was acquired by
the Baptists. The Catholics, too, were impressed with this growth. They opened
their own day school at Lodge Grass in 1911 and another on the upper end of
the Bighorn valley in 1920. As these schools expanded, enrollment at the
reservation boarding schools dropped. In the fall of 1917, for example, only 41
of the 100 spaces at the Crow Agency boarding school were taken.[28]

This proliferation of day schools did not occur without conflict. Petzoldt
resisted Catholic forays into Lodge Grass to recruit students, and he lost no
opportunity to lure parishioners from St. Xavier into his church. The rivalry
between the two groups reached a peak in the fall of 1917 when the Baptist day
school opened ten miles upriver from St. Xavier. Oscar Lipps, a veteran government investigator found that 16 of the new school's 21 students had spent
the previous school year with the Jesuits. Lipps reported that "the Indians had
held a big meeting and had renounced the Catholic faith and agreed to leave the
church and join the Baptist church." He added that area residents "wanted to
get from under the domination of the government and of the Catholic priests."
Not surprisingly, Petzoldt defended his action by claiming that he had acted "in
response to the popular demand of the Indians themselves. . . ."[29]

The success of the Petzoldt mission meant that there would be two formidable Christian outposts on the reservation. By 1904, when the Lodge Grass day
school opened, St. Xavier had been a community center for nearly a generation.
Its lay organizations and its round of religious holidays and community activities formed an important part of social life in the Bighorn valley. Similarly, as
the Baptist day schools spread across the reservation, they also became social
centers for the families who brought their children in to be educated. Neither
group would succeed in turning "the Crows into doves" as Father Prando had
envisioned without coming into conflict with the other. "As it is," wrote Lipps,
"there is only strife, dissension and bitter feeling where the truly Christian
spirit should prevail. As long as present conditions continue, none of the schools
can do their best work."[30]

As the competition between Christian groups accelerated, there appeared to

[28] For a sketch of Lodge Grass Baptist history, see Joe Medicine Crow, "80 Years Along the Jesus
Road," n.p., October 14, 1984, copy in Medicine Crow Papers, Little Big Horn College Archives, Crow Agency, Montana. For the timing of Catholic day schools, see Watembach, "A
Medieval Model of Church," 160–170. An indication of the enthusiasm Lodge Grass people felt
for the day school is the report of the district's first field matron, written at the end of the
school's first year. Jeanette Woodruff reported that children "gathered around the school house
shortly after six o'clock in the morning." Jeanette Woodruff to Commissioner of Indian Affairs,
August 15, 1905, Item 2, Box 7, RCIA-FRC, Seattle.
[29] See Oscar Lipps to Commissioner of Indian Affairs, September 21, 1917, Item 15, Box 60,
Inspector's Reports, 1917–1923, RCIA-FRC, Seattle.
[30] Lipps to Commissioner of Indian Affairs, September 21, 1917.

be a corresponding increase in public expressions of traditional Crow beliefs. The reasons for this are unclear. Perhaps the controls over tribal life were slackened as missionaries trimmed their ambitions. Perhaps individuals who survived the terrible population losses of the 1880s and 1890s gained new confidence after 1900 as district communities took shape and the death rate began to decline. Or perhaps what appears to be a rebirth of traditional culture in the early twentieth century is only a reflection of improved government vigilance – perhaps these activities had continued throughout the reservation era, but were only reported in the twentieth century when government agents began monitoring the details of tribal life. At any rate, a wide variety of activities, from social gatherings to religious ceremonies appear in the written records of the early twentieth century, suggesting a revival of faith in Crow traditions.

In the increasingly authoritarian atmosphere of the reservation, one important influence on tribal behavior was the attitude of government officials. These men strictly prohibited activities such as vision quests and sun dances, which they could identify as religious. In 1914, agent W. W. Scott even turned down Berkeley anthropologist Robert Lowie's request for a reenactment of a sun dance, declaring that such "scientists, naturalists, historians and other kinds of fakirs . . . want to see the Indian as he was and not as he is." Nevertheless, Scott and his fellow agents were willing to allow gatherings they considered purely "social." Crow leaders, in turn, were quick to exploit this exception, arguing that their dances and ceremonies were "innocent" and did not challenge their adherence to Christianity or their loyalty to the United States.[31]

Less than three years after Sword Bearer was gunned down on the banks of the Little Bighorn, Henry Williamson's gruff replacement, Agent M. P. Wyman, invited the commander at Fort Custer to Crow Agency for a Fourth of July parade. Wyman promised that the Crows would "be out in full dress." The parade would be led by the agency police (including Captain Boy That Grabs and officer Fire Bear) and would march from "the camp" across the Little Bighorn through the agency compound, in front of the agent's quarters and back across the river. Wyman's letter made it clear, however, that this peaceful reenactment of Sword Bear's ride was only the beginning of the day's events. "After the procession returns to the camp," he added, "there will be a grand dance by nearly all of the adult Indians." Following the dance, "there will be horse racing by Indians and any others who may desire to participate." Urging the commander to attend, the enthusiastic Agent Wyman closed with an ironic question: "Do you expect to bring any artillery with you . . . ?[32]

---

[31] Agent's Annual Narrative and Statistical Report, Crow Agency, 1914.
[32] M. P. Wyman to General James Brisbin, July 2, 1890, Item 4, Box 14, RCIA-FRC, Seattle. The following year Wyman's letter promised "sham battles" and "other amusements" in addition to dancing and horse racing. Wyman to Col. A. K. Arnold, June 29, 1891, Item 4, Box 15, RCIA-FRC, Seattle.

Officially sanctioned events of this kind made it clear to the Crows that community gatherings and traditional dancing would not be disrupted if they coincided with an American holiday. With the assurance that events were secular, or that they corresponded to some aspect of "civilized" life, government officials and most missionaries would approve of them and find them mildly interesting. The Fourth of July quickly became a fixture in the reservation calendar, with Indians in each district gathering for several days to dance and visit. In the fall, communities often gathered first in October to celebrate the harvest (no matter how meager the crop) and then again in November for Thanksgiving.

In December, Christmas and the coming of the new year usually meant that dances would take place for over a week. Tribal policemen were frequently ordered to break up dances that went beyond the limits set by the agent, but his rules were often difficult to enforce. On Christmas Eve, 1903, for example, Agent Samuel Reynolds wrote the subagent at Pryor that he had just learned the Crows in his district were planning to dance for ten days. "I hardly believe this is true," exploded Reynolds from his desk sixty miles away. "I hope that you will see your Indians quit by Sunday, and see that they go to their homes," he added. Nevertheless, it is difficult to imagine how his lieutenant could have enforced the order. Three years later Reynolds replied to an inquiry regarding the Crow celebration of Christmas with disgust: "Our Indians have usually spent their Christmas holidays in dancing and feasting. They have no more conception of what the day means than they have of their Fourth of July. . . ."[33]

Among the other holidays where dancing was allowed were George Washington's birthday, Easter, the onset of the spring planting season, and Decoration Day. In addition to these eight holidays, prominent leaders such as Plenty Coups and Pretty Eagle were occasionally granted permission to host a dance in their district or to visit another district where a dance would be held in their honor. As with the rules governing the celebration of holidays, however, the decisions of these peaceful but determined leaders were often difficult to contradict. For example, in the summer of 1903 the clerk at Crow Agency wrote to the subagent in the Bighorn valley that Pretty Eagle had just told him that the agent – who was away for a few days – had promised the chief "a dance. . . . I

---

[33] Samuel Reynolds to J. P. Van Hoose, December 24, 1903, Item 5, Box 29; and Reynolds to Commissioner of Indian Affairs, March 13, 1906, Item 2, Box 7; both in RCIA-FRC, Seattle. The persistence of the Christmas celebrations can be observed in Reynolds to "The Farmers" December 1, 1909, Item 5, Box 29; and Field Matron's Report, Lodge Grass, December 29, 1923, Item 16, Box 109, file 140; both in RCIA-FRC, Seattle. The field matron wrote, "The Indians are camping at St. Xavier and Black Lodge in spite of the fact that the weather at this time of year is never favorable for camping and when they know there is always sickness and death among the small children and babies and all get colds and bronchial trouble that usually last till spring or becomes chronic and tuberculosis."

leave the matter entirely to your judgement," the clerk wrote, "as I have not been instructed in the matter."[34]

The content of these district celebrations is difficult to reconstruct from government records, but it is clear that they were not all the same. They all involved drumming, singing and the wearing of traditional costumes. They generally lasted several days and involved assembling and feeding large groups of people. But each dance had a specific focus and was hosted by a different group of sponsors. Agent Samuel Reynolds, who frequently told his superiors that he had the "dance craze" under control, described the main groups in a 1909 letter to headquarters. He reported that the Crow dances "are the tobacco dance, the owl dance, the buck dance and the gift dance." While other activities may have been added to this basic list, it represents the essential repertoire of tribal ceremonies in the early twentieth century.[35]

Anthropologist Robert H. Lowie began conducting field research among the Crows in the summer of 1907. He lived with the German-speaking station master at Lodge Grass, but spent his days travelling the reservation, interviewing men and women about their traditions. He described the owl dance as a "purely social dance" which the Crows acquired from Plains Indian neighbors. In the dance a group of drummers was encircled by two concentric groups of men and women. Men would select a partner and the two would dance "in a clockwise glide" with their hands around each other's waists. "I consider it the most harmful of any of the dances," Agent Reynolds reported.[36]

What Reynolds called the "buck dance" was probably what Lowie and other observers called the "hot dance," a men's dance which other Plains tribes called the "grass dance" or "Omaha dance." While it was reserved for men and controlled by a group of four societies, the hot dance was the centerpiece for gatherings involving the entire community. Membership in the hot dance societies was open to all men, but acquisition of the proper regalia required "gifts" to senior members. Once admitted to a club, individuals were expected to treat their fellow members generously. "The four modern clubs were largely mutual benefit organizations," Lowie wrote. "If anyone had to do a certain amount of work on his farm land, all his associates came to help him."[37]

The Crows apparently learned the hot dance from their old kinsmen the Hidatsa sometime in the late nineteenth century, so it was not strictly a "religious"

[34] Fred Miller to Connolly, July 25, 1903, Item 5, Box 28, RCIA-FRC, Seattle. In 1924, a district subagent wrote from Lodge Grass that "the Indians put in five days counting Sunday in their celebration of decoration day. They did not decorate anything except themselves with paint and feathers." See Farmer's Weekly Report, Lodge Grass, June 7, 1924, Item 15, Box 86, RCIA-FRC, Seattle.

[35] Samuel Reynolds to Commissioner of Indian Affairs, September 6, 1909, Item 2, Box 8, RCIA-FRC, Seattle.

[36] Lowie, The Crow Indians, 93; Reynolds to Commissioner, September 6, 1909.

[37] Lowie, The Crow Indians, 208.

event. Nevertheless, the dance involved a hierarchy of officers, the playing of a sacred drum and, according to Lowie, the ritual eating of ceremonially prepared dogs. Performed by men in a specially prepared lodge, the hot dance appeared to be a completely pacific celebration of male leadership. Men were center stage and unarmed. "What impressed me particularly in the hot dance performance," Lowie wrote of a ceremony he witnessed in 1910, "was the lavish generosity with which members gave away property of all kinds to aged and destitute tribesmen, or to alien visitors. . . . I once saw a man strip himself to his gee-string before a large crowd, giving away all his clothing."[38]

Acts of generosity were also the focus of other dances observed by government agents. These were likely giveaways of food or goods sponsored by individuals to honor a special event or a departed family member. (Such occasions also provided an opportunity for families to supply food and gifts to less well-off kinsmen.) Not surprisingly, agents like Samuel Reynolds, who were horrified by the idea of hard-earned cash and government-issued property being given away, made frequent attempts to ban the practice. (Reynolds reported in 1909 that the gift dance was "done away with entirely.") Nevertheless, it persisted. The subagent at Pryor wrote in the fall of 1923, for example, that a delegation from the Bighorn had recently arrived for a visit. Their hosts celebrated for a week, he wrote, "and these Indians gave away practically all of their horses. This is, of course, one of the old Indian customs . . . It seems to have an intoxicating effect on them when they begin to give things away and they do not seem to know when to stop. . . ."[39]

In memoirs published late in his life, Tom Yellowtail recalled the rise of what he called "pow-wow dancing" in the years before World War I. While noting that these dances became popular "in place of our sacred dance ceremonies," Yellowtail noted that most of the "old warriors" participated in them and that the "special pipe ceremonies and prayers were always observed." In the 1920s Yellowtail and several friends formed a dance society devoted to reviving older Crow dances, and he believed it encouraged others to explore the tribe's traditions. The lesson of this effort, Yellowtail later mused, was that "Indians have many things that are so much better than anything the white man has. They can really be uplifted by their own sacred things, but they do not seem to realize it."[40]

While dancing and dance societies were the most prominent form of traditional cultural expression during the early twentieth century, they frequently

[38] Ibid., 209.

[39] Reynolds to Commissioner, September 6, 1909; Farmer's Weekly Report, November 19 to 24, 1923, Pryor District, Item 15, Box 86, 139F. Both RCIA-FRC, Seattle. The modern giveaway is described in Rodney Frey, *The World of the Crow Indians: As Driftwood Lodges* (Norman, University of Oklahoma Press, 1987), 46–48.

[40] Michael Oren Fitzgerald, *Yellowtail: Crow Medicine Man and Sun Dance Chief* (Norman: University of Oklahoma Press, 1991), 25, 28.

inspired participation in other Crow traditions. The hand game, a traditional guessing game involving drumming, singing and winning with "strong medicine," was often played when groups of families gathered together in the winter. These contests frequently involved betting and were therefore frowned upon unless organizers could show the authorities that the teams were playing for honor and prestige rather than dollars. In the summer, horse racing would take the place of the hand game, prompting similar assurances that the contestants were simply curious as to the speed of their horses. Traditional mourning practices involving self-mutilation and healing ceremonies which contradicted modern medicine were a feature of district gatherings and frequently were condemned by the authorities. Plenty Coups himself was accused by the Pryor subagent of being "one of the greatest advocates of the Indian medicine stuff" in 1923 and threatened with punishment.[41]

IV

For the Crows who came of age in the early twentieth century, the ceremonial complex Agent Reynolds called "the tobacco dance" was probably the most important ritual practiced on the reservation. The cultivation and harvesting of a rare variety of tobacco had of course played a central role in tribal life in the nineteenth century. Frequently noted by travellers, the ritual had been carried out under the direction of the Tobacco Society, which maintained a number of chapters and contained a broad membership drawn from each of the tribe's bands and clans. The survival of the ceremony into the twentieth century was an achievement in itself, but equally important was the symbolic place tobacco planting maintained in the minds of the Crows. Medicine Crow, the young band leader who had settled at Lodge Grass in 1884, told anthropologist Robert Lowie that the sacred tobacco was the tribe's "means of living."[42]

During his summers at Lodge Grass, Robert Lowie spoke to a number of

[41] For a long discussion of the evils of the hand game, see Sam Lapointe to C. H. Asbury, March 1, 1922, Item 15, Box 83, File 131; for mourning practices, see Farmer's Weekly Report, Pryor, April 16 to 21, 1923, Item 15, Box 86, 139F; for accusation levied against Plenty Coups, see Farmer's Weekly Report, Pryor, January 29 to February 3, 1923; all in RCIA-FRC, Seattle. The way these activities were connected to community gatherings was made clear by the Big Horn subagent's report for April 1923. He wrote that "the Catholics were celebrating Easter week and most of the Indians were camped around the church attending services during the day and dancing and playing hand games at night." Farmer's Weekly Report, Big Horn, April 7, 1923, Item 15, Box 86, File 139, RCIA-FRC, Seattle. Plenty Coups and other leaders also enjoyed the excitement of horse racing. In fact the Pryor leader maintained a race track near his home. See F. H. Abbott to Plenty Coups, October 23, 1909, Plenty Coups Papers, Plenty Coups Museum, Pryor, Montana.

[42] See Peter Nabokov, "Cultivating Themselves: The Interplay of Crow Religion and History," (Ph.D. Dissertation, University of California, Berkeley, 1988), 395. For a chronicle of nineteenth-century references to tobacco planting, see ibid., 349–351 and chapter 14.

Crow men and women about the Tobacco Society. While the anthropologist found variations in some of their accounts, he wrote later that "there is a quite general consensus of opinion . . . that in early times the membership of the society was small and that older people predominated." This situation had changed dramatically in recent years, he was told: "More and more people joined, so that about 1910 perhaps a majority of the Indians, even young people, were members." Lowie counted thirty chapters of the society on the reservation, but he noted this number frequently changed as groups merged and split from one another. Among the most important were the strawberry chapter (centered in Lodge Grass and led by Medicine Crow and Old Dog), the weasel chapter in Pryor (reportedly led by Sword Bearer's sister, Muskrat, and which counted Gray Bull, Bell Rock and Lowie's principal informant, James Carpenter, among its members), the yellow tobacco chapter (with members like Shot In The Hand from Bighorn) and the otter chapter, which Crazy Head had joined when he returned from his imprisonment at Fort Snelling in 1888.[43]

Because the Tobacco Society was growing so rapidly in the first decades of the twentieth century, adoption – the process by which members brought outsiders into the organization – had come to figure prominently in its activities. Adoption involved a series of winter rituals and "song-givings" in which couples were trained for their summer initiation. Sometime early in the twentieth century, the latter event came to be performed during Fourth of July festivities. Agents like Samuel Reynolds who wanted to control Crow "dancing" usually were unaware that the "interesting" Indian celebrations of American independence held each summer were actually designed to add members to an ancient tribal order, and that there was a connection between these "approved" activities and the winter dances the government tried so often to suppress.[44]

It is not difficult to imagine the urgency with which Tobacco Society members carried out their duties. Struggling to sustain their communities in the face of disease and relocation, eager to match the successes of rival chapters and convinced that broad membership would build strong bonds between tribesmen, members drew newcomers to their winter adoption dances and the summer ceremonies. With similar motives, initiates in the society would flock to the adoptions, happy to be included in this most distinctive of tribal rituals. One example of the latter case is suggested by an agent's response to a petition from one Sebastian Bear Claw, who requested release from the agency guard house so that he could nurse his sick mother. Agent Asbury responded: "Reliably informed mother was not ill. Was going to hold a tobacco dance at

---

[43] Robert H. Lowie, "The Crow Tobacco Society," *Anthropological Papers of the American Museum of Natural History*, 21 (1924), 135.

[44] Lowie, *The Crow Indians*, 279–280; "The Tobacco Society of the Crows," 195. Fred Miller called the tobacco ritual "interesting" in Fred Miller to Charles D. Curtis, February 23, 1903, Item 4, Box 22, RCIA-FRC, Seattle.

Photographer Richard Throssel reported that these men and women seated around a fire inside a large, ceremonial tipi were mixing tobacco seeds in preparation for the Tobacco Society's spring planting ritual. The stakes to the right of the fire may be emblems of various Tobacco Society chapters. Courtesy of American Heritage Center, University of Wyoming.

which Sebastian was to be a leading character. Sebastian was not permitted to go."[45]

Regular references to Tobacco Society activities in the written record, together with the fact that the society has survived to the present day, make it clear that the group continued through the early reservation era. On the other hand, there is very little information available about the details of the group's activities. The Crows themselves saw no reason to publicize the society, and the agents' files usually contain little more than letters claiming that the dance had been suppressed. One exception to this pattern is a rich trove of correspondence which passed between Crow Agency and the Pryor substation during the winter of 1922–3. It offers a glimpse of how deeply the tobacco adoption rituals

[45] Cope to Asbury, December 9, 1920, Item 15, Box 80, File 125, RCIA-FRC, Seattle (agent's comment was written across the top of the letter). Another account of official opposition to the tobacco society can be found in testimony taken at Crow Agency in 1910 in which Curley and Sees With His Ears were most outspoken. See Central Classified Files, Crow, 150, file 18844–1910, LR-OIA, RG 75, NA.

affected this community and how difficult it was for even the most determined federal agent to stop them.

In the fall of 1922, Sam Lapointe, an Indian boarding school graduate from the Rosebud Sioux Reservation, was serving as the subagent or district farmer for the Pryor district. In late November he reported to headquarters that 23 families were camped at the most remote end of Pryor canyon. "They claim they are there getting out wood for the winter," Lapointe wrote, but actually the camp "was being maintained by the faction known here as the 'Catholic Indians'. . . . This camp has been there the most of this fall and we have been trying to break it up and send them home." The subagent reported that he had issued an order for the camp to move and returned the next day to find that the group had "simply moved to another site." Even though he had only one policeman assigned to his district, Lapointe pledged that he would "break up this camp if it is the last act of my life." To this Christian Indian the gathering was a beacon of immorality:

> Beaver Dances, sort of an animal worship dance, have been danced four or five nights a week . . . Gambling games have been going on night after night up at this camp, and when asked in regard to the games they all deny that any such games have been carried on. But it is a known fact that last week for five nights steady this game of "Hand Game" was played.[46]

Perhaps this group attended the Catholic church in Pryor, or perhaps they simply opposed the recently arrived Baptists. Lapointe did not explain his label, but the "Catholics" were clearly a social division within the community rather than a purely Christian group. The local priests opposed the Tobacco Society's activities as well as gambling games.

Two weeks later on December 4, Lapointe reported that he had broken up the camp and sent everyone home. At Christmas the group had reassembled, however, and doubled in size as the Baptists staged their own dances and celebrations. "The Baptist people had several days and nights of it," he wrote "and the Catholic Indians had a whole solid week of beaver dances and camping for their celebration. I think according to what I hear today they are still celebrating." The enthusiasm apparently persisted, for three apparently Baptist Indians from Pryor – Annie Big Day, Emma Bellrock and Austin Lion Shows – wrote the agent in February asking him to stop the "traveling around one house to another for beaver dancing. . . ." Their protests, together with Sam Lapointe's repeated threats against the group, finally brought a response from the community's unofficial leader, Plenty Coups.[47]

---

[46] Farmer's Weekly Report, November 20 to 25, 1922, Item 15, Box 86, Folder 139, RCIA-FRC, Seattle. For a description of the beaver dance, compiled during the 1920s, see Leslie B. Davis, *Lifeways of Intermontane and Plains Montana Indians in Honor of J. Verne Dusenberry*, Occasional Papers of the Museum of the Rockies, No. 1 (Bozeman: Montana State University, 1979), 43–56.

[47] Farmer's Weekly Report, December 25 to 30, 1922, Item 15, Box 86, and Annie Big Day, Emma Bellrock and Austin Lion Shows to Asbury, February 28, 1923, Item 15, Box 83, both in RCIA-FRC, Seattle.

"The old people have only one dance left," the seventy-three-year-old chief wrote, "and that is the 'Beaver Dance' and we do not ask the younger people to take part in this dance, but it is the only dance of our fathers left to us and that is about all the enjoyment the older Indians have." Plenty Coups closed with the surprising (and probably duplicitous) statement that he was "satisfied" with Sam Lapointe's performance as subagent. He had clashed with the stiff-necked farmer on a number of occasions, but he suggested here that he would cooperate with Lapointe if the policemen would leave his dancers alone.[48]

Agent Asbury's response to Plenty Coups took up the chief's diplomatic tone. Pointedly listing the subagent as the recipient of a carbon copy, Asbury agreed that if the dance were performed by "older people" who got together once a week on weekends "so that it does not interfere with the school," there would be no reason to stop it. "We do not object to recreation," he told the old man. Sam Lapointe was furious. "Call it a recreation or anything you may wish," he wrote in his next report to Asbury; "it is at best a very bad habit." He added:

> Can we Christianize a man by preaching Mohammedanism to him? No more can we civilize these Indians by allowing paganism and heathenish dances to prevail. . . . My special objection to these dances is the so-called "Beaver Dance" which is purely a religious animal worship dance and they are adopting our school children into this dance every time they dance it. . . .

The agent's willingness to allow "recreation" at Pryor was an admission that he could not control every aspect of Crow life. It was also an opening for tribal leaders. As with the celebration of national holidays, the argument that a ceremony was "recreational" would qualify it as "harmless" and permissible. "I do not feel that an Indian dance which is free from immoral and licentious features is necessarily any worse than a white person's dance," Asbury wrote.[49]

Not surprisingly, reports from Pryor continued to mention beaver dances and Tobacco Society activities. At the end of June 1924, one year after Lapointe's campaign against the "Catholic" camp, he wrote that "practically all the Indians of this reservation came by the latter part of the week and are camping on Plum creek." As the Fourth of July public adoption ceremonies drew near, no doubt tobacco society chapters from across Crow country had converged on the Pryor district.[50]

The persistence of various forms of traditional cultural expression gives

[48] Plenty Coups to C. H. Asbury, Item 15, Box 83, File 131, RCIA-FRC, Seattle.
[49] C. H. Asbury to Chief Plenty Coos (*sic*), February 26, 1923, Item 15, Box 83, File 131, 1918–1923; Farmer's Weekly Report, March 5 to 10, 1923, Item 15, Box 86, File 139; C. H. Asbury to Sam Lapointe, February 26, 1923, Item 15, Box 83, File 131, 1918–1923; all in RCIA-FRC, Seattle.
[50] Farmer's Weekly Report, June 23 to 28, 1924, Item 15, Box 87, File 139, RCIA-FRC, Seattle.

This 1908 photograph shows a group of families gathered in camp for a giveaway, the distribution of food and household goods that Crows organized to honor a relative or mark an important event. The woman standing in the doorway of her tipi to the left may be the focus of the ceremony. Courtesy of American Heritage Center, University of Wyoming.

evidence of remarkable determination on the part of Tobacco Society leaders, hot dance organizers and others, but it also reveals a shifting dynamic in the religious life of the Crow community. Physically unable to monitor all aspect of Crow life, and lacking a single Christian sect which might enforce a new moral code on the tribe, tribal agents and district farmers were forced to recognize that the reservation contained a variety of religious and quasi-religious groups. Perhaps the most vivid example of this reality is a letter addressed to Austin Lion Shows from the Pryor subagent barely a year after Lion Shows had written to Agent Asbury condemning the beaver dances taking place in his district. "I understand there was a dance at your place last night," the subagent wrote, "as there has been every night for some time . . . It seems hard to believe that such a thing would be possible in a Christian land and among Christian men and women as you all profess to be."[51]

[51] R. C. Holgate to Austin Lion Shows, December 30, 1924, Item 15, Box 83, File 131, 26–1924, RCIA-FRC, Seattle. Holgate, a physician, succeeded Lapointe as Pryor subagent during 1923.

Situations such as these made it clear that traditional cultural expressions would continue despite the arrival of Christianity on the reservation. The Pryor subagent's closing lines to Lion Shows also indicate that the government had no choice but to exercise a degree of tolerance. Warning that "some action" would have to be taken to avoid having his dances "suppressed by law," he allowed that "you may have dances on *Friday* and *Saturday* nights *but on no other nights of the week*." The letter follows precisely the tone of another letter, written a decade earlier, in which a Crow agent had defended his tolerance of traditional gatherings. "It has always seemed to me," W. W. Scott wrote in the winter of 1912, "that to prohibit the dances entirely would be arbitrary and even unjust to the Indians. . . ."[52]

The peyote ritual, which was introduced onto the Crow Reservation in 1910, formed the final element in the tribe's emerging religious diversity. Used for centuries in the lower Rio Grande valley, the peyote cactus (*Lophophora williamsii*) was introduced to the Cheyennes and Comanches of Oklahoma in the 1880s. There it formed a basic part of a new ceremony that combined elements of Christianity and traditional Indian religious practice. The ritual took place at small meetings where communicants gathered under the direction of a "roadman" to sing and pray to Jesus, God and the peyote itself. Consuming the peyote plant might produce individual visions, but its essential function was, in the words of a modern scholar, to stimulate "religious feeling and a sense of good fellowship and group respect and understanding."[53]

According to anthropologist Omer Stewart, Leonard Tyler, a Cheyenne graduate of Carlisle and a devoted follower of the peyote ritual, carried the ceremony from the Southern Cheyennes in Oklahoma to the Northern Cheyennes in Montana sometime in the 1890s. It was during this same period that peyotism was first observed in the Great Lakes, the Southwest and on the Canadian plains. While Frank Bethune, a successful mixed-blood farmer from the Reno district, is generally credited with bringing the ceremony from the Northern Cheyennes to the Crows in 1910, he and his colleagues did not attract the notice of the Indian Office until 1918 when agent Asbury reported that "the use of peyote is just being started on this reservation."[54]

Less than four years after this first official notice, however, Asbury concluded that "the use of peyote has gained considerable foothold among the

[52] Holgate to Austin Lion Shows, December 30, 1924, emphasis in original; W. W. Scott to Commissioner of Indian Affairs, December 24, 1912, Item 14, Box 54, RCIA-FRC, Seattle.

[53] Omer C. Stewart, "Peyotism in Montana," *Montana: The Magazine of Western History*, 33, 2 (Spring 1983), 5. For a fuller history of the religion, see Omer Stewart, *The Peyote Religion* (Norman: University of Oklahoma Press, 1987).

[54] Asbury to H. A. Larsen, November 13, 1918, Item 15, Box 79, File 122-2, Peyote, RCIA-FRC, Seattle. For the story of Bethune's role, see Stewart, "Peyotism in Montana," 7. Asbury later wrote that he thought peyote had been introduced "about 1912." See Asbury to Ruch Shonle, September 17, 1923, Item 15, Box 79, File 122-2, Peyote, RCIA-FRC, Seattle.

Crows." Reports of peyote use were coming in from every district on the reservation. As one might expect, it appears to have begun in the Little Bighorn (closest to the Northern Cheyennes) and moved quickly west. In the spring of 1919, the subagent at Lodge Grass reported that thirty-five people (fifteen of them Cheyennes) had recently gathered at the home of Tom Stewart for an all-night session. At the same time, the subagent in the Bighorn valley was sure that "the peyote has not got over on the Bighorn," and his counterpart at Pryor noted that "the Indians at the Pryor district do not use it."[55]

While missionaries condemned the early peyote activists as "indolent, unprogressive, reactionary and of shady character," the ritual seems to have appealed first to educated young men, many of them mixed bloods, and to have been opposed most firmly by the older generation of tribal leaders. This na-tional pattern was apparent among the Crows. Among the early supporters of peyote were Ralph Saco and Sits Down Spotted in the Bighorn district, Tom Stewart and Joe Cooper at Lodge Grass, Louis Bompard at Black Lodge and Bethune at Reno. Each of these men had identified themselves as Christians and were active farmers. All but Sits Down Spotted had been educated in government or mission schools. (Stewart's father had served as the interpreter for the Crow leaders who travelled to Washington, D.C., in 1880 and been present at the agency when Sword Bearer made his "raid" there seven years later.) Plenty Coups was the most outspoken opponent of the new faith, but Holds The Enemy, Big Medicine (a tribal policeman) and Bellrock also signed petitions calling for the prohibition of the peyote cactus. While they divided on political issues, these four older men found the new movement (and its leaders) equally threatening to their authority and standing within the tribe.[56]

Believing peyote to be an addictive drug, government agents struggled to eradicate it as soon as it appeared. Unfortunately for them, however, high-speed rail service and parcel post delivery made shipment of the cactus from Texas and Oklahoma to Montana a simple operation. Crow Agent Calvin Asbury was a determined opponent of this practice. In 1920, he met with South Dakota Congressman Henry L. Gandy, the chief sponsor of the first federal proposal to ban the interstate shipment of peyote, and in succeeding years he lobbied hard

---

[55] Asbury to M. K. Sniffen, July 26, 1922, Item 15, Box 79, Peyote; Asbury to Commissioner of Indian Affairs, Response to Circular, April 1919, Item 15, Box 79, File 122–2, Peyote; all in RCIA-FRC, Seattle.

[56] W. A. Petzoldt to Asbury, April 18, 1919; for peyotists, see "Peyote Party at St. Xavier"; Barney Old Coyote to Asbury, February 28, 1922; all filed in Item 15, Box 79, File 122–2, Peyote. Statements by Big Medicine and Plenty Coups which essentially repeat the government's oppo-sition to peyote can be found in Big Medicine to Secretary of the Interior, February 24, 1921; and "The Pryor District Crow Indian Council Resolution, February 12, 1921, both in Item 15, Box 79, Peyote. For James Carpenter's involvement, see Cope to Asbury, February 13, 1922, Item 15, Box 79, Peyote. All of the above are in RCIA-FRC, Seattle. For the profile of a "progressive" peyotist on the Northern Ute Reservation, see David Rich Lewis, "Reservation Leadership and the Progressive–Traditional Dichotomy: William Wash and the Northern Utes, 1865–1928," *Ethnohistory* 38 (Spring, 1991), 124–148.

for passage of a similar state statute. His efforts in Congress failed, but the Montana legislature approved a prohibition law in February 1923. Six years later, after Crow peyotists showed that they could circumvent the Montana act by shipping the cactus to Wyoming and then driving across the state line to retrieve it, Asbury succeeded in persuading the Wyoming legislature to pass an identical measure in that state.[57]

Despite Asbury's determination, the peyote ritual continued to have a wide following. A month after the Montana legislature passed its prohibition act, for example, Bird Above, a fifty-six-year-old farmer, who, like his brother Sits Down Spotted, had lived in the Bighorn valley since the relocation of the agency, wrote a letter to the commissioner of Indian affairs. Ostensibly he wrote to congratulate the commissioner for his condemnation of traditional dancing. He reported that dances generally lasted four days and people there "give lots of things away and blow what money they got. . . ." But Bird Above also wrote that the missionaries ruins our Indians [sic] by letting people camp and travel about. His solution for this apparent chaos was the peyote faith:

> I have found an innocent religion which . . . most of the Indians are follow-
> ing. We stay home and have our little meeting Saturday nights and on till
> Sunday noon and we do not leave our home no time . . . We do not go
> away to visit no place for big Indian pow-wow and give things away. We
> do not believe in that at all. We believe in stay home and look after of farms
> and home and have our little prayer meeting right in our home.

Like other peyotists across the country, Bird Above preached monogamy, hard work and abstinence from alcohol. His argument was difficult to counter, especially when evidence began to accumulate disproving the government's assertion that peyote was addictive and debilitating. The dedication of its followers, as well as their willingness to debate the virtues of peyote with government officials, ensured that the peyote ritual would remain a part of Crow life despite the efforts of prohibitionists. A modern resident of the Crow Reservation typifies this fact. Recalling a confrontation with the Crow agent in the early 1930s, he chuckled as he repeated the man's threat to jail him if he broke the prohibition law. "If you arrest me," he responded, "any time you release me I think I will go to the peyote meeting. . . . You can arrest me all you want . . . I like it; its God's word and I'll stick with it."[58]

V

By the middle years of the 1920s the Crow community appeared to have reasserted its traditional, pluralistic approach to religion. The reservation was a

---

[57] Asbury's prohibition activities are well documented in Stewart, "Peyotism in Montana," 11–12.
[58] Bird Above to Commissioner Burk (sic), March 17, 1923, Item 15, Box 83, File 131, RCIA-FRC, Seattle; Interview with George Takes Gun, August 10, 1987.

mosaic of competing and overlapping spiritual systems. Baptists and Catholics struggled to keep pace with one another, while all the time they seemed to be losing members to the peyote ritual or to an array of traditional Crow ceremonies and dances. Membership in the various religious organizations was fluid; people shifted allegiances and attended two or three forms of ritual at once. Rather than settling into orderly rows of doves, Father Prando's Crows had persisted in pursuing divine power wherever it appeared.

Such appearances were frequently unexpected. In 1923, one of Chief Pretty Eagle's daughters, Nellie Stewart, and her husband Joe (the older brother of the Lodge Grass peyotist Tom Stewart) travelled to Miles City, Montana, to attend a camp meeting conducted by Aimee Semple McPherson, the founder of the Angelus Temple in Los Angeles, California. Pentecostal missionaries had previously counted Nellie among their converts, but her meeting with the radio evangelist impressed her so deeply that she accepted an invitation to come to California to study with McPherson. The Stewarts and three others drove to Los Angeles in the summer of 1924; after three weeks of study, Nellie was baptized by McPherson and sent back to Montana to minister to her tribe.

Nellie Stewart conducted pentecostal services for her Black Lodge neighbors and other followers until her death in 1937. Her group combined traditional Crow beliefs with evangelical Christianity, placing special significance in Nellie Stewart's visions and the songs she received from spiritual beings. There were pentecostalists among the Crows in the 1920s and 1930s, and their existence demonstrates the increasing openness with which the tribe treated new religious ideas. By the 1920s there were so many competing faiths and so active a group of Crow believers, that new groups could form easily, and individuals could select their own path of spiritual salvation.[59]

It was clear that the coercive and contentious atmosphere of the pre–World War I era had disappeared. Unable to ban traditional dancing or to eradicate traditional practices, local missionaries adopted a stance of patience and tolerance toward nonbelievers. The sale of Indian lands to outsiders produced an increase in the reservation's non-Indian population and the subsequent opening of public schools in several districts. This change reduced the enrollment in the church-sponsored day schools and further undermined the authority of the reservation's all-white Christian hierarchy. As enrollments declined, struggles between Catholics and Baptists for school children also faded into memory. "Something has happened," Pryor Subagent Sam Lapointe wrote early in 1923; "the Indians have, for a time, it seems, put away their religious differences and seem to be getting along very nicely. . . ."[60]

[59] Timothy P. McCleary, "Akbaatashee: The Oilers Pentecostalism Among the Crow Indians," M.A. Thesis, University of Montana, 1993, 49–50. Thomas and Joseph Stewart were listed as sons of Thomas Stewart in the 1887 tribal census. See Item 17, Box 154, RCIA-FRC, Seattle.

[60] Farmer's Weekly Report, Pryor, January 15 to 20, 1923, Item 15, Box 86, File 139, RCIA-FRC, Seattle.

Persecution of peyote use continued, but without much success. The first test of the 1924 Montana prohibition statute came in the fall of that year when a middle-aged farmer from Lodge Grass, Big Sheep, was arrested and convicted in a local county court. Early in 1925, while Big Sheep's conviction was being appealed to the state supreme court, he and eight other Crows (including Tom Stewart and Frank Bethune) joined with a group from the Northern Cheyenne Reservation to incorporate themselves as the Native American church of Montana. Their action was patterned after (and no doubt influenced by) actions taken by Oklahoma peyotists to defend their ritual on constitutional grounds. The Montana supreme court announced that it would hear the case, but remanded it to the county for a more complete hearing on several issues. That hearing never took place; local officials dropped the charges against Big Sheep in March 1926.

Despite ongoing harassment by local agents, Crow peyotists continued to practice their faith. They also became more aggressive when defending it. Barney Old Coyote, for example, a Catholic Carlisle graduate who had long been considered a "progressive" leader in the Bighorn, described himself as "neutral" on the issue in 1922 and was ostracized by the church. Undaunted, he spoke out in 1929 against the proposal that Wyoming should pass its own prohibition statute. "You have killed our game," he told reporters in Sheridan; "you have substituted your civilization for ours until we have only one right – and that one right is embodied in the constitution of the United States. It is the right of adoring God." Old Coyote stopped short of identifying himself publicly as a peyotist, stressing instead the right of tribal members to worship as they chose.[61]

The theme of free choice was also reflected in a series of responses filed by district subagents with agency headquarters late in 1926. Agent Asbury had circulated an Indian Office memo asking, among other things, for information regarding Indian attendance at church and other community activities. Every district reported at least one active church, and all but Black Lodge and Pryor noted that their churches were large enough to serve the entire community. When asked to describe community activities, however, the subagents were less precise. At Reno, "church, parties and dances" were listed, but at St. Xavier in the Bighorn valley a disgusted Sam Lapointe remarked that there were "none to speak of. They have their dances," he added, "and a few go to church on Sundays."[62]

A similar survey in 1929 tried to be more statistical, but its conclusions were

[61] For 1922 statement, see Barney Old Coyote to Asbury, February 28, 1922, Item 15, Box 79, File 122–2, RCIA-FRC, Seattle; 1929 statement quoted in Denver *Post*, March 16, 1929. The latter quotation is cited in Stewart, "Peyotism in Montana," 14, and is filed with Item 16, Box 97, File 027, RCIA-FRC, Seattle.

[62] The written comments are contained in "Statistical Data for General Superintendent's Circular No. 5," January 27, 1927, Item 16, Box 103, RCIA-FRC, Seattle.

the same. The Bighorn reported that 100 of the 350 Crows in the district attended the Baptist mission while only 50 were regulars at St. Xavier. "The rest," the subagent wrote, "attend peyote." Reports from the other five districts were similar. All reported some church attendance, from a high of nearly 100% at Reno (nearest the agency headquarters) to a low of approximately 25% at remote Wyola. Multiple membership appeared to be the rule across the reservation. The Black Lodge subagent wrote glumly that the Indians in his district "dance frequently, some few go to church and many play rummy in the pool hall."[63]

An ironic coda to this description of multiple religious activity is contained in a report filed by the embattled Sioux subagent, Sam Lapointe, from St. Xavier in early January 1926. In November he had written in despair, "We seem to have lost control of them"; now, he seemed to offer confirmation of that fact:

> The Indians, both factions (i.e., Baptist and Catholic), danced from two or three days prior to Christmas until January 3, Sunday, when they broke camp. I know from experience that at least some of the missionaries tried all they could to prevent this sort of a Christmas celebration and that is not saying that this office laid idle on the subject, but it seemed the more we tried to prevent it the more they tried to hold it and of course they won. . . . Discouraging if you really want to do some good to and for these Crows, but of course, if indifferent, well, its alright.

While participating in a Christmas gathering and following the reservation's regulations regarding allowable times to dance, the Bighorn Crows had also had an opportunity to socialize and celebrate their own, distinctive traditions. Lapointe added, "At least one half of all their best work horses were given away to visitors."[64]

VI

In his recent portrait of the Crow worldview, anthropologist Rodney Frey argues that tribal members understand the cosmos as a giant wagon wheel in which "the spokes represent the various peoples and religions of the world, each unique unto itself." At the center is the hub, "the pervasive Maker, who is shared and touched by all." Frey contends that modern Crows see every spoke – every religious or cultural expression – to be equally connected to God.

[63] For district response to the social survey questionnaire, see Item 16, Box 100, File 051, Statistics, RCIA-FRC, Seattle.

[64] Farmer's Weekly Report, Big Horn, November 23 to 28, 1925; Farmer's Weekly Report, Big Horn, January 4 to 9, 1926; Item 15, Box 87, Farmer's Weekly Reports, 1925–1927, RCIA-FRC, Seattle.

Frey illustrates this point by recalling an interview with a peyotist who displayed for him a prize peyote button which was never consumed. "This is who I pray to when someone in my family is sick or in need of something," the peyote man told Frey. When the cactus button was turned over, the visitor saw something more: "Glued to the reverse side is a picture of Jesus."[65]

By the end of the 1920s, the Crows had incorporated a variety of new religious ideas into their community life. Instead of the competition and suppression of the early twentieth century, the tribe's religious and cultural life was marked by a variety of overlapping religious sects. As had been the case in the nineteenth century, religious groups were considered open-ended and mutually supportive. Membership in a traditional ceremonial group or a peyote community could fluctuate, or individuals might shift their allegiances from one group to another. In addition, membership in a Christian organization did not preclude participation in the Tobacco Society, a singing or hot dance group, or loyalty to the peyote ritual. At the end of a process of intense regimentation and proselytizing, the Crows seemed to have retained their preference for a plural approach to religious expression and to have stamped their modern existence with the values of their collective past.

Religious institutions on the Crow Reservation had come to resemble Frey's wagon wheel: each was a vehicle for spiritual involvement and group association, and allegiance to one way did not prevent individuals from appreciating another. The Baptist and Catholic churches, the Native American church, the Tobacco Society and the hot dance organizations had been transformed collectively into tribal institutions. As such they could cement family and clan ties, focus the activities of reservation districts and protect their followers from outsiders. The Crow people and their gods were once again intertwined.

[65] Frey, *The World of the Crow Indians*, 150, 158.

8

Leaders in a new arena

We Crow Indians are the owners of this reservation. The other tribes surrounding us, their reservation is not a real reservation for the reason they have fought against the government and have been placed by the government on a reservation. . . . This land is really ours. We would like to do as we wish on this reservation. . . . We want to be like the timber that is being hewed down with an ax, and after that the second growth comes up, and we want to be the same as that.

Bull Robe, 1909[1]

I

In January 1884, as he prepared to move Crow Agency down from the Stillwater valley to the Little Bighorn, Agent Henry Armstrong wrote his superiors in Washington about how he intended to govern his charges once they had arrived in their new home. "As soon as we get firmly established at the new location," he wrote, "it is my intention to institute a simple government and to call all the people together, men, women, and children, rich and poor, sick and well, and explain it to them. . . . The chiefs and headmen have had all the talk they need," he added, "but the great body of the Crows have never had these matters explained to them fairly." Armstrong's plans contained a contradiction that would characterize the government's approach to Crow leaders for the next three decades. Newcomers to Montana and outnumbered by their charges, government men like Armstrong found that the cooperation of the tribe's "chiefs and headmen" was essential to the smooth running of the reservation. Whether their goal was the relocation of the agency or the introduction of farming, it was far more effective to negotiate cooperation than it was to rely on brute force. On the other hand, the Indian Office and its local supporters were determined to undermine the community's indigenous leadership and replace it with "a simple government" representing "the great body" of the tribe. From 1884 onward, then, agency administrators struggled to reduce the power of the local chiefs without creating undue resistance or complete chaos.[2]

[1] "Transcript of Testimony Taken in the Investigation of Conditions on the Crow Reservation," Central Classified File, Crow Agency, File 150, LR-OIA, RG 75, NA (hereafter cited as CCF, Crow, 150), 18844-10.
[2] Henry Armstrong to Commissioner of Indian Affairs, January 11, 1884, Item 2, Box 1, RCIA-FRC, Seattle.

The chiefs and headmen faced a similar contradiction. They wanted to *maintain* their authority as tribal leaders, but they knew this would be impossible unless they were flexible and accommodating. The struggles of the early reservation years, culminating in the death of Sword Bearer, presented the chiefs' dilemma in bold relief. In 1887, men like Pretty Eagle and Plenty Coups sought to pay homage to the young medicine man while avoiding a hopeless confrontation with the assembled bluecoats. They needed the support of "the great body of the tribe" in order to maintain their positions of influence, but they could not rule in opposition to the power of the United States.

In the generation following Sword Bearer's death, the interests of federal officials, tribal leaders and a variety of groups within the reservation community combined to produce a new version of Crow leadership. Through force and exhortation, government agents altered the dress, family life, religious practices and livelihood of reservation residents. At the same time, the admission of Montana to statehood and the rapid expansion of its non-Indian population severely limited the actions and freedom of Crow leaders. In the process, these leaders lost the opportunity to achieve military glory or exercise the broad political power they had wielded in the nineteenth century. Nevertheless, Crows from every corner of the reservation continued to think of themselves as citizens of a distinctive community and to prefer indigenous leaders to external ones. In the crucible of a new and constricted environment, Crows continued to produce their own leaders and to follow their own, locally generated political agenda. In a world where the pathway to leadership could no longer include success in raiding, hunting and horse capturing, reservation residents succeeded in creating and sustaining an indigenous political system.

Just as the evolution of European politics can be tracked through dramatic events – revolutions, elections and coups – so the history of the Crow political system in the first decades of the reservation era reveals itself most clearly in a series of crises that tested and altered it. Four of these crises mark the decades from Sword Bearer's death to the relatively peaceful days of the 1920s. Two are land sales: the decisions in 1890 and 1899 to exchange hundreds of thousands of acres of Crow country for cash and other federal benefits. Each sale delivered temporary wealth to the Crow community, but each was accompanied with irretrievable losses that challenged the credibility of tribal leaders. The third event was the "Helen Grey Affair," in which charges of corruption threatened both the local agent and the authority of the established chiefs. In its aftermath, the chiefs took dramatic steps to incorporate the views of new groups into the political system and to establish more effective systems of maintaining their position. Finally, a twelve-year struggle over a proposal to "open" all remaining tribal lands to outside settlement exposed tribal leaders to a succession of confrontations in both Montana and Washington, D.C. Its resolution was marked by the passage of the 1920 Crow Act, a striking victory both for the leaders who engineered it and for the reservation political system that produced them.

In 1909, when Bull Robe declared to a visiting official from Washington, D.C., that the "Crows really owned" their reservation, he reminded the outsider of a constant feature of tribal life. In the twentieth century, no less than at the treaty grounds in 1868 or among the campfires of 1805, Crow leaders equated authority within their community with control of their land and resources. The persistence of one created a claim to the other. When the thirty-seven-year-old leader from Black Lodge referred to people like himself as "the second growth" that, like their fathers, might "do as they wish on this reservation," he was engaging in more than rhetorical fancy. Bull Robe's father, Three Wolves, had belonged to Spotted Horse's band in the first days of Crow Agency. Three Wolves may well have been present when "Spot" had confronted Captain Armstrong on the banks of the Little Bighorn, and the son – a teenager at the time – surely knew of the incident. From his home on the banks of the Bighorn, downriver from St. Xavier, Bull Robe had witnessed the continuation of Crow family life, the persistence of the community's religious values and the continuing contest between government dreams and local realities. It was not surprising that he saw himself as part of a new generation of leaders, springing up in the image of their predecessors.[3]

II

The summer of 1890 brought disastrous weather to eastern Montana. Long periods of drought interspersed with brief but violent hail storms produced empty wells and a hopeless harvest. Agent M. P. Wyman, a former railroad foreman who had replaced his Republican predecessor when the Cleveland administration distributed the spoils of victory the previous spring, reported in early September that the only cash on the reservation was in the hands of Crows who carried supplies from Custer station to the agency or those who were lucky enough to have some hay to sell to the army or to local cattlemen. The crops, he wrote, "were either completely ruined or badly injured." The farms the allotting agents had confidently begun laying out in the 1880s seemed to be turning into dust, and the few Crows who had shown an interest in agriculture had become discouraged. Even the location of the Indians' allotments was a problem, for the surveyors had identified their boundaries with wooden stakes and holes. Now he observed, "The stakes are rotted and lost or the holes filled."[4]

[3] Bull Robe is listed in the 1887 census as the son of Three Wolves. See Item 17, Box. 154, RCIA-FRC, Seattle (family 597). The list of Crow bands compiled in the early 1880s lists Three Irons as a member of Spotted Horse's band. See Item 21, Box 156, RCIA-FRC, Seattle (Band 22).
[4] *ARCIA*, 1890 (Serial 2841), 115, 116.

On September 27, 289 "chiefs and headmen" – encompassing the full spectrum of tribal opinion and political position from Fire Bear to Deaf Bull – met to draft a petition asking for an increase in their weekly ration of beef. Such requests had been sent to Washington before, but this year their agent reported that conditions were desperate. In a supporting letter, Wyman emphasized that the Crows "have nothing from their farms and naturally feel discouraged." He reminded his superiors that the tribe's request did not require an increase in federal support. The request was that "a portion of the funds received from grazing of stock on this reservation be applied to the purchase of additional beef." The petitioners expressed a willingness to farm, promising that they would require support only until they could "produce crops in sufficient quantity" on their own.[5]

The reply from Washington was both foreordained and unexpected. As it happened, on September 25, 1890, two days *before* the 289 chiefs and headmen had met at Crow Agency to draft their petition, Congress had authorized the Indian Office to negotiate with the Crow Indians for the purchase of all their land west of Pryor Creek. While the tribe awaited a response to their petition, a commission was being appointed to meet with them in council. On November 27, a time when tribal leaders had hoped they would already be enjoying their new rations, the three new commissioners arrived at Crow Agency, ready to exchange American cash for nearly 2 million acres of the upland country in the Clarks Fork and Stillwater River valleys. Hungry, and grieving the loss of dozens of their kinsmen to disease, hundreds of families began to converge on the Little Bighorn to take part in the council.[6]

It took over a week for a representative group of nearly 400 adult males to assemble at Crow Agency. In the interim, the commissioners learned that Plenty Coups and other leaders from Pryor were vehemently opposed to the sale. This was not surprising since the new reservation boundaries would bring white settlement to within a few miles of Plenty Coups's home and promised to end the decades-old partnership of the Pryor leader and the cattlemen who grazed their herds on the tribal lands south of nearby Billings. As they awaited the council, the commissioners also discovered that a number of Little Bighorn chiefs, particularly Old Dog and Spotted Horse, were strongly in favor of the new agreement because it promised them immediate cash for distant lands they rarely visited. They were told that Pretty Eagle, settled midway between the two ends of the reservation, was undecided.[7]

When the Crows held their first session with the commissioners on Saturday

---

[5] The petition, dated September 27, 1890, is filed as 30877–1890, LR-OIA, RG 75, NA. Wyman's letter of support is Wyman to Commissioner of Indian Affairs, September 30, 1890, Item 2, Box 3, RCIA-FRC, Seattle.
[6] For the commission's authorization, see 26 U.S. Statutes at Large, 468; the commission's report is in Senate Executive Document 43, 51st Congress, 2nd Session, 1890 (Serial 2818), 6–26.
[7] Senate Executive Document 43, 6.

morning, December 6, the chiefs and headmen were on the defensive. Their divisions were obvious and their lack of resolve was clear, so they tried to delay or adjourn the proceedings. An uncomfortable Plenty Coups spoke first. He reminded the commissioners that he had been "talking for" his people for over a decade. He had always been cooperative and loyal to the government, but, he told the men from Washington, this request was too much:

> If you white men put in all your money to buy that land you would not pay all it is worth. . . . I don't want to have bad feeling against Indians or whites, but I want my country to remain. If there is anything you love and I want to buy, you won't sell it. The Great Father buys and buys from me and this time I won't do it.

These sad but stirring words sent a wave of excitement through the council. For a moment it appeared that a united front might be established against the commissioners. Speaker after speaker endorsed the Pryor chief's stand. When his turn came, Pretty Eagle chimed in by calling up one of the tribe's favorite images. He told the commissioners that "the Crows have never been fools like other Indians and the Great Father ought to go and bother them people instead of coming and bothering us."[8]

But Plenty Coups and Pretty Eagle could not control the council. Soon the leaders from the Little Bighorn, no doubt encouraged by the commissioners who had spent several days with them prior to the start of the meeting, rose to endorse the government proposal. Ironically, the first to speak in support of the sale was Spotted Horse, the young chief who had disrupted Armstrong's work at the Little Bighorn six years earlier and who had frequently challenged the agent's authority in the first years of the new reservation. Harking back to the Sword Bearer incident when he had decided to keep silent and remain neutral, Spotted Horse declared that "for three winters I have kept still and said nothing. I have made up my mind when the Great Father sends anyone here I will take sides with the Great Father. Today is the day." The ex-rebel acknowledged that the commissioner's price was too low, but he predicted that the sale would go through. Speakers from Bighorn and Black Lodge quickly rose to agree.[9]

Fearing both a loss of the land and a dramatic loss of face, Plenty Coups responded by bringing the meeting to a sudden halt. Outraged by the commissioners' willingness to acknowledge Spotted Horse and his Little Bighorn people, Plenty Coups charged that "these people have bloodied their hands in war." He went on, portraying himself and his kinsmen at Pryor as the government's most reliable allies:

---

[8] Ibid., 11, 12.
[9] Ibid., 12, 13 (Sorrel Horse spoke from Big Horn and Two Leggings from Black Lodge).

In my country you can't find four young men you ever had in prison. My people never pointed their guns towards the whites. . . . These people on the Little Horn have always had trouble among themselves. Mine do not. . . . I don't want my people to get mixed up in such a crowd as this. The Commissioners had better go home.

The meeting erupted into confusion and was rapidly adjourned.[10]

Plenty Coups threatened to leave for home, but the commissioners urged him to stay and, on reflection, he must have realized that the sale could go forward without him. Among other things the Pryor chief must also have considered was the recent experience of the Sioux in Dakota Territory who had recently been bullied into a massive land sale. Those proceedings were instructive as well because as they unfolded the government's representatives showed themselves quite willing to pit one tribal group against another. Plenty Coups understood that if Spotted Horse could be rehabilitated in the government's eyes, there was no reason why he himself could not be deposed. When the Crow council reassembled on the following Monday morning, the veteran warrior rose quickly and spoke bluntly. "What will you give for the land?" he asked. The commissioners immediately raised their initial $800,000 offer to $900,000 and offered to purchase 2,500 head of cattle for a tribal herd. The increase allowed the defeated leader to rescue some of his stature before the crowd. "You see these people here," Plenty Coups replied, "I could hold them a good while but they will do as the Great Father wishes."[11]

With agreement assured, other headmen rose to air their grievances and proposals. Crazy Head, now out of prison, rose to ask that income from the sale be used for the construction of day schools so that Crow children could "come home at night." Medicine Crow asked that Indians be allowed to butcher their own stock without the permission of the agent. Two Leggings asked for cheaper prices at the trader's store, and several men who had settled on the ceded lands reminded the commissioners that they were now entitled to compensation for relocating to the diminished reservation. The final document responded to all of these requests. In addition, of the $900,000 sale price, $275,000 would be used to construct irrigation canals to support Indian farming and $552,000 would provide a yearly annuity of $12 per person for twenty years. Finally, the government promised to construct a blacksmith shop, a grist mill and a permanent subagency near Plenty Coups's home at Pryor creek.[12]

Plainly, for Plenty Coups and other chiefs interested in preserving their political power there were several lessons to be learned from the 1890 land sale. The tribe had been unprepared for the negotiations, and it entered them from

[10] Ibid., 13.
[11] Ibid.
[12] Ibid., 2–5. The agreement was ratified by Congress on March 3, 1891 (26 U.S. Statutes, 1039). The final agreement also provided for a grist mill and blacksmith at Bighorn.

a position of weakness. The commissioners easily exploited differences within the group and weakened the leaders who might have rallied a successful resistance. In the midst of disagreements and disunity, no chief had sufficient stature to speak for the entire assembly, and there was no mechanism for establishing a tribal consensus. Without that consensus any opponent – even one so trustworthy as Plenty Coups – could be labeled a malcontent. The commissioners had short memories. Plenty Coups's past loyalty and Spotted Horse's past opposition meant nothing in the face of a congressional call for additional land sales. The bargaining on the last day of the council indicated that a forceful leader like Plenty Coups could win concessions from the authorities, but only when those concessions did not contradict the government's central objectives and when the tribal leader appeared to speak for a large (and potentially disruptive) segment of the community.

While records of their private deliberations are impossible to reconstruct, it seems clear that the men who aspired to tribal leadership in the ensuing decade learned the "lessons" of the 1890 land sale. They insisted on the rapid implementation of the concessions contained in the agreement, reminding the local agent repeatedly, for example, of his commitment to the construction of day schools and district grist mills. The chiefs also tried to maximize their involvement in the administration of the reservation so as to prevent being manipulated or surprised by directives from Washington. Tribal policemen, for example, were assigned to each district, and while they were formally under the jurisdiction of the agent at Crow Agency, local leaders such as Plenty Coups and Medicine Crow referred to these men as "their" policemen. Leaders like Spotted Horse frequently insisted as well that Crows who had returned from off-reservation boarding schools should become agency employees. In short, they agreed with what Plenty Coups told a visiting inspector in the spring of 1899: "I want our agent to look after our interests."[13]

Insisting on a role in reservation affairs was not only a way of sharing some of the agent's power. Men like Plenty Coups spoke out because they also wanted to position themselves for future deliberations between the U.S. government and the Crows. They wanted to ensure that those negotiations would involve them as the legitimate government of the tribe. One agent wrote to a subordinate in frustration in 1892 that the local chiefs should be told "that the Great Father wants every one of his Indian children to talk for themselves." Despite this effort to ignore them, however, men like Plenty Coups knew from experience that at moments of crisis or conflict the government's men would find the chiefs to be useful allies. They had learned that lesson in 1887 and their insight was repeated many times in the following years. For example, Plenty

[13] Arthur M. Tinker to Secretary of the Interior, June 7, 1899, enclosure, 12; 27761–1899, LR-OIA, RG 75, NA. The same transcript contains numerous references to agency employment, tribal police and the need for day schools.

Coups wrote to the "Great Father" in the winter of 1901, saying, "I want you to do something; I want you to do it for me. . . . I want [the] Indian agent and all the boss farmers to stay longer. I have nothing against them." The Pryor chief knew that an agent in fear of losing his job would welcome such an endorsement.[14]

<h1 style="text-align:center">III</h1>

The Crow chiefs were prepared for their next encounter with a land sale commission. In the summer of 1896, Congress authorized three men to negotiate with three Montana tribes for the purchase of "unused" areas within their reservations. The group began with the Flathead Reservation, so Crow leaders had time to ready themselves for the negotiations. As they awaited the arrival of the government men, the tribe's leaders learned that the commission initially considered resettling the Northern Cheyennes on their reserve and cutting their communal lands in half by opening up large strips of territory across the northern and southern boundaries of the Crows' land to white settlement. Their agent discouraged the former idea, but when the commission first arrived at Crow Agency in the fall of 1898, they proposed the large land cession to the tribe as the starting point for negotiations.[15]

Confident that he could rally united opposition to the proposal, Plenty Coups addressed the commissioners when they met in council on October 31. "You have told me something and now I am going to tell you something," the chief declared. Referring to provisions of the 1890 land sale that had yet to be implemented (such as the construction of day schools and the payment of larger annuities), Plenty Coups indicated that there would be no new negotiations until all the old obligations were fulfilled. "When you have made these settlements to the Indians, then you can come back and I and my people will talk to you about these lands that you now want." In contrast to 1890, no tribal members spoke up for the commissioners. Pretty Eagle and Spotted Horse quickly endorsed Plenty Coups's demand and then there was silence.[16]

One more innovation stopped the commissioners dead in their tracks. Plenty Coups and the others council speakers brought forward a group of young men who had recently returned to the reservation from extended terms in government schools. "Here gathered near me you see the boys we sent to school,"

[14] M. P. Wyman to C. G. Knidler, February 1, 1892, Item 5, Box 27, RCIA-FRC, Seattle; Plenty Coups to Great Father, December 15, 1901, 75436–1901, LR-OIA, RG 75, NA.

[15] J. W. Watson to C. G. Hoyt, Secretary, Crow and Flathead Commission, November 1, 1898, RCIA-FRC, Seattle.

[16] "Proceedings of Council with Crow Indians," filed as 45587–1899, LR-OIA, RG 75, NA, October 31, 1899, 7–8.

Spotted Horse pointed out; "they are young men now and can read and write; they are men now that we look on with confidence." One of the returned students, Carl Leider, stepped forward and announced, "This is the first time in the history of the Crows we younger men have been allowed a voice in the Crow council." Leider went on to read an itemized list of promises broken, payments missed and annuities delayed. The commissioners were stunned. Said one, "This is the first time since I have dealt with Indians that they ever gave me anything on a piece of paper!" Promising to "do our very best to satisfy you," the befuddled commissioners agreed to postpone any further discussion of land sales until the spring of 1899.[17]

The departure of Agent E. H. Becker that spring (after barely a year in office) delayed a resumption of negotiations, but by August his successor was in place and the commissioners had prepared a response to Carl Leider's indictment. A tribal council assembled on August 8 for what turned out to be a five-day session, the longest in the tribe's history. At the outset the government's negotiators understood that they were facing a representative body and that the Indians had assembled to hear a response to their October demands. After a long review of the tribe's complaints and his efforts to correct past errors, Commissioner Charles Hoyt declared that "we come to you today and state that we have looked up these matters and that nearly all are settled or will be settled in a few days. And now we expect you," he continued, "to fulfill your promise to come and talk plainly to us about these lands."[18]

Following those hopeful words, the commissioners repeated their proposal to purchase all of the reservation south of Lodge Grass and north of the confluence of the Bighorn and Little Bighorn Rivers. They claimed the sale would leave the Crows "all of your most valuable land" and promised that, as in 1890, any Indians wishing to remain on ceded lands would be entitled to retain their individual homesteads there. The government men avoided mentioning a specific price for this purchase, but they painted an attractive picture of tribal cattle herds, fenced pastures, grist mills and day schools. This initial presentation ended with a distribution of beef to the entire assembly and an invitation to the Crows to "talk this thing all over among themselves" before delivering their response.[19]

Three leaders – Pretty Eagle, Spotted Horse and Plenty Coups – delivered the tribe's reply on the second day of the council. Totally consistent and obviously well rehearsed, the men from the Pryor, Bighorn and Little Bighorn valleys acknowledged the commission's attempt to straighten out the tribal accounts, but insisted that no sale discussions could take place until all claims had been resolved. Plenty Coups insisted that the group would not accept

[17] Ibid., 12, 9.
[18] Ibid., August 8, 1899, 4.
[19] Ibid., 7, 8, 10.

promises. "After the back payments are paid we will come back and we will talk to you about buying this land," he said, adding that he would employ his own experts to verify the government's figures: "I will get my boys . . . young fellows who are educated – get them together and have them see that all the back payments are paid. . . ." The tribe's new agent, a former merchant from Billings named John Edwards, accused the leaders of acting like "boys," but they ignored him. "If people have anything for sale," Pretty Eagle lectured the white men, "if they do not want to sell for the price offered, these other people can take away what they want to sell – the people who want to buy say that belongs to you and I cannot buy and they go off."[20]

On the third day, the commissioners attacked the chiefs directly. "Our instructions from Washington are to talk with all of the Indians," Charles Hoyt announced, "to let all the Indians have a voice in the matter . . . and then when a majority of the Indians – half of all the Indians come to one mind, then it is a trade. . . ." The implications of Hoyt's statement were spelled out a few minutes later when Agent Edwards stepped forward to announce that "the last train that came in" had brought in $10,000 in treasury drafts to settle the last outstanding claim for back payment of grazing fees. "Here in my hand is the money," Edwards crowed; "when this treaty is decided . . . I will begin to pay this money." If the chiefs were going to obstruct the sale, the commissioners would unabashedly go over their heads with greenbacks. As the agent stuffed the notes back in an envelope, Carl Leider translated his words and the group adjourned until three o'clock in the afternoon.[21]

Edwards's threat worked. Beginning the afternoon of the third day, and continuing for two additional days, the council saw the commissioners and the tribal leaders wrestle over boundary lines and prices. First, Takes Wrinkle, Two Leggings and a group of River Crow headmen from the Black Lodge district offered to sell the far northeasternmost corner of the reservation for $1.50 per acre and a promise that Fort Custer (which the army had abandoned a year earlier) be refurbished and opened as a district school. Second, after rejecting the River Crow offer as too small, and considering, perhaps, that the lands around Lodge Grass were the home territory of Spotted Horse and Medicine Crow, Commissioner Hoyt announced that he had decided "it is perhaps not for the best interests of the Indians to sell the southern part of the reservation." Attention then focused on the portion of the reserve lying north of the Black Lodge settlements at the confluence of the Bighorn and Little Bighorn.[22]

On August 11, the fourth day, Plenty Coups and his colleagues expanded slightly on the River Crows' offer, but he and a succession of speakers (including

[20] Ibid., August 9, 1899, 8, 10.
[21] Ibid., August 10, 1899 (morning), 8, 9.
[22] Ibid., August 10, 1899, afternoon session, 1–3, 12, 13.

Medicine Crow and Spotted Horse) insisted that this northern area was worth $2 per acre. Again, the commissioners faced a united front, and, again, they threatened to undermine the authority of the chiefs in order to win a larger concession. "When we have a majority of the names of the Crow Indians," Commissioner Hoyt declared, "no matter whether Plenty Coups' name is on it or not, or Pretty Eagle's or not, that it is a deal. Every name upon this paper counts as one." The negotiator then proposed enlarging the proposed sale still further so that it would amount to just over 1 million acres and, disingenuously suggested dropping all talk of per acre prices: "We will give you for this land," he stated with a straight face, "one million of dollars."[23]

On the final day of the council, the commissioners pressed their advantage by calling on Big Medicine, the captain of the reservation police and a River Crow with relatives at Black Lodge, to make the opening speech in support of the government's offer. He was followed by Officer Fire Bear, the slayer of Sword Bearer (who promised to "do whatever Big Medicine says") and Big Ox, a band leader from Black Lodge. Apparently convinced that the chiefs had pressed their claims as far as possible, Plenty Coups agreed to the proposed new boundaries but continued to insist on $2 per acre. Pretty Eagle rose immediately afterwards to second his colleague. "I will follow what the rest of them have said whether they talked crooked or straight," the Bighorn leader declared. This mixture of pride in their effort and resignation at the government's ultimate power was also reflected in the brief statement Deaf Bull rose to make towards the end of the final day's session. The recalcitrant rebel of the 1880s, weak and near death, observed that "if one man wants to do anything, or tries do to anything, or says anything, he will be the same as one stick – anyone can break it. . . . My head men and my head chiefs here have told you that we would sell this land and I will agree to whatever they have said."[24]

Despite the fact that the agreement eventually forwarded to Congress called for payment of only slightly more than $1 per acre, the Crow leaders who stood up to Commissioner Hoyt and Agent Edwards could see the value of their united stance. Unlike the divided and indecisive headmen of 1890, the tribal leaders of 1899 were a formidable political machine. Obviously planning in advance who would speak and what the group's position would be, Plenty Coups, Pretty Eagle and Spotted Horse had managed to keep their districts united and quiet. How formidable their machine was becomes even more apparent when one examines who signed the final agreement when the five-day council ended on August 12.

Even though 518 adult male Crows put their mark of approval on the accord

[23] Ibid., August 11, 1899 (morning), 1–2; (afternoon), 16, 17–18.
[24] Ibid., August 12, 1899 (morning), 1, 2, 3, 9. Big Medicine had been a policeman for most of the 1890s; he was made captain in 1898. For more on him, see Peter Jensen, "Big Medicine," *Gun Report*, vol. 37, no. 6 (June 1967), 22–23.

When he posed for this portrait at the turn of the century, Deaf Bull had long since given up his role as recalcitrant enemy of the Indian Office. While he often claimed to be "the only real Indian" left among the Crows, he cooperated with Plenty Coups and other leaders in negotiating sessions with the government. Courtesy of Buffalo Bill Historical Center, Cody, Wyoming. Gift of Forrest Fenn.

in 1899, there are 162 men listed as heads of households in the following year's federal census who did not. Of this group of 162, 119 were later assigned allotments on the reservation. A review of the location of those allotments reveals that 60% of them were in the portion of the reservation closest to the lands sold in 1899. It would seem that a majority of the men who refused to sign the 1899 agreement lived close to (or perhaps previously had lived on) the area being sold. In other words, not only did Plenty Coups and his colleagues bargain on behalf of the tribe, but they appear to have been successful in orchestrating a coalition of followers whom they could deliver to the signing table once the council was over. Their power could even overpower a group of disaffected family heads who quietly opposed the final agreement.[25]

The 1899 land sale demonstrates the resourcefulness, as well as the vulnerability, of an emerging reservation leadership. Operating as a kind of presidium, a small group of chiefs representing the major reservation districts resolved their differences and offered outsiders a united "Crow position" on a public issue. They successfully incorporated young school graduates into their system, and they had the ability to enforce their decisions on an unhappy or indifferent constituency. While centered on men with some claim to status as warriors, the presidium which acted so effectively in 1899 was a product of the reservation environment. The leaders who had come to the fore in the aftermath of Sword Bearer's death understood that they had to be as persistent and as efficient as the white people they faced across the negotiating table. The group's efficiency was limited, however, for it frequently rested on personal prestige and common opposition to further sales of reservation land. The next crisis would demonstrate the limits of this presidium system and would force it to evolve yet again into something new.

IV

The third critical event in the evolution of Crow political leadership began with the arrival of a genteel white woman at the agency train station in the fall of 1906. Helen Pierce Grey was a muckraker, and she arrived at a moment of difficulty.

In 1902, Spotted Horse, the fifty-two-year-old Lodge Grass leader who had evolved from reservation "renegade" to chief in the course of the 1880s and 1890s, died. Two years later, Pretty Eagle, the eldest of the presidium speakers,

---

[25] Compilations are based on the manuscript census returns for 1900, the land sale agreement itself (filed with the council proceedings as 45587–1899, LR-OIA, RG 75, NA, and the "List of Crow Allotments," n.d., Item 53, Box 199, RCIA-FRC, Seattle. The 1900 census lists 582 male heads of household of whom 420 appear on the 1899 land sale agreement.

died at the age of fifty-eight. Also in 1904, the 1899 land sale was unilaterally altered and ratified by a Congress that happily ignored Indian protests. At the urging of budget conscious committee members (and spurred into action by a recent Supreme Court decision that recognized the legislative branch's "plenary power" over Indian affairs), Congress eliminated the government's obligation to pay the tribe directly for the one million acres to be opened to settlers, substituting instead a promise to pass on filing fees collected from homesteaders to the tribal treasury. Not only did this change violate the hard-fought agreements reached at the 1899 council, but it promised that payment for the ceded area would be slow and inadequate. (By 1910 only 150,000 acres had been sold, generating $300,000 for the tribe; 1,000,000 acres remained unclaimed.) The changes offered encouragement to Montana merchants and real estate interests, however, who had been lobbying for the ratification of the Crow agreement for years. Local businessmen eagerly applauded as the former Crow lands were finally opened to throngs of white settlers in the summer of 1906. As Helen Grey began her visit to the newly diminished reservation, lots in the boom town of Hardin, Montana, near the site of old Fort Custer, were being advertised in newspapers across the West.[26]

Internally, new strains were beginning to appear among members of the tribe, as well as in relations between tribal leaders and government officials. Despite their general poverty, differences were beginning to emerge between Crow leaders (who enjoyed the friendship of local stockmen) and their followers (who often struggled to raise enough food to feed their families). Plenty Coups benefitted most conspicuously from his position, as he succeeded in winning grazing leases for cooperative white stockmen and enjoyed friendly relations with the local agent. Tension on the reservation increased in 1902 when Samuel G. Reynolds, a no-nonsense young bank executive from Billings became tribal agent and initiated a program of Indian self-sufficiency. He cut off all rations and pressed the government's allotting agents to complete their work as rapidly as possible. Early in his tenure Reynolds also abolished agency farms on which many tribesmen had worked collectively under the agent's

---

[26] For a discussion of the changes in the 1899 land sale agreement and its impact on tribal revenues, see House Report 1494, Part 2, "Views of the Minority," 61st Congress 2nd Session, 9–11. The first issues of Hardin's weekly newspaper were filled with stories of Helen Grey and the imminent opening of the reservation. See Hardin, *Herald*, February 14, 21, and March 13, 1908. The following account of Helen Grey's involvement in Crow politics draws heavily from my "Building a Future on the Past: Crow Indian Leadership in an Era of Division and Reunion," in Walter Williams, ed., *American Indian Leadership in the Twentieth Century* (Manhattan, Kans.: Sunflower Press, 1981), 76–84. See also Donald L. Parman, "A White Man's Fight: The Crow Scandal, 1906–1913," in Ronald Lora, ed., *The American West: Essays in Honor of W. Engene Hollon* (Toledo, Ohio: University of Toledo Press, 1980), 73–96. Note that the ages given in the narrative are from the 1887 tribal census; while the earliest reliable enumeration available, it does contain errors.

supervision, and announced that he would discontinue the practice of meeting the tribe in the "common and useless pow-wow or council."[27]

Established figures on the reservation seemed vulnerable to criticism. Big Medicine, the chief of the agency police, was especially unpopular. Born in 1857, Big Medicine was slightly younger than Medicine Crow and Plenty Coups, but unlike those two leaders, could make no claim to being a prereservation warrior or traditional chief. He was a River Crow who had spent most of his young adulthood as an army scout. He arrived on the Little Bighorn sometime in the 1880s and settled close to Fort Custer. Never popular, Big Medicine did not appear to have been an object of scorn like his predecessor, Boy That Grabs, or Fire Bear, the capturer of Sword Bearer. Nevertheless, Reynolds's authoritarian style earned the police captain substantial resentment. Big Medicine was an experienced army employee who saw to it that the agent's orders were dispatched and followed, that children were in school and, with rations now abolished, that his kinsmen worked in their fields. According to Reynolds, Big Medicine took seriously the task of "arousing indolent Indians."[28]

Three months before Helen Grey arrived, Holds The Enemy, Pretty Eagle's thirty-seven-year-old son, and other Bighorn leaders demonstrated the depth of local opposition to the police captain by taking the unprecedented step of circulating a petition calling for his dismissal. The young men sent the marks and signatures of 174 Crows "against Big Medicine" to Plenty Coups with the request that the chief "do all you can for us." None of the older tribal leaders – Medicine Crow, or Plenty Coups himself – signed the petition, but several surprising names appeared. Among these were Sees With His Ears and He Knows His Coups, two veterans of the Sword Bearer incident who now lived at Black Lodge and Bighorn; Three Irons, formerly a member of Bear Wolf's band which had traveled frequently to Sioux country twenty years earlier; several young educated Crows (including Philip Ironhead and James Carpenter); and Ben Spotted Horse, the thirty-three-year-old son of the former Lodge Grass leader.[29]

It would appear that generational and political rivalries might now test the

---

[27] *ARCIA*, 1906 (Serial 5118), 252. On rations, see *ARCIA*, 1905 (Serial 4959, 4960), 238; on the abandonment of district farms and the reemphasis on allotment, see *ARCIA*, 1902 (Serial 4458), 229. For a description of Reynolds and his career, see a memoir by his daughter: Carolyn Reynolds Riebeth, *J. H. Sharp Among the Crow Indians, 1902–1910* (El Segundo, CA: Upton 1985), 13, 30.

[28] *ARCIA*, 1906 (Serial 5118), 254.

[29] Petition: Sharp Nose and Holds The Enemy to Chief Plenty Coups, July 7, 1906, Plenty Coups Papers, Plenty Coups Museum, Pryor, Montana. Carpenter's father was white and his mother a Piegan who settled with the Crows. He had briefly attended Hampton Institute. See Robert H. Lowie, "My Crow Interpreter," in Joseph P. Casagrande, ed., *In the Company of Man: Twenty Portraits of Anthropological Informants* (New York: Harper Torchbooks, 1964), and U.S. Indian Agent to H. B. Frissell, October 22, 1903, Item 4, Box 22, RCIA-FRC, Seattle.

power Plenty Coups, Big Medicine and the presidium of chiefs had wielded so effectively in 1899. The extent of that rivalry was clarified soon after Helen Grey stepped off the train at Crow Agency. A partner in an Omaha, Nebraska, news bureau, the middle-aged journalist described herself as a "western free lance correspondent" who had worked in Minnesota and Denver before taking on her present assignment. She came to the Crow reservation on the suggestion of the editor of *Collier's Weekly* to observe the tribe's annual harvest fair and to write a profile of a tribe that was supposedly making a smooth transition to "civilization." She originally expected to stay only a few weeks, but after hearing complaints from the Indians and rumors of agency corruption, she decided to settle in for the winter.[30]

Grey's chief informants on the reservation were the young, disaffected residents of the Lodge Grass and Bighorn districts. She lived for a month at the Crow Agency boarding school, but soon moved to Lodge Grass where she was taken in by Frank Gordon, a white man who had married into the tribe, and a group of young men: Ben Spotted Horse, James Carpenter, Joe Cooper and Fred Geisdorf. These men all belonged to a society called the Crow Indian Lodge, which they and Cooper's half-brother, George Pease, had formed some years earlier. Made up largely of boarding school graduates, the Crow Indian Lodge (also referred to by its initials "CIL") advocated greater commercial freedom for the tribe's farmers and ranchers and was hostile to Agent Reynolds and his restrictive regime. (Carpenter and Spotted Horse had signed the petition against Big Medicine the preceding summer.) During the winter Grey also met with other Crow Indian Lodge members who were older and less well educated. These included men like Packs The Hat, a forty-seven-year-old Lodge Grass farmer, and Spotted Rabbit, a Bighorn resident who was a former follower of Sword Bearer and another signer of the July petition.

Perhaps the highlight of Grey's initial interviews was a trip to the Bighorn district and a meeting with Holds The Enemy, Pretty Eagle's son. The journalist later reported that Holds The Enemy "is the chief of the Crow Indians . . . as he was introduced to me by a delegation of about one hundred from all the districts, including Pryor, as their chief." The Crow Indian Lodge also operated in Bighorn, where, as at Lodge Grass, it attracted returned students like Philip Iron Head as well as disaffected older members of the tribe.[31]

Grey's hosts had two major grievances. First, they wanted to get rid of Samuel Reynolds. They resented his authoritarian style and were angered by

[30] See Helen Grey to Commissioner of Indian Affairs, n.d. (presumably mid-1907), Bureau of Indian Affairs, CCF, Crow, 150, 71908–07.

[31] Statement of Helen Grey, CCF, Crow, 150, 71908–07, 6. See also, Leo Bad Horse to Helen Green (*sic*), March 18, 1907; Helen Grey to Matthew Sniffen, n.d. (postmarked December 4, 1907); all in Correspondence of the Indian Rights Association (hereafter cited as IRA Mss.), Reel 19.

his apparent efforts to open tribal land to white settlement. They questioned his administration of cattle and farming leases and accused him of helping land developers purchase blocks of land assigned by allotting agents to dead Indians. According to Reynolds's critics, this practice, which was technically legal, had enabled a Nebraska real estate company to acquire most of the lots in the new town of Hardin, Montana, and later resell them for a substantial profit. Second, these critics demanded the cancellation of large grazing permits that had recently been granted to Charles Bair and Frank Heinrich, well-connected local stockmen who had long been friendly to both the reservation's agent and its presidium of chiefs. Grey's informants charged that the two men overstocked their pastures and allowed their herds to trample and destroy Indian farmland.[32]

In March 1907, Grey attended a meeting of the Crow Indian Lodge in Lodge Grass where the group's grievances against Reynolds were reviewed and a vote was taken to send a delegation to Washington, D.C., to appeal for help. The same gathering dismissed George Pease as president of the CIL and replaced him with his half-brother, Joe Cooper. Angered by the rising chorus of protests against him, Reynolds ordered Grey off the reservation. She retreated to Sheridan, Wyoming, expecting to be joined shortly by five Crow Indian Lodge leaders who were to accompany her to Washington. Before they could act, however, the five – Spotted Rabbit, Holds The Enemy, Joe Cooper, Packs The Hat and Yellow Brow – were arrested by Big Medicine on the grounds that they could not leave the reservation without the permission of the agent. The men were held briefly and released with the understanding that they would remain at home.[33]

Convinced now that she was on the trail of a major story, Grey embarked for Washington alone. There she was able to arrange short audiences with President Theodore Roosevelt, Secretary of the Interior James R. Garfield and Indian Commissioner Francis Leupp, himself a former newspaperman. By now the seriousness of her charges and her access to the nation's newspapers made Helen Grey a figure to be reckoned with. Roosevelt and Garfield decided that an investigation was warranted, but they stopped short of turning the matter over to one of the Indian Office's regular investigators. Instead, Secretary Garfield decided to send Z. Lewis Dalby, a Virginia lawyer who served as his private secretary, to Crow Agency to study the situation personally. Dalby left Washington for Montana on May 18.[34]

---

[32] Some of these grievances were outlined in articles Grey probably inspired in the Sheridan *Post*. See issues for March 19 and June 7, 1907.

[33] See "Hearings Before the Committee on Indian Affairs, U.S. Senate on S. 2087, to Incorporate a Company for Breeding Horses on the Crow Indian Reservation, Montana, and for other purposes and on S.2963 for the Survey and Allotment of Indian Lands Now Embraced Within the Limits of the Crow Indian Reservation, In the State of Montana, and the Sale and Disposal of All Surplus Lands After Allotment," *Senate Document 445*, 60th Congress, 1st Session, 276, 554–556 (hereafter cited as "1908 Hearings").

[34] The departure date is mentioned in Reynolds to Helen Pierce Grey, May 18, 1907, Item 4, Box 24, RCIA-FRC, Seattle. The details of Dalby's appointment are in 1908 Hearings, 385–390.

The day before Dalby left, Agent Reynolds arrested Helen Grey and expelled her from the reservation. She had returned to Crow Agency in late April with permission to "attend ceremonial dances," but according to the agent she used the occasion to continue meeting with Crow Lodge leaders. "She assailed your office and ours to the Indians," Reynolds wrote to Commissioner Leupp the next day, "and so worked them up that they were on the edge of violence." Undaunted by the agent's action, the journalist insisted that she had the support of the entire tribe. She threatened to return again.[35]

As Grey and her allies awaited the arrival of Inspector Dalby, Big Medicine and his supporters began working to rally support for Reynolds and the agency status quo. With the assistance of the agent, they attempted to form a new men's club, the "Elk Lodge" and to use it counteract the advances of the CIL. Reynolds later claimed that the lodge was formed early in 1907 as a burial society to "provide mutual benefit" and to end the practice of self-mutilation which was a traditional part of Crow mourning. Despite this innocent official rationale, however, the group had a remarkably pointed entrance requirement: "The Indian promises to obey the laws of his country, rules and regulations governing his reservation . . . and that he will live [an] honorable and upright life." In the context of an intensifying controversy over the authority of the tribal police and the agent's definition of an "upright life," these qualifications were clearly intended to attract the most obedient residents of the reservation. Most Crow employees of the agency belonged to the Elks, including Carl Leider, the mixed-blood supporter of Plenty Coups who had risen to prominence during the 1899 land sale negotiations.[36]

Another facet of the Elk Lodge was suggested by missionary J. G. Burgess, a Reynolds critic, who claimed that the agent had been adopted into the Black Lodge chapter of the "Night Hawks," a hot dance drum group, and that the agent, in turn, had invited the dancers to a barbecue at Crow Agency where he urged them to join his new lodge. Burgess also charged that subsequent gatherings at Bighorn and Black Lodge had been held "to counteract the influence of the CIL, which was at that time under the influence of Mrs. Grey and favorable to her." While impossible to corroborate (the agency superintendent would hardly report his membership in a traditional dance club to Washington, D.C.), Burgess's charges square with a variety of other facts. Most Elks were from the Black Lodge district, Big Medicine's home territory, and an area with little regard for the recognized tribal leaders, all of whom were Mountain Crows. "It seems," said Sees With His Ears, a former follower of Sword Bearer

---

[35] Reynolds to Commissioner of Indian Affairs, May 18, 1907, 47356–1907, LR-OIA, RG 75, NA (copy in Item 2, Box 7, RCIA-FRC, Seattle).

[36] Reynolds to Commissioner of Indian Affairs, January 13, 1908, RCIA-FRC, Seattle. Lieder also worked as cattleman Frank Heinrich's agent among the Crows, arranging leases and making rent payments to individuals. See "Report on the Crow Indian Reservation," by Z. Lewis Dalby, CCF, File 150, Crow, 71908–07, 10.

who lived in Black Lodge, that "Plenty Coups and his aggregation seem to take a road off from the tribe, and do not keep in touch with the tribe, and this makes the younger people dissatisfied." Sees With His Ears was an active Elk member, as was Two Leggings, a district elder active in several traditional religious groups. As they expanded, the Elks tapped support that ran wider and deeper than simple affection for Samuel Reynolds and his definition of an "upright life."[37]

Just as nineteenth-century warrior societies had competed for the loyalty of promising young men, the two lodges now vied for support in the struggle over political leadership on the reservation. Big Medicine urged that Joe Cooper and "those boys . . . should not be heard," while putting forward as his followers similarly educated young men like Alexander Upshaw and Frank Shively, both agency employees. Philip Ironhead, who signed himself vice-president of the Bighorn Crow Lodge revealed the intensity of the competition in a letter written to his counterpart at Lodge Grass just before Inspector Dalby's arrival on the reservation. "The Elks are getting numerous," he warned, "and we must by all means prevent them from getting ahead of us in numbers. So we thought best to get in more members; old as well as the young. We want you to do the same. . . ."[38]

Inspector Dalby arrived at Crow Agency on May 23. He ordered Reynolds to allow Grey back on the reservation so that she could prepare her testimony, and he began soliciting statements from tribal leaders and government employees. He had his first full-scale meeting with the dissidents a week later when he travelled to Lodge Grass. The trip coincided with the district's annual tobacco planting ceremony, a coincidence which might account for the presence of Plenty Coups at this first conference, as well as for the obvious tension that surrounded the encounter. Medicine Crow, who had held himself aloof from the controversy, and whose Tobacco Society chapter was responsible for the Lodge Grass tobacco garden, was also present.

---

[37] J. G. Burgess to Z. Lewis Dalby, June 24, 1907, CCF, Crow, 150, 71908–07; Transcript of Testimony Taken on the Crow Reservation, Montana, Commencing October 25, 1909, Part I, 18844–10, LR-OIA, RG 75, NA, 8. For more on Lieder and other "loyal" mixed bloods, see testimony of Big Medicine in 1908 Hearings, 335, 336.

[38] 1908 Hearings, 336; Philip Iron Head to Frank Shane, May 13, 1907, IRA Mss., Reel 19. Later, in July, Helen Grey wrote to Holds The Enemy, "Give my greetings to the boys and tell them to stand by the C.I.L. though Reynolds intends to break it up because he knows what he can do." Grey to Holds The Enemy, July 12, 1907, CCF, Crow, 150, 71908–07.

During the same period that Helen Grey was involved in political rivalry on the reservation, Alexander Upshaw (a member of the pro-Reynolds Elk Lodge) was serving as the principal local contact for Edward S. Curtis, the Seattle photographer who was embarked on his monumental project to photograph all the major native groups in North America. See Mick Gidley, "Three Cultural Brokers in the Context of Edward S. Curtis's *The North American Indians*," in Margaret Connell Szasz, *Between Indian and White Worlds: The Cultural Broker* (Norman: University of Oklahoma Press, 1994).

Wearing their official badges and arrayed behind their leader Big Medicine, these Crow policemen were important allies of Agent Samuel Reynolds when they posed for this portrait in 1908. Courtesy of American Heritage Center, University of Wyoming.

The inspector spoke to a gathering of about sixty tribesmen. Already convinced that Grey was a "muckraker," Dalby insisted that the Crows speak to him directly and not through the journalist. He assured the crowd that he would listen, but he warned that anyone making unsubstantiated charges would be punished. The next day, Plenty Coups and Joe Cooper told the inspector they were prepared to drop their association with Helen Grey, providing she were allowed to leave the reservation without being investigated or harassed by the Indian Office. Dalby agreed, but when he returned to Lodge Grass the following day, Grey disrupted the meeting and tried to rally her supporters. At that point, Dalby later reported, he "turned to Mrs Grey and said to her again that she was still free to go without compulsion if she would . . . She refused to go and defied me to arrest her." Dalby ordered the tribal police to place her under arrest and put her on the next train for Wyoming.[39]

Dalby continued his investigation during June and July. He explored Grey's

[39] 1908 Hearings, 389–408; Dalby to Garfield, June 1, 1907, File 5–1 (Part 1), Indian Office, Crow, Investigation, Records Group 48, National Archives, Washington, D.C. (hereafter RG 48, NA). Dalby's account of his confrontation with Grey is in Dalby to Secretary of the Interior, June 8, 1907, CCF, Crow, 150, 71908–07, 11.

specific charges, but as he moved across the reservation it became clear that he was inclined towards Agent Reynolds's view of things. He ordered the Crows to return to their homes and to stop meeting in councils. He criticized the missionaries and reformers who had corroborated Grey's charges. He also relied on the agency police for information and support. Most telling, however, was his conduct during a private meeting with Plenty Coups in June at Pryor. "I had everyone else excluded from the room," Dalby later recalled. "I said: 'Now Plenty Coups, you have played into the hands of Mrs. Grey . . . I will pass it by this time because it has not done any harm; but I want you to understand that your position here as chief is not an official or necessary position. You have such influence as the Department of the Interior is willing that you should recognize.'" A few days after this confrontation, the secretary of the interior himself passed through the Yellowstone valley on his way to Oregon for a summer holiday. He sent the chief the following note from Billings:

> It is my earnest wish that from this time on none of you have any communication with Mrs. Grey. It is my further wish that you follow the advice given you by Mr. Dalby, the Inspector, and Mr. Reynolds, the Agent. The charges made against Mr. Reynolds were malicious and false. He has my confidence, and I ask that you give him yours. If you have any just cause for complaint, you need not go to any outside person. . . . Nothing but harm to you and your people can result from such trouble and agitation as has resulted from Mrs. Grey's visit.[40]

No one was surprised when Dalby's report appeared in August, exonerating Reynolds and condemning Grey. Divisions continued within the tribe, but the Elk Lodge now appeared to have gained an upper hand. A Billings clergyman reported in October that the Crow Indian Lodge "is being persecuted by the Indians of the other side now in many ways. They taunt them and laugh at them and tell them they can't get any favors. As a consequence the feelings are intense."[41]

Assured of Reynolds "favor" the Elks could celebrate their victory in the traditional Crow way – through taunts and jokes directed at their rivals. The

---

[40] 1908 Hearings, 412–413; James Rudolph Garfield to Plenty Coos (*sic*), June 26, 1907, Plenty Coups Mss. Later in 1907, the photographer Edward S. Curtis, who had spent considerable time among the Crows, advised Secretary Garfield that the government should cooperate with Plenty Coups. Garfield passed the letter on to Dalby who replied, "I agree . . . as to the desirability of using Plenty Coups' influence, *provided Plenty Coups exerts that influence for good*. But if Plenty Coups does not exert his influence for good, he should be dealt with exactly as any other Indian. This is substantially what I said to Plenty Coups himself." See Curtis to James R. Garfield, November 21, 1907; and Dalby to Garfield, November 22, 1907, File 5–1 (Part 2), Miscellaneous Correspondence, Dalby Investigation, Indian Office, Crow Investigation, RG 48, NA.
[41] B. Z. McColloch to Welsh, October 19, 1907, IRA Mss., Reel 19.

Crow Lodge responded in kind, but theirs was a losing proposition. Missionary Burgess at Crow Agency reported that during the annual fair in October, the CIL had a procession "with floats and a band wagon with CIL in white on the sides." Despite their brave showing, however, Burgess reported that Reynolds's critics "are becoming discouraged and worn out as there seems no help in sight."[42]

By December, when a Helena grand jury began hearing charges that Helen Grey had illegally solicited money from the Crows for her initial trip to Washington, D.C., it seemed that Reynolds, Big Medicine and their allies were going to succeed in their campaign to discredit the journalist. The agent declared a smallpox quarantine around the reservation to prevent any of Grey's allies from appearing in court, and he moved forward with the support of the state's Republican political leaders. In a plea to the Philadelphia-based Indian Rights Association, Grey reported that she expected to escape indictment, but that the agent's critics on the reservation were completely intimidated. "It is now too late," she reported. "Fred Geisdorf, an intelligent half-breed, . . . writes that the president of the Lodge Grass Crow Indian Lodge is in the Agency guard house. Joe Cooper returns with the expectation of the same. Mr. Reynolds openly says he will punish every Indian who has taken part against him." Grey did escape indictment, but she was ordered not to return to the reservation, and the new year began with the tribe seemingly fixed on a downward spiral of recrimination and disunion.[43]

Caught between the agent and his critics, tribal leaders seemed locked in what was now a familiar dilemma: to side with Reynolds and lose all semblance of independence or to stick with Grey and become impotent. Remarkably, their response once more was to seek out some other ground on which to stand. Fortunately, the Indian Office bureaucracy soon provided Plenty Coups and his fellow chiefs and head men with the perfect issue with which to rebuild their political support and rehabilitate their authority: yet another assault on Crow lands.

---

[42] Burgess to Welsh, October 22, 1907; IRA Mss., Reel 19. The Crow Indian Lodge produced yet another petition during the summer of 1907. This was a request for a new investigator on the grounds that the group had lost confidence in him. None of the major chiefs signed the document; it carried only thirty-six signatures. The Crow Tribe of Indians to the President, July 7, 1907, CCF, Crow, 150, 71908–07.

[43] Grey to Matthew Sniffen, December 20, 1907, IRA Mss. Following the grand jury examination in December, Grey renewed her attacks on Reynolds and his ties to local businessmen. She was supported in her campaign by the local Democratic party (future U.S. Senator Thomas J. Walsh was her attorney before the grand jury) and opposed by the Republican establishment. One particularly outraged Republican was former agent John Edwards, who in 1907 had become State Senator Edwards of Forsyth, Montana. When Edwards found the editor of the Democratically oriented Billings *Inquirer* selling his newspapers in Forsyth, he knocked him through a plate glass window. See Burgess to Cooper, December 6, 1907, and December 16, 1907, IRA Mss., Reel 20.

V

Early in February, 1908, Inspector James McLaughlin, former superintendent at Sitting Bull's Hunkapapa Sioux Agency at Fort Yates, North Dakota, and now the Indian Office's toughest negotiator, was dispatched to Crow Agency to win approval for the disposition of all remaining tribal land. Now that the allotment of the reservation was complete (and the reservation's leaders in disarray), McLaughlin's superiors believed the time was right to arrange for a final purchase from the tribe. Speaking to a gathering of fifty-nine "leading men" of the reservation, the bearded inspector struck an aggressive note: "The increasing white population of this great country demands additional lands as homes for settlers," he told the group. "I am telling you the naked truth when I say that I believe that there will not be a foot of surplus Indian reservation land in the United States that will not be open to settlement in the near future."[44]

Despite the short notice and contentious atmosphere, the Crow reaction to McLaughlin's proposal was uniform. Plenty Coups spoke first. "I do not want to bargain with the Government or anyone else to dispose of our lands," he declared; "the land is mine and I do not want to sell it at all." As other men rose to respond it rapidly became obvious that the sharp, internal divisions of the previous two years had disappeared. Bell Rock, whom Dalby had indicated would succeed Plenty Coups if the Pryor leader were deposed, spoke next. "I do not want any more bargains or sales," he cried, "and I want you to take my words direct to the President." The Lodge Grass and Bighorn dissidents were represented by Medicine Crow and Spotted Rabbit. They too rejected the government's proposal. Big Medicine, the agent's most stalwart supporter, was diplomatic but clear: "Among my people," he explained, "many of the women are in a pregnant condition and expect to have healthy children, and we need our land to share and share alike in the making of allotments." Even the detested Fire Bear, the policeman who killed Sword Bearer, declared, "We . . . all refuse to consent to the opening of our reservation."[45]

The solid wall of opposition facing James McLaughlin reflected the lessons Crow leaders had learned during the previous year's upheavals. They did not bring back the presidium system of the 1890s. Instead, in the aftermath of Helen Grey's investigations tribal leaders set out to construct ways of encompassing and managing dissent within the community. The principal method of accomplishing this goal was a system of district representation that began to appear when major issues came before the tribe. Initially, this approach was used to select delegates to travel to Washington in 1908 to testify in opposition

---

[44] 1908 Hearings, 776.
[45] Ibid., 771, 772, 773, 774.

to the proposed sale of surplus land. The group contained prominent leaders of the Crow and Elk lodges, such as Joe Cooper and Big Medicine, as well as men from Pryor, Reno, Lodge Grass, Black Lodge and the Bighorn.

The position of one delegate on that journey, James Hill, a thirty-three-year-old former student at the Carlisle Indian School who farmed in the Bighorn district, summarized this new Crow unity. In the future, Hill told the Senate Committee on Indian Affairs, "The reservation that is going to be thrown open is one of the principal things that we are going to use . . . We are going to use every foot of that land . . . and we do not want to sell it at all." Under the force of necessity, leaders from Plenty Coups to James Hill understood that to preserve their own community's independence, future Crow leaders would have to represent the land as well as their kinsmen and immediate supporters. To do this, they would have to build a following among people who represented all the interests and points of view contained within the boundaries of the reservation. To continue an older system based on personal prestige and influence was to leave themselves open to manipulation by outsiders; to construct a new method of leadership, rooted in the support of every district within their territory, would be the price of defending their homeland.[46]

Rivalry between the Elk and Crow Lodges continued during the remainder of 1908. In October, Joe Cooper reported that the Crows were gaining ground and the Elks shrinking in reaction, but others claimed that Crow Lodge members were defecting to the Elks in hopes of landing jobs at the agency. Opposition to any further land sales continued to unite the tribe, however, and the inauguration of President Taft, along with appointment of a new secretary of the interior and commissioner of Indian affairs early in 1909 offered the chance that a shift in personnel would reduce political tensions on the reservation. In July 1909, the new commissioner, Robert Valentine, invited Matthew Sniffen of the Indian Rights Association to travel to Crow Agency to look again at the issue of reservation administration and to hear the Indians' complaints. Taft's secretary of the interior, Richard Ballinger, visited the reservation during that same summer, and in October he dispatched E. P. Holcomb, the Indian Office's chief supervisor to conduct a new round of hearings at the agency. "The

---

[46] 1908 Hearings, 521. The Sheridan *Post* reported a brief diplomatic ceremony which occurred at the conclusion of the Senate hearings into the Grey affair. Plenty Coups marched to the front of the committee room at the head of his delegation and informed the Indian Affairs Committee chair, Moses Clapp of Minnesota, that his judicious handling of the proceedings had earned him a gift. The newspaper continued:

> Chief Plenty Coups then took from one of his followers a huge war bonnet, which had been the chief's insignia of rank and worn by him whenever he went into battle. He said that he was now a man of peace and that the bonnet was of less value to him on the reservation than it would be to the senator in congress. . . .

See Sheridan *Post*, April 17, 1908.

situation at Crow is now full of possibilities," the Indian Rights Association's Sniffen wrote in September.[47]

Inspector Holcomb's hearings began on October 25, 1909, and lasted for nearly three weeks. Assisted by Sniffen and held principally in the carpenter shop at the agency, they provided a broad cross-section of the tribe an opportunity to express their views on reservation life, the sale of tribal lands and a variety of other topics. Little of the information contained in the more than 600 pages of testimony generated by the hearings was new. Agent Reynolds and Big Medicine were accused of sins from adultery to grand larceny and local stock- and cattlemen were pilloried for cheating the tribe and corrupting its leaders. Running through this rhetoric were references to the Crow and Elk Lodges, but the exact membership of these groups had begun to grow vague. Joe Cooper and Big Medicine remained the most prominent speakers for each organization, but few others were eager to claim them as allies. The interests of each group – and their membership – seemed uncertain and subject to change.[48]

Two Leggings, who had been identified as president of the Elks a year earlier, now attacked Agent Reynolds and the tribal police, declaring that "I want all this administration at the agency removed . . . and good men put in their place." Plenty Coups, who had attended Crow Lodge meetings even though he remained officially neutral, was now identified with the agent and his Elk allies. In response, Crow Lodge members began equating all the older men with the Elks. Holcomb asked one of them, "Have the CIL members decided that the old chiefs are too old to govern them?" "Yes sir," was the reply. Having momentarily blunted the congressional attack on their lands, and lacking any other overriding issue to unite or divide them, Crow leaders appeared unsure of themselves and in need of some mechanism for fashioning a unified stance. The 1909 hearings provided an opportunity for them to begin constructing that mechanism.[49]

On November 3, Scolds The Bear, one of the policemen who had arrested Helen Grey at Lodge Grass in 1907, momentarily departed from the hearing's familiar pattern of charges and countercharges when he observed that the Crow and Elk Lodges "started out with good intentions," but that a "certain white woman came here and spoiled everything." Scolds The Bear went on to say that

---

[47] Cooper quoted in B. Z. McCulloch to Sniffen, October 12, 1908, IRA Mss., Reel 20; see also "Testimony of George No Horse," CCF, Crow, 150, 18844–10. Part II, p. 89; Sniffen to Miss Mateer, September 7, 1909, IRA Mss., Reel 21. A sour assessment of Valentine's actions can be found in two letters from former inspector Z. Lewis Dalby to his old boss, James R. Garfield, dated November 19 and December 6, 1909, both in Container 110, James R. Garfield Papers, Library of Congress.

[48] For the arrangements made prior to Holcomb's arrival, see Samuel Reynolds to E. P. Holcomb, October 19, 1909, Item 4, Box 26, RCIA-FRC, Seattle.

[49] See "Transcript of Testimony," CCF, Crow, 150, 18844–10, Part 1, 61; and ibid., Part 2, 276; and Sniffen to Mateer, November 17, 1909, IRA Mss., Reel 21.

he wanted "to see all this confusion laid aside, and the whole tribe work together towards advancement." The following evening, Scolds The Bear's observation became the basis for a resolution of the conflict between the two lodges and a surprising end to the hearings. Plenty Coups and other older leaders were present at the November 4 session, but most of those who spoke that night were younger, educated Crows who seemed momentarily to seize the initiative. James Carpenter and Joe Cooper, consistent leaders of the Lodge Grass Crow Indian Lodge, began the evening by attacking Big Medicine and denouncing the Elk Lodge in familiar terms. "I am an Indian," the balding Cooper declared, "and I am for my people."[50]

The longest speech of the evening was given by Russell White Bear, a twenty-eight-year-old former Carlisle student who had returned to the reservation in 1903 to farm and to teach at the Pryor boarding school. White Bear ignored the complaints which began the hearings and focused instead on the divisions within the tribe. "We don't seem to know what the trouble is," he observed, but he added that unity promised more than the victory of one group over the other. Sensing, perhaps, that the group was ready for a new departure, White Bear invited the assembled dignitaries to heal their differences:

> Now as we are sitting here tonight we can get up and shake hands with one another and be altogether as one people. If we can get together as a body and be that way, if we make a demand to the government, then the government will listen to us and will consider the demand we make if we are one.

After reviewing the problems before them, White Bear asserted that a united tribe could dictate its policies to the government rather than the other way around. Educated Crows could be put in charge of the agency bureaucracy, he suggested, and the local agent could act as "our lawyer." The young teacher implored his audience, "Right now this very minute let us quit and shake hands and take each other by the arm and hold each other up. . . . Do not consider anyone as a CIL, and do not consider anyone as an Elk, forget that, and consider yourselves all as Crow Indians. Remember that you are Crow Indians."[51]

Rising so quickly that one might suspect that it had been prearranged, Plenty Coups, Yellow Crane and Bell Rock – all old warriors now in their sixties – gave brief speeches accepting White Bear's invitation. They were followed by Curley, a former scout from Black Lodge who had been an Elk leader. Dramatically removing the campaign button which many lodge members now wore, Curley declared that he did so "as a sign that I am putting down the differences between us. . . ." Leaders from both sides began coming forward, placing their buttons on the table before Holcomb. Only Cooper hesitated. "This is a big

---

[50] See "Transcript of Testimony," CCF, Crow, 150, 18844–10, 478.
[51] Ibid., 452, 474, 476.

Sitting shoulder to shoulder, Plenty Coups and Big Medicine (sitting to the chief's right and wearing his broad-brimmed policeman's hat) offer an image of tribal unity in this photograph taken about 1910. Also included in this tableau are younger, short-haired men recently returned from school and other supporters from across the reservation. Courtesy of Museum of the Rockies, Montana State University.

trouble," Holcomb told him, "and it takes a big man like you, Joe Cooper, to meet such an emergency." Placing his button on the table, Cooper replied," I surrender this night as General Lee did."[52]

For the remainder of the Holcomb hearings the call for tribal unity emerged as a rallying cry and was rapidly joined by a desire to form a new kind of tribal council that would hear all points of view, but speak with one voice. In Lodge Grass, two days after Cooper's "surrender," One Star, a former tribal police-man who had been fired after criticizing Big Medicine and the Elks, avoided attacking his old enemy and noted instead that since "we have no chief of this district," he and his neighbors should be allowed "to appoint three of our own men whom we choose [who] will represent us at these councils." Holcomb agreed. "I think it would be an excellent idea if you could get together among

[52] Ibid., 482, 488. The next day Holcomb wrote a personal letter to Cooper congratulating him on his concession which said in part, "I trust that the nobility of your act will be appreciated by all the members of the tribe, and that the spirit that prompted you will grow...." Holcomb to Joseph Cooper, November 6, 1909, filed with, "E. P. Holcomb, Supervisor, Submits the Results of his Investigation....", CCF, Crow, 150, 18844–10.

yourselves to let each district elect two or three members . . . who would represent that district in the councils of the tribe."[53]

Accelerating pressure on the Crows to sell more of their land encouraged the move toward the formation of some kind of representative tribal government. Tensions continued between leaders of different districts, as well as between elders and returning students, and the "agency crowd" and those who resisted contact with the government. Nevertheless, the political struggles of the "Helen Grey affair" ended the period when a tribal presidium could lead through personal influence and turned the tribe sharply towards representative democracy.

Agent Reynolds was too optimistic when he wrote that the Holcomb investigation "has been the means of settling . . . factional differences" within the community, but the basis for a new unity seems to have been established by the time the inspector filed his report in on March 7, 1910. Big Medicine, Fire Bear and a number of unpopular tribal judges were dismissed, and the two lodges faded from view. While cleared of wrongdoing, Reynolds soon resigned and returned to his job as cashier of a Billings bank. In the aftermath of these departures, it appeared that tribal members now saw the management and protection of their reservation as a collective responsibility.

Six months after Holcomb's report was filed, in September 1910, a group of Crow leaders gathered to form the first tribal business committee. While later condemned by the reservation's new agent as "the creation and tool of the worst element of our Indians," this group made clear than in the aftermath of the Grey affair, the Crows understood the value of a representative body as a place to air the community's differences and forge a consensus on the future. Its first officers were the former Crow Indian Lodge leader, Joe Cooper, and another young mixed blood man who had recently returned from Carlisle: George Washington Hogan. The next decade would put this new instrument of leadership to active use.[54]

VI

The final political crisis of the early reservation era was a struggle to protect the tribe's communal lands that culminated in the passage of the Crow Act of June 1920. The effort to "open" the reservation to outsiders began in the midst of

[53] Ibid., Part 3, 385; Part 4, 12, 13.
[54] Reynolds to Commissioner of Indian Affairs, November 15, 1909, Item 2, Box 8, RCIA-FRC, Seattle. For Holcomb's report, see "E. P. Holcomb, Supervisor, Submits the Results . . . ," CCF, Crow, 150, 18844–10. For comment on 1910 committee, see W. W. Scott to Commissioner of Indian Affairs, January 12, 1911, Item 14, Box 50, Council Proceedings, 1911–1913, RCIA-FRC, Seattle. The minutes of the first business committee meeting, taken by George Washington Hogan, are in CCF, Crow, 057, 89531–1910.

Despite Superintendent Scott's objection to Cooper and the other early committee members, the Indian Office insisted that he work with the group. See Commissioner of Indian Affairs to Scott, March 2, 1911, CCF, Crow, 057, 89531–1910. Other correspondence in this file discusses the activities of the committee during its first year of work.

the Helen Grey affair when Inspector McLaughlin swooped down on a divided tribal leadership, waving a copy of a land sale agreement that was already before Congress. It continued through three separate attempts by Congress to impose a "sale" on the tribe and did not end until a group of Crow delegates, assisted by their Washington attorneys, hammered out compromise legislation and lobbied it to passage. When the Crow Act became law, it was both a bulwark against the wholesale expropriation of tribal lands and a monument to the tenacity and inventiveness of the reservation's new political leadership.

In 1908, when Medicine Crow responded to the government's first offer to buy the Crow "surplus" lands, he offered something different from previous speakers. Instead of simply rejecting James McLaughlin's proposal out of hand, he turned to three young men and asked them to help devise some compromise. Motioning to Frank Shively, Carl Leider and James Hill, Medicine Crow said, "I call upon you to devise a plan whereby we may have some lands retained for the raising of horses and cattle. We put you in school to learn the white man's way and be able to help us when we are in straits like this. It is up to you . . . You understand how to do things." As others spoke in support of the Lodge Grass chief's idea, it was clear that the assembled "leading men" understood that resistance alone would not defeat the proposal to bring white settlers on the reservation. As they had so many times in their past, the Crows looked for a tactic that would allow them to win their objective without having to make a frontal assault on their enemies. In each of the three attempts to force a bill onto the tribe, Crow leaders worked to maneuver their opponents to the bargaining table.

The first effort to "open" the reservation was sponsored by Montana Senator Joseph Dixon in December 1907. Modeled after the ratified version of the 1899 land sale agreement, the Republican lawmaker's proposal called for opening 2.5 million acres of unallotted Crow lands to homesteading. The government would pay nothing for the land, but would pass all homesteading fees on to the tribe. At the council called by James McLaughlin in February 1908 to discuss the proposal, tribal leaders objected both to the sale itself and to the fact that the government would not be obligated to pay the Crows for the land it acquired; it would only "act as trustee for said Indians to dispose of said lands and to pay over the proceeds received from the sale thereof only as received." Despite its adamant opposition, however, the council acted on Medicine Crow's suggestion and sent Plenty Coups and a group of five educated young men to Washington to present their views.[55]

The 1908 delegation was diplomatic (Plenty Coups called on President Roosevelt and presented him with a war bonnet) but firm. They sought out the assistance of the Indian Rights Association's Washington lobbyist, Samuel

[55] Dixon's bill was S.2963, 60th Congress, 1st Session. It was discussed in *Senate Report 581*, see esp. 4. The delegates sent in early 1908 were Plenty Coups, Carl Leider, Frank Shively, James Hill, David Stewart and Horace Long Bear. See S Doc 445, 60th Congress, 1st Session (Serial 5260), 786.

Brosius, and made the most of the negative publicity surrounding the investigation of Agent Reynolds. This assistance, coupled with their uniform opposition to the measure, succeeded in burying it in a house committee until the final days of the Sixtieth Congress. When a last-ditch effort to resurrect the bill failed and Congress adjourned in March 1909, missionary J. G. Burgess, wrote that the Crows "have learned that unity is strength, that sticking to a thing through thick and thin will prevail and that there were white people outside of the reservation who really care for and will help the Indian."[56]

Before Dixon could file his bill for a second time, the Crows took the offensive. Early in 1909 several Crow leaders contacted Charles J. Kappler, a Washington attorney who had served for a time as clerk to the Senate Indian Affairs Committee and who had begun to represent tribes with complaints against the government. Kappler is best remembered as the author of the first official compilation of all ratified Indian treaties, but in 1909 he was preoccupied with his Indian clients, a group that included the Osage and Chickasaw. The reasons for the Crows' initial approach is unknown, but with proposals for the opening of their lands apparently proliferating, they were obviously eager to bolster their position in the nation's capital. By the end of June 1909, a petition asking that the firm of Kappler and Merillat be appointed "to represent them in their claims before the Congress and the government departments" had been signed by Holds The Enemy, Plenty Coups, Big Medicine and 141 others and was on its way to the Indian Office. "I am confident, Agent Reynolds wrote in a covering letter, "that the granting of their request will be a benefit to the Indians."[57]

---

[56] Burgess to Sniffen, March 16, 1909, IRA Mss., Reel 21. The account of Plenty Coups's call on President Roosevelt is in the Hardin *Herald*, April 24, 1908. (Recall that the chief also gave a bonnet to the chair of the Indian Affairs Committee on the same trip. See note 46, above.) See also Brosius to Sniffen, May 28, 1908, and Grey to Brosius, May 1908, IRA Mss., Reel 20.

[57] Reynolds to Commissioner, June 28, 1909, Item 2, Box 8, RCIA-FRC, Seattle. The petition, dated June 17, 1909, is in Container B122, Indian Affairs File-Kappler and Merillat, Part 1, Robert Lafollette Papers, Library of Congress (hereafter cited as Lafollette Mss.).

In making this request, tribal leaders may have acted on the suggestion of Helen Grey, who was now living in Washington and who had urged them to hire a lawyer, or they may have contemplated filing a suit before the U.S. Court of Claims. Grey opposed the Kappler and Merillat firm. See Grey to Herbert Welsh, March 1, 1909, IRA Mss., Reel 21; Council minutes of February 18, 1909, enclosed in Reynolds to Commissioner, September 30, 1909, Item 2, Box 8, RCIA-FRC, Seattle. According to the council minutes, Plenty Coups said, "Every now and then I hear of a tribe of Indians getting a big chunk of money on some old land matter. They have taken a big lot of country from the Crows that we were never paid for. . . ." In June of 1909, Two Leggings wrote to the secretary of the interior that "we went a lawyer in whom we have confidence to look after our interests." (Two Leggings to Secretary of the Interior, June 11, 1909, IRA Mss., Reel 21.) Another possibility is that Kappler and Merillat were suggested by Robert Lafollette, then a member of the Indian Affairs Committee. See Brosius to Sniffen, December 30, 1909, IRA Mss., Reel 21.

Finally, there may well have been some contact between the Crows and Oklahoma groups who had already retained Washington attorneys. Quanah Parker, for example, had worked closely with attorney William T. Shelley during the struggle to block the seizure of Kiowa and Comanche lands. See William T. Hagan, *Quanah Parker: Comanche Chief* (Norman: University of Oklahoma Press, 1992), 94–100.

Plenty Coups travelled to Washington in August 1909 on another matter, but he also met with Kappler and his partner, Charles H. Merillat, for the pair sent a letter to the "Chief of the Crow Tribe" at Pryor a few weeks after his return home. Kappler and his partner expressed an interest in representing the tribe and suggested that the Crows "might take some steps at this time which would enable it to act speedily upon a contract with us when the time is ripe and the conditions favorable. . . ." Specifically, Kappler and Merillat noted that "many of the Indian tribes have an arrangement whereby all of the tribe are represented through what are called business committees which are selected among the members of the tribe." They added that two representatives might be elected to such a committee from each of the reservation's six districts and that "the time of the Crow fair would be a good time to have a general council meeting and pass a resolution" creating such a group. Enclosed with the letter was a draft resolution authorizing the Crow business committee, "if this letter meets the approval of the tribe."[58]

The Crows, still divided between Elks and the CIL, delayed acting formally on their lawyers' suggestion until the 1910 Crow fair. Nevertheless, all parties agreed that the tribe should press ahead with its request for legal representation before Congress. When the Sixty-First Congress assembled in December 1909, the Indian Office had still not approved Kappler and Merillat, so a general council simply dispatched its own delegation to Washington. Local whites, determined not to suffer a second defeat, protested. As the Hardin *Herald* declared in a front page editorial, "We do not believe that the desire of some shiftless Indians . . . should have . . . the first consideration of our representatives." With another battle building, a general council passed yet another resolution in March 1910 authorizing Joe Cooper and Frank Shively "to make and execute" and agreement with the Kappler firm. The three men signed the contract in Washington at the end of March and forwarded it to the Indian Office for approval.[59]

On April 16, 1910, Indian Commissioner Robert Valentine rejected the Crow

[58] Kappler and Merillat to Plenty Coups, September 17, 1909, Plenty Coups Mss. Plenty Coups travelled to Washington to be present at the opening of bids for cattle leasing, where he probably met the lawyers who were already acting on the Crows' behalf. See Reynolds to Plenty Coups, July 20 and 23, 1909, Item 4, Box 26, RCIA-FRC, Seattle.

[59] The Indian Office's indifference to the tribe's desire for an attorney is reflected in Commissioner Robert Valentine's letter to Plenty Coups, dated August 3, 1909, that insisted that the "most important" thing the tribe could do to help itself would be to "work and become self-supporting." Plenty Coups Mss.

    Hardin *Herald*, December 17, 1909, February 11, 1910; tribal resolution, March 22, 1910, and contract dated February 10, 1910, both in Container B122, Indian Affairs Files, Crow-Kappler and Merillat, Part 1, Lafollette Mss. Apparently the discrepancy in the council action and the contract dates is a result of the fact that the February contract was quickly disqualified since it did not have council endorsement. A second contract was sent to the Indian Office on March 30, 1910; a copy of it could not be found in the archives. See Kappler and Merillat to Commissioner, March 30, 1910, Container B-122, Indian Affairs Files, Crow-Kappler and Merillat, Part 1, Lafollette Mss.

contract with Kappler and Merillat. "There is no apparent necessity for counsel for the Crow Indians," Valentine wrote. The commissioner's action had little effect on the tribe's relationship with the law firm. In March, the attorneys had accompanied Frank Shively, Joe Cooper and George Washington Hogan when they met with Senator Dixon to attempt a compromise on the opening of the reservation. The three young men had been authorized to remain in Washington after the remainder of the Crow delegation returned home. In April (following Valentine's rejection of the tribe's contract with the law firm), Dixon himself presided over what he called "many long and detailed hearings" (some of which may have taken place in the Kappler and Merillat offices), which produced a substitute measure that took a new approach to the tribe's surplus lands. Instead of opening up unallotted areas to white settlement, the substitute called for the division of all remaining tribal land into individual shares that would be distributed to tribal members. Some restrictions would apply to the sale of these shares, but all of the income from them would go to their individual owners. Dixon's new proposal also stipulated that all mineral rights would be retained by the tribe and administered by the Indian Office.[60]

The Dixon substitute bill passed the Senate in May 1910, but when it reached the lower chamber, Montana's lone representative, Republican Charles Nelson Pray of Great Falls, succeeded in replacing it with the original, 1907 bill, which would have simply opened all unallotted lands to homesteading. Kappler and Merillat, still acting without authorization, testified against the measure before the House committee, but Pray, who came to Congress from an area where support for opening Blackfeet, Gros Ventre and other reservation lands was strong, persisted. The congressman declared that there was "no earthly reason why any more lands should be given to the Indians." To accept the proposal of the tribe's lawyers, he added without irony, "would result in perpetuating the reservation and the tribal relationship." Despite such determined opposition, however, the Crows continued to benefit from the work of Kappler and Merillat, and the support of both the Indian Rights Association and Congressman Pray's Democratic party rivals. The latter saw the "defense of the Crows" as an opportunity to embarrass the Republicans and support the Indians' right "to a voice in the mode whereby his large tribal holdings shall be disposed of. . . ." With this coalition in place, Pray's bill was defeated in two separate roll call votes in June 1910 and March 1911.[61]

Resisting Pray's assaults in 1910 and 1911 was a vindication of the Crows'

---

[60] Valentine to Kappler and Merillat, April 16, 1910, Container B-122, Indian Affairs File-Crow, Kappler and Merillat, Part 1, Lafollette Mss.; Brosius to Sniffen, March 10, 1910, and Kappler and Merillat to Sniffen, April 15, 1910, IRA Mss., Reel 21. The senate report on Dixon's substitute bill is Senate Report 526, 61st Congress, 2nd Session (Serial 5583).

A long defense of Kappler and Merillat's role in these negotiations was presented in a letter from the firm to Oscar Lawler, Assistant Attorney General, June 2, 1910, IRA Mss., Reel 21.

[61] *Congressional Record*, June 20, 1910, 61st Congress, 2nd Session, 8560–8561; *House Report 1495, Part II*, "Views of the Minority," 61st Congress, 2nd Session, 16.

unorthodox (and unauthorized) techniques. Tribal leaders continued to communicate with Kappler and Merillat despite the fact that the Indian Office would not approve a contract with them. Writing in March 1911, for example, the lawyers suggested passing resolutions of gratitude to the Democratic leadership and sending a detailed response to Congressman Pray's speeches to the Interior Department "which can be presented to Congress when it again assembles." The Indian Office deeply resented this independence. Agent Reynolds's replacement, W. W. Scott, wrote to headquarters that "this correspondence with our Indians is productive of much annoyance to this office and is detrimental to the Indians." Kappler and Merillat replied by continuing to send Agent Scott carbon copies of all its letters to tribal leaders.[62]

Because of the tribe's steady opposition (and also, perhaps, because of the silent happiness of the cattlemen leasing unallotted land on the reservation), Congress did not consider seriously any further land sale agreements until 1915. In the summer of that year, Montana's Democratic senator, Henry L. Myers (who was up for reelection the following year), began meeting with Yellowstone valley constituents to plan another assault on the Crows' unallotted lands. Acknowledging that "opposition in the East" made obtaining passage of such legislation difficult, Myers promised a compromise bill. Tribal leaders began preparing for another campaign. In August, Plenty Coups and sixty-two other Crow men from Bighorn and Pryor sent a petition to the commissioner of Indian affairs asking "all kindly and honestly disposed people" to support them in their "last stand." In September, tribal leaders met in Hardin with both Senator Myers and Wyoming's newly elected Democratic Governor, John Benjamin Kendrick. Kendrick, a Sheridan rancher who would leave the governorship in 1917 to enter the U.S. Senate, was obviously present to buttress the efforts of his fellow Democrat. But the centerpiece of Myers's gathering was what the Hardin *Herald* called "an extended speech" by a young boarding school graduate from Lodge Grass named Robert Yellowtail. Not yet thirty years old, Yellowtail mustered legal and moral arguments to urge the politicians to abandon their plans for a new bill. While the Hardin reporter summarized rather than reported Yellowtail's words directly, he conceded that the young man was "quite an orator." His performance foreshadowed the appeals Crow leaders would make to outsiders for decades to come: tribal lands could not be taken without the permission of the tribal government.[63]

[62] Kappler and Merillat to Plenty Coups ("Dear Friend"), March 6, 1911, and March 16, 1911, Container B-122, Indian Affairs File, Kappler and Merillat, Part 2, Lafollette Mss. (both also in Plenty Coups Mss.); Scott to Commissioner of Indian Affairs, March 25, 1911, Item 14, Box 50, Council Proceedings, RCIA-FRC, Seattle; and Kappler and Merillat to W. W. Scott, March 18, 1911, Plenty Coups Mss. The tribal business committee responded to Pray's charges in a resolution passed on April 19, 1911; see Plenty Coups Mss.

[63] Plenty Coups and Sixty-two others to Commissioner of Indian Affairs, August 25, 1915, Plenty Coups Mss.; Hardin *Herald*, September 3, 1915.

But Myers and his Democratic colleague, Thomas J. Walsh of Helena, forged ahead. In December 1915, the two senators introduced a proposal to open all of the unallotted land west of the Bighorn and east of the Little Bighorn to homesteaders. Even though the sponsors promised that the tribe would retain the unallotted lands between the two rivers as a communal grazing area, the reactions to his bill were an echo the struggle of 1908–10. A general council of the tribe met to "vigorously protest" Myers's efforts; Charles Kappler appeared at the Senate hearing on the bill to argue the tribe's position; and the Indian Rights Association issued a special pamphlet condemning this attempted "raid on the Crow Indian lands." In addition, the Indian Office, which had previously favored the Dixon and Pray proposals (and which continued to deny approval of Kappler and Merillat), now opposed the idea of further land sales. "There is no urgent necessity for the opening of this reservation," Assistant Commissioner Edgar Meritt told the Senate Indian Affairs Committee.[64]

During the summer of 1916 Crow leaders called a general council to prepare for what they assumed would be another battle over the Myers proposal in the next session of Congress. Evan Estep, the Crow agent, noted that the session ran until midnight on August 4, but that the tribe voted unanimously to oppose any further opening of tribal land. "There was much talk and some of it was rather firey," Estep wrote in his diary, "but the most of them knew what they wanted and stayed until they got it." Readying themselves for an end-of-session attempt to pass the bill, the tribe also held district elections in January 1917 to select a delegation to represent them in Washington. Plenty Coups headed the group as "delegate at large," and he was accompanied by fourteen others, two

---

[64] The Myers bill, S. 2378 (64th Congress, 1st Session), was filed on December 16, 1915, but the tribal council knew in advance of the proposal and met in November to condemn it. For its resolution, see, "Opening of the Crow Indian Reservation," Hearing, December 13, 1916, 5–8. Kappler's statement is in ibid., Part 2, June 23, 1916, 134 (copy filed as Item 15, Box 81, "Acts of Congress and Proposed Legislation), RCIA-FRC, Seattle. The Indian Rights Association pamphlet, entitled "A Threatened Raid on Crow Indian Lands," was published in Philadelphia on January 5, 1916 (copy in Plenty Coups Mss.). Meritt's statement is in "Opening of the Crow Indian Reservation," Hearing, June 23, 1916, 138.

Kappler and Merillat was still operating without a contract approved by the Indian Office. See Charles Kappler to Plenty Coups, December 29, 1915, and June 17 and 23, 1916, and Cato Sells to Charles Kappler, June 12, 1916, Plenty Coups Mss. In addition, Container B-122, Kappler and Merillat File, Part 1, in Lafollette Mss. contains correspondence in the period from 1910 to 1915 on the issue of the law firm's status as representative of the tribe.

The tribal council's resolution, passed in November 1915, added a new argument to its previous position, the fact that white Montanans discriminated against Indians and were not ready for the integration of the races: "a chasm exists between the two people, evidently because of racial feeling, the white man feeling much superior to the Indian, therefore unfit for his association, as evidenced by the fact that Jim Crow tables are in existence in both Hardin, Montana, and Crow Agency, Montana; that the public schools of Wyola and Lodge Grass have refused to admit Indian children who were eligible by reason of their legal status and were shown the greatest of racial hatred." See "Opening of the Crow Indian Reservation," Hearings, December 13, 1916, 6.

each from Black Lodge, Reno, Lower Bighorn, St. Xavier, Lodge Grass, Pryor and Wyola. Among the delegates were Packs The Hat, James Carpenter and Spotted Rabbit, former Crow Indian Lodge activists, as well as former Elks such as Two Leggings and several young returned students. The latter group included Jack Stewart, brother of the former agency interpreter and peyote leader; Barney Old Coyote, a former teacher at the Catholic day school in the Bighorn district; Arnold Costa, the son of Plenty Coups's old comrade Coyote That Runs; and the outspoken Robert Yellowtail.[65]

When the Crow delegates arrived in Washington in late January 1917, they maintained their opposition to further land openings in several sessions with the Senate Indian Affairs Committee. The group also used the occasion to raise several additional issues: complaints over the administration of the federal irrigation project on the reservation, a request that Agent Estep be replaced and a proposal that Crows be hired to fill all the Indian Office jobs on the reservation. Wrote one observer, "The keenness and persistence of Senator Walsh in advocacy of the measure were without avail." Walsh and his colleagues failed to bring the Myers bill to the Senate floor.[66]

With American entry into World War I in the spring of 1917, agitation for the opening of Crow lands was drowned out by the call to increase the nation's military might and to increase food production. With factory work and the first military draft since the Civil War absorbing the nation's manpower, Montana's congressional delegation had difficulty convincing lawmakers that land-hungry settlers were eager to flood into the Yellowstone. For the next two years tribal leaders and Montana politicians maneuvered for advantage, but little could be accomplished without congressional action. The chief advantage this situation provided the Crows (other than a pause in the relentless battle to protect their unallotted lands) was practice in mobilizing local opinion. The ease and self-confidence with which reservation leaders would call councils, confer with attorneys and prepare petitions for Congress or the president was a constant irritant to the Indian Office. In the wake of one such petition, one exasperated agency superintendent wrote of the Crows, "About the worst possible calamity that can befall them is for a 'man from Washington' to come here and stir them all up. . . ."[67]

In early 1919, with Germany defeated and concern for economic recovery

---

[65] Agent's Diary, August 5, 1916. The results of the January elections are recorded in the entry for January 16, 1917. On January 19, Estep noted that "five of the delegates indulged in haircuts" in preparation for the trip. The diary is Item 22, Box 156, RCIA-FRC, Seattle.

[66] See Brosius to Sniffen, January 23, 30 and February 23, 1917, IRA Mss., Reel 32. In later years Robert Yellowtail frequently told of his confrontation with Senator Walsh during this 1917 trip to Washington, D.C. His story forms a vivid part of "Contrary Warrior," the 1983 documentary made of his life.

[67] Evan Estep to Commissioner of Indian Affairs, July 9, 1917, CCF, 10322, 1917, Crow, 174–1, Box 4691.

replacing the inflation-driven prosperity of the war years, Montana's congressional representatives renewed their assault on the Crows' "surplus" lands. But chastened by their decade of defeat, the state's white politicians shifted tactics. At a February hearing on yet another version of the Dixon–Pray–Myers–Walsh proposal, the Senate's Indian Affairs Committee assured tribal delegates gathered before them that no measure would pass without their approval *provided* the Crows could agree on a bill that would end the practice of communal land-ownership on the reservation. The committee gave the tribe until the next session of Congress – due to begin in late summer – to produce their own legislation. Throughout its struggle against Dixon, Walsh and the others, Crow leaders had insisted that the tribe was willing to negotiate. They had claimed that they were willing to divide the reservation into large, individual shares so as to keep its property in Indian hands. Now Congress was calling them on their offer. "It looks like Congress has made up its mind to pass some kind of law changing the status of this land," Agent Calvin Asbury wrote Plenty Coups on March 10; "it is up to the tribe to get the best they can." Three days later, Robert Yellowtail wrote the Pryor chief in a similar vein: "Congress has given us this one more chance and if we don't take advantage of it, it simply means that they will do as they please in the matter."[68]

This unprecedented congressional ultimatum forced tribal leaders to confront a split within their ranks that had often been obscured as they battled against a common foe. Older men like Plenty Coups, Big Medicine and Two Leggings – often called "long hairs" by their opponents and the Indian Office – opposed any alteration of existing reservation boundaries or ownership patterns. In a speech the Pryor leader gave at several places on the reservation in March and April 1919, Plenty Coups put it simply: "The white people, my friends, must not take anything away from me and I do not want to take anything away from them. . . . I want the lessees, both cattle and sheep, to continue just as before," he added. "I do not want to divide the reservation yet." Younger and more comfortable with economic competition, Yellowtail and his educated allies – sometimes called "short hairs" or "boys" – saw the division of all tribal lands among tribal members as the only way to hold off white settlement. Moreover, dividing the reservation into individual shares

[68] Asbury to Chief Plenty Coups, March 10, 1919, Item 15, Box 78, "Delegates to Washington, 1919," RCIA-FRC, Seattle; Robert Yellowtail to Plenty Coups, March 13, 1919, Plenty Coups Mss.

See also correspondence from Victor Evans, the Washington attorney who had been representing the Crows since 1917. Victor Evans to the Crow Tribe, February 19, 1919; and Victor Evans to Chief Plenty Coups, February 20, 1919, both in Plenty Coups Mss. The hiring of Evans is described briefly in the Hardin *Herald* for June 15, 1917.

The delegation to Washington reported on its trip (and the Senate's ultimatum) in a meeting held at Crow Agency on March 7, 1919. See Chairman of Crow General Council to Commissioner of Indian Affairs, March 7, 1919, Item 15, Box 67, "Opening of Reservation, 1918–1919," RCIA-FRC, Seattle.

would provide an opportunity to reduce the power of the Indian Office in their country. For Yellowtail and his allies, distributing the unallotted lands among tribal members would have the effect of granting the Crows – whom he claimed were still "held in bondage" – their freedom.[69]

Through the summer of 1919, a wide and largely undocumented debate took place across the reservation. Led by Plenty Coups, the "long hairs" insisted that the whites could be defeated one more time if the tribe united behind their position. Their opponents declared that now was the moment to seize the initiative and reach an agreement. On August 7, Assistant Commissioner of Indian Affairs Edgar Meritt attempted to break this impasse when he stopped briefly at Crow Agency and spoke to a large crowd. While claiming that, "I am not here to tell you what to do," Meritt agreed that Congress would probably act during the next session. "If we do not get legislation enacted to allot this reservation to the Crow Indians, sooner or later they will get legislation which will throw open part of this reservation to homesteaders." Plenty Coups was not present for Meritt's address, but he was at Crow Agency four days later when 153 tribal members gathered for a general council. By this point the old chief must have been persuaded that the younger men would have their way, for he began the proceedings by declaring his support for a complete division of tribal lands.[70]

Following Plenty Coups's capitulation, the council quickly came to agreement over a bill to divide the unallotted lands among tribal members. Based largely on the proposal they had first developed with Charles Kappler in 1910, the Crows insisted on granting allotments to everyone who had been born since the end of allotment in 1905, called for the retention of mineral lands as tribal property and provided for the division of all tribal assets. The council selected a delegation made up of district representatives and notified the Indian Office that it was ready to present its plan to Congress. Significantly, the seventy-two-year-old Plenty Coups elected to stay behind, symbolically leaving the remaining political chores to the new generation of reservation politicians led by Robert Yellowtail. The group testified in September, the bill passed the Senate in October and it won approval in the lower house on April 22, 1920.[71]

[69] "Speech by Plenty Coups, March 25, 1919," Item 15, Box 67, "Opening of Reservation, 1918–1919"; See also Asbury to Commissioner of Indian Affairs, April 11, 1919, Item 15, Box 78, "Delegates to Washington, 1919"; both in RCIA-FRC, Seattle. Yellowtail's reference to "bondage" occurs in many places. See, e.g., Senate Report 219, 66th Congress, 1st Session (Serial 7590), 10.

[70] "Remarks of Hon. E. B. Meritt, August 7, 1919," Item 15, Box 67, "Opening of Reservation, 1918–1919," File 70–2, RCIA-FRC, Seattle.

[71] "Proceedings of General Council," August 11, 1919, Item 15, Box 67, "Opening of Reservation, 1918–1919," File 70–2, RCIA-FRC, Seattle. The 1920 Crow Act was filed as S. 2809 by the Crows' old enemy, Thomas Walsh. For a legislative history, see Senate Report 219, 66th Congress, 2nd Session (Serial 7590), House Report 468, 66th Congress, 1st Session (Serial 7593), and House Report 789, 66th Congress, 2nd Session (Serial 7653). The act became Public Law 239.

The Crow Act remains a subject of debate, controversy and litigation. Did it mark the Crow leadership's surrender to its greedy white neighbors? Or was it a clever way to hold off the wholesale looting of the tribal domain? In hindsight, the law did not reverse the tide of white settlement or the relative growth of non-Indian economic power in the Yellowstone valley. Senator Walsh got his bill and was rewarded by his constituents with two additional terms in the Senate. (He died in office in 1933.) Nevertheless, the new law contained a number of protections that, even though not entirely unprecedented, would encourage other tribes to follow the Crows' path of resistance and negotiation. These included the retention of mineral rights under tribal control, the transfer of all tribal land to individual ownership and a strong Indian voice in the implementation of the entire undertaking. And, while they would be held separately, reservation lands would only be lost as quickly as Indians themselves parted with them – they would not be placed in the public domain as a unit in the same way the area north of Black Lodge had been in 1904. In fact, following the passage of the Crow Act, no further large-scale land openings would be approved by Congress.[72]

At least as important as the provisions of the law itself, however, was its impact on the evolution of Crow political leadership. The passage of the Crow Act reflected the sophistication and durability of leaders who, since the founding of Crow Agency, had been working to develop a system for making decisions and sustaining a consensus in a settled and fixed environment. Crow leaders adapted to the emergence of district communities within the reservations, responded to events which threatened to undermine and divide them and mastered the art of finding new allies and capturing new strategies. All of these innovations were essential features of the tribe's long struggle to avoid the seizure of their lands.

VII

With Plenty Coups absent, the Crow's 1919 delegation to Washington lacked the familiar presence of an aging, nineteenth-century warrior. Instead the group was led by Robert Yellowtail, about the same age as Plenty Coups had been when he first came to the white man's capital in 1880 and as unlikely a spokesman as the young warrior had been when he had travelled east with Pretty

---

[72] Of course, as historian Janet McDonnell has noted, "By 1921 the era of large scale allotment work was drawing to a close," so the Crows cannot be credited with stopping land seizures. On the other hand, emphasis shifted in the 1920s to providing allotments for landless Indians and questioning the idea that tribal lands should inevitably serve the interests of non-Indian settlers. The Crows played a major role in shaping that debate. See Janet A. McDonnell, *The Dispossession of the American Indian, 1887–1934* (Bloomington: Indiana University Press, 1991), 9–11.

Eagle and other tribal elders. When negotiations over the details of the Crow
bill were completed, Yellowtail was selected to make a closing comment before
the Indian Affairs Committee. His statement articulated the tribe's new sense of
national self-consciousness and clarified the role Crow leaders would seek to fill
in the years to come.

Yellowtail began by observing that President Woodrow Wilson had recently
returned to the United States from the Versailles peace conference and would
soon lay his proposals for a new approach to world peace before the very men
who were deciding the fate of the Crows' unallotted lands. Yellowtail noted that
Wilson's achievements meant that the United States was now committed to the
principle of self-determination for all people, "no matter where they live, nor
how small or weak they may be, or what their previous conditions of servitude
may have been. . . . I and the rest of my people sincerely hope and pray that
[the president] will not forget that within the boundaries of his own Nation are
the American Indians, who have no rights whatsoever." Speaking now not as an
advocate of assimilation or commercial enterprise, but as a tribal representative
clearly feeling the weight of his community's expectations upon him, Yellowtail
compared the Crows to the "small and weak" peoples of the world:

> Mr. Chairman, I hold that the Crow Indian Reservation is a separate, semi-
> sovereign nation in itself, not belonging to any State, nor confined within
> the boundary lines of any State of the Union, and . . . no Senator or any-
> body else, so far as that is concerned, has any right to claim the right to tear
> us asunder by the continued introduction of bills here without our consent
> and simply because of our geographical proximity to his State or his home,
> or because his constituents prevail upon him so to act; neither has he the
> right to dictate to us what we shall hold as our final homesteads in this our
> last stand against the ever-encroaching hand, nor continue to disturb our
> peace of mind by a constant agitation to deprive us of our lands, that were,
> to begin with, ours, not his, and not given to us by anybody.[73]

Yellowtail's words neatly encompassed the political changes that had taken
place within the Crow community over the preceding three decades. His capture of Woodrow Wilson's universalist ambitions brilliantly translated the Crows'
political ideals into terms other American politicians could not ignore. At the
same time, Yellowtail and his colleagues spoke in defense of a culture "not
given to us by anybody," a tradition that was indigenous, distinctive and determined to remain that way. Plenty Coups and the long hairs would surely have
applauded his words.

Facing powerful opponents and unprecedented new conditions, Crow leaders

---

[73] Senate Report 219, 66th Congress, 1st Session (Serial 7590), 8–9. For reports of the "success"
of the delegates' efforts, see Victor Evans to Plenty Coups, September 23, 1919, and Calvin
Asbury to "The Crow Indians," October 8, 1919, Plenty Coups Mss.

in the years before 1920 had reinterpreted their role within their own homeland while managing to present a continuous set of objectives to outsiders. Surviving division and authoritarian rule, the community's chiefs and headmen had evolved into the "second growth" of tribal leadership Bull Robe had described a decade earlier: leaders who could articulate community interests in a new environment. Crow leaders had entered a new arena, pioneered a method of forging community consensus and devised a method for carrying the day.

9

Making a living: the Crow economy, 1890–1920

Senator Paynter: Do you hope the time will come when the tribe can manage that property themselves without the aid of the government?

Mr. Shively: When it comes to that, of course, we want a title to that land. The whole tribe is one; then if it comes in progress in our work toward civilization, learning the methods of doing things just like the other people, we want to retain that land and get a title to it....

Senator Curtis: You have a title to it now.

Mr. Shively: Have we?

Senator Curtis: Why, certainly; it is a treaty reservation. It is your land, but the Government has the power to do as it pleases with it with reference to opening it up. If it thinks it is to the best interest of the tribe, it will do so; but the land now, so far as the title is concerned, is in your tribe, or in the Government in trust for your tribe.

Mr. Shively: Oh.

Senator Curtis: But it is really owned by the Indians.[1]

I

This exchange between Frank Shively, graduate of the Carlisle Indian school and office clerk at Crow Agency, and two U. S. senators took place during the hearings over the 1908 Dixon proposal to open the reservation to white home-steaders. The positions outlined by Shively and the senators typified the divergent perspectives of Crows and government officials regarding the economic future of the reservation. When they relocated the tribe onto the dusty flatlands of the Pryor, Bighorn and Little Bighorn valleys, Henry Armstrong and his military and missionary colleagues had insisted that their goal was to help the Crows become self-supporting actors in the local economy. They nurtured ambitious dreams of acting "in the best interests of the tribe" so that individual Indians could make a living in a world where white settlers would replace the buffalo and cash would replace barter. Unspoken in those dreams, however – as it hovered silently behind Senator Charles Curtis's contorted explanation of

[1] Senate Document 445, 60th Congress, 1st Session (Serial 5260), 204, 209.

tribal title – was the assumption that the Crows would enter the economic world of twentieth-century America as obedient wards of the state and its minions. Curtis and his colleague, Kentucky's Thomas H. Paynter, suggested (and other officials made clear) that in the future tribesmen would make their living as individual players in the American market economy, not as partners in an Indian corporate entity. Further, they would participate in the economy as laborers who took orders from whites and learned new technical skills in government schools, not as entrepreneurs with resources to exploit and choices to make. They would be society's dependents, relying on federal officials and local business leaders to direct them, not active decision makers with the freedom to shape new enterprises or define new roles for themselves in the emerging regional enterprises of the northern plains.

As Frank Shively's words suggest, the Crows had different expectations. Harassed by an onrushing tide of hostile settlers, and suddenly abandoned by the wild game that had sustained them for generations, Crow families at the end of the nineteenth century were eager to learn new ways of making a living. Having adapted to the plains region centuries earlier, and profited for a time from the arrival of the horse, the gun and the fur trader, it seemed reasonable for tribal members to expect that their community might use its skills and its remaining resources to sustain itself through a new season of change. Because Frank Shively had seen more of American enterprise than most Crows, his expectations might have been more precisely drawn than those of his kinsmen, but his desire to "retain that land" and use it for "the whole tribe" reflected a common conviction. As in the areas of family life, religion and politics, the community appeared eager to explore ways of sustaining (and even reshaping) its subsistence traditions in a new setting and adapting itself to the least objectionable aspects of the onrushing industrial economy.

But the government officials and local business leaders who came forward in the early twentieth century to shape the economy of the Yellowstone valley were remarkably resistant to Crow beliefs and expectations. Despite the tribe's desire to use its collective resources in the world of enterprise, Indian Office officials and local business leaders continued to argue that the group had no future in a world of banks and railroads. Ironically, men who prospered in an increasingly collective and corporate business environment insisted that the Crows divide their assets into individual shares and content themselves with life on the margins of the region's marketplace. While Crows were willing – even eager – to learn new skills and acquire a facility with cash, outsiders continually stressed the importance of cultural lessons such as individualism, obedience and the love of daily toil. Henry Armstrong and his successors required the tribe to surrender both its past and its remaining collective assets as the price for participating in a new set of economic relationships. The necessity of earning their daily bread, one agent wrote in 1896, would be "an everpresent and a silent but powerful force" for progress.[2]

II

Differences in expectation and a steady refusal to allow for significant Crow participation in the local economy characterize the economic history of the Crow Reservation in the first decades of the twentieth century. Government men recognized a distinctive Crow attitude towards business affairs, but they could not bring themselves to take it seriously. Instead, they professed puzzlement. On the one hand, they recognized the tribe had a great deal of experience with trade and the uses of money. "There are many shrewd dealers in this tribe," the gruff agent M. P. Wyman reported in 1889. He noted that the Crows "realize fully the value of money and demand and obtain a fair equivalent for whatever they may sell." On the other hand, Wyman wrote a few years later (and here the puzzlement becomes apparent), he had "never seen a tribe more attached to their traditions and older customs than the Crows." The community's determination to resist the economic role authoritarian figures like Wyman laid out for them was interpreted by their "guardians" as yet another sign of its backwardness. "Beyond a disposition to labor and earn money, which they exhibit to a marked degree," Wyman wrote to his superiors, "they do not favor progress in our civilization." As community members struggled to farm, raise cattle and maximize their earnings on tribal assets, they were constantly measured by the non-Indians' standards of "civilized" behavior, found wanting and declared ineligible to function as their neighbors' economic equals.[3]

Indifference to the Crows' economic wishes and hostility to their actions produced a self-fulfilling prophecy. Pronounced "hostile" to the white community's definition of "progress," Crow farmers and ranchers had neither the freedom nor the support they needed to compete in the economic arena. As a result they failed to win even the modest victories that had characterized their adaptation to other aspects of the reservation environment. When Agent Armstrong led the tribe out of the Stillwater valley, the Crows were the largest population group in the Yellowstone valley and they controlled a vast storehouse of natural wealth. By the turn of the century, the growing city of Billings alone contained as many people as the Crow Reservation. Following the 1904 land sale and the creation of the border town of Hardin, thousands of white settlers were literally at the Indians' door. Hardin sprang quickly to life, becoming

[2] J. Watson to Commissioner of Indian Affairs, January 6, 1896, Item 2, Box 4, RCIA-FRC, Seattle.
[3] *ARCIA*, 1889 (Serial 2725), 223; Wyman to Commissioner, March 4, 1892, Item 2, Box 3, RCIA-FRC, Seattle.

the county seat for Bighorn County in 1912 and an important rail depot for the farmers and ranchers of southeastern Montana. It evolved into a local cross-roads, a place where politicians and businessmen sought votes and customers. It became a center of a local economy that functioned without the participation of the Crow tribe. As meager as they might appear several decades later, the town's banks, newspapers, farm implement dealers and commercial enterprises easily outshone the tiny tribal enterprises that struggled to survive next door on the reservation. By 1920 the disparity between the economic power of the Indian and non-Indian communities of the Yellowstone valley had grown so large that it was impossible for members of the tribe to make a living in their homeland without playing the minor, dependent role white officials had so long held out for them.

How did this happen? How could a community of fewer than two thousand people who were so successful in winning concessions from religious and polit-ical leaders fail to penetrate a market economy with a resource base of 3 million acres of land and tens of thousands of dollars in federal subsidies? In an age when businessmen operated without regulation or taxation, how could a com-munity which, as Senator Curtis noted, had title to its lands, lose its ability to feed and clothe itself? In short, how could a community that was simultane-ously founding new villages, creating new forms of worship and developing new systems of political leadership find itself unable to form the business enterprises necessary to sustain itself into the future?

Reviewing the history of Crow land ownership between 1890 and 1920 pro-vides an initial answer to these questions. The tribe began this period with a reservation of more than 3.4 million acres. By 1920, slightly less than 2 million of that total remained in collective ownership; 1.1 million acres had been sold in 1904 and more than 400,000 acres had been allotted to individual tribal members. Virtually all of the tribe's remaining unallotted acres were held by non-Indian stockmen under leases approved by the Indian Office. Only a tiny fraction of the reservation – 6,200 acres in 1915 – was actually being farmed by Indians. In addition, by 1920, more than 10% of the reserve's 542,000 acres of allotted lands had been sold. Even individually owned property was passing out of Crow ownership. Reservation lands were gradually being turned into cash. Rather than providing employment for tribal members or a testing ground for tribal entrepreneurs, Crow country was generating dollars for individual survival.

Table 4 traces both the size and the disposition of tribal income for this same period. It indicates that tribal income was substantial for most of the early twentieth century.In 1915, for example, 1,700 tribal members could have drawn between $250 and $300 per person from a communal treasury enriched by grazing leases, land sales and income from the collectively owned herds of horses and cattle. With many government employees at the time earning annual

Table 4. *Tribal income and expenses, 1908–1920 (dollars)*

	1908	1910	1915	1917	1920
Income					
Land sales	90,788	291,873	357,982	60,000	n.a.
Lease revenue	150,000 (est.)	159,250	150,000	n.a.	285,000
Stock sales	0	0	0	0	150,000
Total	240,788	451,123	507,982	60,000	435,000
Expenses					
"Reimbursements"	76,129	104,835	110,000	n.a.	460,000
Annuity payments	58,368	53,196	35,377	644,550	170,000
Total	134,497	158,031	145,377	644,550	630,000

Note: Reimbursement for 1920 includes funds for Crow hospital and local schools.
Source: Agents Annual Narrative and Statistical Report.

salaries of $500, one can imagine Crow families surviving quite well on shares of this size. But Table 4 also indicates that tribal monies were not simply distributed on a *per capita* basis. In 1915, for example, only $35,000 ($20 per person) was paid out to tribal members. Large annual appropriations were made to "reimburse" the U.S. government for the cost of managing the Crow Reservation, as well as to pay for the construction of irrigation canals in the Pryor, Bighorn and Little Bighorn valleys. While the tribe's assets were creating a substantial flow of cash, they were not making a living for its members.

The decisions to lease or sell Crow lands and to divert tribal income into "community expenses" (such as constructing an irrigation system to support intensive, commercial agriculture) determined the tribe's economic course in the early twentieth century. By using their property to generate cash and invest in their own community, the Crows were casting their lot irretrievably with the agricultural economy of the northern plains. As that economy prospered, their income would presumably increase. In the short run, cash would provide access to the local economy. Over the longer term, the diversion of tribal income into education and irrigation was a vital capital investment. If these investments produced a more productive work force and prosperous farms, then the diversions would have been wise. If they did not, these investments would be exposed as foolish and the tribe's dependence on any remaining cash income would be compounded.

By 1920, the decision to translate tribal assets into cash and to divert tribal income into collective investments had produced a situation in which the Crow community could no longer chart an independent economic course. Despite their ability to participate in the local economy as consumers, Crows had little success using their cash to become independent merchants or business people. At the same time, their educational system had not produced an effectively trained work force, and their staggeringly expensive irrigation system was passing slowly out of their control. Unlike the areas of family life, religion and politics, where new institutions and new traditions grew up on the foundation of the past, the task of making a living brought few victories and little pride. In social and political affairs, the community had been able to shape a distinctive future; in business affairs it had not.

To describe a situation is not to explain it. The descent of the Crows into economic dependency fulfilled the expectations of government officials who had insisted that the tribe's members learn to earn "their daily bread," and it served the interests of local non-Indian farmers and ranchers. Together these expectations and interests had facilitated the transfer of tribal resources to non-Indians – either by encouraging the lease or purchase of reservation land, or by justifying opening the tribe's irrigation system to non-Crows. This transfer of assets provided local non-Indian business people with a new opportunity for profit, and obviously, those individuals and their elected representatives were eager to take every advantage of the situation presented to them. Nevertheless, it is not obvious that a community with the ability to defeat congressional land-grabbers for a decade, or to fend off successive waves of missionaries and pious reformers, would necessarily be overwhelmed by an assault on its resources. How could a community that displayed such resiliency in other aspects of life become so economically exploited?

The economic decline of the Crows is most evident when one focuses on two broad areas of economic activity: farming and ranching. In each category, Indian efforts to function independently were overcome by the economic expectations of agents and policy makers as well as by the economic interests of their white neighbors. At least in the Yellowstone valley, the unregulated, free market of America's great age of industrial innovation did not permit the evolution of tribally based economic enterprises. At the same time, the requirement that they make a living in modern America transformed the Crows from isolated self-sufficiency to a marginal and dependent status which linked them tenuously, but inescapably to the United States and its industrial economy.

III

In the wake of the Sword Bearer incident, the Crows experienced a more authoritarian reservation administration than they had known in the contentious first years of Crow Agency's existence. Missionaries and boarding schools expanded their operations and intruded into the daily life of most families, but the principal aim of agency officials was the development of Indian farming. In the 1880s, cooperative men like Medicine Crow and Sits Down Spotted had been praised for their willingness to take up the plow, but in the 1890s such cooperation was demanded of everyone. The message young Crows received was that they must conform to the government's approach to farming in order to make a living.

Apparently the irony of white newcomers teaching an indigenous people how to survive in their homeland did not occur to the government men. Writing in early 1891, for example, Agent Wyman, the former railroad official who labored to make the agency operate according to his schedule, declared that "wagons and farming implements will only be issued to those Indians who remain at home and keep their places in order." Those who disobeyed and left the reservation not only would lose the agent's assistance, but would be denied rations and would serve a term in the guard house. By the turn of the century, this philosophy had expanded to include the idea that stopping support from the agency would actually help *promote* Indian farming. "I am convinced that the initiation and carrying out of such a measure," Agent Watson wrote in 1896, "is absolutely necessary to make these Indians self-supporting."[4]

To facilitate an expansion of farming activity, as well as to place Crow farmers under more direct supervision, the agents started cooperative farms in each reservation district. "The Indians pursue farming principally upon the large-tract system," Agent E. H. Becker wrote in the summer of 1898. Under this system, district farmers supervised gangs of Crow laborers and divided their crop according to the number of days each person worked. Under this system, wheat, oats and hay were raised for sale at Fort Custer and on the local market. While it is difficult to be precise about the productivity of this system, it appears to have been successful. Table 5 presents the wheat production at four district farms in 1895 and 1896. Recalling that these farms also produced oats and hay suggests that Crows could expect to derive at least some of their income from agricultural sources.[5]

By 1899, the Crows had used some of the income from the 1890 land sale to finance the construction of their own flour mill at Crow Agency. By 1900 the tribe was able to process its own wheat into flour. Because the district farms produced a surplus, the Indian Office arranged for the Crows to supply the

---

[4] M. P. Wyman to C. C. Knidler, February 26, 1891, Item 5, Box 27, RCIA-FRC, Seattle; and Watson to Commissioner of Indian Affairs, January 24, 1896. In a letter to the Lodge Grass district farmer, Watson declared that the Indians of the Little Bighorn would not work on their farms *unless they are thoroughly shaken up* (emphasis in original). He went on to tell the farmer to "let them understand there is a guard house here for all who won't or don't work, and the lodgers will be put at hard work here under police." See Watson to A. A. Campbell, April 8, 1896, Item 4, Box 17, RCIA-FRC, Seattle.

[5] *ARCIA*, Crow, 1898 (Serial 3757), 188; Stouch to Commissioner of Indian Affairs, May 18, 1898, Item 2, Box 5, RCIA-FRC, Seattle.

Table 5. *Wheat production at four district farms, 1895–6*
(bushels)

	Bighorn	40 Mile	Pryor[a]	Black Lodge
1895	40,998	40,730	16,105	20,000
1896	17,377	36,240	15,000	52,060

[a] 31,105 reported for two-year total.

nearby Northern Cheyennes with part of their flour ration at market prices. As in other transactions, Crow farmers were credited with a portion of the sale corresponding to their labor in the wheat fields. Reviewing the sales receipts for 1899, a number of familiar names appear. At the low end, Two Leggings, Deaf Bull, Spotted Horse and The Bread each were credited with producing about 500 lbs. of flour. While this was a relatively small amount, it is striking that these older men, some of whom had actively opposed the government and its program, were involved in the farming program. Younger, educated men produced more. Political activist Joe Cooper, for example, was credited with over 1,400 lbs. of flour, and Louis Bompard, the resettled Assiniboin man who would become a leader of the peyotists in the Black Lodge district, produced nearly 3,400 lbs. Most productive were George Pease (9,817 lbs.), the Reverend Bond's old assistant at his boarding school who now lived on a farm on Soap Creek, and Sits Down Spotted (14,437 lbs.), a thirty-six-year-old Catholic convert who had been among the first in the Bighorn valley to take up farming.[6]

Like non-Indians, Crows approached farming with varying levels of skill and aptitude. Nevertheless, it was clear at the end of the 1890s that the tribe was not opposed to the idea of making a living and deriving income from agriculture or to the doctrine of hard work. Despite this willing attitude, however, Crow farmers did not continue to find success after the 1890s. For just as these Montana tribesmen appeared to be succeeding as farmers, they were overwhelmed by better-financed non-Indian competitors and impoverished by an agricultural project undertaken by their guardians in the Indian Office.[7]

[6] E. H. Becker to J. C. Clifford, May 12, 1899; J. E. Edwards to J. C. Clifford, October 19, November 22 and December 22, 1899, Item 14, Box 19, RCIA-FRC, Seattle. The willingness of nomadic Indian people to adapt quickly to the necessity of farming is illustrated with unique insight in Robert Paschal Nespor, "From War Lance to Plow Share: The Cheyenne Dog Soldiers as Farmers, 1879–1930s," *Chronicles of Oklahoma*, 65 (1987), 42–75.

[7] In general, the fate of Crow agriculture follows closely the general history described in Leonard Carlson, *Indians, Bureaucrats, and Land: The Dawes Act and the Decline of Indian Farming* (Westport, Conn.: Greenwood, 1981). Carlson's argument that competition and market forces, not an inherent Indian disinterest, doomed Native American agriculture is made cogently in Leonard A. Carlson, "Federal Policy and Indian Land: Economic Interests and the Sale of Indian Allotments, 1900–1934," *Agricultural History*, 57 (January 1983), 33–45.

Within months of the founding of Crow Agency, Henry Armstrong wrote to his superiors about the obvious need for irrigation canals in the valley. The arid reservation lands were cut by creeks and rivers which it seemed could easily be diverted to Indian pastures and gardens. "We must have irrigating ditches," he reported in the summer of 1884. "Without them our farming operations must be a partial failure nearly every year and almost an entire failure one-half of the years." Armstrong proposed using tribal funds (income from land sales and cattle leases) to construct a series of three or four ditches at Lodge Grass, Reno, Soap Creek on the upper Bighorn and at Pryor. "It is a mistake to hoard the moneys belonging to the Indians," he wrote; "their moneys ought ... to be used to push the Indians forward as rapidly as possible by making permanent improvements. . . ." Armstrong's modest suggestion touched off more than twenty years of canal construction on the reservation, activity which raided and weakened the tribal treasury while ultimately undermining and destroying Indian farming.[8]

Between 1884 and 1891 approximately $200,000 was spent to construct ditches at the mouth of Lodge Grass Creek, along the Little Bighorn just south of Crow Agency, and on the Bighorn above Fort Custer. By modern standards of engineering these early ditches were crude; they lacked concrete headgates and, because they did not maintain an even grade, they quickly filled with weeds and sediment. While the original irrigation system might have been sufficient for district farms alone, external pressure to allot the reservation and sell off the "surplus" lands, together with the persistent desire to make every Crow an individual, "self-supporting" farmer, drove Armstrong's successors to contemplate an expansion of his original plan. The first opportunity for expansion occurred in 1890, when federal officials inserted language in that year's land sale agreement stipulating that $275,000 of the proceeds be spent on the construction and maintenance of an irrigation system. Following Congress's approval of this agreement, the Indian Office sent Walter H. Graves, a civil engineer, to Crow Agency.

Graves was thrilled with what he saw. Sunny skies, thousands of acres of dry, uncultivated land, and a network of streams and rivers fit together in his mind like a natural trinity. The engineer first proposed expanding the Lodge Grass ditch and constructing another channel parallel to the Little Bighorn from the agency to Fort Custer, eight miles away. Together, Graves declared, these ditches would create enough irrigable farm land "to supply all of the Crows with their allotments." But the engineer had $275,000 to spend and no one in Washington to limit his ambitions. In his initial report to the Indian Office he went on to recommend three additions to the government's original plan. He

[8] *ARCIA*, 1884, 154; Armstrong to Commissioner of Indian Affairs, November 22, 1884, 22905–1884, Special Case 190, Crow, LR-OIA, RG 75, NA.

Three Crow farmers, photographed about the time of World War I, probably in the Black Lodge district near Hardin. Pretty Horse, Lois Bompard and Top of the Moccasin are pictured here as they cut and bind their hay crop. Courtesy of Montana Historical Society.

called for new ditches to be constructed along Pryor Creek, a channel between Soap and Rotten Grass Creeks in the Bighorn and finally, a grand capstone: a massive, thirty-five-mile canal running along the east side of the Bighorn River from the mouth of the canyon (near the site of old Fort C. F. Smith) to a point just above Fort Custer. He was confident that all of this new construction could be paid for with tribal funds. Graves promised that the Bighorn canal would irrigate 35,000 acres of land and would "easily rank among the largest and best constructed irrigation works in the country."[9]

Financed by the new land sale agreement, construction began on Graves's dream in the summer of 1892. By the fall of 1896, as the fifth season of labor drew to an end, the engineer could report that $257,599 had been spent constructing all of the shorter ditches and five miles of the Bighorn canal. Two years later, in the spring of 1898, Graves had completed another seven miles of the canal and used up all the available funds. Work was suspended until another

[9] Walter Graves to Commissioner of Indian Affairs, July 29, 1891, 28345–1891; October 8, 1893, 39981–1893; September 1, 1896, 35775–1896; and March 10, 1898, 14162–1898; all in Special Case 190, Crow, LR-OIA, RG 75, NA.

appropriation of $120,000 from the tribal account was made by Congress early in 1899. Other appropriations in 1901, 1903 and 1904 brought the canal project to completion in April 1905. Following that date funds continued to be drawn from the tribal treasury to refine and maintain the system, so that by 1919 the Crows had spent $1.9 million to irrigate their reservation.[10]

The scale of the Crow irrigation project dramatically altered agricultural expectations on the reservation and in the surrounding counties. Supported by the income from land sales and fueled by the dreams of engineers and local boosters, battalions of Crow laborers had constructed a state-of-the-art irrigation system that far outstripped their needs and managerial capacities. Not only would Graves's complex of headgates, canals and ditches irrigate more than 73,000 acres of land, but it would continue to cost in excess of $100,000 per year to operate and maintain. According to one estimate compiled in 1917, the maintenance of the tribal irrigation system accounted for "nearly half of the expense of running the Crow reservation." Graves himself underscored the importance of these annual appropriations, writing during one campaign for more funds that "without proper supervision, no irrigating ditch will remain for any length of time in a serviceable condition. It is no more possible to utilize a self-operating ditch, and secure satisfactory results, than it is a self-operating railroad." The project had become – as another historian has called a similar effort mounted on the Blackfeet reservation at about the same time – "an end in itself."[11]

Crow leaders opposed a grand irrigation scheme, but their protests were routinely discounted and ignored. At a meeting in 1892, for example, Plenty Coups, Spotted Horse and several others had insisted that they wanted "small ditches" built. Plenty Coups agreed that Walter Graves "has a good heart," but he worried that the project would "cost too much money, more money than the Crows want to give up for it." Once Graves's expanded project began, however, its use of Crow labor gave federal officials a powerful argument for tribal members who worried about their own survival more than the dwindling tribal treasury. As a result, when requests for additional tribal funds came before councils in the early twentieth century, most Crows viewed the project from the

---

[10] Graves to Commissioner of Indian Affairs, September 1, 1896, 35775–1896; W. B. Hill to Commissioner of Indian Affairs, April 10, 1901, 25893–1901; ibid., February 19, 1903, 11777–1903; October 20, 1904, 81803–1904; and April 21, 1905, 32257–1905; all in SC 190, Crow, LR-OIA, RG 75, NA. The 1919 figure is from House Document 387, 66th Congress, 2nd Session, 3.

See also three histories of the Crow irrigation project, unsigned but apparently prepared by Agent Watson in the late 1890s, in Item 88, Box 244, RCIA-FRC, Seattle.

[11] "Memorandum in Relation to Irrigation Matters to Special Agent Linnen, Special Agent Brown and Supervisor West," June 14, 1917, Item 15, Box 60, "Inspector's Reports, 1917–1923," RCIA-FRC, Seattle; Graves to Commissioner of Indian Affairs, August 10, 1895, 45636–1895, SC 190, Crow, LR-OIA, RG 75, NA; Thomas R. Wessel, "Agriculture on the Reservations: The Case of the Blackfeet, 1885–1935," *Journal of the West*, 18 (1979), 17–24.

perspective of day laborers rather than landowners. They voted to approve the appropriations to protect their construction jobs.[12]

As a condition of agreeing to divert their resources to irrigation instruction, Crow leaders had insisted that all construction would be carried out by Indian crews. As a result, hundreds of tribal members found steady work in the 1890s as teamsters and excavators for Mr. Graves. The jobs were popular. Medicine Crow, for example, declared in 1895 that "I was one of the first to get a scraper, and you still see me working on the ditch. I do not want to see anyone else but Crows on the ditches." With steady pay, Medicine Crow and his kinsmen could work together, live at the ditch camp and buy their necessities from the local trader. The skilled jobs available on the irrigation project were an attractive alternative to the regimentation of the district farms and the loneliness of solitary agriculture. Walter Graves reported that at the height of construction as many as 300 Crows and their teams would appear at his headquarters, ready to go to work.[13]

The extent of the tribe's enthusiasm for construction work was made clear in the spring of 1898 when, inevitably, the implementation of Graves's grand design outstripped the available tribal resources. When it became clear that work on the Bighorn canal could not continue, a tribal meeting was called at St. Xavier, the settlement closest to the project's "ditch camp" along the Bighorn. The gathering drafted a petition to the Indian Office which made plain their dependence on wages and the prospect of farming on irrigated land. It noted that government rations were not limited to the elderly and infirm and that Fort Custer, their principal market for hay and agricultural produce, was being closed. "If you cannot help us to get money so that we can water our lands and raise crops, we shall soon be without anything to eat," the petition declared, adding, "it will then cost the government more money to feed us . . . than it would now take to finish our ditches so that we can feed ourselves." Signing the petition were 113 Crow men, including Plenty Coups, Pretty Eagle, Carl Leider and Sits Down Spotted.[14]

Despite the statement that the canal project would help the Crows feed themselves, tribal members viewed the enterprise solely as a source for jobs. Their lack of involvement in the design of the irrigation project, as well as its overwhelming scale, undermined their sense of ownership. This alienation grew more evident as the pace of construction eased after 1905. The need to "get money" continued, of course, but now the Crows possessed an attractive asset:

[12] For Plenty Coups's comment, see Council Proceedings, August 27, 1892, SC 147, Crow, LR-OIA, RG 75, NA.
[13] "Verbatim Report of a Council Held at the Irrigation Ditch Camp, Big Horn Valley, Crow Indian Reservation, Montana, October 28, 1895," 11543–1896; Graves to Commissioner of Indian Affairs, August 9, 1895, 45680–1895; both in SC 190, Crow, LR-OIA, RG 75, NA.
[14] Petition of Crow Indians, April 4, 1898, enclosed in 18471–1898, SC 190, Crow, LR-OIA, RG 75, NA.

irrigated agricultural land. Moreover, the completion of the allotment process and the press to cede their "surplus" lands raised the possibility of transforming some of this asset into cash. Tribal members found that selling the allotments of deceased relatives provided ready income and avoided the problem of subdividing inherited real estate into unproductive pieces. Local whites, pointing out that less than 10% of the irrigable land in the Crow project was being farmed by Indians, noted that opening unallotted, irrigable land to whites would provide income to offset the cost of maintaining the intricate network of ditches and headgates. And local businessmen seeking support for additional irrigation projects on the lands ceded in 1899, urged the Indian Office to lease all uncultivated lands within the irrigation project. Led by Samuel K. Hardin himself, the real estate investor whose name now graced the town that stood near the old site of Fort Custer, local merchants argued that it was difficult to find settlers for their new town as long as 80% of the Crow system was underutilized.[15]

The excitement of irrigating vast stretches of eastern Montana, the tribe's increasing dependence on wage labor and the tides of cash that swept over the irrigation project conspired to saddle tribal members with a difficult choice. Either they farmed their irrigated allotments in the most productive way possible to generate cash for living expenses and to pay the annual maintenance assessments due on all irrigated land, or they would turn their property over to eager whites who would do it for them. In the years before World War I, many Crow farmers faced this dilemma, and the local agent stood ready to advise them. In the same summer as the Bighorn canal was completed, for example, Samuel Reynolds told his superiors that "I feel that now is the time to crowd the work and keep them busy and interested in their individual homes and improvements."[16]

Reynolds's reference to "individual homes and improvements" reflects another consequence of the irrigation project. The pervasive rhetoric of commercial agriculture, together with the increased value of irrigated Crow lands, encouraged government officials to view the tribe's old district farms as both unproductive and unattractive. In the aftermath of construction, Crows would be "crowded" to settle on individual tracts of land as well as to "keep busy" in an effort to maximize the return on their farms. For Reynolds, the community's

[15] In June, 1919, the Indian Office reported that 6,945 acres of the 73,686 irrigable acres on the Crow Reservation were being cultivated by Indians; 7,001 acres were being cultivated by whites. More than 80% of the area covered by the irrigation project lay uncultivated. For a discussion of the impact of the Crow project on area development, see Director, United States Geological Survey, to Secretary of the Interior, June 8, 1905, 47085–1905, SC 190, Crow, LR-OIA, RG 75, NA. For Hardin's position, see Samuel K. Hardin to Secretary of the Interior, March 22, 1905, 43374–1905, SC 133, Crow, LR-OIA, RG 75, NA.

[16] Reynolds to Commissioner of Indian Affairs, September 13, 1905, 74759–1905, SC 190, Crow, LR-OIA, RG 75, NA.

goal was neither individual subsistence (because the Crows were considered generally too backward to use the irrigation system) nor prosperity for their district (because the district farms were now anachronistic). He made it clear that the community's goal should now be the acquisition of cash.

Reynolds and his successors put increasing emphasis on the sale of lands held in the names of deceased tribal members and the leasing of all other unallotted, irrigated areas. These innovations would provide heirs with income, introduce non-Indian farmers onto the reservation and provide tribesmen with funds they could use for their own irrigated farms. Reynolds organized the first purchases of these so-called dead Indian allotments in September 1906. The initial sales attracted little attention, but the agent told his superiors a few years later, "As the Indians awakened to the fact that interest in inherited lands meant money to them they are now showing zeal in presenting their claims." Within five years a new, largely white-owned town was being laid out at Lodge Grass, and non-Indian settlers and investors (including ex-agent Reynolds) were trickling into all parts of the reservation and exercising control over the tribe's resources.[17]

Allotment and the inexorable movement towards commercial agriculture carried a few prominent Crows to prosperity. Plenty Coups, for example, was regularly praised as "the most progressive Indian on this reservation." His two-story frame house sat next to his orchard of fruit trees, at the center of his wheat and hay fields. "I wish," Commissioner Cato Sells wrote the old chief in 1915, that "every Crow Indian would emulate your example and do as you are doing in this respect." Similarly, Medicine Crow cultivated his fields in Lodge Grass and maintained a close relationship with the agency. Other successful farmers included Louis Bompard at Black Lodge, whose barns, garden and outbuildings won regular praise from the agent, and younger, educated men such as Richard Wallace, James Carpenter and Robert Yellowtail.[18]

---

[17] Reynolds to Commissioner of Indian Affairs, February 4, 1909, Item 2, Box 8, RCIA-FRC, Seattle. See Hardin *Tribune*, March 24, 1911. In December, 1906, Reynolds wrote his superiors that the newly irrigated lands of the Big Horn should be advertised for lease in "the leading Eastern Farm journals." He added, "I consider that if these lands can be leased for a term of not less than five years for one dollar per acre or more that we will be getting out of them all that it is possible to get for the Indians." Reynolds to Commissioner of Indian Affairs, December 28, 1906, 23–1907, LR-OIA, RG 75, NA.

[18] Fred Miller to Commissioner of Indian Affairs, September 6, 1909, Item 2, Box 8, RCIA-FRC, Seattle; and Cato Sells to Chief Plenty Coups, June 2, 1915, Plenty Coups Mss. For Medicine Crow and Carpenter, see, respectively, Reynolds to A. L. Babcock, Hardware, April 9, 1903, Item 4, Box 22, and Fred Miller to A. M. Stevenson, March 18, 1908, Item 4, Box 25, both in RCIA-FRC, Seattle.

There are several reports from this period of Plenty Coups' "store" where he distributed both food and tools. This informal establishment no doubt mixed traditional chiefly generosity with modern merchandising. See, e.g., Julia M. Seton, *The Pulse of the Pueblos: Personal Glimpses of Indian Life* (Santa Fe: Seton Village Press, 1939), 160.

Hay, wheat and oats were the most common and most successful crops on the reservation. Most of the oats and hay were consumed by tribal livestock (and, before 1898, by the stock at Fort Custer), but the wheat crop was regularly milled at the agency grist mills. For most of the period 1890 to 1910, the tribe produced over 300,000 lbs. of flour each year for the Northern Cheyenne Reservation and for use in the agency school. At a contract price of $2.25 per 100 lbs., however, this amounted to a tribal income of less than $5 per person. While the Crows had other sources of income (individuals sold agency-milled flour on the open market), these figures indicate a community functioning at a subsistence level rather than producing a large cash income. This observation is confirmed by a note from a man named White Tree to Plenty Coups in the winter of 1916. In addition to complaining about the long winter and a recent series of snowstorms, White Tree pleaded for relief from the annual charges imposed on him for the maintenance of the irrigation system. "Its high for some folks," he wrote, "and they can't afford to pay for it all."[19]

Despite the publicity enjoyed by Plenty Coups and the other successful farmers, White Pine was a more typical example of tribal prosperity than the head man from Pryor. Only a small percentage of the newly irrigated lands were cultivated, and farm produce provided only a small part of tribal income each year. Land sales continued regularly after 1906, largely because Crow farmers were continuously short of cash. Government officials lamented the subsequent drop in Crow landownership, but they satisfied themselves that the new, non-Indian owners would provide an energetic model for the remaining tribal farmers we well as a source of employment for the landless.[20]

As a result, by 1915, despite moments of optimism and occasional references to model farmers, government officials had concluded that the Crows were unsuited to commercial agriculture and unfit to manage their own economic affairs. In 1912 the local agent had noted that "I consider the future of the Crows as farmers very encouraging," but by 1916, Montana's Senator Walsh told his colleagues in Washington that the tribe's irrigation project was deteriorating because "the Indians have never been agriculturalists. They have been hunters for buffalo and they do not take to agriculture. . . ." In this atmosphere,

---

[19] Reynolds to Director of Census, October 13, 1904, Item r, Box 23, RCIA-FRC, Seattle; White Tree to Plenty Coups, February 11, 1916, Plenty Coups Mss. White Tree was evidently a Crow, but his name does not appear on any tribal census.

[20] Reynolds to Commissioner of Indian Affairs, March 28, 1907, 31523–07, LR-OIA, RG 75, NA (on land sales); Reynolds to Commissioner of Indian Affairs, April 5, 1905, 27198–05, LR-OIA, RG 75, NA (on need for cash); Reynolds to George H. Pease, December 29, 1909 (on desire for fee patent), Item 4, Box 26, RCIA-FRC, Seattle. In the fall of 1916 one of the Indian Office's "Last Arrow" ceremonies was held at Crow Agency. Tribal members who had received fee patents for their land came forward to receive their deeds after firing the "last arrow" of their old life and putting on the work clothes of a Montana farmer. See Agent's Diary, June 21 and October 27, 1916, Item 22, Box 156, RCIA-FRC, Seattle.

Crow landowners received little encouragement to retain and develop their remaining assets.[21]

A final measure of pressure on Crow farmers was applied during World War I when a boom in commodity prices brought forth a new demand for "underutilized" farm lands. Within weeks of President Wilson's appearance before Congress to request a declaration of war against Germany, representatives of the Great Western and Sheridan Sugar companies appeared at Crow Agency offering to lease all the available irrigated areas on the reservation for beets. Despite the fact that none of the tribe's political leaders was involved in these negotiations, an agreement was reached to rent more than 20,000 acres of Crow lands for ten years. During the ensuing growing season the Hardin *Tribune* was filled with stories praising the mechanized cultivation of this immense tract. This coverage reached its peak one day in August 1918 when a gang of fifteen tractors broke 355 acres of prairie, establishing, the paper declared, a "World's Plowing Record." The editors added breathlessly that the event had been witnessed "by a large number of people from all over the country, among them the editor of *Country Gentleman* magazine."[22]

Despite the excitement surrounding these large wartime leases, Crow leaders opposed them on the grounds that, as one delegation declared, "such leases will materially affect the immediate control and use" of the allotted lands included within them. In addition, as outsiders gained access to reservation lands, it became more difficult for tribal leaders to argue against the various "surplus" land sale agreements that Montana's congressional delegation were bringing before Congress. The rhetoric of patriotism and commercial enterprise was difficult to overcome. When the business committee refused to approve the wartime leases in the summer of 1918, their agent urged the Indian Office to ignore the protests. "This great project should not depend upon the prejudice or bias of any one or two Indians who may be able to control a vote of the council," he declared. A year later, after his superiors had taken his advice, Agent Calvin Asbury declared happily that "we will have practically all of the agricultural land of this reservation in crops before long."[23]

[21] *Agent's Narrative and Statistical Report*, Records Group 75, National Archives, Washington, D.C. (hereafter cited as *ANR*), Crow, 1912, 3; "Hearings on S.2378," part 4, December 13, 1916 (Washington, D.C.: Government Printing Office, 1916), 16.

The pattern of declining Indian control over economic affairs is traced for another Montana reservation in Michael A. Massie, "The Defeat of Assimilation and the Rise of Colonialism on the Fort Belknap Reservation, 1873–1925," *American Indian Culture and Research Journal*, 7 (1984), 33–49. For the same pattern on a Utah reservation during the years prior to World War I, see Martha C. Knack, "Interethnic Competition at Kaibab During the Early Twentieth Century," *Ethnohistory*, 40 (1993), 212–245.

[22] Hardin *Tribune*, June 7, June 21, July 5, August 30, 1918. See also entry in Agent Estep's diary for May 18, 1917, on lease negotiations, Item 22, Box 156, RCIA-FRC, Seattle.

[23] Hardin *Tribune*, March 14, 1919; Calvin Asbury to CIA, March 23, 1918, Item 15, Box 78, "Delegations to Washington, 1917–1918," RCIA-FRC, Seattle; and *ANR*, 1919, 11.

IV

In 1883, the last of the buffalo disappeared from the Yellowstone valley. The vast herds that had kept William Clark and his party awake as he camped atop Pompey's Pillar in 1806 were now gone, leaving no trace of their former presence in the vast grasslands of the northern plains. As new settlers arrived in the region, it seemed obvious that domesticated livestock could take the place of the vanished bison. Rail lines running from the Yellowstone to Minneapolis and Chicago ensured that the cattle, sheep and horses raised in Montana would find their way to market, and the burgeoning populations of these industrial cities guaranteed that once the animals arrived and were processed, they would find a ready market.[24]

Cattle were distributed to Crow band leaders within weeks of the tribe's arrival at the Little Bighorn in 1884, and these men quickly turned the animals out onto the vacant prairies to fatten. Almost as quickly, non-Indian stockmen began passing through the reservation on their way to the Northern Pacific railhead or spending entire seasons foraging across the tribal pasturelands. As a result, both individual and communal cattle ranching was a continuous feature of reservation life from the 1880s onward, even though both competed with non-Indian stockmen who rented Crow land and often occupied the most attractive grazing areas.

Crows maintained significant herds throughout the early decades of the twentieth century. Between 1898 and 1905, for example, the agents' annual reports indicate that about 4,000 tribally owned cattle were grazing within the boundaries of the reservation. In addition, an estimated 25,000 horses also shared the tribal pastures. While these totals indicate that the tribe's herds were a significant source of food and income (and horse herds an ongoing bone of contention with federal officials who felt they were destroying the range), they were dwarfed by the commercial outfits that leased the reservation's unallotted lands.[25]

Crow leaders frequently complained about the presence of non-Indian-owned cattle on the reservation, but by the end of the 1880s they recognized that the herds would not disappear and that their owners were willing to pay cash for the right to use tribal pastureland. Furthermore, in the aftermath of the Sword

---

[24] For a general overview of Indian ranching, see Peter Iverson, *When Indians Became Cowboys: Native Peoples and Cattle Ranching in the American West* (Norman: University of Oklahoma Press, 1994), especially chap. 4.

[25] A record of cattle shipments by tribal members from the relatively prosperous summers of 1898, 1899 and 1900 confirms the impression that Crow ranching was not commercially significant. Only twenty-four Crow ranchers shipped more than 3 head of cattle during this period, and only one of these – Sees A White Horse – shipped more than 10. During this same period nearly 600 head of cattle were shipped from the tribal herd, but the income from those sales produced about $20 per person for the entire period. See Item 42, Box 174, 1898–1900 (Beef Book), RCIA-FRC, Seattle.

Bearer incident, men like Plenty Coups and Pretty Eagle saw the granting of grazing leases as a way of establishing relationships with powerful whites, thereby enhancing their personal prestige and providing intermittent employment for their followers. In early 1888 three lease agreements were made with men who had the personal endorsement of district leaders: J. A. Campbell (with Pretty Eagle), Nelson Story (with Plenty Coups) and Samuel Hardin (with Old Dog). While the chiefs valued the food these men gave them to pass out among their followers, and benefitted from the jobs they offered the young men of their districts, the Indian Office identified non-Indian cattle as a source of dollars. "You have a large amount of grass on your lands," M. P. Wyman told Plenty Coups in early 1890. "You cannot use it, but others can. And under proper control it will yield you a great many thousand dollars yearly. I don't think you can afford to lose it."[26]

At first the interests of Crow leaders and government officials converged. Each spring, a general council assembled to review the reservation's grazing leases and to discuss problems with stockmen and trespassers. Within a few years, three additional lessees had been added, and the bulk of the unallotted land on the reservation was occupied. But beginning in 1891, the Indian Office insisted that decisions on leasing be made in Washington, D.C., by bureaucrats who would simply award permits to the highest bidders. Despite some support from tribesmen who claimed that Plenty Coups and Pretty Eagle "get all the money" from the leases themselves, the tribe's leaders were able to demonstrate that most Crows opposed this change, preferring that their "friends" continue on the reserve. A council in the spring of 1891 demanded the reinstatement of the present lessees and a recognition of the chiefs' wishes.[27]

When the Indian Office insisted on putting the leases out for bid, M. P. Wyman, the Crows' agent, appealed the decision personally to the commissioner. In a passionate twenty-five-page letter, Wyman – whose previous career with the Northern Pacific Railroad had brought him into close contact with local stockmen – listed the evils that would surely accompany the government's plan. Easterners willing to overgraze the Indian rangelands would probably make the high bids, and these new lessees, unfamiliar with the northern plains, would ruin the tribe's unfenced pastures and alienate the Indians. Wyman explained that the tribe looked upon the current lessees "with more than friendly interest," adding that "the idea that the 'Great Father' will actually take such action as will compel these men ... to leave the land that the Crows always feel

---

[26] "Proceedings of Council," April 27, 1888 Item 2, Box 2, RCIA-FRC, Seattle; and "Report of Conversation Between Plenty Coups and Agent Wyman," February 20, 1890, filed with Wyman to Commissioner of Indian Affairs, March 3, 1890, 7432–1890, LR-OIA, RG 75, NA.
[27] The issue of leasing to the highest bidder was the principal subject of a tribal council on March 15, 1890, Item 2, Box 3, RCIA-FRC, Seattle. The order to base leases on an open bid process is contained in Secretary of the Interior to Commissioner of Indian Affairs, March 20, 1891, Item 4, Box 15, RCIA-FRC, Seattle.

that they own . . . seem[s] very strange indeed." In reply, Commissioner (and former preacher) Thomas Jefferson Morgan rebuked Wyman for his out-spokenness and repeated the order to solicit bids for permission to graze. The agent obeyed, but could not resist adding in a final note that "those chiefs who have expressed themselves so freely will be informed of the impression their words made." When the bids were opened in June, only two of the Crows "friends" – Samuel Hardin and J. A. Campbell – were awarded leases.[28]

Beginning in 1891, the Indian Office went ahead with its plan to divide the reservation into five grazing districts. These districts were unfenced, and each one surrounded Indian allotments and farms. The leases stipulated, however, the five-mile strips along each major river and stream were reserved for Indians. The agreement noted that "any trespass of stock within the limits of these strips will be considered sufficient cause for the immediate removal of the cattle from the Reservation." The 1891 leases were renewed in 1894 for an additional three years, and then in 1895 for five years. At that time, a sixth grazing district was created along Pass Creek, near Wyola, and let to E. L. Dana, a powerful Montana rancher. This bidding process became routinized and predictable. No cattleman was ever evicted from "his" range once the system was set up in 1891.[29]

In the same way that the Crow irrigation project relegated the Crows to the status of observers in their own economic development, the establishment of leasing districts and the bid system created an economic engine the tribe could not control. Generating tens of thousands of dollars annually, grazing leases quickly became an essential prop for the tribal treasury. Money from this source supported modest annual annuity payments and stimulated the rise of the tribal Business Committee. At the same time, the cattle leases gave local stockmen a long-term hold on tribal resources. Men like Samuel Hardin and E. L. Dana built barns, corrals and bunkhouses on tribal land, fenced in areas they needed for their operations and watered their Hereford cattle at reserva-tion streams and irrigation ditches. The result was an ongoing tension between dependent Indian "landlords" and powerful non-Indian tenants.[30]

While E. L. Dana and Frank Heinrich constructed fences along the exterior boundaries of the reservation in their grazing areas, little effort was made by the reservation lessees or the Indian Office to separate the grazing districts from Indian allotments or to keep non-Indian cattle the stipulated five miles from major reservation water courses. As a result, Agent J. E. Edwards wrote in the

[28] Wyman to Commissioner of Indian Affairs, May 1, 1891, 16696–1891; and ibid., May 18, 1891, 19533–1891, both in SC 133, Crow, LR-OIA, RG 75, NA.
[29] ARCIA, 1891 (Serial 2934), 269 (a summary of all cattle leases is contained in the body of the commissioner's report). See also "List of Leases of Grazing Privileges in Force . . . ," October 8, 1897, Item 2, Box 4, RCIA-FRC, Seattle.
[30] For the similar experiences of another Montana tribe during this period, see Wessel, "Agricul-ture on the Reservations."

summer of 1899 that "the Indians are damaged on these permits to the extent of an almost total loss of their hay on these five mile strips, cattle tramping and eating it off." In addition, lessees typically did not consult local residents when they erected fences or corrals – or even sublet portions of their pasture to others – leaving the Crows to protest in their wake. Finally, the absence of any enforcement of lease provisions encouraged an atmosphere of lawlessness in which unauthorized cattle were turned onto the reserve, cattle thieves raided the herds from the Bighorns and rode stolen stock off into Wyoming and overgrazing was common.[31]

With grazing leases running for from three to five years, there were few opportunities to alter or oppose them. Nevertheless, in 1905, when the permits for the five major reservation pastures came up for renewal, tribal leaders made an attempt to reassert control over the process. In January, a "council" of middle-aged band leaders led by Holds The Enemy, Plenty Coups, Medicine Crow and Two Leggings requested the retention of E. L. Dana, C. H. Bair and Frank Heinrich on the grounds that they purchased Crow hay, settled damage claims quickly and had "done their utmost to prevent the stealing of Indian stock by outsiders." As they had in the 1890s, these district leaders wanted to build their association with individual stockmen rather than simply take the highest bid. Plenty Coups, for example, wrote separately to the secretary of the interior about Charles Bair, the sheep man whose stock occupied much of the Pryor valley. "When Indians have been hungry, he has fed them," the chief explained. "When they have had hay, he has bought the hay to help feed his sheep; he has bought much hay from the Indians that he did not need. . . ."[32]

In April, Plenty Coups and Big Shoulder Blade went to Washington to emphasize their commitment to Bair, Dana and Heinrich. With this support, and the endorsement of Agent Reynolds, the Indian Office granted four-year leases to the three named by the council, as well as to sheep men Lee Simonson and James Ash of Absarokee, Montana. One unsuccessful bidder, a powerful Helena stockman who had offered more for one district than Charles Bair,

---

[31] J. E. Edwards to Commissioner of Indian Affairs, August 26, 1899, 41055–1899, SC 133, Crow, LR-OIA, RG 75, NA. See also E. H. Becker to Commissioner of Indian Affairs, July 29, 1898 (on failure to consult); J. E. Edwards to Commissioner of Indian Affairs, August 5, 1899 (on complaints regarding fencing and unauthorized stock); ibid., August 26, 1899 (on violation of five-mile strip provision) and November 21, 1900 (on unauthorized grazing); all in Item 2, Box 5, RCIA-FRC, Seattle. F. M. Heinrich was credited with capturing cattle rustlers at the headwaters of Rotten Grass and Lodge Grass Creeks in 1901, but he quickly parlayed this good deed into a permit to run cattle with the tribal herd in the upland area between the Bighorn and the Little Bighorn. See *ARCIA*, 1901 (Serial 4290), 258.

[32] Reynolds to Commissioner of Indian Affairs, February 20, 1905, 15799–1905 LR-OIA, R675, NA (also found in Item 2, Box 7, RCIA-FRC, Seattle); Plenty Coups to Secretary Hitchcock, April 28, 1905, 34827–1905. A recent memoir of Bair emphasizes his generosity in dealing with Indian lessors. See Lee Rostad, *Fourteen Cents and Seven Green Apples: The Life and Times of Charles Bair* (Great Falls, Mon: C. M. Russell Museum, 1992), 54, 59.

protested the decision, but the Interior Department was firm: "The action taken by the department was in accordance with the wishes of the Indians, and was deemed for their best interests and for the interests of the service, and the same is final."[33]

The renewal of the Heinrich, Bair and Dana leases not only strengthened these individuals' hold on "their" reservation pasturelands, but it associated them more closely than ever with the district band leaders. The ties between these stockmen and the Crow "chiefs" had proven beneficial, but the relationship was both uneven and informal and, like all paternalistic relationships, was doomed to disappointment. Creatures of the cattle market, the ranchers could provide employment for Crow cowboys and a market for Crow hay only so long as these arrangements were profitable; the reservation's headmen could do little to enforce the white men's promises.

While the tribe's relationship with Dana, Bair and the others might prove both profitable and useful in the ongoing struggle over the opening of "surplus" lands, its unevenness ensured that Crows would continue to be dependent on their wealthy tenants. In 1906, for example, Plenty Coups protested to the Indian Office that Bair was exceeding the limit fixed for the number of sheep allowed to graze in his district. "If he has," the chief asked weakly, "I wish he be made to pay for them." The chief had no power to overturn the lease or evict Bair's sheep. Three years later, Two Leggings, another district leader who had supported the 1905 renewals, summarized the tribe's dependent position in a letter to the secretary of the interior. The old warrior presented a long indictment of sheep man Bair, and then paused for a moment of reflection:

> You may wonder why I have so much to say about Mr. Bair and the others. It is because they are rich and have gotten rich off of us Indians. We are poor and have little. They are wealthy and powerful. We want you to help us who are weak rather than those who are strong. They don't need you. We do.

In the nineteenth century, the Crows had been "rich" in horses and kinsmen, "powerful" in warriors and guns. But in the commercial atmosphere of the twentieth century, men like Two Leggings understood that the group's overall economic power had declined and that their future well-being depended increasingly on others. By elevating men like Charles Bair to wealth, the reservation's cattle leasing system – originally conceived as a way of insulating the tribe from the worst effects of the scramble for modern riches – had indirectly

---

[33] "Report of questions asked by Plenty Coups and Big Shoulder Blade . . . in their talk with the Acting Commissioner of Indian Affairs," April 26, 1905, 34827–1905; and E. A. Hitchcock to Commissioner of Indian Affairs, May 18, 1905, 38243–1905; all in SC 133, Crow, LR-OIA, RG 75, NA.

provided independence for tribal leaders and protection for tribal assets, but it had not reversed the flow of economic power away from the Crow community.[34]

The realization that the reservation's sheep and cattle men had become fixtures in the reservation economy probably fueled some of the community's division during the decade leading up to World War I. When Helen Grey began her campaign against the reservation administration in early 1907, much of her fire was aimed at allegedly corrupt ties between local cattlemen and the "agency crowd." The younger, commercially oriented Crows who made up the core of the Crow Indian Lodge, and the older leaders who joined them in opposition to Reynolds and his cronies, resented the established band chiefs. This group also included Crow farmers whose crops had been damaged by unfenced cattle and sheep and those who had been excluded from the lessees' generosity. Unfortunately, these critics of the leasing system had no alternatives to propose, while its supporters insisted that all complaints could be met if the tribe pressed for substantial increases in income when the grazing leases next came up for renewal.

At a council of district leaders in early 1909, Plenty Coups, Medicine Crow, Big Medicine, Holds The Enemy and other older leaders defended the lease system but urged the Indian Office to negotiate a better price for their grazing lands. In 1905 the group had declared that it was "willing that the price be left to the judgement of the Indian Agent," but in 1909 Plenty Coups opened the council by admitting that "we are hard up now and need the money." Moreover, he added, "We do not want this grazing money spent for other purposes but we want it in cash." The younger men and Crow Indian Lodge leaders like Joe Cooper, who had been so much a part of the reservation controversies of the preceding three years, were silent during these discussions and no opposition arose to the renewals. Despite this support, however, Dana was outbid by a new stockman, who, together with Bair, Heinrich and former Crow agent J. E. Edwards, leased the five reservation districts for a total of more than $100,000 per year, nearly tripling the tribe's annual grazing income.[35]

During the next lease period – which was shortened during the 1909 negotiations to three years – commercial interests from the surrounding non-Indian communities penetrated the reservation with unprecedented vigor. Hardin became the county seat of newly organized Bighorn County; the sale of "dead"

[34] Plenty Coups to Acting Assistant Commissioner of Indian Affairs, December 14, 1906, Plenty Coups Mss.; Two Leggings to Secretary of the Interior, June 11, 1909, Reel 21, IRA Mss. From circumstantial evidence such as this, it appears that lease rates on Crow lands were lower than for comparable non-Indian lands.

[35] Reynolds to Commissioner of Indian Affairs, September 30, 1909 (enclosing proceedings of council of February 18, 1909), Item 2, Box 8, RCIA-FRC, Seattle. The bids are summarized in the Hardin *Tribune*, August 27, 1909.

As a footnote to Dana's loss of his grazing lease, the Plenty Coups collection includes a letter from E. L. Dana to the Pryor chief, dated May 24, 1909, which says in part that "it will be all right for you to send me the money you borrowed at some future time when you can more conveniently spare it."

allotments stimulated the growth of white settlements such as the Lodge Grass townsite and allowed cattlemen like Heinrich and Dana to purchase homesteads that could serve as permanent ranch headquarters adjacent to their rented pasturelands. White settlers and white business interests appeared poised to engulf the Crows. And as this tide of non-Indian people and interests rose, it seemed clear that the "rich and powerful" stockmen who had defended them in the past could not prevent the reservation from becoming a community of commercial farms. In this atmosphere of rapid economic change, tribal leaders searched for some other way to participate in the ranching industry.

The young and disaffected men who had risen to influence in the wake of the Helen Grey affair were the first to suggest a way that the Crows might continue to be ranchers without surrendering completely to the local stockmen. Soon after the tribal Business Committee began meeting in 1910, its members discussed the idea of using grazing income for the purchase of cattle for individual tribal members. Supporters of the proposal argued that by developing individually owned herds, the Crows could end their dependence on local white ranchers while continuing to use all of their reservations lands, fending off further attempts to open unallotted lands to homesteaders. In April 1911, the Business Committee passed a series of resolutions outlining this new approach to the Indian Office and demanding a response. A delegation from the group met with Commissioner Robert Valentine the following November and pressed him to act on their behalf.[36]

Meeting with the Crows at Crow Agency during a brief stopover on his way back to Washington, D.C., from a western trip, Valentine invited the group to "speak to me about the biggest things which are in your hearts and in your minds." The response was a torrent of comments on the cattle and sheep industry and uniform opposition to further land sales. Spotted Rabbit and Sees With His Ears, now middle-aged but still reflecting the vigor that had caused them to ride with Sword Bearer twenty-four years earlier, reminded the commissioner that their new Business Committee included "educated boys" and people who are "pretty shrewd." They proposed that ten head of cattle be purchased for every person on the reservation. Significantly, a political opponent of these two speakers – tribal policeman Big Medicine – rose to agree with them. Once he had ten head of cattle, the agency loyalist predicted, he wouldn't "kill them all, nor sell them all, but will always look after them and try to accumulate all he can." The Business Committee had already passed several resolutions and circulated a number of petitions, Spotted Rabbit observed, "but the first thing is the petition for cattle."[37]

[36] For the resolutions calling for a distribution of cattle and opposing the opening of the reservation, see "Minutes of Meeting of the Crow Business Committee," April 19, 1911, Item 14, Box 50, Council Proceedings, 1911–1913, RCIA-FRC, Seattle.

[37] The Honorable Commissioner of Indian Affairs, R. G. Valentine to the Crow Indians on the Crow Reservation, Montana, November 13, 1911, Item 14, Box 50, Council Proceedings, 1911–1913, RCIA-FRC, Seattle, 6, 5, 3, 24.

Valentine understood the tactic. Speaking in reply to the assembled leaders, he said "I understand most of you do not want the reservation open. Now the shortest way to keep Congress from opening the reservation is for you to make use of your land." And clearly, the presence of large numbers of Indian-owned cattle would constitute use. "I venture to make this prediction," the Commissioner declared; "if you, either individually or as a whole were to run one thousand head of stock on these ranges, Congress won't open that land." The commissioner's statement clearly impressed his audience, because Crow leaders repeated it for the next decade. Throughout their struggle to oppose efforts to open the reservation, they returned to the idea that dozens of small Crow ranches would allow them to claim the entire area and hold it for their children.[38]

Not surprisingly, it was the younger, educated members of the Business Committee who pushed the idea of Indian cattle ownership with Congress and the Indian Office. The principal obstacle at first was money. Congress had authorized $240,000 from the 1899 land sale to be spent on a tribal herd. Because the tribe now wanted the funds used to buy additional stock for individual Crows, the Indian Office would not approve the expenditure. But even if it had approved this request, a much larger appropriation was needed if the tribe were to be successful in buying out Frank Heinrich and the other lessees. For this reason, grazing leases were renewed in 1912 even though the Business Committee continued to lobby for increased appropriations and a revision of the 1899 land sale agreement.

Fortuitously, early in 1913 Rodman Wanamaker, a wealthy Philadelphian with a fascination for Indians, made it possible for a Crow delegation to bring the cattle issue home to decision makers in Washington. Wanamaker had succeeded in persuading Congress to authorize a "National Indian Memorial" at the entrance to New York harbor. The dedication of the memorial, which was to consist of a 165-foot-high statue of an Indian welcoming newcomers to America, was scheduled for George Washington's birthday, 1913. Wanamaker's idea was to bring a collection of Indian chiefs to New York City to participate in the ceremonies. His invitation provided an opportunity for several Crows – Plenty Coups, Medicine Crow, White Man Runs Him, Richard Wallace and Robert Yellowtail – to be in the East to lobby Indian Office officials about the cattle situation.

A few days after they had broken the ground for Wanamaker's Indian memorial with outgoing President Taft, this group of older leaders and educated young men gathered in the offices of Acting Commissioner F. H. Abbott to press their request for an appropriation that would allow the tribe to remove the white cattlemen from the reservation. (Woodrow Wilson's appointee to the post, Cato Sells, had yet to take office.) Yellowtail criticized the Indian Office for allowing the reservation's tenants to renew their leases in 1912 with a

[38] Ibid., 20–21.

minimum of advice from the tribe, but Abbott defended the practice. He replied that his "understanding" was "that the Business Committee of the Crow Indians has authorized the Secretary of the Interior to make leases for all of these districts on the Crow Reservation." "We virtually have given him full power to act for us?" Yellowtail asked. The bureaucrat replied, "You have. . . ."³⁹

A week later the group returned to the commissioner's office with a specific proposal. With Yellowtail as spokesman, the delegation requested the appropriation of whatever tribal funds might be available to purchase Frank Heinrich's cattle, all of which ranged in an unallotted wedge of land between the Little Bighorn and Bighorn Rivers. All five delegates spoke in support of the idea. When Abbott suggested buying cattle elsewhere or waiting until Congress amended the 1899 land sale agreement, Medicine Crow was quick to reply: "I have heard of you before," he declared. "I came with the express desire that you make the greatest effort to give us these cattle this spring, to show us that we are going to be on a money-making basis before long, and not put it off as in the past. . . . I want you to get hold of this money and turn it into cattle for us."⁴⁰

Despite the fact that Abbott announced two days later that $400,000 of tribal funds could be used for the Heinrich purchase, the Crow leaders were unsuccessful in their bid to take control of the lessee's herd. The amount was well short of what was required, and the Indian Office would not authorize any expenditure until all the needed funds were in hand. Furthermore, an Indian Office cattle inspector Abbott sent to Montana to review the situation concluded that the tribe should delay its plan for a year or two. He asserted that the Crows were "demoralized" and not prepared to manage cattle on their own. His report also defended Frank Heinrich and noted, "It would not be fair to force him off" the tribal pastures.⁴¹

In the aftermath of the stock inspector's report, it was clear that Heinrich and the other long-term lessees had established themselves so firmly on the reservation that removing them would require more than permission to use tribal funds to buy their assets. Infuriated by the stock inspector's estimation of their competence, Robert Yellowtail asked Agent Evan Estep to call a meeting of the Business Committee. Estep, an Indian Office veteran who relied on a tough, "by the book" administrative style at a number of western agencies, refused.

---

³⁹ "Continuation of Hearing with Delegation of Crow Indians," March 8, 1913, Plenty Coups Mss.
⁴⁰ "Hearing of Crow Indians in the Office of F. H. Abbott, Acting Commissioner of Indian Affairs," March 15, 1913, Item 14, Box 50, Council Proceedings, 1911–1913, RCIA-FRC, Seattle.
⁴¹ The $400,000 authorization is discussed at length in "Conference between F. H. Abbott . . . and a delegation of Crow Indians . . . ," March 17, 1913, Item 14, Box 50, Council Proceedings, 1911–1913, RCIA-FRC, Seattle. The quotations from the inspector's report are taken from Business Committee to Secretary of the Interior, April 30, 1913, enclosed with F. H. Abbott to George W. Hogan, May 26, 1913, Item 14, Box 50, Council Proceedings, 1911–1913, RCIA-FRC, Seattle. Interestingly, the proceedings of the March 17 meeting between the Crow delegation and Abbott indicate that Frank Heinrich's Washington attorney was Lewis Dalby, the man who had been sent to inspect the reservation in 1907.

Yellowtail countered by calling the meeting himself, a violation of conventional reservation procedures. When the group gathered on April 30, 1913, Yellowtail and his younger allies, George Hogan and Russell White Bear, were joined by Spotted Rabbit, Medicine Crow, Sees With His Ears and other older members of the committee. Missing were the Pryor representatives, Frank Shively and Bird Hat, and Sits Down Spotted and Holds The Enemy from the Bighorn. Nevertheless, this "unofficial" meeting produced a manifesto which Hogan and Yellowtail immediately sent to the Interior Department, sidestepping the normal procedure of submitting it to the agent for approval. Estep wrote to Washington afterwards that the document was "a statement by these two boys rather than bona fide minutes of the action of the Committee." Moreover, the agent noted, the fact that the minutes were "not submitted through the regular channel and that the meeting was called without authority . . . the whole proceeding was and is an effort on the part of Yellowtail to take tribal matters in his own hands."[42]

There is no evidence that some members of the Business Committee opposed Yellowtail's action, but the young man's aggressiveness earned him the active opposition of the Indian Office staff. According to Estep and his local colleagues, Yellowtail's stout defense of the stock purchase proposal, as well as the fact that the March 1913 delegation had travelled to Washington without official approval or support, proved the obstinance and foolishness of the Crows. "This incident is in itself a demonstration of the utter futility of our efforts to have the Crows participate in the management of their affairs through the medium of a Business Committee," the agent wrote in June. "The old Indians are credulous in the extreme, and . . . any voice . . . that we concede to the tribe is immediately appropriated by the mixed bloods who are by far the most mischievous and troublesome of all with whom we have to deal. . . . it is absolutely necessary that they be made to understand that they are still wards of the government." Given this situation, Estep declared that putting the tribe in control of its "tribal affairs is premature."[43]

The alignments and attitudes revealed in 1913 persisted to the end of the

---

[42] Agent to Commissioner of Indian Affairs, May 3, 1913, Item 14, Box 50, Council Proceedings, 1911–1913, RCIA-FRC, Seattle. Estep's letter ended with a remarkably revealing comment on the business committee's initiative: "It is necessary to say to you that to allow tribal business to be taken up with your office by the Indians themselves, without consulting this office, would be entirely subversive of all discipline here, and would render us powerless to control them."

[43] Superintendent to Commissioner of Indian Affairs, June 2, 1913, Item 14, Box 50, Council Proceedings, 1911–1913, RCIA-FRC, Seattle. The agent also noted in this letter that Joe Cooper, Russel White Bear, Sam Davis and Robert Yellowtail were the "most mischievous" members of the tribe.

A letter from Robert Yellowtail and Frank Shively to Senator Robert Lafollette, dated April 11, 1913, presented a strong case in favor of funds for tribal cattle herds. It appears to have had the support of the business committee as it was signed by the two men, "duly elected Crow delegates." See Item 14, Box 57, Stock, 1910–1913, RCIA-FRC, Seattle.

decade. Indian Office officials continued to renew the leases of local stockmen and to refuse the Business Committee's calls for a distribution of all reservation cattle to tribal members. The tribal herd grew gradually in size, but the Indian Office managed it without regard to the tribe's desire to assert greater control. One official reply to a tribal delegation that travelled to Washington in 1917 simply declared that "the time has not yet arrived when the herd can be as successfully handled by individuals as it now is by being run as a unit." Commissioner Valentine's brief encouragement, uttered in 1912, was now long forgotten.[44]

V

In the spring of 1912, at a time when families were putting in gardens for the summer, beginning to plan for the July 4 pow-wow at Crow Agency and listening to the gossip about the Business Committee's various attempts to preserve the reservation's current boundaries, a group of young men gathered at Lodge Grass to draft a petition to the commissioner of Indian affairs. Led by three educated political activists who were also members of the local Baptist church – Robert Yellowtail, James Hill and Joe Cooper – the group requested that the Indian Office replace fourteen white employees at the local agency with tribal members. "It is a long established and an undisputed historical truth that when any Nation ever rose above barbarism and primitiveness it was because men of her own blood and bone . . . were able to assume the reigns of guidance and leadership," they wrote. "Precisely what has happened to Nations heretofore, must necessarily happen with us. . . ." By acting immediately, they argued, the Indian Office would be supporting the Crow tribe's "national betterment. . . . The ultimate harvest of the present system has been the squandering of our lands and money perniciously, and the continuity of our stationary detriment."[45]

Knowing that official regulations freed him from any obligation to reply seriously to the proposal, Agent Estep forwarded it to his superiors in Washington with a contemptuous chuckle. "Of course the whole proposition is absurd," he wrote. "The time when the Crows will be able to manage their own affairs is not yet in sight." His reply revealed the stark contrast between the reservation community's desire for some form of "national betterment" and the harsh

[44] E. B. Meritt to Plenty Coups, Russel White Bear, Robert Yellowtail, James Hill and Yellow Brow, Crow Indians, August 31, 1917, Plenty Coups Mss. Frank Heinrich was finally evicted from the reservation for overgrazing his pastures. See "Hearing with the Crow Delegation," March 5, 1918, Item 15, Box 78, Delegates to Washington, 1917–1918, RCIA-FRC, Seattle. Charges of collusion between lessors and tribal leaders also continued to divide the Crows. See, for example, a file of clippings describing accusations against Russell White Bear in 1919, Item 15, Box 80, "Cases for Federal Court, 1916–1920," File 124, RCIA-FRC, Seattle.

[45] "To The Hon. Commissioner of Indian Affairs," May 6, 1912, Item 14, Box 54, "Law and Order," 1912–1914, RCIA-FRC, Seattle.

reality of their economic predicament. Allowed and encouraged to form themselves into villages and small settlements across the reservation's six districts,
Crow people had come to accept their permanent residence on a portion of their
traditional homeland.[46]

Struggling with the authoritarian requirements of missionaries and schoolmasters, the Crows had preserved a measure of individual dignity and religious
tradition while accommodating the arrival of churches and schools. Faced with
daunting political enemies and weakened by declining numbers, they had fashioned a system of reservation leadership which allowed the community to dodge
through its enemies' positions as briskly as a nineteenth-century war party. But
in their efforts to extend this emerging collection of national attributes to the
management of tribal resources and commercial life, Crow innovators like Plenty
Coups, Medicine Crow and Robert Yellowtail had been both overpowered and
ignored. They could not be self-sufficient when they sought ways to make a
living in a system of enterprise designed and ruled by others. They could not
reconcile the past and the present when they failed to retain control over their
inherited assets and were prevented from shaping an effective method of participating in the local economy. If they were to make a living at all, Agent Estep
and his predecessors had made clear, it would be in an occupation defined and
circumscribed by others.

The occupational profile of the Crow Reservation contained in the 1910
federal census confirms this conclusion. The enumerator who filed the return
for the tribe that year listed only two-thirds of the male heads of households as
having a definite line of work. (Female heads of households were almost uniformly ignored.) By implication, the remaining one-third of the tribe's households presumably survived on lease payments, intermittent wage labor and
government rations. Of the 378 Crow male heads of household who reported as
having an occupation in 1910, 135 (40%) were reported as farmers and farm-
workers; 106 (nearly 30%) were involved in ranching, and another 118 (just
over 30%) were listed as wage laborers. The latter group included government
employees, general laborers and people employed for the tribe's irrigation system.
The core of the active Crow workforce was engaged in commercial activities
that were controlled by outsiders. While adapting to the economic necessities of
their day, these household heads do not appear to have overcome a dependence
on cash and commercial transactions whose origins lay beyond their borders. In
short, while capable of managing complex social, religious and political activities, it appeared that circumstances allowed few Crows to "manage their own
affairs."[47]

---

[46] Ibid.
[47] A separate 1910 enumeration for the Crow Reservation is included with the returns for Montana.
A total of 135 male heads of household were reported engaged in "general farm work," 106 in
"Ranching and Stock Raising (two categories)," 38 in "General Labor," 54 in "Government
Labor," 26 in "Ditchwork" and 19 in other miscellaneous categories.

The consequences of the Crows' economic predicament in the years following World War I are best suggested by a tiny incident that occurred in the Bighorn district during Easter week in 1926. According to the local subagent, Sam Lapointe, a man named Kills took a portion of the income he received from the lease of his land to a Hardin bank and exchanged it for a hundred $1 bills. "The next day," Lapointe wrote,

> this same Indian . . . tied every one of these dollars to as many separate sticks as a person would with small flags and in that manner made his whole family, his son and his family, parade in front of all the other Indians so they can see that he is giving away, all of that whole one hundred dollars. . . . I know this family very well. More than half of the time they do not have enough to eat but they can not stand prosperity. According to my record here, Kills and his wife received a trifle over $352 in less than three weeks, just prior to this Easter celebration. If taken care of, this money would have kept them, he and his wife, for a year.[48]

In an atmosphere of economic exclusion, where community self-sufficiency had been denied them and where making a living demanded menial labor, conformity to non-Indian expectations and dependence on the market economy, people like Kills and his family preferred the celebration of community and the traditional Crow value of generosity to the pointless thrift preached by Indian Office functionaries. If tribal members could not participate in economic enterprises on their own terms, they at least had retained the power to reject their "guardian's" expectations.

[48] Farmer's Weekly Report, April 5 to 10, 1926, Item 15, Box 87, Farmer's Weekly Report, Big Horn, 1925–1927, RCIA-FRC, Seattle.

Part Three

Being Crow, 1920–1935

We are not unappreciative of the fact that the Commissioner is endeavoring to try to bring about a situation in which in his mind he thinks of benefit to us. Notwithstanding our appreciation for his efforts, we think the conditions on this reservation are peculiarly suited to our own methods and conditions.

Harry Whiteman, Crow council, May 1934[1]

The passage of the Crow Act in the summer of 1920 marked the Crow community's transition to a settled, community existence. By dividing the reservation into large, individually owned tracts, the new law ended decades of white attempts to dismember the tribe's vast preserve. Produced after years of negotiation between tribal leaders and congressmen, the Crow Act also signaled that local whites could accept the presence of Indian people in modern Montana. Even though missionaries and government bureaucrats continued their work of "uplifting" the tribe, there was a perceptible lessening of pressure on the Crows to abandon their old ways and take up the habits of their pioneer neighbors. And perhaps most important of all, the horrific population losses of the preceding four decades appeared to have ended; during the 1920s the size of the Crow tribe began to increase for the first time since the tribe had left the Stillwater valley.

In 1920, the men and women who had formulated and approved the Crow Act, as well as those who led the community's social and religious activities, were products of the reservation environment. Born after the disappearance of the buffalo and the arrival of the railroad, these people had been educated in government schools, trained in farming, ranching and household tasks and required to support their families with cash. They adhered to laws written in English and occupied homes resting on surveyed land. Even though Fort Custer was abandoned and the old rules against leaving the reservation were now relaxed, Crow families understood their settlements and districts as their homes. The decades of drastic change appeared to be coming to an end; the old life lived only in memory.

In the twentieth century, a series of national institutions – transportation systems, the modern economy, legal structures and government bureaucracies – have become a common presence in Americans' lives. Every citizen experiences

---

[1] "Minutes of the Crow Tribal Council Held May 2, 1934 at Crow Agency, Montana," CCF, Crow, 006, 4894–1934, Part B.

these institutions, even if that experience is oppressive or destructive. Nevertheless, while these institutions have a universal impact, shaping human communities and altering individual aspirations, they cannot create traditions and identities. Those aspects of community life are the product of human experience and of a group's internal dynamics. The emerging stability of reservation life did not diminish the allegiance Crow families and individuals felt towards each other; instead it placed those allegiances in a new context. Being Crow in the years after 1920 meant expressing community values and goals in a modern institutional setting. Allegiance to the society that emerged within that setting was the source of statements like the one quoted above. Speaking before the Crow council in 1934, Harry Whiteman argued that no one was better suited to improve the tribe's condition than its own leaders. Only they could appreciate how current practices were "peculiarly suited" to the tribe's "methods and conditions."

Crows in the 1920s and 1930s lived at the intersection of culture and circumstance; within that zone they defined their identity in the modern era. In it, Crows believed themselves to be a part of a continuous community even though they were products of a new reservation social system and participants in new religious patterns; they followed new leaders and lived their lives within the constraints of new economic realities. To be Crow in the decades after World War I was to inhabit this area of tension and to explore its dimensions.

In the 1920s and 1930s, Crow people were absorbed in the process of "being themselves" amidst the institutions of national life. The experiences of other tribes had little effect on their daily lives. Yet their effort to reconcile culture and circumstance and to assert themselves in a wider world resonated with the experiences of other tribes in other parts of the continent and many of their responses to their predicament pioneered techniques others would employ. While the existence of hundreds of Indian communities in the United States make generalizations difficult, it is striking how many tribes followed the broad outlines of Crow history. Conquered in the nineteenth century and subjected to the reservation regime, they too created new leaders and new patterns of life. And they too emerged alongside the Crows in the 1920s and 1930s, ethnic nations in an increasingly plural society.

10

Stability and dependency in the 1920s

The last ten years somehow or other we have gone back and my people have suffered a great deal. . . . Instead of prospering as we used to, we have lost. My people lease their lands and do not get the right compensation for them. Some of my boss farmers on the reservation are not good. They are not consistent in their work and taking it all in all, I have not been treated and my people have not been treated for the best. Therefore we are the sufferers.

Plenty Coups, 1926[1]

I

The household of James Hill reflected both the pride and the suffering that inspired Plenty Coups's words. Hill's family embodied the upheavals of the Crow past and the relative stability that came to characterize tribal life in the decade following the end of World War I. According to an Indian Office census conducted in 1920, the forty-five-year-old Hill and his thirty-one-year-old wife, Ada Prettyman, had two children and lived in the Bighorn valley on land watered by the tribe's irrigation system. A graduate of the government's industrial training school in Carlisle, Pennsylvania, Hill earned his living as a laborer at the agency and by raising cattle on the tribal pasture. Like most longtime residents of the Bighorn district, he was probably a Catholic. He had selected an allotment within sight of the St. Xavier Mission. Hill had been born in the year of Custer's defeat at the Little Bighorn, but had come of age in the modern world of railroads, mission schools and cash.

This image of stability shifts significantly, however, when one notices that the 1920 census recorded two additional children in the Hill household: Jesse and Amy Prettyman, Ada's children by a previous marriage. Hill's past was even more complicated; widowed before he was twenty-five, he had remarried in 1906. Death continued to stalk him, however. During the next eleven years, Hill and his new wife, Bird Without A Cloud, would bury all four of their children, two boys and two girls. The oldest was four at the time of his death. Perhaps these tragedies contributed to the end of their marriage in 1917. Almost immediately after his divorce, Hill married Ada Prettyman and the two of

[1] Minutes of Council Held August 26, 1926, "Reports of Indian Visiting Inspectors, 1926–1927," Item 15, Box 60, RCIA-FRC, Seattle.

them had a child, William, at the end of the year. This boy lived to be recorded in the 1920 census, but not much longer; he died at the end of the year, just a month short of his third birthday. In the same year James had his first child who lived to adulthood. He was John Hill, the second child recorded in the 1920 enumeration. Three others – Mabel, Clara and Augustine – would be born during the coming decade; all would survive childhood.

Hill owned nineteen head of cattle in 1926, along with an irrigated allotment close to the Bighorn River. A second allotment on the outskirts of Hardin had been sold for cash in 1909. He may also have owned land inherited from his mother and first wife in other parts of the Bighorn valley, but agency records indicate that he was not farming any of his property during the 1920s. Like most of the land around it, his acreage was probably leased to ranchers and cattlemen.

As Hill looked forward to the new decade, he found a number of opportunities open to him. His children could be educated while living at home rather than face the dreary loneliness of boarding school; if he wished, he could participate in tribal rituals like the Tobacco Society dances with a minimum of interference from the local priests or government officials; and tribal politics would give him an opportunity to shape the life of his community. Nevertheless, a survey of living conditions conducted on the reservation in 1923 revealed that Hill and his family lived in a one-room cabin that had neither running water nor an outhouse. It also lacked beds and a dining table. Hill and Prettyman had survived an era of suffering and developed ways to participate in community affairs, but their lives were still conditioned by poverty and dependence.[2]

II

Plenty Coups's description of suffering and the experiences of the Hill household were echoed in the broad contours of tribal life across the reservation. The Crow population rose steadily for most of the years of the 1920s, while the death rate fell; by 1930, there were 1963 Crows living on the reservation, an increase of more than 14%. This increase was greatest among women, and this

[2] James Hill appears on the 1900 census as a widower without children who lived in a tipi with an older couple (perhaps a maternal aunt and her spouse). The 1910 enumeration indicates that Hill married Bird Without A Cloud in 1906 and was the father of Frank and Mattie Hill, both of whom had disappeared by the time of the 1920 census. The 1920 and 1930 Indian Office censuses list him as married to Ada Prettyman and describe the arrival of three children: Mabel (1924), Clara (1926) and Augustine (1929). The death dates of Hill and Prettyman's children can be found in Item 44, RCIA-FRC, Seattle. For Hill's 1926 crop report, see Item 15, Box 90, Industrial Survey, 5 Year Program, 1917–1927, RCIA-FRC, Seattle (report from Bighorn). For the industrial survey of his home, see File 142, Report on Hygenic Conditions of Indian Homes, 1923, Item 15, Box 88, RCIA-FRC, Seattle.

growing pool of potential mothers might well account for the dramatic increase in the number of young people during the decade. The percentage of the population under the age of ten rose from 26 to 30% while the number of Crows under the age of twenty rose from 43 to 49%. Balancing these signs of accelerating growth and stability, were indicators of traditional patterns of behavior as well as rising levels of poverty.[3]

One might expect multigenerational households to disappear in a decade marked by population growth and increased mobility. As Crows like James Hill conformed to "civilized" standards of work and dress, acquired automobiles and sent their children to public schools, it would seem logical for them to live increasingly in cabins and frame houses, away from elders and kin relations. On the surface, it appears that Indian Office records confirm this supposition, for they define a family as a conjugal unit or a single adult and the related children, if any. Using that definition, the agency superintendent reported during the 1920s that there were from 423 to 460 "families" under his jurisdiction. At the same time, however, the superintendent noted that these "families" were living in 305 to 350 "houses" (between 12 and 25% of which were actually tents).

With at least a hundred "families" living without "houses," it seems clear that a great many Crows shared dwellings with people outside the nuclear unit. Elderly adults, childless couples and unmarried men and women lived with their relatives, causing the census taker to count several families in a single dwelling. The fact that a good number of these houses were tents also supports the notion that relatives would gather near a permanent dwelling, perhaps forming a multigenerational compound in which the number of "families" present would greatly outnumber the "houses." For example, in 1927, 1854 Crows were reported to be living in 450 families (average size: 4.1) and 350 houses (average size: 5.3). Households were larger than families; they obviously comprised more than one family group. If for this sample year of 1927 one eliminates the 43 dwellings that were actually tents, the average household size jumps to more than 6, meaning that the average household would contain a "family" plus 2 additional people.

Other data gathered during the 1920s confirms this general outline. For example, "Report on Hygenic Conditions of Indian Homes," conducted by the Indian Office in 1923, described the plumbing and sanitation facilities at each residence as well as the "number of people in the house" and its "number of rooms." Nearly three-quarters of the households had no toilet facilities, and more than half gathered drinking water from rivers or irrigation ditches. The survey also confirmed that households were larger than family groups (in this case the average household size was 4.8, while the 1923 census reported an average family size of 4.1) and indicates the conditions obtaining within them.

---

[3] Unless otherwise indicated, statistics in this and succeeding paragraphs are drawn from *ANR*.

Some 152 of the 181 houses surveyed had three rooms or fewer, and nearly half of the households had 5 or more members.[4]

Two other fragmentary pieces of evidence support the idea that multi-generational households remained the norm among the Crows of the 1920s. First, when the Crow Agency boarding school closed in 1921, the superintendent suggested the huge, vacant buildings be converted into a home for the elderly. Tribal officials replied that they had no need for such a facility. Second, in his annual report for 1927, at the bottom of the page where population figures are entered, Superintendent Calvin Asbury noted, "More than one family often live in the same [house]." He also reported that birth figures were difficult to obtain because "Indians move around so much in summer and other times [it is] hard to get an accurate count."[5]

The persistence of large, multigenerational households ensured the continuation of several community traditions into the 1920s that might otherwise have disappeared. The presence of grandparents, together with the move to educate Crow children in the public schools meant that the tribal language would continue to be spoken in the homes and passed on to a new generation. (The reservation superintendent wrote in 1927 that "not more than 3 or 4% of the children come from homes where the families speak English in the home. . . .") The "crowding" of relations together in small cabins and clusters of tents also provided an opportunity to associate with clan relations and other extended kin. This same crowding also supported the continuation of habits of visiting and travelling, particularly in the summer. "The greatest drawback in trying to teach these Crow Indians to farm is and has been that they will travel, visiting all summer long," wrote an exasperated district farmer in the spring of 1925. He reported that they travelled to the Bighorns and "make the rounds of all the fairs within reach," from Powell and Cody, Wyoming, to Billings, Montana. Reports from other districts regularly noted the absence of Crow families to visit, participate in tribal dances or gather berries in the Bighorn Mountains. None of these reports indicated that these officials were aware of the tribe's

---

[4] See "Report on Hygenic Conditions of Indian Homes, 1923," Item 15, Box 88, RCIA-FRC, Seattle. Because this survey was conducted on permanent dwellings only, the impression these figures convey is understated. All tents are "one room" shelters and many of them were probably erected close to frame houses. Superintendent Calvin Asbury also noted the difference between Crow households and the Indian Office's definition of families in a letter to General Hugh Scott, September 27, 1929, Item 16, Box 109, "Investigation and Inspection," RCIA-FRC, Seattle. Asbury noted that there were 640 families on the reservation but only 251 families in houses, "though the word 'family' in this instance probably meant the head of a family and all relatives living with him"(3).

[5] See Calvin Asbury to Commissioner of Indian Affairs, February 3 and May 8, 1922, CCF, Crow, 806, 10715–1922, quoted in Charles Crane Bradley Jr. and Susanna Remple Bradley, "From Individualism to Bureaucracy: Documents on the Crow Indians, 1920–1945," unpublished manuscript dated 1974, Little Big Horn College Archives, Crow Agency, Montana, 313.

Crow families seldom lived apart from their relatives. This photograph shows a typical pattern in which people lived alongside one another in cabins and tipi, or moved between them with the change of seasons. In any event, this unidentified homestead would likely accommodate more than a "nuclear" unit of parents and their children. Courtesy of American Heritage Center, University of Wyoming.

ancient ties to the Bighorn basin, the high country of the mountains themselves or other traditional hunting and gathering areas.[6]

By the 1920s, social and religious life also reinforced the tribe's customary pattern of multifamily living and summer travel. The Baptist and Catholic churches established a pattern of gatherings and social events to supplement their worship services, and the movement of members between these two groups and the Native American church meant that individuals could participate in several of these schedules at once. Surveys of religious life in the 1920s indicate that the Baptists were strongest in the Little Bighorn districts, while the Catholics retained their majority in the Bighorn and at Pryor, but the reports suggest a fluid and changing membership. The subagent at St. Xavier wrote in 1929

[6] The Agent's comment on language is in Calvin Asbury to Commissioner of Indian Affairs, January 27, 1927, Item 16, Box 103; Farmer's Weekly Report, Big Horn, March 2 to 7, 1925, Item 15, Box 87. See also, reports from Pryor, July 3 to 8, 1922, and April 30 to May 5, 1923; all the above in RCIA-FRC, Seattle.

that 150 district residents attended mission churches, while "the rest attend peyote."[7]

In 1926, the Indian Office circulated an extensive questionnaire regarding "community life" in the six districts of the reservation. Each agency farmer received a list of questions, including "what activities are present in the community life of the Indians?" Only four of the six replies have survived, but these commentaries, together with Superintendent Asbury's summary report, confirm the picture of an active – and distinctly Crow – social life. (By the 1920s, the chief federal officer on the reservation was no longer an "agent." He had become a "superintendent.") The Black Lodge farmer wrote, for example, that his community's activities were "overdeveloped." According to him, the people in his district, which adjoined the town of Hardin, "dance frequently, some few go to church and many play rummy in the pool halls." At Pryor, the subagent was philosophical, but equally derisive: "Very little can be accomplished with the Indians as individuals or families," R. C. Holgate replied. "They are preeminently a group people." When asked in his final report to recommend areas where tribal life could improve, Superintendent Asbury wrote comments which embodied his view of everyday life on the reservation: "Ambition, more staying at home . . . less Indian dances, better homes, more barns, root cellars, wells, more industry and pride should be shown."[8]

III

The rising non-Indian population on the reservation was barely visible in these descriptions. Nevertheless, by 1920 whites had infiltrated most of the districts. Lodge Grass and Crow Agency contained a substantial non-Indian population, and white farmers and ranchers leased or purchased land wherever it was economically advantageous to do so. A rising level of racial tension accompanied this influx of Montana "pioneers." Politically hostile to the tribe and its ambitions, local non-Indians had long favored the opening of Crow lands to homesteading and resisted the integration of Crow aspirations into their plans for Bighorn County's future. Crow children were not admitted to local schools until federal subsidies were provided to enhance the local tax base, adults were frequently discriminated against in the town of Hardin and white community activines did not include Crows unless they were present as dancers, entertainers or opponents of local sports teams. The district farmer at St. Xavier summarized the situation in 1926 when he wrote that "the only whites

[7] File 051, Statistics, 1929, Item 16, Box 100, RCIA-FRC, Seattle.
[8] For district replies, see Statistical Data for General Superintendent's Circular No. 5, Item 16, Box 103, and for Asbury's comments see his letter to the Commissioner of Indian Affairs, dated January 27, 1927, Item 16, Box 103, both in RCIA-FRC, Seattle.

that mix with Indians can be safely traced to the missionaries and that is because they have to. . . . There is no race friction but there are times when race prejudice is very noticeable." Local whites frequently denied these attitudes, but aside from welcoming the notoriety that might accompany a visit to the reservation by the commissioner of Indian affairs or movie star Ken Maynard, they rarely acknowledged men like James Hill.[9]

Economic conditions reinforced this separation of the races, for as the decade wore on the failure of Indian farming and ranching became increasingly evident. While some individual Crows continued to have modest success, the community did not produce sufficient income to become an important factor in the local economy. Tribal members continued to be the nominal "landlords" of their property, but they did not become customers for machinery and durable goods, important sources for bank deposits or economic partners of local whites. Instead the Crows grew dependent on lease income and wage labor while their non-Indian neighbors mechanized their farms and expanded their holdings.

Table 6 presents a profile of Crow income during the 1920s. It includes income paid to individuals (e.g., value of crops raised, wages, payments on leases of individual allotments) as well as to the tribe (e.g., grazing leases, oil and gas leases). The total from both categories is simply divided by the tribal population to produce a per capita figure. Table 6 masks economic inequality within the community – a phenomenon which became increasingly evident during the decade – but it conveys a sense of both the level and the sources of income within the tribe.

Table 6 reveals that during the 1920s Crow income was not heavily dependent on the value of the crops or stock raised by individual tribal members. Both figures dropped by more than 50% during the decade, and at no point did income from these sources represent more than one-third of the community's earnings. The high point came in 1921, when crops and stock earned the tribe over $230,000, 28% of its total income. By 1927, that figure had dropped to

---

[9] See Statistical Data for General Superintendent's Circular No. 5 (St. Xavier), Item 16, Box 103, RCIA-FRC, Seattle.

Agency records contain frequent references to areas where whites and Indians appeared to cooperate: the sale of alcohol, prize fighting and gambling. Hardin saloons were accused of contributing to Crow alcoholism almost from their inception, and each of the incorporated towns on the reservation contained a pool hall. The indefatigable Sam LaPointe wrote in early 1923 that the sale of town lots in Pryor had brought in unsavory whites and set off fits of gambling and prize fighting. The Sioux subagent wrote, "What is the use of trying to teach these Indians the civilized way of life with such influences? I felt as though after all that has happened since the townsite opened up that all of my two years work here has been for nothing, wasted time." See Farmer's Weekly Report, January 1 to 6, 1923, File 139F, Item 15, Box 86, RCIA-FRC, Seattle. For Ken Maynard's visit to Lodge Grass to shoot battle scenes for *Captain of the Strong*, see Hardin *Tribune*, June 17, 1927.

For a modern description of the consequences of these racial divisions in Hardin and Bighorn County, see Orlan Svingen, "Jim Crow, Indian Style," *American Indian Quarterly* 11 (Fall 1987), 275–286.

Table 6. *Crow income, 1921–7*

	1921	1923	1925	1927
Population	1,744	1,777	1,781	1,854
Individual incomes				
Value of crops raised	$174,239	$98,550	$105,000	$86,335
Value of stock sold	56,400	22,600	24,101[a]	18,020[b]
Land sales	81,575	13,578	53,131	51,847
BIA employee wages	22,351	11,180	7,000	23,160[c]
BIA "irregular" wages	19,369	10,000	0	0
Agricultural leases	190,000	180,000	326,066[d]	316,507
Grazing leases	31,000	31,000	167,072[e]	129,483
Oil and gas leases	868	3,000	0	1,580
Lessees' improvements	10,000	10,000	0	0
Other wages			12,434[f]	6,626[g]
				44,200[h]
				2,162[i]
Subtotal	585,802	379,908	694,804	679,920
Per capita	336	214	390	367
Tribal income				
Agricultural leases	18,141	15,000	0	0
Grazing Leases	200,000	140,000	0	13,982
Oil and Gas leases	3,275	15,000	0	3,642
Misc.				1,400
Subtotal	221,416	170,000	0	19,024
Per capita	127	96	0	10
Crow total	807,218	549,908	694,804	698,944
(Individual plus tribal)				
Total Crow per capita	463	310	390	377

[a] 10% of stock value.
[b] Value of "livestock raised."
[c] Value of wages from all sources.
[d] 226,435 acres leased at 1923 rates, $1.14 per acre.
[e] 1,898,551 acres leased at 1923 rates, $0.088 per acre.
[f] 5% of bank deposits.
[g] Interest on bank deposits.
[h] Per capita payments.
[i] Miscellaneous.
Source: Superintendent's Annual Narrative and Statistical Report, Crow Agency, 1920–30.

slightly more than $104,000, 15% of the tribal total. Far more significant was the income derived from the lease of individual allotments and tribal lands. These sources produced well over half the income going to tribal members during the decade. If the Crows had depended only on their own produce for subsistence, their per capita income in 1921 – their most productive year – would have been $132 rather than $463.

The difference between a $463 per capita income and an income of $132 was the difference between subsistence and starvation. In *Middletown*, Robert Lynd and Helen Lynd's classic study of community life in Muncie, Indiana, in the 1920s, the authors estimated that a family of five needed $384 per person to maintain a life of "health and decency." Acknowledging that living costs were vastly different in Indiana and Montana, it is still reasonable to imagine that families of five with incomes of between $300 and $400 per person per year, with no housing costs and few fuel bills, could sustain themselves on the reservation. As a consequence there was little economic incentive for Crow men and women to invest their cash income in farm machinery or to seek long-term employment as wage laborers. The steady, if minimal, income from leases masked the terrible inadequacy of tribal agriculture and provided individuals with little reason to alter the economic patterns established previously. In this atmosphere, white farmers took and sustained the economic advantage.[10]

During the 1920s, the weekly reports of the agency's six district farmers contain ample evidence that the Crows were following their own model of subsistence, regardless of what the government's men demanded. For example, Reg Pearce, the subagent at Wyola, reported in the late summer of 1923 that "most of the Indian crops are ready for threshing, but half of the Indians are out on the mountains picking berries. . . ." A few weeks later Pearce noted that "most of the Indians from Wyola and Lodge Crass are attending the Sheridan fair." The persistence of these activities led one district farmer to reply, when asked what his charges needed to advance, "A little more pep." Gathering, visiting, dancing and hunting were still possible in the economic environment of the 1920s.[11]

Despite the relative stability of lease income during the 1920s, Table 6 reveals that the source of that income shifted during the decade from tribal land to individual allotments. For example, the income from individual agricultural leases rose from $190,000 in 1921 to $316,000 in 1927, while leases on tribal

[10] See Robert S. Lynd and Helen Merrell Lynd, *Middletown: A Study in Modern American Culture* (New York: Harcourt, Brace and World, 1956), Table 7, "Minimum Cost of Living for a Family of Five, 1924," 518, originally published in 1929.

[11] Farmer's Weekly Report, Wyola, August 12, September 9, 1923, File 139, Item 15, Box 86; "Statistical Data for General Superintendent's Circular No. 5, Lodge Grass," Item 16, Box 103; both in RCIA-FRC, Seattle. See also, in the same archive, Farmer's Weekly Report, Bighorn, August 5, 1922, File 139, Item 15, Box 86: "Hay mostly all up . . . most of the Indians gone to the mountains to gather berries."

land dropped from more than $218,000 to $13,000. The reason for this shift was the implementation of the Crow Act, which divided all communal land among tribal members and gave individuals allotments of up to 900 acres each. After 1925, there were no significant sources of tribal income and few opportunities for Crow leaders to wield the kind of economic clout they had asserted in the first years of the twentieth century. Leases with farmers and ranchers were arranged by the Indian Office and, with individual land holdings so small, there was little opportunity for Indian "landlords" to bargain with their tenants.

The history of tribal income during the 1920s underscores the paradoxical quality of reservation life during the decade. A steady and adequate flow of dollars into the reservation supported the consolidation of community life. In the districts created during the previous generation, social relationships, kin networks and marriage patterns stabilized and produced growing families and an increasing population that continued to follow a distinctive way of life. Free from much of the authoritarian rule of missionaries and boarding school administrators, Crow parents and their children were, within limits, able to speak their tribal language, celebrate traditional rituals and experiment with new religious forms. But this same steady income also obscured the tribe's dwindling economic power and the growing distance between Indian and non-Indian farmers and ranchers. The shift to individual leases also silently undermined the authority of tribal leaders and placed Crow landowners at the mercy of outside investors. In the 1920s, dependence on the surrounding, non-Indian economy was the price of cultural persistence.

Nowhere were the crossing trajectories of cultural growth and economic decline better illustrated than in the fate of the tribe's annual agricultural fair. Organized first in 1904 by Agent Samuel Reynolds, who reported that he was seeking "a means of interesting [the Crows] in the work of home building and earning their living from the soil," the event had grown in size and popularity during the decade prior to World War I. It was financed initially by tribal funds, but in later years an elected fair association ran it without a subsidy. Each day of the four- or five-day event began with a parade, and both foot and horse races were prominent features of the program, but the centerpiece of the fair throughout this period was the display of agricultural produce and domestic handiwork. In 1909, for example, over ninety prizes ranging from $25 to $1 were given for success in farming, animal breeding, canning and housekeeping.[12]

Despite its success, it seemed clear from the outset that for the Crows, the principal appeal of the annual fair was not the agricultural exhibition, but the

---

[12] Samuel Reynolds to Commissioner of Indian Affairs, October 25, 1909, Item 2, Box 8. While 1905 was the year of the first successful fair, it was preceded by a failure; see Reynolds to Captain C. G. Hall, December 20, 1906. The program for the 1905 fair, "Industrial Fair of Crow Indians," is in Item 4, Box 23. All of the above are in RCIA-FRC, Seattle.

opportunity it provided for visiting, dancing and politicking. The first meeting of the Crow Business Committee took place at the 1910 fair, and every gathering provided a location for affirming family ties, displaying traditional handicrafts and organizing meetings of religious groups. "It is their week," Agent Reynolds observed, "the only time during the year that they come together in a general body." As the tribe's economic activities were thwarted, the fair's cultural aspects grew in prominence. "The principal difficulty to be encountered in connection with the fair," Reynolds's successor wrote in 1912, "is the intense interest taken by the Indians in their horse racing and dances; an interest which overshadows that of the agricultural exhibits."[13]

During the 1920s the Crow fair all but disappeared. Suspended in 1919 because of a drought, the event took place sporadically over the next ten years. The Pryor and Lodge Grass districts held their own fairs for some of these years, but neither was able to establish itself as a regular feature of community life. The events that did occur featured horse racing and paid little attention to industrial displays. This decline indicated both that fewer Indians were interested in the agricultural aspects of the fair and that other events – taking place beyond the control of the Indian Office – had greater appeal. "It is a fact," Superintendent Asbury wrote in the summer of 1922, "that [a] special effort is being made by both Sheridan and Billings to have a large attendance of Indians" at their annual fairs. In these cities, Crow visitors were provided a special place to camp, encouraged to wear their traditional costumes and left free to enjoy the gathering without Indian policemen looking over their shoulders. They provided a scenic attraction at these local events and contributed to their regional appeal. "I cannot believe this interest [in Indian participation] is prompted by any special love of the Indian," Asbury observed, "but by a keen regard for the money that he spends freely at such times." Two years later he wrote, "The Indians really have no fair of their own."[14]

Indian Office personnel viewed the decline of the Crow agricultural fairs with predictable scorn. Superintendent Asbury wrote in 1922, for example, that "Indians, like children, must have some play time." Such patronizing comments of course encouraged Indian leaders to defend their preferences and to insist on the value of horse racing and on their right to travel where they

[13] Reynolds to Commissioner, October 25, 1909; W. W. Scott to Commissioner of Indian Affairs, July 31, 1912, "Industries, 1910–1913, Item 14, Box 52, RCIA-FRC, Seattle. Tribal leaders also tried to move the fair away from Crow Agency. Commissioner of Indian Affairs Cato Sells vetoed a proposal to hold the fair at Lodge Grass in 1916, in Cato Sells to Richard Wallace, Robert Yellowtail, Curley, Plenty Coos (*sic*), Frank Read and Harry Whiteman, January 12, 1916, Plenty Coups Mss.

[14] For the cancellation of the 1919 fair, see *ANR*, 1920, 13; for cancellation of 1921, see Asbury to Mr. F. V. H. Collins, August 22, 1921, "Indian Fairs," Item 15, Box 82, RCIA-FRC, Seattle; for absence of plans for 1925, see Asbury to J. Clyde Williams, August 18, 1925, Item 15, Box 82, RCIA-FRC, Seattle. Asbury's 1924 comment can be found in *ANR*, 1924, IV, 7.

pleased, even to a Sheridan carnival. But beyond this debate, the shift in the frequency and content of the Crow fairs during the 1920s was a reflection of the tribe's declining economic power, as well as of its resilient, determined commitment to community values and cultural independence.[15]

IV

During the 1920s Crow leaders were aware of their predicament. Proud of the institutions they had created over the preceding generation and confident of their community's determination to follow a distinctive way of life, tribal spokesmen struggled to find solutions for economic and social hardship. Increasingly, this struggle led them to tribal politics. Men who, a decade earlier, had reveled in their confrontations with U.S. authorities now looked for ways to use the political arena to increase their constituents' cash income and protect their community's social and cultural independence. These efforts raised the visibility of politics on the reservation by extending political activity to new areas and, ultimately, by transforming the community's tribal council. In short, a combination of cultural stability and economic dependence energized political life in Crow country during the 1920s.

While confrontations between tribal leaders and the national government continued to occur in the decade after World War I, the most significant political events of the decade occurred at home rather than in Washington, D.C. Interest in local politics deepened as older leaders passed from the scene and competition arose among younger, would-be successors. This competition and the interest it excited were evident at large gatherings, as well as in the daily life of each reservation district. In the districts, the social structure that had taken shape in the first decades of the twentieth century formed the basis for political life; it generated the men and women who would speak in council, as well as the voices that would rise to oppose or veto actions that constituents believed would endanger or undermine the gains of the preceding half-century.

By the 1920s, tribal courts were a prominent feature of district life. Created by federal officials in the late nineteenth century at several other reservations, Courts of Indian Offenses were considered a vital part of the government's law and order program. Judges appointed by the superintendent were charged with enforcing rules laid down by the Indian Office. On its face the system of tribal courts was simply a means of having Indian people police themselves, but at several jurisdictions respected elders took the position of tribal judge and turned the program to their own advantage. Rather than serving as the government's

[15] Calvin Asbury to CIA, July 18, 1922, Item 15, Box 82, "Indian Fairs, 1920–1922," RCIA-FRC, Seattle.

puppets, many of these men used their positions to sustain themselves as leaders in a setting where they might otherwise have slipped into obscurity.[16]

This process operated quite slowly on the Crow Reservation; the first court was not established there until 1901. Until that time, most agents had agreed with M. P. Wyman, who wrote in 1890 that the tribe was not capable of running a court. "All offenses are punished as I deem expedient," the agent reported in 1890, "and the Indians offer no resistance." This pattern changed when Samuel Reynolds appointed Medicine Crow, Two Leggings and Long Tail to the bench. The first two men were respected former warriors from Lodge Grass and Black Lodges, respectively, while the third was a successful farmer from St. Xavier. They were "uneducated and do not speak English," Reynolds noted, but they commanded respect and had "the courage to punish any Indian offender." Despite this endorsement, however, Reynolds and his successors stood ready to remove judges when "any of them show a disposition not [to] perform their duties," and many asserted, including one agent in 1911, that "a modification of their findings is frequently necessary."[17]

Despite these ambiguous origins, however, the tribal courts on the Crow Reservation took on an important role in local affairs. While viewed as instruments of law and order, few conventional crimes came before the tribunals. Major felonies were prosecuted by the local U.S. attorney in federal courts, and several lesser offenses – larceny, assault, extortion – were virtually unknown on the reservation. The bulk of the cases coming before tribal judges were prosecutions for adultery and drunkenness or for offenses committed by people while they were intoxicated. As a result, the focus of the courts became the regulation of community social life rather than the enforcement of a conventional criminal code. Judges became involved in family relationships and social problems such as poverty and alcoholism. Conceived originally as people who would simply enforce the rules, judges evolved in the 1910s and 1920s into government-sanctioned elders who worked to reconcile their oaths of office with individual behavior and the standards of their communities.

Surviving court records allow a glimpse of this Crow tribal court through the career of one of its judges. Born in 1861, Bear Claw was fifty-six in 1917 when accounts of his decisions began to appear in the agency record book. During the next seven years, Bear Claw heard thirty-seven cases, most of them in Lodge Grass, near his home on the Little Bighorn. More than two-thirds of these involved drunkenness or charges of adultery, and several of the balance were related to these offenses. In addition, while Bear Claw's court appeared to be

---

[16] For a description of the courts of Indian offenses, see William T. Hagan, *Indian Police and Judges* (New Haven, Conn.: Yale University Press, 1966).

[17] For the date of the court's founding and a description of its initial operation, see Samuel Reynolds to Commissioner of Indian Affairs, January 2, 1907, Item 2, Box 7, RCIA-FRC, Seattle.

inflexible – only one of these thirty-seven proceedings resulted in an acquittal – most of its sentences were light. The descriptions of the sentences he passed down, as well as the record of how much time each person served, indicate that the judge exercised broad discretion. Prisoners lived at the jail, but the building was never locked, paroles were common and prisoners were frequently released early if they promised to return home. "I do not want to question the action of the court," Superintendent Asbury wrote after one typical conviction in 1921, "but I would regret to keep this man in jail through the harvest season."[18]

The extent to which judges like Bear Claw took on the role of mediator and community elder was also made clear in their handling of repeat offenders. In the records of the Crow tribal court, several individuals appear frequently. While some of these people were arrested several times for drunkenness, others were prosecuted more than once for "adultery," often with the same partner. One young man was convicted of "cohabitation" with the same woman four times in a two-year period. Three of these cases came before Judge Bear Claw. Since the charge of "adultery" was clearly an example of the court enforcing the superintendent's legalistic American standards of morality, these proceedings must have put the tribal judges in a difficult position. (The couple obviously considered themselves married.) Such discomfort might well have been familiar to Judge Bear Claw as he had told the federal census enumerator in 1910 that he had been married five times before the age of fifty. Nevertheless, by sentencing a convicted defendant to a ninety-day term and then releasing him after thirty or sixty, Bear Claw could avoid a "modification" of his findings by the agency staff, maintain his stature in the community, and recognize the relatively minor nature of the crime.[19]

The resemblance of tribal courts to meetings of elders and erring youngsters grows sharper when one notes that none of the people brought before Judge Bear Claw on charges of adultery was older than twenty-five; three of them were teenagers. Similarly, while the age range of those convicted of drunkenness was greater, the punishments were mild. One tribal member found in fact that on his fourth conviction for inebriation the fine had been reduced from $10 to $5. Unencumbered by lawyers, juries or formal procedures, and with agency

[18] Calvin Asbury to I. D. Kephart, July 15, 1921, File 124, "Cases for Indian Court, 1921," Item 15, Box 80, RCIA-FRC, Seattle.

In 1930, Asbury described the treatment of prisoners at Crow Agency: "Prisoners sleep in the jail and they are furnished their meals and work about the agency at whatever labor there may be to do at the time. Their actual labor is under the direction of our yard foreman who handles our miscellaneous work. Prisoners are seldom, if ever locked up. They go to jail and go to bed. In the morning they go to breakfast and report for work. The only time the lock in the jail is used is when we arrest some drunken man or some one who is disturbing the peace and he is kept under lock for one night." See Asbury to Ray A. Brown, August 25, 1930, File 150, "Inspections and Investigations, 1929–1930," Item 16, Box 109, RCIA-FRC, Seattle.

[19] The four prosecutions for adultery occurred on January 21, 1922, October 2, 1922, January 2, 1923, and March 11, 1924. See Item 52, Box 184, RCIA-FRC, Seattle.

personnel rarely present to observe the proceedings, men like Bear Claw worked to reconcile the disputes brought before him by casting themselves in the role of tribal elder. They attempted to represent both the authority of the Indian Office and the traditions of the local community, and in the process they broadened the tribe's political institutions so that they encompassed a wide range of daily life.[20]

Because judges in the 1920s played such a sensitive role in reservation communities, the occasion of appointing someone new to the bench or dismissing a controversial figure from office was an important political event. In 1922, the replacement of Five as the Bighorn district judge by Kills produced a petition signed by fifty district residents, charging the new judge with corruption and favoritism. Five's supporters, who were primarily from St. Xavier and included the children of former Judge Long Tail and Catholic leader Barney Old Coyote, insisted that Kills was "partial to his relatives" and a failure as a farmer. Kills, supported by his neighbors from the upper Bighorn valley, remained in office but apparently stepped down a few years later. Nevertheless, his appearance at the center of an Easter giveaway dance a few years later (see Chapter 9) confirms that he continued to be a central figure in the district.[21]

When a vacancy occurred on the tribal court, both the reservation superintendent and the district's leaders would confer over possible replacements. In January 1924, for example, an opening at Pryor caused the local subagent to hold an informal council at Plenty Coups's home. There five men were nominated for the position and then lectured to by the group about how to conduct themselves in office. According to the subagent who later filed a report of the gathering, the discussion among the district's leaders revealed how deeply they wanted "their" judges to avoid direct punishment and play the role of mediator and elder. "When they were through," the subagent noted, "there was no crime that they could commit but what they demanded of the judge to leave it alone and not try them. . . . They all wanted no laws at all."[22]

Despite their economic reverses and the heavy hand of the Indian Office, the

[20] The convictions for drunkenness that earned decreasing fines were on February 5, 1922, October 11, 1926, and July 5, 1927. See Item 52, Box 184, RCIA-FRC, Seattle.

In a report on tribal courts written in 1930, Asbury noted, "We try to keep our hands off of their decisions; we very seldom attend their hearings . . . and we have found almost always that these judges take their positions seriously. They are conscientious." Calvin Asbury to Malcom McDowell, March 20, 1930, File 023, "Proposed Legislation," Item 16, Box 96, RCIA-FRC, Seattle.

[21] Petition to Calvin Asbury, January 17, 1922, File 124, "Cases for Indian Court, 1922–1923," Item 15, Box 80, RCIA-FRC, Seattle.

[22] Sam LaPointe to Calvin Asbury, January 26, 1924, File 125, "Cases for Indian Court, 1924–1927," Item 15, Box 81, RCIA-FRC, Seattle. After some delay, one of the nominees, Henry Russell, was appointed to the bench. Russell was an educated man in his fifties who frequently served as a translator and confidant of Plenty Coups. See Holgate to Asbury, June 10, 1927, File 125, "Cases for Indian Court, 1924–1927," Item 15, Box 81, RCIA-FRC, Seattle.

Crow Reservation districts were far from inert during the 1920s. Political in-
trigue continued to be an important focus of community activity. The attention
paid to tribal courts was only one example of this phenomenon. Others included the annual (and often more frequent) selection of delegates to attend
tribal business committee meetings or to represent the district in Washington,
district meetings to discuss actions of the Indian Office (such as limits on
dancing or the announcement of arbitrary rules) and situations when district
leaders organized opposition to their local subagent. The most dramatic example of the latter occurred at Pryor where an outspoken district farmer, Sam
LaPointe, found himself transferred to the Bighorn following his campaign to
suppress the Tobacco Society among Plenty Coups and his followers. In all
of these activities, community politicians echoed the words of Reno elder
Stops, who told a district election gathering in 1923 that "we want men for our
[business] committee who are fearless and men who will place the tribe ahead
of everything else. We need aggressiveness. . . ."[23]

V

The campaign to bring Crow complaints before the U.S. Court of Claims
provided another arena where aggressive political leaders could excite their
constituents and cast themselves in the role of community leaders. The idea
of suing the United States for seizing land without compensation and mis-
managing tribal assets was growing in popularity among Indian tribes in the
early twentieth century. Groups in South Dakota, California and Oregon, as
well as several in Montana, had lobbied Congress to approve special jurisdictional bills that would allow them to hire attorneys and seek compensation for
their losses. Crow leaders believed they had a number of potential complaints,
but their principal concern was the fact that in the nineteenth century, the
Indian Office had relocated River Crows to the Mountain Crow Reservation
under the assumption that the 1868 treaty had ceded the traditional River Crow
areas north of the Yellowstone River to the United States. Federal officials
acted on this belief – effectively eradicating the River Crows' title to land north
of the Yellowstone – even though no River Crow leaders had been present at
the Fort Laramie negotiations. Furthermore, Crow leaders pointed out that the
government had never compensated the Mountain Crows for taking the River
Crows in at their new agency.

Tribal members had established relationships with several Washington
attorneys during the struggle over the Crow bill, but it was interest in a possible

---

[23] File 121, Item 15, Box 78, RCIA-FRC, Seattle, contains records of several district elections. For
Stops speech, see Council Proceedings, Reno District, December 31, 1923, "Council Proceed-
ings, 1923," Item 15, Box 77, RCIA-FRC, Seattle. Stops, born in 1869, may have been a son of
Boy That Grabs, the first captain of the Crow Reservation police force.

"River Crow claim" before the Court of Claims that first brought the tribe to Victor Evans in early 1917. After meeting with Russell White Bear and a small group of younger, educated men in Washington, D.C., Evans prepared a contract and dispatched both an associate and the Santee Sioux physician Charles A. Eastman to Montana to win the endorsement of the tribal council. Meeting without the knowledge of Agent Estep, the council approved the agreement in June and submitted it to the Indian Office for approval.[24]

The contract with Victor Evans was rejected by the Indian Office in August 1917, but tribal leaders continued to press their cause. In 1921, a desire for better representation before congressional committees and the Indian Office produced yet another contract. This time a special committee made up of three representatives from each of the six districts selected Edward Horsky, former mayor of Helena, to represent the tribe, but the contract was not approved in Washington. (James Hill was one of the Bighorn representatives on that committee.) Two years later, the Business Committee resolved to return to Victor Evans. Following the failure of this third application, the tribe proposed a contract with the lawyers they had first contacted during the struggle over the Crow bill: Kappler and Merillat. Finally, in July 1926, Congress approved the jurisdictional bill allowing the tribe to litigate its complaints, and in August of the same year, Commissioner Burke approved a contract with Kappler and Merillat to prosecute the River Crow claim.[25]

[24] A copy of the preliminary contract with Victor Evans, dated January 31, 1917, is filed with the Plenty Coups Mss. See also, Victor Evans to Plenty Coups, June 23 and July 25, 1917, Plenty Coups Mss., for discussions of the pending contract.

The agent's lack of involvement in the negotiations with Evans is made clear in Superintendent's Diary, entries for March 14 and 22, April 14, May 31, June 5, 6, 9 and 11, and July 23 and 25, 1917, Item 22, Box 156, RCIA-FRC, Seattle. Agent Estep's contempt for the Dartmouth-educated M.D. came through in this sarcastic comment on June 6: "Dr. Eastman says he is around urging Indians to farm more and as he hobnobbed very much with such scientific agriculturalists as Russell Whitebear, Frank Yarlott, Thomas Medicine Horse and men of that type, I feel sure he is doing an excellent work in this line; he is also explaining to the Indians all about the army registration the day after the registration is over."

[25] See "Remarks of E. B. Meritt, August 7, 1919, File 70–2, Item 15, Box 67 (on Indian Office reluctance to approve a tribal attorney); File 125, Item 15, Box 81 (on election of committee to select a tribal attorney in 1921); "Council Held at Crow Agency, September 20, 1921, File 121, Item 15, Box 78 (proceedings of council selecting Horsky as attorney); Calvin Asbury to Commissioner of Indian Affairs, November 10, 1921, "Religious Customs, Dances, etc.," File 131, Item 15, Box 83 (for Agent's sympathetic analysis of River Crow claim); James Carpenter to Charles H. Burke, December 8, 1921, "Tribal Attorney, 1921–1922," Item 15, Box 81 (presenting arguments in favor of Horsky); Council Proceedings, April 3, 1923, "Council Proceedings, 1923," Item 15, Box 77 (tribal resolution requesting contract with Victor Evans); Proceedings of Crow Tribal Council . . . February 12, 1926, "Council Proceedings, 1924–1927, Item 15, Box 78 (meeting to discuss whom to request as tribal attorney); and Council Proceedings for April 14, 1926, File 121, Item 15, Box 78 (tribal resolution endorsing Kappler and Merillat as attorneys); all in RCIA-FRC, Seattle. See also "Hearing Held November 18, 1921 with Plenty Coups. . . ." Plenty Coups Mss. (See Commissioner Burke's support for the idea of a tribal attorney.)

The jurisdictional act, approved July 3, 1926, is at 44 U.S. Statutes at Large, 807. Attorney

With the filing of their complaint with the U.S. Court of Claims on June 13, 1927, the Crows turned the dispute over to their lawyers. The courts would take thirty-four years to resolve the case (the tribe received $10,000,000 in 1961), but the process of selecting a tribal attorney and winning approval for him from the Indian Office paid much more immediate benefits. By exciting interest in the case through promises of monetary compensation and the prospect of going to court to expose the injustices of the Indian Office, Crow leaders created an issue that cut across district and other boundaries and united the community behind a common cause. Both elders like Plenty Coups and Stops and younger men such as James Hill and James Carpenter supported the effort. They agreed with Knows The Ground, the sixty-year-old leader from St. Xavier, who declared at one of the councils held to discuss hiring an attorney, "Treaties were made by the government and our chiefs during a time when there was hardly any one who could intelligently interpret our language. . . . So we could be very much misrepresented at that time. Now we have some well educated boys in our tribe . . . let this council approve of their wishes."[26]

The River Crow claim also required the tribe to retain a local attorney. Because the litigation was so protracted, involving the preparation of briefs, depositions of tribal elders and substantial historical research, Kappler and Merillat arranged with Hardin attorneys Charles C. Guinn and Dan W. Maddox to collaborate on the case. The presence of these lawyers on the tribe's legal team shifted the tone of local politics. Encouraged that one issue was now before the courts, tribal leaders considered expanding their list of complaints against the government and turning to their local counsel when stymied by the local superintendent. Guinn and Maddox were eager to accommodate them. Within days of his appointment, Charles Guinn appeared at a tribal council meeting to assure Plenty Coups and other leaders that "you have a legal and a just claim" and that "you will be amply paid for a great body of land which has been taken away from you without your consent." Early in the year, before the attorneys had been approved, one elder had stood up in exasperation at a council and condemned the entire effort. "A white man lawyer is no kin to you," he told the group; "so why trouble yourselves about the selection of a

Horsky was frequently accused of bribing the Crows. His biography is contained in the proceedings of a council at Crow Agency on September 19, 1921. See File 121, "Miscellaneous, 1922–1923," Item 15, Box 78, RCIA-FRC, Seattle. The September 19 meeting included Secretary of the Interior Albert Fall, who exchanged in a long colloquy with Russell White Bear and other younger Crows about the necessity of a tribal attorney (16–33). Fall, who was later exposed as corrupt, ended the meeting by declaring, "I do not think you need an attorney to protect you against the Indian Department."

[26] Proceedings of the Crow Tribal Council, February 12, 1926, 2. For reports of the River Crow litigation, see *Crow Nation or Tribe of Indians v. United States, Court of Claims Reports*, Vol. 81, 238–281 (Decided, March 4, 1935); *Crow Tribe of Indians v. United States*, 284 F2nd 361 (1960). See also Bradley and Bradley, "From Individualism to Bureaucracy," 50–59.

lawyer?" The presence of the eager Mr. Guinn at another council meeting a few months later signaled the community's shift towards a very different point of view.[27]

The growing visibility of tribal government and politics on the Crow Reservation in the 1920s was in many respects the consequence of a logical progression of events. The evolution of a distinctive social and religious life in the first decades of the twentieth century, together with the steady tension that had existed between the Crows and their non-Indian neighbors, had produced a group of tribal leaders who saw themselves as the defenders of the community's national interests. Henry Armstrong and the other Indian Office personnel who had governed the community in the nineteenth century of course had assumed that, over time, Crows would become a less distinctive group and that they would eventually give up their collective identity. The workings of the tribal court and the rhetoric surrounding the River Crow claim illustrate how erroneous that assumption was and how far the tribe of the 1920s had diverged from the decultured community Armstrong had envisioned forty years before.

The transformation of the tribal council during this same decade provides yet another example of the Crows' drive towards a distinctive cultural and political identity. When the decade began, the tribal business committee was the reservation's preeminent political body. Fresh from its apparent victory in the struggle over the Crow Act and supported by both older leaders such as Medicine Crow and Plenty Coups and the educated "boys" led by Robert Yellowtail and James Carpenter, the committee seemed to have the support of people in all six districts of the reserve. By 1930 the committee had been replaced by a general council composed of district representatives and any other Crows who wished to attend its meetings. Condemned by the Indian Office as inefficient and susceptible to manipulation, the general council came to be viewed by tribal members as its "traditional" form of decision making.

The success of the Business Committee proved the basis for its undoing. Because the group was perceived as having successfully stood up to various agency and congressional officials and held out against pressure to open tribal land to outsiders, it attracted general participation in its activities. Superintendent Asbury reported in 1921 that "it has been difficult to prevent the [business] committee meetings from merging into a general council in which everybody takes part, and the actions of the voluntary council rather than of the business committee approved." This trend was encouraged by the committee's continued insistence on independence from Indian Office control and the general interest in finding alternatives to the income that was lost when the tribal grazing lands were divided under the terms of the Crow Act. In 1921, the

---

[27] Minutes of Council Held August 26, 1926, 4; Proceedings of the Crow Tribal Council . . . February 12, 1926, 9. Charles Kappler was eventually adopted into the Crow tribe. See Hardin *Tribune*, August 21, 1931, for a description of the ceremony.

committee refused to allow Agency Superintendent Asbury to chair its meetings and it rejected a set of by-laws he had prepared for the group. Also during
1921, the reservation was alive with prospectors who believed they could profit-
ably extract oil from the tribe's marginal reserves. When committee meetings
were devoted to the question of oil leases, interest was intense.[28]

Asbury worked hard to discredit the Business Committee. The group was
dominated by the young, educated men who had risen to prominence in the
struggle over the Crow bill, and the superintendent was eager to dampen some
of their enthusiasm. His first opportunity to do this came in the late summer of
1921 when he assembled forty-four older men to discuss the Business Committee's desire to cancel a series of dubious oil leases which the superintendent had
arranged over the preceding two years. Quickly dubbed the "long hair council,"
this group included Holds The Enemy (Pretty Eagle's son), Curley (the former
Custer scout), Big Medicine (the tribal policeman), and Kills (the later partici-
pant in a giveaway ceremony who was soon to become a tribal judge). It passed
a resolution supporting Asbury's handling of the oil leases and criticizing the
"educated Indians who give us lots of trouble." These statements set off some
of the angriest tribal meetings since the days of Helen Grey and substantially
weakened the Business Committee's hand.[29]

Differences over who had the right to speak for the Crow tribe were the
central feature of a series of general meetings called during the next year to
discuss the tribe's oil reserves, the disposition of the tribal cattle herd and other
questions of economic import. In a session with Commissioner of Indian Affairs
Charles Burke in late August, the "long hairs" were joined by Two Leggings
and Crooked Arm, who said the superintendent "is our only protection" and
urged the assembly to reject the Business Committee's aggressive approach to
oil leasing. Committee advocates accused these elders of giving away "the rights

---

[28] *ANR*, 1921, 14–15. For a discussion of the by-laws, see Proceedings of Business Committee
. . . August 27, 1921, "Council Proceedings, 1921," Item 15, Box 77; and Proceedings of Business Committee, January 21, 1921, File 121, Item 15, Box 77; both in RCIA-FRC, Seattle. For a
discussion of the oil craze, see Bradley and Bradley, "From Individualism to Bureaucracy," 21–22.
      Asbury's attitude towards an assertive, independent council was revealed in a letter to the
commissioner of Indian affairs in 1924. Accused of treating the Crows the way a southerner
treated Negroes, Asbury denied the charge but added, "I rather approve of the comparison with
the attitude of a southerner toward the Negro, for in my opinion, the intelligent southern person
knows the Negro's limitations better than anyone else and is inclined to give him the opportunities to which he is entitled and to give him the respect and treatment that is fitting to his
intelligence and advancement. . . . I admit that with the chronic loafer who will not make use of
his opportunities, I talk plainly to him. To the person who is trying, I am certainly inclined to
encourage him in any way possible." Asbury to Commissioner of Indian Affairs, September 12,
1924, "Council Proceedings, 1924–1927," Item 15, Box 78, RCIA-FRC, Seattle.
[29] See Bradley and Bradley, "From Individualism to Bureaucracy," 15–16; and "Proceedings of
Council held by Commissioner of Indian Affairs, August 27, 1921," File 121, Item 15, Box 77,
RCIA-FRC, Seattle.
      Fittingly, Mrs. Grey reappeared on the Crow Reservation during the summer of 1921 as an
agent for one of the oil interests vying for leases on tribal land. See Bradley and Bradley, "From
Individualism to Bureaucracy," 401.

of the Crow tribe" and obeying the Indian Office "like an oriental slave." Later meetings in September and December continued these themes, but – as had ultimately come clear a decade earlier – there was little interest in a permanent disruption of political life. Instead, each side in the debate frequently noted that it would support a decision by the majority of tribal members. Plenty Coups, for example, who sided with the "long hairs" but who, characteristically, was searching for a middle ground, called on both parties to "work to the good of the majority of the tribe." Alternatively, one Business Committee member protested that his group had always tried to represent the tribe. "We have always sought for the tribal consent and whenever there is an objection raised," he declared, "we always left it to the tribal council to determine for themselves."[30]

These appeals to majority rule accelerated the movement towards a general council form of government. Faced with an increasingly contentious and impoverished electorate, Crow leaders had little else to which they could appeal. The need to protect tribal interests and expand tribal income was growing, and the authority of tribal politicians was regularly questioned by outsiders and internal dissidents. The only way to rise above these crosscurrents was to persuade the group that a particular position represented the fundamental interests of the entire community. Harry Whiteman, a thirty-year-old boarding school graduate, explained some of this dynamic to Commissioner Burke in 1921. "When the rights of the Crow tribe are involved," he explained, "it is worth fighting for. All nations of the civilized world fight for what they deem their rights."[31]

Business Committee representatives continued to be selected in the districts throughout the 1920s, but every time a major issue came before the group, its authority was superseded by a general council. In 1924, a campaign to remove Superintendent Asbury was brought to the floor of a council; in 1926 the general body considered and approved proposals to place the River Crow claim before the courts and to amend the Crow Act. At the end of 1926, when his superiors in Washington suggested reviving the Business Committee to increase efficiency, Asbury reported that the existing group "has almost died for want of interest on the part of the tribe." He added, "They were quite inclined to make every meeting of the business committee a general council participated in by whoever could get to it."[32]

By the end of 1926 when Congress had passed the Crow jurisdiction bill and amended the Crow Act, the Business Committee had all but faded from view. "Meetings were called and the committee sometimes came," Superintendent

---

[30] "Council . . . August 27, 1921," 5, 13; "Council . . . September 19, 1921," 30; "Council . . . September 30, 1921, 12.

[31] "Council . . . August 27, 1921," 15.

[32] Asbury to Commissioner of Indian Affairs, December 30, 1926, "Delegates to Washington, 1924–1927," Item 15, Box 78, RCIA-FRC, Seattle.

Asbury reported in 1929, "but a crowd of those not belonging to the committee came and always wanted to take part in their deliberations." In effect, these meetings and the general meetings called at times of crisis became the general council. Here Crow people gathered to air complaints, resolve differences and set a broad, political agenda for the tribe. Its influence rising and falling with the pace of events, the council became an arena where leaders from different districts would compete for influence with other groups aligned by age, religious affiliation, occupation or economic well-being. Throughout these disputes, however, there was a common adherence to the rhetoric of political and cultural unity. Barney Old Coyote, for example, a young, educated delegate from Bighorn, proclaimed at one 1925 meeting, "Let us have no faction, create no ill feeling and let us all work for the common cause of our people, the Crow Indians." And older men like Stops would reply in a similar vein: "Agree with the boys who are your delegates," he urged one 1926 gathering. "Depend on them; they will guard your interests. They are Crows."[33]

VI

By the end of the 1920s, Crow leaders had succeeded in linking politics to the community's sense of cultural independence. The general council, as well as the courts and district-level political meetings, could be arenas for competition between groups, but they were commonly viewed by participants as opportunities for articulating and defending the tribe's "rights." But how effective were these efforts? How did the energized politics of the 1920s affect the poverty and dependence that had begun to emerge in the tribal homeland after World War I?

Oil was not a solution to Crow poverty. By 1925, 110 of the 143 oil leases on the reservation had been cancelled because the explorers had drilled dry holes. While a dramatic stimulus to tribal politics and a source of endless antagonism and recrimination, the oil business was a bust.[34]

[33] Asbury quoted in Bradley and Bradley, "From Individualism to Bureaucracy," 71; "Minutes of a General Council of the Crow Tribe . . . November 17, 1925, "Council Proceedings, 1924–1927," Item 15, Box 77, 17, RCIA-FRC, Seattle; Proceedings of the Crow Tribal Council . . . February 12, 1926, 6. "Council Proceedings, 1924–1927," Item 15, Box 78, RCIA-FRC, Seattle. Stops was fifty-seven at the time of the 1926 council.

The distance between what men like Old Coyote and Stops envisioned in these meetings and what the Indian Office could understand is revealed in a letter from Superintendent Asbury to his superiors in 1927. Asbury had been asked to comment on the Indian Office practice of refusing to recognize meetings that had not been formally called by the agency superintendent. "I have doubted the advisability of attempting to restrict such meetings," he wrote, "as this office and the Bureau then would be charged with an attempt to dominate and limit their freedom of speech and action, so we let them get together and talk to their hearts' content."

[34] Indicative of how desperate the tribe had become to develop its oil reserves, a council in 1925 agreed to lease a tract of land to a developer without advertisement or competitive bidding. See Council Proceedings, February 21, 1925, "Council Proceedings, 1924–1927," Item 15, Box 78, RCIA-FRC, Seattle.

Despite its poor results, however, the "oil boom" revealed the principal positions within the tribe regarding economic development. The younger, educated men who dominated the 1921 Business Committee were eager to maximize the return on the wells. They were led by George Hogan, James Carpenter, Russell Whitebear and Robert Yellowtail, and their position was neatly summarized by Frank Bethune, a successful mixed-blood farmer and peyote leader from the Reno district who asked one council assembly, "Which hand would you take, either the dollar or the penny? . . . The oil has been produced on the reservation, and I want the dollar and not the penny. I want the one that gives me the most money." The long hair council opposing these men was persuaded that they would be better off allowing the Indian Office to negotiate leases on their behalf. Their priority was not a maximum return, but quick payment. As White Man Runs Him declared in August of 1921, "I want to get some money from the oil before the snow flies on the ground." The older men were cautious about ambitious development projects and long-term investments, but both groups recognized a common need for greater income. When he spoke at the oil leasing councils, Plenty Coups often struck the common ground uniting the two positions: "I want the use of my money so I won't have an empty stomach."[35]

These differences between entrepreneurs and those wanting an immediate payment surfaced again during the early 1920s as the Crows struggled to manage their remaining tribal pastures. Crow cattlemen, particularly those from Lodge Grass whose small herds competed with those belonging to stockmen with large holdings, like Frank Heinrich, cautioned against renting the remaining common lands. Older Crows and people from districts with less involvement in the cattle business cared only about income. When a tribal council meeting in the fall of 1921 discussed whether or not to allow Heinrich another term on the lands between the Bighorn and Little Bighorn valleys, men like Ben Spotted Horse of Lodge Grass urged a negative vote even if it meant forgoing some income. Echoing his father's outspoken defenses of his district a generation earlier, Spotted Horse declared that Heinrich's power must be checked. "Crow people, I ask you to support me," he pleaded. Harry Whiteman from Black Lodge district was not persuaded. "Lodge Grass people seem to work for their own and not for the best interests of the entire tribe," he observed. "We have no other resources than from grazing leases," he added; "it is money the tribe cares for."[36]

After 1922, the only tribal pastures were mountainous areas at the head of the Bighorn and Pryor valleys, but these remained a focus of tribal interest. While some like Ben Spotted Horse continued to warn the tribe against continuing ties with large cattlemen, the pull of a guaranteed income was far more power-

[35] Minutes of Council . . . August 27, 1921, 18, 4, 6.
[36] Proceedings of the Crow Tribal Council . . . November 28, 1921, 7, 5; "Council Proceedings, 1921," Item 15, Box 77, RCIA-FRC, Seattle.

As Plenty Coups neared his eightieth birthday, he retreated from active politics and enjoyed the status of elder statesman. Here he is accompanied at a 1927 commemoration of the Little Bighorn battle by the young, returned student Max Big Man. Courtesy of Smithsonian Institution.

ful. In the fall of 1923, for example, a large council gathered at the time of the Crow fair to discuss extending leases in the Bighorns. While some urged caution and suggested delaying the decision, seventy-four-year-old Plenty Coups suddenly rode into the center of the gathering on horseback and cried, "Close the discussion and let us take a vote." Amid cries of "Take a vote," the assembly voiced unanimous approval for the extension proposal.[37]

Tribal leaders had few other opportunities to affect the grazing process during the 1920s because the bulk of the reservation stock was now ranged on lands owned by whites or leased from individual Crows. Long-time lessees such as Heinrich and Philip Spear purchased allotments to use as homes and headquarters ranches and then rented grazing land from their Indian neighbors. Because these leased ranges were tax-free and flexible (leases could be accumulated during good times and be cancelled during years of drought), they were ideally suited to a business fraught with cycles of boom and bust. In order to protect their positions, these cattlemen frequently paid their "landlords" in advance for their leases and signed lease extensions far in advance of expiration dates. As a consequence, cash-starved Crow landowners, whether they had been judged "competent" (and therefore allowed to negotiate leases on their own) or "incompetent" (required to lease through the agency superintendent), had little leverage over the lessees.[38]

Tribal politicians tried to reverse the Crows' declining hold on lease arrangements in the fall of 1927 when the general council established a lease committee "to oversee, arbitrate and approve leases negotiated by Indian lessors." The group attempted to eliminate the automatic extension of leases, a practice which all but transferred ownership of land to local stockmen, and to enforce a system of competitive bidding. The committee made little headway, however, and by the end of the decade, council leaders were still searching for ways to diminish the power of the lessees.[39]

In a statement before the tribal council in May 1922, Superintendent Calvin Asbury pointed out the growing importance of farming to the Crows. After noting that the tribal cattle herd was nearly gone and the expected grazing lease income was expected to be low, he predicted that "if we depend on the income from oil to buy grub next winter we would be very hungry." His message was

[37] General Council Proceedings . . . September 14, 1923; for an earlier, more cautious approach to the issue, see General Council Proceedings, August 18, 1923; see also Calvin Asbury to Commissioner of Indian Affairs, November 16, 1923; both in "Council Proceedings, 1923," Item 15, Box 77, RCIA-FRC, Seattle.

[38] For a discussion of the individual leasing process during the 1920s, see Bradley and Bradley, "From Individualism to Bureaucracy," 193–202.

[39] Hardin *Tribune*, November 11, 1927. When cattleman Frank Heinrich died in the fall of 1928, he held leases on more than 250,000 acres of reservation land. When Heinrich's estate was distributed, it was disclosed that the cattleman had left $100,000 to Carolyn Reynolds Riebeth, wife of his secretary, E. W. Riebeth, and daughter of his close friend, former Crow Agent Samuel Reynolds. See Hardin *Tribune*, November 2, 1928, and May 10, 1929.

simple: "I can't see very much prospect of money next year except what we earn on our own farms." Unfortunately, despite this energetic rhetoric, the Indian Office did little to foster Indian agriculture during the 1920s. Crows continued to rely on lease income rather than the produce of their own farms for a living; their own production rarely rose above a subsistence level.[40]

In addition to being crippled by the prevalence of agricultural leasing on the reservation, Crow farmers continued to be burdened by the reservation's irrigation system. Not only was the system too big (less than half the reservation's irrigable land was being cultivated in 1923, most of it by non-Indian lessees), but it continued to be a drain on tribal income. Because irrigated lands were more valuable than non-irrigated ones, and because some tribal members held irrigated allotments and others did not, the Crow Act of 1920 had stipulated that everyone holding title to irrigated land would be assessed for the cost of constructing the irrigation system, as well as for annual operation and maintenance expenses. This requirement would have Indians and non-Indians who enjoyed the benefits of irrigation pay for the cost of building and operating the system. Despite its surface logic, however, the new rule transformed the tribe's irrigated land from an unwanted asset to a devastating liability. Crow farmers found that if they held an irrigated allotment, they were required to pay a "reimbursement fee" and an annual "operations and management charge" to cover their share of the tribe's expenditures on their behalf. (The fact that the Crows had not initiated or designed the project had long since been forgotten.) Delinquent fees would be considered a lien against the property at the time of sale. For example, a one-acre allotment with a $40 lien against it that sold for $40 would generate no cash for its owner.[41]

When a congressional committee visited the reservation in August 1925 to explore social and economic conditions there, it was told that "the question of the greatest moment" was the expense of the irrigation system. "Congress . . . makes the charges so heavy," Robert Yellowtail told the group, "that the Indian cannot meet it and, if the Secretary carries out the law, the Indian is going to lose all his land." Tribal leaders (including an irrigation committee appointed by the council in 1927) continued to push for a cancellation of these

---

[40] Minutes of Council . . . May 8, 1922, "Council Proceedings, 1922," Item 15, Box 77, RCIA-FRC, Seattle. For a discussion of the fate of the large Campbell lease, first negotiated during World War I, see Bradley and Bradley, "From Individualism to Bureaucracy," 180–184; and File 54, "Montana Farming Corporation," Item 15, Box 62, RCIA-FRC, Seattle. The latter file contains information on the way Campbell, Superintendent Asbury and stockmen with large holdings worked together to "develop" reservation lands.

[41] For a description of the irrigation system and Crow agriculture, see Bradley and Bradley, "From Individualism to Bureaucracy," 367–380; and Calvin Asbury to Commissioner of Indian Affairs, June 23, 1924, "Inspector's Reports, 1924–1925," Item 15, Box 60, RCIA-FRC, Seattle.

According to the Indian Office, 53,897 acres were irrigable in 1924. Of these, 24,281 acres were actually farmed; 6,650 of the acres used were being farmed by Indians. See Bradley and Bradley, "From Individualism to Bureaucracy," 368.

charges throughout the decade, but to no avail. Both the Indian Office and the Indian Irrigation Service insisted that cancelling future fees would unfairly subsidize one group within the tribe and would penalize the few Crow farmers who had paid their bills in the past. As a result, unpaid assessments continued to rise, and owners of irrigated allotments were forced to either raise sufficient crops to pay their fees or to lease their holdings.[42]

Statistics gathered in 1926 illustrate the consequences of the Indian Office's logic. In that year, 56,000 acres of irrigated reservation land produced crops worth more than $440,000; only about 10% of that amount came from Crows farming their own land. More than 60% of the income produced on irrigated lands was generated by non-Indians who leased Indian allotments; the remaining 30% was earned by non-Indians who had already purchased allotments within the irrigation project. In this atmosphere, there was little reason *not* to continue leasing irrigated land to outsiders or selling it to them outright. Not surprisingly, during the following five years, the percentage of the reservation's irrigated lands owned by non-Crows rose from 23 to 35%.[43]

A number of Crow farmers persisted in their efforts to raise crops during the 1920s, but they continued to play a marginal role in the local economy even though they represented the most prevalent occupation on the reservation. Another industrial survey conducted on the reservation in 1926 revealed that there were 250 farmers in the tribe, a group which cultivated 7,838 acres and produced more than 54,000 bushels of wheat. Most of these farms were quite small, with average sizes ranging from 15 acres per farmer in the irrigated Bighorn district to 76 acres per farmer in Wyola. Wheat was the principal crop, with the most successful farmer on the reservation – Bird Horse – producing more than 1,800 bushels on his Bighorn acreage. Wyola's Carson Yellowtail, another large producer, also cultivated 9 acres of alfalfa and more than 60 acres of hay during this same year.[44]

The contrast between entrepreneur Thomas Campbell – whose wartime leases and gangs of tractors had enabled him to farm more than 20,000 acres of wheat – and his Black Lodge neighbor, The Eagle, raising 632 bushels of wheat and 40 tons of hay on 60 acres is extreme, but it underscores the distance between the mechanized, commercially oriented white farmers who were

---

[42] Memorandum of a Conference . . . August 5, 1925, "Inspector's Reports, 1924–1925," Item 15, Box 60, RCIA-FRC, Seattle. See also W. S. Hanna to Commissioner of Indian Affairs, October 2, 1931, "Proposed Legislation," Item 16, Box 96, RCIA-FRC, Seattle. Hanna's letter indicated that, in 1931, more than two-thirds of outstanding operation and maintenance charges against Indian lands was unpaid.

For a description of the irrigation committee, see Calvin Asbury to Commissioner of Indian Affairs, August 23, 1927, "Inspector's Reports, 1924–1925," Item 15, Box 60, RCIA-FRC, Seattle.

[43] Bradley and Bradley, 374, citing Project Descriptions, Crow Irrigation Project, Mont., July 1, 1931, 40922–1932, Crow 341, LR-OIA, RG 75, NA.

[44] Yellowtail's farm is described in the "Water User's Survey," Box 9064, RCIA-FRC, Seattle.

increasingly evident in the Yellowstone valley and Crow farmers who were raising multiple crops on family farms. The fact that The Eagle was sixty-two in 1926 also suggests that his farm was a household effort, not the product of bank financing, corporate planning or mechanization.

VII

Being Crow in the 1920s required tribal members to adjust to a complex variety of restraints and opportunities. The restraints were most evident in the economic and political realm, where tribal leaders, farmers and stockmen struggled unsuccessfully to reverse a process of domination. Despite their success at fashioning a series of vocal and responsive tribal institutions, Crow politicians could not escape the authority of the Indian Office and Congress. And regardless of the effort and creativity that produced farmers like Carson Yellowtail and Bird Horse, neither these men nor their neighbors and supporters could close the gap between their productivity and that of their better-financed and better-trained non-Indian neighbors.

Amidst a universe of restraints, however, were a variety of new opportunities for community expression. The Crow tribal council became a vehicle for the defense of cultural values and the formation of a distinctive group consensus. Subsistence farming could not compete with large-scale commercial agriculture, but it could be a viable family enterprise and a centerpiece for multifamily households. While isolated, the reservation districts continued to be the focus of daily activities and, with that, continued to sustain Crow kinship ties and support ceremonial life. Being Crow in the 1920s required a sense of balance and flexibility. Where one path was blocked, others opened. Much was lost during the decade, but as the dramatic events of the 1930s would make clear, much had been preserved and accomplished.

11

"Standing for rights": the Crow rejection of the Indian Reorganization Act

> At sundown there was a spectacular parade dance about the camp in which 200 Indian braves in full regalia, fifty of them old Indians in feathered warbonnets, and 150 younger men in porcupine head dress . . . were led by . . . Old Coyote, The Wolf, Yellow Face, Bull That Don't Fall Down, leading Crow chieftains, and Drags The Wolf, and Gros Ventre, all of whom in their early lifetime had taken part in battle.
>
> Description of Fourth of July celebration, Hardin *Tribune*, July 7, 1933[1]

I

This peaceful tableau fulfilled many expectations. From the perspective of the Hardin *Tribune* reporter, the people who paraded before him on the 157th anniversary of American independence were friendly and peaceful. Both the 1,500 Crows who were present and their more than 250 Cheyenne and Gros Ventre guests had spent several days camping in their majestic tipis, feasting on ice cream and performing for white visitors. Moreover, the assembled families appeared content. They danced late into the evening, raced their prize horses in the afternoons and greeted old comrades with food and hospitality. The festival's guest of honor was James Hyde, a career Indian Office administrator who had recently arrived to take up his duties as reservation superintendent. Like the *Tribune* reporter, the tribe's new white "father" must have been pleased to see that the government had apparently succeeded in bringing the Crows through the often violent process of adapting to life in modern America. All that seemed to remain of the unhappy past were picturesque costumes and harmless old warriors.

But within a year of this Fourth of July celebration, these parading Crows would summon the political muscle to force Superintendent Hyde from office and overthrow a new series of reforms imposed on them from Washington, D.C. Echoing the revolution in national politics that was taking place in the

[1] Quoted in Charles Crane Bradley and Susanna Remple Bradley, "From Individualism to Bureaucracy: Documents on the Crow Indians, 1920–1945" (unpublished manuscript, dated 1974), 90; Little Big Horn College Archives, Crow Agency, Montana.

wake of Franklin Roosevelt's recently completed first hundred days in office, dramatic events on the Crow Reservation would reveal how deceptive the surface calm of the 1933 Bighorn parade dance had been and would demonstrate again the resiliency of the people who had gathered that afternoon along the Bighorn. At Crow Agency, as in Washington, a new administration would soon take control of the local Indian Office, and its eager incumbent, Crow political activist Robert Yellowtail, would prove himself no less an insurgent than the New Dealer in the White House.

Yellowtail seized control of the political arena in a way that surprised even his most ardent supporters. But in contrast with national leaders, Yellowtail did not succeed in bringing a series of reforms to the Crow community. Instead, his efforts to win approval for the Indian Reorganization Act, a statute many non-Indian reformers celebrated as the capstone of an "Indian New Deal," ended in failure. Like his predecessors as superintendent, Yellowtail was unable to persuade the Crows that a "reform" emanating from Washington, D.C., had been designed in their best interests. Both Yellowtail's victory in gaining office, and the defeat he suffered in attempting to persuade his kinsmen to alter their institutions of local governance, demonstrated the depth of the Crow commitment to the life they had made for themselves on their reservation. The people who paraded on the Fourth of July in 1933 would applaud Yellowtail's appointment and reject his reforms. They would act as defenders of their community's "rights": privileges they believed were due them by virtue of their membership in the Crow nation.

II

When Robert Yellowtail's predecessor at Crow Agency vacated his office in the summer of 1934, he told the local newspaper, "This is something I never dreamed of." Surely few in the Indian Office would have disagreed with him. Yellowtail had been born in 1888, the son of a Lodge Grass chief named Yellowtail and his mixed-blood wife, Lizzie Shane. In addition to her Crow heritage, the young man's mother could name ancestors who were both Assiniboin and French-Canadian. Her grandfather was Pierre Shane (or Chien), the fur trader who had been with the party of Crow warriors who had raced up the Bighorn valley to greet Lieutenant Templeton at Fort C. F. Smith in 1866. At about the time Robert became a teenager (and, perhaps, at the suggestion of the newly arrived Baptist missionaries in Lodge Grass), he left home to attend Sherman Institute, a federal boarding school in Riverside, California. There, though he chafed under the regimentation typical of the government's institutions, he developed a love of history and American law.[2]

---

[2] Warren L. O'Hara, interim superintendent at Crow Agency, on the occasion of turning over his office to Yellowtail. Quoted in Hardin *Tribune*, August 3, 1934.

When he returned from California, probably in 1910, Yellowtail settled on his allotment south of Lodge Grass, near the new Wyola rail station. The young man arrived back in Montana just as the battle over opening reservation lands to homesteaders began, and his ability to draw on the principles of American law, his ambition to become a successful rancher and his extended family of sisters, in-laws and cousins made him a favorite in the councils and committee meetings that were a frequent feature of reservation life in the years before World War I. His unbending assertion that Crows should control their own affairs also made him a favored counsellor to elders such as Medicine Crow and Plenty Coups; he frequently accompanied them at meetings in both Washington and Crow Agency. He was so assertive, in fact, peppering the commissioner of Indian affairs with suggestions and requests, that one Crow superintendent felt compelled to complain angrily that "I feel I am quite as capable of determining the policy of reservation management as is this half-breed boy."[3]

During the 1920s, Yellowtail continued to be active in Crow politics. He served on the commission that oversaw the implementation of the 1920 Crow Act; he campaigned for Indian citizenship and attempted to organize reservation voters once tribal members began to vote. He worked with the attorneys prosecuting the tribe's case in the Court of Claims and asserted the rights of the reservation community in a variety of spheres, from agency hiring to the expenditure of royalties on tribally owned oil wells. As he declared in a ceremony welcoming Superintendent Hyde to the reservation, treaties and agreements negotiated with federal authorities entitled the tribe to "special rights which we insist shall be respected by the Washington officials and their subordinates in the field."[4]

Yellowtail considered himself a Republican, but he welcomed Franklin Roosevelt's election in 1932, largely because he expected the new administration would reverse its predecessor's approach to Indian affairs. In fact he was so optimistic about the new president that he prepared a letter for the leader of each Montana reservation to sign, calling for consultations with them before the appointment of a new commissioner. Yellowtail and other Crow leaders urged Superintendent Hyde to approve the expenditure of tribal funds to send a delegation to Washington for Roosevelt's inauguration, but they were turned down. Undaunted, Yellowtail set off in his own car with James Carpenter and his brother-in-law, Donald Deer Nose. While in Washington, Yellowtail and his colleagues pressed their request that the new administration seek Indian nominations for the position of commissioner, noting that the high hopes they had held out for Herbert Hoover's famous "Quaker administration" in 1929 had been severely disappointed. Yellowtail and Carpenter's choice was John Collier,

---

[3] Superintendent to Commissioner of Indian Affairs, April 24, 1913, Item 14, Box 52, "Industries, 1910–1913," RCIA-FRC, Seattle.
[4] Hardin *Tribune*, January 15, 1932.

the former New York City social worker who had founded the American Indian Defense Association in 1923 and been an outspoken critic of the Indian Office's policies ever since.[5]

John Collier was a southerner, the son of the Progressive-era mayor of Atlanta, but he left Georgia in 1902 when he enrolled as a freshman at Columbia University and he never returned. After college and a tour of Europe, Collier had been drawn to the settlement house movement and to the work of organizing immigrant communities in the tenements of Manhattan's Lower East Side. During the retrenchments that followed the war, the still-idealistic young man and his family left the city and settled in San Francisco.

Collier was the kind of man who needed a cause, however, and in 1920 he found it. While visiting Taos Pueblo in New Mexico, the "retired" community organizer was converted to Indian affairs. As he learned of the community's religious ceremonialism, Collier was horrified to learn also of the government's determination to "civilize" the group and eradicate its old ways. In Collier's view, such a policy contradicted modern practice in social work by stifling community leadership and depleting the nation's storehouse of cultural wisdom. Indian ways, Collier later wrote, represented America's "Red Atlantis," an undiscovered continent of wisdom and beauty, which should be preserved and protected rather than altered or destroyed. Driven by this conviction, Collier helped found the Indian Defense Association and spent the bulk of the 1920s attacking the allotment policy, intolerant Christian missionaries, and the Indian Office's ossified bureaucracy. As its name implied, the Defense Association urged the government to protect native traditions and nurture the growth of Indian community leadership. Soon after the 1932 election, Franklin Roosevelt appointed Harold Ickes, a prominent Chicago reformer to the post of secretary of the interior. Ickes, who had been a charter member of the Indian Defense Association, quickly named Collier to head the Indian Office.[6]

Upon their return to Montana, Yellowtail, Carpenter and other reservation political leaders began campaigning for the removal of James Hyde as superintendent and the replacement of the entire agency staff with qualified Crows. Yellowtail succeeded in persuading the authorities in Washington to send an investigator to the reservation in July, but the inspector's report was not entirely what the tribal leader had hoped for. B. G. Courtright agreed that Hyde was high-handed and manipulative, but he also described Yellowtail as "totally without principle . . . nervous, high-strung, [and] bad-tempered." Despite his criticism of the Crow leader and several of his political allies, Courtright's words produced results: Hyde was transferred to the Crow Creek Agency in

[5] The Yellowtail trip and its consequences are described in Bradley and Bradley, "From Individualism to Bureaucracy," 91–94.
[6] For a profile of Collier, see Lawrence C. Kelly, *The Assault on Assimilation: John Collier and the Origins of Indian Policy Reform* (Albuquerque: University of New Mexico Press, 1983).

South Dakota at the end of December. But even with this dramatic change behind them, none of the Indian or the non-Indian citizens of eastern Montana were prepared for the news that came in mid-March 1934: Commissioner Collier had taken the unprecedented step of appointing an Indian to supervise his own reservation agency.[7]

Most local whites considered Robert Yellowtail a troublemaker, and by the spring of 1934 it appeared that part of the tribe shared that view. The campaign to unseat Hyde had touched off another round of debate between educated, younger Crows (who supported the effort) and a group of older, long-haired men who rallied to the superintendent's defense. In addition, Yellowtail's growing prominence in local and national affairs had inspired opposition from others of his generation, particularly Russell White Bear and the Reno district's Max Big Man. Big Man was two years younger than Yellowtail, the son of a Gros Ventre father and Crow mother. He had attended the agency boarding school and eked out a living as an independent rancher until hiring on with the Burlington Railroad in 1926. While happy with Collier's decision to put an Indian in the Crow post, Big Man was uncomfortable with the choice of his rival from Wyola. White Bear and Big Man, together with other critics from the educated, relatively successful Crows, were eager to become community leaders themselves and were determined to oppose anyone who overshadowed them. Particularly after the death of Plenty Coups in 1932, these men vied for prestige and aspired to the position of "principal chief" of the tribe.[8]

It is difficult to determine exactly why Yellowtail was appointed superintendent in early 1934, but his activism during the 1920s had surely brought him a sizable reputation among sympathetic whites involved in Indian affairs. He particularly attracted the interest of John Collier and his allies who were beginning to argue that the government's obligation was not to "civilize" Indian people, but to defend their right to live as they pleased. Composed largely of social workers, women's groups, educators and writers, this group was naturally drawn to articulate, tenacious young leaders like Robert Yellowtail. In December 1923, Yellowtail may have encountered Collier when both served on the Committee of 100, a group of experts and Indian representatives assembled by the Indian Office to evaluate the state of federal policy. While the Committee of 100 failed to alter the government's programs or attitudes, disputes that broke out during its deliberations – over religious freedom, land use and tribal governance – continued to emerge during the remainder of the decade. In each of these areas, Collier would have found Yellowtail a sympathetic ally.

During the decade before Roosevelt's election, the Indian Defense Associa-

---

[7] Hardin *Tribune*, March 10, 1933. Courtwright's report is quoted in Bradley and Bradley, "From Individualism to Bureaucracy," 99.

[8] The events of 1933 are summarized in Bradley and Bradley, "From Individualism to Bureaucracy," 90–108.

Plenty Coups at his Pryor home, shortly before his death in 1932. Courtesy of Museum of the Rockies, Montana State University.

tion also won the support of an emerging cadre of professionally trained anthropologists who specialized in the history and traditions of Native Americans. One of the most prominent of this group was Robert Lowie, who had first come to Lodge Grass to study the Crows in 1907. Lowie's principal assistant in his Crow research was James Carpenter, one of the founders of the Crow Business Committee, and a close friend of Yellowtail's. Lowie corresponded with Collier during the first months of the new commissioner's tenure and, here again, Yellowtail's name could well have surfaced.[9]

When Collier announced Yellowtail's appointment in March 1934, the Wyola rancher's supporters called a meeting of the tribal council to adopt a resolution applauding the action. His opponents refused to cooperate. Joining Max Big Man and Russell White Bear in opposition to the resolution were Frank Yarlott of St. Xavier and Harry Whiteman of Black Lodge. All these men had been allies of Yellowtail's at one time or another during the preceding twenty years, but they now resented the superintendent-designate's aggressive tactics and feared that he and his Lodge Grass relatives would run roughshod over groups from other parts of the reservation. Despite the fact that the council passed the resolution supporting Yellowtail by a wide margin, Big Man and the others continued to protest. In response, the idealistic new commissioner in Washington took another unprecedented step. Determined to place a bona fide tribal leader in charge of his own agency, Collier ordered a general referendum on Yellowtail's nomination.

The vote took place on May 4, 1934. In reporting Yellowtail's victory, the Hardin *Tribune* reassured its nervous white readers that the new superintendent "foreswore the ways of his forefathers when he entered the white man's schools and has never returned to them." The newspaper also noted, however, that the new leader continued to defend an Indian's right to "dress, live and worship as he chooses," regardless of his degree of "civilization." The statement captured Yellowtail's appeal to both Indians and whites: he had long been an advocate of democratic decision making, constitutional rights and Indian enterprise, but he was also a product of the social, economic and religious atmosphere the Crows had created on their reservation during his lifetime. The new superintendent insisted that outsiders accept him as a Crow Indian, even as he comforted them with his excellent English and thoroughbred horses.[10]

Yellowtail exactly split the 114 votes from St. Xavier, home of several "long-hair" opponents and his business committee rival Frank Yarlott. He also lost Black Lodge; here the margin was narrower: 43 yes, to 55 no. But that was the extent of the opposition. The new superintendent carried Reno with 60% of the vote and rolled up wide margins everywhere else. The tally at Wyola, his home district, was 62 in favor, 5 opposed; at nearby Lodge Grass, it was 154 yes, 57 no. The vote at distant Pryor, now losing its voice in tribal affairs and perhaps eager for a new patron, was 97 in favor of the appointment and 20 opposed. Despite the organized opposition, the reservation-wide total was 501

[9] See Collier to Robert Lowie, November 20, 1933, and reply, dated December 21, 1933, Box 8, Part 10-A, Robert H. Lowie Papers, Bancroft Library, University of California, Berkeley. Yellowtail was referred to as a member of the Committee of 100 in an article in the Hardin *Tribune*, May 4, 1934.

[10] Hardin *Tribune*, May 4, 1934.

Oddly, despite his brilliant preparations for the August 1934 ceremony in which he would officially become superintendent of the Crow Reservation, Robert Yellowtail had no photographer present to record the event. This snapshot is apparently the only picture taken that day to have survived. It shows the young superintendent taking his oath of office beneath the cottonwood trees that ring the agency headquarters. Courtesy of Dennis Sanders, Hardin, Montana.

yes, and 199 no, a 70% margin of victory, with nearly 80% of the electorate turning out. Yellowtail's rivals remained skeptical, but the vote was a remarkable demonstration of tribal unity. The Hardin newspaper summarized the significance of the vote for anyone who might have missed it: "The result was a landslide."[11]

Reaching into Crow tradition while demonstrating a brilliant flair for modern electoral politics, Yellowtail decided to follow up his election victory with a flamboyant inauguration ceremony. The event took place before 3,000 people on August 3, 1934, on the lawn in front of the agency headquarters building, a spot first surveyed by Agent Henry Armstrong exactly fifty summers earlier, and the site of Sword Bearer's noisy ride through the twilight in 1887. The formal ceremony was preceded by a parade through the streets of Crow Agency.

The new superintendent gathered all the elements of the reservation community around him for his inaugural parade. At the head of the procession marched the Hardin High School band, followed closely by Superintendent Yellowtail and his predecessor, an interim officer named Warren O'Hara. The two men were on horseback and were flanked by three Crows "in full regalia." Riding beside Yellowtail were the tribe's two attorneys, Charles Guinn and Dan Maddox of Hardin, who were followed in succession by the local U.S. commissioner and the president and secretary of the Crow tribal council, James Carpenter and Hartford Bear Claw. Both of these council officers were from Lodge Grass; Bear Claw was the son of the former tribal judge.

Following the front rank of officials, rode the local Indian Office staff, a delegation from the American Legion, a band of aging Crow scouts and then row upon row of representatives from the tribe's clans, dancing societies, school groups and community organizations. Many wore beaded buckskin costumes and headdresses. In all several hundred people joined the parade before it came to a halt in front of a platform that had been erected before the agency headquarters. There Yellowtail and his escort were met by Rev. William Petzoldt, the pastor of the Lodge Grass Baptist Church where the new superintendent worshipped, other local ministers, and a group of local dignitaries. Also present and surely sharing the moment in a state of shock, was Samuel Reynolds, the former agent who was now a successful Billings banker and reservation landowner.

With Russell White Bear and Barney Old Coyote acting as interpreters and masters of ceremonies, the proceedings began with traditional honor songs and Crow prayers in memory of Plenty Coups, Spotted Horse, Pretty Eagle, Medicine Crow and the others who had traced their careers as leaders across the

---

[11] The election results were reported in ibid. and are reprinted in Bradley and Bradley, "From Individualism to Bureaucracy," 109. The newspaper's comment came in its issue of July 27. For a description of the election itself by the Indian Office employee charged with conducting it, see Warren L. O'Hara to Commissioner of Indian Affairs, May 4, 1934, CCF, Crow, 055, 18993–1934.

reservation environment. Attorneys Guinn and Maddox spoke briefly, and then O'Hara introduced Yellowtail. Like the parade that preceded it, the new superintendent's speech touched on several themes in recent Crow history and attempted to gather them into a coherent set of principles. The purpose was both to define a common national identity that might legitimize his tenure in office and to set an agenda for the future.

"Friends," Yellowtail began, "this is our home, this is our domain and this is our country – blessed in many ways. There is no region more favored by nature as a country in which to live well and happily. Nevertheless," he continued, beginning with the Crows' first land cession treaty with the United States in 1851, "our rights as humans were denied. . . . We virtually have lived our lives here as serfs under a bureaucratic dictatorship absolute in power." The new superintendent went on to charge that "during this long autocratic rule, our constitutional rights and other liberties were trampled under foot." He particularly singled out Spotted Horse, who, Yellowtail declared, "never hesitated to demand his human rights," and he recited the times when "greed, avarice and rapacity ran rampant here without a voice in our defense from anyone here or at Washington."

According to Yellowtail, the greatest evil of the past half-century had been federal contempt for Crow "rights." These rights included individual religious and cultural freedoms, as well as the community's right to self-government and independent economic development. Freedom – the right to act in accord with a distinctive cultural agenda, as well as to organize politically – was the key to Crow survival. The new superintendent pointed out that the community had been most successful in maintaining its traditions in areas that were largely free from "bureaucratic dictatorship." These included the social, cultural and religious activities represented in the inaugural parade itself. But, he noted, when the Crows had asserted their political right to self-government, they had continued to be stymied. Here for Yellowtail was the significance of his inauguration as superintendent:

> Today a new rainbow of hope is flashed across the skies of a hitherto dark horizon . . . we find ourselves gathered here today prepared to initiate a . . . home rule program that we lost with the passing of the buffalo and the first treaty we concluded with the government, but which we have just recouped this day. A new era, a new hope and a new deal has dawned for the American Indian.

When he turned from the discussion of home rule to a specific policy agenda, Yellowtail moved from political rights to the development of the tribe's economic resources. Having overcome their serfdom and instituted a government to defend their rights, the superintendent urged his fellow tribesmen to use their new power to assert themselves as ranchers, farmers and owners of vast natural resources. He suggested five new policies: Indian preference hiring in the Indian Office, breaking up the power of large cattlemen by distributing large, "monopoly" leases among several tenants, oil and mineral exploration and the "expeditious" handling of tribal funds. Yellowtail conceded that none of these programs would create an independent tribal economy, but his objective was not economic separation, but the assertion of the community's economic rights. He sought an improvement in the tribe's collective income and well-being; he did not promise a return to the autonomy of an earlier era.

Yellowtail's conclusion returned to politics. "All people," he observed, "have grown better in the proportion that they have grown free and I shall continue to do what little I can in my feeble way to add another flame to the torch of progress for the Crows and the Indian Peoples. . . ." He promised to consult with the tribal council on all matters that came before him and to keep his door open to critics. "This is your domain and therefore your business," he told the Crows gathered before him; "you should be heard at all times on any and all phases of its administration."[12]

With this speech, Yellowtail both celebrated the transformations of the past half-century and identified the principal bulwark he intended to erect in defense of that transformation. By defining the political interests of the Crows as "rights," he was ensuring that they would survive into the future. Remedying the community's economic ills was a pressing concern, but Yellowtail recognized initially the arena where a superintendent could be most effective and where his people had been most successful. Wealth would not necessarily protect the social, religious and community institutions the Crows had erected during the preceding fifty years. The language of community "rights" would. By claiming that "home rule" had returned to the reservation for the first time since the buffalo days, Yellowtail was tying tribal political institutions to the defense of modern Crow culture. Once that connection was made, his mission was clear. As he explained to a group of government officials in Billings two years later, "Every constitutional right that the Crow Indians possess will be most freely accorded them while I am in charge of the Crow Agency."[13]

III

Robert Yellowtail served as superintendent of the Crow Reservation until the Roosevelt administration ended in 1945. Even though he was attacked frequently by his old rivals Russell White Bear, Frank Yarlott and Max Big Man, he managed to retain the support of the tribal council and to balance his

[12] The entire inauguration was described in detail in the Hardin *Tribune*, August 3, 1934.
[13] Remarks of Superintendent Robert Yellowtail before the National Emergency Council, Billings, Montana, April 10, 1936, special case 991, Montana Historical Society.

district, clan and family obligations against the requirements of his position in the federal bureaucracy. But despite his political skill, Yellowtail had little success in alleviating poverty on the reservation. He failed to create an all-Indian agency staff or to generate new income from minerals or oil. And while generally praised for his administrative ability, he had no success in breaking the power of the white tenants who leased the bulk of his tribesmen's land.

Yellowtail's economic foes were formidable, but as his inaugural speech suggested, he and his constituents considered them less important than the enemies of the tribe's political and cultural independence. In the Crow nation's public agenda, "rights" were more important than prosperity. These priorities were brought sharply into focus during the most dramatic political struggle of the 1930s: the battle over the ratification of the Indian Reorganization Act in the spring of 1935.

John Collier's principal objective as Indian commissioner was to apply the ideas of modern social work to Native American communities. He wanted to replace the heavy-handed assimilationist policies of his predecessors with programs that developed the internal political and economic life of each reservation community. He believed that groups of Indians, like neighborhoods of urban immigrants, workers laboring in massive factories or residents of isolated rural communities, needed to develop their own leaders and institutions of governance in order to function effectively in a complex, industrial democracy. In Collier's view, nurturing Indian communities and their political institutions would pay dividends for the entire country; it would demonstrate the extent to which the ignored and neglected members of American society, properly encouraged, could revive themselves and participate actively in national affairs. "The ruin inflicted on Red Indians through the white man's denial of their grouphood is only a special case of something that is universal," he wrote in 1945, adding with characteristic optimism that federal assistance could reverse this process. "The sunken stream can flow again," he declared; "the ravaged desert can bloom, the great past is not killed. The Indian experience tells us this."[14]

Immediately upon taking office, Collier acted on his beliefs by lifting official restrictions on traditional Indian ceremonies and dances, seeking out "progressive" educators to lead native schools, and working on a new piece of comprehensive legislation that would put the relations of Indian tribes and the U.S. government on a new footing. By the end of 1933 he was ready to act. He called a general meeting of Indian reform organizations at the Cosmos Club in Washington, D.C., in January 1934. There he persuaded most of his former comrades from the Indian reform movement of the 1920s to support an approach

---

[14] John Collier, "United States Indian Administration as a Laboratory of Ethnic Relations," *Social Research* 12 (September 1945), 302, 303.

that included ending allotment, consolidating remaining tribal lands into economically viable units and promoting the development of reservation organizations to oversee tribal affairs. Within a month he had produced a draft statute, the "Indian Reorganization Act."

Collier's bill was introduced by Montana Senator Burton K. Wheeler and Nebraska Congressman Edgar Howard on February 12, 1934 – about the same time the commissioner was deciding to name Robert Yellowtail the first Native American superintendent of his own tribal agency. In its initial, fifty-two-page form, the statute was revolutionary: it provided for the organization of tribal governments that would have the power to condemn land, charter businesses and remove Indian Office personnel under their jurisdiction. It also created a national court of Indian affairs and promised large sums for education and the economic development of reservations. Recognizing that his ambitions tested settled routines in both Congress and the Indian Office, Collier began campaigning for the act almost immediately. He rallied sympathetic whites to his cause and organized a series of "Indian Congresses" with representatives of the nation's tribes. During the first months of 1934, he reverted to the tactics that had served him so well in the 1920s: travelling the country, mobilizing his supporters and cultivating the press.

At Crow Agency, much of the early discussion of Collier's idea was obscured by the Yellowtail appointment. Still, the tribal council appointed a committee to review the bill in February 1934 and sent a delegation to the Plains Indian Congress held in Rapid City, South Dakota, in early March. Led by Yellowtail's rivals, Max Big Man and Frank Yarlott, the Crow representatives asked the commissioner to exempt them from the his new scheme. They argued that the Crow Act had granted them such substantial tracts of land that they were not as impoverished as other tribes and they had no need for the protection of the new tribal councils. As Harry Whiteman explained on his return from Rapid City, "We acquired our present rights by continually wedging our way to better things and we are going to keep them."[15]

Trying to generate enthusiasm for his plan, Collier was disappointed, but he assured the Crows that they would not be forced to adopt the law. He told the Rapid City congress that if the Crows or "any other delegation" wanted to be exempted from the act, "we will do all in our power to get them shut out. Of course," he added ominously, "they will have to know, that, as we say, 'you can't have your cake and eat it too.' You can't be both in and out at the same time. . . ." The commissioner was implying that those who refused to follow his plan might not be eligible for federal assistance that flowed to cooperating tribes.[16]

[15] "Brief Summary of a Regular Session of the Crow Tribal Council, March 7, 1934," CCF, Crow, 066, 4894–1934, Part B.
[16] John Collier at Rapid City Congress, March 4, 1934, in ibid.

Despite the commissioner's warning, opposition to his proposal remained firm in Crow country. At a March 7 council meeting (from which Yellowtail was strangely absent), speaker after speaker criticized the bill and repeated Collier's assurance that the tribe would not be required to participate. The opposition centered in the Bighorn and Black Lodge districts, which were most hostile to Robert Yellowtail and was supported by local cattlemen who believed the proposed changes would endanger their hold on Indian pastureland. St. Xavier's Frank Yarlott, for example, argued that the new tribal council would have so much power that it would be a "threat to deprive [the Indians] of the right to live and work with the white race."[7]

A second Crow council in May (again, meeting without Yellowtail) voted narrowly to oppose the Indian Reorganization Act, but Congress approved it in late June, barely a month after the Crow referendum on Robert Yellowtail's appointment as agency superintendent. In its final form, the commissioner's ambitious draft statute had been reduced to a cautious document that focused primarily on reservation administration. Under its provisions, the future allotment of Indian lands was prohibited, and tribes were granted the power to organize themselves into local governments, but few of the powers Collier had asked for were granted. Under the new law tribes could not condemn land, discharge federal employees or participate in a national Indian court system. They were allowed to acquire and "exchange" land, as well as to organize tribal businesses and participate in a revolving economic development fund, but the new, federally approved governments would have little ability to reverse federal action or actively oppose the non-Indian investors who controlled so many of their resources.

Even in its stunted form, the Wheeler–Howard bill represented a dramatic shift in federal policy. Tribes would be supported rather than pulled apart, Indian lands would be restored rather than divided and sold, and Indian communities would be developed and "reorganized" rather than "uplifted" and assimilated. But perhaps most remarkable of all, the Indian Office proposed that the new law apply only to those communities which voted to accept it in special elections. For the first time in American history, Indians would have the opportunity to approve or reject a major government action affecting them. Superintendent Yellowtail was eager to begin the ratification process. He wrote to Collier in October requesting additional copies of the act and promising to

[7] Richard B. Millan, Acting Superintendent, to Commissioner of Indian Affairs, February 15, 1934, "Proposed Legislation," Item 16, Box 96, RCIA-FRC, Seattle; Yarlott quoted in Billings *Gazette*, March 30, 1934, in Bradley and Bradley, "From Individualism to Bureaucracy," 115. In any estimation of the reasons for Collier's appointment of Yellowtail, its potential political impact should be taken seriously. The commissioner surely believed the appointment of an articulate and dynamic Indian leader to a reservation superintendency would help win approval for his bill.

"hold hearings at the various districts on the Crow Reservation and explain the bill paragraph by paragraph so that every Indian will have a thorough explanation of the provisions contained in the bill before the voting takes place." Collier had hoped originally to hold the Crow election in December, but the flood of referenda and the difficulty of distributing information to remote, frequently illiterate communities caused him to delay it until May 18, 1935.[18]

During the fall of 1934, however, as Yellowtail settled into office as superintendent and the campaign to approve the IRA began, the bill's opponents seized the initiative. Big Man, Yarlott and other enemies attended district meetings and peppered the government's representatives with questions and complaints. Much of this opposition was pure political rivalry. As one agency official had written in early 1934, competition between groups was so intense on the Crow Reservation that any proposal that "happened to meet the approval of one group . . . was sure to meet the disapproval of another group for no other reason than the fact that the first group had been pleased with it." Nevertheless, the attacks were effective. Yarlott, for example, frequently referred to the vast powers proposed for tribal governments in Collier's original bill, ignoring the fact that most of these had been eliminated prior to its passage. He charged that Crow landowners would lose their land to a power-mad tribal council, and when told that the law Congress passed would not allow such actions, he protested that their error proved that Yellowtail had not explained the bill properly.[19]

At the end of 1934, concerned that his new appointee might not be able to overcome his opponents, Collier sent Superintendent Centerwall of the neighboring Northern Cheyenne Reservation to Crow Agency to investigate. The superintendent's report, filed in mid-February, was most disturbing. Not only did he describe the power of the opposition, but he noted that its arguments were rooted in the defense of local, community rights. "I have found the Crows very antagonistic toward the bill, Centerwall reported; "the seed of distrust has been deeply sown." Of even more concern was the observation that in his tour of the reservation he was "playing practically a lone hand." Apparently

[18] Robert Yellowtail to Commissioner of Indian Affairs, October 11, 1934; for a discussion of the delay to spring, see Robert Yellowtail to W. C. Centerwall, December 31, 1934; both in "Wheeler Howard Act, Correspondence," Item 16, Box 119, RCIA-FRC, Seattle.
[19] Richard B. Millin to Commissioner of Indian Affairs, February 15, 1934; Bradley and Bradley, "From Individualism to Bureaucracy," 116–118. After meeting with Yarlott and other Crow opponents of the bill, Collier wrote to Yellowtail that "some of the Indians are still under the impression that the original Wheeler–Howard Bill was enacted . . ." (Collier to Yellowtail, May 2, 1935). Yellowtail replied, "Rest assured that the present delegation in Washington have heard all of these discussions but have so far refused to be convinced, and . . . have refused to listen to further discussions upon the subject" (Yellowtail to Commissioner of Indian Affairs, May 6, 1935); both in "Wheeler Howard Act, Correspondence," Item 16, Box 119, RCIA-FRC, Seattle.

Yellowtail had decided to drift into neutrality on the new law. "When time came for discussion of the Wheeler–Howard Bill the superintendent departed for parts unknown and has never attended a single meeting."[20]

For the next three months the commissioner repeatedly asked Yellowtail for assurances that he was campaigning for the act. He telegraphed the superintendent in late February, asking "whether the fullest effort is being made by you and the other agency people." Yellowtail reassured his superiors, but his letters lacked the conviction Collier must have been looking for. The Crow superintendent spoke of distributing information and answering questions, not of persuading reluctant kinsmen or countering his enemies' arguments. Finally, with the vote approaching and Yellowtail still sounding like a dispassionate seminar leader, the commissioner became more direct: "I feel that it is your job to put yourself forcibly into this campaign. It is an administration policy and program and must have the earnest support of the superintendents." He added, "I hope you can put yourself into this campaign."[21]

At the end of April, as preparations for the May 17 referendum neared their end, the superintendent acted. He blanketed the reservation with copies of the Wheeler–Howard bill, defended the measure before several meetings of the tribal council, enlisted local ministers to explain the law from their pulpits and organized a last-minute blitz in which the attorneys Guinn and Maddox, Yellowtail and three neighboring reservation superintendents held simultaneous public meetings in every district. Yellowtail's principal argument in all these settings was that the new law would end the sale of Indian land and consolidate the Crows' remaining property into viable units. As he told the tribal council, "The sale of our lands is what is ruining us, and if continued we will be landless in ten years and beggars on the highways. . . ."[22]

An accomplished politician and stump speaker, Yellowtail might well have been able to turn the tide of the debate had he entered the campaign earlier and more energetically. But as the vote neared, it became clear that the Crow opposition to the Wheeler–Howard bill was not purely a product of political opportunism. By offering to reorganize its tribal government according to a set of regulations emanating from Washington, D.C., the law appeared to strike at the Crows' right to govern themselves. It seemed to attack the "home rule"

[20] W. R. Centerwall to Commissioner of Indian Affairs, February 16, 1935, CCF, Crow, 066, 9566–1935.

[21] John Collier to Robert Yellowtail, February 26, 1935, CCF, Crow, 066, 9566–1935; Collier to Yellowtail, May 10, 1935, CCF, Crow, 006, 9566–1934. This file contains several letters between Crow Agency and Washington, D.C., during the period just prior to the May 17 referendum.

[22] Quoted in Bradley and Bradley, "From Individualism to Bureaucracy," 119, from Council Proceedings, May 17, 1935, CCF, Crow, 16298–1935, For evidence of Yellowtail's last-minute efforts, see Robert Yellowtail to Commissioner of Indian Affairs, November 1, 1934; ibid. April 4, 1935, May 6, 1935, and May 11, 1935; all in "Wheeler Howard Act, Correspondence," Item 16, Box 119, RCIA-FRC, Seattle.

Yellowtail had so recently celebrated in both his election and his colorful inauguration. In February, one of the superintendent's most loyal allies, James Carpenter, explained the Crow perception that the new law violated the tribe's rights in letter to his old friend, anthropologist Robert Lowie. "The bill to my way of thinking is the worst kind of law the Commissioner can enact for the Crows," Carpenter wrote. "It takes all their rights away giving them the dictatorship of his office and officials on the reservation. It sets them back to where the white people were five hundred years ago: *serfs*. There is nothing in the bill that guarantees the Crows their rights. . . . With the little education I have," Carpenter concluded, "I have stood for the Crow and their rights and I will do so as long as I live."[23]

In his final appeals Yellowtail hammered away at his critics and emphasized the law's economic advantages. "We have demonstrated the fact that we have not been able to hang onto our lands," he told a final tribal council meeting on election eve. "Let us fix it now. . . ." The superintendent wired his superiors that same day that he was making a "supreme effort" and hoped "to rout all opposition through sheer argument. . . ." He counted on his supporters at Lodge Grass and Wyola to overwhelm the opposition from other parts of the reservation, but as the polling began, the exhausted campaigner knew he was beaten. Claiming that the vote should have taken place in the fall, Yellowtail wired, "Sentiment was crystallized beyond human endeavor to break . . . am completely worn out. Need some rest."[24]

The results resembled a mirror image of the vote on Yellowtail's nomination in 1934. Out of 801 votes cast (an 80% turnout), only 112 (13%) were in favor of accepting the provisions of Collier's act. Every district rejected it, with the widest margin at a combined polling station for Black Lodge and Reno. There 233 of 245 voters rejected the superintendent's arguments and voted no. Yellowtail himself attributed the defeat to a poorly organized campaign and "the old hostile feeling against the Indian Bureau," but a review of his own inaugural speech would have provided a better clue.

The act infringed on the tribe's hard-fought "freedom" and the "rights" leaders had both defined and expanded over the previous half-century. These ideas were tied closely to the community's sense of independence and nationhood. "We Crows rejected the bill for reasons [of] our interests," James Carpenter wrote later that summer. "We knew what we were doing and prepared to meet the [positive] votes, which we did outvote by a big majority." The vote was not produced by outside manipulators or tribal demagogues: "The Crows have no

---

[23] James Carpenter to Robert H. Lowie, February 26, 1935, Incoming Letters, Robert H. Lowie Papers.

[24] Bradley and Bradley, "From Individualism to Bureaucracy," 120, quoting Tribal Council Proceedings, May 17, 1935; Yellowtail to Commissioner of Indian Affairs, May 17, May 18, 1935, "Wheeler Howard Act, Correspondence," Item 16, Box 119, RCIA-FRC, Seattle.

professionals amongst them but have men with experience and a common education who stand for rights given us under the laws."[25]

<h1 style="text-align:center">IV</h1>

One of the proudest achievements of the Yellowtail administration at Crow Agency was the revival of the annual Crow fair. Moved from late September or October to the last week in August, the event was increasingly staged for outsiders. In 1937, for example, groups of Blackfeet, Gros Ventre, Cheyenne and Sioux joined the white tourists who flocked to the Little Bighorn to witness the dancing and horse racing. Modern automobiles now retraced the paths of Indian raiders and visitors who had come to the Little Bighorn in the 1880s and 1890s. The most dramatic attraction was the daily parade. Wrote a reporter for one travel magazine:

> The most spectacular event of each day was the parade led by "Bobby" Yellowtail, Superintendent of the Crow Reservation. The only note of modernism in the parade was the motor truck which carried the Blackfeet band. All the rest were mounted on horses . . . The Blackfeet band followed Yellowtail in the parade, then the mounted Indian tribes in orderly fashion, each man in full tribal headdress. . . . They proceeded in single file, hundreds of Indians, each dressed differently, in a most magnificent and impressive array reminiscent of former days.[26]

Not only did Yellowtail's presence at the head of the tribal parade recall the march of his ancestors through the Hidatsa villages in 1805, but it represented the presence of a Crow nation in the modern world. Fueled by social, cultural and religious practices that had managed to adapt to a new setting, led by politicians who defended their right to remain independent, Yellowtail and his community defined themselves as people with a country and a distinctive way of life. Their survival and reemergence was not the product of their racial heritage or material setting, but of history: the interaction of traditions, institutions and personalities through time.

Crow history had never been self-generating. Migrations, technological innovations and accident had constantly buffeted and altered the community's sense of itself and its predicament. The arrival of people from Europe in the

[25] James Carpenter to Robert H. Lowie, July 24, 1935, Incoming Letters, Robert H. Lowie Papers. For two model case studies of the Indian Reorganization Act campaign on other reservations, see Donald L. Parman, *The Navajos and the New Deal* (New Haven, Conn.: Yale University Press, 1976), and Thomas Biolsi, *Organizing the Lakota: The Political Economy of the New Deal on the Pine Ridge and Rosebud Reservations* (Tucson: University of Arizona Press, 1992).

[26] G. E. Barrett, "Crow Indians Hold Second Annual Tribal Fair," *Scenic Trails* (October 1937), 10.

Yellowstone valley had shifted the pace, but not the nature, of events. "History," anthropologist Sherry Ortner has written, "is not simply something that happens to people, but something they make – within, of course, the very powerful constraints of the system within which they are operating." Crows had participated in this process despite the suffering and dislocation visited upon them and the "powerful constraints" that continually hovered over their experience. They made their history from the traditions they inherited, as well as from the opportunities that were offered to them by new ideas, new technologies and new allies. The "half-breed boy" in a headdress, astride his horse and carrying an American flag tells us nothing less.[27]

[27] Sherry Ortner, "Theory in Anthropology Since the Sixties," *Comparative Studies in Society and History* 26 (1984), 159.

12

Crows and other Americans

An event is not just a happening in the world; it is a *relation* between a certain happening and a given symbolic system. . . . an event is a happening interpreted. . . .

Marshall Sahlins[1]

I

An event that occurred in Washington, D.C., in the fall of 1921 presents an opportunity to explore the relationship between a "happening" and the interpretations attached to it. Examining this relationship is always appropriate in historical scholarship, but it is especially important at the end of a long narrative that has crossed cultural boundaries and been populated by previously invisible people and events. After all, as Marshall Sahlins has also observed, "What is for some people a radical event may appear to others as a date for lunch." One should be cautious about fitting such events too quickly into an inherited "symbolic system." Rather, by examining the relationship between this concluding happening and the understandings that surrounded it, we might gain a fresh insight into both our story and the symbolic systems surrounding it.[2]

The parade began sharply at 8:30 A.M. The *New York Times* reporter observed that "Washington has witnessed many notable ceremonials, but never one like this." As a military band played "Nearer My God to Thee," the silver-haired president of the United States took his place behind a horse-drawn caisson carrying the remains of an unidentified soldier who had died in France three years earlier, during the final days of World War I.

President and Mrs. Harding stepped off first, followed immediately by Vice President Coolidge and his wife and Chief Justice William Howard Taft. A car carrying the crippled former president Woodrow Wilson and his wife followed close behind. In their wake marched ranks of politicians, veterans, gold star mothers, military bands and delegations from organizations as diverse as the Knights of Columbus, the American Women's Legion and the American Library Association. As they passed the dense crowds lining Pennsylvania Avenue, "men stood with heads uncovered in the presence of the coffin and

---

[1] Marshall Sahlins, *Islands of History* (Chicago: University of Chicago Press, 1985), 153.
[2] Ibid., 154.

silently followed its course as far as the eye could reach." Recalling the tearful funerals of Lincoln, Garfield and McKinley, the *Times* reporter noted that "there were tears today, but most of those who shed them were carried away by the emotion of the symbolism of patriotism which this unknown American embodied."

Just before noon the procession reached its destination, Arlington National Cemetery, in the low hills west of the capital. As more than 100,000 spectators looked on, the coffin was carried to the stage of the cemetery amphitheater. Everyone was in place by 12:00 o'clock. As the hour struck, the audience stood in silence for two minutes, joined by millions of others across the country who paused in simultaneous observances. The singing of "America" brought the period of silence to a close and introduced speeches by the president and other dignitaries. They were followed by a series of international representatives (many of them in Washington for the Conference on Naval Disarmament, which would begin the next week) who presented the unknown soldier with military medals from their governments. Uniformed pallbearers then carried the coffin to a nearby marble sarcophagus, placed it inside and stood at attention as a military chaplain read the funeral service.

After the chaplain had completed his prayers, Plenty Coups stepped forward. Dressed in brilliantly beaded buckskin, carrying a coups stick, and wearing an eagle-feather headdress, the seventy-two-year-old warrior's presence was a stunning match for the European generals and the officers from the Mikado's navy who stood in the front ranks of the audience in their polished boots and gold braid. The huge crowd watched in absolute silence as the Pryor leader – who had first come to Washington with Pretty Eagle and Medicine Crow more than forty years before – removed his war bonnet and laid it on the sarcophagus alongside his coup stick. Ignoring the order that he remain silent during his part of the ceremony, Plenty Coups then turned to the crowd and added his own words to those that had been pronounced earlier. Speaking in Crow, he declared, "I am glad to represent all the Indians of the United States in placing on the grave of this noble warrior this coup stick and war bonnet, every eagle feather of which represents a deed of valor by my race." He added a brief prayer: "I hope that the Great Spirit will grant that these noble warriors have not given up their lives in vain and that there will be peace to all men hereafter." As the old man completed his unauthorized address, a bugler began "taps" and a twenty-one gun salute echoed across the Potomac. His brief appearance, the *Times* reporter noted, was "one of the outstanding features of the whole remarkable ceremony."[3]

---

[3] New York *Times*, November 12, 1921, 1–2. For a description of the two minutes of silence in another city, see Chicago *Tribune*, November 12, 1921, 2. See also John C. Ewers, "A Crow Chief's Tribute to the Unknown Soldier," *American West* 8, 6 (1971), 30–35. Ewers makes clear that Plenty Coups had been told not to speak at the ceremony.

The image of Plenty Coups offering the final blessing at a flamboyant celebration of American patriotism provides an opportunity for viewing the modern history of the Crows in a national context. When he stepped forward to perform his part of the Armistice Day ceremony, the old warrior was both filling a role constructed for him by others and marking an extraordinary individual achievement. Despite his divergence from the official program, he appeared to the public as a loyal ally of American power and a compelling symbol of national unity. He appeared to fit easily into the Armistice Day procession. Nevertheless, Plenty Coups presented himself as the proud representative of a distinctive community who believed in "valor" and obeyed a "Great Spirit." His performance fit the script created for him, but it simultaneously underscored both the survival and persistence of the Crow people. It is possible, therefore, for observers of this incident to view it in two ways: one emphasizing its predictability and patriotic cant, the other recalling the Crow leader's struggle for recognition by both federal authorities and his fellow tribesmen. One view stresses Indian defeat; the other, a kind of victory.

To imagine contrasting interpretations of the Armistice Day celebration is not to suggest that one must choose between them. Rather, to grasp the complexity of that event it is essential to view the two versions together. To do otherwise is to flatten its meaning and distance it from the actors who created it. Moreover, to hold the perspectives of both Plenty Coups and his audience in mind allows one to open an inquiry into the relationship of Crow history – the history that brought the aging chief to Arlington – to the wider story of American society at the turn of the twentieth century.

To construct a multifaceted view of the Arlington "happening," one needs to answer a series of paired questions: Why did American leaders in 1921 choose to have a Crow Indian complete their celebration of wartime heroism, and why would a man like Plenty Coups accept their invitation? What did Americans see in this resilient Crow warrior, and what did he see in them? Exploring such questions allows us to identify the cultural and historical issues being contested by the actors engaged in the Unknown Soldier parade and ceremony. These questions also suggest a way of understanding similar struggles taking place elsewhere in the United States where other ethnically distinct communities interacted with a "symbolic system" that was being constructed to define them. Like the events at Arlington Cemetery, those interactions also produced divergent interpretations of happenings and revealed competing efforts to structure both American culture and its history.

Plenty Coups's appearance at Arlington was a metaphor for the relationship between the Native American experience and the history of United States in the early twentieth century. Playing a limited and tightly scripted role in someone else's ceremony, the chief had little power to alter or affect the events taking place around him. Despite the success of his improvised speech, the

Plenty Coups and Marshall Ferdinand Foch, photographed at Crow Agency, November 28, 1921. The French hero of World War I stopped to visit his fellow warrior a few weeks after their initial meeting at Arlington Cemetery. The event attracted considerable interest in Montana, but the old chief skillfully took center stage and kept the local politicians and merchants in the background. Courtesy Smithsonian Institution.

chief was acutely aware of what he could *not* do or say when he took the floor. On the other hand, Plenty Coups – by speaking, by referring to himself as the representative of his race, and by seizing the opportunity of providing an Indian blessing for the event – turned his assigned role both to his own and to his community's advantage. He used the occasion to celebrate his "noble" Indian past and to promote himself as a politician. (Following his return to Montana, Plenty Coups regularly reminded local officials of the many friends he had recently made in high places. When Marshall Foch of France visited the Little Bighorn a few weeks after Armistice Day, Plenty Coups, artfully shouldered aside the local politicians who assembled to greet him. The hero of World War I had come to see his friend and fellow warrior!) In this sense the Crow leader was broadly representative of Indians who struggled to maintain their visibility and autonomy during the years that bridged the nineteenth and twentieth centuries. The tensions suggested by his Arlington performance mirrored the struggles that were taking place between Indians and other Americans in many parts of the country and foreshadowed conflicts that would burst forward in the decades to come.[4]

But because the funeral of the Unknown Soldier elicited such powerful statements about American nationalism and because Plenty Coups was placed so squarely in the center of its rituals of American unity, the incident also offers an opportunity to consider the chief's performance as a metaphor for early-twentieth-century racial and ethnic relations generally. Other groups were also confined to subordinate roles in the national tableau, and they too pushed at the limits of these assignments in an effort to become visible participants in a plural society. They too sought opportunities in an age of repression. Plenty Coups represents that larger struggle as well as his own.

II

What did American leaders see in Plenty Coups? Between the end of the American Civil War and the end of World War I, both government officials and private citizens worked energetically to sever the bonds connecting Native American communities to their environments and their traditions. This campaign subjected Indian children and their parents to an unprecedented onslaught of schooling and missionization, while it sought to open tribal resources to economic penetration by railroads, commercial farmers and prospectors. Federal Indian policy facilitated this effort by establishing uniform policies for the administration of tribal affairs and mediating between interest groups that competed with each other for access to native communities and their resources.[5]

The events of this fifty-year period produced parallel developments on reservations with widely differing cultural traditions. In the closing decades of the nineteenth century, tribal communities in the Southwest, the Great Lakes, the East and elsewhere – whose residents were separated by outlook, subsistence patterns and geographical conditions – faced an increasingly predictable cast of outsiders who called on native people to give up their distinctive traditions and adopt a common set of "civilized" habits. Collectively, these outsiders and the interests they represented shaped the common outlines of the world twentieth-century Indians would inhabit.

During the 1870s, as warfare ended on the plains, Congress established the first large off-reservation government boarding schools, and the Indian Office

---

[4] For Foch's visit to Crow Agency, see Superintendent to Commissioner of Indian Affairs, November 30, 1921, Box 83, Item 15, File 131, "Religious Customs, Dances, 1918–1923," RCIA-FRC, Seattle.

[5] See Frederick E. Hoxie, *A Final Promise: The Campaign to Assimilate the Indians, 1880–1920* (Lincoln: University of Nebraska Press, 1984). For another perspective on the same years, see Janet A. McDonnell, *The Dispossession of the American Indian, 1887–1934* (Bloomington: Indiana University Press, 1991).

s of coastal cities or had retreated to the sparsely settled interior. During
os and 1890s, however, their little hamlets were besieged by the rapid
of the state's population and the assertion that native land titles were
e or nonexistent. Despite legal appeals and the efforts of a congressional
ission, thousands of California Indians lost their homes. The most dra-
of these dispossessions occurred in 1903 at Warner's Ranch near San
o, where villages of Cupeño, San Luiseño and Kumeyaay Indians were
ed by the U.S. Army and relocated to a reservation in the Pala valley.[7]

ven Indians living in the eastern United States felt a surge of white expan-
during the 1880s. The 11,000 Native Americans who clustered in rural
munities along the Atlantic seaboard found their isolation violated by the
ension of transportation systems and the growth of commercial agriculture.
Massachusetts, the Mashpees of Cape Cod, who in 1869 had lost the legal
otections that had kept non-Indians from purchasing land in their commun-
y, gradually lost their cranberry bogs and ocean-front property to industrial
armers and wealthy Boston vacationers. Native people in North Carolina felt a
different kind of pressure when, in 1885, they responded to the threat of
segregation by persuading the state legislature to recognize them as Indians
rather than as "people of color." As a result they were exempted from the worst
strictures of racial separation.[8]

The great exception to this decade of unrestrained non-Indian expansion
and intrusion occurred in the most isolated region of the continent outside
of Alaska: the American Southwest. There the extension of railroad lines and
mineral exploration dislocated native communities, but relatively little property
changed hands. The Navajos were the most prominent group in this area. Their
population doubled between 1870 and 1900 and they moved peacefully from
hunting and gathering to a new dependence on herding and subsistence agriculture. While the village peoples of the region (the Pueblos of the Rio Grande
valley, Hopi and Zuni) suffered continual pressure on their lands – indeed, it
was at this time that the Hopis and Navajos began their century-long struggle
over a common hunting and grazing area – there were no major land cessions
in the territories of Arizona and New Mexico.

But for the Crows and most Native Americans, the disruptive arrival of non-
Indians during the 1880s forced tribal members to accept life within a set of
fixed and shrinking borders and to function within a cash economy. Indian
people had begun to slip into the orbit of the market economy at almost the
moment of first contact with Europeans, but it was not until the 1880s and

---

[7] See Florence Connolly Shipek, *Pushed into the Rocks: Southern California Land Tenure, 1769–1986* (Lincoln: University of Nebraska Press, 1987).

[8] See Daniel Boxberger, *To Fish in Common: The Ethnohistory of Lummi Indian Salmon Fishing* (Lincoln: University of Nebraska Press, 1989); and Karen Blu, *The Lumbee Problem: The Making of an American Indian People* (Cambridge University Press, 1980).

began to establish uniform standards of ad.
the United States. In 1880, while most Indiar
settlers and government officials, a bureaucrat
the process of assimilating the entire race to no.
government. Despite the variation in its impa
from local settlement was felt in all Native A
people experienced rapid reductions in the amou.
and faced an existence constrained by narrowing

During the same decade that the Crows agreed to
land sale and witnessed the army's ability to mass o
doorstep, tribes in the Great Lakes region were besie
ing to purchase Indian timber and send it down lo
completed rail lines to Chicago, Detroit and Clevela
years in Indian Territory, railroads were allowed to
"civilized tribes" who had been removed to the area
violating half a century of federal protection. At the sar
authorities established new reservations in the territory fo
there from other places in the West. By 1890, there were t
tions in the Indian "homeland" containing nearly seventy gre
Geronimo's tiny band of captured Apaches at Fort Sill, t
Cherokees and Creeks, who occupied large reservations goveri
legislatures and regulated by tribal courts.[6]

The 1880s were also years of dramatic change in the plateau ai
of Washington, Oregon and Idaho. There, inland peoples found
ers and ranchers pressing them to sell their "surplus" lands
communities witnessed the installation of the first fish wheels along
bia River and the first corporate-sponsored fish traps in Puget So
mechanical innovations, together with the transportation available on
completed Northern Pacific Railroad, spurred further population gr
redoubled the pressure on tribal resources. Because the railroad had
effect on plains communities, the entire northern tier of the America
campaigned for statehood. Linked to eastern markets and growing rap
population, the Dakota and Wyoming Territories were as eager to jo
union as Montana, Washington or Idaho; all became states before 1900.

In California, the Indians who had survived the holocaust of the gold
and the first years of American settlement had clung to tiny landholdings on

[6] See Edmund Danziger, *The Chippewas of Lake Superior* (Norman: University of Oklahoma Pre
1987); H. Craig Miner, *The Corporation and the Indian: Tribal Sovereignty and Industrial Civi
ization in Indian Territory* (Norman: University of Oklahoma Press, 1976); Donald J. Berthrong
The Cheyenne and Arapaho Ordeal: Reservation and Agency Life in the Indian Territory, 1875–1907
(Norman: University of Oklahoma Press, 1976); William T. Hagan, *United States–Comanche
Relations: The Reservation Years* (New Haven, CN: Yale University Press, 1976); and Angie
Debo, *Geronimo* (Norman: University of Oklahoma Press, 1976).

1890s that cash threatened to eradicate self-sufficiency as the principal means of subsistence for most tribes. While Crow farmers struggled with grain crops and tried to raise cattle for market, Indians in Massachusetts, New York and North Carolina labored as sailors, domestic servants and field hands, and their counterparts in the Great Lakes survived by fishing, farming and working for wages.

In addition, just as Crow leaders struggled to control the leasing of their land to outsiders, so Oklahoma tribes faced similar concerns with cattlemen who rented immense pastures on the territory's western plains. With the discovery of coal and oil in the territory in the 1890s, the rate of leasing increased dramatically, but as in Montana, tribal leaders had little success maintaining control over their economic "development." The best they could do was bargain for a larger share of the lessors' and developers' profits. The experience of other Plains tribes who engaged in leasing was the same: short-term income provided desperately needed cash for hungry tribesmen but did little to provide long-term economic security.

During the 1880s, energetic government programs to "civilize" the tribes usually accompanied increased economic activity. Not only did boarding schools become a regular feature of reservation life during this period (federal spending for Indian education rose from $75,000 in 1880 to over $2 million in 1895), but missionary efforts increased, local agents insisted on strict rules of conduct for their charges and Indian Office personnel invented new systems for administering and controlling native life. For example, in 1883 Congress authorized the establishment of Courts of Indian Offenses to ensure that tribesmen would adhere to the new regimen of working, attending school and avoiding traditional activities. At the same time both the Protestant Board of Indian Commissioners and the Catholic Board of Catholic Indian Missions worked to raise money for missionary work and to coordinate the efforts of different denominations and orders. Despite the sectarian tensions of the day, these organizations pursued a common commitment to Indian "uplift" and the eradication of tribal cultures. To Indians all these groups appeared as they did to the Crows: as outsiders who disrupted their lives but whose connections to American military power made them impossible to ignore.

The fullest expression of the American government's commitment to undermining the economic and cultural underpinnings of tribal life was the General Allotment Act, signed into law by President Grover Cleveland in February 1887. Anticipated by the allotment provisions of dozens of treaties, the new law gave the president the authority to direct the division of any reservation into individual landholdings. Following this process, the government would acquire the tribe's "surplus" lands for white settlers. As this program was being implemented among the Crows, it was also being imposed on tribes in the Great Lakes, the Dakotas, Oklahoma, the Northwest and parts of the Great Basin. When a final accounting of the law's impact was made in the 1930s, government officials estimated that the Allotment Act had brought about the transfer of over 90,000,000 acres of tribal land to non-Indian ownership.[9]

Plenty Coups could appear at Arlington in 1921 without endangering any of the arrangements non-Indian humanitarians or business interests had made regarding tribal life during the preceding forty years. Like the chief himself, Native Americans were confined and constricted to such an extent that they could not exert themselves militarily or seriously threaten the economies that surrounded their once-vast reservations. The power they had wielded a century earlier – either directly or simply by virtue of their occupation of vast, coveted resources – had now passed into the hands of other Americans. This power shift brought a fundamental change in white attitudes from hostility to sympathy.[10]

In the first decades of the twentieth century, the transition to a more benign view of native people occurred in a number of areas simultaneously. In popular life, for example, the Boy Scout movement (which began in the United States in 1910) incorporated Indian traditions and Indian lore into its rituals and made these subjects appealing to young people who could look forward to a future in which they would never be called to military duty as "Indian fighters." In the world of literature, the decade of the 1920s witnessed the popular and critical success of Oliver La Farge's *Laughing Boy*, a Pulitzer Prize–winning story of a struggling Indian artist and his wife caught between tradition and modernity. And among academics, anthropologist Franz Boas and his protégés, such as Robert Lowie and Ruth Benedict, gradually took control of their discipline, turning it dramatically away from older, evolutionary conceptions of Indians as people who lagged behind Europeans, to the modern academic concept of cultural pluralism. Under the influence of these new ideas, the enmity that had marked most encounters between the two races at the turn of the century was replaced by curiosity and sympathy.[11]

In the years immediately following Plenty Coups's appearance at Arlington, opportunities for the expression of new sympathy for Indians proliferated. A series of government investigations revealed the poverty and dislocation of native life in painful and undeniable detail. Government investigators revealed in 1909 that Indian communities suffered the highest incidence of tuberculosis in the United States, and similar studies in successive years told a similarly grim story regarding other infectious diseases: trachoma, smallpox and influenza. Despite this publicity, however, little was done; only sympathy increased. In 1923, the Committee of 100, appointed by the secretary of the interior (a group which included future Crow superintendent Robert Yellowtail), reported

[9] See Hoxie, *A Final Promise*; McDonnell, *The Dispossession of the American Indian*.

[10] Robert Berkhofer, *The White Man's Indian: Images of the American Indian from Columbus to the Present* (New York: Knopf, 1978), esp. 176.

[11] Ibid., 62–65, 104. On Boas and his students, see the many works of George Stocking, particularly, *Race, Culture and Evolution: Essays in the History of Anthropology* (New York: Free Press, 1968).

that "the great objectives of our benevolent desires have not been attained" and called – unsuccessfully – for increased appropriations for Indian health. Congress created a special investigations subcommittee early in 1928 to gather more information regarding the "condition of the Indians," and later that same year a privately financed study appeared.[12]

Directed by social scientist Lewis Meriam, and written by a team of nine experts who included Henry Roe Cloud, a Winnebago graduate of Yale, this study, published as *The Problem of Indian Administration*, contained data on health, education, economic development, social life and government programs. The results were shocking. For example, Meriam and his staff reported that the infant mortality rate among Indians in the 1920s was more than 190 per 1,000 births, higher than that for both whites (70.8) and blacks (114.1). They noted that native people suffered inordinately from pneumonia, measles and other diseases, but that the government spent only about 50 cents per person per year on health services. Looming over these grim figures were the twin demons of poverty and malnutrition. Nearly half of all Indians had an annual income of under $200, and the government's highly publicized boarding schools spent 11 cents per child per day for food.[13]

Plenty Coups could represent all of these threads. He had survived and flourished as a reservation leader by accommodating himself to government officials and local cattlemen while defending the interests of his local constituents. From the perspective of his hosts at Arlington the chief had demonstrated in his career that military resistance and political obstructionism could not be a part of contemporary native life. He was not an active Christian, but he had been baptized in the Catholic church and had agreed to the construction of schools near his Pryor home. He welcomed the endorsement of local politicians and was comfortable with both cash and rail travel. The audience at the Armistice ceremony could see from the old man's appearance and bearing that he was a Crow Indian, but they could also believe that he belonged to a generation that had made its peace with American expansion and was ready to give way to the demands of "civilization." They could see in Plenty Coups an image of a defeated and colonized people.

III

But what did Plenty Coups see in them? The chief's appearance at Arlington offered him an opportunity to demonstrate that Indian communities had persisted

[12] Francis Paul Prucha, *The Great Father: The United States Government and the American Indians* (Lincoln: University of Nebraska Press, 1984), vol. 2, 847–852. The Committee of 100's work is summarized in House Document 149, 68th Congress, 1st Session, Serial 8273.
[13] The Brookings Institution, Institute for Government Research, *The Problem of Indian Administration* (Baltimore: Johns Hopkins University Press, 1928).

into the twentieth century as viable political and cultural entities. In most reservation settings – as at Crow – the economic and political assaults of the 1880s were met with some form of resistance. Despite the expansion of power and influence that characterized the end of the nineteenth century, native people maintained their integrity – and even a measure of autonomy – through a variety of means ranging from noncooperation, to sabotage (several agents reported that Indians on their reservations followed the Crow practice of destroying surveyor's markers during allotment), to military resistance.

The Sword Bearer incident at Crow Agency was a relatively minor "uprising," but it was echoed in many other communities – in the resistance in Indian Territory led by Chitto Harjo and Redbird Smith, who fought against the forced allotment of their reservations, in the refusal of Geronimo and his followers to accept the rigors of reservation life and in the 1892 decision of Little Bear and his band of Chippewa-Crees to reject the sale of their lands in North Dakota for 10 cents per acre. (The group struck off across the plains on what would be a twenty-year search for a new home. They eventually settled on the Fort Assiniboin military reserve where Rocky Boy's Reservation was created in 1916.) The most dramatic example of native resistance during this period, however, was the Ghost Dance movement which began in 1889.[14]

Initiated in Nevada by a Paiute religious leader named Wovoka (or Jack Wilson), the Ghost Dance religion preached intertribal harmony, sobriety and a return to traditional lifeways. Following instructions received in a vision on New Year's Day, 1889, Wovoka called on his followers to perform a round dance to celebrate his message and to imitate the course of the sun. During 1889 and 1890 word of the prophet's message spread across the West, drawing delegations to his Utah home and widening his circle of influence. Among his most enthusiastic new followers were several groups from the Teton Sioux reservations of western South Dakota. There the fervor of the Ghost Dance movement mixed with resentment over recent forced land sales and the nervous overreactions of white officials to produce a tragic chain of events. First, on December 15, 1890, a group of tribal policemen killed Sitting Bull while attempting to arrest him for supporting the new movement. Two weeks later units of the Seventh Cavalry slaughtered 146 Minneconjou men, women and children at Wounded Knee Creek. Again the official explanation was that the Indians were ghost dancers.[15]

The Ghost Dance religion continued in Utah and elsewhere after the Sioux killings, and other examples of resistance to white authority appeared briefly at

[14] The story of the founding of Rocky Boy's Reservation is ably summarized in William L. Bryan Jr., *Montana's Indians: Yesterday and Today* (Helena: Montana Magazine, 1985), 72–74.
[15] Alice Beck Kehoe, *The Ghost Dance: Ethnohistory and Revitalization* (Fort Worth: Holt, Rinehart and Winston, 1989), provides a useful summary of the movement and an introduction to the literature on it.

other agencies. But the tragedies in South Dakota drove home to the Sioux, as well as to native people generally, the reality of American domination over their dwindling homelands. Despite the humanitarian outrage expressed by American citizens who were sickened by the Wounded Knee carnage, it was clear to Indian leaders – as it had been clear to Pretty Eagle, Spotted Horse and Plenty Coups at the time of the Sword Bearer incident – that direct opposition to government policy would be treated as a challenge to national power and be met with overwhelming force.[16]

In Indian communities across the country in the last decades of the nineteenth century, leaders inhabited a setting where economic change and government policy were constantly undermining their authority and where spasms of federal action provided a constant reminder that overt opposition was futile. At the same time, it was also apparent that within the boundaries of reservations there was a common need for social stability and peaceful administration. These needs created a common desire on the part of both Indians and government officials to sustain some form of indigenous leadership within the confines of the tribes' new homes. In this setting leaders arose who could maintain authority within their own communities while accommodating themselves to a new and oppressive environment. Thus, even though Plenty Coups could represent the defeat of Native Americans before the advancing power of national progress, his growing stature during the last decades of the century also reflected the rise of flexible and inventive political leaders who could offer their followers a measure of protection and political integrity in an extremely restrictive environment.

Each of the new reservation leaders of the 1890s came from a different cultural tradition, and few were as resilient or as creative as Plenty Coups, but as a group they shared his willingness to accept the reality of reservation boundaries and his commitment to defending a community that was emerging within the limits of a new homeland. They were not romantics seeking a return of the buffalo or a rollback of white settlement, but pioneering politicians who marked off an enclave within which they could preserve at least a portion of their community's traditions.

On the plains, Red Cloud among the Sioux and Quanah Parker of the Comanches typified this generation of leadership. Their rejection of violence and resistance to Indian Office authority often alienated them from both the government and their followers, but they tacked their way between the extremes of resistance and accommodation and largely sustained the loyalty of their communities. In the Northwest, the Nez Perce leader Archie Lawyer slowed the government's allotment efforts and struggled to make the best of the

---

[16] For an excellent discussion of the persistence of the Ghost Dance among the Kiowas, see Benjamin R. Kracht, "The Kiowa Ghost Dance, 1894–1916: An Unheralded Revitalization Movement," *Ethnohistory* 39 (1992), 452–477.

land sale agreements that were subsequently forced upon his tribe. Like his colleagues to the east, Lawyer rejected continued military resistance while looking for ways to preserve the autonomy of reservation leaders. In Oklahoma, intertribal conferences organized by leaders such as Pleasant Porter of the Creeks and James A. Norman of the Cherokees sought to blunt the drive towards a new, white-dominated state government by proposing to create a separate, Indian state called Sequoyah. The group succeeded in winning ratification of Sequoyah's state constitution in the fall of 1905, but Congress ignored their effort and abolished tribal governments in the new state of Oklahoma. Cupeño Indians in California suffered a similar defeat when they tried to win confirmation of their Mexican land titles by the federal judiciary. They pursued their struggle to the U.S. Supreme Court, but lost in 1901 when a majority of the justices declared in *Barker v. Harvey* that the group should have presented its complaint to the land commission created soon after California became a state.[17]

Significantly, these attempts to defend a distinctive tribal existence in a context of American expansion frequently relied on the instruments of "civilized" life for their success. The former Lakota war chief Red Cloud, for example, turned regularly to sympathetic whites for support and frequently used newspaper reporters and friendly platforms to appeal over the heads of local government officials in disputes with reservation authorities. These older leaders also allied themselves with young people of Robert Yellowtail's generation to pursue newer forms of action: legal injunctions, petitions and congressional lobbying. Increasingly in the new century, what these Indian politicians saw in government officials and massive crowds such as the ones that gathered on Armistice Day were not the hostile faces of their enemy, but the indifferent expressions of potential supporters.

In Mississippi, for example, sympathy aroused by publicity focused on Indian suffering during the 1918 influenza epidemic and subsequent investigations of desperate poverty among the state's scattered Choctaw communities,

---

[17] See James C. Olson, *Red Cloud and the Sioux Problem* (Lincoln: University of Nebraska Press, 1965); William T. Hagan, *Quanah Parker, Comanche Chief* (Norman: University of Oklahoma Press, 1993; E. Jane Gay, *With the Nez Perces: Alice Fletcher in the Field, 1889-1892*, edited, with an introduction by Frederick E. Hoxie and Joan T. Mark (Lincoln: University of Nebraska Press, 1981), xix–xxv; Angie Debo, *And Still the Waters Run: The Betrayal of the Five Civilized Tribes* (Princeton, NJ: Princeton University Press, 1940), 159–164; Edward D. Castillo, "The Impact of Euro-American Exploration and Settlement," *Handbook of North American Indians, Volume 8: California* (Washington, D.C.: Government Printing Office, 1978), 119–120.

For other examples of political leaders from this era, see Loretta Fowler, "Look at Me, My Hair is Grey," and Thomas R. Wessel, "Political Assimilation on the Blackfoot Indian Reservation, 1887-1934: A Study in Survival," both in Herman Viola and Douglas Ubelaker, eds., *Plains Indian Studies: A Collection of Essays in Honer of John C. Ewers and Wald R. Wedel* (Washington, D.C.: Smithsonian Institution Press, 1982), Smithsonian Contributions to Anthropology, no. 30, pp. 73–93, and 59–72.

together with energetic lobbying by both the tribe and its missionary support-ers, led to the creation of a reservation agency on lands the tribe had formally "ceded" to the United States nearly a century before. Other tribes followed the Crows' path to the U.S. Court of Claims. One of the most ambitious cases initiated before World War I came from the Sioux, who summoned representa-tives from all of the tribe's South Dakota reservations to the Cheyenne River Agency in 1911 to organize a campaign for the return of the Black Hills, seized following fraudulent treaty proceedings in 1876. The group formed a new organization, the Black Hills Treaty Council, hired an attorney and began a seventy-year struggle to restore the hills to Indian ownership. By World War I this kind of activity had produced more than thirty tribal claims before the courts; in 1926 the number of suits had grown so large that the Government Accounting Office created a special Tribal Claims Section to prepare the finan-cial analyses the cases required.[18]

Like their white contemporaries, Indian advocates also turned to formal political organizations to defend tribal and regional interests. In 1912, a conven-tion of delegates from the Haida, Tlingit and Tshimshian communities formed the Alaskan Native Brotherhood to lobby on behalf of the protection of native resources as well as to oppose segregation and discrimination in the territory's schools and businesses. The new organization (quickly joined by the Alaskan Native Sisterhood) was originally sponsored by Presbyterian missionaries, but it rapidly moved beyond social events and religious activities to engage a wide variety of public issues. The Black Hills Treaty Council also transcended its early interest in the Court of Claims. Lead by James Crow Feather, a young, bespectacled boarding school graduate from the Cheyenne River Reservation, the treaty council took up a host of related issues involving reservation govern-ance and cultural freedom.

In New Mexico, another legal challenge to an apparent land seizure served as a rallying point for a group of disparate tribal communities. The boundaries of Pueblo lands in the Rio Grande valley had never been clearly established following the American victory over Mexico in 1848, and this failing had encouraged settlers to ignore native titles and squat on Indian land. Responding to this illegal settlement, the Pueblo communities organized a collective effort to clarify their deeds. Because they were nominally Christian and held their land under fee simple Spanish titles, however, the American courts had tradi-tionally viewed the Pueblos as citizens rather than dependent Indians. The

[18] See Clara Sue Kidwell, "The Choctaw Struggle for Land and Identity in Mississippi, 1830–1918," in Samuel J. Wells and Roseanna Tubby, eds., *After Removal: The Choctaw in Mississippi* (Jackson: University Press of Mississippi, 1986), 64–93; Edward Lazarus, *Black Hills, White Justice: The Sioux Nation Versus the United States, 1775 to the Present* (New York: HarperCollins, 1991); and Harvey D. Rosenthal, "Indian Claims and the American Conscience: A Brief History of the Indian Claims Commission," in Imre Sutton, ed., *Irredeemable America: The Indians' Estate and Land Claims* (Albuquerque: University of New Mexico Press, 1985), 35–71.

Indians' appeal, therefore, was for recognition of themselves as tribal communities, a status that would trigger federal assistance. Their 1913 victory in the
Supreme Court in *U.S. v. Sandoval* further strengthened their intergroup ties
and led in 1922 to the formation of the All Pueblo Council. During these same
years, tribal leaders in Indian Territory continued to organize resistance to
white expansion following the abolition of their reservations and the admission
of Oklahoma to the Union. Among the Cherokees, a conservative religious
group called the Keetoowah Society urged passive resistance and the revival of
old town-square grounds modeled on nineteenth-century ceremonial centers.
Among the Creeks, Chitto Harjo led a similar movement which tried to disrupt
and sabotage the allotment process. U.S. officials harassed and jailed leaders in
both tribes, but resistance continued, fueling opposition to the government's
"civilization" campaign.[19]

A short-lived national version of these early intertribal organizations made
clear the connections Indian leaders maintained with influential non-Indians
and the extent to which Native American arguments regarding their rights were
modeled on the American majority's political ideas. In 1911 a group of educated
Indians and their white supporters organized the Society of American Indians
on the campus of Ohio State University. Membership in the society was limited
to native people, but whites were recruited as "associates," and most of the
organization's activities took place away from Indian reservations. The society
established a journal (*Quarterly Journal*, 1913–15; *American Indian Magazine*,
1915–20) and opened a Washington office. It lobbied successfully on behalf of
the creation of a special court of claims for Indians and improved health care on
the reservations, but it was weakened by divisive religious issues, differences
over the future of the Indian Office, and its failure to win a significant following
among local tribal leaders. Despite its demise in the 1920s, however, the group
brought together a growing cadre of educated, middle-class Indian leaders, such
as Charles A. Eastman (Sioux), Carlos Montezuma (Yavapai), Gertrude Bonnin
(Sioux), Sherman Coolidge (Arapahoe), Laura Cornelius (Oneida) and Arthur
C. Parker (Seneca), and demonstrated some of what was possible in a national
organization.[20]

The advent of the Society of American Indians and the success of groups like

[19] See Willard Rollings, "The Pueblos of New Mexico and the Protection of Their Land and Water
    Rights," in John R. Wunder, ed., *Working the Range: Essays on the History of Western Land
    Management and the Environment* (Westport, Conn.: Greenwood, 1985), 3–24; Sidney L. Harring,
    *Crow Dog's Case: American Indian Sovereignty, Tribal Law, and United States Law in the Nine-
    teenth Century* (Cambridge University Press, 1994), chap. 3; and Debo, *And Still the Waters Run*,
    chap. 5. For a similar group in the Pacific Northwest, the Northwest Federation of American
    Indians, see Frank W. Porter III, "Without Reservation: Federal Indian Policy and the Landless
    Tribes of Washington," in George Pierre Castile and Robert L. Bee, eds., *State and Reservation:
    New Perspectives on Federal Indian Policy* (Tucson: University of Arizona Press, 1992), 110–136.
[20] See Hazel W. Hertzberg, *The Search for an American Indian Identity: Modern Pan-Indian Move-
    ments* (Syracuse, N.Y.: Syracuse University Press, 1971).

the Black Hills Treaty Council not only suggests another area where the experience of the Crows overlapped with other tribes, but it makes clear what a leader like Plenty Coups would have seen in a gathering such as the one at Arlington Cemetery. Men like James Crow Feather argued that the Sioux could reverse their 1876 defeat in court, just as Robert Yellowtail, Russell White Bear, James Carpenter and George Washington Hogan had asserted that the Crows could win compensation for lands lost in 1868 or win a fair return for the rental of their reservation pasture lands. Both groups understood that future success required both a sophisticated grasp of non-Indian institutions and the sympathy of powerful politicians. The decade which saw the formation of the Alaskan Native Brotherhood and the Society of American Indians, as well as the Pueblo victory in the Supreme Court, was the decade of the Crows' struggle to establish a new form of tribal governance, hire an attorney and defend their reservation against homesteaders. Each of these struggles pitted community leaders against outsiders; all of them were successful when the tribe was unified, prepared and speaking a language understandable to legislators and bureaucrats.

At the turn of the century many observers had expected that the scale and brutality of the assault on Indian communities would soon destroy the nation's indigenous cultures. With native lands and resources transformed into commodities the white man could buy or lease, native traditions outlawed or debased, resistance broken and so many native leaders destroyed, it seemed that the continent's indigenous people were entering a period of social and economic domination. Between 1900 and World War I, the Crows had demonstrated the error of such expectations. Even though domination by outsiders took place on an unprecedented scale, these newcomers neither stripped away all the tribe's cultural supports, nor witnessed its extinction. As the death rate declined and communities formed at Pryor, Bighorn and Lodge Grass, tribal members began to see that the community would survive and grow. By World War I, the Crow population was on the upswing, and tribal leaders had begun to lobby for additional allotments to accommodate the hundreds of new births that were taking place among them.

Just as the Crow population decline ended after 1900 and the community began to grow, so the national Indian population gradually expanded in the first decades of the twentieth century. While not every tribe could imitate the Crows' tightly-knit district communities with their clan relations and religious societies, most groups experienced a decline in mortality along with a surprisingly resilient pattern of family life. Communities such as the Hopi, who lived an ordered existence in their multifamily dwellings, sustained most of their ancient social traditions as their population began to recover. Other tribes with a history of intermarriage and flexibility – such as the Ojibwes of Minnesota – maintained these distinctive patterns and experienced a rapid upsurge in population. Over time large-scale intermarriage and migration might undermine a group's coherence and continuity, but in the early twentieth century most American tribes could look back on the assaults of the late nineteenth century and announce that they had survived.[21]

Standing before a vast audience in 1921, an Indian leader like Plenty Coups not only would be looking for potential allies, but also would be demonstrating his own survival. Despite the narrowness of the role prescribed for him, the Crow chief – like similar representatives from other tribes – would be able to show that his language, his values and his community had emerged from the disease and dislocation of the previous generation and could be identified as reflecting a community tied to a continuous cultural tradition.

One of the most distinctive elements of that tradition was religion, and the Crow chief's decision to offer the audience a prayer reflected the fact that this aspect of tribal life was frequently the most recognizable and the most appealing to non-Indians. In fact the religious changes that occurred among the Crows in the first decades of the new century were broadly consistent with those taking place in other Indian communities. Native Americans had long insisted that "religion" and daily life were closely intertwined. As a consequence, there are several points in the histories of most native peoples when political crises have inspired new religious leaders and new rituals. It should not be surprising, then, that the accelerating assault on Indian communities in the 1880s and 1890s helped institute a variety of new religious forms.

The most dramatic innovation began sometime after December 1881, when two rail lines entered Laredo, Texas. From the east, the Texas–Mexican line connected the dusty, Rio Grande town to the gulf port of Corpus Christi. As it cut across southern Texas, the new railroad passed through part of the small area where peyote (*L. williamsii*) will grow in North America. While this east–west road was being completed, Laredo became the southern terminus of a rail line running north to Austin, Texas, and on to Indian Territory. For the first time, peyote buttons, which had been used in religious rituals in the Rio Grande valley for centuries, could be transported cheaply and in bulk to tribes living outside their immediate area of cultivation.[22]

Soon after the rail lines were complete, reports of peyote use in Oklahoma began to proliferate. There, as among the Crows, the "peyote religion" had many elements that suited it to modern Indian life. It was portable, because it focused on the peyote button and did not depend on a specific place or community for its power. It promised to restore the health of participants both through

[21] For a summary of the evidence to support these assertions, see Frederick E. Hoxie, Richard A. Sattler and Nancy Shoemaker, "Reports of the American Indian Family History Project," *Occasional Papers Series*, Vol. 9 (Chicago: Newberry Library, 1992).

[22] Peyote also reached Oklahoma from the Southwest via individual travellers and traders. Quanah Parker apparently obtained the plant from Apaches prior to 1880. See William T. Hagan, *Quanah Parker, Comanche Chief* (Norman: University of Oklahoma Press, 1993), 52.

the ritual itself and through group sanctions against alcohol use. The new rite could also be explained to whites. Peyotists emphasized the Christian-like aspects of their faith (Jesus frequently appeared in prayers and visions) and conducted their "church" business in their new common language, English. At the same time, the peyote ritual had an unmistakable Indianness: it included drumming and singing in the native language, it lasted through an entire night, it was egalitarian, and its object was communion with an unseen, but immediate, spiritual world.

The appeal and mobility of the peyote ritual was unprecedented. Between 1900 and 1920, while the religious use of peyote was becoming common among the Crow and their neighbors, the Northern Cheyennes and Wyoming Shoshones, it was also moving north from Oklahoma to the Winnebagos of Nebraska and Wisconsin and the Ojibwes of Minnesota and west to Taos Pueblo and the Utes of Utah. As at Crow, the peyote ritual in these communities was led by "road men" who trained others to assist them in their work. This first generation of leaders – John Rave among the Winnebagos, Jim Blue Bird among the Sioux and Lorenzo Martinez at Taos Pueblo – were formidable advocates for the new religion. They posed no military threat to U.S. officials, and they accepted most of the Indian Office's regulations concerning the adoption of Anglo-American lifeways. But as they pursued their calling to spread the faith, they began to form a powerful new infrastructure of Native American leadership.

Just as the peyotists among the Crows were challenged by rival groups such as the Baptists of Lodge Grass and Plenty Coups's own followers at Pryor, so other believers on other reservations fell into conflict with both missionaries and defenders of traditional rituals. They responded to these attacks by turning to the American Constitution and the protections it offered against religious persecution. As Comanche leader Quanah Parker told a group of Oklahoma lawmakers who were considering a ban on peyote use, "I do not think this Legislature should interfere with a man's religion. . . ." He repeated this argument frequently during the next two decades, and certainly inspired – although he did not live to see – the 1918 incorporation of the Native American church in Oklahoma, an organization formed "to foster and promote the religious belief. . . in the Christian religion with the practice of the Peyote Sacrament . . . and to teach . . . morality, sobriety, industry, kindly charity and right living. . . ."[23]

The rapid rise of the peyote faith among the Crows and other tribes provides the most dramatic example of religious reorganization among Indian peoples in the first decades of the twentieth century, but it was by no means unique. In

[23] Quoted in Omer Stewart, *Peyote Religion: A History* (Norman: University of Oklahoma Press, 1987) 75, 224.

virtually every Indian community, native leaders attempted to understand their new reservation conditions in religious terms. The ghost dance, for example, which had continued to draw followers even after the killing at Wounded Knee, provided a coherent religious solution to recent events for many groups. During the first two decades of the twentieth century, Jack Wilson continued to sell the red paint which was emblematic of his vision to followers across the Great Basin and Great Plains, and to repeat his message of peace, hard work and sobriety. Among the Indians who persisted in following him were the Kiowas, Comanches and Pawnees of Oklahoma, Sioux groups in Saskatchewan and Shoshone people in Wyoming.[24]

In the Pacific Northwest, two similar visionary movements – the Dreamers and the Indian Shaker church – rose to new levels of influence, offering reservation residents a new kind of hope. While their practitioners could trace these movements' origins to a tradition of regional prophets that had begun long before the arrival of Europeans, twentieth-century Dreamers and the Shakers each began with a new, founding vision. The Dreamers were plateau people, followers of Smoholla (1815?–1895) and Skolaskin (1839–1922); the Shaker church was founded in Puget Sound by a Squaxin man named Squsachtun, or John Slocum (1842–97). Each of these leaders called on his followers to join into congregations of hard-working, sober believers.

Both Smohalla and Skolaskin rejected the Christian and agricultural features of the government's assimilation program. Instead they advocated the preservation of traditional subsistence practices – gathering and fishing – and the adoption of an ascetic, contemplative life. Despite their peaceful message, however, both dreamer prophets and their followers were actively suppressed by federal authorities. Skolaskin was imprisoned at the federal penitentiary at Alcatraz between 1889 and 1892 for subverting reservation discipline, but he returned to the Colville Reservation following his release and continued to criticize both private land ownership and Christianity. By the turn of the century, various forms of the Dreamer faith, often called the Longhouse or Feather religion, had spread across the interior Northwest and were forming both a formidable buttress for native values and a remarkable vehicle for the preservation of native leadership.[25]

John Slocum's vision was pointedly Christian, for it taught that sinners would go to Hell and pious practitioners of the new faith would ascend to Heaven. Also like the Christian missionaries who surrounded them (and the peyotists who were spreading across the plains), Slocum's followers dispatched

[24] See Kehoe, *The Ghost Dance*, chaps. 3 and 4.
[25] Robert H. Ruby and John A. Brown, *Dreamer-Prophets of the Columbia Plateau: Smohalla and Skolaskin* (Lincoln: University of Nebraska Press, 1989).

teachers to surrounding Puget Sound communities. In time, the group also adopted a hierarchy of bishops and priests.[26]

Both the Crows and other Indians also sustained a variety of tribal rituals during the early twentieth century, despite federal bans on the plains sun dance, vision quests, and other forms of native ceremony. Reservation communities continued to value ancient wisdom and to revere elders who had special religious power. Just as Plenty Coups and Medicine Crow pleaded for permission to continue the "harmless" beaver dance, other leaders defended a version of the sun dance that did not include self-torture. In this form the ritual actually spread during this period, moving west to the Utes and Shoshones in Utah and Idaho. In the Southwest as well, other tribes upheld traditions they could defend as inoffensive or purely "cultural."[27]

In the early twentieth century, Native Americans in general, like the Crow residents of Lodge Grass, Black Lodge and St. Xavier, also took part in Christian worship in growing numbers. Indian pastors, such as Philip Deloria among the Sioux, the Nez Perce Billy Williams (who visited the Crows on several occasions) and the many native leaders among the Oklahoma Creeks and Cherokees reaffirmed indigenous values in the context of the white man's faith. They preached the teachings of Jesus, but accepted the existence of distinct Indian communities and encouraged the formation of Indian lay organizations, women's clubs, and service groups. Perhaps the most famous example of this position was the Sioux holy man Black Elk, who labored as a Catholic catechist while struggling to understand a dramatic, youthful vision that formed the basis for his widely read autobiography.[28]

Running close to these religious inventions, survivals and accommodations in the first two decades of the twentieth century were a variety of cultural innovations. Expressed differently and with varying intensity in different places, these expressions of traditional values were apparent in virtually every reservation community in the country. Elsewhere, as at Crow, traditional dance gatherings, pow-wows, community celebrations and tribal fairs allowed groups to gather in explicitly secular settings that local whites would find acceptable. The result was the emergence of a range of "Indian" activities that both reinforced local affiliations and forged new ties among native groups. The grass dance, for

---

[26] Pamela T. Amoss, "The Indian Shaker Church," in Wayne Suttles, ed., *Handbook of North American Indians*, Volume 7: *Northwest Coast* (Washington, D.C.: Government Printing Office, 1990), 633–639.

[27] See Joseph G. Jorgensen, *The Sun Dance Religion: Power for the Powerless* (Chicago: University of Chicago Press, 1972); and Fred W. Voget, *The Shoshone–Crow Sundance* (Norman: University of Oklahoma Press, 1984).

[28] See Raymond J. DeMallie, *The Sixth Grandfather: Black Elk's Teachings Given to John G. Neihardt* (Lincoln: University of Nebraska Press, 1984); and Michael F. Steltenkamp, *Black Elk: Holy Man of the Oglala* (Norman: University of Oklahoma Press, 1993).

example, which in the nineteenth century had been the property of Pawnee and Omaha warriors, was appropriated by Teton Sioux and other Plains Indian communities and made a central feature of intertribal gatherings. Practitioners of the new dance also adopted the Omaha's deer-hair head roaches and feather bustles which quickly became the mark of a "traditional" Indian dancer across the American and Canadian plains. Both of these innovations appeared among the Crows in the 1890s and were a common element in Plains Indian gatherings by the turn of the century.[29]

The grass dance was frequently performed at gatherings called by the government. Assembled to celebrate the Fourth of July, for example, Indian people would win permission to "honor" their national government with a dance. Carrying over the tradition of the warrior societies that had inspired the original dance, the grass dancers also used these occasions to provide for the needy in their communities with generous distributions of food and clothing. Other activities quickly ensued: dancing and drumming competitions, visits from (and return visits to) distant tribes, women's and children's dances and displays of traditional crafts. All of this activity was amplified by rail and automobile transport and encouraged whenever the events occurred near a tourist center.[30]

In the Southwest, tourists riding the Santa Fe Railroad or venturing along the nation's expanding highway system encountered tribal ceremonies that were clearly religious but which were either partially Christian or practiced by groups that were so small and isolated that they were deemed harmless. The Hopi snake dance and the seasonal dances among the Rio Grande pueblos attracted curious visitors and were publicized by local boosters and such magazines as Charles Lummis's Los Angeles–based *Land of Sunshine*. In Tucson, colorful dances performed by refugee Yaquis from Mexico played a central role in reconstituting their religious life in their new homeland and served as an instrument for winning over a cadre of local supporters. Their dramatic performances celebrated the major events in the Christian calendar while appeasing traditional religious deities.[31]

Because the first decades of the twentieth century were marked by religious,

---

[29] William K. Powers, "Plains Indian Music and Dance," in W. R. Wood and Margot Liberty, *Anthropology on the Great Plains* (Lincoln: University of Nebraska Press, 1980), 212–229. For an elaboration of the ways in which cultural celebrations can form the basis for a modern community's identity, see Morris W. Foster, *Being Comanche: A Social History of an American Indian Community* (Tucson: University of Arizona Press, 1991).

[30] For an effective overview of this history, see Thomas W. Kavanagh, "Southern Plains Dance: Tradition and Dynamics," in Charlotte Heth, ed., *Native American Dance: Ceremonies and Social Traditions* (Washington, D.C.: National Museum of the American Indian and Starwood Publishing, 1992), 105–124.

[31] See Marc Simmons, "History of the Pueblos Since 1821," *Handbook of North American Indians, Volume 9: The Southwest* (Washington, D.C.: Government Printing Office, 1979), 206–223; and Edward Spicer, *The Yaquis: A Cultural History* (Tucson: University of Arizona Press, 1980), 243–245.

cultural and political reorganization and revival among Indian communities generally as well as among the Crows, one can imagine that Plenty Coups saw in his audience at Arlington an opportunity to enact simultaneously a number of features of modern Indian life. Because the Crows had pioneered many of the innovations other tribes adopted, and because their experiences were shared by other reservation communities, the old chief could show himself as a successful political leader, a symbol of Indian survival and a representative of an array of religious and cultural traditions. By stepping forward onto the stage at Arlington he enacted the elements of modern Indian nationalism in North America. When Plenty Coups stood before the public, he represented the image of a defeated warrior while he also exemplified the emergence of a new political and cultural self-consciousness among a native people.

Nevertheless, despite his prominence, Plenty Coups's position as a representative of American Indian "nations" at the 1921 Armistice Day ceremony was not understood by his audience to equal that of Marshall Foch or the Mikado's generals. For while considerable political and cultural energy had been expended to produce leaders like the warrior from Pryor, neither he nor his community could exert significant economic or political power in the United States. While his presence signaled that there had been a substantial reorganization of tribal communities in the early twentieth century, his tiny, ritual role also indicated that few steps had been taken towards a reconstruction of the Native Americans' material existence.

In the business world the assaults of the 1880s and 1890s continued into the twentieth century, as did the rising cost of participating in national economic life. As the Crows had learned through the fiasco of their irrigation project and their efforts to farm their reservation, the period from 1900 to 1920 marked the end of rural self-sufficiency throughout most of North America and the final shift of the United States to an urban, industrial economy. The only role available to Crows and other Indians in this new setting was a peripheral and dependent one.

The economic suffering experienced by Native Americans in an age of relative national prosperity was the direct result of government action. In the early twentieth century, for example, the allotment act came to dominate the economic lives of most Indians in the United States. In addition to producing a direct loss of more than 90 million acres through the sale of "surplus" tribal lands, the severalty act pushed Indian people onto small homesteads which they frequently lost once they had received title to them in fee simple. These titles, called fee patents, gave individuals full ownership of their lands, making the property vulnerable to local property taxes and exposing its owners to the entreaties of land speculators and creditors. The practice of issuing these patents to native landowners grew increasingly popular with government officials during the early twentieth century, reaching its peak between 1915 and 1920 when more than 20,000 Indians were forced to accept fee patents to their land, more than twice the number that had been issued since the original adoption of the Allotment Act in 1887. (The fact that the Crows were able to hold off these assaults until the 1920s meant that their situation was different in degree, but not in kind, from that faced by other allotted tribes.)[32]

Like the Crows, other tribes also learned that participation in the white man's economy was an increasingly expensive proposition. If they were to generate profits, for example, Indian crops needed to be produced in large quantities, sold on the open market and delivered to distant customers. Unfortunately, most reservations remained remote from the nation's transportation system, and most Indian farmers did not have access to the machinery, technical expertise and large landholdings needed to produce competitively priced crops. Even Indians with fertile and well-situated land, such as the Yakimas in central Washington state and the Papago residents of irrigated reserves in southern Arizona, were encouraged to join the Crows in leasing their property to whites. By 1920 the Indians who still farmed their reservation lands had little opportunity to produce above the level of subsistence; participation in the larger, market economy was a forgotten dream.

On other reservations as at Crow, ranching frequently appeared to offer Indian communities the most promising opportunities for economic well-being. Cattle and sheep ranching lent themselves to communal effort, and they were ideally suited to the isolation characteristic of many reservations. Nevertheless, during the early years of the twentieth century Indian ranching was marked by repeated failure. White competitors aggressively captured available water and ignored reservation boundaries, so even accomplished ranching communities, such as the Papagos of southern Arizona or the Arapahoes of Wyoming, found it impossible to run profitable herds on their land. On the northern Plains, the Crow pattern was typical. Large non-Indian ranching interests, larger than E. L. Dana or Frank Heinrich, men with ready cash at hand and good contacts in the Indian Office, leased large tracts of reservation land. Ed Lemmon, for example, leased (and fenced) an 865,000-acre area on the Standing Rock Sioux Reservation in 1902. Other cattlemen made similar arrangements at the Rosebud Agency in South Dakota and at Montana's Fort Peck.[33]

In the Pacific Northwest, fishing and farming offered the only viable forms of economic activity, but here too federal actions limited native communities to subsistence-level enterprises and wage labor. Unable to protect their legal right to the region's catch, or to gain access to the capital necessary for industrial fishing, native people in the Northwest were largely confined to manual labor

---

[32] See McDonnell, *The Dispossession of the American Indian*, chaps. 7–9.

[33] See Peter Iverson, *When Indians Became Cowboys: Native Peoples and Cattle Ranching in the American West* (Norman: University of Oklahoma Press, 1994), chaps. 4 and 5; McDonnell, The *Dispossession of the American Indian*, chap. 3.

on farms and in white-owned canneries. Inland areas offered little beyond seasonal employment in the rapidly expanding hops fields and apple orchards. Indian labor gangs moved through Washington, Oregon and British Columbia, just as Crow cowboys worked the local ranches. In neither case did wages relieve the employees' marginal status in the region's economy.[34]

In the Southwest, Navajo sheep herds offered yet another example of a native industry limited by policy to subsistence-level activity. While the Navajo adoption of sheep from the Spanish in the eighteenth century is a mark of cultural innovation, desperate conditions on their vast Arizona and New Mexico reservation meant that Navajos had no opportunity to consider the commercial development of their "crop." Moreover, the government's desire to individualize and "civilize" the Navajo (even though allotment was limited to only a few districts on the reserve) foreclosed any discussion of a communal herd or enterprise. As a result, the image of patient Navajo herders and their expanding herds is one that reflects a local survival strategy rather than engagement in a commercial enterprise.

One area where Navajos did engage in a new commercial venture during the first decades of the new century was in the sale of blankets and silver jewelry. The arrival of the railroad on the reservation (in 1881) and the rising demand for native handicrafts promised an expanding market and escalating prices. Like the Crows, Navajo people quickly adapted to a new commercial opportunity. During the 1880s and 1890s they shifted from mutton to wool production and from small- to large-scale jewelry making. In 1870 there were 3 trading posts on Navajo land; by 1920 there were 144. But Navajo workers – like Crow ranchers – profited little from the growing market. Traders controlled marketing through their access to transportation, and they eliminated competition by holding federally issued licenses. A free market in handicrafts would have run counter to the government's "civilization" program, which was based on the assumption that Indians were "dependent people." In handicrafts as in sheep, cattle, fish and grain, then, native communities demonstrated an ability to function within a market economy, but did not gain the power that would enable them to compete with non-Indians.[35]

In the decades before Plenty Coups's appearance at Arlington Cemetery, the Crows and other tribes in North America began the process of recreating the religious, cultural and political institutions that the Americans had attacked during the assaults of the nineteenth century. In an age of great hardship, they

---

[34] See Daniel Boxberger, *To Fish in Common: The Ethnohistory of Lummi Salmon Fishing* (Lincoln: University of Nebraska Press, 1989), chaps. 2 and 3; and Mourning Dove, *Mourning Dove: A Salishan Autobiography*, Jay Miller, ed. (Lincoln: University of Nebraska Press, 1990).

[35] See Robert S. McPherson, "Naalyehe Ba Hoogan – 'House of Merchandise': The Navajo Trading Post as an Institution of Cultural Change: 1900–1930," *American Indian Culture and Research Journal*, 16 (1992), 23–42.

adapted to institutions and lifeways introduced from the outside, invented new forms of their own and resisted coercive policies when possible. In the process, they laid the foundations for a new version of Indian culture in the twentieth century. The chief's role in the Armistice Day ceremony offered him an opportunity to demonstrate and enact this fact of native survival before a huge crowd. The occasion did not allow him to demonstrate his independence, nor did it provide the Pryor leader with a chance to show off his considerable individual talent. The victory inscribed in his brief appearance on the world's stage could not extend very far beyond symbolism.

IV

But the symbolism embedded in Plenty Coups's appearance extended beyond the realm of Indian affairs. Anthropologists Jean and John Comaroff have written that "colonizers everywhere try to gain control over the practices through which would-be subjects produce and reproduce the bases of their existence . . . and colonization always provokes struggles – albeit often tragically uneven ones – over power and meaning on the frontiers of empire. It is a process of 'challenge and riposte'. . . ." Viewed from their perspective, the Crow chief's performance at Arlington can best be understood not only as a happening with two interpretations, but as an episode in the continuing "challenge and riposte" of Indian–white relations. Indeed, the struggle between Plenty Coups's and his audience's understanding of the event – and, by extension, the parallel struggles that occurred throughout both Crow history and the histories of Indian communities across the country – might best be understood as part of a larger contest over the consequences of colonial rule. It is an incident in which Plenty Coups and his audience might be seen as engaged in "produc[ing] and reproduc[ing] the bases for their existence." This process of cultural production was surely different in the United States than it was in South Africa (the focus of the Comaroffs' study), but the process of resistance and accommodation to colonial rule on the two continents was similar; so much so in fact that the anthropologists' summary description of African colonialism resonates with the experiences of the Crow chief and his tribal homeland: "a long battle over for the possession of salient signs and symbols, a bitter, drawn out contest of conscience and consciousness."[36]

During Plenty Coups's lifetime, the United States had grown from being a rural nation of less than 30 million people to an urban, industrialized society

---

[36] Jean Comaroff and John Comaroff, *Of Revelation and Revolution: Christianity, Colonialism, and Consciousness in South Africa* (Chicago: University of Chicago Press, 1991) Vol. 1, 5, 4. See also George Pierre Castile, "Indian Sign: Hegemony and Symbolism in Federal Indian Policy," in Castile and Bee, *State and Reservation*, 165–186.

with more than 100 million citizens. While immigration had been a constant feature of national life throughout the nineteenth century (the foreign-born portion of the population remained at just under 15% of the total), the country's rapid growth required a flood of immigrants in order to maintain that stable presence. Immigration authorities recorded more than 23 million new arrivals in the United States between 1880, when the Crow chief had first visited Washington, and the year of his appearance at Arlington. As a consequence, the crowds that massed to recognize the Unknown Soldier contained more immigrants than at any time in American history. Native-born citizens were joined by people who had only recently been peasants in Ireland, Germany, Scandinavia, Eastern Europe, Italy, Greece, China, Japan and Mexico.[37]

Historians have differed over the extent to which the immigrant population of the United States changed during these years of massive migration. Contemporary observers, often inspired by bigotry and Anglo-Saxon chauvinism, emphasized the exotic quality of the "new" immigrants from southern and eastern Europe. In the first decade of the twentieth century, these nativists employed negative descriptions of recent, non-Anglo-Saxon arrivals to launch a massive campaign aimed at closing the country's traditional open door to potential new citizens. Their efforts bore fruit with the passage of restrictive immigration laws in the early 1920s. Almost immediately following that campaign, however, scholars began pointing out the consistency of the immigrant presence in national life and the relatively minor observable differences in immigrant background and aspiration over the decades. This debate continues, but both sides would agree that the immigrants who arrived in the United States during the generation before 1920 were drawn from a uniquely wide array of homelands. Unlike Brazil, which drew virtually all of its 3 million immigrants after 1880 from Italy, Spain and Portugal, or Canada, which attracted a like number primarily from Great Britain, the United States contained no single group that could account for more than 17% of its new residents; in fact, it took eight groups to account for 75% of the American total. The American migrants were also increasingly unskilled and destined to labor in the nation's burgeoning industrial cities. Unlike the farmers and craftsmen lured to Australia and Argentina to develop their vast, uncultivated prairies, newcomers to the United States were recruited for its factories, mines and industrial farms.[38]

The new legions of immigrants who made their way to America's industrial cities in the decades before 1930 and found themselves adjusting not only to a unique universe of ethnic groups, but also to some of the 2 million African-Americans who had recently migrated there from the states of the former

---

[37] See Roger Daniels, *Coming to America: A History of Immigration and Ethnicity in American Life* (New York: HarperCollins, 1990), 121–126; and Thomas J. Archdeacon, *Becoming American: An Ethnic History* (New York: Free Press, 1983), 112–142.
[38] Archdeacon, *Becoming American*, 115–135.

Confederacy. Driven by a desire to escape the peonage and oppression that characterized the Jim Crow era, black migrants frequently had to overcome the active opposition of their southern landlords and employers in order to leave. Nevertheless, they persisted and, aided by crop failures in the years just prior to World War I and the wartime boom that ensued, their numbers increased in northern cities. By 1930 more than 20% of the nation's African-American population was living outside of the South, most in urban areas.[39]

Chinese and Japanese immigrants represented a relatively small portion of the tide of newcomers – about 300,000 individuals – but their concentration along the West Coast and in urban areas made them unusually visible and vulnerable. In 1910 more than half of all Chinese lived in cities of over 100,000, while 85% of all Japanese in the country lived in states bordering on the Pacific. Because both groups were early victims of discrimination – America's first immigration restriction law, the Chinese Exclusion Act, was passed in 1882 – they were quick to organize mutual benevolent societies and form themselves into tightly knit communities. The Chinese Exclusion Act prevented that largely male immigrant community from evolving into a stable, self-generating social entity before 1930, but Japanese communities developed farms and fishing enterprises that functioned successfully in the regional economy.[40]

Rail lines reached Albuquerque, New Mexico, from the east in 1880, at about the same time that they were entering eastern Montana. Within a decade, regional spur routes had made possible the opening of coal mines in southern Colorado, timber mills in northern Arizona, large corporate farms devoted to sugar beets and ranches that could now ship their sheep and cattle to stockyards and processing plants in Kansas City and Chicago. These new enterprises drew Hispanic villagers from the old agricultural towns of the Rio Grande valley as well as north from Mexico. Because the international border was not patrolled until 1924, it is impossible to know the exact size of the Mexican migration; most estimates put it at less than 500,000. Nevertheless, the industrialization of the Southwest began a process of population movement that was to continue for the rest of the century. A similar combination of industrial development and new transportation lines also drew more than 800,000 French Canadians across the northern border and into the farms and factories of New York and Massachusetts.[41]

Each of these shifts in population added to the diversity of American life. Despite the many aspects of this history that remain in dispute or unexamined,

---

[39] See Joe William Trotter Jr., ed., *The Great Migration in Historical Perspective: New Dimensions of Race, Class, and Gender* (Bloomington: Indiana University Press, 1991).

[40] Daniels, *Coming to America*, 238–258.

[41] Sarah Deutsch, *No Separate Refuge: Culture, Class, and Gender on an Anglo-Hispanic Frontier in the American Southwest, 1880–1940* (New York: Oxford University Press, 1987), 19–40; Archdeacon, *Becoming American*, 129–130; and Daniels, *Coming to America*, 258–264.

all who have studied it would agree with historian Thomas Archdeacon that the "basic effect of the new immigration was to increase dramatically the heterogeneity of the American population and to make the relationship between its elements enormously complex." Because the groups arrived in large numbers but served industries and institutions they did not control, the multiplying encounters between newcomers and citizens also set off a broad and persistent concern with the nature of membership in American society. "Many Americans," Archdeacon observed dryly, "were troubled by this developing situation. They did not see it as the fulfillment of the nations's destiny but as a threatening departure from the social and cultural homogeneity necessary for unity and stability."[42]

Racial and ethnic conflict thus became a central focus of American politics in the years when the number of new immigrants was on the rise and the nation's cities appeared to have become both chaotic and un-American. New groups struggled to establish their presence within communities controlled by long-time residents, while business leaders and government officials worked to control and administer a rapidly growing set of national institutions. Not surprisingly, then, during the same years when government-sponsored missionaries and school teachers were instructing Crow and other Indian children in the habits of "civilization," voices were rising in Congress and the press calling for restrictions on immigration, for "civics" lessons to teach children uniform standards of patriotism and for more rigorous limits on the granting of citizenship. In the streets these voices were frequently less temperate, as racist, antisemitic and nativist organizations found new members and pressed for more stringent forms of segregation and discrimination.

In this increasingly diverse and contentious environment, ethnic and racial communities responded in ways that roughly paralleled those pursued by the Crows and their kinsmen. They organized themselves into self-help associations and political interest groups that attempted to alleviate the pressure placed on them by employers and hostile politicians, as well as to maintain the traditions they had brought with them to their new homes. A year before the Society of American Indians held its initial meeting in Columbus, Ohio, for example, a similar group of African-American political leaders and sympathetic whites gathered to form the National Association for the Advancement of Colored People. Like the SAI, the NAACP relied on white philanthropists and educated, middle-class members to communicate its concerns; it too was riven with internal dissent and financial worries. Unlike the SAI, however, the NAACP was able to tap a large, national membership and become a permanent force in national politics.

Other groups had similar histories. The Japanese American Citizens League,

---

[42] Archdeacon, *Becoming American*, 142.

the League of United Latin American Citizens and other groups attempted to give voice to group concerns. It is also significant that, as with Native Americans, locally oriented organizations that reflected the concerns of a particular community or region were generally more successful than regional or national groups. These local associations included the Chinese Consolidated Benevolent Association, ethnic mutual aid societies, ethnic insurance and banking associations and local churches. These and other organizations organized for political influence turned to the courts for assistance and looked for ways to advance their causes in the press. Like the Crows, they participated in American institutions and interacted with large, alien institutions in an effort to protect and defend what they asserted were central values or practices within increasingly well-organized communities.[43]

These broadly parallel developments confirm that in the early twentieth century, the nation's ethnic and racial communities shared in the transition that historian Robert Wiebe has described as the movement from a "personal, informal" world to one determined by "the regulative, hierarchical needs of urban-industrial life." It was, he has written, "America's first experiment in bureaucratic order." Like industrialists and government regulators who worried over an unruly, polyglot society, leaders of immigrant groups, African-Americans and others began to think of their communities in relation to the wider world. Because they no longer existed apart from the nation as a whole, it became essential that they be organized, defended and described by a cadre of articulate leaders. At the same time – and ironically as a part of their campaign to defend their particular interests – these communities also adopted and articulated the notion of themselves as tiny embodiments of a national interest. In the midst of the unprecedented size and complexity of modern American society, they saw themselves as smaller versions of the whole: enclaves defined by their articulated traditions, their religious values, their legal interests and their political leadership. Thus, just as the Crows such as Robert Yellowtail came to see their community as a "semisovereign nation" whose borders were defended by leaders and marked off in political struggles, so other communities could understand that the sum of their collective interests (and often their neighborhood or village) defined their identity and their stake in a complicated and contentious country.[44]

This participation in the reordering of American society along ethnic lines had uneven results and frequently horrible consequences. Legally enforced

---

[43] For an excellent discussion of how these organizations functioned in one community, see Lizabeth Cohen, *Making a New Deal: Industrial Workers in Chicago, 1919–1939* (Cambridge University Press, 1990), 54–97.

[44] Robert Wiebe, *The Search for Order, 1877–1920* (New York: Hill and Wang, 1967), xiv. My rereading of Wiebe has been greatly assisted by Kenneth Cmiel's essay, "Destiny and Amnesia: The Vision of Modernity in Robert Wiebe's *The Search for Order*," *Reviews in American History*, 21 (1993), 352–368.

segregation, for example, was a form of "racial reorganization" as much as was the 1915 election of African-American migrant Oscar DePriest, the son of slaves, to the Chicago City Council. It accompanied the complete disenfranchisement of blacks in the South, and it spread its evil tentacles as much by sophisticated political organization and legal maneuvering as it did by intimidation and violence. Similarly, the well-organized successes of Irish-American politicians such as John F. Fitzgerald or Al Smith must be viewed in the same universe as the Jewish quotas at Ivy League colleges, the anti-Catholic bigotry of a remarkably resilient Ku Klux Klan and such violent episodes as the Chicago, Knoxville, and Washington, D.C., race riots of 1919. The racial hatred at large in the United States in the 1920s, and the appearance of such ethnocentric legislation as the National Origins Act offer powerful evidence that the racial progressivism frequently had an ugly face.

Nevertheless, the political leaders who paraded down Pennsylvania Avenue on the morning of November 11, 1921, represented a nation that had begun to incorporate its diversity within a series of new and reformed organizational structures. Far removed from the colonial rulers of South Africa, Americans nonetheless were engaged in a vast and complex process of adjusting diverse traditions to the requirements of a rapidly developing nation state. The "challenge and riposte" embedded in Plenty Coups's appearance represented one group's encounter within the newly constituted whole and in that sense could be grouped with the experiences of delegates who marched behind him that day from the Colored Veterans of the War, the National Catholic War Council or the Jewish War Veterans Association. Like the Crows, these groups had been surrounded and incorporated into the political and cultural institutions of modern America. They too had been forced to accommodate themselves to new geographical boundaries and structures of power which, if not formally imperial, were certainly centralized and far-reaching. These groups' traditions, personal freedoms and available resources differed fundamentally from those of the people of the Little Bighorn, but on this morning they had been drawn into the same parade and into the same enterprise of producing and reproducing the "bases for their existence."[45]

There is a danger in conflating the experiences of diverse peoples. From the perspective of one tribe or ethnic community, it is difficult to detect a point where its experience overlaps with the history of another group. It may also appear foolish to suggest such an overlap. To see a common experience in the anguished struggles of widely separated communities might well be pure sophistry – the examination of distorted shadows on a darkened wall. The danger is

---

[45] For an example of this process at work with another group (and an overview of the literature on the general topic of ethnic reorganization), see April Schultz, "'The Pride of the Race Had Been Touched': The 1925 Norse-American Immigration Centennial and Ethnic Identity," *Journal of American History*, 77, 4 (March 1991), 1265–1295.

greater, however, if we overlook the common experiences of the first Americans who faced this century. To seek out the relationships between them is not to suggest that their histories are identical or obvious. If anything, the story of the Crows should offer compelling evidence that even what might appear at first to be the tiniest of these histories is a complex and open-ended story that leaves us with dozens of unanswered questions. But understanding events in context gives them meaning, and the context sketched out above suggests two concluding observations.

First, in the United States, the expansion of national institutions in the twentieth century has reached deeply into even the most isolated racial and ethnic groups and forced wrenching changes onto peoples often viewed by outsiders as exempt from the processes of history. Participation in an economic and political system that had been thrust upon them, the exploration of new opportunities to express community interests to both constituents and adversaries and the formation of new group structures to defend those interests from attack were all features of Crow life despite the fact that the tribe was severely regimented by government agents and dominated by outsiders. The tribe's engagement with this process and the changes it wrought in their lives suggests that others who began from less distant points in the cultural landscape would have undergone a similar process of change.

Second, if these widely divergent experiences are comparable at all, they tell us that the nation emerging on the Crow Reservation in the first decades of the twentieth century was manufactured by history. While rooted in tradition, the nationalism that mobilized young leaders like Plenty Coups, Spotted Horse or Robert Yellowtail and formed the community that neutralized missionaries and rejected the reforms of John Collier's Indian New Deal had not existed when the Crows had travelled down from the Bighorns in 1884 or first entertained François Antoine Larocque eighty years earlier. It was constructed in their districts, articulated by their new leaders and communicated with the tools the twentieth century had provided. It was the product of their parade through history.

V

E. J. Hobsbawm has observed that nations "are dual phenomena, constructed essentially from above, but which cannot be understood unless also analyzed from below, that is in terms of the assumptions, hopes, needs, longings and interests of ordinary people, which are not necessarily national and still less nationalist." In the twentieth century, both historians and their readers have frequently missed Hobsbawm's insight. They have tended to side with those who see nationalism as an independent force that descends on people from above, sucking up local aspirations and amplifying them until they reach a savage roar that drowns out the voices of ordinary people. Nationalism understood in this way has fueled the dreams of demagogues. But such a perspective misses the fact that ethnic and racial identities have also been formed from below. Bonds of common purpose, loyalty to local institutions and support for local leaders – the elements of a community's sense of nationalism – have also been formed by individuals caught up in a global process of industrialization and institutional transformation. Those who view this process solely from above have failed to understand the extent to which cultural identities are shaped by circumstance, invention and negotiation.[46]

In the United States a focus on national institutions and large bureaucratic structures has similarly obscured the extent to which ethnicity has been shaped locally and unevenly over time. Unaware of, or uninterested in, the intricate stories of ethnic and racial community life that might illuminate this process, Americans have rejected a historical perspective in favor of explanations based on descent. For many, ancestry alone defines and describes the diversity embedded in our nation's past. Assuming that ancestry best describes both identity and community loyalty, this view leaves us with a national narrative written from above. It is a tale in which national structures arise and are manipulated to buttress elite interests and marginalize the aspirations of others. This approach breeds villains and victims who attack and defend stable, "traditional" interests and a constant set of "ethnic" values. As this narrative of Crow history should make clear, viewing a multiethnic national history in this way both obscures and distorts the struggles and inventions of those who made that history in the first place.

The Crows who paraded before their Hidatsa neighbors in 1805, who marched into Fort Laramie in 1868, who followed Henry Armstrong down from the Stillwater in 1884 and who accompanied Robert Yellowtail to his inauguration in 1934 made not only their own but other histories as well. Their energy and creativity shaped and adapted their traditions to new settings, demonstrating as they marched that change can provide opportunities even when it brings suffering and dislocation. Their pioneering steps to shape a nation within the United States found echoes in the experiences of other ordinary people with similar ambitions. The Crows' "gamble with nature" should encourage all Americans to persist in constructing their own communities and organizing their own parades, contributing thereby to the further growth of a plural and democratic nation.[47]

---

[46] E. J. Hobsbawm, *Nations and Nationalism Since 1780: Programme, Myth, Reality* (Cambridge University Press, 1990), 10.

[47] Some of the implications of this final paragraph are explored in David A. Hollinger, "Postethnic America," *Contention*, 2 (Fall 1992), 79–96.

A note on sources

While informed by brief periods of field research and oral history interviews, this book is essentially a work of traditional scholarship, rooted in archives and aimed at the production of a conventional historical narrative. Most of the archival material used here is housed in the National Archives, either at the Federal Records Center for the Northwest Region in Seattle, Washington, or in Washington, D.C. For a guide to the use of those materials, see my "The View from Eagle Butte: National Archives Field Branches and the Writing of American Indian History," *Journal of American History*, 76 (June 1989), 172–180. Other significant manuscript collections include the Plenty Coups Papers, housed at the Plenty Coups Museum in Pryor, Montana, and available on microfilm from the Montana Historical Society; the Robert H. Lowie Papers at the Bancroft Library, University of California, Berkeley, and the American Museum of Natural History in New York and the papers of Joseph Medicine Crow, Eloise Whitebear Pease and Robert Yellowtail at the Little Big Horn College Archives in Crow Agency, Montana. The footnotes to the text will also provide readers with a guide to the secondary literature on the topics covered in each chapter. Nevertheless, anyone who studies Crow history must begin with the writings of Robert H. Lowie. His general work, *The Crow Indians*, published in 1935, forms the tip of an iceberg of scholarly activity, most of which was published in the *Anthropological Papers of the American Museum of Natural History* in the early years of the twentieth century. Writing in Lowie's wake are contemporary anthropologists Fred Voget, Rodney Frey and Peter Nabokov, all of whose works are cited herein. Nabokov's now-classic edition of the memoirs of one Crow warrior, published as *Two Leggings: The Making of a Crow Warrior* (New York: Crowell, 1967; reissued by University of Nebraska Press, Lincoln, 1982), provides an essential perspective on tribal life in the late nineteenth century. With the founding of Little Big Horn College and the availability of outlets for locally generated materials, Crow people have also begun to produce written histories and resource materials. Particularly helpful to me have been *Crow Social Studies: Baleeisbaalichiwee History: Teacher's Guide* and *A Dictionary of Everyday Crow*, both published by the Bilingual Materials Center at Crow Agency in 1986 and 1987, respectively.

Rich photographic resources exist for the study of Crow history. These include the photographic collections at the National Museum of Natural History and the National Museum of the American Indian, both part of the

Smithsonian Institution, the Richard Throssel Papers at the University of Wyoming's Western Heritage Center and the remarkable collection of Fred Miller photographs collected by his daughter and published as *Fred E. Miller: Photographer of the Crows* (Missoula, MN, and Malibu, CA: University of Montana and Carnan VidFilm, 1985).

All of the research notes, files, photocopies, microfilm reels, computer print-outs, interview tapes and correspondence assembled for, or connected with, this project have been deposited in the Little Big Horn College Archives, where, subject to the permission of specific interviewees, they will be available to future researchers. My hope, like the hope of all authors, is that this book opens a subject for further study rather than closes it off.

Acknowledgments

One of the pleasures that accompanied the writing of this book was the opportunity it provided to meet and learn from a large number of knowledgeable people. I am grateful to all of them because I recognize better than anyone else can how much of *Parading Through History* was produced through collaboration rather than individual toil. Thinking back over this project I also realize that the list of people who helped me along the way is so long that I will surely overlook individuals who deserve recognition. I apologize to those I will slight in advance. I also recognize that the errors and oversights that remain in the text are mine.

Members of the Crow community of eastern Montana, particularly the people associated with Little Big Horn College, have encouraged and assisted me throughout the work on this manuscript. Elders Joseph Medicine Crow, Eloise Whitebear Pease and Barney Old Coyote have each assisted me through their writings and conversations as well as their general encouragement. Each has helped me feel welcome in Crow country even though my questions have made it clear that their knowledge of the community's past far exceeds my own. I especially treasure the day Eloise Pease and I retraced the journey her Crow ancestors made from the Stillwater Valley to Crow Agency.

Janine Pease Windy Boy, President of Little Big Horn College, has encouraged this project and welcomed my visits and inquiries. Tim Bernardis, the college Librarian, has been my constant friend, patiently tracking down answers to obscure queries, forwarding notices of new publications, and keeping me abreast of local news. He was also a wonderful host, providing my family and me both housing and the use of his electric NFL football game. Mardell Hogan Plainfeather, daughter of George Washington Hogan and Lillian Bull Shows, has been another wonderful host and mentor. Her introduction to the Crow clan system was especially helpful to me, as was her research into the history of the descendants of Pierre Chien. Mardell's mother graciously agreed to be interviewed as she busily prepared for the 1987 Crow fair, an act of generosity that provided unique insights into several important incidents in Crow history. Former Little Big Horn College faculty member Karen Watembach was my host during an early trip to Crow Agency and served as another patient source of information about Crow traditions and Crow history. Magdalene Medicine Horse and Carson Walks Over Ice, both of the Little Big Horn College Library and Archives, were also of great help as I tracked down questions that seemed to have no answer. I am also grateful to the late George Takes Gun for sharing with me his memories of the early years of the Native American church and to Dale Old Horn, Dan Old Elk, Carolyn Reynolds Riebeth of Hardin and Henry Realbird.

While a fellow visitor rather than a resident of the Crow Reservation, Peter Nabokov has been another steady guide to the nuances and opportunities embedded in this subject. I fear I have not discovered them all, but those that are identified here usually reflect his wisdom. I have also valued the insights and information shared by fellow students of Crow history Fred Voget, Clarence Belue, Peggy Albright, Rodney Frey and Tim McCleary. Like so many other researchers, I am also indebted to Charles and Susanna Bradley for their compilation of materials on Crow history.

The staff of the Newberry Library demonstrated to me during the writing of this book why this institution has been the home for so many scholars and research projects. The matchless collection of books and manuscripts on western Americana assembled by Edward E. Ayer was an essential resource for this book, but I could never have learned what I did from it without the assistance of John Aubrey, Charles Cullen, the late Michael Kaplan, Robert Karrow, Margaret Kulis, Melissa Martens, Bart Smith, Jack Scott, Elizabeth Freebairn, Pat Morris, Meg Bolger and Victor Lieberman. I am also grateful for the assistance provided by Amy Henderson, Ken Kain, Karen Klutho, Eduardo Lopez, Tony Rieck, Josephine Rood and Rebecca Weisz.

The Newberry is the home to a small universe of scholars and researchers, many of whom have helped me along the way. Helga Miz, linguist and outdoorswoman, generously translated the German language letters anthropologist Robert Lowie wrote to his family from the Crow Reservation in the early twentieth century, and Paul Gehl, custodian of the John M. Wing Collection, carried out a similar task with Pierpaolo Prando's letters written in Italian from the Jesuit mission at St. Xavier in the 1880s. Annie Merrit Cochrane helped me compile statistical data, Bruce Fisher spent many hours coding information from Crow censuses, Tom Wilcockson drew the maps for this volume, and Violet Brown, Margret Curtis and Loretta Brown worked both on the project, typing and constructing neat tables from my scribbles, and at the door to my office – fending off interruptions and holding visitors at bay. I have also benefitted from the help of several participants in the Newberry's ACM/ GLCA Humanities Seminar for undergraduates. These included Cary Christie, John Keckhaver and others whom I fear are now middle-aged. Finally, Richard H. Brown, the Library's former Academic Vice-President, watched the evolution of this manuscript with both a critical eye and great good humor. He was supportive, encouraging and patient.

The staffs of several other institutions also helped me with my research. These include the Montana Historical Society, the Plenty Coups Museum,

Eastern Montana College, Montana State University, Northwestern University Library, the Bancroft Library, the National Archives, the Library of Congress and the Federal Records Center in Seattle, Washington. At the latter institution, Joyce Justice and her staff of archivists were particularly helpful and patient. Fred Nicklason and his colleagues at Nicklason Research Associates in Washington, D.C., helped me find solutions to the problem of accessing the Indian Office records for this topic and provided vital help during a critical phase of the book's development. Robert and Eleanor Carriker graciously located and copied materials for me in the Jesuit Archives at Gonzaga University.

Throughout the writing of this book I have benefitted from advice and candid criticism offered by colleagues both in Chicago and elsewhere. William T. Hagan was an early, enthusiastic supporter of my research on the Crows and a generous source of encouragement and support. Henry Binford, Colin Calloway, Rich Edwards, James Grossman, Peter Iverson, Harvey Markowitz, Peter Nabokov, Donald Parman and Mary Beth Rose read all or part of the final manuscript and each offered valuable comments. Others who have read and commented upon earlier versions of the work include Elizabeth Colson, Walter Conser, Raymond J. Demallie, Raymond D. Fogelson, David R. Miller, John H. Moore, Alfonso Ortiz, Peter Powell and Helen Hornbeck Tanner. I am also grateful for the careful proofreading provided by Dr. Ed Peterson and Mary Hanscom. I am grateful to all of these individuals for their insights and encouragement.

Like all those mentioned above, Frank Smith of Cambridge University Press has been patient; he has also believed in my ambitions for this project and has been unflagging in his confidence that at least some of those ambitions might be realized. I thank him for that.

Work on this book was supported by a Rockefeller Foundation Humanities Fellowship and a National Endowment for the Humanities Fellowship for College Teachers and Independent Scholars. Office space during those fellowship periods was generously provided by Northwestern University and Covenant United Methodist Church of Evanston, Illinois, and its former pastor, Donald D. Scott. In addition, I am grateful for the support of the Newberry Library, which made one research trip to Montana possible, and to the National Endowment for the Humanities Travel to Collections Fellowship, which supported another. Both the National Endowment for the Humanities and the Newberry Library also supported an essential period of research at the Federal Records Center in Seattle, Washington, during the summer of 1984. I am also grateful to the University of Wyoming's Western Heritage Center for a research grant that enabled me to examine manuscripts in its collection as well as to draw on local history materials in the Coe Library.

Crow people often say one should measure wealth in relatives, not money. I have grown richer during the writing of this book: my family has grown and my appreciation for them has multiplied. John and Catherine Hoxie provided the personal support necessary for me to spend a summer in the Federal Records Center in Seattle; this book would not have cleared that essential hurdle without them. Through their indomitable spirit, my children – Stephen and Philip Hoskins and Silas and Charlie Hoxie – have helped this manuscript evolve from a story of victimization to what I hope is a tale of adaptation and resilience. And finally, my wife, Holly, to whom this book is dedicated, has helped me understand that all of our stories are connected and that, if we are persistent, we can learn to understand them.

Index